COVER DESIGN . . . more than meets the eye.

Your new copy of *Boone&KurtzBusiness*
represents the first textbook ever to employ
the computer technology capable of creating
a hidden image. This approach, created by
NVision Grafix, Inc. of Irving, Texas, permits
an image to be embedded within a design.
To visualize the embedded image on the
cover, hold the tip of your nose to the cover.
Then, slowly move the book away from your
face to a distance of about 3 feet. As your
focus shifts, the image will appear—an image
depicting one of the major themes of the
book!

BOONE&KURTZBUSINESS

BOONE&KURTZBUSINESS

LOUIS E. BOONE

Ernest G. Cleverdon Chair of Business and Management
University of South Alabama

DAVID L. KURTZ

R.A. and Vivian Young Chair of Business Administration
University of Arkansas

THE DRYDEN PRESS

HARCOURT BRACE COLLEGE PUBLISHERS

Fort Worth Philadelphia San Diego New York Orlando Austin San Antonio
Toronto Montreal London Sydney Tokyo

Editor-in-Chief   Lyn Hastert
Developmental Editor   Daryl Fox
Product Manager   Lise Johnson
Production Manager   Ann Coburn
Production Services   Seaside Publishing Services

Requests for permission to make copies of any part of the work should be mailed to: Permissions Department, Harcourt Brace & Company, 6277 Sea Harbor Drive, Orlando, FL 32887-6277.

Address for Editorial Correspondence
The Dryden Press, 301 Commerce Street, Suite 3700, Fort Worth, TX 76102

Address for Orders
The Dryden Press, 6277 Sea Harbor Drive, Orlando, FL 32887-6277
1-800-782-4479, or 1-800-433-0001 (in Florida)

ISBN: 0-03-010642-7

Printed in the United States of America

4 5 6 7 8 9 0 1 2 3 048 9 8 7 6 5 4 3 2 1

The Dryden Press
Harcourt Brace College Publishers

To Pat and Diane

Preface

Let's use the analogy of a century clock to see just where we are as this course begins. If the twentieth century is viewed in terms of a 24-hour clock, World War I began at 3:21 A.M. World War II ended at 10:48 A.M., and Neil Armstrong walked on the face of the moon at 4:33 P.M. The old Soviet Union disintegrated just after 9:30 P.M., Nelson Mandela was elected president of South Africa at 10:19 P.M., and Atlanta hosts the 1996 Olympics less than an hour before the midnight bell tolls the end of the century.

In looking forward to the remaining months of the 1990s, our century clock reads just past 11:00 P.M. Much of the technological advances that have improved the quality of life for the world—air transportation, television, computers, global telecommunication, miracle drugs—are products of the twentieth century. This century also has seen more than its share of challenges: water and air pollution; wars; depletion of the earth's storehouse of natural resources; efforts to add quality and customer satisfaction to goods and services; human suffering from famine, natural disasters, and the sale of faulty products; unethical actions by people in both the private and public sectors; and the continuing need to provide every person with challenging and rewarding job opportunities.

The mission of *Boone&KurtzBUSINESS* is to introduce these contributions and challenges in a clear and interesting manner. Thumb through the first chapter and you will see how we intend to accomplish this mission. We believe in the value of active learning and we involve the reader at every opportunity. The philosopher Confucius has been quoted as saying, "I hear and I forget. I see and I remember. I do and I understand." Our explanation-and-example approach begins each chapter with an opening vignette of an actual firm that practices the business concepts described in the chapter. Learning aids begin with chapter learning goals and end with an annotated summary of them linked to all testing materials. The students' business vocabulary is developed with the aid of an end-of-chapter self-quiz covering important key terms. High-quality illustrations and special focus boxes enhance the written materials. At the end of every chapter is a multimedia case illuminated by video materials designed specifically for that section.

Much of our focus in the text is directed to the fundamental changes occurring in today's business world, changes that will affect our lives as we enter the new century. Terms appearing regularly in daily news reports are integrated with the business concepts in the text. Examples include:

- empowerment
- downsizing
- information superhighway
- work-force diversity
- strategic alliances
- privatization
- GATT
- NAFTA
- home-based work
- outsourcing
- reinventing the corporation
- cross-functional teams
- the glass ceiling
- productivity
- total quality management (TQM)
- European Union
- benchmarking
- relationship marketing
- financial supermarkets
- virtual reality
- critical thinking
- corporate culture
- customer satisfaction
- online computer services
- interactive media
- the Internet

Another feature of the book is currency. *Boone&KurtzBUSINESS* is as up-to-date as today's publishing technology allows. In an ongoing effort to present the very latest developments, the book continued to be updated even as it went to press. The result is a finished product that offers examples as recent as:

- the impact of the O. J. Simpson case on the use of celebrity endorsers
- the recent Major League Baseball strike
- Atlanta's plans to host the 1996 Olympics

BOOK FEATURES

This edition provides both the professor and the student with state-of-the-art instructional materials. These range from traditional lecture and testing supplements to interactive, multimedia presentation software and displays.

Career Preparation

A major thrust of the book resulted from listening to our own students and to students on dozens of college and university campuses that we visited over the past three years. Students throughout the United States and Canada expressed to us their concerns about finding jobs when they graduate. These concerns are so important that we have made a major commitment to addressing them.

Students of the mid-1990s are pragmatic. They know how important it is to start early in career preparation, to match their individual abilities and interests to specific career alternatives, and to create an academic plan to help them secure that first job on their career path. But they need help in accomplishing this objective.

The first business course is a perfect setting in which to begin career preparation. As the student is exposed to many different aspects of the world of business throughout the course, he or she also can begin to consider which areas represent potential careers. In addition to a description of popular business careers in the careers appendix, we have included five profiles of recent business graduates who have begun successful careers in different business disciplines. We also are providing *Business Career Tracks Software*, which includes resume and self-assessment tools. Eric Sandberg, of the DeVry Institute in Atlanta, designed this software and created special business data sets based on extensive interviews with business executives.

The Career Design Exercises included in the software will help the student in deciding on a major; identifying strong skills; determining whether starting a business may be the most appropriate career path; in creating custom resumes that will stand out from others; and in developing communication skills by organizing thoughts through writing. These materials are fully integrated with the text, require no special preparation by the instructor, need no special equipment, and—best of all—are absolutely free with the purchase of a new copy of *Boone&KurtzBUSINESS*.

Integration of Global Business

Any focus on quality and business competitiveness must include *global* competitiveness. Many books attempt to focus on international issues by placing a chapter on global issues at the end of the text, where it becomes a logical candidate for omission when time runs short. Other texts go a step further and add box examples on international topics. Unfortunately, this is not what is meant when instructors plead for an internationally integrated textbook.

In response to this plea, *BUSINESS* takes a truly global perspective. Hundreds of international examples are interspersed throughout the book's 16 chapters. Coverage of global issues begins in Chapter 1 and ends with the Tokyo Stock Exchange case at the end of the book's final chapter. As part of our strategy for making the book a truly global text, we have placed the traditional "international" chapter in Part One as a key component of the general environment for business. The 1990s business executive must think globally—beyond the "us-versus-them" orientation that is so prevalent in current business education.

Teamwork and Communication

Boone&KurtzBUSINESS is the first introductory text to devote an entire chapter to two fundamental concerns of today's business executives: the shift of organizations to working in teams and the importance of effective communication. Coverage includes work teams and special-purpose problem-solving teams, cross-functional teams, team development, conflict resolution, oral and written communication, verbal and nonverbal communication, international business communication, and communication technology.

Quality and Customer Satisfaction

Another first for this book is a separate chapter focusing on the role of quality in business success. Instead of a narrow conception of quality as affecting only production processes, Chapter 6 shows how total quality management can be applied throughout the organization, from human resource management and finance to marketing and information. The importance of employee involvement, empowerment, training, and teamwork in achieving world-class quality to provide customer satisfaction is examined as well.

Technology

Global economic leadership is related closely to the productivity of a nation's business sector, and its people and productivity, in turn, are spurred by technological advances. The importance of technology is stressed in the very first chapter of the text and continues in each of the book's 16 chapters. Special focus boxes in every chapter demonstrate the contributions of technology to our standard of living. Topics include voice recognition, scanners, virtual reality, databases, videoconferencing, pen notebooks and flash technology, customer service technology, paperless manufacturing, geographic systems, and fiber optics.

Fewer Chapters

At 16 chapters, *Boone&KurtzBUSINESS* is the shortest major book available for the first business course. The book's length and number of chapters are intended to match the time constraints of a one-semester or one-quarter course. Our objective is to permit the instructor to cover all of the text in a single term without facing the dilemma of what important topics to omit when using a text with simply too many chapters and pages to cover.

Focus on Diversity, Ethics, and Social Responsibility

Discussion of ethical, societal, and environmental concerns begins in Chapter 1 and continues throughout the text. Each of the chapters in Part One devote major coverage to these topics. More specific coverage is included for each business function, including human resource management, production, marketing, and finance.

The varying dimensions of diversity—multicultural diversity, gender, age, ethnic backgrounds, the physically and mentally challenged—are discussed in *Boone&KurtzBUSINESS*. The videocase for Chapter 8, "Valuing Diversity at Xerox," describes programs established by this progressive firm to reap the benefits of diversity.

Emphasis on Small Business and Entry-Level Management

Too often, students are introduced to businesses of only one size: large corporations. *Boone&Kurtz BUSINESS* recognizes students' growing interest in small business and the many career opportunities found in organizations other than corporate giants. A balanced presentation of applications and examples from hundreds of both small and big businesses is maintained throughout the text. Discussions of business careers in the career appendix focus on career opportunities in small businesses as well as in larger organizations. In addition, Chapter 5 devotes major coverage to entrepreneurship, small business, and franchising.

Numerous business professors have pointed out to us that most business students will find their first jobs at the supervisory management level. However, most textbooks tend to focus on top-management decisions, activities, and problems, and to neglect discussion of first-line supervisory management. The book provides detailed coverage of first-line management in Chapter 7 and includes many examples of supervisory management activities and concerns.

Integrating Print and Video Technologies

Technological advances are having a profound effect on college and university teaching. In recent years, publishers have been barraged with requests from professors for integrated video materials that are tied closely to business concepts discussed in the text. *Boone&KurtzBUSINESS* has responded to these requests by providing integrated video cases, a laser disk, and an extensive video package. Each of the 16 text chapters features a video case that uses real-world examples, on-location footage, special effects, and state-of-the-art graphics to present basic concepts introduced in the chapter.

The end-of-chapter video cases and the accompanying videos feature a variety of small- and medium-sized organizations. They also focus heavily on international business, on service firms, on organizations founded and managed by minority entrepreneurs, and on such important concepts as quality, ethics and social responsibility, and valuing diversity. In response to instructor requests for shorter-length videos, all videos are now between 10 and 15 minutes in length. The following video cases are included:

Chapter 1	Lincoln Electric
Chapter 2	The Dollars and Cents of Recycling
Chapter 3	Jamaica: Paradise Lost?
Chapter 4	Ampex
Chapter 5	Samuel Adams Lager
Chapter 6	The Japanese Distribution System
Chapter 7	Middle Management: Twenty-first Century Dinosaur?
Chapter 8	Strength in Diversity: Xerox
Chapter 9	American Worker—Japanese Boss
Chapter 10	Sea World
Chapter 11	Global Marketing
Chapter 12	Stewart Warner
Chapter 13	Paint by Numbers
Chapter 14	Springfield Remanufacturing Corp.
Chapter 15	Duracell International
Chapter 16	The Tokyo Stock Exchange

The *Instructor's Resource Manual* provides the following materials for each video case: teaching objectives, a listing of chapter concepts illustrated in the video, video warm-up questions and exercises, a detailed outline of the video, answers to video case questions in the text, video recap, experiential exercises, and a multiple-choice quiz. These superb instructional materials for the video cases were prepared by Gayle Marco of Robert Morris College and Anthony Lucas of the Community College of Allegheny County.

SUPPLEMENTARY MATERIALS

The Dryden Press has spared no expense to make this the premier textbook on the market today. Many instructors teach large classes with limited resources. Supplementary materials provide a means of expanding and improving the students' learning experience. The teaching/learning package provided with the book is designed specifically to meet the needs of instructors facing a variety of teaching conditions and to enhance students' experience in their first business course.

Test Bank

For most instructors, the single most important part of any teaching package is a test bank, comprised of questions that accurately and fairly assess student competence in subject material. Prepared by Dr. Thomas Lloyd at Westmoreland County Community College, the *Boone&KurtzBUSINESS Test Bank* provides 2,500 multiple choice, true/false, matching, and essay test items. A separate essay question is included for every learning goal in the text.

The test items have been reviewed and class tested to ensure the highest quality. Each question is keyed to chapter learning objectives, is rated for level of difficulty, and is designated either as factual or application so that instructors can provide a balanced set of questions for student exams.

Computerized Test Bank

The *Boone&KurtzBUSINESS Test Bank* is available for IBM and Macintosh computers and is free to adopters. The *Computerized Test Bank* allows instructors to select and edit test items from the printed test bank as well as add an unlimited number of their own questions. Up to 99 versions of each test can be custom-printed.

Instructor's Resource Manual

The authors devoted a major effort to developing this critical instructional tool. In preparing the *Instructor's Resource Manual*, we benefitted from the advice offered by Blane Franckowiak of Tarrant County Junior College. The *IRM* contains the following sections for each chapter:

- Annotated Learning Goals
- Key Terms
- Lecture Illustration Files
- Answers to Review Questions
- Answers to Discussion Questions
- Answers to Video Case Questions
- Supplemental Case
- Controversial Issue
- Experiential Exercises
- Guest Speaker Suggestions
- Term Paper Suggestions
- Transparency Teaching Notes

Complete instructions for the Career Design Software also are included to assist instructors in maximizing the effectiveness of the Career Design Exercises. Each exercise is accompanied by a list of specific student benefits, a summary, sample instructions to the exercise, lists of discussion ideas, and suggestions for grading student exercises.

Computerized Instructor's Resource Manual

An *IRM* disk is available that contains detailed lecture outlines for each chapter. This allows instructors to insert class notes and customize course lectures. The software is available in WordPerfect for IBM.

Supplemental Modules

Modules on the subjects of quality, diversity assessment, and business math provide additional coverage and address the desires of instructors who wish to further emphasize any of these areas.

Learning Guide

The *Learning Guide* is invaluable in helping students master business concepts. Each chapter includes a brief outline, experiential exercises, a self-quiz, cases, and short-answer questions. Also included are crossword puzzles at the end of each chapter. *Learning Guide* solutions appear at the end of the guide, rather than in the *Instructor's Resource Manual.* The *Learning Guide* was prepared by Professor Doug Copeland of Johnson County Community College.

Transparency Masters and Acetates

A set of approximately 150 full-color transparency acetates is available for adopters of the book. Each transparency acetate is a striking graphic representation or advertisement that illustrates key concepts discussed in the book. Also available are over 100 transparency masters focusing on concepts—and sometimes on actual figures—discussed in the text. Teaching notes are included for both the transparency acetates and the transparency masters.

Computer Simulation

The *Chopsticks Simulation Game*, created by Professors Eugene J. Calvasina, James Leon Barton, Jr., Ava Honan, Richard Calvasina, and Gerald Calvasina of Auburn University in Montgomery, Alabama, challenges students to develop and experience the business concepts presented in the book. It gives students an opportunity to utilize decision-making tools frequently used in business. The game is accompanied by an *Instructor's Manual* that provides game instructions and student worksheets. The simulation game is available on disk for use with the IBM PC.

The Boone & Kurtz Business Disk and Computer Cases Supplement

These innovative components of the *Boone&Kurtz BUSINESS* instructional resource package are designed to assist business professors who want to include analytical problems as homework assignments or to use such tools as the microcomputer in the basic business course. Both are available free to adopters of the text. The *Computer Cases Supplement* includes more than 75 business problems with solutions that focus on concepts discussed in each chapter. Solutions to each case are included with the *Business Disk*. The *Business Disk* contains complete programs for computer cases and is available to adopters for use with the IBM PC.

Business Career Design Software

This excellent software created for students by Eric Sandburg provides them with interactive exercises coordinated with each part of the text. After completing one or two questionnaires or activities, students can use the software program to help measure their current level of awareness and capabilities and then to obtain personalized advice for making the most of various options and improving skills.

Portfolio of Business Papers

A *Portfolio of Business Papers* has been assembled to help students understand the variety of official documents required in a modern business organization. Authentic business papers are available with complete teaching notes for professors who use *Boone&KurtzBUSINESS* in their classes. The papers were edited by Professors Spencer Mehl of Coastal Carolina Community College and Nikki Paahana of the DeVry Institute of Technology.

Laser Disk

The Dryden Press once again is shaping business education by being the first publisher to offer a business laser disk. The disk includes graphic and textual elements from the textbook and support materials integrated with video and animation sequences to provide a dynamic, easy-to-use mutimedia presentation of fundamental business concepts.

ACKNOWLEDGMENTS

The authors are extremely grateful for the insightful comments of the following colleagues who reviewed all or part of the manuscript:

Robb Bay, Community College of Southern Nevada
Robert J. Cox, Salt Lake Community College
Judson Faurer, Metropolitan State College of Denver
L. Milton Glisson, North Carolina A&T State University
Don Gordon, Illinois Central College
Douglas G. Heeter, Ferris State University
Paul Hegele, Elgin Community College
Tom Heslin, Indiana University at Bloomington
Vince Howe, University of North Carolina at Wilmington
Geraldine V. Jolly, Barton College
Dave Jones, La Salle University
Kenneth Lacho, University of New Orleans
Thomas Lloyd, Westmoreland County Community College
Martin St. John, Westmoreland County Community College
J. Robert Ulbrich, Parkland College
W. J. Waters, Jr., Central Piedmont Community College
Tom Wiener, Iowa Central Community College
Gregory J. Worosz, Schoolcraft College

Special thanks also go to our research associates, Jeanne Harris, Jeanne Lowe, Donna Walker, and Jamie Gunsaulis, for their invaluable assistance. We are especially indebted to Wendy Caster and Alice Fugate, who dedicated many hours to the book's completion.

Last, but not least, we thank our good friends at The Dryden Press and Seaside Publishing Services: Ann Coburn, production manager, who never let the schedule slip; Pat Bracken and Linda Miller, art directors, who crafted a brilliant teaching tool; Daryl Fox, developmental editor, who played traffic cop and emergency-room physician as the pages and chapters of the book fell into place; and Lynne Bush, whose unfailing attention to detail resulted in the on-time publication of a book of exceptional quality. Additionally, Cindy Robinson's fine free-lance photo research aided our work greatly. We are also grateful to Lyn Keeney Hastert, editor-in-chief, and Lise Johnson, senior marketing manager.

Louis E. Boone
David L. Kurtz

Brief Contents

Contents

PART TWO
GETTING STARTED   69

112 *Competing with Quality*
AT&T is the latest to earn the Baldrige Award
for quality and customer satisfaction.

Chapter 4
Developing a Business
Strategy and Plan   70

Developing the Organization's Mission Statement •
Setting Organizational Objectives • Management by
Objectives • Creating a Competitive Differentiation •
The Planning Process • Planning and the Managerial
Functions • Organizing • Directing • Controlling •
Assessment and Evaluation • SWOT Analysis •
Strategic Business Units • Forecasting • Creating a
Business Plan

Chapter 5
Organizing the Business   92

Forms of Private Ownership • Proprietorships •
Partnerships • Corporations • Mergers • Employee
Ownership • Public and Collective Ownership •
Privatization • Cooperatives • Importance of
Entrepreneurship • Are Entrepreneurs a Different
Breed? • Role of Small Business • Opportunities for
Women and Minorities • Franchising • Small Business
Goes Global • Resources for Entrepreneurs

Chapter 6
The Role of Quality in
Business Success   108

Importance of Quality and Customer Satisfaction •
National Quality Programs • Applying TQM
throughout the Organization • Importance of
Feedback to Quality • Continuous Process
Improvement • Benchmarking • Encouraging
Employee Involvement • Empowerment • Training •
Teamwork

PART THREE
MANAGEMENT: EMPOWERING PEOPLE TO ACHIEVE BUSINESS OBJECTIVES   133

168 *Dual Careers*
SmithKline Beecham accommodates working mothers to reap benefits of a diverse working force.

364 Insurance
Would you buy life insurance from this character?

PART ONE

Business in a Global Environment

CHAPTER 1
Business: Blending People, Technology, and Ethical Behavior

CHAPTER 2
Business: Its Environment and Role in Society

CHAPTER 3
Global and Economic Forces Affecting Business

Business: Blending People, Technology, and Ethical Behavior

Learning Goals

1. Explain what a business is and how it operates within the private enterprise system.
2. Define the roles of competition and of the entrepreneur in a private enterprise system.
3. Outline the basic rights of the private enterprise system.
4. Explain the concepts of gross domestic product and productivity.
5. Identify the degrees of competition that can exist in a private enterprise system.
6. Discuss the major challenges and opportunities facing managers in the late 1990s.
7. Describe the most important qualities managers should possess.
8. Explain the ethical and social responsibilities of business.

Few companies have tried as hard as Levi Strauss to blend talented people, technology, and ethical behavior into everyday business practice. CEO Robert Haas, a great-great-grandnephew of the namesake founder, is working to achieve a grand vision in which his firm is capable of both making a profit and making the world a better place to live. "We are not doing this because it makes us feel good—although it does. We are not doing this because it is politically correct. We are doing this because we believe in the interconnection between liberating the talents of our people and business success."

Independent research bears out Haas's belief. One study found that companies that involve their employees more in decision making tend to earn more profits than companies in similar industries who give employees little power over decisions regarding how they perform their jobs. Other research confirms that diverse work teams—those made up of men and women of different ages and from a variety of cultures—tend to produce better solutions to business problems.

Haas's quest for what he calls "responsible commercial success" has led to a long-term strategy to create a more diverse work force. During the ten years since he became

CEO, Levi Strauss has doubled its percentage of minority managers to 36 percent. Over this same period, the percentage of women managers at Levi Strauss rose from 32 percent to 54 percent. An Hispanic manager runs the South American division, and women head Levi Strauss operations in Mexico and Great Britain.

The presence of a work force made up of a wide variety of cultural groups strengthens the company by ensuring a broader range of viewpoints that reflect the entire marketplace. As Haas puts it, "I'm not a 35-year-old woman. I'm no hip-hopper. I'm not the target customer." A few years ago, this broader viewpoint allowed the company to adjust its "501 Blues" advertising campaign to reach more of the fashion-jeans market. The independent loners shown in early ads appealed strongly to young Caucasians, but not to Hispanics. Levi's Hispanic employees pointed out that those gritty street scenes seemed cold and lonely to Latinos. "Why is that guy walking down the street alone?" they asked. "Doesn't he have any friends?" Following their advice, Levi's launched a new series of ads that focused on family and friends, and 501 sales soared in Hispanic communities.

Levi's commitment to ethical behavior is illustrated by its relationships with product suppliers around the globe. The firm requires all suppliers to follow International Labor Organization standards, which prohibit hiring children under the age of 14. An investigation of a Bangladeshi contractor that discovered boys and girls under 14 on the payroll resulted in an ethical dilemma: The children's paychecks were the sole economic support for their families. As Levi's community-affairs chief Robert Dunn put it, "We don't support child labor. But our intention is not to have a devastating effect on families."

The solution: The contractors agreed to guarantee jobs for these children when they turned 14 and Levi Strauss paid their wages and the cost of attending school until then. It was both an ethically responsible act and a move that would enhance Levi's corporate reputation at a cost of only a few thousand dollars. "In today's world, a TV exposé on working conditions can undo years of effort to build brand loyalty," Dunn comments. "Why squander your investment when, with commitment, reputational problems can be prevented?"

Haas is the first to admit that Levi Strauss does not do everything right. The company was slow to respond to such competitive trends as wrinkle-free jeans; moreover, some retailers criticize its customer service as not timely enough. Haas currently is directing a $500 million improvement of Levi's product-development and distribution systems. He insists, however, that he will continue to work toward his goal of running a truly ethical business. "We are only a few steps along in our journey," he says. "We are far from perfect. We are far from where we want to be. But the goal is out there, and it's worth striving for."[1]

CHAPTER OVERVIEW

They all went into business seeking a piece of the American dream: to own their own company, be their own boss, reap the benefits of their own brain power, time commitments, and hard work, and to give something back to the economic system that had allowed them to realize this dream.

There are many ways to achieve the dream. Jim Mattei founded Checkers Drive-In Restaurants because he believed that fast-food veterans such as McDonald's and Burger King had forgotten their take-out roots and had become overpriced. Mattei's twin drive-thru restaurants accommodated twice as many customers as the industry giants; he also held down restaurant costs by eliminating customer seating. Best of all, his tasty four-ounce hamburgers, priced at 99 cents, were an immediate hit. They set off fast-food price wars in every city where Checkers competed with an established McDonald's or Burger King outlet.[2]

Ron Matsch, a St. Louis recreational facilities designer, responded to several mid-1990s trends with his business. The growing number of two wage-earner households, the desire of parents to spend quality time with their children, and increased interest in fitness led Matsch to found Discovery Zone, a chain of indoor fun centers for children ages 12 and younger. The play areas offer kids a chance to exercise and develop their hand-eye coordination; concession areas sell food and clothing, and cater birthday parties. Every Discovery Zone also houses a Quiet Room, a separate area for adults only, with a TV, reading materials—and lots of coffee.[3]

Martha Morris's big idea resulted from a problem: What to do with all that no-longer-needed hiking and camping equipment she had bought for an outdoor vacation? After discovering that no established market for such used products existed in Minneapolis, she took matters into her own hands and opened her first Play It Again Sports outlet. The store featured both new and used sporting goods. Customers could sell, buy, trade, or consign their "used but not used-up" equipment. Sales skyrocketed and Morris opened another store. Because she didn't have enough money to finance a chain of stores, she decided to offer other business people the opportunity to open their own

> **THEY SAID IT**
>
> "If you can dream it, you can do it."
>
> *Walt Disney (1901–1966)*
> *American film producer*

Play It Again Sports founder Martha Morris turned a problem into a business opportunity attuned to the value-conscious marketplace of the mid-1990s.

Play It Again Sports store in return for a $20,000 fee and five percent of store sales. Today, almost 1,000 outlets operate throughout Canada and the United States, and *Fortune* magazine recently named Play It Again Sports' parent company, Grow Biz International, number one in its ranking of the 100 fastest-growing American companies.[4]

Mattei, Matsch, and Morris are three examples of the thousands of business visionaries who have profited from achieving their dreams. Each built a company that might carry the descriptive label *gazelle*—a small- to medium-sized firm with at least $100,000 in annual sales that is growing at a 20 percent or higher rate every year. Even though these gazelles account for only three percent of all U.S. businesses, they have added nearly five million jobs to the American economy since 1990.

In addition to creating jobs, these businesses serve two other purposes. First, they offer goods and services that provide customer satisfaction for value-conscious consumers of the late-1990s. They also offer alternative career paths for business people seeking an option to working for giant corporations. For example, many of the people who buy and operate Play It Again Sports outlets leave corporate jobs to run

their own business. A company spokesperson describes them as follows: "They're around 40 years old and have a net worth of $300,000. Ninety percent have a college degree."[5]

The ability to realize such dreams is made possible by the private enterprise system. In this chapter, we begin the study of business by examining the fact that today's business is unavoidably global in nature and that quality products offering customer satisfaction are the result of blending technology, people, and ethical behavior. Characteristics of successful managers will be identified and the need to include ethical behavior and social responsibility as important organizational goals will be explored. The starting place is an understanding of the word *business*.

WHAT IS BUSINESS?

What do we think of when we hear the word *business*? Some of us think of our jobs, others think of the merchants they deal with as consumers, and still others think of the millions of firms that make up the world's economy. This broad, all-inclusive term can be applied to many kinds of enterprises. Business provides the bulk of our employment as well as the products we enjoy.

Business consists of *all profit-seeking activities and enterprises that provide goods and services necessary to an economic system.* Some businesses produce tangible goods, such as automobiles, breakfast cereals, and computer chips; others provide services, such as insurance, concerts, car rentals, and lodging.

Business is the economic pulse of a nation, the means through which standards of living improve. The United States leads the world in terms of national output of goods and services on a per-capita basis. By contrast, the typical Japanese citizen enjoys a standard of living only 82 percent as high as that of his or her U.S. counterpart, and Germany's is only 71 percent of the United States's. America's robust standard of living depends on the continuing health and dynamism of its business.[6]

Role of Profits

Profits are a critical ingredient in accomplishing the goals necessary to constantly improve standards of living. **Profits** represent *rewards for the business person who takes the risks involved in blending people, technology, and information in creating and marketing want-satisfying goods and services that provide customer satisfaction.* Even though accountants think of profits as the difference between a firm's revenues and expenses involved in generating these revenues, it is useful to think of profits as serving as an *incentive* for people to start companies, expand them, and provide consistently high-quality, competitive goods and services.

Just as important as profits are the social and ethical responsibilities that successful businesses must meet. This means organizations must act responsibly in their dealings with employees, consumers, suppliers, competitors, government, and the general public if they are to succeed in the long run. We will discuss social responsibility and business ethics more fully in Chapter 2.

Business Concepts in Not-for-Profit Organizations

Even though our definition of business focuses on the operations of firms whose objectives include earning a profit for their owners, it is clear that the business concepts discussed in this text apply equally to those **not-for-profit organizations**—*firms whose primary objective is something other than returning profits to their owners.* The 1.3 million not-for-profit businesses operating in the United States employ almost 11 million people (including volunteers) and generate an estimated $300 billion in revenues each year. This sector includes museums, libraries, religious and human-service organizations, secondary schools, many health-care facilities, colleges and universities, symphony orchestras, fraternal organizations, and thousands of other groups, such as government agencies, political parties, and labor unions.

Even though not-for-profit organizations have service objectives not keyed to profitability targets, they still must secure sufficient revenues in the form of membership fees, ticket sales, donations, and grants

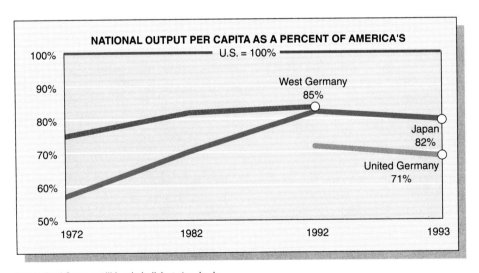

The United States still leads in living standards.

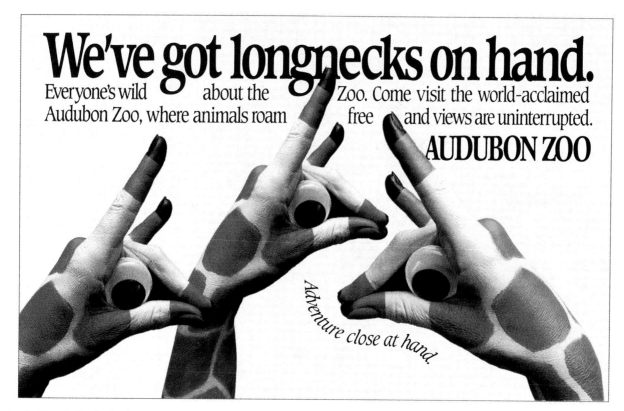

We've got longnecks on hand.

Everyone's wild about the Zoo. Come visit the world-acclaimed Audubon Zoo, where animals roam free and views are uninterrupted.

AUDUBON ZOO

Adventure close at hand.

Application of effective business concepts has replaced the "nation's worst" label at the New Orleans Audubon Zoo with a Top Five ranking.

to cover their costs. They also deal with the same kinds of issues facing their profit-seeking counterparts: developing objectives aimed at serving their constituencies; planning; building an effective organization; attracting, training, and motivating an effective work force; acquiring financing to improve physical facilities; and offering goods and services aimed at providing satisfaction to their customers, clients, and patients.

The remarkable turnaround at the Audubon Zoo is a good example. Two decades ago, this New Orleans zoo ranked at the bottom of the nation's zoos in terms of physical layout, quality of life for the animals who lived there, and the educational and recreational benefits offered to zoo visitors. Embarrassed by the ranking, city officials committed themselves to correcting these problems and making the zoo one of the city's primary tourist attractions. Today, the Audubon Zoo has undergone a renaissance. New attendance records are set every year, and soaring revenues are being reinvested in further improvements. Revenues aren't the only factor soaring on New Orleans' west side: Audubon Zoo recently was ranked among the five best zoos in the United States.

THE PRIVATE ENTERPRISE SYSTEM

An appropriate place to begin our study of business is to describe the economic system to which most U.S. and foreign businesses belong. The **private enterprise system,** or capitalism, is *an economic system founded on the principle that competition among firms determines their success or failure in the marketplace and that this competition, in turn, best serves the needs of society. Competition* is the battle among businesses for consumer acceptance. Sales and profits are the yardsticks by which such acceptance is measured. In fact, we feel competition is so important that numerous state and federal laws have been passed to strengthen its role. These legislative acts, called *antitrust laws,* preserve the advantages of competition by prohibiting attempts to fix prices and monopolize markets.

In the private enterprise system, firms continually must adjust their strategies, product offerings, service standards, and operating procedures; otherwise, competitors may gain larger shares of the industry's sales and profits. Consider the retailing industry. At one time, Montgomery Ward was a major force in retailing, but Sears beat Montgomery

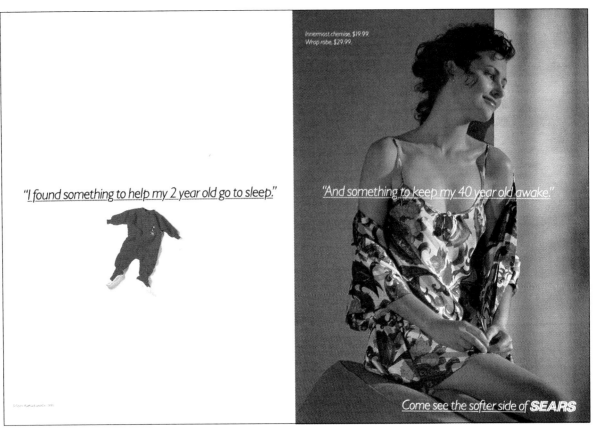

"I found something to help my 2 year old go to sleep."

Innermost chemise, $19.99.
Wrap robe, $29.99.

"And something to keep my 40 year old awake."

Come see the softer side of **SEARS**

Sears's growth strategy involves convincing customers that the retail giant is a source of more than just appliances, hardware, and infant wear.

Ward to take over a major share of the market. In the early 1990s, Sears was overtaken by Wal-Mart, which is not only the nation's largest retailer, but is expanding rapidly into Canada, Mexico, and even into Hong Kong and the People's Republic of China. In the meantime, Sears is attempting to strengthen its competitiveness by eliminating unprofitable activities such as its annual catalogs and featuring new fashion items and well-known electronics and appliance brands to enhance its image as a one-stop source for meeting customer needs.

Competition is the mechanism that guarantees the private enterprise system will continue to offer goods and services that provide high living standards and sophisticated lifestyles. Even not-for-profit organizations, like the American Cancer Society, must compete for contributions with other not-for-profit groups, such as the American Heart Association, the local symphony, or your own college or university. Similarly, government agencies like the U.S. Air Force compete with private industry in attempting to employ qualified personnel.

> **THEY SAID IT**
>
> "Some see private enterprise as a predatory target to be shot, others as a cow to be milked, but few are those who see it as a sturdy horse pulling the wagon."
>
> *Winston Churchill*
> *(1874–1964)*
> *British statesman*
> *and prime minister*

Basic Rights of the Private Enterprise System

Certain rights critical to the operation of capitalism are available to citizens living in a private enterprise economy. These include the rights to private property, profits, freedom of choice, and competition.

The right to *private property* is the most basic freedom under the private enterprise system. The private enterprise system guarantees people the right to own, use, buy, sell, and bequeath most forms of property, including land, buildings, machinery, equipment, inventions, and various intangible properties.

The private enterprise system also guarantees business owners the right to all *profits* (after taxes) earned by the business. Although business is not assured of earning a profit, its owner is legally and ethically entitled to it.

Freedom of choice means that, under a private enterprise system, citizens are free to choose their employment, purchases, and investments. They can change jobs, negotiate wages, join labor unions, and choose among many different brands of goods and services. People living in the capitalist nations of North America, Europe, and other parts of the world are so accustomed to this freedom of choice that they sometimes forget its importance. The private enterprise economy maximizes human welfare and happiness by providing alternatives. Other economic systems sometimes limit freedom of choice in order to accomplish government goals, such as increasing industrial production.

The private enterprise system also permits *fair competition* by allowing the public to set rules for competitive activity. This is why the U.S. government has passed laws to prohibit "cutthroat" competition—excessively competitive practices designed to eliminate competitors. It also has established ground rules that outlaw price discrimination, fraud in financial markets, and deceptive practices in advertising and packaging.

How the Private Enterprise System Works

Capitalism, like other economic systems, requires certain inputs if it is to operate effectively. Economists use the term **factors of production** when they refer to *the four basic inputs of natural resources, capital, human resources, and entrepreneurship.* Not all firms require the same combination of these factors, but each business uses a unique blend of the four inputs.

Natural resources refer to everything useful as a productive input in its natural state, including agricultural land, building sites, forests, and mineral deposits. People who provide these basic resources required in any economic system receive *rent* as a factor payment.

> ### THEY SAID IT
>
> "America is not like a blanket—one piece of unbroken cloth, the same color, the same texture, the same size. America is more like a quilt—many pieces, many colors, many sizes, all woven and held together by a common thread."
>
> *Jesse Jackson
> (1941–   )
> American civil rights
> leader*

Capital, the key resource of technology, tools, information, and physical facilities, frequently determines whether a fledgling computer firm, like Compaq or Microsoft, becomes an industry leader or remains small. *Technology* is a broad term that refers to such machinery and equipment as production machinery, telecommunications, and basic inventions. Information, frequently improved by technological innovations, is also a critical factor, since both management and operative employees require accurate, timely information in order to perform their assigned tasks effectively.

Money is necessary to acquire, maintain, and upgrade a firm's capital. These funds may come from investments of company owners, profits, or loans extended by others. Money then can be used to build factories; purchase raw materials and component parts; and hire, train, and compensate workers. Persons and firms supplying capital receive the factor payment of *interest.*

Human resources, the third factor of production, include the millions of managers and other employees of the world's businesses. Anyone who works, from Jack Welch, the chief executive officer of General Electric Corp., to a self-employed gardener, is a human resource. In return for supplying companies with their managerial and other skills, human resources receive the factor payment of *wages* or *salaries.*

The final production factor is **entrepreneurship,** *the taking of risks involved in creating and operating a business.* The entrepreneur is the risk taker in the private enterprise system, the person who identifies a potentially profitable opportunity and then devises a plan and forms an organization to achieve that goal. Some entrepreneurs set up entirely new companies; others revitalize already-established firms. If they are successful in their efforts, entrepreneurs receive the factor payment of *profits.*

Successful entrepreneurs also receive considerable satisfaction of a nonmonetary nature. Gianna "Gigi" Dekko Goldman is a good example. In 1990, she quit her marketing job at Minnesota-based Minnetonka to start a business selling picture frames to retail giants Dayton Hudson and Saks Fifth Avenue.

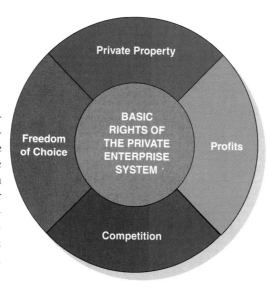

Private Property

Freedom of Choice

BASIC RIGHTS OF THE PRIVATE ENTERPRISE SYSTEM

Profits

Competition

fecting customers. When an HP customer calls with a problem, it automatically is routed to the most appropriate of the firm's four global customer-support centers, depending on the time of day. Often, in complex situations, time can present an obstacle; but for HP employees, finding a solution is an on-going project. At 6:00 P.M. California time, for instance, the assignment moves to the Australian staff and work continues without a hitch.[8]

The five largest U.S. exporters are Boeing, General Motors, General Electric, IBM, and Ford. Coca-Cola, sold in 195 different countries, is an excellent example of a global product. Over 80 percent of the firm's annual profits come from international sales. Kellogg's Corn Flakes are a popular breakfast choice in Great Britain and hundreds of other nations. By expanding its operations beyond its U.S. base, the cereal giant has access to a global marketplace of 5.6 billion inhabitants.

The United States is also an attractive market for foreign competitors. Its size, combined with the standards of living enjoyed by American consumers, has motivated such foreign companies as Mercedes-Benz, Sony, and IKEA to set up production and distribution facilities here. In addition, foreign firms have purchased such well-known companies as Saks Fifth Avenue, 7-Eleven convenience stores, Barnes & Noble book stores, MCA Records, and Universal Studios.

Even the smallest domestic operation is likely to be affected by foreign competition and to depend on foreign suppliers for needed raw materials and finished-goods inventories. Petrofsky's, a St. Louis neighborhood bakery, was able to develop a market for its newly-invented method for quick-freezing uncooked bagel dough by exporting bagels to Japan. The Japanese bagel favorite, cinnamon raisin, produced

Seeing few women executives in corporate America and worried that becoming a mother might lower chances of advancement, Gigi Goldman left her marketing job to found Gianna International.

Today, Gianna International in Rowayton, Connecticut, has more than $1 million in annual sales. A big plus to being her own boss is having a flexible lifestyle, says Goldman, 34. "I wanted to continue my career in an aggressive way, but I also wanted to be a mom."[7]

The entrepreneurial spirit lies at the heart of the private enterprise system. If no one took risks, there would be no successful businesses, and the current economic system could not exist. We will discuss the role of the entrepreneur in more detail in Chapter 5.

TODAY'S BUSINESS IS A GLOBAL BUSINESS

It is virtually impossible to travel outside the United States and fail to observe the internationalization of business. Golden arches, FedEx delivery trucks, and Coca-Cola cans are almost as familiar in Moscow as in Milwaukee. Foreign firms are responsible for building every videocassette player in America. Walkmans offer portable entertainment to music lovers from Tokyo to Toronto to Tijuana.

Global businesses, such as Hewlett-Packard, link their international operations to work on problems af-

Kellogg's cereals are household favorites on every continent.

sales of $1.5 million per year, prompting Petrofsky's to sell its domestic business to Quaker Oats and open retail bagel shops in Tokyo.[9]

Productivity: The Key to Global Competitiveness

To compete in a global marketplace, a nation's economy must be productive. **Productivity** is a measure of efficiency. It can be defined as *the relationship between the number of units of goods and services produced and the number of inputs of human and other resources necessary to produce them.* It is a ratio of output to input and can be calculated for a nation, an industry, or a single firm. When a constant amount of inputs generates increased outputs, an increase in productivity has occurred.

Total productivity considers all inputs necessary to produce a specific amount of outputs. Stated in equation form, it can be written as follows:

$$\text{Total Productivity} = \frac{\text{Output (goods or services produced)}}{\text{Input (human/natural resources, capital)}}.$$

Many productivity ratios focus on only one of the inputs of the equation: labor productivity, or the output per worker-hour. An increase in labor productivity means that the same amount of work produces more goods and services.

A widespread measure of a nation's productivity is its gross domestic product. **Gross domestic product (GDP)** is *the sum of all goods and services produced within a nation's boundaries.*

Productivity is a widely used method for measuring a company's efficiency; in turn, the total productivity of a nation's businesses has become a measure of its economic strength. The first U.S. census, conducted in 1790, revealed that 50 percent of the labor force was engaged in agriculture to feed the nation. Today, less than three percent of the work force not only feeds the nation, but also generates food surpluses for consumers throughout the world. Technological innovations, a growing work force, and infusions of capital to construct more efficient equipment and production facilities have combined to sustain economic growth and improved standards of living for American workers.

Even though the United States continues to lead the world in productivity, the growth of such economies as Germany, Japan, and many Pacific Rim nations has aroused fears that productivity problems may occur in the near future. Concerns have been expressed about the tendency of many American managers to focus too much on short-term goals instead of developing long-range strategies for competing worldwide. News reports of plant closings and work-force reductions often end with discussions of the need to invest more in long-term research, development, and innovation.

Statistics tell a different story. In 1993, for instance, the U.S. standard of living rose 1.9 percent, compared with only 0.9 percent in Japan. U.S. investment in plants and equipment jumped 11.8 percent, compared with a plunge of 8.5 percent in Japan. Recent data reveals that Germany's growth rate has been lower than America's for some 15 years.[10]

Meanwhile, the focus is shifting to service-sector productivity. Over 70 percent of U.S. jobs are now in services, the largest share of any nation. But, as the chart shows, service jobs have been growing even faster overseas. The rapid growth in manufacturing productivity has reduced the share of the labor force needed in the manufacturing sector and prompted workers all over the industrial world to move into services industries. Fortunately, the United States appears to be even further ahead of the pack in service-sector productivity. A recent McKinsey & Co. comparison of U.S. productivity in information and four other service industries with that of Germany, Japan, France, and Britain concluded that U.S. levels are substantially higher. A big reason for the lead is service-company investments in computers, telecommunications networks, and other technologies, enabling their employees to become even more productive.[11]

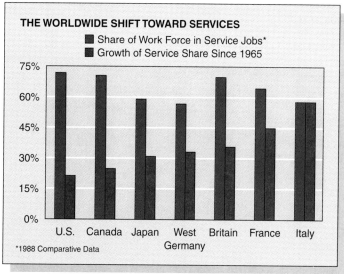

THE WORLDWIDE SHIFT TOWARD SERVICES
■ Share of Work Force in Service Jobs*
■ Growth of Service Share Since 1965
*1988 Comparative Data
U.S. Canada Japan West Germany Britain France Italy

How Businesses Compete

Four basic degrees of competition exist in a private enterprise system: pure competition, monopolistic competition, oligopoly, and monopoly. We can classify firms on the basis of the relative competitiveness of their particular industry.

Pure competition involves *many firms in an industry close enough in size that no single company can influence the prices charged in the marketplace.* Pure competition involves similar products that cannot be differentiated from those of competitors. In a purely competitive market, it is relatively easy for a firm to enter or leave that market. Agriculture is probably the closest example of pure competition (although government price-support programs make it somewhat less competitive) and wheat is an example of a product that is similar from farm to farm.

Monopolistic competition is a *market situation where firms are able to differentiate their products from those of competitors.* You can see monopolistic competition operating when you watch advertisements that try to persuade you to choose one brand over another. Monopolistic competition gives a firm some power over the price it charges. Think about retail stores,

---

DID YOU KNOW?

China has only one telephone per 100 people.

Approximately one-third of the world's inhabitants eat with knives and forks, another third with chopsticks, and the final third with their hands.

U.S. businesses have even managed to sell snowplows to the desert dwellers of Saudi Arabia to remove sand from driveways.

The thumb and forefinger circle "okay" sign used in the United States signifies money in Japan, zero in France, and is a vulgar gesture in Latin America.

In Great Britain, the hood of a car is called a bonnet and the trunk a boot. Windshields are called windscreens, flashlights are torches, and undershirts are known as vests. Even words get new spellings: color is spelled colour, tire becomes tyre, and theater is theatre.

---

where prices can vary among different brands of aspirin, toothpaste, or gasoline.

Oligopoly is a *market in which there are few sellers.* In some oligopolies, such as steel, the products are similar; in others, such as automobiles, they are different. The huge investment required to enter the market tends to discourage new competitors. But the primary difference between oligopoly and the previously mentioned types of competition is that the limited number of sellers gives the oligopolist more control over price. In an oligopoly, the prices of competitive products are usually quite similar because substantial price competition would lessen every firm's profits. Price cuts by one firm in the industry typically are met by all competitors.

Monopoly is a *market situation in which there are no competitors.* Since the Sherman and Clayton Acts prohibit attempts to monopolize markets, nearly all the monopolies in the United States are government-regulated monopolies, such as public utilities. Firms selling electricity and natural gas are regulated by state agencies in the United States. These agencies administer many aspects of the regulated monopolies, including pricing and profits. In a pure monopoly, a firm would have

---

		Types of Competition		
Characteristics	**Pure Competition**	**Monopolistic Competition**	**Oligopoly**	**Monopoly**
Number of competitors	Many	Few to many	Few	No direct competitors
Ease of entry into industry by new firms	Easy	Somewhat difficult	Difficult	Regulated by government
Similarity of goods or services offered by competing firms	Similar	Different	Can be similar or different	No directly competing goods or services
Control over price by individual firms	None	Some	Some	Considerable in a pure monopoly; little in a regulated monopoly
Examples	Small-scale farmer in Pennsylvania	Blockbuster Video	Alcoa	Detroit Edison

substantial control over pricing, but in a regulated monopoly, pricing is subject to rules imposed by the regulators. There are few directly competitive products in a regulated monopoly, and entry into the industry is restricted by the government. In fact, in some states, a public utility periodically must seek voter approval to continue its service.

Most nations of the world contain examples of each type of competition. For example, most businesses in the Czech Republic were state-owned and, until recently, enjoyed monopolies in their respective industries. Today, the Czech economy can be described as an oligopoly that is evolving toward monopolistic competition, as more and more Czech entrepreneurs start small, privately owned businesses. Says Prime Minister Vaclav Klaus, "Three years ago my two sons, at the time 21 and 16, had never in their lives entered a private grocery shop, butcher shop, hairdresser. Today, within a mile of where we live, there probably is not one state-owned shop, cafe, or service."[12]

Nowhere is China's rapid move to capitalism more evident than in Guangdong Province, Hong Kong's closest neighbor of 66 million people. Guangdong's brand-hungry consumers, with the highest incomes in all China, $3,900 annually, can buy Adidas and Reebok sneakers ($95 to $130), Quaker oatmeal ($4.50), Skippy peanut butter ($4), Coke and 7-Up (50 cents per can), and Van Heusen shirts ($16). Fast-food fanciers can purchase Happy Meals from the nearest McDonald's outlet.[13]

BUSINESS OPPORTUNITIES AND CHALLENGES IN THE LATE 1990S

Every period in history has posed particular challenges and obstacles to business, and the current era is no ex-

Ronald McDonald, children's second most-identifiable character (Santa Claus is number one), symbolizes McDonald's for Guangdong boys and girls.

ception. The way that we respond to these challenges today will have a significant impact on America—and the world—tomorrow.

Importance of Partnerships and Strategic Alliances

Traditionally, successful firms were headed by visionaries who bested competition in the marketplace to build their organizations. A growing trend of the late 1990s is for firms to improve their competitiveness by teaming up with other companies to create **strategic alliances,** *partnerships formed to create a competitive advantage.* These long-term partnerships often cross national borders, and can involve any size of company, from the tiniest business to two or more industrial giants. Nowhere are strategic alliances more common than in the telecommunications industry, where U.S. competitors AT&T, MCI, and Sprint are forming alliances with national telephone companies throughout Europe, Central and South America, and Asia in an attempt to achieve global dominance.

Some companies form alliances with transportation carriers to improve moving and storage operations and make joint decisions about physical distribution. Transportation giant Consolidated Freightways has established Menlo Logistics to offer its clients a means of shortening response time and cutting both inventory and transportation costs. By assuming responsibility for everything from dedicated warehousing and shipping to inventory control and order fulfillment, Menlo lets CF customers focus on running their business.

Many strategic alliances involve "partnering" arrangements between suppliers and business customers to develop mutually beneficial initiatives, such as designing new products or trouble-shooting existing ones. For instance, Japan's Honda formed a strategic alliance with U.S. firm Donnelly Corporation to craft an improved type of exterior mirror for Honda cars. As a first step, Honda sent over several engineers to work with Donnelly engineers to improve the efficiency of two Donnelly plants. The resulting savings reduced costs by two percent a year. Then, Donnelly built an entirely new factory, incorporating many of these improvements, and began making Honda's exterior mirrors. The partnership has grown from $5 million in sales the first year to an estimated $60 million in sales by 1997. Both companies plan to make their strategic alliance a permanent arrangement that will benefit each of them. As one Honda manager says, "To Honda, *long term* means forever—assuming you're doing the job."[14]

Strategic alliances abound in many industries. Bailey Controls, which makes control systems for factories, links its computers to Montreal-based Future Electronics and Long Island-headquartered Arrow Electronics to exchange inventory and sales forecast information. Scott Paper negotiates discounts with its suppliers in exchange for a certain level of guaranteed business. Betz Laboratories, which supplies industrial water-treatment chemicals, also provides professional expertise to its partners. A team of Betz engineers works with engineers from customer AlliedSignal to identify ways to improve water purity in AlliedSignal's factories while reducing costs. By using recycled water, for instance, the company was able to save 300 gallons of water a minute; changes like this added up to $2.5 million in annual cost reductions. While this means AlliedSignal will buy fewer water-treatment chemicals, Betz's role as exclusive supplier ensures that its sales to the company will more than double.[15]

Consolidated Freightways uses advanced information technologies in its strategic alliances with firms requiring help in running their distribution networks.

Importance of Quality

While the United States has invented many high-quality items through the years, lately other nations, such as Japan, have developed a reputation for making outstanding products. Business leaders now emphasize the importance of total quality management, a commitment to quality as a crucial business goal for an entire company. It is vital for the United States to develop high-quality goods and services in order to attract new customers. It is also important to maintain quality on a long-term basis to keep those customers coming back for more.

Motorola's strategic alliances, for example, include a strong emphasis on quality. First, the company looks for potential partners that share its corporate focus on quality. It then fosters this approach by requiring partners' employees to take classes at Motorola University in total quality management and customer satisfaction. Even after being chosen as partners, suppliers must maintain rigorous quality standards; Motorola teams tour their factories every two years and grade them against competitors in terms of quality and timeliness. In addition, Motorola managers rate suppliers every month on an index combining cost and quality, and compare their performance against that of competitors.[16]

Quality can be more difficult to provide and measure in service industries than in manufacturing. Indeed, a recent study of the airline industry shows that overall industry quality has slipped over the past four years. Quality measures in air transportation include a wide variety of factors, such as on-time performance, baggage handling, the rate at which passengers are "bumped" from flights, and frequency of low fares. The study rated Southwest Airlines as number one in overall quality; its on-time percentage is 90 percent, for example, compared to an industry-

BUSINESS STRATEGY

How Hampton Inns Offer Quality and Customer Satisfaction by Securing Guest Feedback

One of the best ways to attract and retain customers is to find out what they want and give it to them. That is how Hampton Inns has remained competitive in the lodging industry.

Memphis-based hotel and gaming firm Promus Co. is looking closely at how and why customers choose Hampton Inns, one of its subsidiaries. Its most recent effort to lure more customers to its national chain has been to offer guaranteed refunds to customers who are dissatisfied with their stay for any reason. In 1993, Hampton Inns refunds amounted to $1.1 million—a small price to pay for developing a positive reputation and creating customer loyalty and satisfaction. The new refund policy also generated an additional $11 million in revenues for the chain.

Guest surveys have proven the new policy to be very persuasive, and Hampton Inns management believes it is a win-win situation for everyone. Promus and Hampton Inns are happy, customers are happy, and employees are happy. Under the new policy, everyone from the maids to front-desk clerks now are empowered to grant refunds. Job satisfaction and employee morale have improved;

turnover at the chain fell from 117 percent to a remarkable 50 percent.

A review of guest complaints helps Promus identify areas that need improving. One of the most frequent complaints at its Embassy Suites hotel chain was not being able to get irons and ironing boards when they were needed. Promus always had staffed its hotels with service people who spent their entire time delivering irons from room to room, but no amount of employee training or system planning was successful in providing customers instantly with irons upon request.

When Promus planners examined the problem more closely, they dis-

covered that the chain could put a board and iron in every Embassy Suites room for a cost of roughly $80. By depreciating the expense over four years, the cost would average $20 a room and a total cost of $475,000 per year on the expense side of the account ledger. "We have literally no problems now from an area that was one of the largest complaint generators," says Mark C. Wells, Promus' senior vice president for marketing.

SOURCE: Wells quotation from David Greising, "Quality: How to Make It Pay," *Business Week,* August 8, 1994, 57.

wide average of 82 percent.[17] In Chapter 6, we will take a closer look at the importance of quality in achieving business success.

Importance of Technology

Technology involves *the application to business of knowledge based on discoveries in science, inventions, and innovations.* Technological breakthroughs such as videotelephones, orthoscopic surgery, and bullet

trains result in new goods and services for consumers, better customer service, lower prices, and improved working conditions. Technology can make products obsolete—cassette tapes and CDs, for example, wiped out the market for vinyl record albums—but just as easily can open up new business opportunities.

One in three U.S. households currently contains a personal computer. The number grows to a staggering 68 percent in affluent households headed by college graduates.[18] To address this addition to the typical family's inventory of electronic equipment, a group of

PERCENT OF HOMES CONTAINING COMPUTERS BY EDUCATION AND FAMILY INCOME	$20,000		$30,000–$49,000		$50,000+	
	College Grad	Non Grad	College Grad	Non Grad	College Grad	Non Grad
Has PC in home	30	15	47	30	68	48
Uses modem	10	2	14	4	21	12
Cable-TV subscriber	50	57	61	64	76	74
Has video camera	20	17	28	33	45	51

entrepreneurs introduced a new magazine in 1994: *Family PC.*

This year, companies around the world will spend over $13 billion to buy computer hardware and software. Many of these purchases will involve building new computer networks and expanding existing networks that link employees, suppliers, and customers. Computer networks and electronic mail (E-mail)— a system for sending and receiving written messages through computers—permit a more direct exchange of information within organizations, bypassing formal corporate hierarchies.

Technological developments like networks provide three major benefits for organizations. First, they speed up business operations by allowing people to exchange information and make decisions much more quickly. Second, they bypass functional boundaries; people in different departments can communicate directly rather than going through formal channels. Finally, computer networks allow people with diverse skills to work together. "To develop complex products, you need lots of people with specialized knowledge, working together in a little virtual department," says John Manzo, vice president of engineering at Pitney Bowes.[19]

Changes in technology can create whole new industries and new ways of doing business. Technological innovations, ranging from voice recognition and scanners to advanced fiber optics and on-line services play such an important role in advancing a nation's standard of living that they are featured in every chapter of the text. Next, we will consider two recent technological developments: interactive media and the Internet.

Interactive Media.   Interactive media combine computers and telecommunications to create software that users can direct themselves. Imagine shopping for an apartment on your computer. Want

to see the living room? The screen shifts to that room, allowing you to look around, then goes into the kitchen and on into the bedroom and inside the closets. Want to go to the mall without leaving home? Simply key in the name of the store you want to "visit" and you control the simulated travel up and down the aisles, pausing to examine specific items, determine their sizes and prices, and even place an order. Industry analysts predict that such interactive media soon will become a major player in businesses that together generate more than $300 billion annually in the United States alone. These industries include video games, videotape rentals, cable TV, catalog shopping, TV shopping, and books and periodicals.

Interactive media are likely to affect the future of advertising, too. The SoftAd Group, located in Mill Valley, California, creates interactive marketing materials for clients such as Ford, Abbott Laboratories, and glass manufacturer PPG Industries. Two SoftAd programs have been developed to help viewers learn more about Ford vehicles and the advantages of windows made from PPG glass. Interactive ads like these allow customers to experiment with colors and styles, explore different options, and ask for more information.[20]

The Internet.   More and more businesses are tapping into the Internet, a web of 30,000 computer networks connecting universities, research institutions, not-for-profit and for-profit organizations, and individuals. In 1991, only 144,000 commercially registered computers were linked to the Internet; today there are almost 600,000, and the number continues to grow (see chart). Thirty-five percent of business users use the Internet to communicate with colleagues, while 26 percent use it to stay in touch with customers. Other uses include education, communication with government agencies, and tapping into

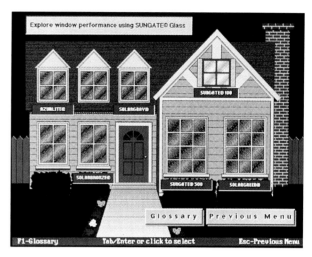

Hawking Fords and PPG glass via interactive advertisements developed by the SoftAd group: Digital glitz combined with lots of information to help with complex buying decisions

the Internet's numerous on-line forums and news groups.[21]

For Alberto Martin, owner of California nightclub Alberto's, the Internet is a great way to publicize upcoming attractions. Martin sends regular on-line messages about the club's specialty, music from Latin America and Africa, to Internet news groups interested in those topics. Internet users with the right computer equipment even can listen to samples from the work of musicians scheduled to play at Alberto's. One day, for instance, Martin announced electroni-

cally that Brazilian stars Gilberto Gil and Caetano Veloso would be performing; in 24 hours he had sold 200 tickets to the event.

The Internet also can help companies solve problems much more quickly. Greenville Tool and Die, a small auto-industry supplier located in Michigan, used to fix software problems in its computer-controlled machinery by mailing a package of computer tapes overnight to its software company in Boston. Solving the problem, and getting corrected tapes back, often took several precious

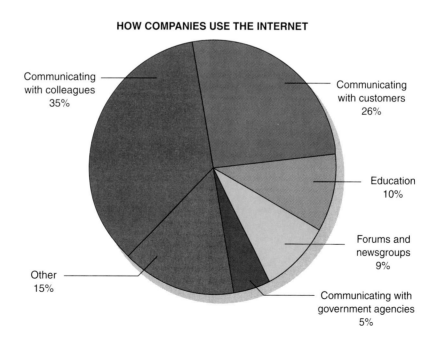

HOW COMPANIES USE THE INTERNET

Communicating with colleagues 35%
Communicating with customers 26%
Education 10%
Forums and newsgroups 9%
Communicating with government agencies 5%
Other 15%

Virtual Reality

Your business is thriving, so you hire an architect and an ergonomical engineer and set out to make the perfect work space. During the first office walk-through, you are delighted with the gigantic windows flooding natural light into the drafting room. You also are pleased with the assorted colors and varied heights of cubical dividers that keep the clerical area from looking too regimented. But you are disappointed that the dark walls in your office overwhelm the simple furniture you prefer. No problem: Just ask the architect to change the computer program—you have been walking in virtual reality.

Or perhaps you are being trained to assemble computer parts in a sterile room. The protective clothing and gloves you wear are unfamiliar, and you drop an expensive component on the floor. That is, you drop an expensive *virtual* component; with no harm done, you continue practicing your new skills.

Virtual reality quickly has matured from its start as a clumsy entertainment curiosity. In early virtual-reality systems, the user donned a large mask or helmet that provided images and sound and a cumbersome sensor-heavy Data Glove. The systems provided changing points of view and some sensory feedback as the user moved head and hand, but the grainy images changed slowly and awkwardly. New technology, however, includes advanced liquid-crystal displays and the Cyber Finger, a wristband that actually responds to the electrical signals sent out by muscles in the user's hand and fingers.

Start-ups like Worldesign are developing virtual-reality technology for use by commercial customers, such as utilities.

The potential of virtual and enhanced reality grows as technology advances. Colt Virtual Reality Ltd. has developed Vegas 2, which provides a library of virtual people. It is used with software from Dimension Ltd. that allows the modeling of emergencies. With this system, an engineer can examine where best to put the exits in a department store, based on the behaviors of virtual shoppers, with their virtual children and even virtual wheelchairs, after a (virtual) fire breaks out.

Using enhanced reality, users wearing special glasses can see whatever is in front of them as well as the enhanced reality image, which might be a pattern or instructions to be followed. A surgeon can have a patient's magnetic resonance imaging scan projected onto the patient's shaved head, allowing exact tumor location.

Virtual and enhanced reality can provide flying lessons on the ground, wind-tunnel testing for computer-generated airplane models, and a way to explore the inside of a molecule.

Due to limitations in current technology, computer speed, and money, some forms of virtual reality will appear later than others, if ever. However, Roy Latham, president of Computer Graphics Systems Development says, "By the year 2000, I believe we will have real-time virtual environments in the home."

SOURCE: "Virtual Reality Gets Real," *Inc.,* July 1994, 31.

days. One night, Greenville employees were so frustrated by a software glitch that they sent an electronic appeal for help via the Internet to the man who originally wrote the software—who happened to live in New Zealand. The software writer promptly fixed the problem and zapped the solution back in time for work to start the next morning.[22] In Chapter 10, we will take a closer look at how various technologies can help business people make better decisions.

Importance of Focusing on People

Earlier, we noted that people are a crucial input to any economic system. Ironically, perhaps, the growing importance of technology makes it even more important for organizations to make effective use of human resources. Computer networks allow employees to work together directly and pool their collective knowledge. This tends to flatten the organizational hierarchy, creating a more informal organization.

More and more organizations are discovering the benefits of teamwork, in which employees work together on a project. At Lotus Development, software writers in Asia and Europe team up via computer networks with their American colleagues to develop new products. It used to take Lotus three to four months to create a Japanese version of a new English-language software package; thanks to international teamwork, it now takes three to four weeks.

Teamwork allows organizations to reap the benefits of a wide range of employee skills. Insurer Marsh & McLennan, for instance, assembles teams of specialists in different areas to handle projects. A broker in Madrid who wants to insure a Spanish oil and gas company might call together a team consisting of industry experts from the New York headquarters and specialists in secondary markets from London. Team members work together for the duration of the project to share knowledge about the oil and gas industry and suggest ways to spread the risk. When the job is finished, the team disbands as members join other teams to cooperate on other initiatives.

Empowerment also requires employees to develop greater aptitude for analyzing situations and making their own decisions. Westin Hotels, for instance, has created a set of skill standards for recruiting, hiring, training, and retaining its 35,000 employees. Hotel managers identified 14 key characteristics that effective employees must possess, no matter what their organizational rank. In addition to technical competence, these skills include the ability to show initiative, a commitment to quality, and good communication skills. Since Westin began screening for employees who possess these skills and the ability to manage themselves, its employee turnover rate has fallen dramatically.

Importance of Outsourcing

Another fast-growing trend in business is *outsourcing*, in which a company farms out one or more of its in-house operations to a preferred vendor with a high quality level in those particular task areas. Outsourcing can save money because a company does not have to hire additional staff to perform those functions, thereby producing savings on salaries and benefits, while freeing existing personnel to do other tasks. For example, a firm may outsource its warehousing, payroll, delivery services, or data-processing operations. Eastman Kodak has outsourced its computer operations to IBM; large oil companies often outsource cleaning and maintenance work on oil refineries.[23]

In Chapter 3, we will look at outsourcing as a way to enter foreign markets. In Chapters 7 and 8, we will examine different management styles and how outsourcing can enhance the productivity of an organization's human resource. Chapter 9 will explore the importance of teamwork and communication skills in building an effective organization.

THE MANAGER OF THE LATE 1990S

Leadership is a trait that has long been admired. As Italian statesman Niccolo Machiavelli remarked 500 years ago, "There is nothing more difficult to take in hand, more perilous to conduct, or more uncertain in its success than to take the lead in the introduction of a new order of things."[24]

What qualities will the successful manager of the future need? Among the most important will be the ability to manage change, create and sustain a vision of how an organization can succeed, apply critical thinking and creativity to business challenges, and manage an increasingly diverse work force.

THEY SAID IT

"It doesn't matter if a cat is black or white, so long as it catches mice."

Deng Xiaoping (1904–   ) Chinese prime minister

Need for a New Type of Manager

Once, managers were encouraged to be "organization men," grey flannel suit wearers who worked in a world of strict dress codes and rigid hierarchies. To be successful today, however, an organization must remain flexible and open to change. Businesses must be able to update technologies, identify new marketplace needs, create new goods and services, and stay ahead of global as well as domestic competitors. This creates a need for a new type of manager who can serve as a change agent—one who can perceive the need for change and can manage the change process successfully.

Factors that require organizational change can come from both external and internal sources; successful managers must be aware of both. External forces might include feedback from customers, developments in the international marketplace, economic trends, and new technologies. Internal factors might arise from new company goals, employee needs, labor-union demands, or problems in production lines.

Management at Fujitsu Corporation, for example, perceived a need for greater computer power to improve aerospace research in order to become more competitive. Fujitsu worked with officials at Japan's Science & Technology Agency to build a huge supercomputer that achieves the world's fastest computing speed for aerodynamic simulations. Fujitsu uses the computer to help design aircraft and perform other scientific calculations. Tohru Amano, a research director at the agency, believes that investment in sophisticated computers is a crucial way to prepare for future changes, too. "In the coming century," he predicts, "the world will need these tools to cope with new scientific parameters."[25]

Need for a Vision

A second important managerial quality is **vision,** *the ability to perceive marketplace needs and what an organization must do to satisfy them.* Thomas Edison, the famed inventor of thousands of products ranging from the electric light bulb to the phonograph and motion picture, was such a person. Not only did he have the ability to make great technological breakthroughs, but he also never forgot to focus on *salable solutions* to very real problems. As he put it, "Anything that won't sell, I don't want to invent. Its sales is proof of utility and utility is success."[26] Other well-known visionaries include:

- Fred Smith, who conceived of a nationwide overnight package delivery service with a sorting hub in Memphis, called Federal Express;
- Anita Roddick, whose natural skin products and cosmetics produced and packaged in an environmentally conscious manner are the basis of The Body Shop global chain of retail outlets; and
- Wally Amos, a pioneer in producing and marketing premium-priced, high-quality gourmet cookies in the United States and abroad.

When it comes to vision, few business people can match entrepreneur Edward Tuck. An electrical engineer who flies planes as a hobby, Tuck recently conceived the idea of building a network of hundreds of low-orbiting satellites to facilitate global communication. After all, a huge potential market exists: 50 percent of the world's population lives at least two hours away from a phone.

Tuck has been joined by two other entrepreneurs who also are known for possessing vision: William Gates, who started software manufacturer Microsoft, and Craig McCaw, who founded McCaw Cellular. The three plan to build a huge system of 840 low-orbit satellites—almost three times the number of satellites currently orbiting the earth. The system, called Teledesic, will provide videoconferencing, interactive media, and other information services to subscribers around the world.

Although Teledesic will cost $9 billion to build, it offers a totally new level of service to subscribers. Teledesic customers will be able to send and receive an almost unlimited amount of voice, data, and video information.[27]

Importance of Critical Thinking and Creativity

Critical thinking and creativity are essential qualities in a good manager. **Critical thinking** refers to *the process of determining the authenticity, accuracy, and worth of information, knowledge claims, or arguments.* Perhaps a simpler description would define it as "informed skepticism." Critical thinkers do not just accept what they hear or see at face value; they evaluate the information and form their own conclusions.[28]

Creativity is *the development of novel solutions to perceived organizational problems.* Creativity always has been a valuable skill in business. Swiss engineer George de Mestral noticed that burrs stuck to his wool socks because of their tiny hooks, and invented Velcro. Leonardo da Vinci's idea for a helicopter came from watching leaves twirl in the wind.

Similarly, Clarence Birdseye observed a natural phenomenon and developed a process that led to his founding of General Foods. As a fisherman and fur trader in Labrador, Birdseye found that fish that are pulled out of the water through holes cut in the ice froze instantly in air temperatures below 40°. When thawed, though, the fish were tender, flaky, and moist—the next best thing to fresh fish. Subsequent quick-freezing experiments with caribou, geese, and even heads of cabbage proved equally satisfactory. A decade later, Birdseye cashed in his life insurance policy and used the money to design a sophisticated

THEY SAID IT

"It is better to light a candle than to curse the darkness."

Chinese proverb (motto of the Christopher Society)

HOW TO DEVELOP CRITICAL THINKING AND CREATIVE SKILLS

OPEN YOUR MIND

- Become aware of the need to be more creative.
- Recognize your routine patterns of thought and behavior.

PUT YOURSELF IN SOMEONE ELSE'S SHOES

- Pretend you are a customer of a particular company and think of five things you would do to improve it.
- Repeat the exercise from the viewpoints of a sales representative for that company, an employee, and a dissatisfied customer.

PUT THE ISSUES IN REVERSE

- Name good ways for a company to *lose* customers.
- Name good reasons for *not* buying a product.
- List ways a company could destroy a good relationship with a customer or supplier.

FORCE CONNECTIONS

- Select six photos of dissimilar items. Number the photos, roll a pair of dice, match the two numbers with the pictures, and create a statement that explains how these two items could be "connected" to create a new product or service.
- Select 50 nouns at random from a dictionary. Write each word on a card, shuffle the cards, draw two, and make a connection between the resulting pair of words.

LOOK FOR INSPIRATION IN NEW PLACES

- Take a different route to school or work. What do you notice?
- Look for new product or service ideas in unusual places: an airport, doctor's office, theater, sporting event. What other possible sources can you think of?

SEEK MULTIPLE SOLUTIONS

- Choose a routine task that you perform frequently. Ask yourself, "How else could I do this?" "What might happen if I did it another way?"

quick-freeze machine. In so doing, he created a multibillion-dollar industry, gave farmers the incentive to grow crops for a year-round market, and—in the case of frozen orange juice—created a product where none had existed before.[29]

Successful managers design an organization to encourage creativity and critical thinking. These organizations tend to be loosely structured; employees frequently have overlapping responsibilities, work in teams, and enjoy a great deal of flexibility in carrying out assignments. Managers in such companies encourage employees to learn new skills and experiment with new approaches; they reward innovation but do not punish people for making honest mistakes in the process.

James Collins, a professor at the Stanford Business School who has studied a number of innovative companies, compares creative, critical thinkers to clockmakers, as opposed to timekeepers. "A timekeeper churns out product without any thought of where he's headed," explains Collins. "A clockmaker builds a company to last. He or she isn't wedded to any single product or idea. . . . Entrepreneurs should have a vision for their company first, then experiment, sometimes unsuccessfully, with ideas."[30]

Reaping the Benefits of Diversity

The old stereotype of the WASP (white Anglo-Saxon Protestant male) as a fixture in the work place and the marketplace is a far cry from the reality of the late 1990s. **Diversity,** *the blend of persons of different genders, ethnic backgrounds, cultures, religions, ages, and* *physical and mental challenges*, continues to enrich our culture and our modern business practices.

Enlightened managers recognize the gains their organizations receive from encouraging all of their employees to contribute. In fact, our economy depends on it. By the year 2000, nearly 85 percent of the people entering the U.S. work force will be women, minorities, and immigrants. Over this same period, the percentage of white males in the labor force is expected to shrink from 51 percent to 45 percent.

Several studies have shown that diverse employee teams and work forces tend to perform better and come up with better solutions to business problems than homogeneous groups do. As we saw in the opening story to this chapter, feedback from Hispanic employees helped Levi Strauss fine-tune its marketing to the Latino population.

Diversity is also a trend outside the United States. As more companies engage in global production and marketing, they tend to hire employees from an ever-wider range of cultures and backgrounds. Matsushita Corporation, for instance, employs 254,000 people in Japan, but it also hires 99,000 people in 150 factories located in 38 other countries. Each factory reflects the customs and work practices of its host country. In Matsushita's Malaysian factories, for example, company cafeterias serve Chinese, Malaysian, and Indian foods. The firm accommodates Muslim religious customs by providing prayer rooms and allowing two prayer sessions on each work shift.[31]

We will discuss diversity further in Chapters 2 and 8. In Chapter 9, we examine it in relation to employee work teams.

DOING WELL BY DOING GOOD

In recent years, headlines have publicized the unethical conduct of several well-known business people.

What Would You Do for Money?

Ex-CIA agent Aldrich Ames is accused of selling secrets to the Soviet Union for $2.5 million.

Representative Dan Rostenkowski, under indictment on 17 federal counts, allegedly embezzled $500,000 in public funds.

Hillary Clinton used friends to make a $100,000 profit in commodities trading.

James Jett is accused of making phantom trades at Kidder Peabody, perhaps accumulating as much as $350 million in false profits.

Securities trader Michael Milken served time in prison after being convicted of securities-related violations. The federal government investigated high-level managers at respected financial firm Salomon Brothers after they were accused of unfair bond trades that cost investors around the world more than $100 million.[32]

Despite the headlines, however, the fact remains that most business people believe in the principles of ethics and social responsibility. **Business ethics** refer to *the standards of business conduct and moral values.* They involve the right and wrong actions that arise in any work environment. While sometimes a conflict may appear to exist between decisions that are ethical and those that are practical or profitable, it is nonetheless essential for companies to evaluate their ethical responsibilities in decision making.

As we saw in the chapter introduction, companies' relationships with their suppliers may lead to ethical dilemmas. Like Levi's, many firms may find that their vendors are violating labor laws by underpaying workers and forcing them to work in poorly lit, dangerous conditions. The garment industry includes roughly 22,000 small contractors, many of which pay employees less than minimum wage. To make sure that its suppliers pay their employees minimum wage and overtime, Patagonia audits contractors' timecards several times a year. Managers at Guess? collect weekly reports from their clothing contractors to monitor their wage and overtime payments.[33]

Social responsibility is *a management philosophy that highlights the social and economic effects of managerial decisions.* For instance, business decisions can impact the environment. We are becoming increasingly aware that the earth's resources are not limitless. In fact, it is possible for us to run out of natural resources, or to pollute our water and air so badly that it will affect the way we live. (Just ask people in downtown Mexico City, where the air is so filthy that many residents suffer from chronic coughs and bronchitis.)

Protecting the environment is a social responsibility of business today and an important corporate objective.

Enlightened business managers must find creative ways to make a profit without damaging the environment. A good example of attempts to protect our fragile ecosystem is the banning of CFC refrigerants that threaten the ozone layer. Since 1994, automobile air-conditioning systems have been redesigned to use CFC-free coolants.

Social responsibility also includes addressing the needs of employees and the general public. As more women enter the work force, and as more children come from single-parent families, child care and elder care are becoming crucial needs. At the present time, a relatively small percentage of firms offer child- and elder-care help to employees, whether through subsidies or by sponsoring day-care centers at the work site. Firms providing such programs, however, have found that they reduce employee absenteeism and turnover, and serve as effective recruiting tools.

A growing number of lending agencies are discovering that it is possible to meet both their fiscal and their social responsibilities. The Dominican Republic-based Ademi Bank allocates a certain percentage of its lending to poor would-be entrepreneurs who devise business plans with a reasonable chance of success. One customer is Cristina Narcisa Nunez, who used an Ademi loan to start an open-air button factory outside Santo Domingo. Today, her factory's 26 employees generate average monthly sales of $18,000 from buttons cut from coconut shells and then shipped to Italian clothing makers. Nunez enjoys the independence of running her own company. "You have to love it because it's yours," she says.[34] In Chapter 2, we will explore business ethics and social responsibility in greater detail.

WHAT'S AHEAD

The study of business is an exciting, rewarding field involving a global landscape that always is changing. Now that we have introduced some basic terms and issues in the business world of the late 1990s, let's identify several major themes that we will encounter in the remainder of this book. Throughout the text, we discuss six major issues crucial in the coming years:

- Ethics and social responsibility
- Diversity

- The importance of technology
- The need for improved productivity and continuous improvement in quality
- The importance of well-trained human resources who are empowered to make decisions about their work, flexible enough to succeed in different work areas, and work well with people from different departments inside the organization
- Global competitiveness.

Each of the essential business activities and functions—developing objectives and creating plans; establishing an effective work force; fostering teamwork and communication; obtaining and using needed information; and producing, marketing, and financing the firm's output—are the subjects of the following 15 chapters. We begin our study of business by examining the business environment and its responsibilities in Chapter 2.

SUMMARY OF LEARNING GOALS

1. **Explain what a business is and how it operates within the private enterprise system.**
   Business consists of all profit-seeking activities and enterprises that provide the goods and services necessary to an economic system. The United States has a capitalist economy, a private enterprise system in which success is determined by competition among business firms.

2. **Define the roles of competition and of the entrepreneur in a private enterprise system.**
   Competition is the battle among businesses for consumer acceptance. It is a critical aspect of the private enterprise system that helps to determine which companies succeed. An entrepreneur is a risk taker, someone who finds a profitable opportunity and forms a business to fill that need. Profits are the financial rewards achieved by successful entrepreneurs and business people.

3. **Outline the basic rights of the private enterprise system.**
   Certain basic rights are available to citizens living in a private enterprise economy: the right to private property; the legal and ethical right to any profits that might result from an enterprise; the freedom of choice in purchases, employment, and investments; and the right to set ground rules for competitive activity.

4. **Explain the concepts of gross domestic product and productivity.**
   Productivity, the relationship between the number of units of goods and services produced and the number of inputs of human and other resources necessary to produce them, is a measure of the efficiency of production. Productivity gains are important to a country's economic health because they lead to higher living standards and greater global competitiveness. A widespread measure of a nation's productivity is its gross domestic product (GDP). As more and more industries compete in a global marketplace, productivity will become an even more crucial factor in a nation's economic health.

5. **Identify the degrees of competition that can exist in a private enterprise system.**
   The four basic degrees of competition in a private enterprise system are pure competition, monopolistic competition, oligopoly, and monopoly. In pure competition, products are similar, there are many firms in a particular industry, and firms are close enough in size that no one company can influence prices. In monopolistic competition, firms are able to differentiate their products from those of competitors, giving companies some control over the prices they can charge. Oligopoly is a market in which there are few sellers, so the firms have more control over prices. Monopoly involves a situation in which a firm has no competitors, so it has substantial control over its prices unless they are regulated by the government.

6. **Discuss the major challenges and opportunities facing managers in the late 1990s.**
   Challenges include
   1. the possibility of forming strategic alliances with other firms to create a competitive advantage;
   2. an emphasis on quality as a crucial business goal for an entire company;
   3. investments in technology that speed up business operations, bypass functional boundaries, and allow people with diverse skills to work together;
   4. the need to make effective use of human resources through teamwork, empowerment, and training; and
   5. the growth of outsourcing, which can save a company money while offering important business opportunities.

   Two important technological developments are interactive media and the Internet.

7. **Describe the most important qualities that managers should possess.**
   Among the most important qualities for managers are the ability to manage change, create and sustain a vision of how an organization can succeed, apply critical thinking and creativity to business challenges, and manage an increasingly diverse work force. Factors that necessitate organizational change can come from both external and internal sources; successful managers must be aware of both. Successful managers design an organization to encourage creativity and critical thinking. Multicultural diversity always has been a fact of American life, as new immigrants and cultures continually enter U.S. society. Furthermore, as more companies engage in worldwide

production and marketing, they tend to hire employees from an ever-wider range of cultures, ages, genders, and backgrounds.

8. Explain the ethical and social responsibilities of business.

Most business people believe in the principles of ethics and social responsibility. Business ethics deals with the right and wrong actions that arise in any work environment. Social responsibility is a management philosophy that highlights the social and economic effects of managerial decisions. Ethical and social responsibilities involve being aware of how business decisions can impact the environment, employees, and the general public.

KEY TERMS QUIZ

business ethics · productivity · technology
strategic alliance · vision · entrepreneurship
diversity · pure competition · not-for-profit organization
monopoly · private enterprise system · profits
critical thinking · social responsibility · oligopoly
business · monopolistic competition · gross domestic product (GDP)
creativity · factors of production

business 1. All profit-seeking activities and enterprises that provide goods and services necessary to an economic system.

profits 2. Rewards for the business person who takes the risks involved in blending people, technology, and information in creating and marketing want-satisfying goods and services that provide customer satisfaction.

not-for-profit organization 3. Organization whose primary objective is something other than returning profits to their owners.

private enterprise system 4. Economic system in which success or failure is determined by how well firms match and counter the offering of competitors.

factors of production 5. Basic inputs into the private enterprise system, including natural resources, labor, capital, and entrepreneurship.

entrepreneurship 6. Taking risks to set up and operate a business.

productivity 7. The relationship between the number of units of goods and services produced and the number of inputs of human and other resources necessary to produce them.

GDP 8. Sum of all goods and services produced within a nation's boundaries.

pure competition 9. Situation in which there are many firms in an industry and none can influence market prices individually.

monopolistic competition 10. Situation in which firms differentiate their products from those of competitors.

oligopoly 11. Market having few sellers and substantial entry restrictions.

monopoly 12. Market situation in which there are no direct competitors.

strategic alliance 13. Partnerships formed to create a competitive advantage.

technology 14. The application to business of knowledge based on discoveries in science, inventions, and innovations.

vision 15. The ability to perceive marketplace needs and what an organization must do to satisfy them.

critical thinking 16. The process of determining the authenticity, accuracy, and worth of information, knowledge claims, or arguments.

creativity 17. The development of novel solutions to perceived organizational problems.

diversity 18. The blend of persons of different genders, ethnic backgrounds, cultures, religions, ages, and physical and mental challenges.

business ethics 19. Standards of business conduct and moral values.

social responsibility 20. Management philosophy that highlights the social and economic effects of managerial decisions.

OTHER IMPORTANT TERMS

antitrust laws   human resources
capital   natural resources
competition

REVIEW QUESTIONS

1. Define profit and explain its role in the private enterprise system.
2. What roles do entrepreneurs play in the private enterprise system? What type of people become entrepreneurs?
3. Discuss the basic rights upon which the private enterprise system is based. How does each right contribute to the effective functioning of the private enterprise system?
4. Identify and describe the components of the private enterprise system.
5. What is meant by the term *productivity*? Why is productivity an important public issue today? How might American businesses foster greater productivity?
6. The four basic degrees of competition are pure competition, monopolistic competition, oligopoly, and mo-

nopoly. Match these types with the businesses listed below:
   a. Chevron
   b. Southwestern Bell Telephone
   c. Wal-Mart
   d. Sid Olsen's 640-acre farm in southern Minnesota
7. What can a company gain from forming a strategic alliance?
8. Why are critical thinking and creativity important characteristics in a manager?
9. Explain the benefits of hiring a culturally diverse work force.
10. Is it realistic for a profit-seeking company to "do well by doing good"? Defend your answer.

DISCUSSION QUESTIONS

1. Apply the creativity exercises suggested in the chapter to a problem you have experienced at school or work. What solutions can you devise?
2. Profit sometimes has been described as the regulator of the private enterprise system. Discuss the meaning of this comment.
3. The chapter presents a list of challenges that the United States must face in order to remain competitive in international business. Suppose the president of the United States gave you the political power to address these challenges. Describe the steps you think the United States should take.

4. Have you ever been in a situation in which you felt yourself to be a minority? Describe how you felt. What could other people who were present have said or done to make you feel more a part of the group? Relate this situation to steps that managers could take to manage a diverse work force effectively.
5. Comment on this statement: "All organizations must serve their customers or clients in some way if they are to survive."

VIDEO CASE: Lincoln Electric

This video illustrates how effective human resource programs have allowed this manufacturer of arc welding machines and motors to compete successfully throughout the world. It is included on page 409 of Appendix D.

Solution to Key Terms Quiz

1. business **2.** profits **3.** not-for-profit organization **4.** private enterprise system **5.** factors of production **6.** entrepreneurship **7.** productivity **8.** gross domestic product (GDP) **9.** pure competition **10.** monopolistic competition **11.** oligopoly **12.** monopoly **13.** strategic alliance **14.** technology **15.** vision **16.** critical thinking **17.** creativity **18.** diversity **19.** business ethics **20.** social responsibility

CHAPTER 2

Business: Its Environment and Role in Society

Learning Goals

1. Discuss the competitive issues that the United States faces in an increasingly global economy.
2. Explain how government regulates business.
3. Summarize the relationship between supply, demand, and price.
4. Describe how the social-cultural environment can impact business.
5. Discuss ways in which the technological environment can affect business.
6. Outline business's responsibilities to the general public.
7. Identify business's responsibilities to customers.
8. Describe business's responsibilities to employees.
9. Explain business's responsibilities to investors and to the financial community.

Approximately 30 percent of the U.S. population smokes; these smokers consume over 550 billion cigarettes every year. And here's another fact: Lung cancer is a major killer in the United States, and 96 percent of the people who die from it are cigarette smokers.

These gloomy statistics explain why the tobacco industry has found itself the unwilling focus of a controversial debate on business ethics. Cigarette manufacturers long have claimed that there is no proven connection between lung cancer and smoking. They also deny making any attempt to market cigarettes to children and teenagers. Surely, they say, companies operating in a free enterprise system should be able to make and market their products without government interference.

Opposing this viewpoint are many public interest groups, consumer advocates, and health-care professionals, such as the American Medical Association (AMA). Numerous medical studies have shown a relationship between rates of smoking and the incidence of lung cancer and other diseases. Reports published in the *Journal of the American Medical Association* have accused tobacco marketers of deliberately targeting children and teenagers in much of their advertising; indeed, most smokers do start the habit during their teenaged years. Surely, say antismoking advocates, business has an ethical responsibility not to market products that are so clearly harmful to the public health. Dr. Thomas Houston, AMA director of preventive medicine and public health, urges physicians "to get the general public enraged at what the tobacco industry is doing to their health."

One of the most vociferous antismoking crusaders is Representative Henry A. Waxman of California, who claims that the effects of tobacco use cost the U.S. health-care system $50 billion a year. Tobacco usage, says Waxman, is "the single, most preventable factor in the rising costs of health care. Until we improve control of tobacco use, it is going to be difficult to control medical costs."

Waxman believes the government should toughen legislation to discourage tobacco use. Noting that the industry spends more than $4 billion a year to promote its products, he has proposed a bill called the Tobacco Education and Child Protection Act that would impose further restrictions on tobacco marketing. Among other prohibitions, the act would restrict tobacco advertising in connection with athletic and music events and mandate stern new warnings on tobacco packaging, including the blunt "Cigarettes can kill you."

Waxman also wants to impose a stiff tax of $2 a pack on cigarettes, a proposal supported by AMA President Dr. Joseph Painter. Says Painter, "As the price of tobacco goes up, the number of people who use it decreases"; he notes that tobacco consumption in Canada fell drastically after the Canadian government imposed higher taxes.

Among the points of disagreement is whether cigarettes are truly addictive. Opponents contend that nicotine, a key ingredient in cigarette smoke, is a potent addictive substance. Cigarette manufacturers, for their part, claim that cigarettes are not addictive, that smokers smoke because they want to and can stop any time they wish. Until recently, they also could point out that nicotine's addictiveness never had been scientifically proven.

Waxman, however, claims that Philip Morris, maker of the popular Marlboro cigarettes, blocked publication over a decade ago of a study that proved just that. At that time Philip Morris employed psychologist Victor DeNoble to do research on nicotine. DeNoble's experiments demonstrated that laboratory rats exposed to nicotine seemed to crave more of the substance. He wrote an article on his research, submitted it to the journal *Psychopharmacology*—and then withdrew it. His decision not to publish, he wrote the journal editor, was "due to factors beyond my control." DeNoble tried again to publish the article three years later, after he had left Philip Morris, and again withdrew it; a letter from a coauthor refers to an injunction by Philip Morris against publication of the article.

Waxman charges that Philip Morris executives blocked DeNoble's article because they feared it would provide ammunition for stricter government regulation. "The nation's largest tobacco company has had relevant information for years about the important role nicotine plays in preventing smokers from quitting," Waxman alleges. "Despite this, the tobacco industry has denied that nicotine is addictive. . . . Rats aren't open to ads or to peer pressure. Now what do you think the cause of their addiction to cigarettes is?" Executives at the company deny that they got an injunction against DeNoble's paper.

The debate continues, as officials at the Food and Drug Administration ponder whether the government should begin regulating tobacco products as a drug, and more research studies bear out DeNoble's conclusions. William Corrigall of the Addiction Research Foundation in Toronto believes that nicotine "is clearly addictive in people. People [like rats] will increase their workload to get nicotine. They will pay more for cigarettes. They will smoke outside in snow storms and rainstorms."[1]

CHAPTER OVERVIEW

Most of us would agree that business should be ethical and socially responsible. Business people in all industries need to think seriously about the environment in which they operate and the role that they play in society.

This chapter begins by describing five major forces that affect the business environment; these forces are important because they provide the frame of reference within which business decisions are made. We will examine major challenges that impact the competitiveness of the United States in the global market and discuss the role of social responsibility and ethics in business decision making. We will conclude by considering the responsibilities that business owes to the general public, its customers, employees, investors, and the financial community.

THE ENVIRONMENT FOR BUSINESS

It is crucial for business people to monitor trends and developments in the business environment continually. There are five major environmental factors that impact business: competition, regulation, the economy, the social/cultural environment, and technology. Note that some of these factors are beyond a business person's control, while others can be changed; a manager who is concerned about a specific piece of legislation, for example, can lobby against it.

Competitive Environment

As we move toward the year 2000, the world is shifting toward an increasingly global economy. As an illustration, consider the annual number of international telephone calls placed to and from the United States; over the past decade, this number has soared from 500 million to almost 2.5 billion each year.[2] This development changes the competitive environment for business, both in the United States and in other countries. While companies may be powerhouses at home, in this expanded worldwide setting, they become less significant. The big challenge today is for the United States to develop its ability to compete in a global market.

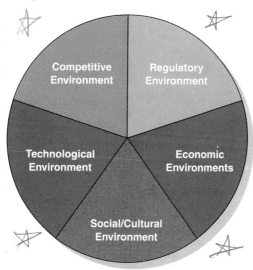

The environmental factors impacting business

Traditionally, a firm's competitiveness depended on its ability to keep its costs down. If it could produce something more cheaply, then it could price products lower and "out sell" the competition. A company's competitiveness also was linked to the resources available in its particular geographic location. Today, however, we are seeing a shift from competition based on costs to competition based on many factors, including product design, product development, and efficient use of technology. Firms succeed or fail based on the quality and service that they provide. Improvements in technology and transportation have made companies independent of their locations. Information can be passed around the world; workers in Ireland or the Bahamas can process data gathered in Asia, for instance, and transmit it to the United States with the touch of a button.

We will examine several competitive issues in an increasingly global economy. These issues include researching and developing better products, improving quality and service, improving the competitiveness of the work force, and improving organizational flexibility.

Researching and Developing Better Products. A crucial factor in keeping America competitive is **research and development,** *the scientific process of developing new commercial products.* R&D, as it often is called, can create totally new industries (such as airplanes and automobiles in an earlier day) and can dramatically change already existing industries (think about how computers have transformed so many people's jobs).

Designing and developing a winning new product is not easy. Only one of every 20 to 25 ideas ever actually leads to a new product—and out of every 10 or 15 new products, only one becomes a commercial hit. However, companies that invest wisely in R&D are able to develop new products efficiently, before competitors beat them to market. Chrysler, for instance, developed its affordable Neon car in 31 months at a cost of $1.3 billion, which is low by industry standards.[3]

Improving Quality and Customer Service. Vital to global competitiveness are improvements in product quality and customer service. Says Jack Welch, chief executive of General Electric, "If you can't meet a world standard of quality at the world's best price, you're not even in the game." M. A. Hanna, a polymer maker with $1.3 billion in annual sales, invested in new computerized systems to speed up the company's production process, reduce inventory, and cut the amount of

New products may replace existing technologies or transform them radically, as RCA hopes to do with its digital satellite system. Large, unsightly satellite dishes would give way to 18-inch mini-dishes like the one pictured here.

TECHNOLOGY

Businesses thrive on information the way mammals thrive on oxygen; without it, they'd die. The development of sophisticated computer databases has allowed more access to more information more quickly than dreamed possible even 20 years ago. Most importantly, databases allowed data to be easily grouped, categorized, cross-referenced, and examined.

Databases are particularly useful to research businesses. Databases that can be accessed by telephone include *Dialog,* which specializes in business information and features TRW Business Credit Profiles and On-line, and the *Economic Bulletin Board* (run by the U.S. Department of Commerce), which includes census, industry, and general economic statistics. Databases that are available for purchase on CD-ROM include *Moody's Company Data,* which features financial information on 10,000 businesses, and *IBID,* which lists all books in print for booksellers.

Databases can be developed from scratch to meet specific goals. In Franklin Park, Illinois, the library and chamber of commerce set up a database of Franklin Park businesses.

What started as little more than a mailing list grew to a major information base with extensive indexes. The database is used by customers, wholesalers seeking to supply local stores, and advertisers.

Fingerhut, a catalogue retailer with over 13 million customers, relies on its own extensive database to tailor its sales efforts to the particular wants, needs, and habits of its shoppers. First Fingerhut assembles some 1,400 pieces of information on each household, ranging from past purchases and income to the birthdays and sexes of the children. Then statisticians predict future purchases of customers based on their past histories. Using this information to generate individualized promotions and specialty catalogues, Fingerhut efficiently matches customers to the items they are most likely to buy. For instance, a greeting from Fingerhut to parents before a child's birthday includes information on age-appropriate toys for sale plus the promise of free gifts. It's no surprise that Fingerhut is the fourth largest mail-order company in the United States.

Some commercial databases fill extremely specialized niches. One type is used by employers who need to prove that they turned down a job applicant based on skills and job requirements rather than the applicant's sex or race or disability. These databases include complete, detailed job descriptions (sometimes based on the U.S. Department of Labor's *Dictionary of Occupational Titles*) that can be edited to fit the needs of a particular employer.

An old cliche says that love makes the world go 'round. Another says that money makes the world go 'round. Nowadays, however, it may well be information that keeps the globe turning.

SOURCES: Jim Bessen, "Riding the Marketing Information Wave," *Harvard Business Review,* September–October 1993, 150–160; Michael P. Cronin, "Choosing Job-Description Software," *Inc.,* February 1993, 30; Patrick Marshall, "On-Line and on Track," *Inc.* (Special Issue: "The Office Technology Advisor"), Fall 1992, 42–47; and Bob Watson and Lawrence Boyle, "The Growth of a Business Directory," *RQ,* Fall 1992, 10–13.

scrap from its factories. These improvements have paid off; over the past four years, the firm has reduced by one-third the amount of working capital necessary to earn a dollar of sales. Lexus and Infiniti have stolen market share from German and American luxury cars by offering better quality at prices that average 40 percent less.

Another important aspect of competitiveness is **customer service**—*the aspect of competitive strategy that refers to how a firm treats its customers.* Competitive firms make it as easy as possible for customers to order and receive their products. Notes Robert Immerman, founder of Ohio-based InterDesign, which sells small plastic items to retailers, "In the seventies, we went to the post office to pick up our orders. In the early eighties, we put in an 800 number. Late eighties, we got a fax machine. In 1991 . . . we added electronic data interchange." These days, InterDesign receives

more than half of its customers' orders via computer links; errors in order entry and shipping have become relatively rare. As the error rate falls, however, customers' expectations rise. Immerman comments, "We had 50 weeks perfect with a big chain. Then one week we missed part of the order for one item on a long list—and they're on the phone wondering what's wrong."[4]

Improving the Competitiveness of the Work Force. More and more, human resources are replacing factories and machines as a decisive competitive factor. "The only way we can beat the competition is with people," notes Robert Eaton, CEO of Chrysler. "That's the only thing anybody has. Your culture and how you motivate and empower and educate your people is what makes the difference." It is important for a company to create a culture that encourages employees to innovate and follow up on new ideas. Companies then must be able to move new ideas through development and into the marketplace quickly.

Just adding new equipment is not enough; workers must be able to use it effectively. Employees must be able to control, combine, and supervise work operations, and they must be motivated to provide the best quality and service possible. The skills that are demanded of the U.S. work force are changing; effective workers in a global economy will be able to ask questions, define problems, combine information from many different sources, and deal with topics that stretch across disciplines and cultures. Indeed, the best way for Americans to prepare for a global economy is to become as educated as possible and to continue that education throughout their lives.[5]

Improving Organizational Flexibility.
"Management today has to think like a fighter pilot," says consultant Fred Wiersema. "When things move so fast, you can't always make the right decision—so you have to learn to adjust, to correct more quickly."

This is true even for a venerable company like General Electric Lighting, founded in 1878. For years, GE viewed fellow U.S. company Westinghouse as its principal rival—until Westinghouse sold its lamp division to the Dutch firm Philips Electronics. As John Opie, GE Lighting's chief executive, recalls, "Suddenly we have bigger, stronger competition. They're coming to our market, but we're not in theirs. So we're on the defensive." Opie reacted quickly by purchasing European firms, such as Hungary's Tungsram and Britain's Thorn EMI. Today, GE holds 18 percent of Europe's lighting market and is moving into Asia through a joint venture with Hitachi. Five years ago, less than 20 percent of GE Lighting's sales were made outside the United States; today more than 40 percent come from abroad, and Opie predicts that this figure will rise above 50 percent by 1996.[6]

Regulatory Environment

Government regulates competition and competitors as well as specific business practices. Government control takes two broad forms: the regulation of industry and the enactment of statutes. A **regulated industry** *is one in which competition is either limited or eliminated, and government monitoring substitutes for the market controls.* Examples of regulated industries are found in public utilities and other industries closely tied to the public interest, where competition would be wasteful or excessive. For example, only one electrical power company can serve a given market. The large capital

investment required to construct a pipeline or electric transmission line or to build and operate a nuclear power plant makes this type of regulation appropriate. But the lack of competition sometimes can cause deterioration in services and performance.

The second form of government regulation, enactment of statutes, has led to both state and federal laws affecting competition and various commercial practices. The accompanying box summarizes major federal laws and how they impact different aspects of American business.

Deregulation, *the movement toward eliminating legal restraints on competition in various industries,* has the potential to reshape the legal environment for business significantly. The trend started with the Airline Deregulation Act, which encouraged competition among airlines by allowing them to set their own rates and to add or subtract routes based on their profitability. Other industries that have been deregulated include railroads, trucking, and handguns.

Deregulation can have a substantial impact on businesses. For example, the Airline Deregulation Act has led to the merger or acquisition of several airlines. Because airlines now are free to select their routes, many have pulled out of smaller markets. As a result, commuter airlines have grown significantly. Commuter airlines such as Britt, Hensen, and Horizon now serve as passenger feeders to major airlines operating out of major airports.

A huge investment is required to construct, service, and maintain a city's electrical plant.

IT'S THE LAW

Laws Maintaining a Competitive Environment

1890   Sherman Antitrust Act
Prohibits restraint of trade and monopolization; delineates maintenance of a competitive marketing system as national policy

1914   Clayton Act
Strengthens Sherman Act by restricting such practices as price discrimination, exclusive dealing, and tying contracts that may substantially lessen competition or tend to create a monopoly

1914   Federal Trade Commission Act
Prohibits unfair methods of competition; established Federal Trade Commission, an administrative and investigative agency

1938   Wheeler-Lea Act
Amends the FTC Act to further outlaw unfair or deceptive business practices; gives FTC jurisdiction over false and misleading advertising

1950   Celler-Kefauver Antimerger Act
Amends the Clayton Act to include major asset purchases that will decrease competition in an industry

1978   Airline Deregulation Act
Grants considerable freedom to commercial airlines in setting fares and choosing new routes

1980   Motor Carrier Act and Staggers Rail Act
Significantly deregulates the trucking and railroad industries by permitting them to negotiate rates and services

Laws Regulating Competition

1936   Robinson-Patman Act
Prohibits price discrimination in sales to wholesalers, retailers, or other producers; prohibits selling at unreasonably low prices to eliminate competition

1993   North American Free Trade Agreement (NAFTA)
International trade agreement between Canada, Mexico, and the United States that facilitates trade by removing tariffs and other trade barriers among the three nations

Laws Protecting Consumers and Ensuring Equal Opportunity

1906   Federal Food and Drug Act
Prohibits adulteration and misbranding of foods and drugs involved in interstate commerce; strengthened by the Food, Drug, and Cosmetic Act (1938) and the Kefauver-Harris Drug Amendment (1962)

1961 Title VII of the Civil Rights Act (as amended by Equal Employment Opportunity Act of 1972 and the Civil Rights Act of 1991)
Prohibits discrimination in hiring, promotion, compensation, training, or dismissal on the basis of race, color, religion, sex, or national origin; the employer must prove it did not engage in discrimination

1963 Equal Pay Act
Requires equal pay for men and women working for the same firm in jobs that require equal skill, effort, and responsibility

1967 Fair Packaging and Labeling Act
Requires disclosure of product identification, name and address of manufacturer or distributor, and information on the quality of contents

1967 Federal Cigarette Labeling and Advertising Act
Requires written health warnings on cigarette packages

1968 Age Discrimination in Employment Act (as amended)
Prohibits discrimination against anyone aged 40 or over in hiring, promotion, compensation, training, or dismissal

1970 National Environmental Policy Act
Establishes the Environmental Protection Agency to deal with various types of pollution and organizations that create pollution

1972 Consumer Product Safety Act
Created the Consumer Product Safety Commission with authority to specify safety standards for most consumer products

1973 Vocational Rehabilitation Act
Requires government contractors and subcontractors to take affirmative action to employ and promote qualified disabled workers; includes federal employees and persons with communicable diseases, such as AIDS

1990 Nutrition Labeling and Education Act
Requires food manufacturers and processors to provide detailed nutritional information on the labeling of most foods

1991 Americans with Disabilities Act
Protects the rights of people with disabilities; prohibits discrimination against the disabled in public accommodations, transportation, and telecommunications

1993 Brady Law
Imposes a five-day waiting period and a background check before a hand gun purchaser can take possession of a gun

1993 Family and Medical Leave Act
Requires covered employers to grant up to 12 weeks of unpaid, job-protected leave to eligible employees

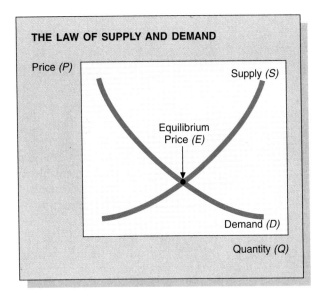

THE LAW OF SUPPLY AND DEMAND

Price *(P)*

Supply *(S)*

Equilibrium
Price *(E)*

Demand *(D)*

Quantity *(Q)*

Critics of deregulation often point out the negative effects of the trend. Some say deregulation may lead to higher prices as competitors are eliminated. Others suggest safety may be sacrificed in the name of competition.

Economic Environment

Economics *is the social science of allocating scarce resources and is a study of people and their behavior.* Economists seek to understand the choices people make in using these scarce resources. We all make economic choices every day when we decide what products to buy, what services to use, and what activities we will fit into our schedules.

There are two sides to the study of economics: microeconomics and macroeconomics. *Microeconomics* deals with the study of "small" economic units, such as individuals, families, and companies. Although these economic units may be small, their economic choices may be international in scope. Even individual consumers may become involved in international trade by deciding to buy products made in other countries. International trade is thus part of the study of microeconomics.

The other branch of economics, *macroeconomics*, deals with broader issues, like the overall operation of a country's economy (*macro* means "large"). Macroeconomics addresses questions such as how to maintain adequate supplies of the resources people want. What do we do if demand for scarce resources exceeds the supply? What government pol-

icies will be most effective in improving our standard of living over time?

Two important principles of economics, both micro and macro, are supply and demand. **Supply** *refers to sellers' willingness and ability to provide goods and services for sale in a market.* **Demand** *refers to buyers' willingness and ability to purchase these goods and services.*

The relationship between supply and demand determines another feature: price. As the quantity of a particular product increases, the supply goes up; as the price of that product increases, demand for it goes down. The law of supply and demand states that prices *(P)* in a market are set by the intersection of these supply *(S)* and demand *(D)* curves. The point where the curves meet, known as the *equilibrium price (E)*, is the prevailing market price at which one can buy that item.

If the actual market price is different from the equilibrium price, people tend to make economic choices that return the prevailing price to the equilibrium amount. For instance, if sellers lower their prices below equilibrium, buyers are likely to snap up all of the available supply quickly. As sellers get more of the item, they are likely to mark up the price so they can increase their profits. On the other hand, if merchants mark their prices too high, buyers will purchase less of the product. Sellers will end up competing with each other for customers by lowering their prices to the point where they can sell all of their supply, which is the equilibrium price.

Changes in economic policy can open up new markets. India's economy, for example, has long suffered from strict government regulation of many industries. Government officials issued licenses that gave certain firms exclusive rights to provide specific goods and services, while high tariffs excluded foreign competitors. By limiting the supply of goods and services, the government curbed competition and kept prices high. Recently, the government has eliminated many of these controls, with the result that many Indian firms are exploring new lines of business. "Before, we were in heavy industry because that's where the government let us go," explains Krishan Kumar Modi, head of the manufacturer Modi Group, "but our future is clearly in consumer goods." Through a joint venture with Walt Disney Company, Modi is starting a cable TV service that will broadcast Disney films and TV shows in Hindi and English. He also is hiring and training thousands of salespeople who will sell his products door-to-door across India.[7]

THEY SAID IT

"What is good for the country is good for General Motors, and what is good for General Motors is good for the country."

*Charles E. Wilson
(1890–1961)
chairman, General
Motors Corporation
and U.S. secretary
of defense*

Social and Cultural Environment

As a nation, the population of the United States is becoming older since our birthrate is falling. We are concerned about the environment and about buying products that are ecologically friendly and that reduce pollution. We value time at home with family and friends, watching videos, and eating microwaved snacks. These are the types of events that shape the social-cultural environment of business.

Business people must be sensitive to society's changing values and shifts in demographics, such as population growth and age distribution. These changing variables affect the way consumers react to different products and marketing practices. One important trend is the growing popularity of goods and services that offer convenience and speed; another is the growing importance of cultural diversity. The United States is a mixed society composed of various submarkets, each of which displays unique values and cultural characteristics and differs by age, place of residence, buying behavior, and buying preferences.

World markets for aluminum and other raw materials have been drastically altered by the break up of the U.S.S.R. Prior to the 1990s, most of Russia's aluminum supply was used by the Soviet military. As demand within the U.S.S.R. was cut, worldwide supply increased, driving down prices and causing U.S. suppliers to cut production.

One submarket that is growing in importance is the disabled. General Motors, for example, targets disabled consumers by sponsoring the GM Mobility Assistance Center, which has a toll-free telephone line. Center staff can help callers identify local driver assessment centers and local companies that provide adaptive driving devices or vehicle modifications. They also can provide advice about appropriate GM cars and trucks for specific disabilities. GM reimburses disabled buyers up to $1,000 toward the cost of adapting their vehicles.[8]

International Business and the Social-Cultural Environment.
The social-cultural context for business decision making often is more pronounced in the international sphere than in the domestic arena. Learning about culture and societal differences among countries is pivotal to a firm's success abroad. Business strategies that work in the United States often cannot be applied directly in other nations.

For example, Anglo-Dutch company Unilever owns the largest manufacturer of soaps and detergents in India. The company's traditional advertising strategies are ineffective in small Indian villages, which lack the media available in larger cities. Thus, much of its advertising in rural India is carried by a fleet of video trucks, which pull into villages and present movies interspersed with Unilever commercials.

Social-cultural factors also influence the types of products a company makes. Whirlpool builds giant ovens especially for consumers in Africa and the Middle East, who may want to roast an entire sheep or goat for dinner. The company also builds small, brightly colored refrigerators for Asian customers, many of whom keep their refrigerators in their living rooms for reasons of space and status.[9] Whirlpool is clearly responding to social-cultural factors in its product development strategy.

Technological Environment

The final environmental factor we will consider is the technological environment. New technology results in new goods and services, improvements in existing products, better customer service, and often lower prices through the development of more cost-efficient production and distribution methods. Technology can quickly make products obsolete—compact disks, for example, have virtually replaced long-playing vinyl records—but can just as quickly open up new business opportunities.

Technology even has spawned entirely new industries. Computers, lasers, and xerography all have resulted in the development of new industries in the past 40 years. More recently, advances in human genetics have led to the formation of a dozen small

Whirlpool refrigerators in a Bangkok showroom

companies, each competing to develop marketable applications for biogenetic research. Scientists at Sequana Therapeutics in La Jolla, California, are working on a shampoo that they hope will deliver genes for promoting hair growth directly to bald scalps. Workers at Boston-based Millenium Pharmaceuticals are trying to turn genetic data about obesity and diabetes into pills that will help those conditions.[10]

Applying new technologies in creative ways may give a firm a definite competitive edge and open up new markets. When Ellen Peck heard that 90 percent of the people who used computer network Internet were men, she knew there was a market for a female-oriented on-line service. "All I heard was that women don't use on-line services," Peck recalls. "It was like a joke. Two shoe salesmen go to a tropical island. One calls his office and says, 'I'm coming back tomorrow—no one here wears shoes.' The other one calls his office and says, 'Don't expect me back for a month—no one here wears shoes!' " Peck and telecommunications consultant Nancy Rhine started Women's Wire, a computer network that offers 240 on-line conferences and information resources. Women's Wire currently has 1,300 subscribers; Peck expects the subscriber list to reach 10,000 within a year.[11]

> ## DID YOU KNOW?
>
> A global survey of managers showed the environment as the number one issue for the 1990s.
>
> Singapore has strict laws against littering, spitting, and the importation of chewing gum.
>
> By the year 2000, 15 percent of the population of highly industrialized nations will be over age 65, as compared with less than 5 percent for the typical developing nation.
>
> Chinese companies have made several unfortunate brand-name choices for products intended for export to the United States. High on the Chinese list of "What Not to Name a Product" are Fang Fang lipstick, White Elephant batteries, and Pansy men's underwear.

THE ROLE OF SOCIAL RESPONSIBILITY AND ETHICS IN THE BUSINESS ENVIRONMENT

Many business decisions can involve making decisions about what a company "owes" to society. As you will recall from Chapter 1, we define social responsibility as a management philosophy that highlights the social and economic effects of managerial decisions.

Why should a company worry about being socially responsible? Because it does not operate in isolation. In fact, we can think of a business as a set of relationships involving its suppliers, distributors, customers, employees, and other firms—all of the people who somehow are affected by that company's operations. Ultimately, every company interacts with national systems in communications, transportation, education, and health care, as well as global systems of trade agreements, monetary exchanges, factor costs, and environmental restraints.

This means that social and ethical problems, at both national and international levels, affect every company. Many important social issues, such as drug abuse, alcohol abuse, ethnic and gender discrimination, and pollution, can impact any of these relationships. For instance, social problems affect the quality of a firm's most valuable asset: its work force. Drug abuse and alcoholism can make workers less healthy; discrimination against women and various cultural groups may restrict the educational opportunities that these workers receive. This can lead to major financial problems for business. Thus, any steps that a firm can take to resolve social problems can, in turn, help its employees—and improve its bottom line. Perhaps Jim Casey, founder of United Parcel Service (UPS), said it best nearly 50 years ago: "Are we working for money alone? If so, there is no surer way not to get it."[12]

In addition to dealing with broad social issues, business people may be required to resolve specific ethical questions. In Chapter 1 we learned that business ethics deals with the right and wrong actions that arise in any work environment. Sometimes a conflict exists between an ideal decision and one that is practical under certain conditions, but it is nonetheless important for companies to evaluate their ethical responsibilities in decision making. Businesses that fail to do so may find the penalties severe. Recently, consumers and attorneys general in over 40 states accused Sears, Roebuck automotive centers of misleading customers and selling them unnecessary parts and services. While the company denied any intent to defraud customers, CEO Edward Brennan admitted that its compensation systems and lack of monitoring could have "created an environment in which mistakes did occur." Sears ended up refunding customers' money and offering coupons to those who had pur-

chased certain auto services during a two-year period. The total cost of the settlement was an estimated $60 million.

Many firms find ethics training to be valuable. After being investigated for fraud and mismanagement, aerospace and defense contractor Martin Marietta instituted a companywide program of ethics training. Training for senior executives focuses on the challenges of ethical decision making and balancing multiple responsibilities and priorities. Training for all employees includes access to an "ethics network" by which workers can report their concerns anonymously. Executives believe that the ethics program has improved Martin Marietta's relations with the government and with auditors. They also feel that publicity about the program has helped the company win more contracts.

Top-level executives are the source of ethical decision making. It is important for employees to know that ethics and social responsibility are a priority for the firm. Suggestions for achieving an ethical corporate culture include:

Develop a written code of ethics.
Make the code as specific to the company as possible.
Establish an anonymous reporting procedure for internal problem solving.
Involve all employees in identifying ethical issues.
Include ethical decision making in employees' performance appraisals.
Publicize executive priorities and efforts related to social issues.[13]

TO WHOM IS BUSINESS RESPONSIBLE?

Just what does business owe to society? A company, after all, must make money in order to survive in the marketplace. If it goes bankrupt, many people could suffer, including employees, customers, and their families. What happens when, in order to stay in business, a company does things that could be considered harmful?

The social responsibilities of business can be classified according to relationships a business has with the general public, customers, employees, investors, and the financial community. Many of these relationships stretch beyond national borders. We will look at each of these categories in the rest of the chapter.

> **THEY SAID IT**
>
> "I make my money by supplying a public demand. If I break the law, my customers, who number hundreds of the best people in Chicago, are as guilty as I am. The only difference between us is that I sell and they buy. Everybody calls me a racketeer. I call myself a businessman. When I sell liquor, it's bootlegging. When my patrons serve it on a silver tray on Lake Shore Drive, it's hospitality."
>
> *Al Capone
> (1899–1947)
> American gangster*

Responsibilities to the General Public

Businesses have responsibilities to the general public including dealing with public health issues, protecting the environment, and developing the quality of the work force.

Public Health Issues.
Public health concerns include—but are not limited to—issues such as smoking, substance and alcohol abuse, and AIDS.

As we saw in the opening story to this chapter, smoking has many documented health risks: smoking is one of the three top risk factors involved in heart disease and stroke.[14] Furthermore, spouses and co-workers of smokers are also in danger, since their exposure to so-called "secondhand smoke" increases their risk for cancer, asthma, and respiratory infections. As a result, many employers have banned smoking in the work place.

Alcohol abuse and substance abuse are also serious public health problems in the United States. Motor vehicle accidents are a major killer, and many serious crashes are caused by drunk drivers. Alcohol abuse has been linked to serious diseases, such as cirrhosis of the liver. For these reasons, public opposition to alcohol advertising is growing steadily. Many consumers view both alcohol and tobacco advertising as socially irresponsible. Some brewers have tried to counter these arguments by sponsoring advertising campaigns that promote moderation.

AIDS represents a different type of challenge to business; while no one accuses industry of causing AIDS, firms nonetheless must deal with its consequences. AIDS (acquired immunodeficiency syndrome) is a fatal disease that breaks down the body's ability to defend itself against illness and infection. What is especially dangerous about AIDS is the long time (typically five years) between first exposure to the

NOW MIGHT BE A GOOD TIME TO BRING UP A DELICATE SUBJECT. DRINKING.

LET'S STOP UNDERAGE DRINKING BEFORE IT STARTS.

Many advertisements sponsored by Anheuser-Busch and other brewers deal with the issue of drinking by minors, a perennial problem.

AIDS virus and actual development of the disease. While people during this period may not show any symptoms of AIDS and probably don't even know they have it, they are still carriers who can give the disease to someone else. It is this large pool of unknown carriers that accounts for the rapid spread of the disease. In 1982, only 1,013 cases of AIDS were reported; today there are over 200,000.[15]

The rapid spread of AIDS means that companies will increasingly find themselves educating their employees about it and dealing with employees who have the deadly disease. Health care for AIDS patients can be incredibly expensive, and small companies could have trouble paying these health-care costs. Do companies have the right to test potential employees for the AIDS virus? Some people feel this violates the rights of job applicants. Others feel that firms have a responsibility not to place those with AIDS in jobs where they could possibly infect others. These are difficult questions in which a business must balance the rights of individuals against the rights of society in general.

Protecting the Environment. Ecology and environmental issues continue to be important to the public. **Ecology**—*the study of the relationships between living things and their environment*—is now a legal as well as a societal issue for managers to consider.

Pollution. Pollution—*tainting or destroying a natural environment*—is the major ecological problem today. Pollution can come from many sources; when we burn fossil fuels, such as coal and oil, for energy, carbon dioxide and sulfur enter our atmosphere. Both of these chemicals cause environmental problems. The extra carbon dioxide collects in the atmosphere and traps heat, leading to the so-called *greenhouse effect* that allegedly is affecting the earth's temperature and its ability to support life. During this century, the amount of carbon dioxide in the atmosphere has soared; we are burning more fossil fuels than ever before. Many scientists fear that this could result in global warming, with disastrous results.

Meanwhile, the sulfur from fossil fuels combines with water vapor in the air to form sulfuric acid. The rain that results is called *acid rain*. Acid rain kills fish and trees and can pollute the groundwater from which we get our drinking water. In the northeastern United States, rain and snow are now about 100 times more acid than normal. Acid rain is also dangerous because wind can carry sulfur all over the world. Sulfur from factories in the United States is damaging Canadian forests, and pollution from London smokestacks is destroying the forests and lakes of Scandinavia.[16]

The Recycling Solution. Every time we throw away a plastic box, a newspaper, or a glass bottle, we are adding to the world's trash problem. Garbage just never seems to die; it stays intact in landfills for years, and we're running out of places to put it.

An important solution is **recycling**—*reprocessing used materials so they can be reused.* Recycling could provide much of the raw material we need for manufacturing, but we need to do a lot more of it. 40 percent of the garbage produced by a typical American household consists of paper; just recycling your daily newspaper could save four trees every year.[17]

Electric cars, once a science-fiction solution to pollution, are being designed, tested, and marketed by the major automakers in response to both consumer demand and new state regulations.

We can divide the complex topic of energy into both short-term and long-term issues. In the short run, the problem is one of **conservation**—*preserving our declining energy resources.* We have seen that burning fossil fuels damages the environment. In any case, our supplies of these fuels are limited and will run out eventually. In addition to conserving current energy sources, we need to develop long-term solutions to supplying energy by using alternative energy sources. Nuclear power, wind, sun, synthetic fuels, and even garbage and other waste products all have been suggested as substitutes for fossil fuels.

Carmakers, for instance, are developing electric cars that they hope will eventually replace standard, fossil-fuel-burning vehicles. California regulators have mandated that by 1998, two percent of the vehicles sold in the state must be electrically powered.

New York and Massachusetts will require electric vehicles the year after that, and ten other states, plus the District of Columbia, are considering similar laws. Ted Morgan, president of U.S. Electricar Inc., is working to develop engine-less electric cars, but not for consumers. "That's the market the Big Three [automakers] will go after," he says. Instead, Morgan plans to develop fleets of electric cars for utilities and the U.S. Postal Service.[18]

Developing the Quality of the Work Force. In the past, a nation's wealth often has been thought to consist of its money, production equipment, or natural resources. A country's true wealth, however, lies in its people; an educated, skilled work force is its most valuable asset. It is becoming increasingly clear that, in order to remain competitive, American business must assume more responsibility for developing the quality of its work force.

Between now and 2000, most new jobs will require a college education. Many professions will demand ten years of study beyond high school, and even the least-skilled jobs will require a certain level of reading, computing, and thinking. Business must encourage students to stay in school, continue their education, and develop their skills. Companies also must encourage employees to learn new skills both to help themselves and to help the company remain competitive.

Companies have a responsibility to integrate disadvantaged groups into the economy. A recent survey by the National Organization on Disability, for instance, shows that two-thirds of disabled Americans between the ages of 16 and 64 are not working, even though the overwhelming majority of them would like to be employed. Private employers are often effective providers of cost-efficient training programs that can play a key role in giving these workers a "second chance." Marriott International sponsors a program called "Bridges . . . from School to Work," which helps young people with disabilities make this transition. Marriott offers paid internships for special-education students in their last year of high school. Approximately 500 students enroll in these internships every year; more than 80 percent of those who complete the internships receive offers of permanent jobs.[19]

ETHICS AND SOCIAL RESPONSIBILITY

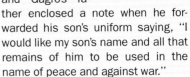

Benetton

Since the business environment and its impact on the firm is largely beyond the control of individual managers, most companies take special care to avoid problems that might derail an otherwise successful strategy. Little wonder that they continue to shake their heads about Benetton. Let's face it: Benetton, the Italian clothing company with over 7,000 retail outlets in 110 countries, marches to the beat of a very different drummer. It *courts* controversy. Explains creative director Oliviero Toscani, "Controversy is proof we've achieved our [communication] objective: to take the role of protagonist in the confrontation of ideas on important topics. We want to put an image out there to create a healthy dialogue, not sweep issues under the rug."

Benetton's messages feature eye-catching, occasionally unforgettable visions, such as Queen Elizabeth as a black woman; Spike Lee as a white man; a man named David Kirby surrounded by his loving family as he dies of AIDS; rows of crosses in a military cemetery; a nun kissing a priest; rows of colored condoms; and the blood-stained uniform of Marinko Gagro, who was killed fighting in Bosnia-Herzegovina. The images are typically photographed in clear, vivid, bright colors, and the Benetton logo sits quietly in a corner of each one.

As might be expected, responses to these messages have been, well, *mixed*. In Britain, an angry royalist who painted over the windows of six Benetton stores explained, "If Benetton can black the Queen's face, we can black their windows." The picture of the nun kissing the priest received so much negative response in Italy that Benetton stopped using it. The *Los Angeles Times* refused to show Gagro's bloody uniform, saying it didn't want to subject earthquake-shaken Angelenos to more bad news. The Vatican newspaper called the same picture "advertising terrorism."

Many critics have accused Benetton of exploiting people to sell clothing. However, the families of David Kirby and Marinko Gagro disagree. The Kirbys volunteered to share how much they loved their son in an effort to change attitudes toward people with AIDS, and Gagro's father enclosed a note when he forwarded his son's uniform saying, "I would like my son's name and all that remains of him to be used in the name of peace and against war."

Despite criticism, Benetton continues to produce success in the marketplace. Its communications are so connected to provocative issues that its customers have come to expect this from their brand. The various controversies don't seem to have hurt Benetton's bottom line; after-tax profits grew 12.6 percent in 1993 to $132 million.

SOURCES: "Benetton: The Next Era," The Economist, April 23, 1994, 68; Gary Levin, "Benetton Ad Lays Bare the Bloody Toll of War," Advertising Age, February 21, 1994, 38; Sara Gay Forden and James Fallon, "Benetton's Colors Spark U.K. Ire," Advertising Age, March 30, 1993, 19; and Lisa Lockwood, "Benetton Again Stirring It Up with Latest Ad," Advertising Age, February 16, 1994.

Responsibilities to Customers

Consumer demands are another social-responsibility issue facing business. **Consumerism**—*the public demand for business to consider consumer wants and needs in making its decisions*—is a major social and economic movement. Ralph Nader is a leading force in this trend.

Since the emergence of consumerism a few decades ago, consumer groups have sprung up throughout the country. Some concentrate on an isolated situation, such as rate hikes by a local public utility, while others attack broader issues. The net effect has been passage of numerous consumer protection laws. There is little doubt that more such laws will be passed in the years ahead that will have a big impact on business.

Consumerism is based on the belief that consumers have certain rights. President Kennedy outlined these rights as the right to be safe, the right to be informed, the right to choose, and the right to be heard. Much consumer legislation is based on these statements. In fact, many companies go to considerable effort to ensure that consumer complaints receive a full hearing. Ford Motor Company, for example, has set up a consumer appeals board to resolve service complaints.

> **THEY SAID IT**
>
> "Start with what is right rather than what is acceptable."
>
> *Peter Drucker (1909–   ) American business philosopher and author*

Responsibilities to Employees

Business's responsibilities to its employees are far ranging. Issues include family leave, equal employment opportunity, multicultural diversity, sexual harassment, and sexism.

Family Leave.   As the number of families with two wage earners increases, conflicts between employees' responsibilities at home and at work may clash. Employees care for elderly parents or relatives, while others find themselves juggling child care or other family crises with the demands of their jobs. **Family leave**—*giving employees a leave of absence from work in order to deal with family matters*—has become an important issue for many workers.

The Family and Medical Leave Act of 1993 requires all businesses with 50 or more employees to provide up to 12 weeks of unpaid leave annually for employees who have had a child, are adopting a child or becoming foster parents, who are caring for a seriously ill relative or spouse, or who are seriously ill themselves. Workers must meet certain eligibility requirements and their employers must continue to provide health benefits and guarantee that employees will return to equivalent jobs.

Detailed regulations provided by the Labor Department will govern implementation and enforcement of the law. One headache will be reconciling inconsistencies between the federal law and the laws of the 11 states that already have some form of family leave. Another problem may be assessing the impact of compliance on small businesses.[20]

Ensuring Equal Employment Opportunity.

The Civil Rights Act (1964) ruled that discriminatory practices are illegal, and Title VII of the act prohibits discrimination in employment. The **Equal Employment Opportunity Commission (EEOC)** *was created to increase job opportunities for women and minorities and to help end job discrimination based on race, color, religion, sex, or national origin in any personnel action.* Minorities defined by the EEOC include African Americans (not of Hispanic origin), Hispanics, Asians or Pacific Islanders, and Native Americans or Alaskan Natives.

The EEOC can help an employer set up an **affirmative action program** *to increase job opportunities for women, minorities, the disabled, and other protected categories.* Such programs include analyzing the present work force and setting specific hiring and promotion goals with target dates in areas where women,

minorities, and others are underutilized. Penalties for violations can be imposed.

The goals of the EEOC have been strengthened by passage of the Equal Pay Act (1963), the Age Discrimination in Employment Act (1967), the Equal Employment Opportunity Act (1972), the Pregnancy Discrimination Act (1978), and numerous executive orders. The Americans with Disabilities Act (1991) protects the rights of people with disabilities; the Vietnam Era Veterans Readjustment Assistance Act (1974) protects the employment of both disabled and able-bodied Vietnam-era veterans.

Encouraging Multicultural Diversity.

The American work place is changing. By the year 2000, women will make up about 47 percent of all workers, while minorities and immigrants will hold 26 percent of all jobs. By the end of the decade, white males will account for only 32 percent of those entering the work force.

The racial and cultural blend within a society, referred to as **multicultural diversity**, has always been part of American culture, as new immigrants enter and become part of U.S. society. The challenge for U.S. business is to learn how to manage diversity creatively, to benefit from the different viewpoints, experiences, and talents of the various cultures in our society.

Dealing with a culturally diverse work force means understanding what motivates employees and how they function best. Developing a better understanding of people's cultures and behaviors will help business people manage culturally diverse staffs more effectively. Respecting employees' cultural differences is a vital part of management in the 1990s.

Sexual Harassment.

Sexual harassment refers to *inappropriate actions of a sexual nature.* Legally, there are two categories of sexual harassment: (1) unwelcome advances and requests for sexual favors that affect promotions and raises; and (2) a "hostile" work environment in which an employee feels hassled or degraded because of unwelcome flirting, lewd comments, or obscene jokes. The courts have ruled that allowing sexual materials, such as pin-up calendars and pornographic magazines, in the work place can create a "hostile" atmosphere that interferes with an employee's ability to do a job.

Sexual harassment is a major problem for business. Over 10,000 complaints are filed with the Equal Employment Opportunity Commission every year—double the number of five years ago. Research shows that 90 percent of *Fortune* 500 firms have dealt with complaints about sexual harassment. More than a third of them have been sued at least once; a quarter of them have been sued repeatedly. Sexual harassment is estimated to cost the average large corporation $6.7 million a year in investigation costs, legal fees, and so forth.

The Civil Rights Act of 1991 gave more employees the ability to fight sexual harassment. For the first time, women (and men) were able to win damages for intentional sexual harassment. The law also allowed judges to force the losing party to pay the fees of the winner's expert witnesses, an often crucial—but expensive—component of winning a complex harassment case.

It is important for employers to resolve sexual harassment problems in-house, avoiding lawsuits if possible. Many firms have established antiharassment policies and employee-education programs. A recent survey of 600 major companies found that 50 percent of them planned to increase the amount of sexual harassment prevention training they offer to managers and employees. Effective harassment prevention programs include (1) issuing a specific policy prohibiting sexual harassment, (2) developing a complaint procedure employees can follow, (3) creating a work atmosphere that encourages sexually harassed staffers to come forward, and (4) investigating and resolving complaints immediately and taking disciplinary action against harassers.[21]

Sexism. Sexual harassment is often part of a much bigger problem: sexism. **Sexism** refers to *discrimination against either sex, but it primarily occurs against women.* Some examples of sexism are blatant: a woman being paid less than a male colleague to perform the same job or a male employee being promoted over a female with more experience. Other instances are more subtle: The only female in a work group may not be introduced to a client or doesn't get a work assignment when a manager passes them out.

Sexism is a global issue. A United Nations study found that women, who account for over half the earth's population, do two-thirds of the world's work, earn one-tenth of the world's income, and own one-tenth of the world's property. The 1993 *U.N. Human Development Report* concluded that no country offers its female citizens opportunities comparable to those enjoyed by their male counterparts.

One important issue concerns equal pay for equal work. In the United States, women who work full time earn 71 percent of what full-time male workers earn; women high-school graduates earn less than men who quit school before the ninth grade. In industrialized nations worldwide, women's pay averages just two-thirds that of men's. Many women find the route to corporate success is blocked by a *glass ceiling* of discrimination. There are several reasons for this; one is that many corporate jobs rely on recruitment by word of mouth and networking, which tends to exclude women and minorities. Women often have less access to training and development programs. Managers' stereotypes can make things worse: managers may assume that a woman with children would not be interested in transfers or promotions that require longer hours. Executive search firms may compound the problem by focusing on white males.[22]

> **THEY SAID IT**
>
> "The worst crime against working people is a company which fails to operate at a profit."
>
> Samuel Gompers
> (1850–1924)
> American labor leader

Responsibilities to Investors and the Financial Community

There is probably no place where the public expects a higher level of business ethics than in the arena of financial transactions. Just because a business practice is legal doesn't mean that it is also ethical. When it comes to business's responsibilities to investors and the financial community, the public expects behavior that is *both* legal and ethical. Ethical business behavior is not just something that sounds good on paper. When business does not meet its social responsibilities, it can hurt hundreds or even thousands of people.

Unethical business practices in stock and bond trading can injure people who lose their investments or their jobs. Irresponsible investments can hurt millions of consumers. By the 1990s failure rates of banks and savings and loan institutions (S&Ls) were the highest they have been since the 1930s depression. All too often, the reason was too many high-risk investments. Banks used their deposits to finance real-estate developers, Third World governments, and corporate leveraged buyouts. When these parties could not repay the loans, the banks went under.

So far the federal government has covered all depositors' losses at federally insured failed banks and

S&Ls. However, this has meant passing out billions of dollars, and the government agencies that cover the debts are running out of money. Ultimately, taxpayers will end up paying for these unwise investments.

SUMMARY OF LEARNING GOALS

1. **Discuss the competitive issues that the United States faces in an increasingly global economy.**

The world is shifting toward an increasingly global economy. This development changes the competitive environment, both in the United States and in other countries. The big challenge today is for the United States to develop its ability to compete in a global market. Currently, there is a shift from competition based on costs to competition based on factors, such as product design, product development, and efficient use of technology. Firms also will succeed or fail based on the quality and service that they provide. Competitive issues that the United States faces include researching and developing better products, improving quality and service, improving the competitiveness of the work force, and improving organizational flexibility.

2. **Explain how government regulates business.**

Government regulates competition and competitors as well as specific business practices. Government control takes two broad forms: the regulation of industry and the enactment of statutes. A regulated industry is one in which competition is either limited or eliminated, and government monitoring substitutes for market controls. The enactment of statutes has led to both state and federal laws affecting competition and various commercial practices.

3. **Summarize the relationship between supply, demand, and price.**

Supply refers to sellers' willingness and ability to provide goods and services for sale in a market. Demand refers to buyers' willingness and ability to purchase these goods and services. The relationship between supply and demand determines another price. As the quantity of a particular product increases, the supply goes up; as the price of that product increases, demand for it goes down. The law of supply and demand states that prices *(P)* in a market are set by the intersection of these supply *(S)* and demand *(D)* curves. The point where the curves meet, known as the equilibrium price *(E)*, is the prevailing market price for that item.

4. **Describe how the social-cultural environment can impact business.**

Business people must be sensitive to society's changing values and to shifts in demographics, such as population growth and age distribution. These changing variables affect the way consumers react to different products and marketing practices. The United States is a mixed society composed of various submarkets, each of which displays unique values and cultural characteristics and differs by age, place of residence, buying behavior, and buying preferences. The social-cultural context for business decision making often is more pronounced in the international sphere than in the domestic arena.

Learning about culture and social differences among countries is pivotal to a firm's success abroad. Business strategies that work in the United States often cannot be applied directly in other nations.

5. **Discuss ways in which the technological environment can affect business.**

New technology results in new goods and services, improvements in existing products, better customer service, and often lower prices through the development of more cost-efficient production and distribution methods. Technology can quickly make products obsolete, but can just as quickly open up new business opportunities and industries. Applying new technologies in creative ways may give a firm a competitive edge and open up new markets.

6. **Outline business's responsibilities to the general public.**

The responsibilities of business to the general public include dealing with public health issues, protecting the environment, and developing the quality of the work force. Public health issues include smoking, secondhand smoke, alcohol and substance abuse, and educating employees about AIDS. Businesses also should take steps to reduce their impact on the environment (working to minimize pollution, acid rain, and the greenhouse effect; supporting recycling; and conserving and developing our energy resources). Companies must remain alert to changes in environmental regulations, since the laws can change quickly. Additionally, it is important to business to develop the quality of its work force, since a well-educated, skilled work force is a nation's most valuable asset.

7. **Identify business's responsibilities to customers.**

Business's most readily identifiable responsibilities are related to its customers. These responsibilities have been heightened by the consumerism movement, which is based on the idea that consumers have certain rights. According to President Kennedy, these consumer rights are to be safe, to be informed, to choose, and to be heard.

8. **Describe business's responsibilities to employees.**

Relations with employees are some of the most significant social responsibility and ethical issues facing contemporary business. Issues include family leave, equal employment opportunity, sexual harassment, sexism, and managing a culturally diverse work force.

9. **Explain business's responsibilities to investors and the financial community.**

There has been considerable publicity in recent years about business's social and ethical responsibilities to investors and the financial community. Important topics include honest securities trading and responsible investing.

KEY TERMS QUIZ

research and development   demand   family leave
customer service   ecology   Equal Employment Opportunity Commission (EEOC)
regulated industry   pollution   affirmative action program
deregulation   recycling   multicultural diversity
economics   conservation   sexual harassment
supply   consumerism   sexism

economics ___ 1. The social science of allocating scarce resources.

demand ___ 2. Refers to buyers' willingness and ability to purchase products.

ecology ___ 3. The study of the relationship between living things and their environment.

family leave ___ 4. Giving employees a leave of absence from work in order to deal with family matters.

research and development ___ 5. The scientific process of developing new commercial products.

consumerism ___ 6. Refers to the public demand for business to consider consumer needs in making decisions.

customer service ___ 7. The aspect of competitive strategy that refers to how a firm treats its customers.

conservation ___ 8. Refers to the preservation of declining energy resources.

regulated industry ___ 9. An industry in which competition is either limited or eliminated, and government monitoring substitutes for market controls.

recycling ___ 10. The reprocessing of used materials for reuse.

supply ___ 11. Refers to sellers' willingness and ability to provide products.

deregulation ___ 12. The elimination of legal restraints of competition.

pollution ___ 13. Refers to tainting or destroying a natural environment.

sexism ___ 14. The discrimination against either sex, primarily occurring against women.

multicultural diversity ___ 15. Refers to the racial and cultural blend within a society.

EEOC ___ 16. The federal commission created to increase job opportunities for women and minorities and to help eliminate job discrimination.

affirmative action program ___ 17. A program set up by businesses to increase opportunities for women and minorities.

sexual harassment ___ 18. Refers to inappropriate actions of a sexual nature.

OTHER IMPORTANT TERMS

acid rain   greenhouse effect

REVIEW QUESTIONS

1. What is meant by the terms *social responsibility* and *business ethics*? Cite an example of each. Discuss the current status of social responsibility and business ethics in U.S. industry.

2. How does government regulate both competitive and specific business practices? Describe several federal laws with which business people should be familiar.

3. Distinguish between microeconomics and macroeconomics. Describe some issues involved in each.

4. What is meant by deregulation? What are its advantages and disadvantages?

5. What contributions can American business make to the job skills of the work force? How does the United States compare to other industrialized nations in regard to worker training?

6. Explain the importance of R&D in global competitiveness. How does the United States rate in regard to R&D expenditures?

7. What are business's responsibilities to the general public? Cite specific examples.

8. Distinguish between sexual harassment and sexism. Cite examples of each. How can these problems be avoided?

9. On what fundamental rights is consumerism based? How has the recognition of these rights improved the contemporary business environment?

10. What is meant by multicultural diversity? Discuss its implications for American business.

DISCUSSION QUESTIONS

1. Describe specific steps you can take to make yourself a more competitive employee in a global economy. What classes would you like to take? In what areas would you like to get more experience? Share your opinions with the class.

2. Choose a foreign country and a specific occupation (perhaps the job you would like to have after you finish school). Research how that country trains people to hold that particular job. What role does the government play, if any, in this training? Are private companies involved? How does it compare to the career training available in the United States?

3. Respected economist Milton Friedman believes that social responsibility is not really the concern of American business. He says, "There is one and only one social responsibility of business—to use its resources and engage in activities designed to increase its profits so long as it stays within the rules of the game, which is to say, engages in open and free competition, without deception or fraud."[22] Other business scholars argue that com-

panies have the obligation to become involved in social responsibility issues such as those discussed in this chapter. What is your opinion? What arguments do you feel either support or disprove Friedman's position? Explain your answer.

4. Suppose that you own a small company with 12 employees. One of them tells you in confidence that he has just found out he has AIDS. You know that health care for AIDS patients can be disastrously high, and this could drastically raise the health insurance premiums that your other employees must pay. What are your responsibilities to this employee? To the rest of your staff? Explain.

5. Describe the major social and ethical issues facing the following:
   a. Automobile manufacturers
   b. Real-estate developers
   c. Detergent manufacturers
   d. Drug companies selling products used to treat AIDS
   e. Managers of stock brokerage firms

VIDEO CASE: Is There Cash in Our Trash?

The video case for this chapter discusses the economics of recycling and can be found on page 409 of Appendix D.

Solution to Key Terms Quiz

1. economics 2. demand 3. ecology 4. family leave 5. research and development 6. consumerism 7. customer service 8. conservation 9. regulated industry 10. recycling 11. supply 12. deregulation 13. pollution 14. sexism 15. multicultural diversity 16. Equal Employment Opportunity Commission (EEOC) 17. affirmative action program 18. sexual harassment

CHAPTER 3

Global and Economic Forces Affecting Business

Learning Goals

1. Explain the importance of international business.
2. Identify the different types of economic systems.
3. Discuss the economic concepts involved in international business.
4. Explain why nations tend to specialize in certain goods.
5. Name the different levels of involvement in international business.
6. Explain countertrade.
7. Identify the main obstacles confronting global business.
8. Explain multinational economic integration.
9. Distinguish between a global and multinational strategy.

What is the most popular sport in the world? Baseball? Football? Basketball? If you guessed any of these, try again: The globe's best-loved athletic pastime is soccer. If you didn't know that, take heart, because soccer has always excited more interest abroad than in America. Indeed, a recent poll found that fewer than 17 percent of U.S. respondents had any interest in watching a soccer match, either in person or on TV.

In the global arena, however, soccer is a winner, and the World Cup, the quadrennial tournament that determines the game's international champions, is the world's single largest sporting event. Thirty-one billion people watched the 1994 World Cup television broadcast, compared to 16.6 billion viewers for the 1992 Olympic Games—and a paltry 253 million spectators for last year's Super Bowl.

Given America's relative lack of enthusiasm, the United States seems like an odd choice to host the fifteenth World Cup. (The same poll cited above also revealed that only 25 percent of U.S. respondents even knew what the World Cup was.) From a marketing standpoint, however, the choice makes a lot of sense. Sports marketing is a huge business, and multinational firms appreciate the enormous global exposure that comes from association with this event. They also view the fifteenth World Cup as an opportunity to win new converts in the United States. Says Alan Rothenberg, president of the U.S. Soccer Federation, "Our plan is to open the world's largest market to the world's most popular sport."

Eleven companies signed up as official sponsors of the 1994 World Cup, and eight became marketing partners, paying millions of dollars for various levels of national and international rights to advertising, promotions, and exclusivity by product category or territory. At least 15 firms registered as official suppliers of goods, services, and equipment, and more than 50 were licensed to sell World Cup-related merchandise. This list does not include numerous other companies that sponsored promotions in various regional markets.

For some companies, such as The Coca-Cola Company, the World Cup has long played an important role in global business strategy. The firm has been the World Cup's exclusive soft-drink sponsor since 1978 and has served as an official sponsor for the last five tournaments. "To the worldwide Coke system, this dwarfs any other event," says Bruce Kirkman, vice president of Coca-Cola USA. The company ran promotional programs in over 50 nations and manufactured a special series of commemorative bottles and cans. Promotions included contests that gave fans the chance to buy or win souvenir posters, pins, soccer balls, glassware, clothing, game tickets, and trips to World Cup matches.

An event of this magnitude can provide the ideal introduction for a new product. Appropriately, The Coca-Cola Company chose this time to unveil its new sports beverage, PowerAde, and dubbed it the official sports drink of the World Cup. A million free samples of PowerAde were handed out. The company hopes that PowerAde eventually will win 20 percent of the $1.2 billion sports-drink market.

Another official sponsor is MasterCard, which sees the World Cup as its entree to international markets. "We were perceived as being dramatically behind our global competitor, Visa, and we were looking for something to raise our brand awareness," explains Pete Hart, former CEO of MasterCard International. In addition to sponsoring the games, MasterCard signed up two soccer greats, Britain's Bobby Charlton and Brazil's Pele, to promote its card. Since its affiliation with the World Cup, MasterCard's name recognition around the globe has skyrocketed.

General Motors' GMC Truck Unit, on the other hand, hopes that World Cup sponsorship will help it reach new customers in the United States. Demographic studies show that more than 11 million American kids under age 18 are actively involved in soccer. Many women also are involved in the sport, both as players and as coaches. Other fans include Asian-Americans and Latinos, groups with strong cultural ties to soccer's international heritage. Fans in Los Angeles' Korea Town eagerly follow the career of Asian star Kim Joo-Sung. In Jackson Heights, New York, a predominantly Colombian neighborhood, men have been known to don blond wigs to imitate the tresses of popular midfielder Carlos Valderrama. Eighty thousand Team Mexico fans crowded into Pasadena's Estadio de las Rosas recently to cheer an exhibition match. In the Los Angeles area alone, there are more than 40 Latino adult soccer leagues consisting of about 70 teams each. GMC's sponsorship is part of a broad strategy to target female and Hispanic consumers—two segments in which it has relatively low market share. "We have to understand the changing country that we live in, and address the changing customer base," says vice president Roy Roberts.

Brazil may have won the 1994 World Cup, but the real winners are the businesses that sponsored the event, which generated sales of $300 million. Says Rothenberg, "The effect is going to be the lasting elevation of soccer to a higher position as a sport and as a business in this country."[1]

CHAPTER OVERVIEW

Benjamin Franklin once said, "No nation was ever ruined by trade." Today, most business people would agree with the eighteenth-century statesman. At one time, the international aspects of business mattered to only a few U.S. firms; for most, the domestic market was all they needed. Today, though, the various economies of the world are growing closer all the time.

Since 1987, exports have accounted for 55 percent of all U.S. economic growth. Economists predict that the passage of the North American Free Trade Agreement (NAFTA) and the expansion of Asian, Latin-American, and Eastern-European markets will make global trade even more important to the U.S. economy in coming years.[2] The top emerging markets for U.S. companies can be measured by the growth in American exports to those regions. Exports to Eastern Europe grew 42 percent in one year; also growing are U.S. exports to Central America, South America, China, and Asia.

We can divide international business into three major activities: **exporting** *(selling domestic goods and services abroad)*, **importing** *(purchasing foreign goods, raw materials, and services)*, and *foreign production* (making goods and supplying services in a foreign country for sale there or in other countries). In this chapter, we will see how these activities form patterns of trade and world business.

ALTERNATIVE ECONOMIC SYSTEMS

Many people forget that a large part of the world lives under economic systems other than capitalism. The number of countries with other systems makes it important to learn the primary features of these alternative economies. This text does not concern itself with political questions, but rather with the economic aspects of socialism, communism, and mixed economies.

Communism

"The theory of Communism may be summed up in one sentence: Abolish all private property"—so wrote Karl Marx in 1848. Marx's writings form the basis of communist theory. He believed that workers were being exploited by the upper classes. Ultimately, according to Marx, this would lead to a class struggle that would make way for a new world order called **communism.** ~~All property would be shared by the people of a community~~ (hence the name *communism*) under the direction of a strong central government.

Marx felt that, ultimately, a nation's people should own all of the country's productive capacity, but conceded that the central government would have to operate businesses until a classless society could evolve. He felt that this classless society would be based on the idea, "from each according to his abilities, to each according to his needs." This means that each individual should contribute what he or she can to society, but that the society's resources should be distributed to its citizens according to their needs rather than their contributions. Obviously, this represents a very different approach from the capitalist idea of paying people according to the work they perform. While such a system benefits those who are unable to work, it also takes away much of the incentive for workers to do their jobs well, since pay is not necessarily tied to performance. Under communism, the central government owns the means of production, and

EMERGING MARKETS FOR U.S. COMPANIES
Share of U.S. export growth

Eastern Europe	42.0%
Central America	26.0%
South America	20.0%
China	18.0%
Other Asia	13.0%
Africa	11.0%
Middle East	10.0%
East Asian NICs*	6.5%
Former Soviet Union	6.0%

* NIC = newly industrialized countries
SOURCE: DEPARTMENT OF COMMERCE

THEY SAID IT

"A day will come when you, France; you, Russia; you, Italy; you, England; you, Germany—all of you nations of the continent, will, without losing your distinctive qualities, be blended into a . . . European fraternity . . ."

Victor Hugo
(1802–1885)
French novelist

the people, in turn, work for state-owned enterprises. The government determines what people can buy because it dictates what will be produced.

Many nations adopted communist economic systems during this century in an effort to improve the quality of life for their citizens. In practice, however, communist governments often gave people little or no freedom of choice in selecting jobs, purchases, or investments. Continuing economic troubles led to the collapse of some communist governments, such as those of the former Soviet Union and Eastern Europe.

The Former Soviet Union

Many formerly communist nations now are going through dramatic changes. Perhaps the most exciting changes have occurred in the republics that formerly comprised the Soviet Union. These new nations are trying to restructure their economies by introducing Western-style capitalism and private enterprise. By decentralizing economic planning and providing more incentives for workers, they hope to shift their communist-based economies to market-driven systems.

Part of this effort involves converting defense factories to plants that produce badly needed consumer goods. One military factory converts tanks into fire engines and bulldozers, while another plant that once manufactured trucks for carrying missiles now fits those trucks to transport chilled beer. One creative community turned a missile into a water tower.

These changes have opened up new business opportunities for Westerners, too. Western and former-Soviet firms have started about 700 joint ventures (jointly owned companies). In the true spirit of capitalism, the post-Soviet government has hired the Wall Street investment banking firm Bear, Stearns to advise them on the most profitable way to sell state-owned businesses to private buyers. Polaroid has started a joint venture to make and sell instant cameras. In a $3 billion deal—the largest ever between a Russian and U.S. company—PepsiCo agreed to barter, or exchange, soda for ships and vodka. The Fiat Group has made the largest investment of any Western company so far ($5 billion); it plans joint ventures to produce 900,000 cars in Russia and 250,000 compacts in Poland each year. And formerly communist couch potatoes now can enjoy the area's first commercially sponsored TV show: a one-hour version of MTV, which beams rock music (and advertisements for American products) into 88 million households each week.

Other Eastern European countries are starting to "go capitalist." More than a half-million new private companies have been founded in Poland. Multinational companies are showing an interest as well. Coca-Cola is building the first of 11 planned factories in Poland, while ABB, a Swedish-Swiss manufacturer of locomotives and industrial equipment, has formed three joint ventures. In the Czech Republic, private owners have taken over several small businesses; Volkswagen, General Electric, and Westinghouse are investing in companies in both the Czech Republic and Slovakia.

What Is Ahead for Communism?

Despite these sweeping changes, the governments of Eastern Europe and the former Soviet Union still face tremendous economic and political challenges. Inefficient businesses that once were supported by government subsidies now are forced to watch expenses and, in some cases, to cut costs by cutting staff. Some companies have shut down entirely, putting workers out of jobs. (For 60 years, the communist government insisted that there was no unemployment in the Soviet Union. Recently, however, the republics have established several unemployment offices, admitting that a problem does exist. In fact, over nine percent of Russia's citizens are out of work.)

A continuing problem is the inefficient distribution system for various products, including food. Farm produce is harvested from the fields, packed into trucks and railway cars, and hauled to city warehouses. By the time it reaches population centers, the food may be rotten—in which case it is packed up and returned to the farms for fertilizer. Russian distribution still is controlled largely by a handful of government officials. Shortages of food, housing, and most other products continue to plague the population, driving up prices.

Socialism

As we have seen, under communism there is no private property at all, and the central government owns and operates all factors of production. **Socialism,** another major economic system, is related to communism in that *the government owns and operates key industries* that are considered vital to the public welfare, such as transportation, utilities, and medicine. However, *private ownership is allowed for industries that are considered less crucial*, like shops and restaurants. Socialists believe major industries are too important to be left in private hands; they feel that government-owned businesses are more efficient and can serve the public better. Until recently in Mexico, for instance, the government owned the nation's banks and telephone system. In France, one-third of the country's industrial production still comes from state-owned firms.

Socialist economies usually follow some master plan for using the nation's resources. Workers are free to choose their employment, but the state often encourages people to pursue careers in areas where the public need is greatest. As a result, most citizens work for government enterprises. The management of these government-run businesses may change often, according to which politicians are in power. Many top business positions may be awarded through political patronage, rather than according to a manager's ability.

Why would a country choose socialism over capitalism? Perhaps because governments in socialist countries may provide services that capitalist governments do not, such as low-cost health care for citizens. Privately funded health care, like the United States has, can be expensive for both individuals and for companies that provide medical insurance for their employees.

Socialist economies also may provide more support for the unemployed. In Israel, for instance, an unemployed worker gets 75 percent of his or her salary for six months, no questions asked. After six months, some workers are eligible for continued payments, computed on the basis of what is necessary to support their families. The Israeli government offers other benefits, too, such as financial support for new immigrants.

The price for such benefits can be steep: socialist countries often have high income taxes, because somebody has to pay for the handouts. This causes some highly paid workers, often skilled professionals, to leave for other countries (such as the United States) in search of lower tax rates. It may be, too, that such practices can take away people's incentive to work;

> **THEY SAID IT**
>
> "Canada is a country whose main exports are hockey players and cold fronts. Our main imports are baseball players and acid rain."
>
> *Pierre Trudeau (1919–) Prime minister of Canada*

Clinton's Dilemma

In 1994, social responsibility and ethics were hotly debated subjects at the international level. President Clinton gave himself a deadline of June 4 (the fifth anniversary of the Tiananmen massacre, in which Chinese leaders responded to peaceful protest by killing protesters) to decide whether to renew China's most-favored-nation (MFN) status.

Clinton was in an awkward situation. On one hand, during his campaign for the presidency he had vowed not to extend China's MFN status unless the country showed vast improvement in human rights, such as ending exports made by prison labor, allowing *Voice of America* radio broadcasts to be heard, and accounting for political prisoners. On the other hand, U.S. businesses, large and small, insisted that Clinton keep trade flowing with the world's most populous country. The freedom and safety of a billion Chinese people hung in the balance, as did the jobs and financial security of hundreds of thousands of Americans.

Clinton needed to balance human rights and economics. In addition, since he was having foreign-policy difficulties in Bosnia, Rwanda, Haiti, and Cuba, Clinton needed a political success overseas.

There was no clear road to follow,

and Congress, the media, and other countries weighed in with differing interpretations of the situation. "Stripping China of its MFN status would . . . devastate the Chinese economy and imperil Beijing's model economic reform program," said *U.S. News & World Report.* "Getting [tough] on China would only [make] things worse," proclaimed *Newsweek.* Some analysts suggested that Clinton simply announce that China had met his goals and then renew MFN status without losing face; however, the arrest in April of dissident Wei Jingsheng worked against that tack. *Business Week* claimed that "delinking" MFN status from human rights actually would *improve* the situation in China, arguing that increased capitalism and affluence inevitably would lead to more freedom for its people.

In contrast, Mike Jendrzejczyk of Human Rights Watch lamented, "The Chinese government seems determined to prevent economic reform from leading to political reform," and Chinese exile Fang Lizhi argued, "As Japan and Germany bloodily illustrated in this century, nationalism plus economic might without human rights is not the road to democracy; it is the road to fascism." A third point of view, offered by representatives of various Southeast Asian countries, was that the very idea of individual

rights is a Western concept not relevant to Asian peoples.

Clinton finally decided to extend China's most-favored-nation status, winning both praise and criticism for his move. For instance, while many Asian countries were pleased, some European aircraft manufacturers complained. They didn't want to compete with U.S. aircraft companies in the huge Chinese market. Will Clinton's decision lead to affluence and human rights in China? Only time will tell.

SOURCES: Amy Borrus and Joyce Barnathan, "China's Gates Swing Open," *Business Week,* June 13, 1994, 52–53; Henrik Bering-Jensen, "Shortsighted China Policy Yields Dilemma for Clinton," *Insight on the News,* June 13, 1994, 14–16; Joyce Barnathan, "China: Is Prosperity Creating a Freer Society?" *Business Week,* June 6, 1994, 94–99; Joe Klein, " 'Hard' vs. 'Soft' vs. 'Viral' Power," *Newsweek,* June 6, 1994, 39; Douglas Harbrecht and Amy Borrus, "China: Can He Save Face?" *Business Week,* April 18, 1994, 56–57; Fang Lizhi, "Call Beijing's Bluff on Human Rights," *New Perspectives Quarterly* (Spring 1994): 62–63; and Susan V. Lawrence, "How Not to Pressure China," *U.S. News & World Report,* January 31, 1994, 55.

after all, why work when you can make almost as much by not working? Some Israeli government officials, for instance, claim that the country's generous benefits contribute to its high rate of unemployment; people do not bother to apply for available jobs.

Mixed Economies

In practice, most countries do not have a "pure" economy—all one type or another. Instead, they have a **mixed economy,** *an economy with a combination of government ownership and private ownership.*

The proportions of private and public enterprise vary widely in mixed economies, and the mix is always

changing. Presently, several countries are *converting government-owned companies into privately held firms,* a trend known as **privatization.** Countries may privatize state enterprises to improve their economies, believing that private corporations can manage businesses more cheaply and more efficiently than government units can. Sometimes, unloading these enterprises can raise badly needed cash for a government. Great Britain's government raised more than $23 billion by selling all or part of many state-owned businesses to private owners, including British Airways and aircraft engine maker Rolls-Royce.

Many European countries are privatizing industries as they move toward forming a unified economic community. France now allows private

System Features	Capitalism	Communism	Socialism	Mixed Economy
Ownership of enterprises	Businesses are owned privately, often by a large number of people. Government ownership is minimal.	The government owns the means of production with few exceptions, like small plots of land.	Basic industries are owned by government, but small-scale enterprises can be owned privately.	A strong private sector exists along with public enterprises in a mixed economy. The private sector is larger than that under socialism.
Rights to profits	Entrepreneurs and investors are entitled to all profits (minus taxes) that they earn. However, they are expected to operate in a socially responsible manner.	Profits are not acceptable under communism.	Profits officially exist only in the private sector of socialist economies.	Entrepreneurs and investors are entitled to private-sector profits, although taxes are often quite high. State enterprises also typically are expected to break even or to provide a return to the government.

Comparison of Economic Systems

companies to own up to 49 percent of a state-owned industry or bank. Renault, France's state-owned auto maker, issued a quarter of its capital to the Swedish company Volvo in return for a similar stake in Volvo. Italy has agreed to sell some of its airline routes, currently belonging to state-owned Alitalia, to privately owned carriers. The London-based European Bank for Reconstruction and Development, created by Western nations to foster Eastern European business reforms, is scheduled to be privatized.

Similarly, Mexico has started an economic reform program that has privatized more than a thousand state-owned companies, including the Telmex phone company and 18 national banks. The government also introduced a healthy dose of competition by deregulating the trucking industry—which used to make a $500 million profit each year for 15 powerful families. Today, post-deregulation has allowed trucking rates to drop by one-fourth, and 21 percent more trucks are on the road.

Economic Concepts Involved in International Business

The main patterns of international business result from a combination of economic and political factors.

DID YOU KNOW?

Each billion dollars' worth of U.S. exports creates more than 20,000 jobs.

The U.S. gesture of sliding a finger across the neck (to slit one's throat) means "I love you" in Swaziland.

To make a sale of construction vehicles in Venezuela, Caterpillar had to take iron ore in payment. The ore was shipped to Romania in exchange for men's suits which were then sold in London for cash.

French fries never are labeled as such in France. Even at a Parisian McDonald's outlet, you'll have to ask for *pommes frites.*

To understand trade and world business, let us first look at such concepts as balance of trade, balance of payments, and exchange rates.

Balance of Trade. A country's **balance of trade** is *the relationship between its exports and imports.* If a country exports more than it imports, it has a favorable balance of trade, called a *trade surplus.* If it imports more than it exports, it has an unfavorable balance of trade, or a *trade deficit.* By the mid-1990s, the United States averaged a trade deficit of about $117 billion. Despite this enormous figure, the United States is the top exporter in the world, with a record $448.2 billion in exports annually. The world's second-largest exporter is Germany, followed by Japan, France, and Great Britain.[3]

Balance of Payments.
A nation's balance of trade plays a central role in determining its **balance of payments**—*the overall flow of money into or out of a country.* Other factors affecting the balance of payments are overseas loans and borrowing, international investment, profits from such investments, and foreign aid. A favorable balance of payments, or *balance of payments surplus,* means that more money is coming into a country from abroad than is leaving it. An unfavorable balance of payments,

System Features	Capitalism	Communism	Socialism	Mixed Economy
Management of enterprises	Each enterprise is managed separately, either by its owners or by people who represent the owners. Government interference is minimal.	Centralized management of all state enterprises is a traditional feature of communism. Management is subject to centralized plans (3- to 5-year plans). Planning now is being decentralized.	A significant degree of government planning exists in socialist nations. State enterprises are managed directly by government bureaucrats.	The management of the private sector is similar to that under capitalism. Professional managers are also common in state enterprises.
Rights of employees	The rights to choose one's occupation and to join a labor union have long been recognized.	Employee rights traditionally were limited in exchange for a promise of no unemployment.	Workers have the right to choose their occupations and to join labor unions. However, the government influences career decisions for many people.	Workers have the right of job choice and labor-union membership. Unions in these countries are often quite strong.
Worker incentives	Considerable incentives exist to motivate people to perform at their highest levels.	Incentives are emerging in communist economies.	Incentives usually are limited in state enterprises, but do exist in the private sector.	Capitalist-like incentives exist in the private sector. Incentives in the public sector are more limited.

or *balance of payments deficit*, means that more money is leaving the country than entering it.

Nations with a deficit normally try to solve this problem by reducing their dependence on foreign goods, reducing investments abroad, devaluing their currency, or increasing their exports. Often these steps involve making politically controversial moves that may reduce the demand for foreign-made goods and also may lead to higher prices and greater unemployment. For instance, while cutting back the number of Japanese cars imported into the United States would reduce the number of imports, it would also end up raising the price of each imported vehicle.

Exchange Rates. A nation's **exchange rate** *is the rate at which its currency can be exchanged for the currencies of other nations.* A currency's exchange rate usually is quoted in terms of other important currencies. For example, the U.S. dollar bought about 100 Japanese yen and 1.54 German marks in late summer, 1994, while the Canadian dollar was worth about 75 U.S. cents.

Exchange rates can have a major impact on a nation's economy. Changes in exchange rates can wipe out or create a competitive advantage quickly, so they

are a big consideration in whether or not to invest abroad. If the dollar rises in price relative to the yen, for instance, this means that a dollar will buy more yen. Japanese products become less expensive, Japanese imports increase, and U.S. firms face greater competition.

Devaluation describes *the fall of a currency's value relative to other currencies or to a fixed standard.* Devaluation of the dollar makes U.S. goods sell for less abroad and lowers costs for visiting foreigners. If the dollar buys fewer yen, this increases the price U.S. consumers pay for Japanese products and decreases the amount of competition for U.S. firms. It also makes it more expensive for American companies to buy assets abroad, but less expensive for foreign firms to purchase American assets.[4]

International exchange rates are based on a system called *floating exchange rates*, where currency traders create a market for the world's currencies based on the countries' trade and investment prospects. In theory, this means that exchange rates are free to fluctuate, or "float," according to supply and demand. In practice, exchange rates do not float in total freedom. Countries often intervene to adjust their own exchange rates. Also, some currency blocs exist within which exchange rates are linked to each other, and many governments practice protectionist policies that seek to "protect" their economies from trade imbalances. A disadvantage of the floating-rate system is that exchange rates are highly sensitive to every bit of new information that could affect business. For the most part, however, the floating-rate system works well, and it appears that it will continue as the global basis for determining exchange rates.

Specialization among Nations

Nations usually benefit if they specialize in certain products or commercial activities. By doing what they do best, they are able to exchange surplus domestic output for foreign-made products that are needed. This allows a higher standard of living than would be possible if the country tried to produce everything itself.

However, specialization has its dangers if taken too far. Many less-developed countries depend on one or two primary commodities, such as grain and copper, to earn foreign currency to pay for imported goods. If the price of their main good declines, it becomes much more difficult to import needed goods and services. Other problems can occur when a country depends on foreign nations to supply something that is critical to its economy. For instance, oil is important to the U.S. economy because it helps to fuel our cars and machinery. Much of our oil comes from Middle Eastern countries, so wars and political unrest in that area of the world endanger our oil supply.

Absolute Advantage. A country has an *absolute advantage* in the marketing of a product if it has a monopolistic position or it produces the good at the lowest cost. Examples of absolute advantage are rare because few countries are sole suppliers, and because rapidly changing economic conditions can wipe out advantages in production costs.

When it comes to gem-quality diamonds, for instance, South Africa traditionally has had an absolute advantage, since it had a rare domestic source of these gems. However, the discovery of diamond deposits in other areas of the world—such as Canada—has removed South Africa's absolute advantage.

Comparative Advantage. A more practical approach to international specialization is that of *comparative advantage*. A country has a comparative advantage in an item if it can supply that item more efficiently and at a lower cost than it can supply other goods, compared to other nations. For example, if

country A can produce a certain good three times as efficiently as country B, and it produces a second product only twice as efficiently as country B, then country A has a comparative advantage in the first item. Country B, even though it produces the second good less efficiently than country A does, has a comparative advantage in this item because that is the one it is relatively more efficient at producing. Worldwide, the greatest supply of both products will result when each country specializes in producing the good where it has a comparative advantage, that is, country A producing the first good and country B producing the second.

Countries tend to follow this pattern of specialization. A tropical nation, such as Costa Rica, may specialize in agriculture, due to its climate and inexpensive labor. U.S. exports, on the other hand, reflect America's comparative advantage: the fact that it is a highly industrialized country with good natural and agricultural resources. The United States tends to export manufactured items (aircraft parts, electrical machinery), food products (grain and soybeans), and some natural resources (coal).

Self-Sufficiency. Some countries prefer to be self-sufficient rather than specializing and trading. Many Central American nations have tried to remain self-sufficient, although this pattern is changing. Other countries seek self-sufficiency only in commodities they regard as strategic to their long-run development, such as energy in the United States; but a few—Israel, for example—try to be self-sufficient in regard to many national-defense items. These countries see the noneconomic advantages of self-sufficiency as being more important to the national welfare than the economic advantages of specialization.

Getting Started in Global Business

Global business involvement is an evolving process for many firms. For example, a small company might start exporting on a limited scale, then expand its overseas efforts as management gains experience and confidence in its ability to operate effectively abroad. The company later may move to even greater degrees of global involvement.

Four levels of involvement in world business are direct and indirect exporting, foreign licensing, overseas marketing, and international production and marketing. As a firm becomes more active internationally, both the risks and the degree of control over marketing increase.

Top U.S. Exporters and Exports

Exporter	Major Export Product	Amount ($ billions)	Export	Amount ($ billions)
Boeing	Commercial aircraft	$17.5	Agricultural products	$42.2
General Motors	Motor vehicles and parts	14.0	Computers and office equipment	27.0
General Electric	Jet engines and turbines	8.2	Aircraft	26.3
IBM	Computers	7.5	Electrical machinery	32.2
Ford	Motor vehicles and parts	7.2	General industrial machinery	18.5
Chrysler	Motor vehicles and parts	7.0	Power-generating machinery	18.0
McDonnell-Douglas	Aerospace products	4.9	Specialized industrial machinery	16.7
Philip Morris	Tobacco, beverages, and food products	3.8	Motor vehicle parts	16.8
Hewlett-Packard	Computers	3.7	Scientific instruments	14.4
DuPont	Specialty chemicals	3.5	Coal and other fuels	11.3

Direct and Indirect Exporting. Exporting firms produce goods at home and sell them abroad. Many companies engage in *indirect exporting*, often without realizing it, when their products are part of another good that is exported. Electronic components are a common example.

When a firm actually seeks export business, it is engaging in *direct exporting*, the most common form of international business. The company must devote both capital and managerial resources to this effort. Frequently, a firm will coordinate its export operation with an in-house "export manager," or it may hire an outside company specializing in export promotion.

While the exporters shown in the table are large corporations, it is not necessary for a firm to be big in order to become a successful global exporter. A recent *Inc.* magazine survey of small companies shows that 38 percent of them are involved in direct exporting; they derive an average of 15 percent of their sales from overseas markets. According to the Commerce Department, firms with fewer than 20 employees account for 12 percent—about $30 billion—of total U.S. exports.

Foreign Licensing. Foreign licensing refers to a contract in which a firm allows a foreign company to produce and distribute its products or use its trademark, patent, or processes in a specific geographic area. It is a low-cost way for firms to enter new markets. Licensing also provides local marketing information and distribution channels and avoids protectionist barriers.

Overseas Marketing. When a firm gets involved in overseas marketing, it establishes a foreign sales office. The parent company directly controls all foreign marketing, even though the goods and services may come from a variety of sources, such as domestic plants, licensees, or subcontractors.

Sometimes the choice between licensing and overseas marketing can be an important one. When PepsiCo first entered India, it did so via foreign licensing. At first the strategy worked well; within three years Pepsi won 25 percent of India's soft-drink market. However, their archrival, The Coca-Cola Company, countered with an overseas marketing coup: it acquired the distribution network and sales offices of Parle Exports, an Indian firm that controls 60 percent of the country's beverage market. While The Coca-Cola Company will continue to control Indian marketing operations, the pre-established distri-

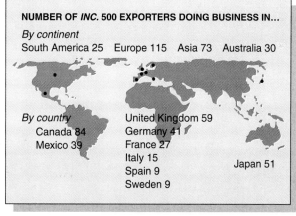

NUMBER OF *INC.* 500 EXPORTERS DOING BUSINESS IN...

By continent
South America 25   Europe 115   Asia 73   Australia 30

By country
Canada 84
Mexico 39
United Kingdom 59
Germany 41
France 27
Italy 15
Spain 9
Sweden 9
Japan 51

For the world. By the world.

Boeing is America's leading exporter, and has been for the last three years. Airlines in more than 140 countries fly Boeing airplanes. But we are a major *customer* as well as a major *supplier*. For example, we buy goods and services from some 39,000 firms with facilities and employees in every state in the U.S. and in 34 nations around the world.

Information on Boeing's role in the global economy: write to Corporate Communications, P.O. Box 3707, MS 10-16, Seattle, WA 98124-2207.

BOEING

Boeing products alone account for more than 65 percent of the United States' $26.3 billion aircraft export market.

bution network gives it a big advantage in covering the large country.[5]

International Production. Total global business involvement occurs when a company produces as well as markets its products abroad. A firm may enter foreign markets in this way by starting a subsidiary or acquiring an existing firm in the country where it is expanding. Sometimes, too, a company will enter into a **joint venture** with a local firm or government, *sharing the operation's costs, risks, management, and profits with its local partner.* The way in which a company enters a new market may depend on political factors. America's trading relations with other nations may vary according to whether it grants these countries *most-favored-nation (MFN)* status, which means that

Pepsi's advantage over Coke in India dried up when Coca-Cola bought Parle Exports.

these countries are subject to the same, relatively low import duties. For instance, many American firms waited until President Clinton renewed China's most-favored-nation trade status before entering the market. Caterpillar Inc. quickly formed a joint venture to build hydraulic excavators in China; Caterpillar managers expect the Chinese market to bring in $2 billion by the year 2000.[6]

Outsourcing, the practice of contracting production and other business services to outside firms, was introduced in Chapter 1. In many cases, these outside firms are foreign-based. For example, major shoe manufacturers, such as Nike and Reebok, contract much of their production to workers in Asia. Many of Hewlett-Packard's best-selling computer printers are assembled and packaged in Asia.

Countertrade

Sometimes it is difficult to tell who is selling and who is buying in international trade because of the practice of **countertrade,** or *international bartering agreements in which an exporter must buy something in order to sell something.* Some degree of countertrade is involved in an estimated 15 to 30 percent of all international trade.

Countertrade typically is used when the buyer has limited foreign exchange, so payment must be made in terms of other goods. On occasion, however, the buyer pays for the goods, and the seller agrees to purchase other merchandise from the buyer or find a customer for the products. Often countertrade may be the only way a firm can enter a particular market. Many developing countries simply cannot obtain

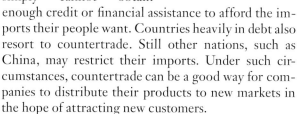

A recession in Europe has contributed to EuroDisney's $1 billion loss.

enough credit or financial assistance to afford the imports their people want. Countries heavily in debt also resort to countertrade. Still other nations, such as China, may restrict their imports. Under such circumstances, countertrade can be a good way for companies to distribute their products to new markets in the hope of attracting new customers.

Multinational Corporations.   A **multinational corporation** is *a firm with major operations outside its home country.* Many of America's largest multinationals are oil, auto, or chemical companies. *Foreign direct investment* occurs when a firm invests abroad in order to create or expand a permanent interest in an enterprise. Usually such an arrangement gives a company some degree of control over its operations.[7]

Barriers to International Business

The opening of the Channel tunnel has removed one of the physical barriers between England and France.

Various barriers to conducting effective world business exist. Some are minor and easily overcome; others are nearly impossible to bridge. In any case, business executives must expect and learn to handle a multitude of problems in attempting to reach world markets.

Cultural Barriers.   To succeed in foreign markets, firms must understand cultural factors, such as language, education, social values, religious attitudes, and consumer habits. Many Asian cultures place great emphasis on personal relationships as a crucial part of doing business. This helps explain, for example, why Japan has been so successful in forming business ties with Pacific Rim nations.

Cultural factors also help explain why Euro-Disney, Disney's huge theme park near Paris, has been less successful than its counterparts in the United States and Japan. Disney management expected European tourists to behave like Americans, who bring their families to spend a week at a time in Florida's Disney World hotels. However, Europeans' per-capita income is lower than that of Japanese and American tourists, and they prefer to spend it on long vacations. Many EuroDisney visitors are day-trippers who made a brief stop and returned to their Paris hotels in the evening. Another problem is that, unlike snack-happy Americans, Europeans like to eat their meals at set times; long lines formed in front of park restaurants when everyone stopped for lunch at 12:30. Once the tourists got inside, they were less than pleased to discover that the eateries did not serve beer or wine. Complicating the situation were French employees who resented Disney's U.S.-style rules forbidding facial hair, makeup, and fingernails longer than 0.2 inches.[8]

Physical Barriers.   A variety of physical barriers also can affect world trade. Location can make a big difference: it is easier for Japan to do business with Pacific Rim nations than it is for the United States, because Japan is much closer geographically. For the same reason, many American businesses are investing money and moving operations to Mexico rather than to Asia. While investment opportunities in Latin America are tremendous, U.S. companies may face other physical barriers, such as poor roads, mountainous terrain, and uncertain transportation systems.

Lifting of the U.S. trade embargo against Vietnam has opened up a market of 71 million potential consumers of American goods.

Other barriers to trade may be less visible, but important nonetheless. For instance, American elec-

trical products run on a different type of electric current than those in Europe. Different time zones also can make it difficult to do business with other countries. Stockbrokers in the United States who deal with foreign stock exchanges often have to start work early and work late to include worldwide business hours.

Tariffs and Trade Restrictions.   Global commerce is affected by tariffs and related trade restrictions. These restrictions include import quotas, embargoes, and exchange control.

Tariffs.   A **tariff** is *a tax levied on products imported from abroad.* Some require a set amount per pound, gallon, or other unit; others are figured on the value of the good. Tariffs can be classified as either revenue or protective. A *revenue tariff* is designed to raise

---

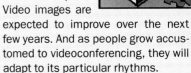

TECHNOLOGY

Videoconferencing: Eliminating Physical Barriers

Walter Hubbard, group vice president for carpet products at BASF's Fibers Division, frequently confers with BASF employees at 24 locations worldwide. Once these meetings required exhausting and expensive airplane rides; now Hubbard travels only as far as the videoconferencing room. As Hubbard convenes with people all over the world, he views them on a large computer monitor and hears them through loudspeakers—and they see and hear him as well. Hubbard says that BASF travel costs have gone down 40 percent.

Women's clothing manufacturer Liz Claiborne uses a videoconferencing hookup from New York headquarters to factories in Sri Lanka and Indonesia. Through this system, clothing in Asia can be immediately approved by executives in North America. Travel and overnight delivery costs are eliminated, and time is saved.

Similarly, videoconferencing allows centralized employee interviewing and training, as well as instantaneous troubleshooting; no longer must a factory in location A

lose a day of work to broken machinery while the expert repairperson flies out from location Z. As an additional benefit, videoconferencing requires workers to prepare carefully for meetings and to minimize casual conversation, since facilities are usually available for limited periods of time.

Although videoconferencing has changed the way business is done, it is far from perfect. The technology, although getting less expensive, is costly; the video images are jerky; there is a time delay between speaking and being heard; and, ironically, because video meetings are so easy to arrange, some executives find themselves spending more time, rather than less, in conference.

In addition, videoconferencing requires new behaviors by participants, who need to wait extra seconds before talking to make sure that the previous speaker is finished; to wear dark colors, which read well on the video monitor; to identify themselves and address each other by name each time they speak, for clarity; and to refrain from sudden movements, which blur the video image.

Many of these problems are already disappearing. Companies that don't want to pay for their own equipment can use public videoconferencing facilities, which are available

from companies such as Sprint. Video images are expected to improve over the next few years. And as people grow accustomed to videoconferencing, they will adapt to its particular rhythms.

No one claims that videoconferencing is ideal for all uses. For instance, it is not useful for sensitive negotiations that require close attention to voice quality, body language, and other subtle signals. In addition, many employees view business trips as welcome breaks in routine, and the airlines are certainly not pleased that thousands of people will no longer need to take millions of trips.

Nevertheless, any technology that saves days of employee work time and thousands of dollars is here to stay. *Black Enterprise* magazine says that industry analysts predict that videoconferencing will soon be "as commonplace as the fax machine."

SOURCES: Carolyn M. Brown, "Next Best Thing to Being There," *Black Enterprise,* February 1992, 53–54, and Louis E. Boone and David L. Kurtz, *Contemporary Business Communication* (Englewood Cliffs, NJ, Prentice Hall, 1994), 684–688.

funds for the government. Revenue tariffs were a major source of U.S. government revenue until the early twentieth century. A *protective tariff*, which is usually higher than a revenue tariff, is designed to raise the retail price of imported items and improve the competitiveness of domestically made goods. Countries sometimes protect their "infant industries," and their related jobs, by using tariffs to bar foreign-made products.

Trade Restrictions.   There are other ways of restricting trade besides the use of tariffs. An *import quota* sets a limit on the number of certain products that can be imported. The objective of such quotas is to protect domestic industries and their employees or to preserve foreign exchange. For instance, there are quotas restricting the number of Japanese cars and trucks that can be brought into the United States. This is complicated by the fact that many Japanese firms have assembly plants in the United States. A new law, which recently took effect, requires content labels on cars and trucks weighing 8,500 pounds or less, detailing where the parts are made. Content is measured by the dollar value of the components, not by the labor cost of assembling the vehicles. This change is expected to raise the apparent foreign content of many cars assembled here.[9] While this may not directly affect the number of automobiles imported, it heightens the already-present trade tensions between the United States and Japan.

The ultimate quota is the *embargo*, a total ban on imported or exported products. Embargoes typically are used for political rather than economic purposes. Until recently, U.S. businesses were unable to do business in Vietnam due to the United States trade embargo against that country. Within a week after the embargo ended, more than 34 American firms had entered the Vietnamese market. The Coca-Cola

Company lined up two joint ventures, for example, and Mobil Oil bought a 38 percent stake in the Blue Dragon oil field 150 miles southeast of Ho Chi Minh City.[10]

Foreign Trade Zones

Many countries have special areas where foreign goods may be held or processed and then re-exported without incurring further duties. *Foreign trade zones* often are located at major ports of entry to a country, as well as near important production facilities inland. Such zones are useful to both the government that maintains the zone and the foreign firms that use it. For foreign companies, the trade zone offers a convenient location near a major market without all of the costs normally associated with exporting products. They can import their merchandise, store it in the zone, and process, change, test, or demonstrate it without paying duties. Duty payments come due only if the exporter actually ships its goods from the foreign trade zone into the target market. For the host country, the zone provides jobs for the people who process the merchandise in that area.[11]

Exchange Controls.   Foreign trade also can be regulated by using *exchange controls*, under which firms can buy and sell only through the central bank or other designated government agency. The government then can allocate, expand, or restrict access to foreign exchange in accordance with national policy.

Exchange controls can be used selectively to reduce the importation of specific products or the operation of particular companies. (Sometimes countries do this to restrict the inflow of goods considered as luxuries or as unnecessary.) Such regulations can be difficult for firms to deal with because they can affect free trade in components or supplies for other products, or for overseas production. Often a company will have to negotiate with government officials to agree on what can and cannot be brought into the country.[12]

Exchange controls are not restricted to less-developed countries. Britain, for example, had some form of exchange controls from the time of World War II until the early 1980s.

GATT and the Move toward Free Trade

While trade restrictions and tariffs continue to affect the flow of global commerce, the overall trend has been toward free trade. The **General Agreement on Tariffs and Trade (GATT)** is *an international trade*

GATT notwithstanding, the French continue to restrict imports of U.S. films and TV programs, in spite of their popularity.

IT'S THE LAW

Webb-Pomerene Export Act: (1918) Exempts from antitrust laws certain combinations of U.S. firms acting together to develop export markets. The intent is to give U.S. industry economic power equal to that possessed by a cartel, a monopolistic organization of foreign firms. This is important because foreign firms frequently cooperate with each other in ways that would be illegal for U.S. firms under domestic antitrust law. Companies operating under Webb-Pomerene must not reduce competition within the United States and must not use unfair methods of competition.

Export Trading Companies Act: (1982) Encourages formation of export trading companies by eliminating some antitrust barriers and allowing banks to participate in such enterprises. An export trading company is any type of organization that seeks to expand exports.

Foreign Corrupt Practices Act: (1978) Forbids U.S. firms from bribing foreigners to buy their goods and services. Enacted in the wake of numerous reports of companies doing just that, the law also requires businesses to set up adequate accounting controls to monitor internal compliance. The law provides for penalties against both the company and the official involved. Firms can be fined up to $1 million for violations, while the individuals implicated face $10,000 fines and up to five years in jail.

accord that has sponsored a series of negotiations that have reduced worldwide tariff levels. The most recent negotiations, the so-called Uruguay Round, produced a new General Agreement that became effective in 1995.

The goal of the new agreement is to stabilize worldwide currencies and prevent protectionist laws that restrict international trade. Other goals include protecting patents and copyrights, lowering trade barriers for services, and improving methods for settling trade disputes. Economists estimate that, by 2005, the new GATT could create 2 million U.S. jobs and increase the United States' gross domestic product by as much as $350 billion. However, they caution that the agreement still permits many national trade barriers that will have to be worked out in the future.[13]

Political and Legal Barriers

Firms operating abroad often are hindered by local politics and laws. Indonesia's government, for example, prohibits foreign firms from creating their own wholesale or retail distribution channels, which forces outside companies to use Indonesian distributors. Brazilian laws require foreign-owned manufacturers to buy most of their supplies from local vendors. Clearly, managers involved in international business must be well versed in legislation affecting their industry if they want to compete in today's world marketplace.

As mentioned earlier, many U.S. firms have started doing business in China since that nation's MFN status was renewed. The renewal has opened up new markets to AT&T, for example. The Chinese government plans to spend $41.4 billion on telecom-

munications during the next six years, and AT&T is competing against European and Japanese rivals for several contracts. William Warwick, CEO of AT&T China, believes that the MFN renewal gives AT&T an advantage: "By removing the uncertainty, it strengthens our position," he says. A U.S. official in Hong Kong agrees: "There was a subtle resistance to having a long-term supplier relationship with the U.S. firms. That's going to disappear."[14]

Legal Framework for International Business

The legal environment for U.S. firms operating abroad has three dimensions: U.S. law, host-country law, and international requirements. All firms operating in the United States are subject to comprehensive business legislation. In addition, their international operations also are subject to various trade regulations, tax laws, and import-export requirements.

International Trade Requirements. International requirements can be seen in the various agreements existing among nations. The United States has many *friendship, commerce, and navigation (FCN) treaties* with other nations. Such treaties include many aspects of international business relations, such as the right to conduct business in the treaty partner's domestic market. Other international business agreements concern product standards, patents, trademarks, reciprocal tax treaties, export control, international air travel, and international communications.

Originally set up to coordinate international financial relations, the *International Monetary Fund (IMF)* lends money to countries that require short-

While AT&T's expansion into China reflects its overall global strategy, the services it provides can help other businesses develop a global strategy as well.

term assistance in conducting international trade. The IMF has played a major role in overseeing agreements between the debtor countries and their lenders to renew their loans while ensuring repayment. The *World Bank* was established to make long-term loans for economic development projects. In addition, the Export-Import Bank of the United States helps U.S. businesses meet the financing conditions necessary for exporting overseas. All of these financial institutions help to facilitate international business activity.

The legal requirements of host nations strongly affect international marketers. Japan, for example, often is cited as having complex import requirements. Other nations, such as Mexico, put various restrictions on foreign ownership of their business sectors. The majority of international business people realize the importance of obeying the laws and regulations of the countries within which they operate. Violations of these legal requirements constitute setbacks for international business as a whole and should be carefully avoided.

Dumping. **Dumping,** *selling goods abroad at a price lower than that charged in the domestic market,* is prohibited in many countries. U.S. law requires that imported items be sold for at least production costs, plus ten percent overhead and a minimum eight percent profit margin. If dumping is proved, punitive trade restrictions may be assigned to the dumped products.

Firms dump products for a variety of reasons, but usually it is to increase market share. This is similar to predatory pricing in the domestic market, since dumping undersells rivals and can force them out of business. Also, when a country's domestic market is too small to support an efficient level of production, the large U.S. market becomes a tempting target for dumping. Alternatively, a firm might dump surplus goods or technologically obsolete products overseas.

Dumping has become a controversial issue in the global marketplace; since the mid-1980s, over 40 nations have created their own antidumping laws, many of them modeled on U.S. legislation. Since that time, the number of dumping complaints worldwide has risen to roughly 2,000. Many economists feel that the U.S. laws make it too easy to prove dumping, and indeed, the Commerce Department finds dumping in over 90 percent of all the cases it investigates.[15]

Multinational Economic Communities

Since World War II, there has been a trend toward multinational economic integration by various means.

The simplest approach is to establish a **free trade area** in which *participating nations trade freely among themselves without tariffs or trade restrictions.* Each maintains its own tariffs for trade outside this area. A **customs union** *sets up a free trade area, plus a uniform tariff for trade with nonmember nations.* In a **common market,** or *economic union, members go beyond a customs union to try to bring all government trade rules into agreement.* These partnerships meet with varying degrees of success. We will discuss two such efforts: NAFTA and the European Union.

NAFTA.   The North American Free Trade Agreement (NAFTA), which became effective in 1994, created a free-trade zone with the United States, Canada, and Mexico. By eliminating all trade barriers and investment restrictions between the three nations over the next 15 years, NAFTA opens up a market of 360 million people who produce and consume $6.7 trillion in goods and services.

As with many other free trade issues, NAFTA is controversial. Opponents to the pact fear employers will move their production facilities to Mexico, where hourly wages average $2.35, compared to $16.14 in the United States. Environmentalists point to the pollu-

tion generated by Mexican plants, which usually do not meet the same safety and environmental impact standards that are required of U.S. companies. Supplemental agreements were negotiated addressing these issues.

Those who support NAFTA feel the agreement will bring more jobs and economic growth for Americans, Canadians, and Mexicans. Proponents of free trade argue that the United States has everything to gain from a more prosperous southern neighbor. Even before the agreement was signed, American companies already were doing business south of the border. "Mexico is the third largest market for U.S. exports [after Canada and Japan], and number one in terms of growth," says consultant Philip Roussel, who notes that exports to Mexico have risen 18 percent annually in recent years. Both Canada and Mexico are major purchasers of American vehicles, electrical products, and machinery. As Mexico grows wealthier, the argument goes, its citizens will spend even more.

Many business people feel that American-style customer service and quality will give U.S.-made products a competitive edge in the future. Mexicans, says ethnic-marketing consultant Armando Gutierrez, "think U.S. products are the best in the world." Ex-

Although much of the furor over NAFTA has centered around jobs, in reality it will have little impact on the number created or lost in the United States.

U.S. Trade with NAFTA Partners					
U.S. Trade with Mexico			**U.S. Trade with Canada**		
Top Exports (in billions)	Electrical products	$4.3	**Top Exports** (in billions)	Road vehicles	$17.6
	Road vehicles	3.6		Electrical products	7.9
	Machinery	2.8		Industrial machinery	4.9
	Telecommunications	1.6		Office machines	4.8
	Office machines	1.1		Power generators	4.2
Top Imports (in billions)	Electrical products	$4.8	**Top Imports** (in billions)	Road vehicles	$25.6
	Petroleum	4.6		Petroleum	6.6
	Road vehicles	4.3		Paper products	6.1
	Telecommunications	2.9		Metals	3.6
	Vegetables, fruits	1.4		Electrical products	3.6

plains Brian Brisson, an assistant commercial attaché with the U.S. Embassy in Mexico, "Mexicans tend to rank service, the personal touch, right up there with price. They want attention before, during, and after the sale." This is why John Lopez, who manages Mexican accounts for Vista Chemical Company's Latin American division, spends 60 percent of his time in Mexico. "There are plenty of flights from Houston, so I get down there all the time," says the Colombian-born Lopez. "We're not selling a commodity, we're selling a product that requires a lot of technical support. That means I need to be as close to the customer as possible."[16]

European Union. Perhaps the best-known example of a common market is the European Union. The potential of the European Union is tremendous: 12 countries, 335 million people, and a market of $5.53 trillion are involved.

To achieve its goal of a "borderless Europe," the union is working to erase barriers to free trade among its members. This is a highly complex process that involves standardizing business regulations and requirements, standardizing trade duties and value added taxes, eliminating customs checks, and creating a standardized currency, known as the European Currency Unit (ECU). Europe's economic borders were technically dissolved on December 31, 1992, although true economic integration will not take place for several more years.

Consider the difficulty of standardizing a currency when large differences exist between the strengths of the members' various economies. Another problem is the persistence of cultural traditions that have existed for centuries. For example, Belgium is a small country, but it contains three distinct cultures: Dutch consumers in the north, French-speaking people in the south (who view themselves as Wallonians rather than Belgians), and a small German community in the southeast.[17]

Developing a Global Business Strategy

In developing an international business strategy, managers can choose from either a global or multinational strategy. A **global strategy** *uses a standardized product and marketing strategy worldwide.* The same product is sold in essentially the same manner throughout the world. The Ford Motor Company is applying a global strategy by merging its U.S., European, Asian, and Latin American operations into one huge organization, with the goal of creating standardized categories of cars to be sold worldwide. Ford management hopes to reduce the company's costs dramatically by having to engineer products only once, rather than multiple times for different markets.[18]

Ford hopes success with the Contour, its latest world car, will give it the capital it needs to expand into China and India.

Under a **multinational strategy,** *each national market is treated differently.* Firms develop products and marketing strategies that appeal to the customs, tastes, and buying habits of particular national markets. Software maker Microsoft pursues a multinational strategy by creating products for specific markets, such as software that can read Japanese characters. Microsoft also staffs its overseas sales and distribution operations with local workers. "The local employees understand the bureaucracy and how to get through the red tape, which is usually much worse than in this country," explains Charles Stevens, general manager for worldwide business strategy. "They also understand the customer." Over the past five years, international sales have risen from 45 percent to 55 percent of the company's annual revenues.[19]

SUMMARY OF LEARNING GOALS

1. **Explain the importance of international business.**
   Since most national economies are closely linked today, international business is growing in importance. Exports account for 55 percent of all U.S. economic growth. Economists predict that the passage of NAFTA and the expansion of Asian, Latin American, and Eastern European markets will make global trade even more important to the U.S. economy in coming years.

2. **Identify the different types of economic systems.**
   Many Americans forget that much of the world lives under economic systems other than capitalism, primarily communism, socialism, and mixed economies. Communism, as proposed by Karl Marx, is a classless economic system in which private property is eliminated and goods are owned in common. Socialism is an economic system in which the basic industries are owned and operated by the government, and private ownership of some small businesses is permitted. A mixed economy is one in which businesses and industries are publicly and privately owned in various combinations.

3. **Discuss the economic concepts involved in international business.**
   Economic concepts involved in international business include the balance of trade (the difference between exports and imports), and balance of payments (the difference between inward and outward cash flows), and the exchange rate. International exchange rates are based on a system of floating exchange rates, where currency traders create a market for the world's currencies based on the countries' trade and investment prospects.

4. **Explain why nations tend to specialize in certain goods.**
   Countries usually benefit if they specialize in certain products or commercial activities. A country has an absolute advantage in making a product if it holds a monopoly or produces the good at the lowest cost. It has a comparative advantage if it can supply the product more efficiently or at a lower cost than it can supply other products. Some countries refrain from specializing because they want to be self-sufficient, particularly in certain strategic areas.

5. **Name the different levels of involvement in international business.**
   The four levels of involvement in international business are direct and indirect exporting, foreign licensing, overseas marketing, and combined foreign production and marketing.

6. **Explain countertrade.**
   Countertrade refers to negotiated bartering agreements to facilitate exports and imports between countries. It often is used when a buyer has limited foreign exchange. In other instances, a seller agrees to buy certain products from the purchaser in order to expedite the original sale. The practice of countertrade is expected to grow in the future.

7. **Identify the main obstacles confronting global business.**
   A wide variety of obstacles face world business. Examples include physical and cultural barriers, tariffs and trade restrictions, and political and legal obstacles. Physical barriers, such as geographic distance or poor transportation systems, can affect world trade. Cultural barriers (language and different business customs) also can be a problem. Trade restrictions, such as tariffs, import quotas, embargoes, and exchange controls, may discriminate against particular products, companies, or nations. Other barriers to trade include different national laws and marketing requirements, as well as political factors.

8. **Explain multinational economic integration.**
   Multinational economic integration is the removal of barriers to the movement of goods, capital, and people. Three formats, with increasing levels of integration, exist: the free trade area, the customs union, and the common market or economic union.

9. **Distinguish between a global and multinational strategy.**
   In developing an international business strategy, managers can choose from either a global or multinational strategy. A global strategy uses a standardized product and marketing strategy worldwide; the same product is sold in essentially the same manner throughout the world. Under a multinational strategy, each national market is treated differently. Firms develop products and marketing strategies that appeal to the customs, tastes, and buying habits of particular national markets.

KEY TERMS QUIZ

balance of trade
tariff
balance of payments
free trade area
devaluation
multinational corporation

General Agreement on
Tariffs and Trade
(GATT)
countertrade
exchange rate
customs union

socialism
dumping
mixed economy
common market
multinational strategy
communism

importing
privatization
exporting
global strategy

_____ 1. An international bartering agreement in which an exporter must buy something in order to sell something.

_____ 2. An international accord that has sponsored a series of negotiations on tariffs and trade restrictions.

_____ 3. The worldwide use of a standardized product and marketing strategy.

_____ 4. Selling domestic goods abroad.

_____ 5. The relationship between a country's exports and imports.

_____ 6. An economic system that advocates government ownership and operation of all basic industries.

_____ 7. Buying foreign goods and raw materials.

_____ 8. A corporation that operates on an international level.

_____ 9. A strategy whereby each national market is treated differently.

_____ 10. The rate at which a country's currency can be exchanged for other currencies.

_____ 11. An economic system having a mix of government ownership and private enterprise.

_____ 12. A tax levied against imported products.

_____ 13. The trend to substitute private ownership for public ownership.

_____ 14. The flow of money into and out of a country.

_____ 15. A form of economic integration that maintains a customs union and seeks to bring other trade rules into agreement.

_____ 16. A form of economic integration in which a free trade area is established for member nations and a uniform tariff is imposed on trade with nonmember nations.

_____ 17. Selling goods abroad at a price lower than that charged in the domestic market.

_____ 18. The reduction in value of a country's currency.

_____ 19. An economic theory, developed by Karl Marx, under which private property is eliminated and the means of production are owned in common.

_____ 20. A form of economic integration in which participants agree to trade among themselves without tariffs or trade restrictions.

OTHER IMPORTANT TERMS

absolute advantage
cartel
comparative advantage
embargo
exchange control
Export Trading Companies Act
(1982)

floating exchange rates
Foreign Corrupt Practices Act (1978)
foreign direct investment
foreign production
foreign trade zones
friendship, commerce, and navigation
(FCN) treaties

import quota
International Monetary Fund (IMF)
joint venture
most favored nation (MFN)
outsourcing
Webb-Pomerene Act (1918)
World Bank

REVIEW QUESTIONS

1. Is it possible for a nation to have a favorable balance of trade and an unfavorable balance of payments? Defend your answer.
2. Differentiate between private enterprise, communism, socialism, and mixed economies. Discuss the current status of each of these economic sytems.
3. Explain how exchange rates are established. What factors can affect them?
4. Distinguish between the concepts of absolute advantage and comparative advantage.
5. Identify the levels of involvement in international business and give an example of each.

6. What is meant by countertrade? Why do you think this has become such an important part of international business?
7. How do firms with a multinational strategy operate in the global marketplace?
8. Describe three types of barriers that firms may face in international business. Give an example of each.
9. Explain the difference between a revenue tariff and a protective tariff. What type of tariff is the United States most concerned with today? Why?
10. Describe the three basic formats for multinational economic integration.

DISCUSSION QUESTIONS

1. Keep a diary of your purchases for a week. How many of the items you bought were foreign made? Discuss what you have learned from this exercise.
2. For over 30 years, the United States has enforced a ban on trade with Cuba for political reasons. Given the change in the former Soviet Union, should the United States now resume trade with Cuba? What would be the advantages and disadvantages of doing so? Explain your answer.
3. The People's Republic of China is scheduled to resume control of Hong Kong in 1997. As a result, many Hong Kong business people and other educated citizens have emigrated to other nations, such as Canada and Aus-

tralia. Discuss the impact of this situation on international business.
4. Analyze a government-owned business in the United States—perhaps even in your own community. How does its government-owned status make it different from businesses that are privately owned? Do you think that it would be more or less efficient if it were privatized (or would it make any difference)? Explain your answer.
5. Compare advertisements from two multinational firms, one of which uses a global strategy while the other employs a multinational strategy. Which strategy do you think is more effective? How does this choice of strategy affect each firm's products and marketing?

VIDEO CASE: Jamaica—Paradise Lost

The video case for this chapter discusses the effects of the International Monetary Fund's policies on the economy of Jamaica and can be found on page 411 of Appendix D.

Solution to Key Terms Quiz

1. countertrade 2. General Agreement on Tariffs and Trade (GATT) 3. global strategy 4. exporting 5. balance of trade 6. socialism 7. importing 8. multinational corporation 9. multinational strategy 10. exchange rate 11. mixed economy 12. tariff 13. privatization 14. balance of payments 15. common market 16. customs union 17. dumping 18. devaluation 19. communism

Getting Started

CHAPTER 4

Developing a Business Strategy and Plan

Learning Goals

1. Differentiate between strategic and tactical planning.
2. Identify the components of a mission statement.
3. Define objectives and how they differ from the mission statement.
4. Explain competitive differentiation and identify methods businesses use to create it.
5. Explain SWOT analysis and how it is used in corporate planning.
6. Describe SBUs and give examples.
7. Define forecasting and differentiate between quantitative and qualitative forecasting.
8. List the methods of forecasting.
9. Outline the components of the business plan.

Bill Gates has a plan. Although Microsoft, the company he founded and runs, is enormously successful, with annual revenues of $4.5 billion and $2.5 to $3 billion in cash on hand, Gates knows that the world of computing constantly evolves, shifts, and even mutates. While today's computer industry centers on the desktop computer, tomorrow's will not *have* a center; instead, wired and wireless high-speed networks will move computing from the office onto the so-called "information superhighway." Gates plans for Microsoft to dominate that superhighway.

Gates's objectives for Microsoft include developing programs for the computers that will link people to movies and information and shopping services and everything else the superhighway will offer. Whether PCs, digital televisions, geographical information systems, or inventions yet undreamed-of, all computers need software, and Gates wants the bulk of that software—if not all of it—to be made by Microsoft. Says Gates, "Our software will be used in business, in the home, in the pocket, and in the car. We're making a big bet on that."

While Gates's objectives are large, he knows that they will be reached step by step. For instance, Microsoft is striving to make its software simpler to use and less intimidating to people who are not computer literate, a necessary task for the success of Gates's vision.

Analysts point out that dominating the information superhighway will be easier said than done, and Microsoft has its weaknesses as well as its strengths. The software program Windows NT is far from a runaway best seller and Chicago (an updated Windows

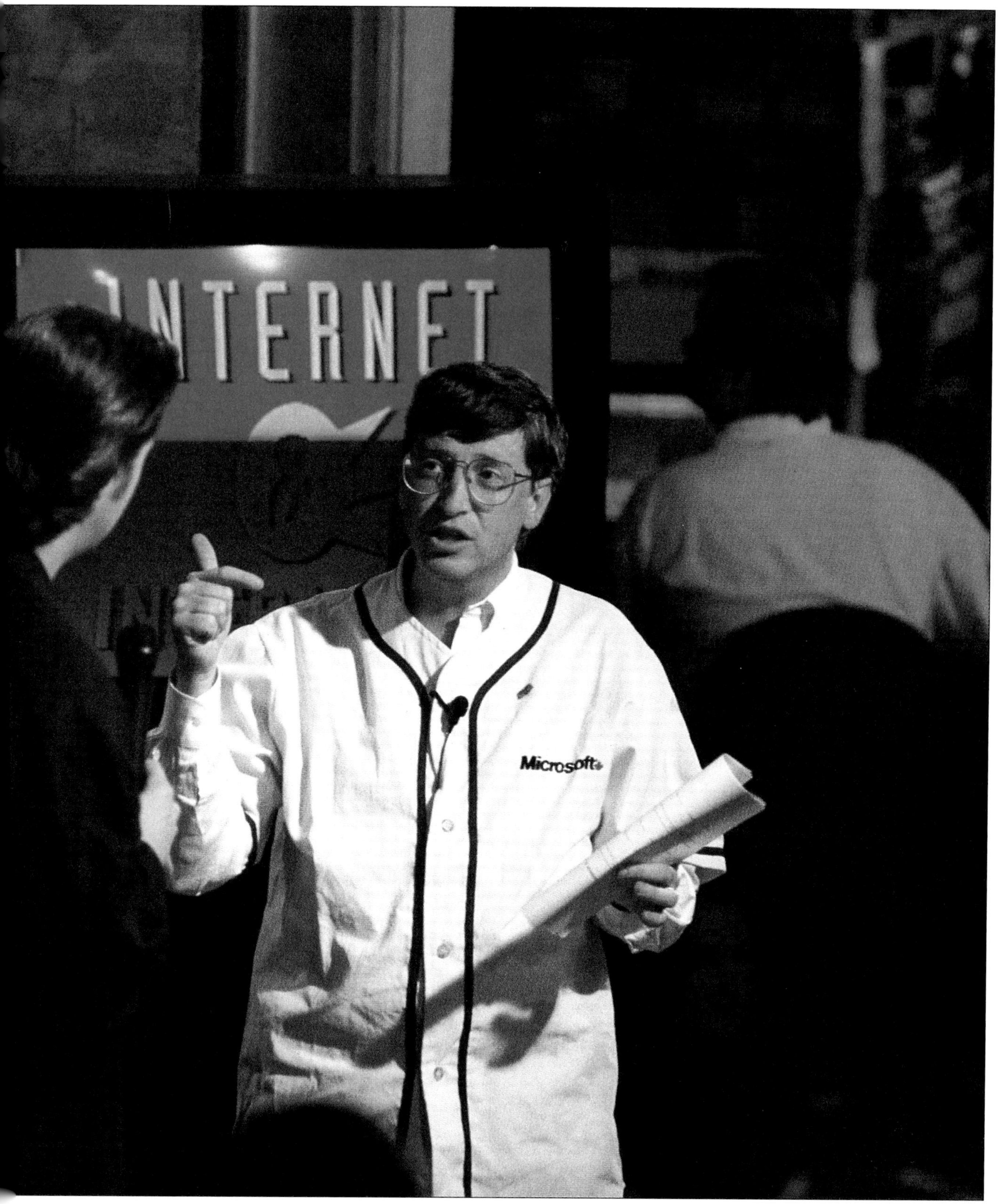
INTERNET
Microsoft

operating system) was released behind schedule. The unveiling of Winpad, Microsoft's software for personal digital assistants, has been delayed again and again. In addition, while success at the level to which Gates aspires requires partnership with other companies, being a partner is not Microsoft's—or Gates's—forte. Although Microsoft has deals with Tele-Communications Inc. (TCI) and Rogers Communications, an agreement among Microsoft, TCI, and Time Warner fell through when Time Warner found Microsoft's demands unreasonable. Analyst William M. Bluestein of Forrester Research says that some companies believe that when negotiating with Microsoft, "you want to keep your hand on your wallet." Bluestein also compared Gates and TCI chair John C. Malone working together to "two scorpions in a bottle."

Yet it is a time of virtually unlimited opportunity for Microsoft, and Gates plans to take full advantage. Emphasizing research, Gates lavishly funds top-notch people to develop the technology of the future. (Microsoft's development budget exceeds $600 million.) Microsoft's staff is not limited to computer experts; the payroll includes linguists and special-effects whizzes, plus specialists in other fields that might contribute to Microsoft's future. The mission of all these people is to make real Gates's vision of a global telecommunication system run by Microsoft software.

No company exists in a vacuum, and Microsoft faces some serious threats. Competition is tough, and companies such as Novell and AT&T would like nothing better than to run Microsoft right off the information superhighway. In addition, there have been legal threats against Microsoft. In 1994, Microsoft paid $120 million to Stac Electronics after Stac sued Microsoft for copyright infringement and won (although Microsoft mitigated that loss by entering into a partnership with Stac). Also in 1994, the Justice Department got Microsoft to agree to a consent decree that banned some of the software giant's sales practices. The decree also gave the Justice Department the right to monitor Microsoft's compliance for six and a half years.

Gates is pragmatic about the realities of the computer industry, saying that the average new project has "less than a 50 percent chance of working," and he knows that one generation's computer colossus can be the next generation's struggling also-ran. For Gates, the appropriate response to the uncertainties of the coming information superhighway is simple: stay at the head of the pack vying for the fast lane. Says Gates, "Companies in this business have often lost their way. We will not fall short for not having an expansive view of how technology can be used."[1]

CHAPTER OVERVIEW

In this chapter, we discuss how companies, like Microsoft, develop a business strategy and plan. First, a company writes a mission statement, which includes what product it plans to provide, its potential customers, and its philosophy of business. Next, a company sets its objectives—that is, the major goals that it hopes to meet over the short or long term. Establishing these objectives leads to the company's next step: creating a competitive differentiation, whether by hiring and keeping the best workers, producing high-quality output, inventing a unique product, streamlining logistics, reducing costs, or utilizing the finest in computer technology.

Next, the organization makes specific plans to meet its objectives. Strategic planning involves the establishment of actions and the allocation of resources, whereas tactical planning includes implementing the activities specified by the strategic plans. Tactical planning tends to be shorter term than strategic planning. Both types of planning are necessary to achieve organizational objectives.

One specific form of planning relies on SWOT (Strengths and Weaknesses, Opportunities and

> **THEY SAID IT**
>
> "The time to repair the roof is when the sun is shining."
>
> *John F. Kennedy (1917–1963) 35th president of the United States*

Threats) analysis, a process that was carried out in the opening story on Microsoft. The strategic business unit is another important planning tool, as a company splits itself into logical divisions, each with its own objectives and planning.

Planning must be underpinned by forecasting, which is figuring out the likely financial status of a company, based on its objectives, over the short and long term. Forecasting can be qualitative (based on people's opinions and judgment) or quantitative (using mathematical formulas based on historical data and different business theories). Various methods of forecasting are described. The chapter concludes with a summation of how to create a business plan.

DEVELOPING THE ORGANIZATION'S MISSION STATEMENT

Before plans and strategies are formulated, it is necessary to determine a company's larger purpose. By developing a **mission statement,** *a written explanation of a company's aims,* a company can define its general goals and rationale. The mission statement may include what goods or services are to be provided and what the market will be, as well as information on treatment of employees and the company's belief system or values.

Mission statements may be written by a company's founder as the company is set up, or they may be developed based on input from management and workers alike. As companies grow and change, mission statements may be rewritten to reflect new goals and attitudes. Mission statements generally are aimed at guiding the people within a firm, but they also can be used to inform customers of a company's point of view.

Office-furniture manufacturer Haworth Inc., of Holland, Michigan, uses a long mission statement that discusses principles ("Haworth competes enthusiastically in a free enterprise system"), customer satisfaction ("We listen to our customers and understand their changing needs"), human resources ("Our corporate culture offers a participative environment that supports teams and individuals"), and dedication to quality ("At Haworth we combine smart thinking with hard work to eliminate wasted time, effort, and materials").[2]

Coffee retailer Starbucks sums up its mission in 87 words:

"To establish Starbucks as the premier purveyor of the finest coffee in the world while maintaining our uncompromising principles as we grow. Starbucks accomplishes this mission with the help of five guiding principles:
1. *Provide a great work environment and treat each other with respect and dignity.*
2. *Apply the highest standards of excellence to the purchasing, roasting, and fresh delivery of our coffee.*
3. *Develop enthusiastically satisfied customers all of the time.*
4. *Contribute positively to our communities and our environment.*
5. *Recognize that profitability is essential to our future success."*[3]

Once the mission statement is written, the next step is to establish organizational objectives.

SETTING ORGANIZATIONAL OBJECTIVES

Objectives *are guideposts that managers use to define standards of what the organization should accomplish in such areas as profitability, customer service, and employee*

(TOP) Goals – long range, broad in nature Strategic

(MID) objectives – short range, specific in nature, time line, tactical

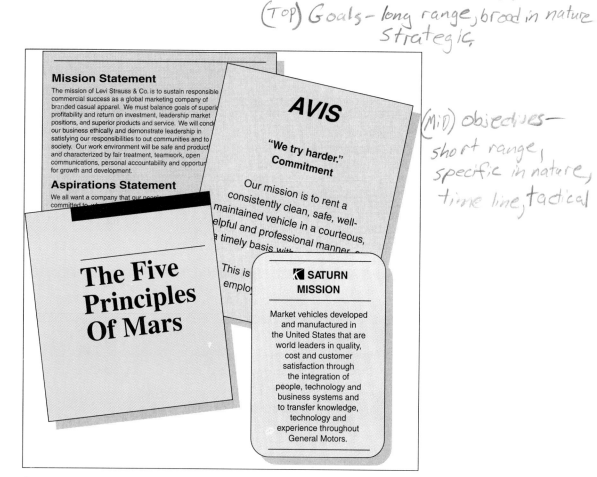

Samples of four mission statements

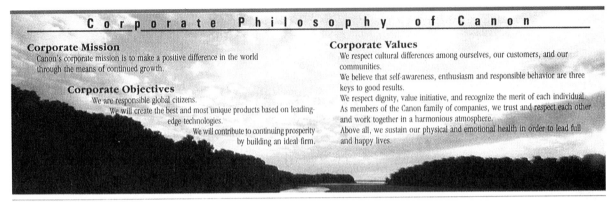

Corporate Philosophy of Canon

Corporate Mission
Canon's corporate mission is to make a positive difference in the world through the means of continued growth.

Corporate Objectives
We are responsible global citizens.
We will create the best and most unique products based on leading-edge technologies.
We will contribute to continuing prosperity by building an ideal firm.

Corporate Values
We respect cultural differences among ourselves, our customers, and our communities.
We believe that self-awareness, enthusiasm and responsible behavior are three keys to good results.
We respect dignity, value initiative, and recognize the merit of each individual.
As members of the Canon family of companies, we trust and respect each other and work together in a harmonious atmosphere.
Above all, we sustain our physical and emotional health in order to lead full and happy lives.

Canon

By specifying its corporate mission and values, Canon, a global giant in computers, copiers, and other office products, develops more specific objectives to guide its operations.

satisfaction. In general, more and more businesses are setting objectives other than profitability. As consumer concern about environmental issues mounts, many firms find that becoming environmentally responsible pays off with customers. Other businesses channel some of their profits into socially responsible causes, such as funding educational programs and scholarships. Managers continually evaluate performance in terms of how well the organization is moving toward its objectives.

Functions of Objectives

In contrast to the mission statement, which delineates the company's goal in general terms (as in Starbucks' stated aim to "apply the highest standards of excellence to the purchasing, roasting, and fresh delivery of our coffee"), objectives are more concrete ("go to extreme lengths to buy the very finest *arabica* coffees available on world markets—regardless of price").[4] The activities and decisions at all levels of a company are influenced greatly by the objectives of the organization, which serve three important functions: providing direction, setting standards, and providing motivation.

Providing Direction. By specifying end goals for the organization, objectives direct the efforts of man-

agers. For example, General Electric identified the "need for speed" as a primary objective for staying competitive in a rapidly changing global marketplace. GE identified four factors to meet this goal.

The company started with meetings—called "Work-Outs"—attended by employees from all areas and levels of the company. Employees were encouraged to pinpoint problems, bring up ideas, and suggest solutions. From this process came improved self-confidence for all workers, leading to GE's vision of a company without boundaries in which departments work together rather than independently of each other.

Setting Standards. Objectives function as standards for the manager since they offer tangible benchmarks for evaluating organizational performance. Without such standards, the manager has no means of deciding whether work is good or bad. If performance appears unsatisfactory, management can refocus the organization in the direction of its objectives.

Providing Motivation. Finally, objectives encourage managers and workers to do their best. A certain percentage of defect-free products, for example, might be set as a goal, and bonuses, profit sharing, or other incentives can be linked to accomplishing it.

IDENTYFYING PRIMARY OBJECTIVES AT GENERAL ELECTRIC

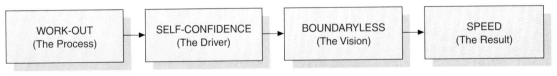

WORK-OUT (The Process) → SELF-CONFIDENCE (The Driver) → BOUNDARYLESS (The Vision) → SPEED (The Result)

MANAGEMENT BY OBJECTIVES

As well as defining the goals of the entire company ("increase sales 13 percent"), objectives also can be used at the level of the individual employee ("reduce output errors by 5 percent"). A widely used management technique aimed at improving worker motivation and performance is **management by objectives (MBO).** *MBO encourages employees to participate in setting their own goals, lets them know in advance how they will be evaluated, and bases their performance appraisals on periodic analyses of their progress toward agreed-upon goals.* An estimated 200 of the largest 500 industrial firms in the United States currently use some form of MBO.

The MBO approach was popularized in the early 1950s by management writer and consultant Peter Drucker, who described it this way:

> "The objectives of the district manager's job should be clearly defined by the contribution he and his district sales force have to make to the sales department, the objectives of the project engineer's job by the contribution he, his engineers, and draftsmen make to the engineering department. . . . This requires each manager to develop and set the objectives of his unit himself. Higher management must, of course, reserve the power to approve or disapprove his objectives. But their development is part of a manager's responsibility; indeed, it is his first responsibility."[5]

Steps in MBO

The five-step sequence used by most MBO programs is as follows:

1. Each employee discusses the job description with the manager.
2. Together, they set short-term performance goals.
3. The employee meets regularly with the manager to discuss progress toward the goals.
4. Intermediate checkpoints are established to measure progress toward the goals.

5. At the end of a defined period, both the manager and the worker evaluate the results of the worker's efforts.

Through the MBO process, the manager and the employee reach an understanding about the employee's major areas of responsibility and required level of performance. This understanding forms the basis of the worker's goals for the next planning period (usually six months).

Employee goals should be in numerical terms whenever possible—for example, reducing scrap losses by 5 percent or increasing sales of pocket calculators by 15 percent. Once these goals are established and agreed upon, the worker is responsible for achieving them.

At the end of the period, there is a formal review in which the worker and the manager discuss performance and determine whether the goals were achieved. They analyze any unmet goals, devise corrective measures, and set new goals.

Benefits of the MBO Process

The chief purpose of management by objectives is to improve employee motivation. Since workers participate in setting their goals, they know both the job to be done and precisely how they will be evaluated. An MBO program also can improve morale by improving communication between employees and managers. In addition, it enables workers to relate their performance to overall organizational goals. Finally, it serves as a basis for decisions about salary increases and promotions.

Problems Inherent in MBO

The success of MBO programs is affected greatly by the degree of management support and involvement. In addition, management must make a conscious

STEPS IN MANAGEMENT BY OBJECTIVES

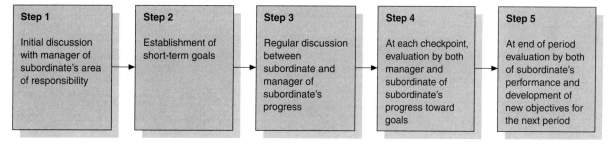

Step 1	Step 2	Step 3	Step 4	Step 5
Initial discussion with manager of subordinate's area of responsibility	Establishment of short-term goals	Regular discussion between subordinate and manager of subordinate's progress	At each checkpoint, evaluation by both manager and subordinate of subordinate's progress toward goals	At end of period evaluation by both of subordinate's performance and development of new objectives for the next period

effort to avoid overburdening the MBO system with too much paperwork and record keeping. A potential problem is that, in many organizations, workers' goals constantly change. In such situations, it is difficult to measure results accurately.

Some managers have difficulty in communicating with individual employees and in formulating short-term performance goals. However, when goals are assigned rather than agreed to, the result is typically resentment and lack of commitment on the part of the employee. MBO will succeed only where both managers and subordinates feel comfortable with it and are willing to participate in it.

CREATING A COMPETITIVE DIFFERENTIATION

Once a company has developed a mission statement and set objectives, it still faces the challenge of competing with other companies with similar missions and objectives. A company may do this by selling more of its product, cutting overhead, increasing efficiency, and instituting internal improvements that allow greater profit per sale.

A **competitive differentiation** is *any aspect of a company or its performance that makes it more successful than its competitors.* Methods of creating a competitive differentiation include improving management of human resources, using total quality management, developing new products, improving logistics within the company through just-in-time techniques, utilizing up-to-date technology, and reducing overhead and prices. An individual company may use more than one of these techniques.

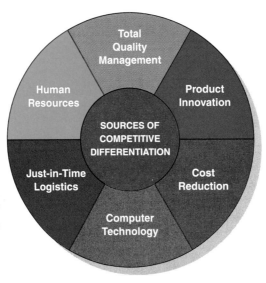

Human Resources

Starbucks CEO Howard Schultz never has forgotten being financially insecure. "My dad was a blue-collar worker," he explains. "He didn't have health insurance or benefits, and I saw firsthand the debilitating effect that had on him and on our family." Schultz determined never to treat workers the way his father was treated. This determination motivated Schultz to provide Starbucks employees with a benefits plan unprecedented in the retail service industry, where many

workers are part-time and turnover is traditionally high. Starbucks employees who work more than 20 hours a week receive health insurance, including preventative medical, vision, and dental coverage, plus stock options and, of course, coffee.

Says Schultz, "More than half of our retail sales force is part-time workers. That tells me that the majority of our customers are coming into contact with part-timers. How we treat our people is directly related to how we treat our customers and to the quality of our product. It's inarguable that our part-timers are key to the company's success."

Employee turnover at Starbucks is less than 50 percent; for food retailers, the usual rate is over 100 percent. Since Starbucks provides extensive training for each worker, says Schultz, "the longer an employee stays with us, the more we save." In addition, employee pilfering is low.

Schultz feels that employee loyalty is one of Starbucks' main strengths, and says that, when the workers became stockholders, "All kinds of [employees] started coming up with ways to save money and improve productivity." He adds, "Our only sustainable competitive advantage is the quality of our work force. We're building a national retail company by creating pride in—and a stake in—the outcome of our labor."[6]

Another company that has built a competitive advantage through human resources is USA Truck. The long-haul trucking industry suffers worker turnover rates of up to 200 percent per year, but USA Truck has reduced attrition to only 85 percent, saving close to half a million dollars each year through lowered recruiting and training costs. Why do truckers stay with USA Truck? Because they are treated well.

In 1989, Breck Speed, now chairman, and Robert Powell, now president, along with four other USA Truck managers, bought the company from Arkansas Best Corporation. They saw that turnover was costing the company too much money, so they asked the drivers what would make them stay with the company. USA Truck vehicles now have antilock brakes and air-ride suspensions; the drivers' dormitory features private showers; schedules are arranged so that drivers get home every two weeks rather than every six; and supervisors treat truckers with respect and concern. Says USA driver Carlton Curry, "Some outfits talk to you like you're a dog, but it's first class here, man."

Since new drivers are the most likely to quit, USA Truck allows them to accompany experienced drivers on their first runs; they are given easier productivity standards and relaxed mileage quotas. Also, new truckers are not routed to congested destinations, such as New York, until they have gained experience.

This is not to say that being a trucker for USA Truck is easy; drivers are required to be on time to the hour, and they can lose their jobs by being late just twice in one year. Nevertheless, by treating employees well, USA Truck has seen profits rise, with the company's operating ratio shrinking to 87 percent, considerably lower than the industry's 95 percent average.[7]

The comfortably cosmopolitan atmosphere of Starbucks keeps its customers coming back. Its benefits package and training plan keep its employees loyal.

Total Quality Management

As noted in Chapter 1, total quality management (TQM) is a competitive method based on setting quality as a strategic objective and viewing the organization as an entire system with all members contributing to the final results. With TQM, workers are trained to be more assertive and knowledgeable. Through quality circles, in which groups of up to ten employees meet voluntarily as often as once a week, workers get the opportunity to define, analyze, and solve quality-related problems.

TQM requires that quality be part of the process from start to finish; this includes investing money up front so that products are made correctly the first time. Although TQM costs more at first, the expenses associated with poor product quality, such as downtime, repairs, rework, and employee attrition, are lessened considerably. In TQM, one definition of "quality" is "pleasing the customer"; customers are considered to be partners.

Product Innovation

Business competition in the world of video games can be as aggressive as "Mortal Kombat" itself. In this multibillion-dollar industry, customers quickly tire of yesterday's hit and avidly seek tomorrow's sensation, as video-machine manufacturers grapple for a larger market share.

Sega, Nintendo, Sony, Atari, and 3DO now are fighting it out to rule the video marketplace. Nintendo engaged Sega in a price war in Europe, scarring both companies' bottom lines, and all companies have seen current sales suffer as customers wait for improved technology. In short, video entertainment technology is an industry that demands constant product innovation.

Sega has a history of taking product innovation seriously. Founder David Rosen started Sega in the 1950s as an import/export firm, but soon became entranced with technology. He developed booths that took customers' pictures and delivered a finished photo within minutes, then he moved on to coin-operated mechanical games, the ancestors of today's video games. Sega's creation "Periscope" was credited with saving the mechanical-game industry, and Rosen became convinced that the way to a customer's heart and wallet was through exceptional technology.

In keeping with this belief, Sega invests $200 million on research and development each year. Its latest innovation, currently code-named Saturn, utilizes state-of-the-art compact-disc and cartridge technology with capabilities superior to current CDs and cartridges.

Sega CEO Hayao Nakayama sees a need for even further product innovation. "Newcomers will charge in," he says. "There will be excessive competition. Creativity will run into a wall. Games will become boring. What are you going to do?"

Sega's answer? Virtual-reality theme parks. Today's computer graphics present the creation of haunted houses or airplanes, ski slopes or tornadoes, so Sega will try to provide thrills while keeping overhead low. Where Magic Mountain features expensive rides taking up hundreds of acres of land, Sega's virtual-reality theme parks will offer the same excitement in technology-equipped capsules only a few dozen square feet big.

Like all other computer, video, and entertainment companies, Sega wants its own hunk of the information superhighway. Again, Sega is relying on product innovation; the company hopes to make interactive TV and the ability to download video games available. Sega's slogan reflects just where it wants to be in the climb to market dominance: "Welcome to the Next Level."[8]

TECHNOLOGY

Pen Notebooks and Flash Technology

All businesses, new and old, must choose the appropriate computer system based on their computing requirements and financial resources. Once initial decisions are made, businesses must then monitor their computer use to determine the right time to update equipment. Yet this all may be easier said than done. New developments in technology occur so frequently that some computers are old-fashioned by the time they leave the manufacturer, and a business may feel pressured to always purchase the newest, and therefore most expensive, equipment. But buying cutting-edge technology can be problematic, as some inventions never live up to their hype.

One innovation that initially offered less than advertised was pen computing. Pen computers accept handwritten input, theoretically offering keyboard-shy users a chance to join the computer revolution. However, people's writing varies widely, and early pen computing software couldn't detect the sometimes minute differences between "c" and "e" or "i" and "l." Pen computers may someday be as ubiquitous and useful as cellular phones or fax machines, but businesses that invested in the first models did not get their money's worth.

In contrast, flash technology may genuinely be a computing miracle. Flash memory chips, which replace hard disks, combine the flexibility of random access memory with the longevity of read-only memory. These chips are lighter than hard disks, use less electricity, and never "crash." They've been described as "close to the ideal memory." However, the design of flash memory chips will continue to evolve for years, and it may be difficult for businesses to determine the best time to upgrade their computers when next year's flash technology will be even better.

In the midst of this whirlwind of constantly changing technological wonders, the Gillette Company discovered that, for its employees, less can be more. Gillette salespeople use handheld, pen-based computers on sales calls. These devices have 20-megabyte hard drives, 2,400 characters-per-second modems, and DOS 3.3; in the high-tech world of today, they are the equivalent of writing with a quill dipped in ink. Yet these easy-to-use computers, which allow Gillette reps to check off boxes rather than input data with a keyboard or by hand, are exactly right for the many first-time computer users in the Gillette sales force. And their ability to transmit data to a central database via phone jacks allows Gillette to form daily summaries of sales in different stores and locations.

While some businesses, particularly those that use computers in manufacturing and design, may need to purchase new technology almost continually, others may find that "last year's model" works just fine. The challenge is to match the computer technology to the user and the work being done.

SOURCES: Tony Seideman, "On the Cutting Edge," *Sales & Marketing Management,* June 1994, 18–23; Roberta Salvador, "What's New in Pen Computing?," *Electronic Learning,* March 1994, 14; Richard Brandt, "The Coming Firefight Over Flash Chips," *Business Week,* February 1, 1993, 68; and Gregory T. Pope, "Memories Are Made of This," *Discover,* January 1993, 94.

Just-in-Time Logistics

Just-in-time (JIT) logistics is a method of streamlining manufacturing or service provision by eliminating wasted time and space. By reducing "non-value-added time" (for instance, the time a partially assembled product sits on a table awaiting a missing part or a finished product is stored in a warehouse) and boosting "value-added time," JIT decreases overhead and increases profits.

Although JIT may sound appropriate only to large manufacturing companies, it can be helpful for the smallest service business as well. For instance, a self-employed electrician can benefit from the JIT approach. By limiting the parts kept on hand, arranging appointments with no wasted or "non-value-added time" in between, and striving to do a perfect job the first time out, the electrician will improve his or her income through JIT methods.[9]

Still, JIT has a role in major corporations. Chrysler's Jefferson North plant, in Detroit, embraced JIT with great success. Expensive parts are delivered to the plant only six hours before they are used, thereby cutting overhead, plus Chrysler requires that suppliers deliver parts in the order they will be used. In addition, Chrysler workers are encouraged to be self-directed. As a result of these procedures, Chrysler won *Modern Materials Handling*'s Productivity Achievement Award in Manufacturing. In addition, while Jefferson North initially had one daily shift that manufactured 100 Jeep Grand Cherokees each day, its two shifts now produce 3,600 cars each week.[10]

JIT has its critics as well as its supporters. Economist George Newman writes, "Transportation costs rise sharply as you switch from carload to less-than-carload shipments, from rail to truck, from public to private carrier. . . . If a batch is faulty, you may discover it too late, and in any case you have no backup stock to substitute. You have no safety cushion against any unpreventable disruption due to bad weather, traffic tie-ups, or strikes, leading to a snowballing of your losses." As for JIT's strengths, Newman points out that working in partnership with suppliers, streamlining procedures, and raising quality expectations are all just basic good-business procedures.[11]

Computer Technology

Many firms benefit from advances in computer technology. Mail-order companies keeping databases on people's buying habits tailor their mailings to the most responsive audience. Bookstores track inventory and find out instantly which distributor has the book a customer is seeking. A retailer checks in seconds whether a buyer's credit card is good. Computers allow employees in different cities to work together on a sales proposal while looking at the same "paperwork" on their computer screens. With computers, movie makers create images so real that the animation cannot be differentiated from film.

The Great Atlantic & Pacific Tea Company (A&P) supermarket chain is just one business that has created a competitive differentiation through computer technology. With A&P's Bonus Saver program, customers receive extra discounts by running a card with a magnetic strip through the cash register; while the customers get bargains, A&P keeps track of their buying habits. A&P then uses this information to guide its centralized buying process, which allows it to negotiate lower prices from suppliers and use fewer employees. The usual risk of centralized buying—that the chain will ignore the needs of shoppers in particular neighborhoods—is eliminated since A&P's database reveals exactly who buys what and where. Customers benefit when their preferred items, including ethnic foods and local favorites, are available at good prices, and A&P benefits from the resultant customer loyalty.[12]

Cost Reduction

One method of creating a competitive differentiation simply is to charge less for the product. The challenge becomes discovering how to offer low prices yet still make a profit. Wal-Mart solved this problem by insisting on the lowest possible prices from suppliers. Its guaranteed everyday low pricing (EDLP) entices people into the store, without the need for expensive advertising campaigns. Many other retailers, such as Dillard's, also have adopted EDLP as a basic business strategy.

THE PLANNING PROCESS

Once the mission statement has been developed, the objectives defined, and the competitive differentiation determined, it is time to plan the actions that will allow the company to anticipate the future and achieve company objectives. **Planning** involves making decisions about the activities the organization should perform; how big it should become; the production, marketing, and financial strategies it should use; and the resources it will need. In other words, *planning answers the questions of what should be done, by whom, where, when, and how.*

Planning is a perpetual process. When a business is being started, managers may focus the majority of their time on planning. Later, as business conditions and laws change, the business will need to change as well. Therefore, companies must monitor their operations frequently and make necessary adjustments to their plans. The computer industry, for example, changes rapidly, so Hewlett-Packard managers seek innovations in order to remain competitive. When plans were being made to develop a desktop laser printer for the office market, Dick Hackborn, HP's executive vice president for desktop computer products, remembers, "We realized we had an emerging technology converging with an unmet user need." Plans were made, revised, and amended before HP finalized the printer that positioned the company in the top spot in the industry.[13]

Ongoing analysis and comparison of actual performance with company objectives enables the company to adjust plans before problems become crises. Accomplishing other managerial functions also depends on sound, continual planning.

Types of Planning

Planning can be classified on the basis of the scope involved. Strategic planning, tactical planning, operational planning, and adaptive planning are the primary categories.

Strategic Planning. The most far-reaching type is **strategic planning,** *the process of determining the primary objectives of an organization, adopting courses of action, and allocating the resources necessary to achieve those objectives.* The strategic planning process is reflected in the firm's mission statement. For example, Kansas Gas and Electric Company defines its mission simply: "Provide excellent service to customers and a profit to shareholders." Strategic plans tend to be both broad

> **THEY SAID IT**
>
> "Plans are nothing; planning is everything."
>
> Dwight D. Eisenhower (1890–1969)
> 34th president of the United States

and long-range, focusing on those organizational objectives that will have a major impact on the organization over several years.

When strategic planning becomes too vague, the resulting plans are often ineffective or irrelevant. Intel CEO Andrew Grove says, "You look at corporate strategy statements, and a lot of them are such pap. You know how they go: 'We're going to be the world class this and a leader in that, and we're going to keep all our customers smiling.' " Grove has found that a strategy statement is valuable only if used as a constant guide for the actions of managers and workers.[14]

Tactical Planning. Tactical planning *involves implementing the activities specified by the strategic plans.* Tactical planning tends to focus on the current and near-term activities required to implement overall strategies. Although strategic and tactical planning have different time frames, both must be integrated into an overall system designed to achieve organizational objectives.

Operational Planning. Operational planning *creates the work standards that implement tactical plans.* This involves choosing specific work targets and the right employees to carry out the plans. Operational plans often are stated in terms of quotas, standards, or schedules. For example, the management of a major publishing house expects its sales representatives to make 20 customer contacts per day, with the first one at 8:00 A.M. or earlier.

Adaptive Planning. Planning, whether strategic, tactical, or operational, needs to be fluid enough and forward-looking enough to adapt to changes in a business's situation and environment. To succeed, companies must emphasize focus and flexibility in making plans; that is, companies must include **adaptive planning.** *Focus* means figuring out and then building on what the company does best. *Flexibility* means developing scenarios of future activities to be ready to take advantage of opportunities when they occur.

For example, if a company's main customers are baby boomers who are new parents, plans should be made for the eventual aging of the consumer base. Alcohol, cigarette, and candy manufacturers must consider the changing mores and growing health consciousness of their customers when making plans. A company with international markets must plan for changes in the strength of the dollar versus other currencies.

Contingency Planning

One of the more contemporary aspects of planning is **contingency planning,** which refers to plans to resume operations as quickly and as smoothly as possible after a crisis while fully communicating what happened to the public. Contingency planning involves two components: business continuation and public communication. Many firms have developed management strategies to speed recovery from accidents, such as airline crashes, factory fires, chemical leaks, oil spills, product tampering, and product failure. Contingency planning is more important now than ever; over half of the worst industrial accidents in this century have taken place since 1977.

Many firms designate a crisis manager to be in charge of handling emergencies that may arise and to create an effective crisis-prevention program. When such an event occurs, it is essential that the firm involved tell the truth. Accepting responsibility, even though it may hurt short-term profitability, is critical, since early honesty means so much in the court of public opinion. When A. H. Robins Co. decided to fight a $4.6 billion lawsuit on its Dalkon Shield intra-uterine contraceptive, the federal court judge made this point in a rebuke to Robins management: "You have taken the bottom line as your guiding beacon and the low road as your route. That is corporate irresponsibility at its meanest."[15]

The crisis manager also must ensure that the firm faces the public and makes amends. These may range

Types of Plans		
Type	**Description**	**Example**
Strategic	Establish overall objectives; position the organization in terms of its environment; can be short- or long-term.	British Petroleum's plans to achieve its growth objectives through mergers and market expansions.
Tactical	Implementation of activities and resource allocations; typically short-term.	B. Dalton's Christmas gift book selection mail-out.
Operational	Use of quotas, standards, or schedules for implementing tactical plans.	Standards for handling employee grievances within 48 hours of receipt.

Planning at Different Management Levels

Primary Type of Planning	Managerial Level	Examples
Strategic planning	Top management	Organizational objectives; fundamental strategies; long-term plans.
Tactical planning	Middle management	Quarterly and semiannual plans; departmental policies and procedures.
Operational planning	Supervisory management	Daily and weekly plans; rules and procedures for each department.

from product replacements to payments of medical or monetary claims. Finally, the underlying cause of the problem must be determined and systems established to make certain that it does not recur. Hiring a highly regarded, independent research group to deduce the cause of the problem frequently is recommended as a method of ensuring objectivity.

Perhaps an even greater responsibility for the crisis manager is to minimize the possibility that emergencies will occur in the first place. Effective crisis-prevention programs include providing special training to keep workers alert to dangers; delegating decision making and authority in a crisis to those who run the operation; improving internal communication systems; avoiding overworking employees; and ensuring that technology does not take away workers' ability to evaluate a situation. The most effective policy for crisis prevention is to give employees information at the right time, plus to give them adequate training in handling emergencies and decision making.[16]

Planning at Different Organizational Levels

Although managers spend some time in the act of planning virtually every day, the total time spent and the type of planning done differ at different levels of management. In general, members of top management, including the board of directors and the chief

> ### DID YOU KNOW?
>
> Puerto Rican Chevy dealers complained about the name chosen for a new GM model: the Nova. Although the word literally means "stars," it sounds like the Spanish phrase *no va*, which means "No way. It doesn't go." GM wisely changed the name to Caribe in Latin America.
>
> KFC Corp. franchises needed major adjustments when they expanded into Hong Kong. The Chinese, known as fastidious people who typically use warm, damp towels to clean their hands after eating, were mystified by Kentucky Fried Chicken's "finger-lickin' good" slogan.
>
> A Japanese colleague who responds by saying "yes" to your suggestion, question, or advice isn't necessarily agreeing with you. It means "I hear you" or "I understand what you are saying." Similarly, you will rarely hear the word "no" from a Japanese. The closest is likely to be a sad face and the response, "It will be very difficult."
>
> In India and Bulgaria, shaking your head sideways means "yes," but nodding means "no."

executive officer, spend a great deal of time on long-range planning, whereas middle-level managers and supervisors focus on short-term tactical planning. Employees at all levels can benefit themselves and the company by making plans for meeting goals.

Planning and the Managerial Functions

Each step in planning gets more specific than the last. From the global mission statement to the general objectives to the specific plans, each phase must fit into a comprehensive planning framework. The framework also must include small functional plans, aimed at individual employees and work areas and relevant to individual tasks, which fit within the overall framework, allowing the objectives to be reached and the mission to be achieved. Planning is a key managerial function and planning activities extend into each of the other functions—organizing, directing, and controlling.

Organizing. Once plans have been developed, the next step typically is **organizing.** *Organizing is the means by which management blends human and material resources through a formal structure of tasks and authority.* It involves classifying and dividing work into manageable units by determining specific work activities necessary to accomplish organizational objectives, grouping work activities into a logical pattern or structure, and assigning activities to specific positions and people.

Included in the organizing function are the important steps of staffing the organization with competent employees capable of performing the necessary activities and assigning authority and responsibility to these individuals. Organization is discussed in more detail in Chapter 5 and staffing in Chapter 8.

Xerox CEO Paul Allaire changed his organization to be more market driven. Allaire won his job after successfully restructuring Rank Xerox, the London-based subsidiary, where he cut staff by 40 percent and reduced costs by $200 million.

Xerox's Stamford, Connecticut, headquarters next felt the effects of Allaire's management restructuring. In one year, an informal Xerox team comprised of accounting, sales, distribution, and administration employees saved the company $200 million in inventory costs. The team was organized to accomplish specific goals for a particular period of time and was disbanded after it succeeded. By reducing the power of the traditional hierarchical organization, Xerox cut back its bureaucracy, allowing all employees to participate more in the planning process.[17]

Directing. Once plans have been formulated and an organization has been created and staffed, the task becomes that of **directing,** or *guiding and motivating employees to accomplish organizational objectives.* Directing includes explaining procedures, issuing orders, and seeing that mistakes are corrected.

The directing function is most important at the supervisory level. If supervisors are to "get things done through people," they must be effective leaders. However, middle and top managers also must be good leaders and motivators, and they must create an environment that fosters such leadership.

Controlling. Controlling *is the function of evaluating the organization's performance to determine whether it is accomplishing its objectives.* The basic purpose of controlling is to determine how successful the planning function has been. The four basic steps in controlling are to establish performance standards; monitor actual performance; compare actual performance with established standards; and, if performance does not meet standards, determine why and take corrective action.

The control function is well illustrated by New Jersey-based Becton Dickinson and Company, a medical equipment manufacturer. Becton Dickinson found itself losing its competitive position, so it decided to restructure to encourage cross-functional teamwork among employees. Today, Becton Dickinson enjoys a highly competitive position in the market thanks to employee teams that set goals and achieve them.

Becton Dickinson encourages workers to get involved in business decisions. Some employees form self-management teams to expand their contribution to the company's growth. One group volunteered to manage a production line at a Maryland facility. The team, at first, focused on such basic issues as production schedules and work-flow adjustments. Then, as enthusiasm for the program grew, they became involved in more sophisticated control projects, like analyzing defects and recommending solutions. Within three months, productivity increased by 20 percent while quality improved 30 percent.[18]

ASSESSMENT AND EVALUATION

Throughout the planning process, it is continually necessary to assess organizational resources and evaluate risks and opportunities, since developmental and marketing plans can be influenced by both internal and external pressures. Production, marketing, finance, technology, and employee talents are some of the internal resources that need to be monitored frequently and evaluated for both strengths and weaknesses. Objectives and functional plans then can be oriented toward a company's strengths, with other objectives aimed at overcoming the company's weaknesses.

Organizations also must monitor outside factors, including environmental legislation, technological developments, successes and failures of competing companies, and changing social trends. In addition, uncontrollable factors, such as the weather and the value of the dollar relative to other currencies—and their effects on the availability of supplies and the viability of foreign markets—must be assessed frequently.

SWOT Analysis

SWOT analysis is *an organized method of assessing a company's internal strengths and weaknesses and external opportunities and threats.* SWOT allows the formulation of a practical approach to planning based on a realistic view of a company's situation.

When strengths and opportunities mesh, a company has leverage in the marketplace. A hypothetical example would be a sun-protection products manufacturer, who is well stocked with high-strength sunscreen when TV weather reports start announcing UV ratings as a regular feature.

On the other hand, when external threats assail a company's weaknesses, the company has a problem to deal with. This would occur if, when UV ratings start being publicized, a sun-protection products manufacturer already has focused its line by producing and heavily advertising suntan lotion, rather than sunscreen, having judged that consumers no longer are taking the skin cancer threat very seriously. (Note that one company's opportunity can be another company's threat.)

In cases where opportunity knocks but a company's weaknesses render it unable to answer, a constraint exists. In such a case, a sun-protection products manufacturer finds itself limited by lack of inventory and cash just as newly publicized UV ratings motivate more consumers to purchase sunscreen.

The combination of an outside threat with an inside strength is called a vulnerability. This might occur to the manufacturer if their top-selling sunscreen becomes the focus of false rumors that it contains carcinogens.

Any company can be assessed through SWOT analysis at any point in its history. Microsoft was discussed in terms of its strengths, weaknesses, opportunities, and threats at the opening of the chapter, and Walt Disney Co., along with its latest project, Disney's America, a proposal to build a historical theme park in Virginia, can be analyzed the same way.

Disney's strengths constitute an impressive list. Besides its theme parks in California and Florida, Disney also owns 254 retail stores and a professional hockey team. Disney's library of animated movies, including *The Lion King* and *Aladdin*, seems likely to be profitable for decades to come. In 1993, Disney also added independent film company Miramax to its substantial holdings. With Disney's America, the company hoped to call on years of experience at running theme parks.

Disney's weaknesses make a smaller list, but nonetheless a significant one. Euro Disney has been unsuccessful enough to cause Disney's first quarterly loss in close to ten years. In addition, Disney chair Michael Eisner's health problems, following the death of President and Chief Operating Officer Frank Wells, point up the fact that Eisner has not chosen an heir apparent. Such instability could hurt all Disney projects. The fate of Euro Disney is a reminder that the company is capable of making judgment errors.

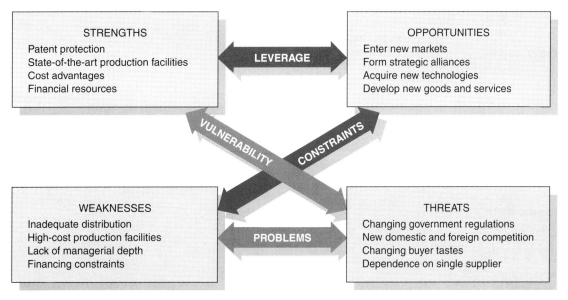

The basic premise of SWOT analysis is that taking a critical internal and external view of reality will lead the manager to select the appropriate strategy for accomplishing the organization's mission.

Opportunity is everywhere Disney looks. Plans include new hotels, a water adventure park and stadium in Orlando, and a Westcot Center in Anaheim. The state of Virginia offered Disney $163 million in incentives to locate its America theme park there.

However, many Virginians, as well as many outside historians and writers, criticized the idea of a theme park in the midst of historic battlefields. A group called Protect Historic America published an ad, labeled "The Man Who Would Destroy American History" (referring to Eisner), which pointed out the damage the park might do to Americans' sense of history and to Virginia's "gentle rolling hills." Says the ad, "It's about who we are as a nation and what we stand and fight for. And that's just not something you can buy or sell." This criticism was such a serious threat that the Disney organization decided to withdraw the plan to build America.[19]

Strategic Business Units

One technique for evaluating and assessing the present success and future plans of a firm is to break the company down into **strategic business units (SBUs).** *Each SBU is its own organization, with its own personnel, objectives, and products—and its own planning.* As discussed at the start of this chapter, Microsoft has expansive and varied goals. Microsoft's advanced technology division seeks to supply the software for TV-top boxes that plug users into digitized movies and TV shows and for computers so small that they might be worn like wristwatches. The consumer software division focuses on consumer-oriented "edutainment" CD-ROM disks. And the basic research division concentrates on such challenges as developing "natural language" programs that understand English.[20] SBUs are a useful tool in evaluating business performance since it relates outcomes to the specific goals of a unit.

FORECASTING

Forecasting *is the estimation or prediction of a company's future sales or income.* Forecasts can be short term (under one year), intermediate (one to five years), or long

This pastoral Virginia setting was the proposed location of Disney's controversial "America" theme park. Although its original plans were shelved, Disney is said to be seeking another site, possibly also in Virginia.

term (over five years). They can be **qualitative** *(subjective)* or **quantitative** *(based on historical data and mathematical methods).*

Forecasts are important because they guide the planning process and help decision making. On the other hand, they are also problematical, as they can become outdated and incorrect as a result of changes in consumer spending habits, unexpected moves by competitors, and the like.

Qualitative Techniques

Let's look at qualitative forecasting techniques first. They include sales-force composite, managerial opinion, jury of executive opinion, the Delphi technique, and buyer surveys.

Sales-Force Composite.
With this technique, salespeople are asked to forecast short-term sales based on their extensive knowledge of their territories. Results are compiled by district, by region, and nationally. The sales-force composite is useful, but limited. Although salespeople may not be able to anticipate changes in the competitive marketplace, they might be naturally reluctant to make forecasts that add to their sales quota. Because of these limitations, the sales-force composite is best used in tandem with other forecasting methods.

Managerial Opinion.   During budgeting and planning stages, a manager may be asked to predict the sales results in his or her particular units. Although managers are likely to know their operations well, they may feel pressured, much as salespeople do, to bias their predictions one way or another. Some managers will underestimate their predictions so that they can surpass the forecast easily and look good; other managers may overestimate their predictions to get more staff and a larger budget. In any case, even the most straightforward of managers can be just plain wrong.[21]

Jury of Executive Opinion.   The jury of executive opinion averages the forecasts of top executives from

Forecasting Methods		
Type	**Explanation**	**Examples**
Qualitative	Subjective estimate or prediction of future events or outcomes.	Customer surveys; sales-force estimates; opinions of key executives and industry experts.
Quantitative	Estimates or predictions of future events or outcomes based on statistical techniques.	Test markets; trend analysis; exponential smoothing.

all divisions. This technique works better with experienced managers who are well informed about sales and changing trends. The jury of executive opinion, which is particularly suited to short-term forecasting, is useful in the development of new products.

Delphi Technique.   The Delphi technique uses an anonymous panel of individuals from both outside and inside the company. Each person is sent a questionnaire, then the answers are compiled and averaged. Instead of just using that data, another questionnaire, adjusted to account for the answers received thus far, is sent out. The technique is not considered complete until a consensus is reached. Although an expensive and lengthy process, the Delphi technique can forecast technological advances and long-term company success.

Buyer Surveys.   Another form of forecasting relies on information culled from buyer surveys, based on mailed questionnaires and telephone or personal interviews. This expensive technique has some serious limitations; people may not reveal their true buying habits, and, even if they plan to make a certain purchase, ultimately they may not do so. Buyer surveys are best used for short-term or intermediate forecasting for companies with a limited customer base.

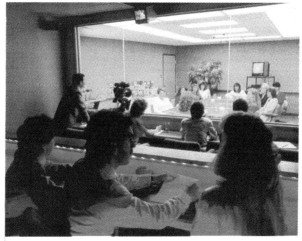

Find out what hundreds of researchers already know...

Focus Suites is like no other facility you've ever tried.

• The expertise of our professional recruiters is unsurpassed in this industry.
• We have three separate, totally private 3-room suites.
• These extraordinary suites are available for the same cost or less than that of an ordinary facility.

Call today for a competitive bid on your next qualitative research project. Once you've tried us, you'll never be satisfied with an ordinary facility again.

The Right People... The Right Price... The Right Place

FOCUS Suites of Philadelphia

One Bala Plaza, Suite 622, 231 St. Asaphs Road
Bala Cynwyd, PA 19004 (215) 667-1110

Independent research firms, such as Focus Suites of Philadelphia, aid the process of surveying buyers by conducting group interviews with a cross-section of prospective buyers.

Quantitative Forecasting

The second category of forecasting techniques is quantitative in nature. Test markets, trend analysis, and exponential smoothing are included in this group.

Test Markets.   Companies sometimes distribute new products in limited test areas. Management then can assess the best prices, promotional strategies, and packaging for their products. The success of a product in a few areas often can be extrapolated to a larger region or the whole country. Test marketing is expensive and risks tipping off competitors as to a company's plans, but is essential in many instances.

Trend Analysis.   Trend analysis is a mathematical approach to forecasting that assumes that the trends of the past will continue in the future. If, for instance, sales of a particular item have been increasing at ten percent each year, trend analysis assumes that the ten percent growth will continue. This approach has two major limitations: it requires extensive historical data, and it is unable to predict shifts in market direction.

Exponential Smoothing. Exponential smoothing is a form of trend analysis that considers recent historical data as more important than older data. Therefore, it is a more realistic indication of future sales.

Other Forecasting Components

Other helpful components of forecasting include environmental and industrial forecasting. Environment forecasting focuses on outside considerations, such as consumer confidence, governmental attitudes, and currency exchange rates; while industry forecasting judges how well the industry is doing on a whole. Industrywide forecasts may be available from trade associations and their related publications.

CREATING A BUSINESS PLAN

Written business plans provide an orderly statement of goals for ready reference at all times. They give a sense of purpose to the organization, and they provide guidance, influence, and leadership. They readily communicate ideas about goals and the means of achieving them to associates, employees, and others. Plans set standards against which achievements can be measured.

Planning usually works best if the whole organization participates. Planning can combine ideas and communicate information while making everyone a part of the team.

The **business plan** may be informal and kept completely within the mind of the manager or business owner, or it may be formal, with written copies and schedules and deadlines. It may be used only by people inside the organization, or it may be used to communicate the business's goals to banks or financial backers. There is no single form for the plan to take, but almost all plans include the time frame, money involved (both income and outflow), and units of achievement (subjective and numerical). The business plan also should include methods used to achieve goals, procedures to be followed, and values the organization holds important. Planning should contain forecasts as well as forethought. Perhaps most importantly, plans always should be open to revision.

If you are starting a business, the process of writing the business plan forces you to examine the business thoroughly and objectively. It is almost impossible to create a market for goods or services without considering the various marketing ramifications. The marketing section of the plan should include an analysis of the target market, the competition, and the plans for distribution, advertising, pricing, and location. It should cover the background of the industry and industry trends as well as the potential of the new venture. It also should point out any unique or distinctive features of the business and explain the reasons for a particular start-up date.

The plan should include an operating plan forecast, a plan for obtaining capital, and a description of how funds will be spent. In addition to the standard financial statements, a business plan ought to contain an analysis of when the break-even point will occur. Plans written to obtain funding should provide resumes of the principals in the business.

The executive summary should be the first item in the plan, although ideally it will be the last part written. The executive summary contains the who, what, why, when, where, and how of the business plan in brief.

The introduction to the plan should be a general statement of the concept, purpose, and objectives of the proposed business, along with an overview of the industry. It gives a brief description of your education, experience, and training and should refer to the resume(s) included later in the plan.

Before writing a plan, answer some questions: How would you explain your idea to a friend? What is the purpose of your business? In what way is your idea different from existing businesses? What is the state of the industry you are entering? Who is your customer or what is your client base? How will your goods or services be marketed? How much will you charge? How will you finance your business? What qualifies you to run this business?

Give special attention to what you intend to call your business. Does the name reflect the business's goals? Is it already registered by someone else? Does it have any hidden meanings to other people? What does it mean phonetically in other languages? Is it offensive to any religious or ethnic group?

Trade journals are an excellent source of industry-related information. The Small Business Administration and the local library also can assist you with your research. In addition, it helps to talk to suppliers in the industry and to local licensing authorities. How many similar firms have succeeded? How many have failed? Why? What risks are specific to your industry?

> **THEY SAID IT**
>
> "Business is like war in one respect. If its grand strategy is correct, any number of tactical errors can be made and yet the enterprise proves successful."
>
> *General Robert E. Wood (1879–1969) president, Sears, Roebuck & Company*

BUSINESS STRATEGY

The Best-Laid Business Plans . . .

No matter how well developed, a business plan is just words unless it is backed by action. Take the goals established by Michael Carpenter when General Electric Chief Executive Jack Welch assigned him to save the securities firm Kidder Peabody, a money-losing G.E. subsidiary, in 1989. Among its other problems, Kidder Peabody had been forced to close down its risk arbitrage division after being implicated in insider trading.

Carpenter's business plan included making the most of Kidder employees, limiting overhead, and developing a positive corporate culture. The most important goal to Carpenter was emphasizing integrity, which he called steps "one through ten." Despite his straightforward plan, by 1994 Carpenter was unemployed, and a new scandal at Kidder Peabody resulted in the first quarter in 13 years in which G.E.'s profits decreased.

What happened between 1989 and 1994? Joseph Jett, a Kidder Peabody trader, allegedly invented some $350 million in nonexistent profits in order to increase his bonus. Taking advantage of a bookkeeping system that treated exchanges as sales, Jett is alleged to have made an estimated $35 *billion* in false trades.

Where was Carpenter as the situation unfolded? *Fortune* magazine argues that Carpenter certainly was not busy emphasizing integrity as he had promised. According to *Fortune,* Carpenter had not even attained the license legally necessary to manage Kidder Peabody until he had been on the job for over four years. In addition, according to *The Wall Street Journal,* under Carpenter's watch, bond trader Neil Margolin allegedly concealed $10 million in losses for over a year, and Vice President Clifford Kaplan was discovered to be working simultaneously for another company. On the whole, *Fortune* argues, Carpenter's leadership was one of "high turnover and low morale, of unlicensed and uninformed executives, of high risk gambles in the bond markets."

Some experts disagree with this interpretation. An anonymous G.E. executive defends Carpenter: "In the G.E. system, it's the chief financial officer and his staff who are responsible for guarding the financial gates." (However, Kidder Chief Financial Officer Richard O'Donnell says, "This is a complex issue involving a whole group of departments and processes.")

Other financial experts join *Fortune* in blaming Carpenter. An anonymous source in *The Wall Street Journal* asks, "Where were Kidder's controls?" In a letter to the *New York Times,* Interpublic Group of Companies Vice President Eugene P. Beard writes, "When profits for transactions . . . are astounding, . . . then [they] require more scrutiny than a simple random review." Unnamed G.E. officials in *The Wall Street Journal* say that Jett could not have pulled off his alleged scam if company leaders had been paying attention, while some experts claim that Carpenter paid attention only to the bottom line. (Carpenter denies this, asking in *The Wall Street Journal,* "is all we're concerned with making a buck? No. Categorically, no.")

While the full details of this scandal may never be known, it is possible that Carpenter might have avoided disaster by simply following his own business plan.

SOURCES: Terence R. Paré, "Jack Welch's Nightmare on Wall Street," *Fortune,* September 5, 1994, 40–48; Eugene P. Beard, "Missing the Red Flags at Kidder," *New York Times,* September 4, 1994, 9 [letter]; Carol J. Loomis, "G.E. Stumbles," *Fortune,* May 16, 1994, 14; "How Will Welch Deal with Kidder Scandal? Problems Keep Coming," *The Wall Street Journal,* May 3, 1994, 1, 6.

What are the typical markups? Expenses? Profit percentages?

The marketing part of your plan is the core of your business rationale and must answer many questions. Who is your market? What is the profile of your average customer, including age, sex, family size, annual family income, location, buying patterns, and reasons for buying from your business? What is your competitive advantage? How will you determine the price of your goods? Where will your business be located? Who are your direct competitors?

Marketing plans must consider rental, leasing, or purchase costs and explain the influence of traffic volume, neighboring businesses, demographics, parking, accessibility, and visibility. Labor costs, utility access and rates, police and fire protection, zoning restrictions, and other government rules and regulations also must be discussed.

Other topics to be included are whether the firm will be a sole proprietorship, partnership, or corporation; when it will be necessary to hire employees and what their job descriptions will be; the lines of authority in the business; a risk-management plan, including detailed information on insurance; what suppliers you will use and how you have assessed their reliability and competence; and whether you will extend credit to your customers.

The financial part of the business plan requires particular attention to detail. If you are using your plan as part of a request for financing, your banker will look at your management skills and experience, the risk, your collateral, and your ability to repay a loan. If you are writing a plan to obtain venture capital, however, the venture capitalist will look at profits and upside potential and not so much at downside risks.

If you have made certain assumptions in the body of your plan, tie them into the financial section. If you plan two retail outlets, for example, your cash-flow projections should show how you are going to pay for them. The bankers or investors analyzing your plan may not know whether it costs $250 or $25,000 to install an exotic high-tech part, but they do know that a telephone system for 50 people costs more than $250 per month. Carelessness with seemingly insignificant variables can undercut credibility.

Itemize expenses on a month-by-month basis; do not simply project an annual amount. If you have $100,000 in costs, don't assume that this means more than $8,000 each month. Some expenses will be paid monthly and some annually. If you have a lot of annual payments up front, you will be running back to your financiers in the first month to explain why your cash-flow projection was off. This is not a good way to start.

Your plan must include all assumptions you are making about the conditions under which you intend to operate. It also should include detailed profit-and-loss and cash-flow projections.

After you have assembled your business plan, add a table of contents so that the reader can turn directly to those parts of the plan that are of most interest. Make sure the plan is presented in an attractive and professional format.

SUMMARY OF LEARNING GOALS

1. **Differentiate between strategic and tactical planning.**
   Strategic planning involves the establishment of actions and the allocation of resources, whereas tactical planning includes implementing the activities specified by the strategic plans.

2. **Identify the components of a mission statement.**
   A mission statement is a written explanation of a company's purpose and aims. It may include what products are to be produced and what the market will be, as well as information on treatment of employees and the company's belief system or morals.

3. **Define objectives and how they differ from the mission statement.**
   Objectives are guideposts that define standards for what the organization should accomplish in such areas as profitability, customer service, and employee satisfaction. In contrast to the mission statement, which delineates the company's goal in general terms, objectives are more concrete.

4. **Define competitive differentiation and identify methods businesses use to create it.**
   A competitive differentiation is any aspect of a company or its performance that makes it more successful than its competitors. Methods of creating a competitive differentiation include management of human resources, total quality management, product innovation, just-in-time logistics, efficient up-to-date technology, and reducing overhead and prices.

5. **Explain SWOT analysis and how it is used in corporate planning.**
   SWOT analysis is an organized method of assessing a firm's internal strengths and weaknesses and external opportunities and threat. SWOT provides a realistic view of the company's position and is used in the overall planning process.

6. **Describe SBUs and give examples.**
   Strategic business units are divisions within the organization, each with its own executives, workers, objectives, products, and planning. Disneyland and the Mighty Ducks are SBUs of Walt Disney Co.

7. **Define forecasting and differentiate between quantitative and qualitative forecasting.**
   Forecasting is the estimation or prediction of a company's future sales or income. Qualitative forecasting is subjective and relies on the judgment and opinions of managers, the sales force, customers, and others. Quantitative forecasting is based on historical data and mathematical methods.

8. **List the methods of forecasting.**
   Qualitative techniques include the sales-force composite, the managerial opinion, the jury of executive opinion, the Delphi technique, and buyer surveys. Quantitative techniques include test marketing, trend analysis, and exponential smoothing.

9. **Outline the components of the business plan.**
   The business plan includes the executive summary, the marketing plan, the financial plan, evaluations of the business owner and/or manager and of the industry, and a discussion of the business's organization and structure.

KEY TERMS QUIZ

tactical planning
strategic planning
mission statement
qualitative forecasting
business plan
management by objectives (MBO)
objectives

SWOT analysis
directing
operational planning
quantitative forecasting
organizing
competitive differentiation
contingency planning

forecasting
controlling
adaptive planning
planning
strategic business units (SBUs)

_____ 1. Planning for short-term implementation of current activities and the related resource allocation.

_____ 2. A program designed to improve motivation through employee participation in goal setting and defining factors used in performance evaluations.

_____ 3. Refers to planning that allows changes in response to new developments in the business's situation and environment.

_____ 4. Anticipating the future and determining the best courses of action to achieve company objectives.

_____ 5. Refers to planning for emergencies.

_____ 6. Evaluating the company's performance to determine whether it is accomplishing its objectives.

_____ 7. A written explanation of a company's purpose and aims.

_____ 8. Refers to any aspect of a company and its performance that makes it more successful than its competitors.

_____ 9. Determining the overall strategy and resource allocations necessary to reach intermediate and long-term objectives.

_____ 10. Refers to guiding and motivating workers to accomplish organizational objectives.

_____ 11. Refers to work standards and tasks that implement tactical plans.

_____ 12. The process of blending human and material resources through the design of a formal structure of tasks and authority.

_____ 13. Guideposts in defining what the business aims to achieve in areas such as profitability, customer service, and social responsibility.

_____ 14. Refers to forecasting based on subjective judgment and experience.

_____ 15. Divisions within a company, each with its own management, workers, objectives, products, and planning.

_____ 16. The analysis of a business based on its internal strengths and weaknesses and external opportunities and threats.

_____ 17. The description of the business's goals and the means for achieving them.

_____ 18. Refers to forecasting based on mathematical models.

_____ 19. The estimation or prediction of a company's future sales or income.

OTHER IMPORTANT TERMS

buyer surveys
constraint
Delphi technique
everyday low pricing (EDLP)
exponential smoothing
jury of executive opinion
just-in-time logistics (JIT)

leverage
problem
sales-force composite
total quality management (TQM)
trend analysis
vulnerability

REVIEW QUESTIONS

1. Distinguish between strategic and tactical planning. Identify instances of each at Wal-Mart.
2. What is a mission statement? Identify the primary components.
3. How do objectives differ from mission statements? Cite specific examples.
4. What is meant by competitive differentiation? How do firms implement it?
5. What is SWOT analysis? Apply SWOT analysis to a local firm.
6. Explain the concepts of leverage, problems, constraints, and vulnerability as they relate to SWOT analysis.
7. Explain the SBU concept. Cite specific examples for a firm with which you are familiar.
8. Differentiate between quantitative and qualitative forecasting. Also, identify the time period used in forecasting.
9. Outline the major types of forecasting procedures. Define each of these methods.
10. What is a business plan? What elements are included in a business plan?

DISCUSSION QUESTIONS

1. You have decided to start one of the following businesses: an importing/exporting firm, a music store, a delivery service, a supermarket, or a clothing store. Choose one and write a mission statement for your business.
2. How might the business you selected create a competitive differentiation?
3. How might SWOT analysis and SBUs help your business?
4. As the owner of the business selected above, what forms of forecasting would you use?
5. Write a brief business plan for the business you picked. Include strategic plans, tactical plans, operational plans, adaptive plans, and/or contingency plans, as appropriate.

VIDEO CASE: Ampex

The video case for this chapter illustrates how lack of strategic planning hurt Ampex in the video-recording market and can be found on page 412 in Appendix D.

Solution to Key Terms Quiz

1. tactical planning 2. management by objectives (MBO) 3. adaptive planning 4. planning 5. contingency planning 6. controlling 7. mission statement 8. competitive differentiation 9. strategic planning 10. directing 11. operational planning 12. organizing 13. objectives 14. qualitative forecasting 15. strategic business units (SBUs) 16. SWOT analysis 17. business plan 18. quantitative forecasting 19. forecasting

CHAPTER 5

Organizing the Business

Learning Goals

1. Identify and explain the three basic forms of business ownership.
2. Compare the advantages and disadvantages of the forms of business ownership.
3. Discuss the levels of corporate management.
4. Explain how private ownership, public ownership, and collective ownership (cooperatives) differ.
5. Explain the vital role played by entrepreneurs and small businesses in the global economy.
6. Define small business and identify the industries in which most small firms are established.
7. Compare the advantages and disadvantages of small business.
8. Describe resources that are available to entrepreneurs.
9. List the advantages and disadvantages of franchising.
10. Outline the popular methods of small business operation in the global market.

In 1971, Joseph Montgomery was a full-time Wall Street analyst and part-time biking enthusiast who was unimpressed with the bikes he saw in shops. Montgomery saw big opportunities in the bicycle industry, which he believed was dominated by old-fashioned, unexciting products.

That year he started his own company, Cannondale, to design and manufacture state-of-the-art bicycles. State-of-the-art bikes take money, however, and at first Montgomery lacked enough capital to begin building them. For the next 12 years Cannondale made and sold bicycling accessories, while its founder experimented with various bicycle designs.

Eventually, Montgomery made enough money to start building his own designs, starting with an all-aluminum, large-diameter, welded-frame model. Since then, he has transformed his little start-up company into the country's leading manufacturer of up-scale bicycles. In the past four years, its revenues have tripled to over $100 million. Five percent of those revenues come from Japan, where sales jumped more than 50 percent last year alone. Cannondale is now the most popular American bike sold in that country.

While Montgomery is pleased with Cannondale's success, he is aware that such tremendous growth brings its own problems. He worries that, as it expands, the company

could lose its entrepreneurial, risk-taking flavor. He has organized the company in a way that he hopes will maintain its small-company strengths, even as it becomes a world leader in its industry.

Central to Cannondale's organization is a focus on quality and innovation. Montgomery designed its factories to be flexible, allowing the company to rethink and retool constantly. As Montgomery explains, "If your reason for living is innovation, making products for a lot of different niche markets, then the name of the game is reinventing your product all the time." The company makes 37 models of bicycles, and redesigns 90 to 95 percent of them each year. Cannondale frames are hand-welded from aluminum parts that are cut by computer-assisted machines in Pennsylvania factories. The machines are linked electronically to corporate headquarters in Connecticut, allowing designers at computer keyboards to reshape bicycles hundreds of miles away.

Another feature of Cannondale's organization is its close ties to bicycle dealers. Unlike most of their competitors, Montgomery and his son, Scott, bypass distributors and work directly with cycling stores. "Your voice gets weaker and weaker as you go through layers," explains Scott Montgomery. "Your service levels get worse; communication becomes slower."

Recently, for example, Joseph Montgomery invited Vermont bike retailer Zandy Wheeler to visit a Cannondale factory. During lunch, Wheeler mentioned that his staff spent too much time preparing Cannondale bikes for sale. Before he left the building, Cannondale employees showed up to demonstrate additional parts that could be preassembled before shipping. Wheeler was impressed: "I'd like to do more business with people who are that committed," he commented.

Even in Japan, which has well-established networks of intermediaries, Cannondale bypasses regional distributors and sells directly to retailers, who welcome the novel strategy. "They know that with every level of distribution comes a level of service breakdown," Scott says. By working directly with bicycle dealers, Cannondale can pocket profits that otherwise would be absorbed by distribution costs. It also can gain firsthand knowledge of what sells in Japan. When retailers noted that their customers wanted bikes that were smaller and more brightly colored than American models, Cannondale used this information to tailor its products more closely to local tastes.

The Montgomerys also work to maintain direct communication and a small-company attitude among their own employees. Originally, they considered a sales goal of $120 million for the current fiscal year, but decided to scale the number down, lest it strain the company's resources or damage the quality of the products. Meanwhile, Joseph Montgomery continues to visit the firm's assembly lines two days a week. When a small company expands, he explains, "you don't get in your car and go to the beach. You come down here and roll up your sleeves and make sure that these people understand that you care as much as you did when you were making half or a third as many bikes."[1]

CHAPTER OVERVIEW

Every business, be it General Electric or a neighborhood Mexican restaurant, must choose the type of legal ownership that best meets its needs. This entails considering many variables, including financial resources, financial liability, and the skills of the people involved.

In this chapter we will look at the advantages and disadvantages of the three major forms of private business ownership and will discuss the importance of entrepreneurship and small business, both in the United States and in the world economy.

Forms of Private Ownership

There are three major forms of private business ownership: sole proprietorships, partnerships, and corporations. Sole proprietorships are the most common, accounting for 69 percent of all U.S. businesses.

Ownership Structure of U.S. Business

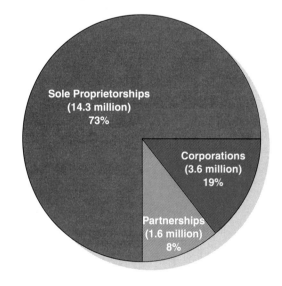

Most businesses in the United States are sole proprietorships, possibly because it is the easiest type to form.

Advantages and Disadvantages of Each Form of Private Ownership		
Form of Ownership	**Advantages**	**Disadvantages**
Sole Proprietorship	1. Easy to form and dissolve 2. Owner has control over all aspects 3. Owner retains all profits after taxes *tax only once*	1. Unlimited financial liability 2. Financing limitations 3. Management deficiencies 4. Lack of continuity
Partnership	1. Easy to form 2. Complementary management skills 3. Expanded financial capacity	1. Unlimited financial liability 2. Interpersonal conflicts 3. Lack of continuity
Corporation	1. Limited financial liability 2. Specialized management skills 3. Expanded financial capacity 4. Economies of larger-scale operation	1. Difficult and costly to form and dissolve 2. Tax disadvantage 3. Legal restrictions *ownership and control* ** seperation of ownership and control.*

Each form of ownership has its strong points—and at least a couple of drawbacks.

Partnerships make up 10 percent of U.S. firms, and corporations comprise the remaining 21 percent.

Sole Proprietorships

The most common form of business ownership, the **sole proprietorship,** is also the oldest and the simplest because *there is no legal distinction between the sole proprietor as an individual and as a business owner.* The business's assets, earnings, and debts are those of the owner. Although sole proprietorships are common in a variety of industries, they are concentrated primarily among small businesses, such as repair shops, small retail outlets, and service organizations.

Sole proprietorships offer advantages not found in other forms of business ownership. They are easy to form or dissolve and give the owner flexibility and the right to retain all profits after taxes. There are advantages and disadvantages to each of the forms of private ownership.

A minimum of legal requirements make it easy to go into and out of this form of business. Usually the only legal requirements for starting a sole proprietorship are registering the business or trade name at the county courthouse and taking out any necessary licenses. Ownership flexibility is another advantage; the owner can make management decisions without consulting others, take prompt action when needed, and keep trade secrets where appropriate.

A disadvantage of the sole proprietorship is that the sole proprietor is financially liable for all debts of the business, and its financial resources are limited to the owner's personal funds and money that can be borrowed. Financing limitations can keep the business from expanding. Another disadvantage is that the owner must be able to handle a wide range of management and operational tasks; as the firm grows, the owner may not perform all duties with equal effectiveness. Finally, a sole proprietorship lacks long-term continuity, since death, bankruptcy, retirement, or change in personal interests can terminate it.

Partnerships

Another option for organizing a business is forming a **partnership,** *an association of two or more persons who operate a business as co-owners by voluntary legal agreement.* Partnerships have been a traditional form of ownership for professionals offering a service, such as physicians, lawyers, and dentists. A **joint venture** *is a partnership formed for a specific undertaking.* For example, Johnson & Johnson is exploring the Korean market for baby-care products via Johnson & Johnson Korea, a joint venture with Korean firm Dong-A Pharmaceuticals.

Partnerships are easy to form; as with sole proprietorships, the legal requirements involve merely registering the business name and taking out the necessary licenses. Another advantage is the opportunity for professionals to combine complementary skills. Partnerships also offer expanded financial capability through the combined resources of the partners. They also usually give greater access to borrowed funds than do sole proprietorships.

Like the sole proprietorship, most partnerships have the disadvantage of unlimited financial liability. Each partner is responsible for the debts of the firm, and each is legally liable for the actions of the other partners. Partners must pay the partnership's debts from their own funds if those debts exceed the partnership's assets. It is also much harder to break up a partnership than it is to dissolve a sole proprietorship. Rather than simply withdrawing the business's funds, the partner who wants out must find someone to buy his or her interest in the firm.[2]

Corporations

A **corporation** *is a legal organization whose assets and liabilities are separate from those of its owner(s)*. It can be formed only with the approval of the appropriate state agency. A **stockholder** *is someone who acquires shares of stock in a corporation,* thereby becoming a part-owner of the business. When all or a majority of a corporation's stock is owned by another corporation, it is a **subsidiary** *of that corporation*, which is usually called the *parent company*.

Corporate ownership offers considerable advantages. First, because corporations are considered separate legal entities, the stockholders have limited financial risk; if the firm fails, they lose only the amount they have invested. The limited risk of corporate ownership is reflected clearly in the names used by firms throughout the world: "Incorporated" or "Inc." (United States); "Limited" or "Ltd." (Canada and the United Kingdom); "Proprietary Limited" or "Pty. Ltd." (Australia); "Aktie Bolag," or "stock company" (Scandinavia).

Other advantages of corporations are that they can draw on the specialized skills of several employees, unlike sole proprietorships and partnerships where managerial skills usually are confined to the abilities of the owners. Expanded financial capability, another advantage, allows a corporation to grow and become more efficient than if it had been set up as a sole proprietorship or partnership. People outside the business may invest in it by buying shares of stock, and the corporation's size and stability may make it easier for a business to borrow additional funds. A large corporation can finance projects internally by transferring money from one part of the business to another. Longer manufacturing runs usually mean more effi-

Levels of Management in a Corporation

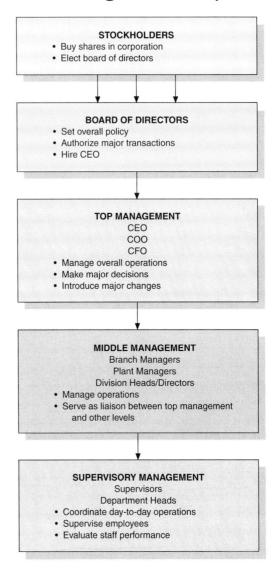

Levels of management in a corporation are often defined by job function.

cient production and lower prices, thus attracting more customers.

A disadvantage of incorporation is that, as a separate legal entity, a corporation is subject to federal and state taxes on its profits. In addition, any dividends—payments to stockholders from profits—also are taxed on an individual basis. Additionally, corporate ownership involves many legal problems not encountered by sole proprietorships and partnerships. The number of laws and regulations affecting corporations has increased dramatically in recent years.[3]

Many states allow business owners to organize as a *limited liability company (LLC)*, which combines the corporate advantage of limited liability with the favorable tax treatment of a partnership. An LLC is governed by an operating agreement similar to a partnership agreement, but it reduces partners' liability for the actions of the other business owners.[4]

Corporate Management

There are generally several levels of management in a corporation. The stockholders elect a **board of directors,** which becomes *the governing authority for the corporation.* Members of the board—many of whom are non-employees—set overall policy, authorize major transactions involving the corporation, and hire the chief executive officer (CEO). The CEO and other members of top management set corporate policy, make most of the major corporate decisions, and manage the overall operations of the company. The next level is middle management, which coordinates the operational functions of the company and serves as a liaison between top management and lower levels. The bottom tier of management includes supervisory managers, who coordinate the day-to-day operations of the firm, supervise employees, assign specific tasks to the staff, and are

> ### THEY SAID IT
> "It is more admirable to be in business for yourself than to work for somebody else."
> *H.L. Mencken (1880–1956) American editor*

often responsible for evaluating employees' job performance.[5]

Trends in Corporate Ownership

Corporate ownership has been in a state of flux in recent years. Many well-known firms have become part of another corporation as a result of mergers or acquisitions, or have been split into smaller units.

A **merger** *refers to two or more firms that combine to form one company.* In an **acquisition,** *one firm purchases the property and assumes the obligations of another company.* For instance, Viacom recently bought out Paramount.

Employee ownership is increasingly common in the late 1990s. From Weirton Steel and Avis Rent-A-Car to United Airlines, organizations are seeking to survive in a competitive marketplace by turning all or part of ownership over to the people who run the business. In such cases, the corporate organization remains in place, but a large percentage of the stockholders also work for the company. Today,

United Airlines employees recently became majority owners of the company.

"UNLEASH THE ENTREPRENEURIAL SPIRIT. IT CAN TURN YOUR COMPANY AROUND."

Many corporations are seeking to unleash the entrepreneurial spirit of their employees by running divisions as if they are small businesses.

employee ownership represents $60 billion in corporate stock. Nowhere is the trend more visible than in the airline industry.[6] Fifty-five percent of UAL is employee-owned; employees own 45 percent of TWA stock; and employees own at least five percent of Northwest, Alaska Air, Delta, Southwest, and USAir.

Public and Collective Ownership

One alternative to private ownership is some form of **public ownership,** *in which a government unit or its agency owns and operates an organization.* In the United States, local governments often own parking structures and water systems. Public ownership may come about because private investors cannot be found for a project or because certain functions of a project, such as municipal water systems, are considered so important to the public welfare that they are publicly owned.

Public ownership remains common abroad, despite a general trend toward *privatization,* in which privately owned firms take over functions that used to be performed by publicly owned companies. Chile has

> **THEY SAID IT**
>
> "Entrepreneurs are the forgotten heroes of America."
>
> Ronald Reagan
> (1911–   )
> 40th president of
> the United States

sold off several public companies in the last decade. Mexico sold stock in Telefonos de Mexico, its national phone company. The largest block of stock went to a consortium that included Southwestern Bell and France Telecom as well as to Mexican buyers.

Another alternative to private ownership is a **cooperative,** *an organization whose owners band together to operate all or part of their industries collectively.* Cooperatives often are created by large numbers of small producers that want to be more competitive in the marketplace. Well-known cooperatives include Sunkist Growers, Ocean Spray cranberries, and Recreational Equipment Inc., the nation's largest consumer cooperative.

THE IMPORTANCE OF ENTREPRENEURSHIP

An **entrepreneur** *is the risk taker in the private enterprise system, a person who seeks a profitable opportunity and takes the necessary risks to set up and operate a business.* Entrepreneurship and a strong small business sector always have been the backbone of any private enterprise system. They provide the competitive zeal that keeps the system effective. The U.S. government encourages the development and continuity of these firms by enacting antitrust legislation that maintains the competitive environment in which such companies thrive. A federal agency, the Small Business Administration, was set up in 1953 to assist small firms.

Entrepreneurship is more popular than ever: Two million businesses were started in a recent year. In 1987, only about three percent of people who lost corporate jobs started their own firms; today that number has tripled.

These statistics suggest the vital role that entrepreneurs and small-business owners play in contemporary business. Aside from the many services they provide to consumers, these organizations also help other businesses function more efficiently. Many small firms serve as suppliers to large corporations; AT&T, for example, buys $1.5 billion of goods and services from more than 100,000 small companies every year. "The small companies have advantages," says Patricia Cox, AT&T's director of global procurement. "They have lower costs, lower overhead, and they tend to be specialists." [7]

THE ROLE OF SMALL BUSINESS

A **small business** *is a firm that is independently owned and operated, is not dominant in its field, and meets certain size standards for its income or number of employees.* Besides these characteristics, a small business has limited capital resources and fewer than 400 employees.

Small businesses are more common than one might think: 95 percent of all enterprises in the United States are firms with less than 50 employees. Twenty percent of the companies started recently are one- and two-person operations. For instance, there are 47,000 consultancies in the United States that hire three or fewer people; this number has doubled in a two-year period. [8]

Small Business: Strengths and Weaknesses

Small businesses are not simply smaller versions of large corporations. Their legal organization, market position, staff capability, managerial style and organization, and financial resources generally differ from bigger companies, which gives them some unique advantages.

Small firms are usually the first to offer new concepts and new products in the marketplace; Federal Express and Apple Computer are classic success stories. Small companies often can be more flexible than large corporations, allowing them to tailor their services to the needs of their customers. They can provide a product more cheaply than large firms because they have small staffs and lower overhead costs.

Certain types of industries and markets lend themselves better to smaller firms. Large companies may choose not to pursue limited markets because high overhead costs force them to set minimum sales targets, but this situation provides substantial opportunities for small, lower-cost competitors. Economic and organizational factors may dictate that an industry consist essentially of small firms; upscale restaurants are an example.

THEY SAID IT

"To open a business is very easy; to keep it open is very difficult."

Chinese proverb

Survival Rate of Businesses (Shown as %)	Years of Survival		
	<2	2-4	4-6
Total, All Industries	76.1	47.9	37.8
Construction	77.1	45.6	35.2
Manufacturing	78.7	56.2	46.2
Transportation, Communication, Public Utilities	75.7	46.2	37.0
Retail Trade	75.6	48.1	37.0
Finance, Insurance, Real Estate	74.2	46.2	36.0
Services	75.4	46.5	37.3

Although small businesses have fewer resources, the first years are hard on all businesses.

Small firms sometimes have a variety of disadvantages, including poor management, inadequate financing, and government regulation. Small firms can be more vulnerable during a recession, since they have fewer resources to fall back on. On average, nearly 62 percent of all businesses dissolve within the first six years of operation.

While these problems can be overcome, it is important to think carefully about all of these issues before starting a company.

Often, small companies fail because the people who start them are ill-prepared as managers, with little training or education in running a business. They may be so excited about their projects that they neglect paperwork and fail to write a business plan. Government regulation can also create problems: the Small Business Administration estimates government paperwork costs small firms billions of dollars each year. Larger firms with substantial staffs usually can cope better with the blizzard of required forms and reports.

Inadequate financing is yet another leading cause of small business failures. Of the financial obstacles that face small companies, uneven cash flow is the biggest problem. This may be because many companies start with inadequate capital and lack the resources to carry them through difficult periods.

Small Business Opportunities for Women and Minorities

Many small businesses are started by minorities and women, possibly because they feel their opportunities will be better if they work for themselves rather than for somebody else. A breakdown of the types of businesses typically owned by women, African Americans, Hispanics, and other minorities shows that service and retail firms are the most common types owned by each group.

These companies have a tremendous economic impact. For example, businesses owned by women employ more of the U.S. population than all of the companies in the *Fortune* 500. According to the U.S. Census, there are 49 metropolitan areas where woman-owned businesses have sales of more than $1 billion a year. Hispanics form the nation's largest group of minority business owners; during the past ten years, the Hispanic population grew by 53 percent in the United States, and the number of Hispanic-owned firms doubled. During the same period, companies owned by African Americans grew by

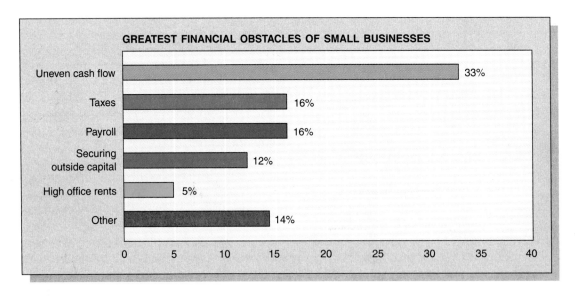

The greatest financial obstacles facing small businesses.

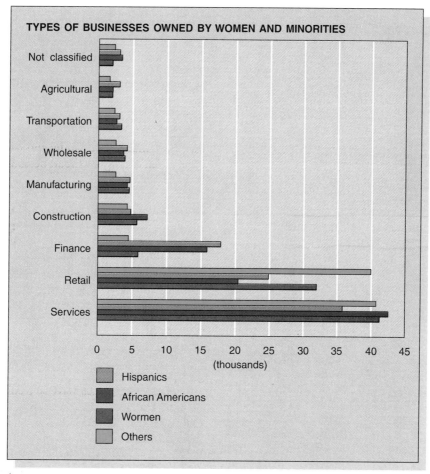

TYPES OF BUSINESSES OWNED BY WOMEN AND MINORITIES

Legend:
- Hispanics
- African Americans
- Wormen
- Others

(thousands)

Businesses owned by minorities and women contribute a great deal to the overall economy.

38 percent, and their revenue more than doubled (compared to a revenue rise of 55 percent for all U.S. businesses).[9]

Franchising

The franchising concept has played a major role in the growth of small business. **Franchising** *is a business agreement that sets the methods a dealer can use to produce and market a supplier's good or service.*

The dealer, or **franchisee,** *is a small-business person who is allowed to sell a good or service of a supplier, or* **franchisor,** *in exchange for some payment* (usually a flat fee plus future royalties or commissions). Total

African-American entrepreneurs have sought opportunities in many global markets, including Japan. Frank Brooks of Brooks Sausage Company sells millions of dollars worth of pork patties to McDonald's in Japan for its popular teriyaki pork sandwich.

costs can vary widely; average start-up costs for a Subway Sandwiches franchise are $70,000, versus $610,000 for a McDonald's and $694,280 for a Hardee's. The franchisor typically provides building plans, site selection help, managerial and accounting systems, and other services to assist the franchisee. The franchisor also provides name recognition for the small-business owner who becomes a franchisee. This image is created by advertising campaigns to which the franchisee typically contributes.

The concept is growing rapidly; by the year 2000, total sales from franchising are expected to top $1 trillion in the United States. Franchising is also

BUSINESS STRATEGY

Threads 4 Life

T. J. Walker and Carl Jones decided to go into retailing when they heard friends talking about starting ethnic-clothing stores. The two friends traveled to New York City and walked around Brooklyn and Queens to see what urban kids were wearing; Walker toted a sketch pad and jotted down ideas. They pooled their savings to start Threads 4 Life, which designs and sells $70 million worth of colorful, urban-inspired clothes each year. While the company's primary market is young African Americans, many white teenagers buy the clothes too, and sales are taking off in Europe and Japan as well. As Jones says, "Black kids are setting the trends in fashion."

SOURCE: Brian Dumaine, "America's Smart Young Entrepreneurs," *Fortune,* March 21, 1994, 34–48. © 1994 Time Inc. All rights reserved.

popular overseas. Franchised sales in Australia, for example, currently amount to $32 billion a year, and are expected to hit $50 to $60 billion by the end of the decade.[10]

Swisher International illustrates how the franchising system works. Swisher sells bathroom-cleaning franchises for $35,000 plus 11 percent of the franchisee's sales. Franchisees get an exclusive territory of 500,000 people (additional territories can be purchased for $10,000). In exchange, Swisher provides two weeks of training, handles all accounting and purchasing, and even answers the phone (unanswered calls are shifted to Swisher headquarters in Charlotte, North Carolina, where a receptionist places the message in a voice-mail system). Some Swisher franchisees make over $100,000 a year.[11]

Franchising: Strengths and Weaknesses

The franchising concept does not eliminate the risks for someone considering a small-business investment; it merely adds alternatives. In fact, the failure rate of franchises is close to that of independent businesses.[12]

Existing franchises have a performance record on which the prospective buyer can make comparisons and judgments. In addition, a widely recognized name gives the franchisee a tremendous advantage. Car dealers, for instance, know their brand-name products will attract a given clientele. A franchise also gives the small-business owner a tested management program and often offers valuable business training. The prospective franchisee usually does not have to worry about setting up an accounting system, establishing quality-control standards, or designing employment application forms.

On the negative side, franchise fees can be expensive. Good franchises with tested management systems, proven performance records, and widely recognized names usually sell for more than those without such benefits. Prospective franchisees must decide whether the expenses involved are fair compensation for what they will receive. Another potential drawback is that the franchisee is judged by what his or her peers do. A strong, effective program of managerial control is essential to offset bad impressions created by unsuccessful franchises.

Familiar American fast-food franchises are becoming a common sight in many foreign cities. This KFC outlet is in Toyota City, Japan.

SPEECH RECOGNITION

Cost-conscious entrepreneurs and small-business managers are now warned: a particular brand of thief is hanging out in airports and other public locations, stealing long-distance phone codes by watching business travelers at pay phones punch in their numbers. These criminals may not be able to enjoy their ill-gotten gains much longer, thanks to companies such as Sprint.

The weapon being used by this telecommunications giant is a computer "speech-recognition" system that allows access only to the caller who has the right password *and* the right voice. Sprint's computer also keeps a list of ten preset numbers for each user, and a simple "call office" or "call home" makes the connection.

Sprint's system is simple because it requires the computer to recognize only a few words. But much more sophisticated speech-recognition systems are already in use, and they promise to change the ways people at every level of the organization and every degree of computer literacy use computers.

IBM makes 95 to 98 percent accuracy claims at 70 or more words per minute for its Personal Dictation System. All the user need do is speak into a microphone. The system uses context to distinguish between such homophones as *here* and *hear* and contains a vocabulary of 32,000 words. Users can add their own personal macros; for example, the word *letter* might cue the software to set preselected margins for letterhead and insert a return address. The program's main limitation is that, during setup, the user must read an entire short story out loud to acquaint the computer with his or her particular accent. This not only makes the system difficult to share, but a cold or sore throat can require software retraining.

Today's speech-recognition systems are far from perfect; in one case, a system heard "make your pets old" when the user said "make your text bold." Most systems require that the user speak relatively slowly, with careful enunciation and pauses between words. Although most of the problems will eventually be solved by improved technology, there is still the very human dilemma of people in an office being disturbed by co-workers talking out loud to their computers all day.

Nevertheless, speech-recognition programs will save work and money for business people ranging from company-founding entrepreneurs to office workers. They are likely to be particularly popular among computer users who don't type and aren't comfortable using a mouse, physically-challenged workers, and people who need to use computers while keeping their hands free.

SOURCES: Wendy Pickering, "Computer: Take a Memo," *Datamation,* January 7, 1994, 51–62; Barbara Kantrowitz, "Hey Computer, Do My Taxes," *Newsweek,* March 7, 1994, 48; Hewitt D. Crane and Dimitry Rtischev, "Pen and Voice Unite," *Byte,* October 1993, 98–102; William S. Meisel, "Talk to Your Computer," *Byte,* October 1993, 113–120; and Gene Bylinsky, "At Last! Computers You Can Talk To," *Fortune,* May 3, 1993, 88–91.

Small Business Goes Global

With the development of a worldwide economy, more small firms are going global. Licensing, franchising, and exporting through intermediaries are three possible ways for small- and medium-sized companies to enter the international market.

Under a licensing agreement, one firm allows another to use its intellectual property—such as trademarks, patents, or technical knowledge—in exchange for royalties. For instance, a firm that has developed a new type of packaging might license the process to other companies abroad.

DID YOU KNOW?

In order to register a new car in Japan, you must show proof of having a parking space.

In Japan, Ronald McDonald is called Donald McDonald since it is easier to pronounce.

Korea and Hungary score consistently among the top nations when comparing student achievement in math and science. Hungarian citizens claim the world's literacy title: over 98 percent can read and write.

Labor unions routinely serve on most corporate boards in Europe.

Franchising can be another way for small firms to enter foreign markets. Worldwide, franchising is expanding rapidly; it is growing 2.5 percent a year, compared to an overall global growth in business of 2.3 percent. Approximately 15 to 20 percent of U.S. franchise companies have overseas outlets. Canada is the biggest market for U.S. franchises, followed by Japan, continental Europe, Australia, and the United Kingdom.[13]

Sometimes export success comes from exporting through intermediaries that can provide services small companies cannot afford on their own. An **export management company** *is a domestic firm that specializes in performing international* *marketing services as commissioned representatives or distributors for other companies.* Another option for small firms wishing to export is to work with an **export trading company,** *a general trading firm that plays a varied role in world commerce by importing, exporting, countertrading, investing, and manufacturing.*

Resources for Entrepreneurs

The **Small Business Administration (SBA)** *is the principal government agency concerned with small U.S. firms.* The SBA provides financial assistance, aids in government procurement matters, and offers management training and consulting.

The SBA provides a variety of services and publications. It maintains toll-free telephone numbers and on-line computer programs to answer questions. Its hundreds of business publications can be ordered for little or no cost, and its conferences and seminars are widely available. Management consulting is also conducted through a variety of programs.

Some small businesses are physically going global. Law-school buddies Adam Haven-Weiss and Andrew Badner chose Budapest for their first New York Bagel store and plan to expand.

SUMMARY OF LEARNING GOALS

1. **Identify and explain the three basic forms of business ownership.**

   The three legal forms of business ownership are sole proprietorship, partnership, and corporation. Sole proprietorship, a business owned and operated by a single person, is most common. A partnership is operated by two or more people as co-owners. A corporation is a legal entity separate from its owners.

2. **Compare the advantages and disadvantages of the forms of business ownership.**

   The advantages of sole proprietorships are (a) retention of all profits, (b) ease of formation and dissolution, and (c) ownership flexibility. The disadvantages are (a) unlimited financial liability, (b) financing limitations, (c) management deficiencies, and (d) lack of continuity. The advantages of partnerships are (a) ease of formation, (b) complementary management skills, and (c) expanded financial capability. The disadvantages are (a) unlimited financial liability, (b) possible interpersonal conflicts, (c) lack of continuity, and (d) complex dissolution. The advantages of corporations are (a) limited financial liability, (b) specialized management skills, (c) expanded financial capability, and (d) economies of larger-scale operation. The disadvantages are high taxes and legal restrictions.

3. **Discuss the levels of corporate management.**

   Stockholders own the corporation, the board of directors governs it, and top management is responsible for its actual operation. Middle management coordinates

the operational functions of the company and serves as a liaison between top and lower levels of management. Supervisory managers coordinate the day-to-day operations of the firm, supervise employees, assign specific tasks to the staff, and often are responsible for evaluating employees' job performance.

4. **Explain how private ownership, public ownership, and collective ownership (cooperatives) differ.**

   Private ownership refers to ownership by an individual or individuals, regardless of whether the organization is set up as a sole proprietorship, partnership, or corporation. One alternative to private ownership is public ownership, in which a government unit or its agency owns and operates an organization on behalf of the population served by the unit. Another alternative to private ownership is the cooperative, which provides for collective ownership of production, storage, transportation, and/or marketing activities.

5. **Explain the vital role played by entrepreneurs and small businesses in the global economy.**

   Entrepreneurs and small businesses play an important part in the private enterprise system. They provide independence and bring competitive fervor to the economy. Small firms account for the bulk of all U.S. commercial enterprises and provide a major portion of national output and employment.

6. **Define small business and identify the industries in which most small firms are established.**

   A small business is one that is owned and operated independently, does not dominate its market, and meets a variety of size standards for its income or number of employees. Small companies are found in nearly every industry, including farming, retailing, services, and high technology.

7. Compare the advantages and disadvantages of small business.

Small businesses have some distinct advantages over larger competitors, including ease of introduction of innovations, the ability to provide better service and lower costs, and the ability to fill isolated niches. They also have disadvantages, including poor management, inadequate financing, and government regulation.

8. Describe resources that are available to entrepreneurs.

The Small Business Administration (SBA) is the principal government agency concerned with small U.S. firms. The SBA provides financial assistance, aids in government procurement matters, and offers management training and consulting.

9. List the advantages and disadvantages of franchising.

The advantages of the franchising approach to small business are access to performance records on which to make comparisons and judgments, a widely recognized name, and tested management systems. Disadvantages include the high cost of buying and starting some franchises, as well as the restrictions that come from fitting into a corporate culture that has already been established. Another disadvantage is that when some franchise outlets fail, this can affect consumers' attitude toward all the outlets.

10. Outline the popular methods of small business operation in the global market.

With the development of a worldwide economy, more small firms are going global. Licensing, franchising, and exporting through intermediaries are three possible ways for small- and medium-sized companies to enter the international market. Export management companies and export trading companies can provide specialized services that small firms cannot handle themselves.

KEY TERMS QUIZ

corporation
board of directors
partnership
subsidiary
sole proprietorship
joint venture
stockholders

small business
merger
acquisition
cooperative
entrepreneur
franchising
public ownership

franchisee
franchisor
export management company
export trading company
Small Business Administration (SBA)

board of directors 1. The governing body of a corporation elected by the stockholders.

public ownership 2. An enterprise owned and operated by a governmental unit.

franchising 3. An agreement that sets the methods a dealer can use to produce and market a supplier's good or service.

export management companys 4. A firm that performs international marketing services as commissioned representatives or distributors for other companies.

sole proprietorship 5. Refers to ownership (and usually operation) of an organization by one person.

corporation 6. A legal entity with authority to act and have liability separate and apart from its owners.

export trading company 7. A trading firm involved in importing, exporting, countertrading, investing, and manufacturing.

franchisor 8. A supplier of a franchise that provides various services in exchange for a payment by the franchisee.

acquisition 9. A procedure in which one firm acquires the property and assumes the obligations of another firm.

franchisee 10. A small business person who is allowed to sell the goods or services of a supplier in exchange for some payment.

joint venture 11. A partnership formed for a specific undertaking.

subsidiary 12. A corporation with all or a majority of its stock owned by another corporation.

entrepreneur 13. A risk taker in the private-enterprise system, specifically a person who creates a new business.

partnership _____ 14. Two or more persons who operate a business as co-owners.

stockholders _____ 15. People who acquire the shares of, and therefore own, a corporation.

merger _____ 16. Refers to two or more firms that combine to form one company.

cooperative _____ 17. An organization that is operated collectively by its owners.

small buisness _____ 18. An independently owned and operated firm which meets certain size standards for income and number of employees.

(SBA) _____ 19. The principal government agency concerned with small U.S. firms.

OTHER IMPORTANT TERMS

employee ownership   parent company
Fortune 500   privatization
limited liability company

REVIEW QUESTIONS

1. Outline the ownership structure of U.S. business.
2. What is meant by a sole proprietorship? Why is it the most popular form of business ownership? Are there any disadvantages to this form of business ownership?
3. What are the advantages and disadvantages of partnerships?
4. How would you define a corporation? What are the advantages of the corporate form of business ownership?
5. What is a cooperative? How does it differ from other forms of business enterprises?
6. Define entrepreneurship and small business. Why are entrepreneurs so important to private enterprise?
7. Outline the advantages small firms have over larger ones. Cite an example of each advantage.
8. Why is financing such a problem for small business? Explain how this disadvantage can be overcome.
9. Name some of the resources that serve entrepreneurs and the small-business sector. Discuss the programs that are available.
10. What is franchising? Why is it such a vital element of the small-business sector?

DISCUSSION QUESTIONS

1. Assume that you and your brother are about to open a family restaurant. What factors would determine your choice of a form of business ownership for a new enterprise? Why?
2. Choose an entrepreneur or small-business owner in your area. Interview him or her about the experience of owning one's own business. What advice would this person give about starting a business? What mistakes do new business owners commonly make? Share your findings with the class.
3. Assume you are involved in establishing the following businesses. What forms of business ownership would you use?
   a. Colorado Rockies (professional baseball team)
   b. Dry-cleaning franchise in Fresno, California
   c. Management consulting firm in Boston, Massachusetts
   d. Small foundry in Warren, Michigan
4. Choose a franchise company that operates outlets both in the United States and other countries. Compare the operations of the U.S. outlets with those in at least two foreign countries. Are they different, and if so, in what ways? (For instance, you could compare the menu of a North American fast-food franchise with its menus in other nations.) If there are differences, explain why you think they exist.
5. What steps are necessary to set up a corporation in your particular state or locality? Do these differ from what is required elsewhere? If so, how?

VIDEO CASE: Samuel Adams Lager

The video case for this chapter illustrates the efforts of entrepreneur Jim Koch to create a niche for his product and is found on page 413 of Appendix D.

Solution to Key Terms Quiz

1. board of directors 2. public ownership 3. franchising 4. export management company 5. sole proprietorship 6. corporation 7. export trading company 8. franchisor 9. acquisition 10. franchisee 11. joint venture 12. subsidiary 13. entrepreneur 14. partnership 15. stockholders 16. merger 17. cooperative 18. small business 19. Small Business Administration (SBA)

CHAPTER 6

The Role of Quality in Business Success

Learning Goals

1. Explain the importance of quality and customer satisfaction in achieving a competitive advantage.
2. Summarize the status of quality programs in the United States, Japan, and Europe.
3. Discuss the role of top management in applying total quality management (TQM) to an organization.
4. Relate TQM to various functions within an organization, including production, human resource management, marketing, information processes, and financial management.
5. Identify the major methods of securing feedback from customers, employees, and suppliers.
6. Describe how organizations can work toward continuous process improvement.
7. Define benchmarking and explain its contributions to quality and customer satisfaction.
8. Identify the components of employee involvement and their impact on quality and customer satisfaction.

The R. L. Drake Company almost went out of business twice. But each time it was saved by quality. The Miamisburg, Ohio, firm was founded 50 years ago by Robert Drake, Sr., an electrical engineer who started building amateur radio components capable of broadcasting as well as receiving signals. Drake's business grew steadily and the company expanded into building shortwave and marine radios.

The 1980s saw Japanese competitors, such as Kenwood, Yaesu, and Icom, enter the amateur radio market, and Drake's sales plummeted. A distributor recommended that the company enter an entirely new arena: satellite receivers. At that time, satellite receivers were a novelty—mostly homemade gadgets of widely ranging quality that were peddled through classified ads.

After studying the market, Drake's managers agreed that a definite business opportunity existed. Not only were most satellite receivers of poor quality, but the market was expected to expand rapidly with the growth of cable TV channels, such as Home Box Office (HBO), that broadcast its programs via satellite. They figured that many consumers would consider a high-quality satellite receiver to be a worthwhile investment—

especially since they could view HBO programming for free—and they were right. By 1985 the company production line was running 24 hours a day to keep up with demand.

Then, in 1986, a second crisis occurred: HBO started scrambling its satellite signal, and other cable channels, from Cinemax to CNN, quickly followed suit. Virtually overnight, Drake's primary market evaporated. In one year, sales fell 60 percent and the company was forced to lay off two-thirds of its work force. What saved the firm was its reputation for quality. Over the years, the Drake brand had become a respected name among amateur radio operators all over the world. Company engineers quickly designed an export version of its satellite receiver capable of handling 225 channels, five languages, and a range of power sources and band widths. Today, Drake is the only U.S. satellite receiver manufacturer and generates sales in over 30 countries.

Meanwhile, Drake's management detected a renewed interest in shortwave radio among both U.S. and foreign consumers. Although Japanese firms dominated the market, Drake CEO Ronald Wysong was unimpressed with their quality. "We felt the Japanese shortwaves were high-priced, high-margin, and some of the equipment wasn't very good." So the U.S. firm returned to its roots by introducing a high-quality tabletop model at a competitive price.

The Drake R8 shortwave solved the nagging problem of interference from other stations with five built-in filters, each of which focuses on the desired signal more precisely than the last. Helping to hold down costs was Drake's decision to put its money into improving the radio's capabilities, not its appearance. After all, their research showed that shortwave customers almost always choose performance over style. Says electronics retailer Robert Hatter, "The thing looks like it was made in someone's garage, but if you close your eyes, you'll find it's a top notch performer that's giving the Japanese a run for their money."

Most of the savings on styling is reinvested in customer service, a vital component of Drake's quality reputation. Wysong set up several toll-free telephone lines to facilitate service and encourage customer feedback. These communication channels also are used to slash marketing costs, since one-third of all sales are by phone directly to the Drake factory.

The cost savings also help Drake keep prices competitive and customers happy. Says Drake dealer Fred Osterman, "The R8 is our most popular tabletop receiver by far. There isn't even a close second now."

After two close calls, R. L. Drake is profitable again. Forty percent of each year's sales occur outside the United States, with Africa and the Middle East its largest export markets. Revenues are rising steadily, fueled by the firm's reputation for quality products and excellent customer service. To quote Lawrence Magne, publisher of *Passport to World Band Radio*, "We feel Drake is the best at any price."[1]

CHAPTER OVERVIEW

Managing for quality to provide complete customer satisfaction is essential for surviving and thriving in today's competitive global marketplace. Like R. L. Drake, many U.S. companies have learned the hard-won lesson that long-term success requires delivering superior-quality goods and services at good value. Quality-conscious companies, such as R. L. Drake, involve employees in finance, production, marketing, and every business function in understanding and satisfying customer needs and wants. In fact, companies committed to quality are so customer-focused that they manage their businesses according to their customers' definition of quality. Stew Leonard's, the Norwalk, Connecticut-based supermarket, has their philosophy etched on a large boulder at the store's front entrance. "Rule 1: The customer is always right," says the motto. "Rule 2: When the customer is wrong, reread Rule 1."

> **THEY SAID IT**
>
> "Quality in a product or service is not what the supplier puts in. It is what the customer gets out and is willing to pay for. Customers pay only for what is of use to them and gives them value. Nothing else constitutes quality."
>
> *Peter Drucker (1909–) American business philosopher*

This chapter discusses the role of customer-focused quality in building competitive advantage. To help you understand why the issue of quality is a critical challenge facing U.S. as well as foreign firms, we begin by examining the importance of quality and customer satisfaction, and look at quality programs in the United States, Japan, and Europe. We then discuss ways to apply total quality management to each function of the organization and to obtain feedback. Finally, we examine the critical quality issues of continuous process improvement, benchmarking, and employee involvement.

IMPORTANCE OF QUALITY AND CUSTOMER SATISFACTION

Quality describes *the degree of excellence or superiority of an organization's goods and services.* Quality is a broad term that encompasses both the tangible and intangi-

WE ASKED TOP FINANCIAL ANALYSTS HOW THEY'D INVEST $10,000. BUT THEY NEVER GOT BACK TO US.

Shown left to right: K75, $6,790; R 100 GS, $8,090; K75 S, $9,590; R 100 R, $8,540

One minute they were talking leveraged buyouts, the next they were gone. Was it the distinctive styling? The state-of-the-art engineering? Or just that with each of these four awe-inspiring BMW motorcycles going for under $10,000, they had found the most fulfilling investment of all? As long as there's open road, we may just never know.

 FOR THE WORLD AHEAD.

Satisfied cyclists award the BMW their quality stamp of approval.

ble characteristics of a good or service. Tangible characteristics include such physical traits as durability and reliability. Also included in the overall definition of quality is the intangible component of **customer satisfaction,** *the concept that a good or service pleases buyers because it meets their emotional needs and quality expectations.* The true measure of quality is whether a firm has satisfied its customers. BMW's quality manufacturing offers customer satisfaction to motorcycle purchasers of varying lifestyles; the only commonality is an appreciation of traveling the open road and a desire to spend less than $10,000 for two-wheeled transportation. As author and consultant A. V. Feigenbaum notes, "Quality is what your customers say it is—not what you say it is."[2]

Organizations throughout the world are offering high-quality goods and services to create customer satisfaction through **total quality management (TQM),** *an approach that involves a commitment to quality in achieving world-class performance and customer satisfaction as a crucial strategic objective* for the entire company. In a total quality organization, marketers develop products people want to buy, engineers design products the way customers want to use them, production workers build quality into every product they make, salespeople deliver what they promise customers, information-systems specialists use technology to ensure cus-

tomer orders are filled correctly and on time, and financial managers help determine prices that give customers value.

Does quality pay? Absolutely; studies show that quality programs can boost company revenues by as much as 40 percent, while decreasing production costs 20 to 50 percent, saving 40 percent on space and inventory, cutting production time by as much as 70 percent, and building strong customer loyalty.

At the same time, a growing number of quality-conscious organizations are stressing *return on quality.* Companies focus their efforts to improve quality on measures that produce tangible customer benefits while lowering costs or increasing sales.[3] For example:

> *AT&T measures all quality programs in terms of financial returns. To win approval from top management, proposed programs must yield a 30 percent drop in defects and a 10 percent return on investment.*
>
> *Instead of stressing prompt delivery at any cost UPS is giving drivers free time to talk with customers. The objective is to produce millions in additional sales by improving customer relations and developing new sales leads.*
>
> *Rather than just pushing workers to meet strict package-sorting goals, Federal Express is investing in sorting equipment to cut down on misdirected packages, which can cost the company $50 apiece.*

THEY SAID IT

"When the product is right, you don't have to be a great marketer."

Lee Iacocca (1924–   ) Chairman, Chrysler Corp.

In addition to providing financial returns from reduced costs, increased satisfaction, and added sales, quality-improvement programs are essential if firms are to stay abreast of their competitors. As more companies worldwide apply the principles of total quality management, standards rise. Chey Jong-Hyon, chairman of Korean petroleum products maker Sunkyong Group, notes, "If we merely try to be excellent, our gap with the world's top companies will remain because they keep improving. Only by seeking super-excellence can we reach their level or overtake them." Or, to quote Ram Charan, quality consultant to many of the world's largest companies: "If you're not *better* than the best on a worldwide basis, you're not going to make a living."[4]

NATIONAL QUALITY PROGRAMS

During the past decade, a quality revolution has spread throughout business. More and more firms around the world are realizing that quality programs directly affect company profitability. In fact, they are crucial to an organization's continued existence: A company that fails to provide the same level of quality as its competitors will not stay in business very long.

Quality Programs in the United States

One response to the inroads Japanese and European competitors made in both U.S. and international markets during the 1980s was the creation of the Malcolm Baldrige National Quality Award. Widespread concerns that the quality levels of imported products exceeded American-made products led Congress to establish this prize in 1987 as part of a national quality improvement effort. Named after the late secretary of commerce, the Baldrige Award is the highest level of national recognition for quality that a U.S. company can receive. Its purposes are to promote quality awareness, to recognize quality achievements of U.S. companies, and to publicize successful quality strategies. Each year only two awards can be given in each of three categories: manufacturing, service, and small business. Applicants scoring more than 600 points undergo an on-site evaluation for compliance with the award's standards (see table). Award winners may publicize and advertise receipt of the award so long as they agree to share information about their quality strategies with other U.S. organizations.

THEY SAID IT

"There is only one boss: the customer. And he can fire everybody in the company, from the chairman on down, simply by spending his money somewhere else."

*Sam Walton
(1918–1992)
Founder,
Wal-Mart Stores*

The Baldrige Award has proven successful in motivating American industry by giving companies a goal to shoot for. At DuPont, in fact, so many divisions want to apply that some will have to wait until after the year 2000 to take their turn. Recent winners include Xerox Business Products and Systems (manufacturing), Federal Express (services), and the relatively unknown small business, Globe Metallurgical. Two AT&T divisions—credit card and network systems groups—have won the award.

Since the first Baldrige Award, U.S. firms have made steady improvements in their operations. Average defects per vehicle in American-made cars have fallen from 7.3 to 1.5. A decade ago, eight percent of the steel products made in the United States contained defects, and almost 3,000 U.S.-made computer chips failed for every billion hours of computer usage. Today, the defect rate has plummeted to one percent of steel products and fewer than 100 chips.[5]

Quality Programs in Japan

In an effort to rebuild their industrial base after World War II, Japanese business and industry leaders studied the work of American quality proponents, especially

Winning the Baldrige Award		
Baldrige Award Criteria	**Description**	**Points**
Customer focus and satisfaction	The effectiveness of systems to determine customer requirements and demonstrated success in meeting them	300
Quality and operational results	The results in quality achievement and quality improvement, demonstrated through quantitative measures	180
Human resource development and management	The success of efforts to develop and realize the full potential of the work force for quality	150
Management of process quality	The effectiveness of systems and processes for assuring the quality of all operations	140
Leadership	The senior executives' success in creating and sustaining a quality culture	100
Information and analysis	The effectiveness of information collection and analysis for quality improvement and planning	70
Strategic quality planning	The effectiveness of integrating quality requirements into business plans	60

Firms must score at least 600 points to be eligible to compete for the Baldrige Award—America's highest quality honor.

W. Edwards Deming. By the 1970s, the Japanese had emerged as formidable global competitors. They had achieved a reputation worldwide for goods and services of high, yet affordable, quality.[6]

To show their appreciation for Deming's role in the rebirth of Japan as an economic superpower, the Japanese government created the Deming Prize in 1951. This award recognizes companies and individuals who achieve the most significant gains in quality; it is awarded annually in a ceremony broadcast on national television in Japan. To this day, the Deming Prize remains Japan's most coveted industrial award.

Quality Programs in Europe

The nations that comprise the European Union (EU) represent not only formidable competitors to U.S. firms, but also a sizable export market for goods whose quality levels match EU standards. Contributing to the worldwide interest in quality in the late 1990s are the European Union's **ISO 9000** standards, *international standards for quality management and quality assurance.* Developed by the International Standards Organization (ISO) to ensure consistent quality among the products manufactured and sold throughout the EU nations, the ISO 9000 is a widely recognized quality model. Many European

THEY SAID IT

"Use your own best judgment at all times."

Entire contents of Nordstrom Corp. policy manual

companies now require suppliers to be ISO-certified as a condition of doing business with them. To receive certification, a company must undergo an on-site audit to ensure that documented quality procedures are in place and that all employees understand and follow those procedures. Meeting ISO requirements is an ongoing process; companies are audited briefly once every six months and must complete recertification every three years. ISO 9000 companies are required to limit their purchases to suppliers that also are certified. Roughly 40,000 companies worldwide are ISO-certified. However, this number includes only about 400 U.S. firms and just 48 in Japan.

Like Japan and the United States, the European Union has created its own recognition of excellence in quality, the European Quality Award. The application and assessment process is similar to that of the Baldrige Award, with a focus on customer satisfaction, human resource management, and leadership. Applicants also are assessed on their quality management of resources and their firms' impact on the environment.

As trade barriers among member European Union nations fall, new rules governing the production process are being phased in. These regulations can be highly detailed—specifications for the electrical system of washing machines, for instance, cover more than 100 typed pages—and it is important for U.S. exporters to be aware of them.[7]

APPLYING TQM THROUGHOUT THE ORGANIZATION

Organizations today recognize that improving quality is a critical strategy for building competitive advantage. Within the organization, higher quality leads to increased productivity and lower costs. Externally, quality improvements increase customer satisfaction and lower prices, which in turn boosts market share. Ultimately, a successful commitment to total quality should result in increased earnings and profitability.

TQM often is viewed as primarily affecting production by increasing efficiency on the shop floor. In this section, we will correct this too-narrow view by examining its application to all business functions, including production, human resource management, marketing, information processes, and financial management. The starting place for the creation of a total quality organization is the commitment and involvement of top management.

Top Management Involvement

Effective TQM programs begin with the involvement of top managers who believe that the success of their firm is based on quality and customer satisfaction. As Charles Aubrey, president of the American Society for Quality Control, puts it, top managers "must take a strategic view of quality: setting priorities, identifying what's most critical to the success of the enterprise,

HOW QUALITY IMPROVEMENTS BENEFIT AN ORGANIZATION

Quality improvements impact an organization both internally and externally.

and focusing improvement efforts on the customer. These are decisions that only top management can make."[8]

Quality advocate W. Edwards Deming created a classic set of guidelines for top managers, called his "14 Points for Quality," that encourage managers to view their organizations as systems that use the knowledge and skills of all employees to improve qual-

Deming's 14 Points for Quality

1. Drive out fear.
2. Eliminate quotas and numerical goals.
3. Break down all barriers between departments.
4. Eliminate inspection by building products right the first time.
5. Institute a vigorous education program.
6. Remove barriers that rob workers of their right to pride of workmanship.
7. Institute leadership with the aim of helping people do a better job.
8. Eliminate slogans, exhortations, and production targets.
9. Adopt a new philosophy to awaken managers to the challenge, to learn responsibilities, and to take on leadership.
10. End practice of awarding business based on the price tag. Move toward single supplier and base long-term relationship on loyalty and trust.
11. Improve constantly and forever the system of production, marketing, and service.
12. Put everyone to work to accomplish this transformation.
13. Institute job training.
14. Create constancy of purpose toward the improvement of goods and services to become competitive, stay in business, and to provide jobs.

Deming's 14 Points for Quality Improvement are designed as guidelines for managers in accomplishing quality objectives.

ity. Managers are responsible for communicating the goals of total quality management to all staff members, and for encouraging them to improve themselves and take pride in their work. Research determines customers' needs and wants. This information is then used to design and redesign functional, dependable goods and services; to remove defects by reducing variations; and to build relationships of loyalty and trust with suppliers to improve incoming materials and to decrease costs.

Lee Kun Hee, chairman of Korea's Samsung Corp., motivates his management team to improve quality through applying what he calls "shock therapy." To alert them to the need for TQM, he issued surprise orders for senior executives to fly to Los Angeles and visit local dealers carrying Samsung electronics products. Lee already had talked with these dealers and knew that they would barrage his staff with numerous complaints about product defects and customer-service shortcomings. By moving them out of their offices and onto the firing line, Lee hoped to produce a jolt of reality regarding the firm's quality problems. After all, Samsung, the largest non-Japanese conglomerate in Asia, has seen its earnings drop to $600 million on global sales of $54 billion.

Chairman Lee also has introduced several other innovations. He videotapes his speeches on quality so Samsung's 188,000 employees can hear his recommendations directly, rather than having his words filtered through their supervisors. Samsung executives receive foreign language training and study management style variations that may be present in Samsung's far-flung production and sales facilities. Managers also are required to spend more time with suppliers, customers, and on the production floor with assembly workers. Meetings are limited to an hour, and every important meeting is taped, making managers more accountable for following through on their commitments. The company actively recruits female managers, an unusual practice in Korea. Lee has taken

Samsung CEO Lee (bottom on video) is leading a quality revolution that includes recruiting women managers.

motivation to new lengths by promising to donate 70 to 80 percent of his personal fortune to a foundation that would benefit Samsung employees if the quality program produces measurable results by 1997. Otherwise, he says, he will resign as chairman: "I have staked my honor, my life, and my assets on these changes."[9]

TQM and Production

Early efforts to improve quality in the production process consisted mostly of end-of-the-line inspections: Workers were positioned at the end of the assembly line to weed out finished products that failed to meet quality specifications. While end-of-the-line inspections still are used today, it is increasingly viewed as an approach that is designed backwards. It does nothing to correct the manufacturing errors that created the problems in the first place. In addition, it can be time-consuming and often is ineffective, since inspectors do not always catch defective products. Finally, it is expensive. Samsung's Chairman Lee estimates that every year 6,000 of his firm's 36,000 employees spend their time identifying and then repairing an average of 20,000 defective products.

The quality movement began as an attempt to improve product quality by improving the production process itself. An early approach still used today is **statistical quality control,** *a system using statistical procedures to gather and analyze data to pinpoint and correct problem areas.* It involves developing control charts for detecting variations in the manufacturing process that could produce defective products. By controlling these variations, statistical quality control builds quality into the production process rather than relying on inspection to find defects.

Organizations seeking to improve their own production systems also will demand better quality and quicker response time from their suppliers; they are slashing the number of suppliers with whom they do business. Ten years ago, Xerox bought equipment from 5,000 suppliers. Today, it buys from 500—a 90 percent reduction. Motorola has trimmed its supplier ranks by 70 percent, Digital Equipment by 67 percent, and General Motors by 45 percent. Since Xerox pared its supplier list, it consequently has reduced its reject rate on parts by a factor of 13.

When Boeing began planning its new 777 aircraft, it selected Alcoa to supply special aluminum alloys used in the new plane's wings and outer "skin." Alcoa relied on statistical quality-control charts to monitor key steps in producing these components to make sure the new alloy did not vary at any time from the original design specifications.

Alcoa workers pore over statistical quality-control charts to ensure zero defects in the Boeing 777 wings.

ISO 9000 certification rapidly is becoming a prerequisite for firms doing business in Europe—and for their suppliers. The U.S. chemical giant DuPont learned the importance of these standards recently when it lost a major European order for polyester film to an ISO-certified British firm. That same year, DuPont revised its internal standards to meet ISO requirements.[10]

TQM and Human Resource Management

An organization cannot be any better than its employees allow it to be. Indeed, Baldrige Award recipients often win praise for quality in their human resource management practices. AT&T's Universal Card Services certifies local day-care centers for employees' offspring, helps parents find a qualified care provider for mildly ill children, and offers employees and their families free use of the company health club. Employees needing auto financing can take advantage of the low interest rates offered by AT&T's credit union.

What is the best way to motivate employees to improve quality? When psychologists at the American Quality Foundation studied worker attitudes and behavior, they found key differences between U.S. and Japanese workers. While the Japanese enjoy working toward incremental, step-by-step improvements,

Americans tend to get impatient and look for ways to achieve a single breakthrough. Japanese employees are likely to be more methodical in their search for quality, while U.S. workers tend to be more emotional. Thus, the foundation recommends that managers of American workers motivate them by focusing on major changes rather than small ones, and by encouraging them to feel a sense of individual achievement and personal reward.

Another effective motivational technique involves the concepts of internal and external customers. So far in this chapter we have discussed customer satisfaction in terms of **external customers**—*people or organizations who buy or use another firm's good or service.* However, TQM also emphasizes the importance of **internal customers**—*individual employees or entire departments within an organization who depend on the work of other people or departments to perform their jobs.* For example, a Compaq Computer employee processing an order for a new PC is the internal customer of the Compaq salesperson who completes the sale, just as the person who buys the product is the salesperson's external customer. When employees view their colleagues as internal customers, they are motivated to deliver higher-quality goods and services to their co-workers. They accept the responsibility of helping fellow employees do their jobs better and add further value to the production and marketing processes.[11]

Any department that in some way adds value to the end-user's product is, in fact, an internal customer in need of information. Consider how clearly the product design engineer at a firm, such as Texas Instruments, must understand who the end users are and what needs they have. In this case, the design engineer becomes one of the marketing department's internal customers. If the marketing department does not clearly identify the target customer to the design engineer, it has delivered unsatisfactory customer service.[12]

TQM and Marketing

With TQM, customer satisfaction becomes the primary goal of marketing. As Sam Walton, founder of

BUSINESS STRATEGY

Quality Programs in South Korea

Since the mid-1950s, South Korean business has been a highly successful operation of giant conglomerates that manufacture inexpensive consumer goods ranging from shoes to radios. But the future success of the tiny country will depend on its ability to produce high-quality goods and services and provide customer satisfaction. The World Economic Forum includes South Korea in a 15-member category of newly industrialized nations, but even in that group it ranks only number 6, behind such countries as Malaysia and Chile.

Several large South Korean corporations have undertaken far-reaching quality programs throughout their organizations, from human resource management to inspection processes. Hyundai Motor, the nation's biggest auto maker, successfully entered the U.S. market in 1987, but had trouble competing once consumers discovered the high number of defects in its cars. Hyundai management attacked the problem by developing training programs for everyone involved with producing and distributing its cars.

One quality improvement process Hyundai implemented was to increase the number of times each vehicle is inspected. Each car on its way to America is inspected and test-driven at least three times before being put on the market: first at the factory, then at the U.S. port of entry, and finally at the U.S. dealer's showroom. Any necessary repairs are made immediately. In just two years, Hyundai has jumped from last place in the J. D. Power Consumer Satisfaction Index to the middle ranks, and it continues to move upward.

Samsung is another well-recognized South Korean electronics manufacturer that has realized the importance of quality. CEO Lee Kun Hee tells his employees, "Change everything but your wives and children." Workers who previously had worked 12 and 14 hours a day were placed on 8-hour shifts to improve efficiency and enhance morale. To address the high level of defects, Samsung allows production workers to stop assembly lines when defects occur. As Lee says, making defective products "is cancerous and a criminal act on the part of management."

Daewoo Electronics dramatically reduced product defects and gained domestic share at the expense of its competitors. Internally, Daewoo management began reassigning or laying off clerical workers; externally, the firm began demanding cash refunds from suppliers of shoddy components. Founder and CEO Kim Woo-Choong claims the quality levels of its subcompact cars are now comparable to Japanese models.

SOURCE: Louis Kraar, "Korea Goes for Quality," *Fortune,* April 18, 1994, 153–159.

America's largest retailer, Wal-Mart, once said, "An improvement's not an improvement until your customer knows about it."[13] TQM must focus first and foremost on the customer; quality marketing means customer-driven marketing. This fact is evident from the criteria for the Baldrige Award, where the customer satisfaction score accounts for 300 of the 1,000 total points.

Total quality management impacts the marketing function in several ways. One is product design; quality product decisions involve selecting the tangible and intangible characteristics that allow a good or service to meet customer needs. Products must be designed with changing customer values in mind. Singapore Airlines, for instance, addresses the needs of busy travelers by offering over-ocean fax transmission as a standard passenger service. Its Boeing 747 jets have facsimile machines in the front and rear cabins. The jet's transmitter sends the fax message to a satellite that beams it to ground stations in Singapore, Norway, or England. From there, the message travels via telephone lines to its destination.

TQM also challenges organizations to increase the speed and efficiency of delivering goods and services so customers will receive the right amount, at the right place, and at the right time. A customer-focused distribution strategy leads to higher levels of customer satisfaction. This is why California-based Granite Rock, a supplier of crushed rock and concrete, developed GraniteXpress, a 24-hour automated system for dispensing rock from its quarry. Customers drive their trucks up to a concrete-loading facility and insert a magnetic card to place an order and charge it to their account. In less than ten minutes, the correct amount of rock slides down a chute into the waiting truck. President Bruce Woolpert got the idea from watching people use automatic teller machines: "We thought if they can dispense $20 bills accurately, then we can do that with rock."[14]

TQM also impacts an organization's advertising and personal selling efforts. Advertising for United Parcel Service (UPS) communicates the firm's "tightest ship in the shipping business" slogan by focusing on its speed and dependability. Through ads, news features, and sales presentations, UPS customers learn about the efficiency of the firm's 62,000 neatly dressed delivery people. At each stop, the UPS driver sheds the seat belt, toots the horn, and cuts the engine as he

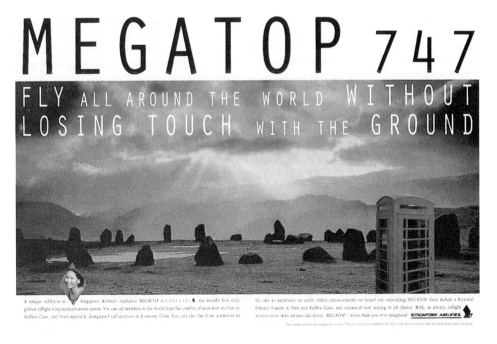

MEGATOP 747

FLY ALL AROUND THE WORLD WITHOUT LOSING TOUCH WITH THE GROUND

Trans-Pacific business travelers can conduct business en route via telephone or fax on Singapore Air.

brakes to a stop. In a single motion, up goes the emergency brake and the gearshift goes into first—ready for takeoff after delivery. A clipboard goes under the right arm and a package under the left. The keys, teeth up, are on the middle finger of the driver's right hand. Then the representative of the world's largest overnight shipping company trots to the office or house at the prescribed three feet per second.

A customer-oriented marketing strategy often includes a guarantee of customer satisfaction. L. L. Bean has built a successful business based on the guarantee stated in every apparel catalog: "Our products are guaranteed to give 100 percent satisfaction in every way. Return anything purchased from us at any time if it proves otherwise." Oakley Millwork Inc., an Illinois-based building-supplies firm, offers an extraordinary guarantee. If a customer orders a product that is out of stock and must be back-ordered, it is free. Clients in the building industry were thrilled with the guarantee. "I directly attribute a 20 percent increase in our sales to that guarantee the year it came out," says owner Glen Johnson.[15]

TQM and Information Processes

Effective information systems can support TQM programs by improving customer service and boosting employees' productivity. This is why U.S. companies spend more than $1 billion a year on computers and related technologies to bolster customer-service departments. In a recent survey of 782 large American and European companies, 70 percent of the respondents identified customer service as the major focus of their investments in technology.[16]

Imagine an international airline that gave your money back if it didn't arrive on time. Now imagine if that airline only took packages.

UPS INTRODUCES THE WORLDWIDE EXPRESS ON-TIME GUARANTEE. We promise to deliver your package on time to hundreds of cities around the world or we'll deliver it for free. Kind of makes you wish we also took people, doesn't it? For guarantee details, call 1-800-PICK-UPS. The package delivery company more companies count on.

Quality commitments and money-back guarantees make UPS the tightest ship in the shipping business.

For years, clerks at American Express had to laboriously type the handwritten numbers on every charge slip—900,000 slips a day—into the company's computer system. Inevitably, clerical errors led to billing errors and angry customers. Then AmEx purchased handwriting-recognition computer systems that can read and process legibly written numbers. The error rate has plummeted, and so has processing time. While the system cost more than $10 million, it is expected to pay for itself within four years. Says Senior Vice President Cliff Dodd, "It is critically important to us."[17]

Whirlpool Corp. recently received a computerized alert when its information system reported several complaints about a new Whirlpool washing-machine model. Several of the machines developed an annoying leak after just a few washloads. Not only did the Whirlpool computer system warn management about the problem, it also provided repair centers with a list of people who had purchased the model. Mechanics were quickly dispatched to make the necessary repairs and keep Whirlpool customers happy customers.[18]

While information technologies can improve customer service, they also can detract from it if badly planned. Voice mail, which began as a communication medium for people within an organization and has evolved into a virtual receptionist for many companies, can save time and money. But, if poorly designed, voice mail can frustrate callers and alienate potential customers, who may decide to call the competition instead. Says telecommunications consultant Tom Hunse, "These days, the [primary] user of voice mail is the [out-of-office] caller. It's not the way you want to treat a customer or client when they call." Hunse suggests the following guidelines for a high-quality voice-mail system.[19]

- Offer callers the option of talking to a human operator at any time during the message.
- Change the message daily to reflect the specifics of your schedule.
- Ask callers to leave a detailed message. This way, the necessary information will be ready when the call is returned.
- Check for messages regularly, at least three times a day. Return all calls within 24 hours.

TQM and Financial Management

Applying TQM to financial management means establishing clear quality goals and linking them to employee compensation and financial returns for the company. For an employee-owned company like Avis, high-quality customer service is linked directly to the

Avis employee-owners receive payoffs by trying harder to serve customers in over 4,800 locations across the globe.

firm's profits—and to long-term returns for its owner-employees. However, a study by the American Quality Foundation and accounting giant Ernst & Young finds that, at more than 80 percent of American companies, quality performance measures play no role in determining senior managers' compensation. Lack of clear, quality-oriented financial objectives can derail projects and waste precious funds.

When Mike Walsh took over as CEO of Tenneco, the giant gas pipeline and automobile-parts manufacturer was generating over $1.3 billion in annual revenues, but also was posting annual losses of $732 million. Walsh immediately instituted financial management measures that revealed a linkage between Tenneco's losses and specific quality problems. These problems included unscheduled downtime due to equipment failures, growing numbers of warranty claims due to defects, insufficient project planning, and inadequate testing and inspection procedures. Says Tenneco President Dana Mead, "We used total quality as an integral part of addressing the crisis. We burned cost-of-quality objectives into the goals for every operating unit." Walsh also changed Tenneco's compensation scheme to link a significant portion of every senior manager's bonus to meeting these objectives. Within three years, Tenneco had reversed its downward spiral and was earning $215 million in operating income annually.[20]

THE IMPORTANCE OF FEEDBACK TO QUALITY

As a first step in improving quality, a company must compile feedback to use in measuring its present performance. **Feedback** consists of *messages returned by the audience to the sender that may cause the sender to alter or cancel an original message.* Feedback can be obtained from three primary sources: customers, employees, and suppliers.

Customer Feedback

Choosing the best way to obtain and measure customer feedback is often a challenging task for management, since *gaps*—differences between actual and perceived quality of goods and services—may exist. Xerox CEO Paul A. Allaire describes such a gap that existed a few years ago at headquarters of the firm that invented the photocopying market: "We were fairly arrogant, until we realized the Japanese were selling quality products for what it cost us to make them."[21]

In a few instances, management receives a positive surprise in learning that a favorable gap exists; that is, their products are better than expected. If firms are to avoid unfavorable gaps, they must go beyond traditional performance measures and focus on exploring what drives customer behavior, then formulate their mission statements, goals, and performance standards based on customer perceptions.

Many companies measure customer satisfaction by monitoring purchasing behavior over a period of time and surveying customers periodically regarding their experiences with company products and service personnel. Xerox's Customer Satisfaction Measurement System tracks the purchase behavior and preferences of 200,000 Xerox equipment owners; results show a 40 percent increase in customer satisfaction over the past decade.

Toll-free telephone lines can be an effective customer feedback system. More than two-thirds of U.S. manufacturers offer toll-free numbers, compared to

CALLING THE HOTLINES: WHAT WE FOUND			
COMPANY	WHAT CALLER RECEIVES	COMPANY REPRESENTATIVE'S PHONE MANNER	CALLER'S TIME ON HOLD
SmithKline	Refund	Cheerful	None
Duracell	Coupon	Sympathetic	None
Kraft General Foods	Coupon	Professional	None
Mars, Inc.	Refund*	Efficient	None
Nestle SA	Coupon	Efficient	None
Warner-Lambert	Refund*	Efficient	None
Gerber	Coupon	Earnest	30 seconds
Frito-Lay	Refund	Cheerful	1 minute
Mattel	Refund	Professional	3 minutes
Colgate-Palmolive	Coupon	Cheerful	3 mins., 46 sec.
Binney & Smith	Coupon	Cheerful	5 minutes
Dow	Refund	Professional	5 minutes

*Consumer gets refund after product is returned

A survey finds that companies with toll-free telephone lines reward complaining customers with a coupon or refund.

just 40 percent a decade ago. One reason for installing these lines and printing the number on packages is that consumers often associate the promotion of toll-free numbers with high-quality goods and services. Also important is the fact that talking to customers yields valuable information. "We get immediate feedback on our products," explains a spokeswoman for Starkist Foods. Toll-free phone lines are "a wonderful research tool," according to Pillsbury CEO Paul Walsh. "If we have a problem with a product, we want to be the first to hear about it."[22] Customer feedback and customer satisfaction measurement are discussed in more detail in Chapter 11.

Employee Feedback

As Federal Express CEO Frederick Smith points out, "Customer satisfaction begins with employee satisfaction." Effective managers take time to solicit and respond to employee feedback. Sam Walton used to ride with Wal-Mart truck drivers and visit stores early in the morning to talk with employees. Thousands of firms ask employees to complete standardized surveys. Another method used for decades by U.S. and Japanese companies is to actively solicit ideas from employees and then reward individuals and teams for their suggestions.

The Ritz-Carlton's employee-feedback programs are one reason why the chain became the first hotel to win the Baldrige Award. Every Ritz-Carlton employee receives more than 100 hours of quality training, double the amount offered by most U.S. companies. The hotel's 13-member quality-management team meets weekly to address quality problems identified by employees. New hires are interviewed on their twenty-first day on the job, and again on their thirtieth day, in order to answer questions and review their progress. These reviews help management evaluate quality performance.[23]

Quality researcher Kathryn Troy suggests that organizations develop a recognition program that honors skilled employees and gives them a chance to tell other employees what they do. "It sounds hokey, but it's successful," Troy explains. "Almost all of the total quality graybeards who have been at it for years have well-established recognition programs. Corning, Xerox, Motorola, and Milliken—they all have them."[24]

Supplier Feedback

Another element of total quality management involves giving feedback to and receiving it from suppliers. This means thinking in terms of customer/supplier partnerships that require members to consider each other as their customers. For example, a manufacturer orders its parts from another company (the supplier) and the two form a partnership. The manufacturer becomes the supplier's customer. In recent years, companies have started to demand higher levels of quality from their suppliers, and suppliers must comply if they want to maintain the business relationship.

Livingston, New Jersey's St. Barnabas Medical Center is one of a growing number of health-care providers who ask all patients to complete a questionnaire on employees, the quality of hospital food, and overall cleanliness. One respondent was pop singer Whitney Houston, who had a baby there. Feedback from Houston and other less-famous patients helps determine the performance of Seiler Corp., the contract-services firm that provides dietary and housekeeping services for St. Barnabas and other hospitals. The feedback also directly affects Seiler's profits, since its fees are tied to these quarterly survey scores. Seiler executives view the arrangement with St. Barnabas as a true partnership, and have invested $1.2 million to update the hospital's kitchen. As Ronald Del Mauro, president of St. Barnabas, comments, "If we're successful, they're successful."[25]

CONTINUOUS PROCESS IMPROVEMENT

In recent years, Japanese quality programs have migrated across the Pacific and are being implemented throughout America and Europe. **Continuous process improvement,** or *kaizen* as it is called in Japanese, is *the process of constantly studying and making changes in work activities to improve their quality, timeliness, efficiency, and effectiveness.* Continuous improvement results in value-added goods and services that meet customer needs and innovations that exceed customer expectations. This process must be ongoing, since customers' needs, wants, and expectations are always changing.

The quality of work processes, to a large extent, determines the quality of the resulting goods and services and can give the organization a competitive advantage. Continuous process-improvement efforts focus on three objectives: reducing cycle time, reducing variation, and eliminating waste.

Reducing Cycle Time

Cycle time is *the time it takes to complete a work process or activity,* from beginning to end. For example, the time it takes to design a conveyor system, handle a

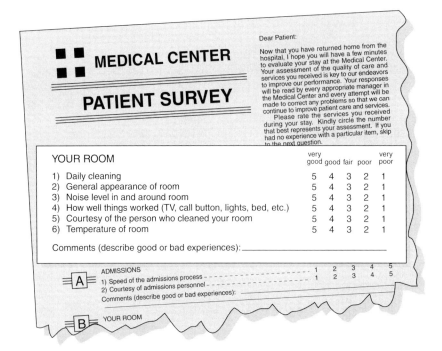

Part of a questionnaire similiar to the one that helps determine how much St. Barnabas pays its vendor of dietary and housekeeping services.

customer inquiry, or create an employee training video all represent cycle time. In each case, the time involved can be reduced through several means. These include simplifying work processes, eliminating steps that do not add value to the product, and bringing individuals from several departments together to work out production inefficiencies that add to cycle time. Such reductions accomplish two important objectives:

- they reduce the time involved in bringing new products to the marketplace; and
- they permit the firm to respond more quickly in filling customers' orders by producing and delivering them quickly.

L. L. Bean, the Freeport, Maine, mail-order firm, is a recognized leader in cycle-time control. Workers use flowcharts to track movements involved in filling customer orders and to eliminate wasted movements. Frequently-ordered merchandise is stored closer to the packing station. Such improvements result in 99.9 percent error-free shipments being filled within a few hours following receipt of each order.[26]

The concept of cycle time is closely associated with a term that has become a business buzz-word of the late 1990s: **reengineering**—the *process of mapping out delivery chain processes in detail to identify areas in which to reduce cycle time or errors by applying technology*

> **THEY SAID IT**
>
> "The difficult we do at once; the impossible takes a bit longer."
>
> *Inscription on the memorial to the Sea-Bees (U.S. Naval Construction Battalions)*

in those key steps. When a company reengineers a process, management systems, job designs, and work flows are evaluated carefully and then are modified in an effort to improve efficiency and reduce cycle time. Ford Motor Company's vendor-payment system kept 400 accounting department employees awash in a sea of paperwork. When top management learned that rival Mazda performed the same work with only five workers in their accounts-payable division, they realized that reengineering was needed. Computers now match receipt records, purchase orders, and invoices and then prepare checks automatically. Today, the same work is performed by only 100 Ford employees and company vendors are paid immediately upon receipt of a shipment.[27]

Wal-Mart's new computer and telecommunications technologies allowed the discount retail giant to reduce dramatically the time lag between ordering products from its vendors and delivering the items to its retail stores. The shorter cycle time resulting from this reengineering allowed Wal-Mart to cut its inventory carrying costs and to pass the savings along to customers in the form of lower prices. The result was a significant competitive advantage for the Bentonville, Arkansas-based firm.

One approach used to map out cycle time and find areas for improvement is the **PDCA cycle**, a *step-by-step process of Planning, Doing, Checking, and Acting.* In the *planning* step, employees analyze their work and determine what changes might improve it. In the *doing* step, they implement these changes. During the *checking* step, they observe the effects of the change. *Acting,* the final step, changes work activities to bring about improvement. Throughout the cycle, employees are asked to examine their own jobs in relation to how it affects customer satisfaction.

Total quality organizations apply the PDCA cycle to all business processes, from planning long-term strategies to adjusting short-term details of customer service. A recent patient survey by administrators at Orlando's Florida Hospital Medical Center found that food service was an important determinant of patients' attitudes toward hospitals, and that 12 percent of their patients had complained about the hospital's food. They used the following PDCA cycle to help resolve the problem.[28]

The PDCA cycle allows employees and management to analyze cycle time and find areas for improvement.

- *Planning.* Staffers analyzed the hospital's food-service operations and found that the inefficient cafeteria tray-line layout sometimes led to food mixups. A patient on a restricted diet might receive a tray intended for one on a regular diet, and vice versa.
- *Doing.* The staff experimented with reorganizing the tray lines to reduce the chances of error.
- *Checking.* They measured the results of the change, and found that complaints about food fell from 12 to 2 percent. Overall patient satisfaction with the food increased, even though the meals themselves tasted the same as they always had.
- *Acting.* The new tray line setup was adopted as a permanent arrangement.

Reducing Variation

All work processes, goods, and services have some degree of variation. This can result from such factors as poor market research, faulty machinery or outdated technology, inadequately trained employees, inefficient work procedures, and defective parts and materials from suppliers.

Product variation in the creation and marketing of services is strongly influenced by whether the service is equipment-based or people-based. Standardization of intangible products is simpler for equipment-based industries like computer time-sharing, motion picture theaters, automated car washes, and dry cleaners. Eliminating product variation is much more difficult for people-based service providers such as lawn-care firms, plumbing and appliance repair firms, recruiting agencies, lawyers, and accountants. In fact, it is sometimes difficult even to assure consistency in the services provided by different employees of the same firm.

Quality programs are used to train employees of both producers of goods and service providers to use statistical controls and problem-solving methods to reduce variations. The goal is to reach the highest possible performance standard, so customers can depend on consistently high quality each time they purchase a good or service.

Effective work processes build quality into a product by reducing variations in production that would cause errors. Clothing manufacturer Healthtex combines well-trained employees, state-of-the-art production machinery, and high-quality materials to produce its long-lasting, fashionable lines of infant wear. This approach of incorporating high-quality levels at the beginning of the production line is much more cost effective than inspecting finished products to spot defects and correct problems.

Eliminating Waste

To economically produce and market goods and services that satisfy customers, quality companies concentrate on eliminating waste. Waste includes any work activity that does not add value to the product.

Wasted time and resources cost companies enormous amounts of money. The *costs associated with poor-quality products and production processes, such as scrap, rework, and loss of customers,* are called the **costs of quality.** These costs have internal and external dimensions. Most internal quality costs are measurable; examples include discarding unusable parts, reworking defective parts, inspecting and discarding faulty goods, redesigning inferior products, and retraining

Healthtex purchasers are assured of product consistency by the production and distribution processes combined with the customer satisfaction guarantees provided by the VF Corporation division.

employees. External costs are more difficult to measure. They include lost sales, missed marketing opportunities, frequent repairs, negative word-of-mouth advertising, bad publicity, and loss of customers to competitors.

Continuous process improvement involves more than making the production line more efficient. Five years ago, Motorola accountants spent 11 days of every month completing the paperwork and financial statements for the previous month's work. By reducing cycle time through streamlining the department's procedures, it now takes two days. Not only does the new system free Motorola accountants to perform other tasks, it reduces dramatically the time required for outside auditors to inspect the company's records, saving Motorola 50 percent in external accounting charges.[29]

BENCHMARKING

What specifically does high quality mean? Is 99 percent defect-free performance satisfactory? In some industries, zero defects is a very real goal. Even a 99.9 percent error-free performance standard would mean that 18 commercial air carriers would crash every day in the United States, the U.S. Postal Service

would lose 17,000 pieces of mail each hour, 500 incorrect surgical operations would be performed each week, and financial institutions would deduct $24.8 million from the wrong accounts every hour.[30]

Most quality-conscious organizations rely on an important tool called **benchmarking.** This approach to creating a world-class organization consists of *identifying how business leaders achieve superior performance levels in their industry and continuously compare and measure the firm's performance against these outstanding performers.*[31] It involves learning how the world's best goods and services are designed, produced, and marketed, and then using the information to help improve the company's own operations. The purpose of benchmarking is to achieve superior performance that results in a competitive advantage in the marketplace.

The five-phase sequence of applying benchmarking begins with planning (see table). In this phase, participants select the companies they want to benchmark and determine how they will collect the needed data. Next comes the analysis phase; team members study their own company practices and compare them with those firms considered best in their industries. The third step, integration, begins with communicating the results of this comparison to the members of the organization. Goals and action plans then are developed to incorporate these superior practices. The

Steps in the Benchmarking Process

Planning Phase

1. Select benchmarking candidates.
2. Identify organizations to use in making comparisons.
3. Select data-collection methods and collect needed data.

Analysis Phase

4. Identify gaps between company practices and industry-best practices.
5. Forecast future performance levels if identified benchmarks are implemented.

Integration Phase

6. Communicate benchmarking findings and gain acceptance.
7. Establish functional goals.
8. Develop action plans.

Action Phase

9. Implement plans and monitor progress.
10. Review benchmarks and replace as needed.

Maturity Phase

- Achievement of leadership position.
- Benchmarking fully integrated throughout the organization.

The ten steps to benchmarking can be applied to all business procedures and practices.

fourth phase, action, involves putting these plans in place and monitoring their progress. The new processes are measured against the benchmarks, which are replaced as needed. In the final stage, maturity, the organization achieves a leadership position in its industry by integrating the best industry practices into all organizational functions.[32]

Planning and Analysis

The benchmarking product should focus on **critical success factors,** *activities and functions considered most important in gaining a competitive advantage and achieving long-term success.* These factors vary among organizations. For one firm, a critical factor might be satisfying customers with excellent service; for another, it might be bringing products to the marketplace faster.

After deciding what to benchmark, a firm must identify other organizations recognized as perfor-

mance leaders. In identifying leaders, companies may look internally, to competitors, or to firms in other industries. In *internal benchmarking,* comparisons are made between similar functions performed in different departments or divisions within the firm. *Competitive benchmarking* involves comparisons with direct product competitors. Reports in magazines, such as *Consumer Reports,* are well-known competitive benchmarks that compare competing brands of products, such as stereos or coffeemakers. The J. D. Power consumer satisfaction rankings compare initial quality assessments of auto purchasers. In *functional benchmarking,* firms make comparisons between the functions of firms in different industries. Benchmarking pioneer Xerox Corp. has benchmarked organizations as diverse as Florida Power & Light (quality programs), American Express (billing and collections), and Mary Kay Cosmetics (warehousing and distribution operations).

Integration, Action, and Maturity

Firms use benchmark findings to implement improvements, such as setting new performance goals, changing current processes by adapting the best practices of the benchmark partners, and measuring the progress of the new work practices. Benchmarking results should be communicated to employees so they understand the reasons for change, the opportunities for improvement, how they can help implement these changes, and how these changes impact the organization's overall business strategy.

For instance, a recent benchmarking project at Xerox concerned the company's cost centers. Management wanted to remake them into money-making profit centers. Employees at the Business Systems Group's logistics and distribution cost center established benchmarks by gathering data on how to operate a successful profit center. Information sources included vendors, other companies with similar cost centers, and noncompeting firms in various industries. This information was used to establish market values for the functions that center employees performed. Based on these values, the staff negotiated service levels with managers of Xerox departments who used the services of the center and then developed level-of-service targets. Finally, the center began marketing its services to outsiders. Within two years, this external business began generating a profit.

Many firms strive for a *zero-defects* standard as a performance goal. H. J. Heinz production facilities use an error-free standard of 99.9997 percent, which translates to 3.4 defects per million units. Xerox uses a standard of one mistake per 1,000 transactions

Efficiency Breakthroughs via Scanners

Before you read further, let's get something straight: scanners are *not* those bar-code-reading devices that automatically record the price of the frozen pizza and six-pack of Cokes at the local supermarket. The scanners being introduced here are special devices that read images and text from paper and then transfer it to digital format. Once stored in the computer, the document can be retrieved or manipulated.

The result is an efficiency breakthrough with immense promise for aiding firms in their quest for quality. Gone are the days of typing lengthy pages into the word processor. For a list price of just over $1,000, a scanner, such as Hewlett-Packard's ScanJet IIcx, can input a page-sized document in eight seconds. In addition to scanning text, today's scanners can aid creators of company newsletters, advertising pieces, annual reports, and visual-aid-filled speeches (to say nothing of artists) by capturing color images for such uses.

Not all scanners are as small, slow, or inexpensive as the HP system. Larger mainframe systems, capable of scanning and accessing tremendous amounts of documentation, also are growing in popularity. Delaware recently invested $2 million in a Wang imaging system to handle the multitude of documents associated with the 280 giant *Fortune* 500 companies headquartered in the state. The system, which currently stores over 3 million documents, has proven to be a money maker. Delaware collects $2 million annually in access fees from individuals and firms who request reprints of these documents.

The efforts by Food and Drug Administration officials to expedite the drug-approval process led them to install scanning technology to manage information. At the local level, Middlesex County, Massachusetts, officials digitized its 25,000 book Registry of Deeds, then began selling access to persons conducting property-title searches. At an annual fee of $100, the system already has generated over $1 million in revenues.

Over 4 million smaller "flat-bed" scanners and large mainframe scanners can be found in offices across the United States. Their proliferation is evidence of the benefits they provide in storing and accessing large amounts of information. Some observers equate their popularity to the abandonment of paper as the primary means of written communication. Whether quality-oriented companies will eventually convert to an all-digital "paperless" office remains to be seen. However, the cost and efficiency of such technologies as scanners offer a viable solution to mounting stacks of documents and the monotony of keyboarding long pages of text into the computer.

This compact, relatively inexpensive Hewlitt-Packard scanner can read into memory a 450-page book every hour.

SOURCE: Neil Weinberg, "Bypassing the Keyboard," *Forbes,* July 18, 1994, 300, 302; and Lori Grunin, "Speed Up, Price Down: Newest HP Scan Jet Is a Winner." *PC Magazine,* January 11, 1994, 48.

recorded by its accounting department, and it is working toward a goal of one mistake per 1 million.

Today, benchmarking is a major component of most firms' quality programs. AT&T, Metropolitan Life, IBM, Marriott, and thousands of other large and small firms use benchmarking as a standard tool for measuring quality. Increased interest in benchmarking has spawned a number of associations, councils, and specialized consulting firms. The American Productivity and Quality Center has organized an International Benchmarking Clearinghouse that offers benchmarking training, a data base of best practices, and conferences to help members share information.[33]

ENCOURAGING EMPLOYEE INVOLVEMENT

Boosting customer satisfaction and promoting companywide quality is usually dependent on **employee involvement,** *practices that motivate employees to perform their jobs better through empowerment, training, and teamwork.* The idea behind employee involvement is to unleash the energy, creativity, and talents of all employees. Bringing out workers' best qualities makes them feel better about themselves and their work. It also helps them to feel a sense of ownership and thus take greater pride in their work.

Empowerment

Empowerment is *the practice of giving employees the authority to make decisions about their work without supervisory approval.* Empowered employees have increased responsibility for implementing the organization's vision and strategy.

Empowerment, training, and teamwork all add to a firm's commitment to quality through employee involvement.

For example, in the production process, empowered assembly-line workers can stop the process when they detect a problem and then find a solution to fix it.

Empowerment taps the brainpower of all employees to find better ways of doing their jobs and executing their ideas. Some quality analysts believe that empowering employees may give U.S. firms an opportunity to pass the Japanese in quality by unharnessing American workers' potential to innovate. Organizations that empower employees nurture their capacity to improve and create. John Wilesmith of Rank Xerox summarizes the major benefit of empowerment as "getting more from your work force, tapping the wisdom and knowledge of every employee, believing that with every pair of hands you hire, you get a free brain."

Empowerment can be a highly effective marketing strategy. Customers appreciate it when an employee has the authority to handle a transaction or complaint efficiently, without having to check with a supervisor. Superior service leaves a lasting impression and personally ties the customer to the company. Hotel chain Ritz-Carlton empowers its front-desk personnel to waive charges from guests' bills if they perceive a problem; housekeepers have the authority to order a new washing machine if they feel the hotel needs one.

Empowerment also can be a powerful competitive weapon. By empowering employees, AT&T's Universal Card Service division gains a value-added competitive advantage in the marketplace. The company gives its telephone representatives, who handle up to 40,000 customer calls a day, the authority to raise customers' credit limits, investigate complaints, and issue new cards without having to contact their supervisors first. Representatives are able to resolve 95 percent of customer concerns in one phone call. Universal Card staffers also can meet on their own to devise solutions for persistent problems.

Empowerment keeps both external and internal customers happy. Universal Card Services garners more than 2,000 commendations a month—either letters or complimentary phone calls—from external customers. Meanwhile, telephone representatives feel their work is important. The company rewards quality work by tying quarterly bonuses and pay raises to how well employees reach their performance goals. The turnover for service reps is exceptionally low—8 percent a year, compared to up to 50 percent in other companies.[34]

Training

In order for an employee to become involved on even the most basic level, a thorough understanding of the job or process is required. Employee training provides workers with a wide range of learning experiences. It begins with management sharing knowledge about the organization's visions, values, and strategies. To help identify with the purpose of their work, employees should be able to answer these questions:

- Who are our major competitors?
- What are our company's strengths and weaknesses compared to competitors?
- How are we performing in measures such as sales, profits, and market share?
- Who are our target customers?
- What are our customers' needs and expectations?

- How satisfied are our customers with our goods and services?

Teaching employees the technical skills needed to measure and monitor the quality of their work is another aspect of training. Technical training, which varies depending on employees' jobs, can involve learning how to use quality tools, such as statistical quality control and problem-solving methods, as well as learning more about customers' needs.

"The training program is one of the reasons that I joined Eastman Chemical," comments market development representative Tom Weaver. All Eastman sales reps go through an extensive six- to nine-month training program, including experience in technical services labs, where they learn to operate the same equipment that their customers use to process Eastman products. "When they go to call on a company, they can talk to the technical person or a lab person and not just walk in and say 'This is what I've got, let's see if it fits,'" explains Ridley Ruth, Eastman's training supervisor.[35]

The importance of quality training is underscored by the huge investments organizations make in educating and developing employees. TQM training alone can cost anywhere from $300,000 for a company with fewer then 3,000 employees to $12 million at a corporation with 13,000 workers.[36]

Teamwork

The final component of employee involvement is teamwork. A *team* is a small number of people with complementary skills who are committed to a common purpose, approach, and set of performance goals. They all hold themselves mutually responsible and accountable for accomplishing their objectives. Quality organizations group employees into teams and teach them team-building skills. The value of these groups is that, by working collectively, employ-

---

DID YOU KNOW?

Avon, an American symbol of capitalism, is a big hit in China. Operating under the name *Ya Fran* (which means "Exquisite Fragrance"), the firm has its own sales force operating in the Peoples Republic. The top Chinese salesperson earned over 30,000 yuan (about $5,600) in a recent month, 200 times the average monthly income of a Chinese worker.

German factory employees work among the least hours a year, but receive the highest wages of any nation.

When Helene Curtis introduced its Every Night shampoo line in Sweden, it renamed the product Every Day since Swedes usually wash their hair in the morning.

A Flemish translation of the General Motors Corp. logo "Body by Fisher" came out "Corpse by Fisher." A literal translation of the Chinese characters used phonetically on the Coca-Cola bottle in China during the 1920s was a perplexing "bite the wax tadpole." Today, the new characters translate as "happiness in the mouth."

Almost half of all patents registered in the United States last year were filed by foreign individuals or organizations. Over 50 percent of U.S. doctoral degrees in engineering granted during the past decade went to non-U.S. citizens; 48 percent in mathematics; 32 percent in business; and 29 percent in the physical sciences.

---

ees produce higher performance levels, respond more quickly, and become more flexible in meeting customer needs.

Three types of employee involvement teams are quality circles, cross-functional teams, and self-managed teams. A **quality circle,** an idea that originated in Japan, is a *small group of employees from one work area or department who meet regularly to identify and solve problems.* A quality circle in one city's police department redesigned the headquarters' layout to provide a private area for detectives to use for conducting interviews. An employee group for camping equipment-maker Coleman Co. suggested design improvements to a propane lamp valve that now saves the company $50,000 a year.

The second type of employee involvement teams, the **cross-functional team,** *involves employees from different departments who work on specific projects, such as developing a new product or solving a complex problem.* When Colgate decided to develop a new automatic dishwashing detergent to be sold throughout the world, it assembled a team of representatives from research and development, manufacturing, product management, and Colgate's European Coordination Group. The result of the cross-functional team's efforts was the introduction of Galaxy Automatic detergent in the 12 countries that account for 95 percent of worldwide dishwasher detergent sales.

The **self-managed team,** the final type of employee involvement teams, is a *group of employees who work with little or no supervision.* Team members schedule their own work, are trained to do other employees' jobs, and are responsible for the quality of their work and are accountable for performance results.

Depending on the objective of the task, teams can range in size from several employees in one work area to hundreds of employees from different company locations around the world. Chapter 9 discusses teamwork in greater detail.

SUMMARY OF LEARNING GOALS

1. **Explain the importance of quality and customer satisfaction in achieving a competitive advantage.**

   Quality describes the degree of excellence or superiority of an organization's goods and services. Customer satisfaction is the concept of a good or service pleasing buyers because it has met their emotional needs and quality expectations. The true measure of quality is whether a business has satisfied its customers. Quality and customer satisfaction directly affect the bottom line and are crucial to an organization's continued existence, both domestically and internationally.

2. **Summarize the status of quality programs in the United States, Japan, and Europe.**

   In the United States, the Malcolm Baldrige National Quality Award recognizes excellence in quality management. The purposes of the award are to promote quality awareness, to recognize quality achievements of U.S. companies, and to publicize successful quality strategies. Only 19 companies have won the award since 1987, but its existence has led to steady improvements in the quality of American products.

   Japan has become a world leader in quality by studying the work of American quality consultants. The Japanese government awards the Deming Prize to companies and individuals who achieve the most significant gains in quality. The European Union has developed the ISO 9000 standards—international standards for quality management and quality assurance that form a widely recognized quality model. Like Japan and the United States, the EU has created its own quality prize, the European Quality Award.

3. **Discuss the role of top management in applying total quality management (TQM) to an organization.**

   Effective TQM programs begin with the involvement of top managers who believe in the importance of quality and customer satisfaction. Managers should view their organizations as systems that use the knowledge and skills of all employees to improve quality. Managers are responsible for communicating the goals of total quality management to all staff members, and for encouraging them to improve themselves and take pride in their work.

4. **Relate TQM to various functions within an organization, including production, human resource management, marketing, information processes, and financial management.**

   The quality movement started as an attempt to improve product quality by improving the production process through statistical quality control. Improving production often means demanding better quality from suppliers. Applying TQM to human resource management involves motivating workers and offering helpful services. An effective motivational technique centers on the concepts of internal and external customers. With TQM, customer satisfaction becomes the primary goal of marketing. TQM impacts the marketing function in several ways, including product design, distribution strategy, promotion, and price. Effective information processes can support TQM programs by improving customer services and boosting employees' productivity. Applying TQM to financial management means setting clear quality goals and linking them to financial returns and employee compensation.

5. **Identify the major methods of securing feedback from customers, employees, and suppliers.**

   As a first step in boosting customer satisfaction, a company must compile feedback and measure its present performance. When measuring customer satisfaction, there may be gaps between expected quality and perceived quality. Some companies measure customer satisfaction by monitoring customers over a period of time. Many use toll-free telephone lines to obtain feedback. Effective managers take time to solicit and respond to employee feedback, either informally or formally, and recognize skilled employees. Exchanging feedback with suppliers means thinking in terms of customer/supplier partnerships. Companies have started to demand higher levels of quality in their suppliers' products, and suppliers must comply if they want to maintain the business relationship.

6. **Describe how organizations can work toward continuous process improvement.**

   Continuous process improvement involves constant studying of work activities and, when necessary, making changes to improve their quality, timeliness, efficiency, and effectiveness. Continuous improvement efforts focus on improving quality by reducing cycle time, reducing variation, and eliminating waste. Reengineering and the PDCA cycle are tools for identifying ways to reduce cycle time and errors.

7. **Define benchmarking and explain its contributions to quality and customer satisfaction.**

   Benchmarking is a process in which an organization continuously compares and measures itself against business leaders anywhere in the world, to gain information that will help it improve its performance. It can be applied to all business procedures and practices. The process of benchmarking includes five key steps: planning, analysis, integration, action, and maturity. Today, benchmarking is a major component of many firms' quality programs.

8. **Identify the components of employee involvement and their impact on quality and customer satisfaction.**

   Employee involvement refers to practices that motivate employees to perform their jobs better through empowerment, training, and teamwork. The idea behind employee involvement is to unleash the energy, creativity, and talents of all employees. Empowerment is the practice of giving employees the authority to make decisions about their work without supervisory approval. Employee training consists of a wide range of learning experiences. The value of teamwork is that, by working collectively, employees produce higher performance levels, respond more quickly, and become more flexible to customer needs.

KEY TERMS QUIZ

feedback
customer satisfaction
total quality management (TQM)
PDCA cycle time
reengineering
cycle time
benchmarking

critical success factors
internal customers
quality circle
statistical quality control
cross-functional team
quality
continuous process improvement

self-managed team
costs of quality
external customers
ISO 9000
empowerment
employee involvement

_____ 1. The degree of excellence or superiority of an organization's goods and services.

_____ 2. The concept of a good or service pleasing buyers because it has met their emotional needs and quality expectations.

_____ 3. An approach that involves a commitment to quality in achieving world-class performance and customer satisfaction as a crucial strategic objective.

_____ 4. International standards for quality management and quality assurance.

_____ 5. A system of locating and measuring quality problems on production lines.

_____ 6. People or organizations that buy or use another firm's good or service.

_____ 7. Employees or departments within an organization that depend on the work of other people or departments to perform their jobs.

_____ 8. Messages returned by the audience to the sender that may cause the sender to alter or cancel an original message.

_____ 9. The process of constantly studying and making changes in work activities to improve their quality, timeliness, efficiency, and effectiveness.

_____ 10. The time it takes to complete a work process or activity.

_____ 11. A process in which existing processes in the delivery chain are mapped out with detail, and technology is applied to key steps to reduce cycle time or errors.

_____ 12. A step-by-step process of **p**lanning, **d**oing, **c**hecking, and **a**cting.

_____ 13. The costs associated with poor quality, such as scrap, rework, and loss of customers.

_____ 14. The process in which an organization continuously compares and measures itself against business leaders.

_____ 15. Those factors most important in gaining a competitive advantage and achieving long-term success.

_____ 16. Practices that motivate employees to perform their jobs better through empowerment, training, and teamwork.

_____ 17. The practice of giving employees the authority to make decisions about their work without supervisory approval.

_____ 18. A small group of employees from one work area or department who meet regularly to identify and solve problems.

_____ 19. Involves employees from different departments who work on specific projects, such as developing a new product or solving a particular problem.

_____ 20. A group of employees who work together on projects with little or no supervision.

OTHER IMPORTANT TERMS

competitive benchmarking
functional benchmarking
gaps

internal benchmarking
return on quality
team

zero defects

REVIEW QUESTIONS

1. Define the concepts of quality and customer satisfaction.
2. How does total quality management help an organization compete more effectively?
3. Compare the Baldrige Award, the Deming Prize, and the European Quality Award. How are they alike? How do they differ?
4. Why is it important for senior management to support quality programs?
5. Distinguish between external customers and internal customers.
6. How can a firm determine whether it is satisfying its customers?
7. What is meant by customer/supplier partnerships?
8. What are the goals of continuous process improvement?
9. What criteria might a firm use to choose a suitable benchmark partner?
10. How can managers encourage employee involvement?

DISCUSSION QUESTIONS

1. Apply continuous process improvement to a service or procedure at your college or university. At the present time, does this service satisfy customers as much as it could? If not, why not? How might you analyze and resolve any problems?
2. During the 1980s, sales of catalog retailer L. L. Bean grew 20 percent a year. More recently, sales growth has slowed to 3 percent a year or less. Meanwhile, returns that once averaged 5 percent of sales have risen to 14 percent. To cut costs, CEO Leon Gorman has cut inventory levels and slowed spending on automation, preferring instead to hire seasonal workers, who now comprise 40 percent of the company's total work force. However, competitors, such as Land's End, are gaining market share. Unlike L. L. Bean, Land's End is investing $5 million in new computer systems and warehouse equipment.

   Develop a quality program that might help L. L. Bean.
3. Identify an organization in your city or state that you consider to be a world-class competitor in terms of quality and customer satisfaction. Defend your choice.
4. In designing its Aurora car, Oldsmobile attempted a new approach to product development. It created assembly-line "stop stations" where groups of five employees work at their own pace to bolt the Aurora body together. Helping the three-year development process was a rotating group of 50 hourly workers and engineers. In the final stages, Oldsmobile formed another group comprised of employees from marketing, public relations, engineering, and manufacturing, as well as several Oldsmobile dealers. This group developed a dealer-training program and an advertising campaign for the Aurora.

   Relate the Aurora product-development process to the chapter's discussion of benchmarking, empowerment, training, and teamwork.
5. Choose two companies that have active total quality management programs. (Possibilities include such firms as Motorola, Xerox, AT&T, and DuPont.) Compare the various initiatives involved in each company's programs. How are they alike? How do they differ?

VIDEO CASE: Ampex

The video case for this chapter emphasizes the importance of corporate mission objectives and strategies. It also illustrates how poorly devised short-term plans can result in long-term problems. It appears on page 414 of Appendix D.

Solution to Key Terms Quiz

1. quality 2. customer satisfaction 3. total quality management (TQM) 4. ISO 9000 5. statistical quality control 6. external customers 7. internal customers 8. continuous process improvement 9. cycle time 10. reengineering 11. PDCA cycle time 12. costs of quality 13. benchmarking 14. critical success factors 15. employee involvement 16. empowerment 17. quality circle 18. cross-functional team 19. self-managed team 20. feedback

PART THREE

Management: Empowering People to Achieve Business Objectives

CHAPTER 7

The Organization and Its Management

Learning Goals

1. Discuss the need for organizational structure, and list the steps involved in the organizing process.
2. Evaluate each of the four basic forms of organization.
3. Identify the skills required for managerial success.
4. Explain the concept of leadership, and identify the three basic leadership styles.
5. Describe the role of intrapreneurship in modern organizations.
6. Explain the impact of downsizing and outsourcing on today's organizations.
7. List the steps in the decision-making process, and contrast programmed and nonprogrammed decisions.
8. Discuss the importance of time management.

The Newes

C hrysler's Neon project was ambitious by any standards. The goal was far-reaching: to design and build an entirely new small car that would replace the Dodge Shadow and Plymouth Sundance models. The target market would be the members of Generation X, the post baby-boomers, both in the United States and abroad.

The $1.3 billion budget sounded impressive, but not when the project leaders began designing entirely new factories and renovating assembly facilities. In addition, some Neon customers would want a two-door version; others would require an automatic transmission. Production facilities and component parts would have to accommodate these different versions of the basic model.

The results surprised everyone. Every Neon that rolled off the assembly line cost Chrysler $500 less than its planners had expected. The final design resulted in a vehicle weighing less than anticipated, which allowed it to surpass its fuel economy targets. Best of all, initial sales in both the United States and Japan were healthy, and the Neon joined a relatively rare category of cars that earn a profit in the first year of production. In Japan, the media even dubbed the car "the Japan killer."

Innovative management played a major role in the project's success. The new Neon was the first vehicle completely designed, processed, and built according to Chrysler's "platform team" concept. This called for extensive employee involvement throughout the project and depended on an unprecedented level of teamwork among Chrysler managers, workers, suppliers, and customers.

The new car project instigated a dramatic change in Chrysler's way of doing business. Managers now are encouraged to give more responsibility to employees. They also are urged to get more involved in design, marketing, and manufacturing issues. Dennis Pawley, Chrysler's executive vice president of manufacturing, notes that he spends only about five hours a week at the office. Most of his time is devoted to visiting plants and monitoring the company's quality programs. "You can't have this kind of culture without having the top guy out there," he says. Downsizing has eliminated two levels of management beneath Pawley, who now delegates more decision making to general managers. As he points out, "If I tried to do everything, I couldn't survive."

The Neon team managers instituted market research at an unusually early point in the development process. Team members took prototypes to malls around the United States and bought hot dogs for shoppers who agreed to critique them. Focus groups offered free pizza to potential customers, who discussed their small-car likes and dislikes. Says Chrysler executive Bob Marcell, "Our goal was to spend an inordinate amount of time on what turns buyers on and what turns them off."

Suppliers also got involved with the project earlier than ever before. All of Neon's major suppliers joined the team three years before the car went into production. They worked with other team members to develop appropriate cost and weight targets. The result was that Neon uses only half as many suppliers and incorporates only one-third the parts of other Chrysler models. While the Shadow and Sundance require 382 different types of fasteners, Neon uses only 190, meaning fewer tools and operations are needed during production, thereby reducing errors. "It's a major improvement over the way things were done in the industry as recently as four years ago," comments Rudy Paluch of Johnson Control Inc., which supplied Neon's seats. "The biggest advantage was that there were no surprises that would increase costs."

Decision-making on the Neon teams was pushed farther down the chain of command than on any previous Chrysler project. Specific components and work processes were developed by small teams headed by first-level managers and product-design engineers. Another innovation was the inclusion of assembly-line workers, who joined the teams three years before the car was scheduled for production. In the past, tooling would be developed by the engineering group, and the first time an operator would see it would be the day he or she showed up on the job.

Managers and workers alike are pleased with the Neon management strategy. Marcell feels that the platform team concept will have a profound effect on Chrysler's organizational structure and the role of its managers. "We're not talking about abdicating leadership," he says. "We're talking about changing the way they lead."[1]

CHAPTER OVERVIEW

Christine Todd Whitman, Barry Switzer, and Leslie Wexner are all managers. Whitman is governor of New Jersey, Switzer is head coach of the Dallas Cowboys, and Wexner is chairman of The Limited chain of retail stores. Managers preside over organizations as diverse as San Diego State University, Mayo Clinic, and a local Taco Bell.

The importance of effective management to organizational success cannot be overestimated. Analyses of small-business failures usually list "poor management" as one of the leading causes. When asked about their career objectives, many students in an introductory business course will reply, "I want to be a manager."

In this chapter we will examine the meaning of management and its universal applications. First, we will identify the three levels of management in a typical organization and will discuss international management issues. We will look at the different types of organizational structures, the skills required for managerial success, the current trends toward downsizing and outsourcing, and the process of managerial decision making. Finally, we will examine the importance of effective time management, and will discuss new career opportunities for displaced managers.

MANAGEMENT PRINCIPLES ARE UNIVERSAL

Management is *the achievement of organizational objectives through people and other resources.* The manager's job is to combine human and technical resources in the best way possible to achieve these objectives. Managers are not involved directly in production; that is, they do not produce a finished product. Instead, they direct the efforts of others toward the company's goals.

The management principles and concepts presented in this chapter apply to not-for-profit organi-

> **THEY SAID IT**
>
> "All humankind is divided into three classes: those who are immovable, those who are movable, and those who move."
>
> *Benjamin Franklin (1706–1790) American statesman and philosopher*

Maybe the best way for a kid to find himself is with a compass.

Life's biggest questions often have the simplest answers. Go figure. Call us at (214) 637-1480.

The troop leader is the first-line manager in the Boy Scouts of America organization.

zations as well as profit-seeking firms. The local library administrator, the head of the Salvation Army, and a Boy Scout troop leader all perform managerial functions similar to those performed by their counterparts in industry. Service-oriented agencies benefit from effective management as much as profit-oriented ones do.

The Management Pyramid

The local Discovery Zone franchise has a very simple organization—an owner/manager, an assistant manager, and a few part-time employees. By contrast, large organizations have a complex managerial structure. Toyota, for example, has a chairman of the board, a president, four executive vice presidents, six senior managing directors, 12 managing directors, as well as a board of auditors. Are all of these people managers? The answer is yes, since they all are engaged in combining human and other resources to achieve company objectives.

Chapter 5 pointed out that a firm's management can be divided into three categories: top management, middle management, and supervisory management.

Although all three categories contain managers, each level stresses different activities. **Top management** is *the highest level of the management hierarchy and is staffed by executives who develop long-range plans and interact with the public and outside entities, like the government.* **Middle management** is more involved than top management in specific operations within the organization. Middle managers are *responsible for developing detailed plans and procedures to implement the general plans of top management.*

Supervisory management, or *first-line management,* includes people who are directly *responsible for the details of assigning workers to specific jobs and evaluating performance* daily or even hourly. Supervisory management is the level at which most people obtain their first managerial experience. They may have such job titles as supervisor, chairperson, department head, group leader, or section chief. In each case, the position involves coordinating the work of operative employees in accomplishing tasks assigned by middle management. The first-line manager is often as much a teacher, expediter, and assistant as a supervisor. Because they interact continuously with members of the work team, effective human relations skills are extremely important.

Effective communication links must exist between all levels of management. It is also important that each level be responsible for the decisions that legitimately should be made at that point in the organization.

At any level, managers need the ability to lead and motivate other people, the ability to work in a team, the skill to formulate and carry out long-range plans, the courage to take risks, and the ability to relate to others. The lack of some of these abilities often prevents people from moving up the managerial ladder.

Managing across Borders

Many firms face an important decision: choosing and training managers to oversee international operations and foreign-based offices. Placing a manager overseas

> **THEY SAID IT**
>
> "Some players you pat their butts, some players you kick their butts, some players you leave alone."
>
> *Pete Rose*
> *(1941–)*
> *American baseball*
> *player and manager*

can be expensive and difficult, both for the company and the manager. Culture shock and the stress of an unfamiliar environment can make it harder for the manager to perform. The prevalence of two-income families complicates matters, since the manager's spouse may not be able to find comparable work in the new country. Says Catharine Tiemann, president of consulting firm Global Human Resource Services, "Companies recognize they have to do more than they've done in the past. They can't just send people over there and forget about them."[2]

Some firms are responding by choosing foreign managers more carefully. AT&T hires psychologists to help pick managers most suited to the challenges of working in a different country. Employees who are being considered for such transfers must take a written test and go through management interviews. In addition, they must complete a self-assessment checklist to judge their own "cultural adaptability." Other companies assist overseas managers and families by boosting the language and cultural training available, finding new jobs for spouses, and paying tuition costs for family members who want to study abroad.

ORGANIZATIONAL STRUCTURE

The functions performed by managers in accomplishing the goals of the organization—planning, organizing, leading, and controlling—were discussed in Chapter 4. *Organizing* was defined as the means by which management blends human and material resources by designing a formal structure of tasks and authority. It is the process of arranging work, dividing it among employees, and coordinating it so plans can be carried out and objectives can be accomplished. It can be seen in sports teams, social clubs, religious groups, and work activities. Even groups of animals—bees, ants, baboons, and beavers—have organization. **Organization** can be defined as *a structured grouping of people working together to achieve organizational objectives*. Three key elements are present in an organization: human interaction, goal-directed activities, and structure.

AT&T SELF-ASSESSMENT TEST OF CULTURAL ADAPTABILITY

	Yes	No
1. Would your spouse be interrupting a career to accompany you on an international assignment? If so, how do you think this will affect your spouse and your relationship with each other?	☐	☐
2. Do you enjoy the challenge of making your own way in new situations?	☐	☐
3. Is securing a job primarily your responsibility? Are you comfortable networking and being your own advocate?	☐	☐
4. Can you imagine living without television?	☐	☐
5. Is it important for you to spend significant amounts of time with people of your own ethnic, racial, religious, and national background?	☐	☐
6. As you look at your personal history, can you isolate any episodes that indicate a real interest in learning about other peoples and cultures? If so, briefly describe them.	☐	☐
7. Do you enjoy sampling foreign cuisines?	☐	☐

	Often	Sometimes	Rarely
8. Has it been your habit to vacation in foreign countries?	☐	☐	☐

	High	Average	Low
9. What is your tolerance for waiting for repairs?	☐	☐	☐

NOTE: Use back of form for detailed responses.

Steps in the Organizing Process

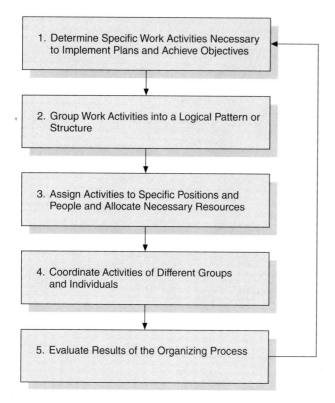

1. Determine Specific Work Activities Necessary to Implement Plans and Achieve Objectives

2. Group Work Activities into a Logical Pattern or Structure

3. Assign Activities to Specific Positions and People and Allocate Necessary Resources

4. Coordinate Activities of Different Groups and Individuals

5. Evaluate Results of the Organizing Process

In the organizing process, managers first determine the specific activities that are necessary to meet the organization's plans and objectives (see chart above). Next, they group these activities into a logical structure, assign them to specific employees, allocate resources for their completion, and coordinate the activities of the assigned personnel. Finally, they evaluate the results and make changes as needed.

For a small business, these steps are relatively simple. The owner-manager of the local dry-cleaning firm employs a few people to sell, to launder and dry-clean clothing, and to make deliveries. The owner usually handles purchasing tasks (detergents, plastic wrappers, etc.). The owner also assigns jobs to employees and personally directs business operations in pursuit of profits and growth. The tasks of coordinating work schedules and training new employees are relatively uncomplicated. Should one employee prove less effective in operating the check-out terminal, he or she can be reassigned to one of the cleaning tasks.

But as a company grows, the need for organization increases. With increased size comes specialization and more employees. Rather than a simple salesperson, the manager employs a sales force; rather than one bookkeeper, an entire accounting depart-

ment is utilized. The large number of personnel and the accompanying specialization make it impossible for one person to supervise all operations. Some formal organization is therefore necessary.

Although a small firm experiences fewer organizational problems than a large one, both must have a formal structure to ensure that people perform tasks designed to accomplish company objectives. In a dry-cleaning company, for example, specific duties are assigned to wrappers, pressers, and other personnel.

As we have seen, the starting point in designing the appropriate organizational structure is to focus on the activities necessary to reach goals. Management analyzes the jobs to be performed and employs people who are both willing and qualified to perform the jobs. Coordinating workers' activities is another important responsibility, because employees must "pull together" if the firm is to operate smoothly.

A well-defined organizational structure also should contribute to employee morale. Employees who know what is expected on the job, who the supervisor is, and how their work contributes to organizational objectives are more likely to form a harmonious, loyal work force.

A company objective of "providing customers with quality products at competitive prices" does not tell a mechanic that production machinery should be inspected regularly and defects repaired. Company objectives are often broad and do not specify individual work activities. Consequently, they must be divided into specific goals for each employee in the organization.

Hierarchy of Objectives

A *hierarchy of organizational objectives* extends from the overall objectives of the entire firm to specific objectives of the firm to specific objectives established for each employee. The broader goals of increasing profitability, sales, market share, and service are broken into objectives for each division, factory, department, work group, and employee. Once this has been accomplished, each person can see his or her contribution to the overall organizational goals. The number of levels in the hierarchy depends on the size and complexity of the firm. Smaller firms usually have fewer levels than larger ones.

Departmentalization

Departmentalization is the subdivision of work activities into units within the organization. This lets individuals specialize in certain jobs and thus become

Various Forms of Departmentalization Used in One Company

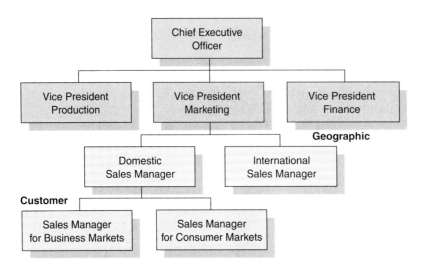

efficient in them. A marketing department may be headed by a marketing vice president and may include sales, advertising, and marketing research. A human resource department may include recruitment, training, employee benefits, and industrial relations.

Five major forms of departmentalization exist: product, geographic, customer, functional, and process. Deciding what bases to use involves balancing the advantages and disadvantages of each. The experience and judgment of top management come into play in such decisions.

Procter & Gamble, the Cincinnati-based manufacturer of household goods ranging from Pringle's potato chips to Crest toothpaste and Tide detergent, divides its organizational structure on the basis of *product departmentalization.* Each division—food products, toiletries, paper products, packaged soaps and detergents, coffee, and industrial foods—is headed by a vice president.

Dillard's uses *geographic departmentalization* for organizing its department stores, as do railroads, gas and oil distributors, and other retailers. Many sporting-goods stores subdivide using *customer departmentalization,* with a wholesale operation serving school systems and retail divisions serving other customers.

Petroleum firms, like Mobil and Texaco, sometimes are divided on the basis of *functional departmentalization,* with exploration, production, refining, marketing, and finance departments. Finally, many manufacturers utilize *process departmentalization,* with separate departments for cutting material, heat-treating it, forming it into its final shape, and painting it.

Delegation

As the organization grows, the manager must assign part of his or her activities to subordinates in order to have time to devote to managerial functions. *The act of assigning activities to subordinates* is called **delegation.** Subordinates to whom the tasks are assigned thus receive *responsibility,* or an obligation to perform those tasks. Along with responsibility goes *authority,* the power to make decisions and to act on them in carrying out responsibilities. Problems can arise if managers delegate responsibility without giving the necessary authority, too. Delegation of authority and responsibility make the subordinate accountable to the supervisor. *Accountability* means employees are responsible for the results of how they perform their assignments and that they must accept the consequences of their actions.

Authority and responsibility tend to move downward in organizations, as supervisors delegate them to subordinates. However, accountability moves up the ranks. The final accountability for employees' performance rests with their managers, who in turn are accountable to their bosses. Therefore, it is crucial for managers to select the best-qualified employees when delegating.

Organization Charts

The authority and responsibility relationships of most organizations are shown in the *organization chart.* In organizations as diverse as major league baseball's

Organization Chart for the Texas Rangers Baseball Club

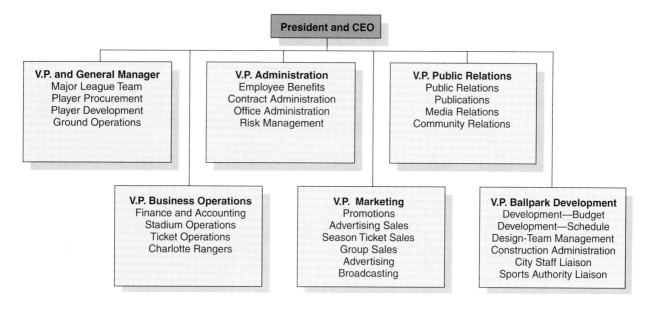

President and CEO

V.P. and General Manager
Major League Team
Player Procurement
Player Development
Ground Operations

V.P. Administration
Employee Benefits
Contract Administration
Office Administration
Risk Management

V.P. Public Relations
Public Relations
Publications
Media Relations
Community Relations

V.P. Business Operations
Finance and Accounting
Stadium Operations
Ticket Operations
Charlotte Rangers

V.P. Marketing
Promotions
Advertising Sales
Season Ticket Sales
Group Sales
Advertising
Broadcasting

V.P. Ballpark Development
Development—Budget
Development—Schedule
Design-Team Management
Construction Administration
City Staff Liaison
Sports Authority Liaison

Texas Rangers and the law-enforcement agency with the same name, this diagram represents a blueprint showing the division of work, chain of command, and departmentalization of activities. It provides all employees with a visual statement of these relationships, enabling them to see how their work relates to the overall operation of the company and to whom they report.

Because the organization chart specifies each area of responsibility and authority, it also can help managers coordinate activities. However, since the chart reflects the organization at only one point in time, it should be updated periodically to reflect changes.

THE DOWNSIZING REVOLUTION

Traditionally, as companies have grown larger, they have become *tall organizations*, with many levels in the management hierarchy. During the 1970s, many organizations grew taller as the number of middle-management positions increased dramatically. The progression from supervisory to middle to top management was a recognized career path for many managers.

More recently, however, organizations have begun **downsizing,** in which *management decides to eliminate layers from the management hierarchy in an effort to reduce costs and make the firm more efficient.* This creates a *flat organization*, with many positions at the same level in the hierarchy.

After World War II, *big* made sense as companies grew rapidly. Technology, for the most part, was limited to typewriters and slide rules. Markets were regulated and largely domestic, and the work force consisted mostly of low- or semi-skilled employees. However, these cumbersome organizational structures are no longer sustainable in today's globalized, high-tech environment.

In recent years, the United States and every other industrialized country began to see the effects of a management revolution. Reports of layoffs and plant closings filled the headlines. IBM and General Motors cut tens of thousands of jobs, Sears closed its non-retail subsidiaries, and American Express lost almost 1 million card customers and its chairman stepped down. America's largest corporations are reshaping the traditionally vertical management hierarchy into a leaner, faster, and more efficient structure. By the early 1990s, a new horizontal management style clearly had emerged in corporate America.

Xerox Corp. illustrates the new leaner management structure. In 1991, the photocopying pioneer dismantled its corporate hierarchy of huge divisions grouped around tasks and replaced it with nine lean divisions organized along product lines. Factory workers were required to assist in designing assembly lines and engineers were given training in finance and marketing. By implementing these bold new management principles, Xerox laid a strong foundation for creating cross-functional teams.[3]

The Cost of Downsizing

Reducing managerial layers requires two components in order to succeed: training and empowerment. By the start of the 1990s, many businesses had begun to downsize and, while easily convinced of the benefits of employee empowerment, did not realize the broad changes that would result and the enormous cost to the firm. IBM alone spent $11 billion to streamline the giant international firm. General Electric downsized, invested heavily in training, and already has begun to reap benefits—revenues have increased from $27 billion to $60 billion and profits have tripled to $4.4 billion.[4]

In a recent survey, 68 percent of executives whose firms have downsized experienced problems they had not counted on. The primary reasons given by respondents for downsizing their firms included reducing overhead (79 percent), increasing customer satisfaction (78 percent), decreasing purchasing and logistics costs (61 percent), and improving employee satisfaction (60 percent). A small percentage stated that increasing market share (13 percent) and profitability (12 percent) were reasons for downsizing.

Job Deaths: 12 Large Downsizings

In their quest for efficiency and survival, many of America's corporate giants have been shedding employees at unprecedented rates. Here are 12 of the largest announced staff reductions since 1991:

IBM	85,000	Nynex	22,000
AT&T	83,000	Hughes Aircraft	21,000
General Motors	74,000	GTE	17,000
U.S. Postal Service	55,000	Martin Marietta	15,000
Sears	50,000	DuPont	14,800
Boeing	30,000	Eastman Kodak	14,000

Any time employees are let go, no matter the number, significant emotional and financial factors enter the picture. Management must overcome the typical barriers that accompany change. Employee unwillingness to believe that change is necessary was listed as the greatest barrier to change (64 percent) in a recent study.[5]

Downsizing remains a controversial issue. Some managers contend that it is a fad, a relatively quick way to cut costs without having to correct inefficient ways of doing business. Others insist that it is a painful but necessary step to remain competitive in a global economy. Between 1983 and 1993, *Fortune* 500 companies eliminated 4.7 million jobs—a quarter of their work force. But some economic experts question whether job cuts and improved productivity go together. A financial analysis of 140,000 factories revealed that while 55 percent of productivity gains came from downsized companies, 45 percent came from companies that were hiring more workers. In addition, management must consider how downsizing affects the workload of remaining employees.[6]

In spite of these criticisms, downsizing in corporate America appears to be paying off. Many companies that suffered in the early stages of restructuring would have been even worse off if they hadn't reduced costs through cutbacks. Most found that downsizing led to improved productivity, enhanced quality and customer service, and a greater willingness to take risks. By selling off its defense operations and computer business and cutting its work force by 30 percent in 1986, Honeywell began restructuring its operations. It recently reported steady earnings and plans to increase annual sales from $6 billion to $10 billion by the end of the decade.[7]

Downsizing doesn't always mean layoffs. Many companies have been able to cut their work force by offering early retirement plans, voluntary severance programs, and reassignment. What is important to re-

Communication technology used to link geographically separated work teams is an important component of Ford's auto design programs.

member is that the decision to downsize must be accompanied by a commitment to quality and growth, not just a reduction in costs. Two important components of successful downsizing are employee empowerment and outsourcing. Empowerment ensures that the employees are able to carry on the operations of the firm; outsourcing allows outside experts to perform functions previously done in-house.

Empowering Employees

As organizations downsize, remaining workers must take on new tasks and responsibilities. As whole management levels vanish, the remaining managers must assume control of more employees than ever before.

Empowering employees—*giving them additional decision-making authority and responsibility*—helps organizations deal with these changes. It frees managers from hands-on control of subordinates and motivates workers by making their jobs more interesting. All too often, traditionally tall organizations have discouraged employees by eliminating much of their power in making decisions affecting their jobs. The challenge of management today is to find ways to encourage creativity and innovation—once a hallmark of the American worker.

As detailed earlier in the chapter, Chrysler Corp. has become a model of restructuring in American business. Where senior management traditionally had been responsible for all decision making, today, six platform teams run the business. Each team includes all individuals involved in production of a specific car, jeep, minivan, or truck. The team makes all decisions associated with its vehicle. Senior management's role consists of ensuring that the team's decisions are in line with company goals. Employee empowerment has enabled Chrysler to cut its product development from four and one-half years to an average of three years.[8]

In addition to providing its design teams with the authority and responsibility for creating auto designs

WE WON'T ASK WHY, JUST WHERE AND WHEN.

If we can ship entire zoos, priceless works of art, and *the* Batmobile, we can ship your cargo. Truth is, we have a fleet of 747s dedicated solely to your needs, twice as much international capacity as any other U.S. combination carrier, and more than a thousand daily departures to cities all over the world. Ship with us. No matter what. No matter where. Call 1-800-NW-CARGO.

NORTHWEST CARGO

Some People Just Know How To Fly.™

Transportation services rank high among candidates for outsourcing.

for the twenty-first century, Ford Motor Co. supplies them with the technology required to convert ideas into actual prototypes. Although Ford's design studios are located in cities as distant as Turin, Italy, and Melbourne, Australia, all are linked electronically to facilitate immediate exchange of ideas and to address problems as they arise.

Outsourcing

Another important development accompanying the corporate downsizing trend is **outsourcing,** *relying on outside specialists to perform functions previously performed by company employees.* Outsourcing began on a small scale, typically with contracting services such as maintenance, cleaning, and delivery. Today, outsourcing has expanded to outside contracting of such fundamental tasks as production of one or more items in the product line, accounting and legal services, and warehousing and transporting finished goods. It has become a major part of competitive strategies used by such U.S. corporate giants as General Motors and

IBM, as well as international firms like Tokyo-based Fujitsu Ltd.

Half of Fujitsu's business comes from the United States, the other half from Europe. So when the firm's import and distribution operation in Western Europe had serious problems with deliveries, management decided to outsource. Fujitsu deliveries to Italy were earning a reputation for taking from two weeks to never arriving at all, so the international computer maker turned deliveries over to United Parcel Service, the world's largest delivery-service company. Italian orders now arrive within four days of the order being placed.[9]

Outsourcing typically is used in service industries ranging from housekeeping (81 percent) to office movers (29 percent). But as the downsizing revolution has grown, so has outsourcing's importance as a quality component in every major industry. The key to success in outsourcing is a 100 percent commitment by both parties. Outsourcing is a partnership in the purest sense of the word.[10]

Outsourcing complements downsizing in a variety of ways. It reduces the need for employees to perform certain tasks. It allows a firm to continue performing the functions it does best, while hiring firms to do other tasks that they are more qualified to handle.

Another benefit of outsourcing is the firm's ability to negotiate the best price from among competing bidders and to avoid the long-term human resource costs associated with in-house operations. Firms that outsource also have the flexibility of changing suppliers at the end of the contract. A firm that decides to contract its transportation needs to a firm, such as Northwest Cargo, can later decide to perform this function with company personnel should the service provided by the outside supplier prove unsatisfactory.

TYPES OF ORGANIZATIONAL STRUCTURE

Organizations can be classified into four main types according to the nature of their internal authority relationships: line, line-and-staff, committee, and matrix. These categories are not mutually exclusive. In fact, most of today's business organizations combine elements of one or more types of organizational structure.

Line Organization

Line organization, the oldest and simplest organizational structure, is *based on a direct flow of authority from the chief executive to subordinates.* The line orga-

Information Technologies: Keys to Twenty-first Century Management

Information technologies have paved the way for the most revolutionary changes in business today. For decades, conventional wisdom held that workers were only necessary to carry out the tasks given to them by managers—those individuals in the organization who were "in the know." Today, however, the roles of workers and managers have been redefined. Top management is becoming increasingly involved in daily operations of the firm and more and more employees are given information beyond the narrow scope necessary to perform their particular tasks.

Information technologies have had the greatest impact on first-level employees who are being empowered to make a greater number of decisions than ever before. This wealth of shared information has removed many of the traditional lines drawn between the levels of organizational management.

The keys to the success of information technologies in improving organizational performance and product quality are training and control.

All members of the organization must be given the information they need, the ability to analyze the data, and the power to act on the information.

Several guidelines for both managers and employees have been suggested for improving the effective use of information technologies. While managers must instill commitment in employees, the worker must be able to act without management direction. Management also must provide training and tools to employees so they can understand how their jobs affect the entire organization. Employees need freedom to organize and schedule work and, since interaction with other employees and groups inevitably will increase, they will need strong interpersonal skills, including the ability to handle conflict. Finally, employees must be compensated according to their performance, which can be based on customer satisfaction or on the accomplishment of specific goals.

Computers and related technologies make it easier for employees to perform tasks once reserved for managers. Charles Chaser, for example, is a line worker at Chesebrough-Pond's factory in Jefferson City, Missouri. In a traditionally tall organization,

Chaser probably would not have had the authority to manage inventory. On a recent day, however, he scanned an inventory report and noted that supplies of a particular nail polish were below the standard 24-day stock level. Deciding that the polish must be selling well, Chaser immediately turned to his computer and typed in instructions for the factory line to produce 400 more units the next morning. He is one of several hundred line workers at the plant who have the authority to schedule their own work loads, track shipments, and perform other functions that used to be done only by factory managers.

As information technologies continue to erase the lines between white- and blue-collar workers, managers' objectives will be to support workers who manage themselves. As Hewlett-Packard manager James M. Barbour puts it, "I see myself more not as a manager, but as a facilitator."

SOURCE: Barbour quotation from James B. Treece, "Breaking the Chains of Command," *Business Week/The Information Revolution 1994,* 112–114.

---

nization is simple. The *chain of command*—the set of relationships that indicates who gives direction to whom and who reports to whom—is clear, so "buck-passing" is extremely difficult. Decisions can be made quickly because the manager can act without consulting anyone other than an immediate supervisor. But an obvious defect exists within line organizations. Each manager has complete responsibility for a number of activities and cannot possibly be an expert in all of them.

This defect is very apparent in medium- and large-sized firms, where the pure line form fails to provide specialized skills so vital to modern industry. Executives in this type of organization become overburdened with administrative details and paperwork and have little time for planning.

> **THEY SAID IT**
>
> "Good management consists in showing average people how to do the work of superior people."
>
> *John D. Rockefeller, Jr. (1874–1960)*

The obvious conclusion is that this structure is ineffective in all but the smallest organizations. Hair salons, "mom-and-pop" grocery stores, and small law firms can operate effectively with a simple line structure. Ford, General Electric, and Boeing cannot.

Line-and-Staff Organization

The **line-and-staff organization** *combines the direct flow of authority present in the line organization with staff departments that serve, advise, and support the line departments.* Line departments are involved directly in decisions affecting the operation of the organization. Staff departments lend specialized technical support.

Line - directly
staff - Indirect

For all practical purposes, the line-and-staff and the newer matrix structures are the only forms of organization capable of meeting the requirements of modern businesses. They combine the line organization's rapid decision-making capability and effective, direct communication with the staff specialists' expert knowledge needed to direct diverse and widespread activities. The line-and-staff form is commonly used in medium- and large-sized firms.

The major difference between a line manager and a staff manager is in authority relationships. A *line manager* forms a part of the main line of authority that flows throughout the organization. Often line managers are involved directly with the critical functions of production, financing, or marketing. A *staff manager* provides information, advice, or technical assistance to aid line managers. They do not possess the authority to give orders or to compel line managers to take action, although they do have the necessary line authority to supervise their own departments. Examples of staff managers in medium- and large-sized organizations include the director of research, the advertising manager, the legal counsel, and the director of engineering.

Committee Organization

Committee organization is the organization structure in which authority and responsibility are held jointly by a group of individuals rather than by a single manager. It typically is used as part of the regular line-and-staff structure.

Examples of the committee structure exist throughout the organization. For example, various firms have used the Office of the CEO concept, in which the duties of the chief executive officer are shared among two or more executives. Typically, the responsibilities are split along functional lines, with one person handling manufacturing, another marketing, and so on. Committees also are used in other areas, such as new-product development. The new-product committee may include managers from such areas as accounting, engineering, finance, manufacturing, marketing, and research. Including representatives from all areas involved in developing new products generally improves planning and company morale because diverse perspectives—production, marketing, and finance—are considered.

But committees tend to be slow and conservative, and decisions often are made through compromise based on conflicting interests rather than by choosing the best alternative. The definition of a camel as "a horse designed by a committee" provides an apt description of some committee decisions.

The Matrix Organization

A growing number of organizations are using the **matrix,** or **project management organization**—a *structure in which specialists from different parts of the organization are brought together to work on specific projects.* Like the committee form, the matrix organization typically is used as a subform within the line-and-staff structure.

The matrix organization is built around specific projects or problems. Employees with different areas of expertise gather to focus on these specific problems or unique technical issues. An identifying feature of such organizations is that some members of the organization report to two superiors instead of one. Project members receive instructions from the project manager (horizontal authority), but maintain membership in their permanent functional departments (vertical authority). The term *matrix* comes from the cross-hatching of the horizontal authority-responsibility flow over the vertical flows of the traditional line-and-staff organization. This type of organization has been used in organizations as diverse as Dow Chemical, Chase Manhattan Bank, Procter & Gamble, Lockheed Aircraft, and the Harvard Business School.

The major benefits of the matrix structure lie in its flexibility and the ability it offers to focus resources on major problems or projects. However, the project manager must be able to mold individuals from diverse parts of the organization into an integrated team. Team members must be comfortable in working for more than one boss.

Delaware-based W. L. Gore & Associates has used a matrix structure since its founding in 1958. The company's 5,600 employees make Gore-Tex waterproof fabric and Teflon products in 35 plants around the world. Employees have no job titles and their compensation is determined largely by evaluations made by co-workers. When one employee wants to take responsibility for developing a particular product, he or she becomes a "product specialist" and recruits other employees to form a team. The team grows as more workers are recruited. Eventually, it breaks up into multiple teams, each of which takes responsibility for performing specific manufacturing tasks related to the new product.

> **THEY SAID IT**
>
> "If anything goes bad, I did it. If anything goes semi-good, then we did it. If anything goes real good, you did it. That's all it takes to get people to win football games."
>
> *Paul W. "Bear" Bryant (1913–1983) American football coach*

Matrix Organization

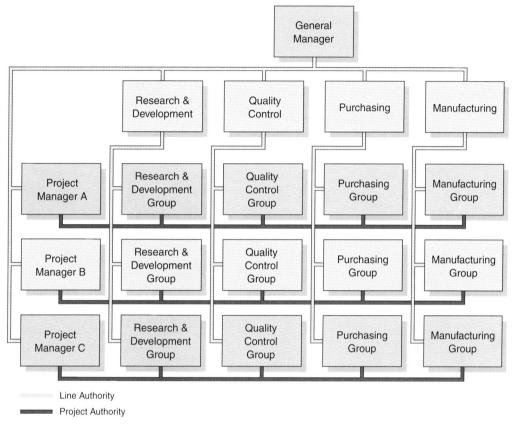

Line Authority
Project Authority

While its matrix organization helps Gore to earn almost $1 billion a year, its decentralization can make communication more difficult, and not all workers like it. "You have to take a lot of responsibility to work here, and not everybody is willing to do that," admits employee Bert Chase. "This place is for people with bound wings who want to fly."[11]

The project-team approach offers built-in flexibility for adapting to a changing business environment. It also provides an outlet for employees' creativity and initiative by gathering hand-picked groups of employees—and perhaps even outside contractors—who possess the right skills for a particular project. When the problem is solved or the project ends, the group dissolves and the employees return to their "regular" jobs. In the future, as the need arises, they may become part of a different group assembled to solve a different problem. General Electric CEO John Welch is a strong advocate of this approach. Says Welch, "What we value most is boundarylessness. It's the ability to work up and down the hierarchy, across functions and geographies, and with suppliers and customers."[12]

Comparing the Four Forms of Organization

Although most large companies are organized on a line-and-staff basis, the line organization is usually the best form for smaller businesses. The committee form is used to a limited extent in major corporations. The matrix approach is used increasingly by both medium-sized companies and large, multiproduct firms to focus diverse organizational resources on specific problems or projects.

SKILLS REQUIRED FOR MANAGERIAL SUCCESS

Face facts: you have agonized several times in the past about whether you have what it takes to be a good manager. Certainly, you have many strengths, but are they the right combination to make you successful, happy, and productive as a manager? Or should you focus your education more toward acquiring narrower

Four Forms of Organization		
Organization Form	**Advantages**	**Disadvantages**
Line	Simple and easy for both managers and subordinates to understand	No specialization
	Clear delegation of authority and responsibility for each area	Overburdening of top executives with administrative details
	Quick decisions	
	Direct communication	
Line-and-staff	Specialists to advise line managers	Conflict between line and staff unless relationships are clear
	Employees reporting to one superior	Staff managers making only recommendations to line managers
Committee	Combined judgment of several executives in diverse areas	Committees slow in making decisions
	Improved morale through participation in decision making	Decisions are the result of compromises rather than a choice of the best alternative
Matrix	Flexibility	Problems may result from employees being accountable to more than one boss
	Provides method for focusing strongly on specific major problems or unique technical issues	Project manager may encounter difficulty in developing a cohesive team from diverse individuals recruited from various parts of the organization
	Provides means of innovation without disrupting regular organizational structure	Conflict may arise between project managers and other department managers

skills that would make you a valued specialist rather than a leader of men and women? The evaluation form shown here has been used by such business giants as Ford, TRW, Xerox, and Boeing to find out how people operate in certain areas, such as teamwork, communications, and embracing technology. Even though it is designed to be completed by managers, their bosses, and coworkers, simply completing it without input from others should offer some insight on how you might rate as a manager.[13]

Every manager, regardless of level in the organization, must possess skills in three basic areas: technical, human relations, and conceptual. Although the importance of each skill varies at different levels, managers use all three types at some time during their careers.

Technical Skills

Technical skills refer to *the manager's ability to understand and use techniques, knowledge, and tools of a specific discipline or department.* An employee in the human resources department, for instance, must understand the technical details of work-place laws. Technical skills are particularly important for first-line managers who frequently are involved with production

employees who operate machinery, salespersons who must explain the technical details of their firm's products, or computer programmers working on a complicated assignment.

In general, as a manager moves up the managerial hierarchy, technical skills become relatively less important. However, top executives in many large organizations often started out as technical experts. For example, a vice president of information systems probably has experience as a computer analyst, while a vice president of marketing might have a background in sales.

Human Relations Skills

Human relation skills are "people" skills involving the manager's *ability to work effectively with and through people.* Human relations skills concern communicating, leading, and motivating workers to accomplish assigned activities. In addition, the ability to interact with superiors and people outside the immediate department or work area is important. The ability to create a work environment in which organizational members will contribute their best efforts is a crucial managerial skill at every level.

Good *communication skills* are an important component of effective human relations. All of us tend to assume that people understand exactly what we mean, but good managers make it a point to check whether their communications come across the way they mean them to. This also involves paying attention to nonverbal communication, such as tone of voice, facial expression, and posture. Studies show that as much as 93 percent of a message's emotional impact comes from such nonverbal signals.

Tommye Jo Daves, manager of a North Carolina Levi Strauss sewing plant, certainly possesses the technical skills for her job. She joined the company in 1959 and worked her way up from seamstress to supervisor to plant manager. However, she finds that human relations skills are far more important in her current job, especially since the plant adopted a matrix organization in which teams of workers are cross-trained to perform 36 different tasks and participate in running the factory. Admits Daves, "Sometimes it's real hard for me not to push back and say, 'You do this, you do that, and you do this.' Now I have to say, 'How do you want to do this?' I have to realize that their ideas may not be the way to go, but I have to let them learn that for themselves."[14]

Conceptual Skills

Conceptual skills refer to the *ability to see the organization as a unified whole and understand how each part of the overall organization interacts with other parts.* These

---

HOW GOOD A BOSS ARE YOU?

Ask the people who work with and for you—as well as your boss—to answer these questions about you. Questions are taken from *The Profilor,* and assessment developed by Personnel Decisions of Minneapolis. Ratings are on a scale of 1 to 5. A 5 means you exhibit a behavior "to a very great extent"; a 1 means "not at all."

The manager:
Develops strategies to help make the organization successful.
- 5 To a very great extent
- 4 To a great extent
- 3 To some extent
- 2 To a little extent
- 1 Not at all
- NA Does not apply

Recognizes broad implications of issues.
☐5 ☐4 ☐3 ☐2 ☐1 ☐NA
Understands complex concepts and relationships.
☐5 ☐4 ☐3 ☐2 ☐1 ☐NA
Analyzes problems from different points of view.
☐5 ☐4 ☐3 ☐2 ☐1 ☐NA
Makes decisions in the face of uncertainty.
☐5 ☐4 ☐3 ☐2 ☐1 ☐NA
Makes sound decisions based on adequate information.
☐5 ☐4 ☐3 ☐2 ☐1 ☐NA
Integrates planning across work units.
☐5 ☐4 ☐3 ☐2 ☐1 ☐NA
Translates business strategies into clear objectives and tactics.
☐5 ☐4 ☐3 ☐2 ☐1 ☐NA
Provides clear direction and defines priorities for the team.
☐5 ☐4 ☐3 ☐2 ☐1 ☐NA
Fosters the development of a common vision.
☐5 ☐4 ☐3 ☐2 ☐1 ☐NA

Acts decisively.
☐5 ☐4 ☐3 ☐2 ☐1 ☐NA
Takes a stand and resolves important issues.
☐5 ☐4 ☐3 ☐2 ☐1 ☐NA
Wins support from others.
☐5 ☐4 ☐3 ☐2 ☐1 ☐NA
Gets others to take action.
☐5 ☐4 ☐3 ☐2 ☐1 ☐NA
Champions new initiatives within and beyond the scope of the job.
☐5 ☐4 ☐3 ☐2 ☐1 ☐NA
Involves others in the change process.
☐5 ☐4 ☐3 ☐2 ☐1 ☐NA
Has the confidence and trust of others.
☐5 ☐4 ☐3 ☐2 ☐1 ☐NA
Shows consistency between words and actions.
☐5 ☐4 ☐3 ☐2 ☐1 ☐NA
Persists in the face of obstacles.
☐5 ☐4 ☐3 ☐2 ☐1 ☐NA
Puts a top priority on getting results.
☐5 ☐4 ☐3 ☐2 ☐1 ☐NA

How you rate
If you score all 4s and 5s, you are viewed as competent. Focus on fine-tuning and making the most of those strengths.
If you score 3 on any item, determine how important the skill or behavior is to your job. If it's important, try to improve.
If you score below 3, it's fix-it time. Target those areas for development.

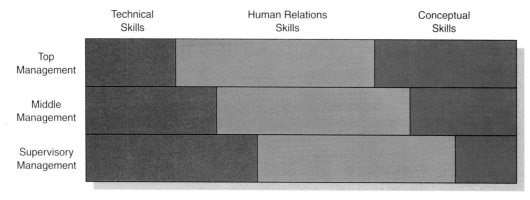

The relative importance of different managerial skills varies at different managerial levels.

skills involve a manager's ability to "see the big picture" by acquiring, analyzing, and interpreting information. Such skills are especially important for top-level managers, who must develop long-range plans for the future direction of the organization.

Levi Strauss & Co. teaches its managers conceptual skills through a series of workshops called Leadership Week. During one workshop exercise, managers are organized into teams, blindfolded, and asked to work together on shaping a piece of rope into a square. Tommye Jo Daves' team failed at this task, but she found the experience worthwhile nonetheless. The most important lessons, she says, were, "You can't lead a team by just barking orders, and you have to have a vision in your head of what you're trying to do."[15]

Managerial Skills: Who Needs What?

All managers within an organization need to possess technical, human relations, and conceptual skills. However, the relative importance of each skill differs for each level of management (see chart). Supervisory managers, who spend much of their time dealing with operative workers, must be strong in technical and human relations skills. They spend relatively little time, however, in long-range planning and other conceptual tasks. Top managers, on the other hand, need strong conceptual skills and human relations ability, but spend little time dealing with technical matters. Middle managers require a blend of all three skills.

In general, conceptual and human relations skills transfer well from one department, company, or industry to another. Technical skills, however, are harder to transfer, due to the unique characteristics and requirements of many such skills. Furthermore, even though people may be great managers within a single functional area (such as engineering), moving into top management may require additional skills.

Their success as top managers depends on their ability to understand the contributions made by all departments, not just the one with which they are most familiar.

LEADERSHIP

Leadership, the most visible component of a manager's responsibilities, is the *act of motivating or causing others to perform activities designed to achieve specific objectives.* Because of the importance of effective leadership in organizational success, it is not surprising that there is a great deal of research into the characteristics of a good leader. Great leaders do not all share the same qualities, but three traits often are mentioned: empathy (the ability to place oneself in another's position), self-awareness, and objectivity in dealing with others.

Leadership research focuses on different styles of leadership and circumstances under which each style might prove successful. This approach to leadership is known as the *contingency theory.* It argues that management should adjust its leadership style in accordance with the situation at hand. We now will examine specific approaches to leadership styles.

Leadership Styles

Leadership involves the exercise of *power*—the ability of one person to influence the behavior of another. This power may result from one or more sources. Leaders secure some power from their position in the organization. As managers, they are responsible for directing the activities of their subordinates. In other cases, their power comes from their expertise and experience: first-line supervisors who were once expert carpenters are likely to be respected by their crew of carpenters. Other leaders secure power from the force of their personalities. Followers of such charismatic leaders may grant them power because they want to please them or become more like them.

The way in which a leader uses available power to lead others is referred to as *leadership style*. A continuum of leadership styles exists, within which we can identify three basic styles. At one end of the continuum are *autocratic leaders*, who make decisions on their own without consulting others. The autocratic leader reaches a decision, communicates it to subordinates, and requires them to implement it. *Democratic leaders*, the second type, involve their subordinates in making decisions. A democratic sales manager, for example, allows sales personnel to participate in setting sales quotas, while an autocratic sales manager simply assigns quotas for each salesperson. The most democratic style of leadership belongs to *free-rein leaders*, who believe in minimal supervision and leave most decisions to their subordinates.

The current trend is toward democratic and free-rein leadership. As U.S. companies downsize and eliminate layers of management ranks, lines of authority become shorter, and the employees who remain must assume greater responsibility. "Whips and chains are no longer an alternative," explains leadership author Warren Bennis. "Leaders must learn to change the nature of power and how it's employed."

Robert Haas, CEO of Levi Strauss & Co., explains how his firm accomplishes this. "What we're trying to do around here is syndicate leadership throughout the organization. In a command and control organization, people protect knowledge because it's their claim to distinction. But we share as much information as we possibly can throughout the company. Business literacy is a big issue in developing leadership. You cannot ask people to exercise broader judgment if their world is bounded by very narrow vision."[16]

Which Leadership Style Is Best?

Appropriate leadership style is a function of the leader, the subordinates, and the situation. In short, the best leadership style is one that adapts to the circumstances at hand. Some leaders are uncomfortable in situations characterized by high participation of subordinates in decision making. Some followers do not have the ability or the desire to assume such responsibility. Furthermore, the specific situation helps determine which style will be most effective. Problems requiring immediate solutions may have to be handled without consulting subordinates. When there is less time pressure, participative decision making may work best.

In many cases, democratic leaders will ask for advice from others but will make the final decisions themselves. A leader who usually prefers a free-rein style may be forced by circumstances to be autocratic in making a particular decision. For example, if there is to be a ten percent reduction in staff, those subject to being fired are not likely to be consulted on who should go.

After devoting many years to research to determine the best types of leaders, experts agree that no single best style of leadership exists. Rather, they contend that the most effective leadership style depends on the power held by the leader, the difficulty of the tasks involved, and the characteristics of the workers. Both extremely easy and extremely difficult situations are handled best by leaders who emphasize the accomplishment of assigned tasks. Moderately difficult situations are handled best by leaders who emphasize participation and good working relations with subordinates.

CORPORATE CULTURE

The most appropriate leadership style depends greatly on **corporate culture,** *the value system of an organization.* Managerial philosophies, work-place practices, and communication networks are included in the concept of corporate culture. Tyson Food's corporate culture is reflected in the fact that everyone—even CEO Don Tyson—wears tan work clothes on the job.

The corporate culture typically is shaped by the leaders who founded and developed the company and by those who succeed them. One generation of employees passes on a corporate culture to newer employees. Sometimes this is part of formal training. New managers who attend McDonald's Hamburger University may learn skills in management, but they also acquire the basics of the organization's

---

DID YOU KNOW?

While U.S. citizens represent the world's largest demand for VCRs, no VCRs are produced in the United States.

In Ethiopia, the time required to make a decision is directly proportional to its importance. This is so much the case that low-level bureaucrats there attempt to elevate the prestige of their work by taking a long time to make decisions. Westerners there are innocently prone to downgrade their work in the local people's eyes by trying to speed things up.

Suppose Lee Woon Chee is the director of your firm's Singapore office. Addressing him as Mr. Chee is like calling your Canadian colleague Mr. Ed or Mr. Bob. He should be addressed as Mr. Lee, since the surname comes first in Chinese and the given name last.

Giving gifts of knives and handkerchiefs in Latin America means you wish hardship on the recipient.

corporate culture. Employees can absorb corporate culture through informal contacts as well, by talking with other workers and through their experiences on the job.

Corporate culture has a major impact on the success of an organization. In organizations with strong cultures, everyone knows and supports the organization's objectives. In those with weak cultures, no clear sense of purpose exists. In fact, the authors of the classic book *In Search of Excellence* concluded the presence of a strong corporate culture was the single common thread among many diverse but highly successful companies, such as General Electric and McDonald's.[17]

INTRA-PRENEURSHIP

Major innovations often have been the domain of small business. In Chapter 5, we learned that many small firms are started by entrepreneurs, risk-takers who set up and operate new businesses. From Thomas Edison's development of the phonograph to the birth of the Apple computer in Steven P. Jobs' garage, the U.S. entrepreneurial sector is the birthplace of hundreds of major industries. Entrepreneurs have given the world such popular consumer products as ballpoint pens, fiberglass skis, Velcro fasteners, and Big Mac hamburgers.

Today, many corporations are encouraging **intrapreneurship,** *entrepreneurial-type activity within the corporate structure.* Although the intrapreneur may begin by assembling a special task force and/or working within the confines of a matrix structure, a successful project may result in an entirely new subsidiary of the corporation. In some cases, a separate company is formed at the outset. While the disadvantages of this approach are identical to those described earlier regarding the matrix organization, the advantages lie in the available financing and necessary manufacturing and marketing expertise already in place in a large company. In addition, the intrapreneuring option permits many firms to retain

valuable entrepreneurially oriented employees who might otherwise leave the company and start their own businesses.

Hewlett-Packard (H-P) is an example of a comany that fosters intrapreneurship. A few years ago, H-P manager Jim Olson became an intrapreneur when he realized that the company was not involved in the rapidly growing areas of television and telecommunications. Following approval by other members of H-P top management, his first step was to recruit a team of engineers and managers, who spent the next several months visiting TV networks, production houses, and trade shows. Team members returned to H-P, plunged into research and design, and created 14 new products in nine months. One is the VidJet Pro, a studio tool that files video images along with the videotape, so customers can see what's on a tape without having to watch it. Other new products include a machine that monitors the quality of video signals, and a video server that feeds movies into interactive TV. The division is building components of high-tech TV systems for Pacific Telesis and Time Warner, and is negotiating deals with other major telephone companies as well. Olson notes that his intrapreneurship arrangement with H-P gave him the best of both worlds: He had the huge company's financial support and expertise, but also had the freedom to innovate. "We're street fighters here," he says. "We're like a start-up."[18]

A manager systematically progresses through each step in the decision-making process to reach a decision ultimately aimed at solving a specific problem or taking advantage of a particular business opportunity.

MANAGERIAL DECISION MAKING

The most important task of a leader is decision making. Managers earn their salaries by making decisions that enable their firms to solve problems as they arise. In addition, managers continually are involved with anticipating and preventing problems. The decision-making process can be described in five steps. In a narrow sense, it can be thought of as simply choosing among two or more alternatives—the chosen alternative being the decision. But in a broader sense, **decision making** *involves recognizing that a problem exists,* *identifying it, evaluating alternatives, selecting and implementing an alternative, and following up* (by getting feedback) on the effectiveness of the decision. Whether the decision to be made is routine or unique (such as a decision to construct a major new manufacturing facility), the systematic step-by-step approach will be effective.

Types of Decisions

We can classify decisions by their relative uniqueness. A *programmed decision* involves simple, common, frequently occurring problems for which solutions already have been determined. Examples of programmed decisions include choosing the starting salary for a computer programmer, determining reorder points for raw materials used in production, and selecting price discounts offered to customers who make large-quantity purchases. Organizations develop rules, policies, and detailed procedures for making such decisions consistently, quickly, and inexpensively. Since such solutions eliminate the time-consuming process of identifying and evaluating alternatives and making new decisions each time the situation occurs, they free managers to devote time to more complex problems.

A *nonprogrammed decision* involves complex, important, and nonroutine problems or opportunities. Because nonprogrammed decisions typically are made in situations that have not occurred before, identifying alternatives, evaluating them, and implementing the best ones become critical tasks. In fact, managers often are evaluated on their ability to make nonprogrammed decisions.

Companies can help employees develop their decision-making skills by rewarding those who are willing to deal with nonprogrammed situations. Consider Sysco, the largest company in the food-service industry, where employees are encouraged to try out new ideas. Charles Cotros, head of Sysco's Memphis unit, noticed that his salespeople spent a great deal of their time driving from client to client. After considering several ways to boost their productivity, he made a nonprogrammed decision to limit sales territories geographically. Cotros knew this decision involved risk. "I'd go home at night and think, 'My God, we're going to lose all our customers and all our salespeople.'" But the new strategy paid off. In six years, his unit's market share grew from 12 percent to 20 percent, and pretax profit margins doubled to 6 percent. "Today about half of [Sysco's] operating companies have geographic sales territories, and more are moving that direction," says Cotros, who has since

been promoted to executive vice president—a signal to other Sysco employees that risk-taking is rewarded.[19]

TIME MANAGEMENT

Managers are busy people who are expected to accomplish a lot of goals in a limited amount of time. **Time management,** or *the effective allocation of one's time among different tasks,* is a key element of managerial success today.[20] The starting point for time allocation is to place a value on working time. In other words, what does your time cost the organization? Once you know the value of your time, you quickly can identify the activities where it is cost effective for you to spend your time.

> **THEY SAID IT**
>
> "Managers must have the discipline not to keep pulling up the flowers to see if their roots are healthy."
>
> *Robert Townsend (1920–   ) Former president, Avis Rent-A-Car*

Time Management Guidelines

Numerous time management guidelines have been suggested over the years. Some of the best known include (1) always leaving at least a quarter of your time unscheduled; (2) assigning priorities to tasks; (3) breaking big jobs into smaller ones; and (4) when taking on something new, giving up something old. Following are some other generally accepted time management ideas.

Establish Goals and Set Priorities. Make a list of your long- and short-term projects. Look at the list regularly and revise it as needed. Arrange the items on the list in order of their importance and then divide items into specific tasks. Then start at the top of the list and get to work. Do not get upset if your priorities change by the hour—just revise your list and get on with the work. Schedule your daily activities on an hour-by-hour appointment calendar.

Learn to Delegate Work. Part of setting priorities is deciding whether you really need to do a project. One management professor notes that there are really only six things a top manager always should do: planning, selecting the team, monitoring their efforts, motivating, evaluating, and rewarding them. Consider delegating the other tasks to a subordinate. Some questions to ask yourself in deciding what to delegate are: Is this project truly necessary? (Will anyone really read this report you're slaving over?) Would this project benefit one of my subordinates? (One of your employees may be eager for the experience and opportunity to try something new.) Is this what my bosses think I should be spending my time on? (If not, can someone else do it instead?)[21]

Office products, such as Day Runner personal organizers, help managers schedule activities on an hour-by-hour daily appointment calendar.

Concentrate on Most Important Activities.
Learn the Pareto Principle of time management: You can achieve 80 percent of your goals in only 20 percent of your time if you work on those tasks critical to the completion of the overall project and avoid those that contribute little to the outcome.

Do Most Important Work When Most Alert.
Work on high-priority items when you are mentally alert and on low-priority items when your energy has ebbed.

Group Activities Together.   Set aside a period of time to read all your mail and answer all your phone calls. This will help you make the most efficient use of your time.

Learn How to Handle Interruptions.   Incoming phone calls, unscheduled visitors, and even the mail can play havoc with your schedule. You can control these interruptions by having your assistant handle all but essential calls when you are working on an important task, by working in another office where no one will be able to find and interrupt you, by setting times when subordinates can talk to you and times when they cannot except for emergencies, and by learning how to deal with long-winded callers. Interrupting yourself also wastes time. Instead of getting yet another cup of coffee or walking down the hall to chat with a friend, try to finish what you are doing, even if the job is difficult or unpleasant. Just think how good you will feel when it's done!

A notebook, computer, pager, and cellular phone help Harriet Donnelly, AT&T managing director of consumer products, manage her time well, no matter what time zone she's in. Donnelly typically leaves her New Jersey home on Monday morning to travel to her other offices in California, Japan, or Europe. Once arrived, she may spend all day in meetings and not return to her hotel room before 9 or 10 P.M. She uses her flight time to prepare presentations on her computer, and stays in touch with headquarters via voice mail and electronic mail. "You can get hooked on working this way," says Donnelly. "It takes away the nine-to-five restrictions that many people are still limited by. The bad part is that I work more hours, but I feel very productive."[22]

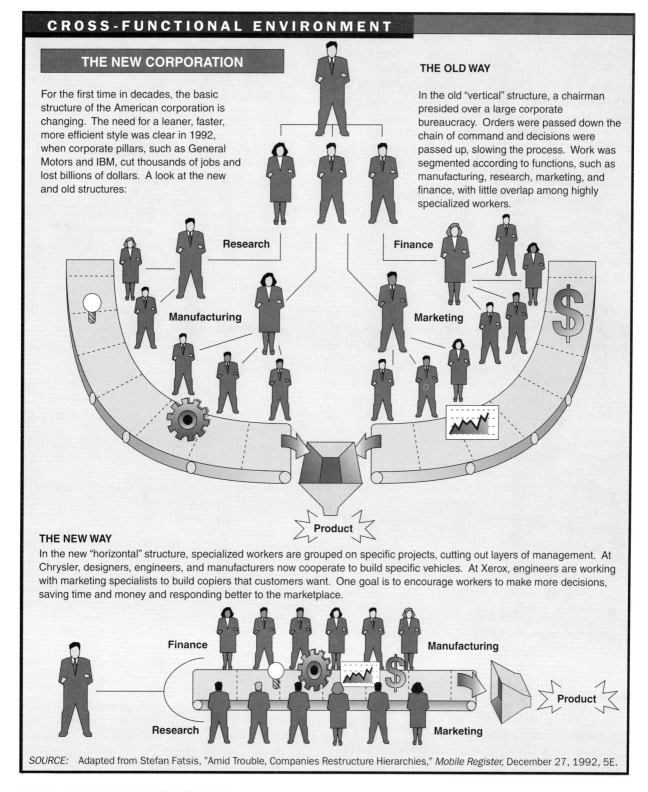

CROSS-FUNCTIONAL ENVIRONMENT

THE NEW CORPORATION

For the first time in decades, the basic structure of the American corporation is changing. The need for a leaner, faster, more efficient style was clear in 1992, when corporate pillars, such as General Motors and IBM, cut thousands of jobs and lost billions of dollars. A look at the new and old structures:

THE OLD WAY

In the old "vertical" structure, a chairman presided over a large corporate bureaucracy. Orders were passed down the chain of command and decisions were passed up, slowing the process. Work was segmented according to functions, such as manufacturing, research, marketing, and finance, with little overlap among highly specialized workers.

Research

Finance

Manufacturing

Marketing

Product

THE NEW WAY

In the new "horizontal" structure, specialized workers are grouped on specific projects, cutting out layers of management. At Chrysler, designers, engineers, and manufacturers now cooperate to build specific vehicles. At Xerox, engineers are working with marketing specialists to build copiers that customers want. One goal is to encourage workers to make more decisions, saving time and money and responding better to the marketplace.

Finance

Manufacturing

Research

Marketing

Product

SOURCE: Adapted from Stefan Fatsis, "Amid Trouble, Companies Restructure Hierarchies," *Mobile Register,* December 27, 1992, 5E.

NEW OPPORTUNITIES FOR MANAGERS

As we have seen, business organizations are undergoing a revolution in structure. The tasks and responsibilities expected of managers within these organizations also are changing, as they manage diverse groups of employees, create flexible work teams, assume broader spans of control, and encourage intrapreneurship. In some cases, downsizing has eliminated many manager's jobs.

While traditional supervisory and middle-management positions might be getting more scarce, other opportunities will be available for those with good management skills. Some middle managers leave large corporations for smaller firms. Another option is to become a *contract manager*, someone on a temporary appointment. Temporary management is a fast-growing area in the United States and Europe, where a manager may contract with an employer to work for a specified period of time.

An increasing number of managers decide to start their own companies. In fact, the number of people who start their own businesses after losing their jobs has tripled since 1987. One example is Monica Castaneda, a former defense contract administrator at TRW. When Castaneda was laid off, she opened a sewing business, making flame-retardant suits for test pilots and embroidered uniforms for race-car drivers. "I thought I'd spend all my time sewing," she says. However, as her business grows, she finds herself delegating the stitchery to others and returning to the skills she honed at TRW. "What I'm really good at is administration and taking care of contracts."

For managers, as for all employees, it is important to remain flexible and develop new skills. Consider Rod Loehr, an engineer who worked for CAE-Link Corp. for 33 years. When the firm closed, the 54-year-old Loehr's job went with it. Before long, he had found an even better-paying job as an engineering manager at Litton Applied Technology. Loehr ascribes his success to his willingness to learn new software and update his skills. "Taking classes helped me get the position I'm in," he says.[23]

SUMMARY OF LEARNING GOALS

1. **Discuss the need for organizational structure, and list the steps involved in the organizing process.**
   The organizing process and its resulting structure form the basis for organizational planning to reach organizational objectives. The need for structure increases as organizations grow in size. Once organizational objectives and plans have been developed, organizing involves the following five steps:
   1. Determine specific work activities necessary to implement those plans and accomplish objectives.
   2. Group work activities into a logical pattern or structure.
   3. Assign activities to specific positions and people and allocate the necessary resources and authority to carry them out.
   4. Coordinate activities of different groups and individuals.
   5. Evaluate the results of the organizing process.
2. **Evaluate each of the four basic forms of organization.**
   Four forms of organizational structure are used: line, line-and-staff, committee, and matrix. The line organization is the simplest form, but it suffers from a lack of specialization by management. This poses a problem for larger organizations. The line-and-staff form assigns authority to line managers and adds staff specialists to provide information and advice. However, conflict can arise between line and staff members if their relationship is unclear.
   The committee form of organization rarely is used as the sole organization structure, but it often is incorporated to some extent within the line-and-staff structure. Because committees can be composed of representatives of a number of areas in the organization, they ensure that each area is represented in the decision-making process. However, they are relatively slow in making decisions, which often end up being compromises among conflicting interests. The matrix form of organization, another subform of the line-and-staff structure, permits large, multiproduct firms to focus organizational resources on specific problems or projects. Because of its "team" approach and the fact that team members are accountable to more than one manager, conflict can occur.
3. **Identify the skills required for managerial success.**
   These three basic managerial skills are technical, human relations, and conceptual. Technical skills, which involve the manager's ability to understand and use techniques, tools, and knowledge of a specific discipline or department, are most important for first-level managers. Human relations skills, which involve working effectively with and through people in the accomplishment of assignments, are important for managers at every level. Conceptual skills, which involve the manager's ability to see the "big picture" of the organization as a whole and how each part contributes to its overall functioning, are relatively more important for top management.
4. **Explain the concept of leadership and identify the three basic leadership styles.**
   Leadership is the act of motivating or causing others to perform activities designed to achieve specific objectives. The three basic leadership styles are autocratic, democratic, and free-rein. The best leadership style depends on three elements: the leader, the followers, and the situation. Today, the general trend is toward greater participation of subordinates in decisions that affect them.
5. **Describe the role of intrapreneurship in modern organizations.**
   The term *intrapreneurship* refers to various attempts to make large organizations more entrepreneurial. Intrapreneurship units achieve the innovative dynamics of a

smaller firm. These units are given free rein (and sometimes financial incentives) to accomplish their assigned objectives.

6. **Explain the impact of downsizing and outsourcing on today's organizations.**

   Downsizing refers to the elimination of one or more layers from the management hierarchy in an effort to reduce costs and make the firm more efficient. This results in a flatter organization structure and requires empowerment of workers to make decisions previously made by their supervisors. Outsourcing is the practice of relying on outside specialists to perform functions previously performed by company employees. Relying on outside contractors to perform needed functions also will simplify the organization by eliminating the need for company employees in these areas.

7. **List the steps in the decision-making process and contrast programmed and nonprogrammed decisions.**

   The decision-making process consists of five steps:
   1. Recognition of problems and opportunities
   2. Development of alternative courses of action
   3. Evaluation of alternatives
   4. Selection and implementation of the chosen alternative
   5. Follow up to determine the effectiveness of decisions
   Programmed decisions involve simple, frequently occurring problems or opportunities for which solutions have been determined previously. Such decisions are made quickly by reference to a rule or procedure, and managers need spend little time in identifying and evaluating alternatives. By contrast, nonprogrammed decisions involve more complex, relatively unique situations. Their solution requires considerable management involvement in identifying and evaluating alternatives.

8. **Discuss the importance of time management.**

   Time management refers to the process of allocating one's time among different activities. Given the variety of goals management is expected to accomplish in a limited amount of time, it has become evident in recent years that time management is a major ingredient in managerial success. The starting point in effective time management is to know what one's time is worth so that it can be allocated in a cost-effective fashion.

KEY TERMS QUIZ

line-and-staff organization
management
downsizing
human relations skills
empowering
conceptual skills
leadership

outsourcing
top management
delegation
time management
corporate culture
line organization
middle management

intrapreneurship
matrix organization
supervisory management
technical skills
decision making
organization

_____ 1. The achievement of organizational objectives through people and other resources.

_____ 2. The highest level of the management hierarchy staffed by executives who develop long-range plans and interact with the public and outside entities, like government.

_____ 3. Those people responsible for developing detailed plans and procedures to implement the general plans of top management.

_____ 4. Those people directly responsible for the details of assigning workers to specific jobs and evaluating their performance.

_____ 5. A structured grouping of people working together to achieve organizational objectives.

_____ 6. The act of assigning activities to subordinates.

_____ 7. Management decision to eliminate layers from the management hierarchy in an effort to reduce costs and make the firm more efficient.

_____ 8. Giving employees additional decision-making authority and responsibilities.

_____ 9. Relying on outside specialists to perform functions previously performed by company employees.

_____ 10. The direct flow of authority from the chief executive to subordinates.

_____ 11. Combines the direct flow of authority present in the line organization with staff departments that serve, advise, and support the line departments.

_____ 12. Structure in which specialists from different parts of the organization are brought together to work on specific projects.

_____ 13. The manager's ability to understand and use techniques, knowledge, and tools of a specific discipline or department.

_____ 14. "People" skills involving the manager's ability to work effectively with and through people.

_____ 15. The ability to see the organization as a unified whole and understand how each part of the overall organization interacts with other parts.

_____ 16. The act of motivating or causing others to perform activities designed to achieve specific objectives.

_____ 17. The value system of an organization.

_____ 18. Entrepreneurial-type activity within the corporate structure.

_____ 19. Recognizing that a problem exists, identifying it, evaluating alternatives, selecting and implementing an alternative, and following up.

_____ 20. The effective allocation of one's time among different tasks.

OTHER IMPORTANT TERMS

accountability	contract manager	organization chart
authority	democratic leaders	organizing
autocratic leaders	departmentalization	power
chain of command	free-rein leaders	programmed decision
committee organization	leadership style	responsibility
contingency theory	nonprogrammed decision	

REVIEW QUESTIONS

1. Explain the statement, "Management principles are universal." Do you agree or disagree?

2. Describe some traits that would make a manager a good candidate for a foreign transfer. Would you be a good candidate for such a transfer? Why or why not?

3. On what level of the management would each of the following persons be listed?
   a. Department head   d. Branch manager
   b. Chief operating officer   e. Mayor
   c. Supervisor   f. Dean

4. Identify and briefly explain the three skills required for managerial success. Which skills are relatively more important for top management? Which are more important for first-line managers?

5. MacDugal's Paper Distributors has long observed St. Patrick's Day as a paid holiday for its employees. Donald MacDugal, company president, noticed that St. Patrick's Day will fall on Wednesday during the next year. He wonders whether the Monday of that week should be declared a company holiday instead. Using

each of the steps in the decision-making process, describe how you would make this decision.

6. Classify each of the following as either a programmed or nonprogrammed decision. Defend your answers.
   a. Determining registrar's office system for processing student requests for dropping and adding courses.
   b. Making a retail store-manager's decision about the number of men's dress shirts to order.
   c. Creating a hospital's procedure for admitting new patients.
   d. Pondering management's decision to relocate corporate headquarters from Detroit to Dallas.

7. What is departmentalization? What are its major forms?

8. Explain why so many organizations have been downsizing and outsourcing during the 1990s.

9. Summarize the major strengths and weaknesses of each type of formal organizational structure.

10. What is meant by corporate culture? Describe the corporate culture of a firm in your area.

DISCUSSION QUESTIONS

1. Describe the skills that you think would be helpful to someone working in a matrix organization. What can you do to prepare yourself for a successful career in such a company? Be specific.
2. Give an example of a firm in your state that should use the following forms of departmentalization. Defend your answers.
   a. Product
   b. Geographic
   c. Customer
   d. Functional
   e. Process
3. The typical professional sports team is owned by wealthy individuals who enjoy being involved with a particular sport. The owners usually make the major policy decisions, but a hired general manager handles other managerial duties. The general manager oversees facilities, equipment, vendors, and personnel matters. He or she also may have responsibility for player personnel decisions such as trades, new-player drafts, and assignment of players to minor leagues. The field manager, or head coach, is in charge of the team's actual performance. This person assists the general manager in matters concerning players. Other personnel employed by professional teams include team physicians, assistant coaches, trainers, equipment managers, secretaries, scouts, and ticket-sales personnel. Draw an organization chart for a professional sports team. Discuss the strengths of this organizational structure.
4. In recent years, U.S. firms have eliminated many management and professional jobs. Discuss how you feel this will affect the U.S. work place in the next decade. Explain how managers displaced by the downsizing trend may be able to take advantage of the growing practice of outsourcing.
5. Napoleon always refused to reply to letters for six months because he believed that most of the problems raised in the correspondence either would be solved or forgotten in that time. Comment on Napoleon's unique approach to time management.

VIDEO CASE: Middle Management: Twenty-first Century Dinosaur?

This video focuses on downsizing the organization of the late 1990s and empowering employees to make decisions previously the responsibility of middle management. It examines the thinning ranks of middle management in many companies. It is included on page 415 of Appendix D.

Solution to Key Terms Quiz

1. management 2. top management 3. middle management 4. supervisory management 5. organization 6. delegation 7. downsizing 8. empowering 9. outsourcing 10. line organization 11. line-and-staff organization 12. matrix organization 13. technical skills 14. human relations skills 15. conceptual skills 16. leadership 17. corporate culture 18. intrapreneurship 19. decision making 20. time management

CHAPTER 8

The Human Resource

Learning Goals

1. Explain the importance of human resource management and the responsibilities of a human resource department.
2. List the different needs in Maslow's hierarchy.
3. Distinguish among Theory X, Theory Y, and Theory Z managers.
4. Explain how recruitment, selection, orientation, training, and evaluation contribute to placing the right person in a job.
5. Explain the concept of job enrichment and how it can motivate employees.
6. Outline the different forms of compensation.
7. Summarize the role of labor unions and list their primary goals.
8. Outline the sources of power, or "weapons," of labor and management.
9. Identify and briefly describe each of the major human resource concerns for the twenty-first century.

Rhino Foods, Inc.
79 Industrial Parkway
Burlington, Vermont 05401
802-862-0252 • 1-800-639-3350 • Fax 802-865-4145

Employee layoffs can be devastating to employee morale, but management may face a "cut costs or else" ultimatum if the survival of the firm is at stake. Cost-cutting efforts have cost hundreds of thousands of jobs this decade in large corporations and small businesses alike. A few firms, however, have found a way for their workers—who might otherwise have been laid off—to continue drawing a paycheck.

Take the case of Rhino Foods, a $5 million specialty-dessert maker based in Burlington, Vermont. When President Ted Castle faced the unpleasant prospect of a temporary layoff recently, he asked his 55 employees to think of solutions to the staffing overcapacity. A series of brainstorming sessions produced an idea that might save 26 workers from unemployment: an employee-exchange program with other distributors and producers in the region.

Rhino's human resource director Marlene Dailey was given the task of identifying possible clients and determining their needs. Ben & Jerry's Ice Cream, Rhino's biggest customer, was one of the first to take on workers—and that's how bakers became order-takers in Ben & Jerry's food-production division.

Since the hiring companies were also Rhino customers, management made it clear to the 26 employees who volunteered to enter the exchange program that they had to perform their new assignments with the same commitment to excellence they had displayed

CHESSTERS
QUALITY FROZEN CUSTARD
FROM VERMONT

at Rhino. Although Rhino would be consulted in any disciplinary decisions, the contracting firms had authority over these employees. As one worker in the program explained, "If we get fired there, we get fired here."

At the beginning, contract lengths were kept short. For example, assignments at Gardener's Supply were limited to three weeks. However, the arrangement worked so well that Gardener's Supply management asked that the contract be extended. Rhino workers earned the same wage as other employees doing the same job. If the contract wage rate was lower than the worker's previous pay, Rhino made up the difference.

Contract workers continued to receive health and dental insurance coverage from Rhino in addition to benefits required by law, such as worker's compensation. A key factor in the program's success was keeping communications open between Rhino and its contract employees. Often these workers later rejoined Rhino with quality improvement ideas. On completing a job at Ben & Jerry's, one worker suggested rotating breaks on the production line.

Rhino's employee exchange program is a win–win situation for the community, the employer, and workers alike. The company was able to reduce its work force temporarily and also avoid losing its well-trained employees. For their part, contract workers frequently learn new skills and remain loyal to the company since they still are employed. President Castle also was able to demonstrate his firm's principles in a tangible way: "The company's relationship with its employees is founded upon mutual trust and respect within an environment for listening and personal attention." This innovative program earned Rhino the 1994 Blue Chip Enterprise Award from the U.S. Chamber of Commerce.[1]

CHAPTER OVERVIEW

The importance of people to the success of any organization is stressed in the very definition of *management:* the use of people and other resources in accomplishing organizational objectives. This chapter addresses the critical issue of human resource management. We will examine the way an organization recruits, trains, and motivates people. We also will discuss employee training, development, and counseling, and will consider issues in labor–management relations. Finally, we will take a look at human resource concerns of the next century, including the opportunities and challenges in managing older workers, two-career couples, part-time employees, and an increasingly diverse work force.

HUMAN RESOURCE MANAGEMENT: A VITAL MANAGERIAL FUNCTION

In this chapter we emphasize people—the human element—and their importance in accomplishing an organization's goals. Most organizations devote considerable attention to **human resource management,** which can be defined as (1) *the process of acquiring, training, developing, motivating, and appraising a sufficient quantity of qualified employees to perform the activities necessary to accomplish organizational objectives;* and (2) *developing specific activities and an overall organizational climate to generate maximum worker satisfaction and employee efficiency.*

> **THEY SAID IT**
>
> "Daughters of lions are lions, too."
>
> *Swahili proverb*

While the owner-manager of a small organization is likely to assume complete responsibility for human resource management, larger organizations use company specialists called *human resource managers* to perform these activities in a systematic manner. The position is becoming increasingly important because of increased competition, growth in the use of outsourcing and part-time workers, a new emphasis on cost control, complex wage and benefit programs, and a changing work force. These human resource managers assume primary responsibility for forecasting personnel needs, recruiting, and aiding in selecting new employees. They also assist in training and evaluation, and administer compensation, employee benefits, and safety programs.

We can view human resource management in two ways. In a narrow sense, it refers to the functions and operations of a single department in a firm: the human resource, or personnel, department. Most firms with 200 or more employees establish such a department. In a broader sense, though, human resource management involves the entire organization, even when a special staff department exists. After all, general management also is involved in training and developing workers, evaluating their performance, and motivating them to perform as efficiently as possible.

The core responsibilities of human resource management include human resource planning, recruitment and selection, training/management development, performance appraisal, and compensation and employee benefits. Trained specialists from the human resource department typically are involved in carrying out each of these responsibilities. However,

A hundred years ago, companies hired workers by posting a notice outside the gate, stating that a certain number of workers would be hired the following day. The notice might list skills, such as welding or carpentry, or it might simply list the number of workers needed. The next morning, people would appear at the front gate—a small number in prosperous times, large crowds in periods of high unemployment—and the workers would be selected. The choices were often arbitrary; the company might hire the first four in line or the four people who looked the strongest or healthiest. Workers operated under a precise set of strict rules. This is one turn-of-the-century example of such a list.

RULES FOR CLERKS, 1900

1. This store must be opened at sunrise. No mistake. Open at 6:00 A.M. summer and winter. Close about 8:30 or 9 P.M. the year round.
2. Store must be swept and dusted, doors and windows opened, lamps filled and trimmed, chimneys cleaned, counters, base shelves, and showcases dusted, pens made, a pail of water and the coal must be brought in before breakfast, if there is time to do it and attend to all the customers who call.
3. The store is not to be opened on the Sabbath day unless absolutely necessary and then only for a few minutes.
4. Should the store be opened on Sunday the clerks must go in alone and get tobacco for customers in need.
5. Clerks who are in the habit of smoking Spanish cigars, being shaved at the barber's, going to dancing parties and other places of amusement, and being out late at night will assuredly give the employer reason to be overly suspicious of employee integrity and honesty.
6. Clerks are allowed to smoke in the store provided they do not wait on women while smoking a "stogie."
7. Each store clerk must pay not less than $5.00 per year to the church and must attend Sunday school regularly.
8. Men clerks are given one evening a week off for courting and two if they go to prayer meeting.
9. After the 14 hours in the store, leisure hours should be spent mostly in reading.

such responsibilities usually are shared with line managers, ranging from the company president (who is involved in overall planning) to first-line supervisors (who may be involved in preliminary interviews with applicants and in employee training), and—in companies practicing worker empowerment—even operative employees on the shop floor. By accomplishing these critical tasks, the human resource department achieves its overall objectives of (1) providing qualified, well-trained employees; (2) maximizing employee effectiveness in the organization; and (3) satisfying individual employee needs through monetary compensation, employee benefits, advancement opportunities, and job satisfaction.

HOW NEEDS MOTIVATE PEOPLE

From his examination of 20 top American firms, Robert Leering, author of *A Great Place to Work*, concludes that any manager can turn a bad work place into a good one through what he calls "the three Rs." The first of these is granting workers more and more *responsibility* for their jobs. The second R involves sharing the *rewards* of the enterprise as equitably as possible. The third R is ensuring that employees have *rights*. These include establishing some kind of grievance procedure, allowing access to corporate records, and giving employees the right to confront those in authority without fearing reprisals.

The presence of the three Rs in an organization should contribute to employee morale. **Morale,** *the mental attitude of employees toward their employer and job,* involves a sense of common purpose with respect to other members of the work group and to the organization as a whole. High morale is a sign of a well-managed organization, because workers' attitudes toward their jobs affect the quality of the work done. One of the most obvious signs of poor manager–worker relations is poor morale. It lurks behind absenteeism, employee turnover, slowdowns, and wildcat strikes. It shows up in lower productivity, employee grievances, and transfers.

Burnout, a byword in business today, is evidenced by low morale and fatigue. The most likely burnout candidates are those who care most about their jobs and the company. They experience burnout when they feel a sense of futility and a lack of accomplishment. Kenneth Pelletier, a stress-management consultant and psychiatrist, believes a manager can inspire workers and prevent burnout by showing appreciation for effort. Appreciation is, according to Pelletier, "the most underestimated benefit."[2]

What factors lead to high employee morale? Interestingly, managers and employees give different answers. In one classic study (see table on next page), managers thought that the most important factors involved satisfying employees' basic needs for money and job security. Employees, however, want to be appreciated, to be treated sympathetically, and to feel like part of a team.

Other studies agree with these results. An Opinion Research Center survey found that many Americans would rather work for a small company than a large corporation. Says one researcher, "This desire is interesting, when you consider that benefits and pay

What Contributes to High Morale?		
Most Important	**Less Important**	**Least Important**
Manager Opinions Good wages	Good working conditions	Tactful disciplining
Job security	Interesting work	Full appreciation for work done
Promotion and growth with company	Management loyalty to workers	Sympathetic understanding of personal problems
		Feeling "in" on things
Employee Opinions Full appreciation for work done	Job security	Promotion and growth with company
Feeling "in" on things	Good wages	Management loyalty to workers
Sympathetic understanding of personal problems	Interesting work	Good working conditions
		Tactful disciplining

Managers and employees have quite different opinions regarding what factors contribute to high morale.

are generally better in big corporations, and most people know that."[3]

Maintaining high employee morale also means more than just keeping employees happy. A two-day workweek, longer vacations, or numerous work breaks easily could produce happy employees. But truly high morale results from an understanding of human needs and the ability of the organization to make satisfying individual needs consistent with organizational goals.

Each of us is motivated to take actions designed to satisfy needs. A **need** is simply *the lack of something useful*. It reflects a gap between an individual's actual state and his or her desired state. A **motive** is *the inner state that directs us toward the goal of satisfying a felt need*. Once the need—the gap between where a person is now and where he or she wants to be—becomes important enough, it produces tension and the individual is *moved* (the root word for *motive*) to reduce this tension and return to a condition of equilibrium.

Let's look at an example. If you have been in class or worked at your job until 1 P.M., your immediate need may be for food. Your lack of lunch is reflected in the motive of hunger. So you move—literally—to address your need by walking to a nearby restaurant where you buy the $2.69 special (hamburger, fries, and soft drink). By 1:20 you have satisfied your need for lunch. Now you are ready to satisfy your next need: getting to your 2:00 class on time! The principle behind this process is that a need produces a motivation, which leads to goal-directed behavior, resulting in need satisfaction.

Maslow's Needs Hierarchy

Psychologist Abraham H. Maslow developed a widely accepted list of human needs based on these important assumptions:

- People are wanting animals whose needs depend on what they already possess.
- A satisfied need is not a motivator; only those needs that have not been satisfied can influence behavior.

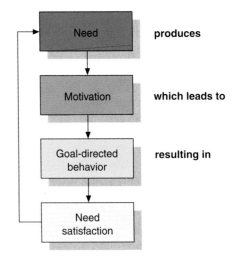

THE MOTIVATION PROCESS

Need   **produces**

Motivation   **which leads to**

Goal-directed behavior   **resulting in**

Need satisfaction

● People's needs are arranged in a hierarchy of importance; once one need has been at least partially satisfied, another emerges and demands satisfaction.

Everyone has needs that must be satisfied before higher-order needs can be considered. On the bottom level of Maslow's hierarchy of needs are *physiological needs*—the most basic needs, such as the desire for food, shelter, and clothing. Since most people in industrialized nations today can afford to satisfy their basic needs, however, higher-order needs are likely to play a greater role in worker motivation. These include *safety needs* (job security, protection from physical harm, and avoidance of the unexpected); *social needs* (the desire to be accepted by members of the family and other individuals and groups); and *esteem needs* (the needs to feel a sense of accomplishment, achievement, and respect from others). The competitive urge to excel—to better the performance of others—is an esteem need and an almost universal human trait.

At the top of the hierarchy are *self-actualization needs*—the needs for fulfillment, for realizing one's own potential, for using one's talents and capabilities totally. Different people may have different self-actualization needs. One person may feel fulfilled by writing a poem, another by running a marathon, and someone else may not attain self-actualization until listed in the *Guinness Book of World Records.* For Steve O'Donnell, a writer with the David Letterman TV show, self-actualization means "a pat on the back, making Dave happy, the thrill of hearing the audience laugh—that's what matters most." Organizations seek to satisfy employees' self-actualization needs, whatever they may be, by offering challenging and creative work assignments and opportunities for advancement based on individual merit.[4]

A major contribution of the needs hierarchy concept is that, for most people, a satisfied need is no longer a motivator. Once physiological needs are satisfied, the individual becomes concerned with higher-order needs. There obviously will be periods when an

MASLOW'S HIERARCHY OF HUMAN NEEDS

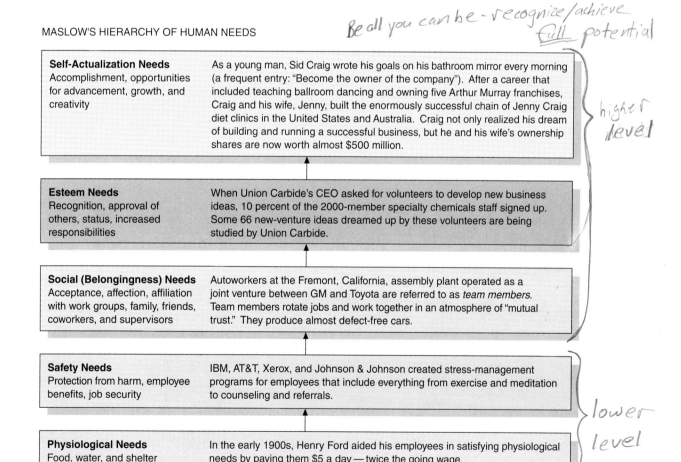

Maslow's hierarchy of needs illustrates the order in which needs are satisfied.

individual is motivated by the need to relieve thirst or hunger, but interest most often is directed toward the satisfaction of safety, belongingness, and the other needs on the ladder.

Theories X, Y, and Z

Maslow's theory became popular with managers because it is relatively simple and seems to fit the facts. (After all, few of us are interested in self-actualization when we're starving.) Business organizations have been extremely successful in satisfying the lower-order physiological and safety needs. The traditional view of workers as ingredients in the production process—as machines, like lathes, drill presses, and other equipment—led management to motivate them with money. Today's managers have been forced to reconsider their assumptions about employees and how best to motivate them.

Psychologist Douglas McGregor, a student of Maslow, proposed the concepts of Theory X and Theory Y as labels for the assumptions that different managers make about worker behavior and how these assumptions affect their management style. **Theory X** *assumes that employees dislike work and must be coerced, controlled, or threatened to motivate them to work.* Managers who accept this view feel that the average human being prefers to be directed, wishes to avoid responsibility, has relatively little ambition, and wants security above all. Such managers are likely to direct their subordinates through close and constant observation, continually holding over them the threat of disciplinary action, and demanding that they closely follow company policies and procedures.

If people behave in the manner described by Theory X, this may be because the organization satisfies only their lower-order needs. If, instead, the organization enables them to satisfy their social, esteem, and self-actualization needs, too, employees may start to behave differently. McGregor labeled this thinking **Theory Y,** *an assumption that workers like work and,*

> ### DID YOU KNOW?
>
> Conducting personal interviews in Belgium or Switzerland requires you to be able to speak four different languages.
>
> Many American recruiters consider a willingness to "look you in the eye" an important personality trait for job applicants. In Japan, though, children are taught never to look directly at a person with superior status. Japanese workers frequently lower their eyes when speaking with superiors as a sign of respect.
>
> At Nissan USA there are no privileged parking spaces and no private dining rooms. The president's desk is in the same room with a hundred other white-collar workers.
>
> Many Spanish offices, shops, and restaurants close for *siesta* between 1:30 and 4:00 P.M. And visitors to Madrid should prepare for late dinners. Restaurants there don't open until at least 9:00 P.M., and *Madrillanos* often sit down to a full-course dinner at midnight.
>
> The cost of living for an international manager is highest in Tehran, Tokyo, and Abidjan; the lowest-cost cities are Warsaw, Harare, Zimbabwe, New Delhi, and Mexico City.

under proper conditions, accept and seek out responsibilities to fulfill their social, esteem, and self-actualization needs. The Theory Y manager considers the expenditure of physical and mental effort in work as natural as play or rest. Unlike the traditional management philosophy that relies on external control and constant supervision, Theory Y emphasizes self-control and direction. Its implementation requires a different managerial strategy that includes worker participation in major and minor decisions previously reserved for management.

The trend toward downsizing, empowering, and increased employee participation in decision making has led to a third management style, labeled **Theory Z.** This approach *views involved workers as the key to increased productivity for the company and an improved quality of work life for the employee.* Theory Z organizations blend Theory Y assumptions with Japanese management practices. Long-term employment for employees and shared responsibility for making and implementing decisions are characteristics of such organizations. Evaluations and promotions are relatively slow, and promotions are tied to individual progress rather than to the calendar. Employees receive varied and nonspecialized experience to broaden their career paths.

The move toward the participative management style that characterizes the Theory Z approach is dramatically reshaping U.S. corporations. As we saw in the last chapter, many companies are adopting the matrix form of organization to reap the benefits of the team approach to solving problems. Increasingly, managers are asking workers how to improve their jobs—and then giving them the authority to do it.

William Malec, chief financial officer of the Tennessee Valley Authority, goes to unusual lengths to learn how TVA workers feel about their jobs. He spends one day every month actually doing the job of one of his 2,000 employees. This practice helps him see the company from an employee's point of view and identify areas for improvement. A stint as a clerical worker taught him that employees had to fill out too many forms to rent a company car; he changed the rules so that they only had to show their company badge and Social Security number. While cleaning offices one night, he learned that janitors wasted a great deal of time plugging and unplugging their vacuum cleaners. He bought them battery-powered sweepers. Explains Malec, "When you get down into their jobs they will tell you things you don't normally hear."[5]

BUILDING THE TEAM

Given the importance of a well trained, high-quality employee team in achieving organizational success, it is not surprising that human resource management is such an important function. The entertainment industry visionary Walt Disney expressed it this way: "You can dream, create, design, and build the most wonderful place in the world, but it requires people to make the dream a reality."

Not just people, but well-trained, well-motivated people are required. The recruitment and selection process plays a major role in convincing such people to become a part of the organization. Writer Leo Rosten made this observation, "First-rate people hire first-rate people. Second-rate people hire third-rate people."

Recruitment is expensive; it can include interviews, tests, medical examinations, and training. The human resource manager must ensure that potential employees have the necessary qualifications for the job, since an employee who leaves the firm after a few months can cost a company up to $75,000 in lost productivity, training costs, and employee morale. A poor employee who stays with the company can cost even more.

To ensure that potential employees have the necessary qualifications for the job and that they either possess needed skills or are capable of learning them, most firms use a six-step approach to recruitment and selection. Rejection of an applicant may occur at any of these steps.

Businesses use both internal and external sources to find candidates for specific jobs. Most firms have a policy of *hiring from within*—that is, considering their own employees first for job openings. If qualified internal candidates are not available, management must look for people outside the organization. Outside sources for potential job applicants include colleges, advertisements in newspapers and professional journals, public employment agencies (such as state employment services), unsolicited applications, and recommendations by current employees.

Management of Sharro, a 700-store international chain of cafeteria-style Italian restaurants, can attest to the importance of hiring—and promoting—from within whenever possible. When the Commack, New York, supplier of lasagna, pizza, cheesecake, and the like, went outside the company for management talent, morale sagged, sales per store declined, and profits fell below expectations. As Mario Sharro admits, "Many of our own people had the qualifications to do the job. It was a case of 'the grass always looks greener.'" Today, Sharro promotes almost exclusively from within and seeks new employees based on recommendations of its work force.[6]

As we saw in Chapter 2, a number of federal and state laws aimed at prohibiting discrimination in hiring practices have been enacted over the last three decades. Failure to follow these requirements may prevent the firm from profiting from the strengths of its own diverse work force; it also can result in stiff penalties and bad publicity. In addition to these laws, employers must be aware of various other legal restrictions governing hiring practices.[7] For instance, some firms try to screen out high-risk employees by requiring drug testing for job applicants, particularly in industries where employees are responsible for public safety, such as airlines and public transportation companies. Drug testing is controversial, however, due to concerns about privacy. Furthermore, positive test results may be inaccurate; traces of legal drugs, such as prescribed medications, may chemically resemble traces of illegal substances. Several states have passed laws restricting drug tests.

The use of polygraph (lie detector) tests is prohibited in almost all pre-hiring decisions, as well as in random testing of current employees. The only organizations that are exempt from this law are federal, state, and county governments; firms doing sensitive

STEPS IN THE RECRUITMENT AND SELECTION PROCESS

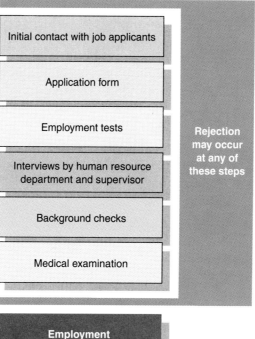

Initial contact with job applicants

Application form

Employment tests

Interviews by human resource department and supervisor

Background checks

Medical examination

Rejection may occur at any of these steps

Employment

work under contract to the Defense Department, FBI, or CIA; pharmaceutical companies handling controlled substances; and security guard services.

Employees, for their part, must be aware of legal restrictions governing their own behavior. For instance, a growing number of communities ban smoking in work places and public areas. Many employers have policies against hiring smokers; some penalize current employees who smoke by charging higher premiums for health insurance and other benefits.

Orientation, Training, and Evaluation

Newly hired employees usually complete an orientation program, which is the joint responsibility of the human resource department and the department in which the person will work. Another major function of the human resource department is developing and maintaining a well-trained, productive labor force. Employee training should be viewed as an ongoing process throughout an employee's tenure with the company.

On-the-job training, in which *employees are trained for job tasks by allowing them to perform them under the guidance of an experienced employee,* is a frequently used method. A variation of this approach is *apprenticeship training,* a program wherein an employee learns a job by serving as an assistant to a trained worker for a relatively long time period. Formal training programs —and particularly apprenticeship programs—are much more common in Europe than in the United States. While U.S. apprenticeship programs currently involve only 200,000 people out of a total work force of almost 120 million, almost 70 percent of Germans enter the work force through apprenticeships. Other differences exist between U.S. and European training approaches. European apprentices start younger (between age 16 and 19, compared

WORKING SMART

You don't have to choose between getting ahead and getting a life.

Working hard to build the life you want. Seeing your dreams and making them happen. At SmithKline Beecham Pharmaceuticals, we call this Working Smart.

With one of the most comprehensive training programs in the industry, SmithKline Beecham Pharmaceuticals will help prepare you to be a successful Professional Sales Representative. Our excellent salary and bonus plan, exceptional benefits, and room to advance all provide you with the incentive to excel.

With the introduction of several new products, we currently have territory openings nationwide. So if you have a college degree, proven success in medical or professional sales, and you're ready to start Working Smart at SmithKline Beecham Pharmaceuticals, send your resume to: P.O. Box 58070, Dept. SW, Philadelphia, PA 19102. We are an Equal Opportunity Employer, M/F/H/V.

SB
SmithKline Beecham
Pharmaceuticals

Pharmaceutical giant SmithKline Beecham features its comprehensive training programs in advertisements seeking applicants for sales careers.

with age 27 in America) and involve many white-collar professions (in contrast to U.S. programs that usually focus on blue-collar trades).[8]

Off-the-job training involves some form of *classroom training,* in which classroom techniques—lectures, conferences, audiovisual aids, programmed instruction, or special machines—are used to teach employees difficult, high-skill jobs. A **management-development program** is *training designed to improve the skills and broaden the knowledge of current and potential managers.* Such programs often are conducted off the company premises. General Motors, Holiday Inn, McDonald's, and Xerox are among the dozens of giant companies that have established college-like institutes that offer specific programs for current potential managers.

Another important human resource management activity, **performance appraisal,** is *the evaluation of an individual's job performance by comparing actual performance with desired performance.* This information is used to make objective decisions about compensation, promotion, additional training needs, transfers, or terminations. Such appraisals are not confined to business. Professors appraise student performance through assignments and examinations, while students appraise instructors by completing written evaluations.

Effective training programs often include both training and performance appraisal. Consider the Hewlett-Packard Interactive Network, which combines a classroom training format with interactive video. H-P instructors present the telecourses in special studios; the information is beamed to Hewlett-Packard offices and factories around the world. Students provide feedback to instructors by speaking into microphones at their desks, or by typing responses into networked computers. Instructors, who have electronic seating charts for each on-line site, provide immediate performance appraisals by polling students; test results can be displayed instantly on computer-generated charts. Since the company began using the interactive network, the cost of new-product seminars has fallen by more than 98 percent. The network is so cost effective that Hewlett-Packard has turned it into a profit-maker by selling the service to other companies.[9]

Employee Compensation

One of the most difficult functions of human resource management is to develop an equitable compensation and benefits system. Because labor costs represent a sizable percentage of total product costs, wages that are too high may result in products that are too expensive to compete effectively in the marketplace. But inadequate wages lead to high employee turnover, poor morale, and inefficient production.

The terms *wages* and *salary* often are used interchangeably, but they do have slightly different meanings. *Wages* represent compensation based on the number of hours worked or the amount of output produced. Wages generally are paid to production employees, retail salespeople, and maintenance workers. *Salary* is employee compensation calculated on a weekly, monthly, or annual basis. White-collar workers, such as office personnel, executives, and professional employees, usually receive salaries.

A satisfactory compensation program should attract well-qualified workers, keep them satisfied in their jobs, and inspire them to produce. The compensation policy of most companies is based on five factors: (1) salaries and wages paid by other companies in the area that compete for the same personnel, (2) government legislation, (3) the cost of living, (4) the ability of the company to pay, and (5) the workers' productivity.

Many employers seek to reward superior performance and motivate employees to excel by offering some type of *incentive compensation*, an addition to a salary or wage given for exceptional performance (see figure). Effective incentive compensation plans reward employees for goals related to quality as well as productivity; ineffective plans can backfire. Robert Rodin, CEO of Marshall Industries, a California-based electronics distributor, admits that his company's old compensation program was counterproductive; he used to reward top performers with cars or trips. Recalls Rodin, "We used to have people shipping ahead of schedule just to make a number or win a prize. In this day of quality, you can imagine our customers were not too happy about getting product early." Today, in addition to their salaries, every Marshall employee earns the same percentage bonus—up to 20 percent of annual salary—based on the firm's profits. While the new compensation plan costs the company 15 percent more than the old one, sales are up $250 million.[10]

FOUR FORMS OF INCENTIVE COMPENSATION

PROFIT SHARING
Bonus based on company profits

GAIN SHARING
Bonus based on surpassing predetermined performance goals

LUMP-SUM BONUS
One-time cash payment based on performance

PAY FOR KNOWLEDGE
Salary increase based on learning new job tasks

These four types of incentive compensation are designed to reward exceptional performance by the individual work team.

Employee Benefits

The typical organization furnishes many benefits to employees and their families besides wages and salaries. **Employee benefits** are *rewards such as pension plans, insurance, sick leave, child care, and tuition reimbursement given at all or part of the expense of the company*. Some benefits are required by law; most employers must contribute to each employee's federal Social Security account. In addition, they make payments to state employment insurance programs that assist laid-off workers and to worker's compensation programs that provide compensation to persons suffering from job-related injuries or illnesses.

One desirable employee benefit is job protection for workers who need emergency time off to care for dependents or for themselves if they are too ill to perform their work. The *Family and Medical Leave Act of 1993* requires covered employers to give up to 12 weeks of unpaid, job-protected leave to eligible employees. The law applies to all public agencies, including state, local, and federal employers and schools.[11]

Other benefits may be provided voluntarily. Examples include health insurance, pensions and retirement programs, paid vacations and leave time, and employee services, such as tuition-reimbursement programs. In 1995, two Marriott hotels in Atlanta joined forces with a local Omni hotel to help solve the 300 percent annual turnover rate among low-income, entry-level employees. They subsidized construction of a round-the-clock child-care and family services center and reserved 80 percent of the slots for low-income employees and their families.[12]

Employee benefits are a large and rapidly growing component of human resource costs. Wages account for only 61 percent of the typical employee's earnings; the other 39 percent takes the form of employee benefits. A major reason why benefit costs have been rising faster than wages and salaries during the past ten years is the soaring cost of medical benefits. Even though employees' vacations and leaves of absence take the biggest chunk of a company's benefits budget, medical costs are increasing much more rapidly.

An increasingly common method of controlling benefits costs is to offer *flexible benefit plans*. This so-called "cafeteria plan" is a system of flexible benefits in which employees are provided with specific dollar amounts of benefits and are allowed to select areas of coverage. They are well-suited for two-income households wanting to avoid duplicate coverage and for single people who do not need a more expensive family insurance plan. Also, their flexible nature permits employees to adjust their benefits packages through various stages of their lives.

A vital employee benefit for all workers is safe working conditions. All employees deserve a safe work place, but every year an estimated 10,000 workers die from on-the-job injuries—about 30 per day. Another 70,000 are disabled permanently from job-related injuries or illnesses. Some of the most dangerous industries are steel, ship-building, logging, construction, and food processing.[13]

Recognition of the importance of a safe work environment led to the creation of the *Occupational Safety and Health Administration (OSHA)*, a federal agency

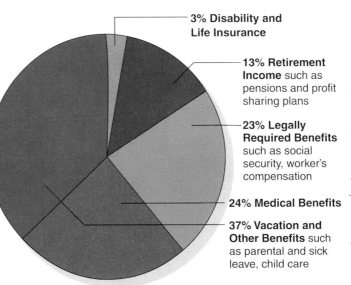

WHERE THE EMPLOYEE BENEFIT DOLLAR GOES

3% Disability and Life Insurance

13% Retirement Income such as pensions and profit sharing plans

23% Legally Required Benefits such as social security, worker's compensation

24% Medical Benefits

37% Vacation and Other Benefits such as parental and sick leave, child care

whose purpose is to assure safe and healthful working conditions for the U.S. labor force. Employers are responsible for knowing and complying with all OSHA standards that apply to their work place. Employees must be informed of their rights and responsibilities under the law.

Job Enrichment

In their search for ways to improve employee productivity and morale, a growing number of firms are focusing on the motivational aspects of the job itself. Rather than simplifying the tasks involved in a job, they seek to enrich the job by making it more satisfying and meaningful. **Job enrichment** involves *redesigning work to give employees more authority in planning their tasks, deciding how the work is to be done, and allowing them to learn related skills or trade jobs with others.*

A recent survey of 77 major companies found that job enrichment plays a crucial role in determining which new products succeed and which did not. Successful product development teams that succeed enjoy full support from top management and are given the authority to manage the project themselves. An example is the team that developed Thermos' popular Thermal Electric Grill that uses a new, clean-burning technology to give food a barbecued taste. According to team member Frederick Mather, "Our reward is that the team owns the project from beginning to end, and that gives us a sense of pride. The real reward is a new product that gets up and flies."[14]

Job enlargement sometimes is used interchangeably with job enrichment, but it differs in that it is merely an expansion of a worker's assignments to include additional, but smaller, tasks. Rather than performing two tasks, a worker might be given four similar tasks. Enlarging a job might lead to job enrichment, but not necessar-

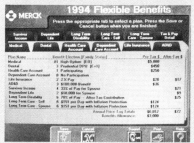

Virtual Personnel

For centuries people have had to adapt to technological changes, from the invention of the wheel to the discovery of electricity and the combustion engine to the proliferation of today's world of computers. In the short run, workers often are left unemployed as machines perform many of the functions previously done by humans. In the long run, the labor force adapts to technological changes and, as new applications are found, new jobs are created.

While most small businesses today still have a person to answer the phone, most medium- and large-sized organizations have changed to computerized telephone systems. More recently, computer technology has moved up the managerial ladder to replace white-collar workers. This new computerized work force is referred to as *virtual personnel.*

U.S. drug giant Merck & Co. began a transition to virtual personnel in its human resource management division back in 1990. At an initial cost of $3 million, Merck converted its universal employee health insurance plan to a flexible package of benefits managed by a new computerized system. Kiosks, resembling automated teller machines with computer screens, were installed, enabling 15,500 headquarter employees to enroll themselves in the plan. Without this system, Merck would have had to double its human resource staff to 40 people.

The project was such a success that Merck invested another $1 million to install 24 more kiosks at each of the firm's 15 U.S. locations. Companywide enrollment took just five weeks and no additional clerical workers were needed.

Employees choose the benefits they want simply by entering their Social Security number and Merck ID number. Since employees can take care of personnel matters themselves, Merck has been able to reassign employees and redesign tasks. Although computers can't counsel employees, they are excellent for routine, programmed clerical tasks.

Plans for new applications are already on the table. The next goal is to merge three systems—payroll, benefits, and personnel records—into one integrated system. This system is expected to save Merck a cool $1.7 million a year.

Virtual personnel will handle many more tasks in the near future. Specialized software soon will allow Merck employees to take care of retirement planning, and the company is considering posting job openings on the system as well.

SOURCE: Carolyn T. Geer, "For a New Job, Press #1," *Forbes,* August 15, 1994, 118–119.

ily. Job enrichment occurs only when the new tasks give an employee greater authority and responsibility for the end result. Enrichment means that employees have more opportunity to be creative and to set their own pace within the limits of the overall schedule.

Flexible Work Schedules

According to a recent study of 7,437 employees, ranging from clerks to managers, the number one stress factor for U.S. workers is time pressure.[15] This helps

Balancing act.

The first computer to understand you don't just have a job. You have a life.

Something fundamental has changed in America. Now it's not just the living you make, it's the life you make. You want to enjoy the things you're supposedly working for. Your family. Your home. Yourself.

At IBM, we know balancing your job with the rest of your life isn't easy. That's why we created the IBM PS/1. A line of computers specially designed to help you do office work at home or run a small business, so you can spend more time with the people you care about most. And if those

people happen to include kids, the IBM PS/1 can help with their homework as easily as yours.

We also know you'd like to improve the quality of your life without compromising on the quality of your computer. So while our new PS/1s are priced to compete with the most affordable computers around, we give you a lot of things no one else can. Like true IBM compatibility. More power than the average office computer, with room to expand. Built-in software and features— including Windows™ or OS/2®—and the ability to

run other popular business and educational software. Not to mention IBM reliability, support and service—not just lip service. And no computer's easier to set up and use.

It may take more than a perfectly balanced computer for you to find that perfect balance in your life. But who knows? You might just do your best work with someone looking over your shoulder.

For a PS/1 retailer near you, call 1 800 IBM-3377.

IBM

IBM, PS/1 and OS/2 are registered trademarks of International Business Machines Corporation. Windows is a trademark of Microsoft Corporation. © 1992 IBM Corp.

New technologies, such as the fax machine, E-mail, and more powerful personal computers make home-based work an increasingly feasible option.

explain why flexible work schedules are a good way for companies to attract and motivate talented employees and enrich their jobs. Flexible schedules include flextime, compressed workweeks, job sharing, and home-based work.

A work-scheduling system that allows employees to set work hours within constraints specified by the firm is called **flextime.** Most employers offering flextime designate certain "core hours" when employees are required to be on the job, such as between 9 A.M. and 3 P.M.[16] Meetings typically are scheduled during these core hours. In general, flextime is more common in insurance, finance, retailing, and government positions than in manufacturing jobs. Its use is more widespread in Europe than it is in the United States; an estimated 40 percent of the work force in Switzerland and 25 percent in Germany have flexible schedules, compared to roughly 12 percent in the United States. Other alternative work-scheduling practices include a *compressed workweek*—where employees work the same number of hours in fewer than the typical five days— and *job sharing*, the division of one job assignment between two or more employees.

More and more companies offer employees a fourth option of **home-based work**—*working the same jobs, but doing the work at home instead of in the*

office. Home-based workers sometimes are called telecommuters because they may "commute" to work electronically by being hooked up via home computer to the company's computer system. Technologies, such as personal computers, electronic mail, and facsimile machines, make working at home easier than ever before.

The number of company employees who work at home rose 15 percent last year to reach 7.6 million. While most home-based workers like the arrangement, some people adapt better than others. At US West Inc., for example, employees who want to become telecommuters must go through a rigorous screening process to make sure they—and their supervisors—will be able to make the arrangement work. Successful telecommuters need to be self-disciplined, reliable, computer literate, and able to do without much supervision; they also need bosses who are comfortable with setting goals and managing from afar.[17]

LABOR–MANAGEMENT RELATIONS

In nations throughout the world, employees have joined together to increase their power to achieve the goals of improved wages, hours, and working condi-

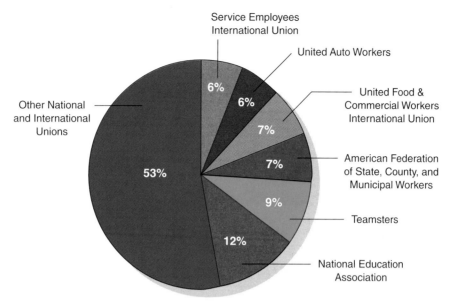

Service Employees
International Union

United Auto Workers

6%

6%

Other National
and International
Unions

United Food &
Commercial Workers
International Union

7%

53%

7%

American Federation
of State, County, and
Municipal Workers

9%

Teamsters

12%

National Education
Association

Almost one in every two U.S. union members belongs to one of the six largest unions.

tions. These efforts have, to a considerable extent, succeeded; today's work place is far different from the one existing at the turn of the century, where child labor, frequently unsafe working conditions, and a 72-hour workweek (six 12-hour days a week) were commonplace.

Today, the people who head organizations that provide necessary goods and services, the people who do the work, and the government organizations that maintain the society comprise the various industrial relationships. With the growing interdependence among nations around the world and the increasing number of multinational corporations, understanding labor–management relations becomes imperative for business students.

Development of Labor Unions

A **labor union** is *a group of workers who have banded together to achieve common goals in the key areas of wages, hours, and working conditions.* Labor unions can be found at the local, national, and international levels. A *local union* represents union members in a specific area, such as a single community, while a *national union* is a labor organization consisting of numerous local chapters. An *international union* is a national union with membership outside the United States, usually in Canada. In the United States, the governing body of most labor unions is the *American Federation of Labor/Congress of Industrial Organizations (AFL/CIO),* a national union made up of affiliated individual unions. The AFL/CIO serves a mediation and political function.

Almost 17 million U.S. workers—15.8 percent of the nation's full-time labor force—belong to labor unions. The 2-million-member National Education Association ranks as the largest union, followed by the Teamsters union with 1.6 million members.

The Collective Bargaining Process

The primary objective of a labor union is the improvement of wages, hours, and working conditions for its members. This goal is achieved primarily through **collective bargaining,** *a process of negotiation between management and union representatives for the purpose of arriving at mutually acceptable wages and working conditions for employees.*

Issues covered in collective bargaining include wages, work hours, benefits, union activities and responsibilities, grievance handling and arbitration, and employee rights and seniority. As is the case in all types of negotiations, the collective bargaining process is one of demands, proposals, and counterproposals that ultimately result in compromise and agreement. The initial demands merely represent a starting point in negotiations. They are rarely, if ever, accepted by the other party without some compromise. The final agreement depends on the negotiating skills and relative power of management and union representatives.

Union contracts, which typically cover a two- or three-year period, are often the result of days and even weeks of discussion, disagreement, compromise, and eventual agreement. Once agreement is reached,

IT'S THE LAW

Government attitudes toward unionism have varied considerably during the past century. These shifting attitudes can be seen in major pieces of legislation enacted during this period.

1932 Norris-La Guardia Act
Protects unions by reducing management's ability to obtain injunctions halting union activities.

1935 National Labor Relations Act (Wagner Act)
Legalizes collective bargaining and requires employers to bargain with their employees' elected representatives.

1938 Fair Labor Standards Act
Outlawed child labor and sets a minimum wage and maximum basic hours for workers employed in industries engaged in interstate commerce.

1947 Labor–Management Relations Act (Taft-Hartley Act)
Prohibits a number of unfair union practices, including requirements that only union members be hired *(closed shop)* and forcing firms to pay for work not done *(featherbedding)*; also permits states to pass *right-to-work laws* prohibiting compulsory union membership.

1959 Landrum-Griffin Act
Requires regularly scheduled elections of union officers by secret ballot and regulates handling of union funds.

1988 Plant-Closing Notification Act
Requires employers to give 60 days' notice before a plant closing or mass layoff.

---

union members must vote to accept or reject the contract. If the contract is rejected, union representatives may resume the bargaining process with management representatives, or union members may strike to obtain their demands.

Once ratified by the union membership, the contract becomes a legally binding agreement for all labor–management relations during the period specified. Some contracts are only a few pages in length, while others can run hundreds of pages.

Settling Union–Management Disputes

Although strikes make newspaper headlines, 95 percent of all union–management negotiations result in a signed agreement without a work stoppage. Approximately 140,000 union contracts are currently in force in the United States. Of these, 133,000 were the result of successful negotiations with no work stoppage. The courts are the most visible and familiar vehicle for dispute settlement, but most disputes are settled by

negotiations. There is real motivation to make negotiations work, since so much time, money, and personnel costs are involved with trial settlements. Dispute resolution mechanisms, such as grievance procedures, mediation, and arbitration, are quicker, cheaper, and less complicated procedurally, and receive less publicity.

The union contract serves as a guide to relations between the firm's management and its employees. The rights of each party are stated in the agreement. But no contract, regardless of how detailed, will eliminate the possibility of disagreement. Such differences can be the beginning of a *grievance*, a complaint—by a single worker or by the entire union—that management is violating some provision of the union contract. Almost all union contracts require that these complaints be submitted to a formal grievance procedure, typically beginning with the employee's supervisor and moving up the company's chain of command. If the highest company officer cannot settle the grievance, it is submitted to an outside party for mediation or arbitration.

Strikes capture the attention of fans, sports-apparel giants, and even the president of the United States.

Mediation is *the process of settling union–management disputes through recommendations of an impartial third party.* Although the mediator does not serve as a decision maker, union and management representatives can be assisted in reaching an agreement by the mediator's suggestions, advice, and compromise solutions.

When disputes cannot be solved voluntarily through mediation, the parties can turn to **arbitration**—*bringing in an impartial third party, called an arbitrator, who renders a legally binding decision.* The arbitrator must be acceptable to the union and to management, and his or her decision is legally enforceable. In essence, the arbitrator acts as a judge, making a decision after listening to both sides of the argument. Ninety percent of all union contracts call for the use of arbitration if union and management representatives fail to reach an agreement.

Weapons of Unions and Management

Although most differences between labor and management are settled through the collective bargaining process or through a formal grievance procedure, both unions and management occasionally resort to weapons of power to make their demands known.

Union Weapons.   The chief weapons of unions are strikes, picketing, and boycotts. The *strike,* or *walkout,* is one of the most effective tools of the labor union. It involves a temporary work stoppage by employees until a dispute has been settled or a contract signed. Although strikes are relatively rare, they do make headlines. Recent examples range from the United Auto Workers strike at Caterpillar to the Major League Baseball strike. Since striking workers are not paid by the company, unions generally establish funds to provide workers' wages, allowing them to continue striking without financial hardships. In the case of the baseball strike, the strike fund came from licensing fees paid by Upper Deck, Topp's, and other firms using the players' likenesses.

Picketing—workers marching at the entrances of the employer's plant as a public protest against some management practice—is another effective form of union pressure. As long as picketing does not involve violence or intimidation, it is protected under the U.S. Constitution as freedom of speech. Picketing may accompany a strike, or it may be a protest against alleged unfair labor practices. Because union workers usually refuse to cross picket lines, the picketed firm may be unable to obtain deliveries and other services. When management at government-owned Air France announced plans to reduce the airline's work force and cut some workers' wages, thousands of Air France employees picketed airports in Paris. The government was forced to back down when the picketing disrupted flights and airport operations.[18]

A *boycott* is an organized attempt to keep the public from purchasing the goods or services of a firm. Some unions have been quite successful in organizing

> **THEY SAID IT**
>
> "You do not lead by hitting people over the head—that's assault, not leadership."
>
> *Dwight D. Eisenhower (1890–1969) 34th president of the United States*

CROSS-FUNCTIONAL ENVIRONMENT

Union Success at Saturn

Saturn began as a General Motors Corp. experiment back in the late 1980s. A task force called the "Group of 99," consisting of 33 managers and 66 union members was assigned the responsibility of designing a car that would be globally competitive in the compact-car market. Today, Saturn is a prime example of what can be achieved when management and employees from diverse functional areas work together.

Everything about Saturn was unusual from the start. GM entrusted the task force with a $3.5 billion budget and a clean slate: They were given no directions on how to design or manufacture the car. Each member of the Group of 99—managers as well as union employees—had an equal voice in the overall assignment.

The task force was divided into smaller work teams responsible for different phases of design or production. Each team studied successful manufacturing and design processes from different businesses around the world. They were free to choose whatever manufacturing process and organizational structure they felt would work best. The final choice was a lean manufacturing operation with an emphasis on teamwork.

Since the early days of mass production, management has controlled factory workers. Not so at Saturn—the workers have complete control. Any Saturn employee can shut down any section of the produc-

tion line to solve a quality problem. No managers are found around the production lines. Work-team representatives, called coaches, coordinate activities with other teams and management.

The team concept is working well for Saturn. Each of the 5,000 employees is involved regularly in managing daily operations and in all strategic decision making. Each team runs its segment of the production line as if it were its own independent business with its own budget and authority to hire fellow team workers.

No personnel department exists at Saturn. Job rotations are determined by work teams. Team members cover for fellow workers who are absent or are out on leave. The team even decides by consensus all personnel matters—management never intervenes.

GM's experiment has proven successful. Employee pride and positive attitudes translate into quality workmanship reflected in the 270,000 new Saturns purchased annually. Last year, 44,000 Saturn owners from across the United States made the trek to Spring Hill, Tennessee, to an annual reunion. Another 100,000 participated in parties and picnics sponsored by local dealers. Even a recent product recall was viewed by customers as a commitment to quality. Thanks to the dedicated employee and management teams, the Saturn dream is now a reality.

SOURCE: John Bissell, "Saturn 'Homecoming': Publicity Stunt or Triumph of Relationship Marketing?" *Brandweek,* August 8, 1994, 18; and Gene Hunt and Don Davis, "Saturn's Brave New World," *Richmond Times-Dispatch,* January 4, 1993, B1.

boycotts, and some unions even fine members who defy a primary boycott.

Management Weapons.   Management also has weapons for dealing with organized labor. In the past, it used the *lockout*—in effect, a management strike to bring pressure on union members by closing the firm. The lockout rarely is used today, unless a union strike has partially shut down a plant.

In recent years, management at organizations ranging from International Paper Company to the National Football League has resorted to replacing striking workers with *strikebreakers,* nonunion workers who cross picket lines to fill the jobs of striking workers. However, management frequently encounters difficulties in securing a sufficient number of replacement workers with the required skills. In some instances, employers have resorted to using supervisory personnel and other nonunion employees to continue operations during a strike.

Management sometimes obtains an *injunction*—a court order prohibiting some practice—to prevent excessive picketing or certain unfair union practices. Injunctions may be used to restrain violence, limit picketing, or prevent damage to company property. Finally, some employers have formed an *employers' association,* a cooperative effort to present a united front in dealing with labor unions.

The Future of Organized Labor

Despite their valuable contributions to working people in nonunion firms as well as organized companies, the future role of labor unions is unclear. Less than two decades ago, over 26 percent of the nation's full-time labor force were union members; today, the union share has fallen to 15.8 percent.[19]

The decline also is occurring in other nations. Unions' share of the work force has dropped from 56 percent to 45 percent in the United Kingdom, from 19 percent to 11 percent in France, and from 31 percent to 25 percent in Japan. Argentina's powerful General Confederation of Workers, which boasted 4 million members 20 years ago, now has split into three factions with a combined total of less than 3 million workers.[20]

Many experts feel that the future of organized labor lies in continuing to build a cooperative relationship with management. The rate of strikes in Great Britain has reached its lowest in over a century. Union workers at Dutch steel maker Hoogovens reached a compromise with managers by agreeing to a wage freeze and early retirement for 600 workers in exchange for job guarantees for the rest. Union members at an Atlanta AT&T facility helped managers design a work-team system that improved phone-repair and quality-control procedures. The new system proved so cost-effective that AT&T moved 100 jobs back to Atlanta from Mexico.[21]

HUMAN RESOURCE CONCERNS FOR THE NEW CENTURY

A number of issues will continue to grow in importance during the remaining years of the twentieth century: adjusting corporate policies to reflect the aging work force, corporate responses to the needs of two-career couples, assisting in breaking the so-called glass ceiling, adjusting to the growing ranks of part-time workers, and managing a more culturally diverse work force.

Older Workers

Along with the aging of the U.S. population is the aging of its work force. The 1960s counterculture slogan "Never trust anyone over 30" is increasingly out of place as the median age approaches 31 and the "over-65s" represent the fastest-growing segment of the population. Federal and state laws prohibit mandatory retirement for most workers, so attempts to reduce company payrolls by eliminating the typically above-average wages and salaries of older, more experienced workers usually involve *financial incentives to encourage voluntary retirement.* These **worker buyout plans** typically include financial packages containing a cash bonus, continuation of such employee benefits as insurance coverage, and higher than normal retirement benefits (to cover the gap between retirement and the onset of Social Security payments).

In addition to reducing company payrolls, worker buyouts may contribute to the morale of remaining workers who see tangible evidence of management's attempts to maintain job security by resorting to a buyout rather than a layoff. Also, unclogging job and promotion opportunities improves the upward mobility of younger employees.

However, business pays a price when it loses older workers. These employees are often the most experienced and knowledgeable, and many employers find that they are simply more effective than less-experienced workers. Some companies reward and retain experienced employees by offering non-financial incentives. Semiconductor manufacturer Intel, for example, copies the faculty practices of many universities by giving its employees an 11-week paid sabbatical every seven years.[22]

Two-Career Households

In 1970, women held only 22 percent of nonclerical white-collar jobs in the United States; today they hold 46 percent. This statistic reflects the increase in two-career households, which have specific job-related needs that must be addressed by employers. These

> **THEY SAID IT**
>
> "The person who knows *how* will always have a job. The person who knows *why* will always be his boss."
>
> Diane Ravitch
> (1938–   )
> American educator

issues frequently arise when a manager, professional staff member, or highly skilled employee is hired from another geographic area. Relocation services for the spouse often are required to attract the new employee. For example, IBM reimburses spouses for up to $500 in job-search expenses. Other firms aid by providing employment leads and financial assistance until the spouse locates a job in the new city.

These services pay off for both employees and employers. Flexible work arrangements, part-time work options, high-quality child care, and parental-leave programs are effective ways for firms to attract, retain, and motivate workers. After Martha Arnold, a business development director at Johnson & Johnson, bore her first child, the company rearranged her schedule and allowed her to work part-time for three years. Today, Arnold is back to working full-time and has been promoted. "If part time hadn't been available, I doubt I would still be with Johnson & Johnson," she says.[23]

An important human resource challenge involves meeting the needs of two-career households when work schedules must change constantly in response to staffing needs. Schedules of employees at Bank of America, for instance, can change monthly based on customer traffic. The bank compensates workers on rotating schedules by increasing their pay and offering expanded referral services for child care and other family-related needs.[24]

The Glass Ceiling

Even though the number of women in professional positions has risen, a recent study shows that women overall hold less than one-third of all managerial jobs. There are even fewer—less than five percent—at the corporate vice-president level.[25]

A U.S. Department of Labor study concluded that it is difficult for women and minorities to advance beyond a certain level within many business organizations. Where this level falls in the corporate hierarchy varies from company to company. It has been coined the **glass ceiling** because it is *an invisible barrier difficult for women and minorities to pass.* "The [corporate] culture is more important than policy," says human resources consultant Rose Jonas. "If the culture doesn't change, nothing will change for women."[26]

The glass ceiling can be broken, however, as shown by the experience of Sara Lee Corp. "We are the largest company in the world named for a woman, a distinction we are proud of," says Chairman John Bryan. "It gives us a little bit of responsibility to be ahead of the curve on women's issues." Since many of the company's customers are women, Bryan notes, he didn't want to have "a bunch of old men sitting around trying to figure out the business." Instead, he set specific targets for hiring women into high-level positions and held managers accountable for meeting those goals. Sara Lee began hiring female managers during the 1980s and has one of the highest percentages of women executives in its industry. Currently, 17 percent of Sara Lee's top 500 managers and 11 percent of its division presidents are women, but Bryan has set new targets. By the year 2000, he wants those figures to be 30 percent and 20 percent, respectively. The women in these positions serve as role models for other employees, according to Judy Sprieser, president of Sara Lee's bakery division. When she tours the company's plants, she says, "Invariably, a woman on the plant line will pull me aside and say, 'We're so excited you're up there.'"[27]

Growing Use of Part-Time Employees

One result of increased automation and downsizing during the 1990s is growth in the number of part-time employees. Sometimes referred to as just-in-time employees, this sector of the U.S. work force has almost tripled since 1970 to

WHERE WOMEN COUNT	
Women as a percentage of officials and managers in major industry categories.	
	% Women
Finance, Insurance, Real Estate	41.4
Services	38.9
Retail Trade	38.5
Transportation, Communication	25.6
Wholesale Trade	20.9
Manufacturing	15.9
Agriculture	14.5
Construction	10.4
Mining	9.8

Women play an even greater role in top management in the 1990s than they did in the past, although they fare better in certain industries, such as finance, insurance, and real estate.

THEY SAID IT

"Why do you think I'm fighting? The glory? The agony of defeat? You show me a man says he ain't fighting for money, I'll show you a fool."

Larry Holmes (1949–) World heavyweight boxing champion, 1978

At Avon, Diversity Has Always Been Our Style.

Our District Sales Managers are wearing makeup from the Avon Tones of Beauty collection. Jewelry by Avon.

For over 100 years, Avon has been a leader in diversity and empowerment – the tools of achievement. We're proud of our strong heritage of commitment to the realization of goals and aspirations. And we're proud to have been honored recently in *Black Enterprise* as one of America's "25 Best Places for Blacks to Work." In this spirit, we salute five of our District Sales

Managers, pictured above. They represent the leadership and entrepreneurism that has inspired thousands of our African-American Representatives to achieve their dreams and fulfill their ambitions. If you're interested in learning more about becoming an Avon Representative or would like to know about our earnings opportunities, just call us toll-free at 1-800-821-0400.

Avon District Sales Managers, pictured left to right: Verna Cox, Philadelphia, PA; Audrey A. Burke, Souk Village, IL; Elisia R. Jorge, Los Angeles, CA; Rhea Jones, Flint, MI; Sylvia Coleman, Atlanta, GA.

AVON

Avon's commitment to diversity and empowerment earned its ranking as one of the 25 best places for African Americans to work.

6.3 million people; internationally, part-time workers in industrialized nations number more than 60 million.[28]

Part-time work today has been created as a result of such management trends as compressed workweeks, job sharing, flextime, and home-based work programs. The need for two-career households and flexibility in the labor force also has contributed to the number of part-time workers. Nationally, the average part-time worker is a 30-year-old woman.

Since part-time wage rates typically are 60 percent of regular full-time wages, companies can reduce their labor costs significantly. Part-time workers usually receive fewer benefits, which reduces yet another major company expense. However, this short-term savings may have negative long-term implications. Overreliance on part-timers may leave the company

without an experienced, well-trained work force, especially in a downsized organization.

Approximately 7,000 temporary work agencies account for 15 percent of all jobs created in the United States. Of these, Milwaukee-based Manpower Inc. is the largest; it is also the world's largest private employer. With over 80,000 employees in 1993, Manpower was responsible for two percent of all new jobs created in the United States.[29]

Managing a Culturally Diverse Work Force

In comparing the current ethnic makeup of our work force with projections for 2050, we discover that the European-American segment of the labor force will decline from 75 percent today to 53 percent by the mid-twenty-first century. The Hispanic population will be the fastest-growing segment of the labor force, more than doubling from 9 percent today to 21 percent in 2050. African Americans will increase to 15 percent from 12 percent today, and Asian Americans will account for 10 percent of the work force in 2050.

What do these numbers mean for managers? Clearly, successful companies will find effective ways to manage and empower this diverse group of workers. Dennis Longstreet faced this challenge when he became president of Ortho Biotech. Says Longstreet, "The first thing you learn is that you can't start a biotechnology company by hiring a bunch of white males from New Jersey. If you want the best people in the field, you're hiring people from universities and small biotech companies—women, Asians, African Americans, very few of whom have ever worked in a corporate environment." Longstreet meets regularly with employee teams called "affinity groups" that allow members of various cultural groups to discuss their concerns. "This isn't about designing a customized approach for every group and every issue," he explains. "It's about listening to people—their problems and their aspirations. . . . Now everything is done in a town-meeting fashion, with them doing most of the talking and me doing most of the listening." Since the affinity group program started, Ortho sales have risen 50 percent, and employee turnover is down by 8 percent.[30]

SUMMARY OF LEARNING GOALS

1. Explain the importance of human resource management and the responsibilities of a human resource department.

Most organizations devote considerable attention to human resource management, which can be defined as (1) the process of acquiring, training, developing, motivating, and appraising a sufficient quantity of qualified employees to perform the activities necessary to accomplish organizational objectives; and (2) developing specific activities and an overall organizational climate to generate maximum worker satisfaction and employee efficiency. A human resource management department is responsible for handling human resource planning, developing job descriptions and job specifications, screening job applicants, developing and administering testing programs, interviewing prospective employees, orienting and training new employees, and administering employee compensation, benefits, and safety programs.

2. List the different needs in Maslow's hierarchy.

Psychologist Abraham Maslow proposed a hierarchy of human needs consisting of physiological needs (food, shelter, clothing), safety needs, social (belongingness) needs, esteem needs, and self-actualization needs. Maslow pointed out that satisfied needs are not motivators.

3. Distinguish among Theory X, Theory Y, and Theory Z managers.

The traditional Theory X manager views workers as being lazy, disliking work, and requiring close and constant supervision. Theory Y assumes employees want to satisfy social, esteem, and self-actualization needs through work as well as through other activities. They emphasize employee self control and self direction. A Theory Z organization is more likely to include long-term employment, shared decision making, relatively slow promotions and evaluations, and varied and non-specialized job assignments. The Theory Z approach emphasizes involved workers as the key to increased productivity and improved quality of work life.

4. Explain how recruitment, selection, orientation, training, and evaluation contribute to placing the right person in a job.

The recruitment and selection process involves locating potential employees, evaluating each application, administering employment tests, arranging for medical examinations, and interviewing. Once hired, the employee completes an orientation program, which is the joint responsibility of the human resource department and the department in which the employee will work. Another major function of the human resource department is developing and maintaining a well-trained, productive labor force. Employee training should be viewed as an ongoing process throughout an employee's tenure with the company. Evaluation is the process of comparing actual performance against desired performance to make objective decisions about compensation, promotion, additional training needs, transfers, or terminations.

5. Explain the concept of job enrichment and how it can motivate employees.

Job enrichment involves redesigning work to give workers more authority in planning their tasks, deciding how the work is to be done, and allowing them to learn related skills or to trade jobs with others. This approach can improve employee productivity and morale by focusing on the motivational aspects of the job itself, and making it more satisfying and meaningful.

6. Outline the different forms of compensation.

A satisfactory compensation program should attract well-qualified workers, keep them satisfied in their jobs, and inspire them to produce. The compensation policy of most companies is based on five factors: (1) salaries and wages paid by other companies in the area that compete for the same personnel, (2) government legislation, (3) the cost of living, (4) the ability of the company to pay, and (5) the workers' productivity. Incentive compensation programs, such as profit sharing, gain sharing, bonuses, or pay-for-knowledge plans, often are added to a salary or wage to reward superior performance and boost employee morale.

7. Summarize the role of labor unions and list their primary goals.

A labor union is a group of workers who have banded together to achieve common goals in the key areas of wages, hours, and working conditions. Labor unions serve an important purpose; workers have learned that, through bargaining as a unified group, they can obtain improvements in working conditions. Union influence has helped to achieve many innovations in business, such as the standard 40-hour workweek, safer working conditions, a guaranteed minimum wage, and the presence of employee-designated members on corporate boards of directors.

8. Outline the sources of power, or "weapons," of labor and management.

Although most differences between labor and management are settled through the collective bargaining process or formal grievance procedures, both unions and management have other ways of making their demands known. The chief weapons of unions are the strike, picketing, and boycotts. Management's weapons are the hiring of strikebreakers, injunctions, lockouts, and employers' associations.

9. Identify and briefly describe each of the major human resource concerns for the twenty-first century.

Current issues in human resource management include: (1) finding cost-effective ways to retain valuable older workers, (2) meeting the needs of two-career households, (3) breaking through the glass ceiling, (4) the growth in part-time employees as a result of increased automation and downsizing, and (5) managing a culturally diverse work force.

KEY TERMS QUIZ

employee benefits   motive   Theory X
morale   human resource management   management-development program
collective bargaining   glass ceiling   flextime
Theory Y   need   mediation
worker buyout plan   Theory Z   arbitration
labor union   job enrichment   home-based work
on-the-job training   performance appraisal

_____ 1. Process of acquiring, training, developing, motivating, and appraising a sufficient quantity of qualified employees to perform necessary activities; and developing activities in an organizational climate conducive to maximum efficiency and worker satisfaction.

_____ 2. The mental attitude of employees toward their employer and job.

_____ 3. Lack of something useful; discrepancy between a desired state and the actual state.

_____ 4. Inner state that directs individuals toward the goal of satisfying a felt need.

_____ 5. Managerial assumption that workers dislike work and must be coerced, controlled, or threatened to motivate them to work.

_____ 6. Managerial assumption that workers like work and, under proper conditions, accept and seek out responsibilities to fulfill their social, esteem, and self-actualization needs.

_____ 7. Management approach emphasizing employee participation as the key to increased productivity and improved quality of work life.

_____ 8. Training employees for job tasks by allowing them to perform them under the guidance of an experienced employee.

_____ 9. Training designed to improve the skills and broaden the knowledge of managers and potential managers.

_____ 10. Defining acceptable employee performance levels, evaluating them, then comparing actual and desired performance to aid in determining training, compensation, promotion, transfers, or terminations.

_____ 11. Employee rewards, such as pension plans, insurance, sick-leave pay, and tuition reimbursement, given at all or part of the expense of the company.

_____ 12. Redesigning work to give employees more authority in planning their tasks, deciding how they are to be done, and allowing them to learn related skills or to trade jobs.

_____ 13. Group of workers united by common goals, such as wages, hours, and working conditions.

_____ 14. Negotiation between management and union representatives concerning wages and working conditions.

_____ 15. Process of settling union-management disputes through recommendations of an impartial third party.

_____ 16. Process of bringing an impartial third party into a union–management dispute to render a legally binding decision.

_____ 17. Work-scheduling system that allows employees to set work hours within constraints specified by the firm.

_____ 18. Program allowing employees to work at home, sometimes linked to their employers by terminals hooked to a central computer.

_____ 19. Financial incentive designed to encourage older employees to retire voluntarily.

_____ 20. Arbitrary barrier that keeps women and minorities from advancing to top management.

OTHER IMPORTANT TERMS

American Federation of Labor (AFL)   burnout   compressed workweek
apprenticeship training   classroom training   Congress of Industrial Organizations (CIO)
boycott   closed shop   employers association

esteem needs	job enlargement	safety needs
Family and Medical Leave Act (1993)	local union	salary
featherbedding	national union	self-actualization needs
flexible benefit plans	Occupational Safety and Health	social (belongingness) needs
grievance	Administration (OSHA)	strike
hiring from within	open shop	strikebreakers
incentive compensation	physiological needs	wages
injunction	picketing	
international union	right-to-work laws	

REVIEW QUESTIONS

1. Explain the primary functions of a human resource department. Which of these responsibilities are most likely to be shared with line departments?
2. Based on Maslow's hierarchy of human needs, which needs are being referred to in the following statements?
   a. "The new General Motors labor agreement will guarantee the jobs of at least 80 percent of all GM workers through 2008."
   b. "This is an entry-level job here at Marx Clothiers, and we pay minimum wage for the first six months."
   c. "We have just organized a company basketball team. Why don't you try out Thursday afternoon right after work?"
   d. "Judy won our Employee of the Month award this month due to her exceptional performance."
   e. "We pay a 20 percent bonus for employees who work the midnight shift."
3. Write brief job scenarios of three people employed in an organization implementing Theory X, Theory Y, and Theory Z management. Relate each of these employees to Maslow's needs hierarchy and list factors that might be used by managers in motivating each employee.
4. Identify several methods of work structuring that should result in job enrichment. Can you think of situations where job-enrichment programs would not be effective? List them and explain your reasoning.
5. Why do many firms follow the policy of hiring from within? What are the problems involved in following such a policy?
6. Compare and contrast the various types of employee-training programs.
7. Distinguish among the major pay-for-performance compensation plans.
8. What is a labor union? List the primary goals of labor unions.
9. Explain the major weapons of unions and management. Describe instances in which each might be used.
10. Why are more firms using part-time workers? Is this trend beneficial or detrimental to U.S. business? Explain your answer.

DISCUSSION QUESTIONS

1. Discuss the issues involved in managing a culturally diverse work force.
2. Consider your most recent (or current) job supervisor. Would you describe this person as a Theory X, Theory Y, or Theory Z manager? Why do you think your boss has adopted this management approach?
3. Discuss the type of compensation plan you would recommend for each of the following:
   a. jewelry repair
   b. retail salesperson
   c. assembly-line worker in an electronics factory
   d. professional athlete
4. Explain why major firms, such as IBM, Sears, Eastman Kodak, and Texas Instruments, operate without unions. Does the provision of job security eliminate the need for unions? Explain your answer.
5. A survey of 2,010 workers performing 23 different jobs conducted by the Institute of Social Research of the University of Michigan gave the following "Most Boring" awards: assembly-line workers, forklift-truck driver, machine tender, and monitor of continuous-flow production. By contrast, these jobs were ranked at the "Least Boring" end of the scale: physician, professor, air traffic controller, and police officer. Identify some common characteristics of each group of jobs that appear to explain their rankings.

VIDEO CASE: Strength In Diversity: Xerox

This video illustrates how this giant corporation recognizes cultural diversity as a competitive advantage. It is included on page 416 of Appendix D.

Solution to Key Terms Quiz

1. human resource management 2. morale 3. need 4. motive 5. Theory X 6. Theory Y 7. Theory Z 8. on-the-job training 9. management-development program 10. performance appraisal 11. employee benefits 12. job enrichment 13. labor union 14. collective bargaining 15. mediation 16. arbitration 17. flextime 18. home-based work 19. worker buyout plan 20. glass ceiling

CHAPTER 9

Teamwork and Communication

Learning Goals

1. Distinguish between the two major types of teams found in organizations.
2. Identify the characteristics of an effective team and the different roles played by team members.
3. Summarize the stages of team development.
4. Relate team cohesiveness and norms to effective team performance.
5. Describe the factors that can cause conflict in teams, and discuss conflict resolution styles.
6. Explain the importance of effective communication skills in business.
7. Compare the different types of communication.
8. Identify and explain several important considerations in international business communication.
9. Summarize important developments in communication technology and how they affect business communication.

The people at Boeing—the world's largest aircraft manufacturer and one of America's leading exporters—are true believers when it comes to the virtues of teamwork. After all, using teams on the new 777 passenger jet project cut the number of engineering hangups by more than half. As Boeing President Philip Condit put it, "Your competitiveness is your ability to use the skills and knowledge of people most effectively, and teams are the best way to do that."

Boeing empowers team members as a means of encouraging them to work together and develop initiative. When the Seattle-based giant set out to design the 777, a massive project involving 10,000 employees and more than 500 suppliers, it created a hierarchy of teams. This structure was designed to pull all of the Boeing work teams together.

The 777 team structure has three layers. At the top is a management team of five or six top managers who are responsible for the plane being built correctly and on time. In the middle is a large group of 50 or so leaders organized in two-person teams and responsible for the 200-plus work teams that have responsibility for specific parts of the plane. These work teams are typically cross-functional groups, each consisting of 5 to 15 workers. Work team examples include the wing team, the flap team, and the tail team.

Communication flows are open within the Boeing team hierarchy, which allows information to move quickly up and down the organization. But management noticed early in the project that information was not moving well horizontally. To correct the problem,

Boeing added a fourth layer of teams called *airplane integration teams*—five groups, each with 12 to 15 people, drawn from the work teams. This layer has access to everyone in the organization. Integration team members also serve as negotiators and arbitrators when necessary to reduce conflicts that sometimes arise among teams in the 777 project.

A few months ago, the integration team was called in to resolve such a conflict after one work team had designed the passengers' oxygen system to be placed in the same spot that a second team had planned to put the gasper, a tiny nozzle that directs fresh air toward the passenger. Within three hours, the three teams had brainstormed an ingenious solution: a special clamp to hold both systems. At the old Boeing, a problem like that probably would not have been caught until the plane was being manufactured.

The contributions of the team approach were obvious in 1994, when the new 777 passenger jet flew its first successful test flight with fewer than half the number of design glitches of earlier programs. The approach is helping Boeing to achieve its goal of a barrier-free enterprise where everyone is working to satisfy the customer.[1]

CHAPTER OVERVIEW

Teamwork was first introduced in Chapter 1 as one of the major business opportunities and challenges of the late 1990s. In Chapter 6, it was discussed as an important component of employee involvement and a means of helping motivate employees to perform their jobs better.

In Chapter 6, we also discussed the contributions of quality circles, groups of employees from the same work area who meet regularly to identify and solve quality-related problems in their area. The matrix organizational structure, a means of blending the expertise of managers and operative employees from finance, engineering, marketing, and other functions to work on specific projects, was described in Chapter 7.

In this chapter, we examine the characteristics of successful teams, discuss sources of team conflict, and explore ways to resolve disagreements that might arise among team members or between teams. We also look at the importance of communication in promoting teamwork, and discuss the factors that facilitate effective communication both inside and outside an organization. Finally, we consider some guidelines for effective international communication and look at the latest developments in communication technology.

TEAMWORK

Being on a team is an important part of growing up. Most of us have joined some type of team—a soccer team, scouts, a debate team, or a drama club—in school. In each case, the purpose of the team either was to perform a certain function or to solve a particular problem. The same holds true for teams in business: Teams are either work teams or problem-solving teams.

As the Boeing experience with the 777 passenger jet project illustrates, employee teams are a growing trend in business, and the ability to work effectively in teams is a more important skill than ever before. A recent survey of the nation's 500 largest corporations found that teamwork is the topic taught most frequently in today's employee training programs.

Some teams, such as the management and work teams at Boeing, work together over an extended period of time. Others collaborate for much shorter periods. For example, CEO Joseph Day of the German–Japanese joint venture Freudenberg-NOK, asks each of his employees to serve on special problem-solving task forces called GROWTTH (Get Rid of Waste Through Team Harmony). Each GROWTTH team spends no more than three days at one of the company's 14 U.S. plants. The task force's assignment is to analyze work processes and make recommendations for improvement. In a typical year, about 40 different teams visit each factory.

Every visit results in several practical suggestions being made and then implemented. Although many deal with relatively small changes, the overall impact of the combined recommendations is significant cost savings and improvements in quality. Says Day, "What we are doing is what any company will have to do to survive a decade from now."[2]

What Is a Team?

As we discussed in Chapter 6, a **team** is *a small number of people with complementary skills who are committed to*

> **THEY SAID IT**
>
> "I get by with a little help from my friends."
>
> *John Lennon (1940–1980) English songwriter and singer*

a common purpose, approach, and set of performance goals. All team members hold themselves mutually responsible and accountable for accomplishing their objectives. Well-known industry examples include:

- *Eastman Chemical,* a Kodak unit that has replaced its senior vice presidents for administration, manufacturing, and research and development in favor of over 1,000 self-directed teams.
- *Motorola,* whose Government Electronics group redesigned its supply-management organization as a process with external customers at the end; team members conduct peer evaluations.
- *Lexmark International,* a former IBM division that replaced 60 percent of its managers in manufacturing and support in favor of cross-functional teams worldwide.
- *Xerox,* which develops new products through multidisciplinary teams. These teams work in a single process, instead of vertical functions or departments.[3]

Teams can be as small as two people, or as large as 75. In practice, however, most teams have fewer than 15 members. What is important is that team members have a common goal and that all of them are working to achieve it.

The benefits from the team approach, coupled with the downsizing of the traditional organizational structure, have produced a virtual rainbow of forms: problem-solving teams, product-development teams, management teams, work teams, quality circles, even *virtual teams* for geographically separated team members who interact via computer. The teams most popular today consist of two species: work teams, which include high-performance self-managed teams, and special-purpose problem-solving teams.

Work Teams and Problem-Solving Teams

The trend in U.S. business toward developing teams began in the 1980s when American management began to address quality concerns in a variety of ways, including forming quality circles in which workers meet weekly or monthly to discuss ways to improve quality. This concept spread like wildfire as such teams demonstrated their ability to help companies cut defects and reduce re-work. By 1987, two-thirds of America's 1,000 largest corporations used these groups. By the mid-1990s, the percentage of major firms using quality circles to solve minor quality problems had declined, primarily due to the fact that the limited scope of activities they focus on typically produces only modest increases in productivity.

THE FIVE SPECIES OF TEAMS

The kingdom of teams can be confusing. Here's a rundown of the most common types.

Virtual Teams
A characteristic of this new type of work team: members talk by computer, flying in and out as needed, and take turns as leader.

Management Teams
Consisting mainly of managers from various functions, like sales and production, this species coordinates work among teams.

Quality Circles
In danger of extinction, this type, typically made of workers and supervisors, meets intermittently to air work-place problems.

Problem-Solving Teams
This most popular of types comprises knowledge workers who gather to solve specific problems and then disband.

Work Teams
An increasingly popular species, work teams do just that—the daily work. When empowered, they are self-managed teams.

The current focus on teams and teamwork has evolved into two basic methods. **Work teams,** used by about two-thirds of U.S. companies, are relatively permanent in nature. They represent a *mid-1990s approach in which small numbers of people with complementary skills perform the day-to-day work of the organization.* A team of Procter & Gamble design engineers with the task of producing a series of new products is an example of a work team. If a work team is empowered with the authority to make decisions about how the daily work gets done, it is described properly as a *self-managed team.* Common tests for a self-managed team are: Can it change the order of tasks? Does it have budgets?

Self-managed teams are most effective when they combine employees with a range of skills and functions. Members are cross-trained to perform each other's jobs as needed. Empowering these teams with the decision-making authority necessary to perform their organizational role usually means permitting them to select fellow team members, spend money, solve problems, evaluate results, and plan future projects.[4]

Thermos' successful Thermal Electric Grill was developed by a self-managed team that included employees from engineering, marketing, manufacturing, and finance. CEO Monte Peterson empowered the team to create a new product that would, as he says, "reinvent the company" by revitalizing its stagnant barbecue-grill sales. Team members took full control of the project, christened themselves the Lifestyle team, and went out into the field to study consumers' cook-out habits. Team leadership rotated according to task priority. When marketing research was most important, the marketing-department representative supervised the group; when it was time to work out the technical design aspects, team leadership shifted to research and development employees.[5]

Problem-solving teams, in contrast, are *temporary combinations of workers who gather to solve a specific problem and then disband.* The special-purpose problem-solving teams differ from quality circles in important ways. Where quality circles are permanent

Thermos' eight-member team developed a new electric grill that, in addition to being cleaner and cheaper than coal- or gas-burning grills, has won four design awards for its beauty and utility.

committees designed to handle whatever work-place problems may arise, problem-solving teams have specific missions that can be broad (find out why customers are not satisfied) or narrow (solve the overheating problem in generator number 4). Once the task is completed, the problem-solving team usually disbands.

Although the *cross-functional team* concept typically is associated with problem-solving teams, individuals from diverse functional backgrounds also can serve as members of more permanent work-team arrangements. Such teams made major contributions to the development of Boeing's 777 wide-bodied jet. Boeing engineers, marketers, and mechanics worked with representatives from key suppliers and customers to ensure that the final product provided optimum value and customer satisfaction. This practical input from Boeing employees, suppliers, and potential purchasers resulted in the creation of an airplane that was unprecedented in its ease of operation, repair, and maintenance.[6]

TEAM CHARACTERISTICS

Teams are capable of increasing productivity, raising morale, and nurturing innovation. However, these benefits result only if the right type of team is chosen for the task to be accomplished. Companies such as DEC, America's second largest computer maker; Nynex, the Baby Bell for New York and New England; and Boeing, the world's largest aircraft manufacturer, all have used teams successfully. Not only is the right type of team necessary, the right people must be on the team. It is important to note that, while 680 of the nation's 1,000 largest companies currently use work teams, only ten percent of the people who work at these firms are on such teams.

Teams consume time, energy, and money. They must, therefore, be formed carefully with several factors in mind. The most important of these factors is to choose the right type of team to accomplish the objective. To be effective, team members should receive training support, strong communication links, and specifics about the jobs they must perform. One major pitfall for many companies using teams is their tendency to create teams when they are not really needed. Some people are better left to work alone and some tasks can be better accomplished by individuals. Before a team is formed, management should analyze the work to be done, decide whether a team approach is preferable, and then select the best type of team.

Effective teams share a number of characteristics. Three of the most important are the size of the team, the roles played by its members, and its diversity.

Team Size

Is there an ideal size for a team? Effective teams can have anywhere from 5 to 12 members, but many proponents of teams believe the ideal size is about 7 people. Groups of this size are big enough to benefit from a variety of diverse skills, yet small enough that members can communicate easily and feel part of a close-knit entity.

Rubbermaid organizes its home-products division into teams of five to seven people, one each from manufacturing, research and development, finance, marketing, and other departments. Each team focuses on a particular product line, such as bathroom accessories. The team approach works so well that Rubbermaid's introduction of new products averages one a day, 90 percent of which achieve their target sales.[7]

While teams smaller and larger than this size also can be effective, they create certain challenges for a team leader. Participants in small teams (two to four members) want to get along with each other, tend to be informal, discuss more personal topics, and make fewer demands on team leaders. Large groups with more than 12 members are a greater challenge for team leaders since decision making becomes more centralized and participants may feel less committed to team goals. Large teams also tend to have more disagreements, absenteeism, and membership turnover. Subgroups may form, leading to possible conflicts among various factions. As a general rule, teams

of more than 20 people should be divided into sub-teams, with each of these smaller groups having its own members and goals.

Team Roles

Over time, team members tend to play certain roles, which can be classified as task specialist or socio-emotional. People who assume the **task specialist role** *devote time and energy to helping the team accomplish its goals.* These are the group members who are active in proposing new solutions, evaluating the suggestions of others, and asking for more information. They may bring up new ideas, summarize the discussion so far, and attempt to energize the group when interest drops. Team members who play a **socio-emotional role** *devote their time and energy to providing support for group members' emotional needs and social unity.* They encourage others to contribute ideas, and they may change their own opinions in order to maintain team harmony. They attempt to reduce group tensions and reconcile conflicts.

Some team members may play a *dual role,* in which they contribute to the team's task and support members' emotional needs at the same time. Those able to assume a dual role may become team leaders because they satisfy both types of needs. And, finally, some people may fall into a *nonparticipator role,* in which they contribute little to either the task or to members' socio-emotional needs.

The challenge for managers is to ensure that teams are balanced with members capable of performing each type of role. Both the task specialist and socio-emotional roles are important, and too much of either type can impair a group's ability to function. Teams filled with task specialists may be productive in the short term but unsatisfying over a longer time period, since team members may become unsupportive and will not convey enough personal concern for each other. Teams filled with socio-emotional types can be satisfying but unproductive, since participants may hesitate to disagree or to criticize each other.[8]

TEAM MEMBER ROLES

TASK SPECIALIST
Devotes time and energy to accomplishing team goals

SOCIO-EMOTIONAL
Devotes time and energy to encourage team harmony

DUAL
Devotes time and energy to task accomplishment and supporting team members' emotional needs

NONPARTICIPATIVE
Makes minimal contributions to either tasks or team members' socio-emotional needs

The Value of Diversity

Several years ago, CEO Ernest Drew of chemical giant Hoechst Celanese organized a conference to analyze the company's corporate culture and suggest ways to change it to improve performance. Attending the conference were the firm's top 125 officers, most of them white males, and 50 women and minorities from the ranks of middle management. The group divided into small problem-solving teams. Some groups were mixed by race and gender, while others consisted almost entirely of Caucasian males. When the teams presented their findings, says Drew, "It was so obvious that the diverse teams had the broader solutions. They had ideas I hadn't even thought of. For the first time, we realized that diversity is a strength as it relates to problem solving. Now we knew we needed diversity at every level of the company where decisions are made."[9]

Several research studies have confirmed Drew's conclusion. At the University of North Texas, for example, the work of culturally diverse teams of business students was compared to that of all-white teams over a period of 17 weeks. By the end of the study, the heterogeneous teams displayed a broader range of viewpoints and produced more innovative solutions to problems than the homogeneous teams.

Since that conference, Hoechst has intensified efforts to hire and train qualified employees regardless of their cultural affiliation. The chemical giant's polyester textile filament division is an example of team success. The division had lost money for 18 years straight, until, in desperation, Drew placed it under the control of a diverse group of managers. Previously the division had concentrated on commodity production, but the new management team decided to target niche markets, such as automotive upholstery shops. They also found ways to improve quality while cutting costs. These days the division is highly profitable, as William Harris, head of worldwide fibers points out: "We tried everything for so many years, but the business did not perform better until we had a diverse management group."[10]

TEAM PROCESSES

Should all companies organize their employees as teams? Actually, no. Not all firms are suited to the team format. Furthermore, while some departments within an organization may thrive using the team con-

cept, others may not. "Teams are great, but some work needs to be accomplished solo," says Kathleen Emery, vice president of the consulting firm Designed Learning Inc. "Be selective. When work makes sense to be done in teams, then do it; when it doesn't, don't. Teams aren't the answer to every situation."[11]

Furthermore, a study of 45 team projects at a dozen major U.S. companies found that certain types of teams are more effective than others, depending on the goal of a particular project. A cross-functional team can be an effective way to develop an entirely new good or service. However, a vertical team from a single department, such as product engineering, may be a better choice if the goal simply is to modify an existing product. Since it takes time for members of cross-functional teams to establish their roles and begin working together productively, such delays could allow a competitor's modifications to reach the market faster.

If management decides to use a team approach, the first step should be to agree on precisely what they want to accomplish. The focus then should move to identifying customer needs and the best ways to achieve customer satisfaction. Management should meet with all employees who are associated with a particular facet of the project to discuss team goals and the best ways to do the work. This may involve restructuring some jobs and cross-training employees to perform more than one task.[12]

Managers can increase the likelihood of forming effective work teams by using a systematic approach. Such an approach (see figure) begins with analyses of successful teams in other organizations and includes team-member involvement in planning and implementation accompanied by built-in flexibility and a willingness to modify plans when necessary. Note that the final step relates to determining an appropriate compensation plan for team members. This can be difficult, since compensation must motivate individual team members while still encouraging them to act as a team. Managers should devote considerable time in selecting the best ways to reward individual achievements and added responsibilities.

A frequently used approach is to give team members a chance to provide input on compensation issues and perhaps make the final decision themselves. Management should avoid using individual incentive programs, such as contests and personal bonuses, since they foster competition rather than cooperation within groups. "Don't set up a reward system that acknowledges individual achievement at the expense of the team," suggests consultant Ron Johnson.[13]

> **THEY SAID IT**
>
> "I didn't say that I didn't say it. I said that I didn't say that I said it. I want to make that very clear."
>
> *George Romney (1907–   ) American industrialist and governor of Michigan*

Stages of Team Development

Once a manager has formed a team, the group goes through five stages of development: forming, storming, norming, performing, and adjourning.

The first stage, *forming*, is an orientation period during which team members get to know each other and find out which behaviors are acceptable to the group. During this early phase, team members are curious about what is expected of them and whether they will fit in. An effective team leader provides time for participants to become acquainted and converse informally.

During the next phase, *storming*, participants' individual personalities begin to emerge as they clarify their roles and expectations. Conflicts may arise as people disagree over the team's mission and jockey for position and control of the group. Subgroups may form based on common interests or concerns. At this stage, it is important that the team leader encourage everyone to participate, allowing them to work through their uncertainties and conflicts. Teams must move beyond this stage in order to become truly productive.

As teams move on, they enter the *norming* stage. Differences are resolved, members accept each other, and consensus is reached about the roles of the team leader and other participants. The norming stage is usually brief, and the team leader should use it to emphasize the team's unity and the importance of its objectives.

1. Study other companies' teams that have successfully met challenges similar to yours.

2. In the planning and implementation process, include appropriate union members, employee representatives, and all team members.

3. Seek and encourage feedback from all participants throughout the process.

4. Set realistic deadlines and distribute training and implementation schedules to team members, management, and others affected by the new system.

5. Be prepared to slow down if the process becomes overly complicated.

6. Regularly evaluate the original plan and make adjustments if necessary.

7. Keep everyone informed of all developments throughout the process.

8. Be prepared to handle team fears, anger, confusion, and resistance.

9. Develop a plan to address compensation issues such as how individual achievement will be acknowledged, how added responsibilities will be reflected in a team member's pay, and how company profits from the project will be shared with team members.

NINE STEPS TO BETTER WORK TEAMS

Next comes the *performing* stage. This phase is characterized by problem solving and a focus on task accomplishment. At this point, team members interact frequently and handle any conflicts constructively. The team leader focuses on task performance and encourages both socio-emotional team members and task specialists to contribute.

The *adjourning* stage occurs as groups disband following completion of a task. During this phase, the focus is on wrapping up and summarizing the team's experience and accomplishments. The team leader may recognize participants' contributions with some type of ritual, perhaps by handing out plaques or awards.[14]

Team Cohesiveness

Teams tend to be most productive when they are highly cohesive. **Team cohesiveness** is *the extent to which team members are attracted to the team and motivated to remain a part of it.* This cohesiveness typically increases when members interact frequently, share common attitudes and goals, and enjoy being together. When cohesiveness is low, morale suffers.

Managers at GM's Saturn Corp. are learning first hand the importance of team cohesiveness. Saturn workers, organized into teams that handle a variety of tasks, enjoy an unusual level of control over operations at the firm's Spring Hill, Tennessee, assembly plant. When the Saturn program first began, these teams were highly cohesive. One reason was that many new hires shared a common interest in becoming part of the Saturn experiment. Another was the company's extensive training program. All new workers received up to 700 hours of training in such team-building skills as conflict management and communication.

Recently, in an effort to cut costs, managers reduced new-employee training to 175 hours, and refocused the training emphasis on job-specific tasks rather than interpersonal skills. Furthermore, a new union agreement commits management to limit new hires to GM workers who have been laid off from other plants. Many of these applicants are less committed to the team concept. "These folks are tougher to integrate into Saturn," admits human resource management chief

Timothy Epps. The resulting tensions have resulted in occasional conflicts among employees and their union representatives, which in turn have led to lower team cohesiveness.[15]

Team Norms

A **team norm** is *a standard of conduct that is shared by team members and guides their behavior.* Norms are not formal, written guidelines; they are informal standards that identify key values and clarify team members' expectations.

In the Saturn project, conflicts among employees reflect differing norms. The original Saturn workers were attracted to the company by the promise of greater cooperation with management and a larger role in running the factory. Many of them share a view of Saturn as a great experiment in labor–management relations. As one assembly worker put it, "We are the future of the American car industry, if it has a future." Opposing this norm is the belief, held by some new hires who had been laid off at other GM plants, that Saturn's labor leaders are allied too closely with its management. While most Saturn employees continue to support the company's innovative labor system, a growing minority—29 percent in a recent

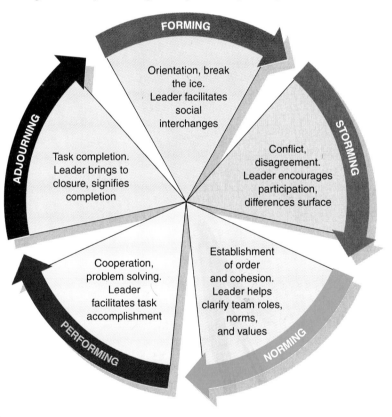

Five stages of team development

TECHNOLOGY

Fax Machines

In their continuing effort to improve communications, a growing number of both giant and tiny firms are expanding their use of the fax machine. Invented over 60 years ago, the fax (short for *facsimile*) machine has experienced widespread acceptance just over the past decade. But, as the chart shows, the advantages of this technology are so significant that even sales of fax machines for home use have exploded since 1989.

As a result of its efficiency, the fax machine's role has expanded beyond a method for mailing a document rapidly. In fact, many firms have begun to use the fax as a primary means of communicating within the company, communicating with clients, and receiving orders from customers.

Toronto-based Technology Partners Inc. developed TravelFax, an automated system for booking travel reservations in conjunction with the Sabre Travel Information Network. The traveler simply faxes a travel-request form, which is automatically processed, and the confirmation then is faxed back to the customer.

Although reaching out to customers and associates via fax is efficient, a persistent problem with fax communication has been increasing cost. In companies that send thousands of faxes a week, the time required to operate the machine becomes costly.

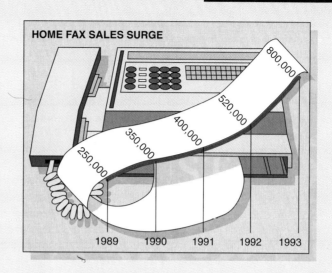

HOME FAX SALES SURGE

250,000 350,000 400,000 520,000 800,000

1989   1990   1991   1992   1993

Until recently, many businesses have relied on third parties to handle their large-scale faxing, costing thousands of dollars. Many firms now use computerized fax services rather than the typical stand-alone fax machines.

Employees of food importer Vie de France Corp., of McLean, Virginia, previously spent 40 hours a week faxing price quotes to its 250 restaurant clients. However, with the installation of a $3,000 local-area network fax server, the orders can be faxed automatically during the evening hours, thus eliminating wasted employee time.

Once considered a separate device, many PCs now are equipped with faxing capabilities. Intel's SatisFAXtion allows the user to fax docu-

ments independently of other work being done on the same computer. These improvements in faxing are resulting in an overall increase in the use of the fax machine for ordinary business communications. At Chemical Bank in New York, a single PC faxes information to 300 separate branch offices.

SOURCES: Rick Fairlie, "Technology Partners Promise Quality Control, Agentless Booking," *Travel Weekly,* September 23, 1993, 26–27; and "25 Breakthroughs that Are Changing the Way We Live and Work," *U.S. News & World Report,* May 2, 1994, 52, 56. Home fax sales figure reprinted from "Home Fax Sales Surge," *USA Today,* August 18, 1994, B1. Copyright 1994, USA Today. Reprinted by permission.

election—support a shift to a more traditional approach.[16]

TEAM CONFLICT

Of all the skills that a team leader must possess, none is more important than the ability to manage conflict. **Conflict** is an *antagonistic interaction in which one party attempts to thwart the intentions or goals of another.* A certain amount of conflict is inevitable in teams, but too much can impair the ability of team members to

exchange ideas, cooperate with each other, and produce results.

Causes of Conflict

Conflict can stem from many sources. It frequently results from competition for scarce resources, such as information, money, or supplies. In addition, team members may have personality clashes, or conflicting ideas about what the team should accomplish. Poor communication also can cause misunderstandings and resentment. Finally, conflict can result when job responsibilities or team roles are unclear.

If not managed properly and promptly, conflict can even destroy a company. Art Nevill founded Refuse Compactor in 1970 and, over the next 20 years, built the company to $7 million in annual sales. However, conflict developed between Nevill and his employees over compensation. Nevill awarded raises to employees he felt worked the hardest. When their coworkers asked for comparable raises, he recalls, "I told them to hustle more. You make me more money, you'll make more money. I'm not about to give raises to people who say, 'Pay me more money or I won't work hard.' That's not American." Nevill felt his system would motivate employees to work harder, but the employees thought he was being unfair. They voted to join a labor union, which presented Nevill with a list of demands. While the union members believed they were fighting for their lawful rights, Nevill perceived the move as an attempt to take control of his company. When he refused their demands, the workers went on strike. The strike dragged on as both sides refused to back down. Eventually, most of the strikers were forced to find other jobs, many of which paid less than their original jobs. Meanwhile, the company's sales fell dramatically. This unresolved conflict brought Refuse Compactor to the brink of bankruptcy.[17]

Styles of Conflict Resolution

Conflict resolution styles represent a continuum, ranging from assertive to cooperative. There is no one best way to manage conflict. The most effective resolution style varies according to the particular situation. Resolution styles include:

- *The Competing Style.* A decisive, assertive approach that might be expressed as, "We'll do this my way." While it does not build team rapport, the competing style can be useful for unpopular decisions or emergencies. It did not work for Art Nevill's situation, however; when he refused to consider employees' demands, he precipitated a strike.
- *The Avoiding Style.* Neither assertive nor cooperative, the avoiding style is most effective when the cause of conflict is trivial or a no-win situation, when more information is needed, or when open conflict would be harmful.
- *The Compromising Style.* A moderate degree of both assertiveness and cooperativeness, this approach works well when two opposing goals are equally important, when combatants are equally powerful, or when there is pressure to achieve some sort of immediate solution.
- *The Accommodating Style.* A high degree of cooperativeness is involved in this style, which can help maintain team harmony. A team member may choose to back down if an issue is more important to others in the group.
- *The Collaborating Style.* A high degree of both assertiveness and cooperativeness characterizes the collaborating style. While this approach can be time-consuming and require lengthy negotiation, it can achieve a win–win situation. It is useful when consensus from all parties is important, or when the viewpoints of all participants must be merged into a mutually acceptable solution.

A team leader can reduce the disruptive impact of conflict by focusing team members on broad goals that go beyond the immediate sources of disagreement. When Thermos CEO Peterson first organized the electric grill group, some participants resisted the idea of working in teams. Peterson dealt with their objections by emphasizing the importance of the project to Thermos' long-term success. "Like a politician, you provide a platform for change and then paint a picture of the difference between winning and losing," he says. "After that, the old barriers break down, and teamwork becomes infectious."[18]

When conflict results from ambiguous or overlapping responsibilities, a team leader can handle it by clarifying participants' respective tasks and areas of authority. The leader may encourage the opponents to negotiate an agreement. This works well if they are able to deal with the situation in a businesslike, unemotional way. Stubborn disagreements may be turned over to a mediator, an outside party who will discuss the situation with both sides and make a decision. As we saw in Chapter 8, disputes between labor unions and management often are resolved through mediation.

Peterson had to act as an informal mediator several times during the development of the electric grill. At one point, the team reached an impasse over price. While the finance and research and development team members insisted it should be priced at $299, members from the marketing department argued that this was too expensive to sell at discount chains like Kmart and Target. Finally, Peterson settled the argument by saying, "Give me a reason why

> **THEY SAID IT**
>
> "If I went back to college again, I'd concentrate on two areas: learning to write and to speak before an audience. Nothing in life is more important than the ability to communicate effectively."
>
> *Gerald R. Ford (1913–) 38th president of the United States*

you *can't* sell it at that price level." When the dissenters were unable to come up with a reason, the $299 price became official.[19]

Perhaps the team leader's most important contribution to conflict resolution is to facilitate good communication. Ongoing communication ensures that team members perceive each other accurately, understand what is expected of them, and obtain the information they need. The better they communicate, the more likely they are to work cooperatively as a team. In the remainder of this chapter, we will discuss the importance of effective communication and will look at how good communication skills promote success, both inside and outside the organization.

THE IMPORTANCE OF EFFECTIVE COMMUNICATION

Communication can be defined as *the meaningful exchange of information through messages*, and it is essential to business. Managers, for example, spend 80 percent of their time in direct communication with others, whether on the phone, in meetings, or in conversation. The other 20 percent is spent on desk work, much of which is also communication in the form of writing and reading.

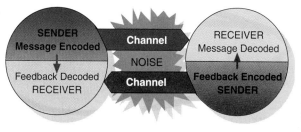

Communication skills are just as important for other business people as well. Consider a few examples. Communication with the marketplace, in the form of market research, helps a company learn what products people want and what changes to make in existing goods and services. Communication among engineers, marketers, and production workers enables a company to create products providing customer satisfaction, while communication through advertising and personal sales presentations creates a favorable image for the company and persuades customers to buy.

Every communication follows a step-by-step process that can be thought of as an interaction among six elements: sender, message, channel, audience, feedback, and context (see figure). First, the *sender* composes the *message* and sends it through a communication carrier, or *channel*. *Encoding* is the translation of a message into understandable terms and in a form capable of being transmitted through the communication medium selected by the sender. There are many channels to choose from, including written messages, face-to-face conversations, and electronic mail. The *audience* consists of the person or persons who receive the message and interpret its meaning. *Decoding* is the receiver's interpretation of the message. *Feedback* from the audience—a response to the sender's communication—helps the sender determine whether the message was interpreted correctly. Every communication takes place in some sort of situational and cultural *context*. The context can exert a powerful influence on how well the process works. A conversation between two people in a quiet room, for example, may be a very different experience from the same conversation held outdoors, on a freezing cold day, next to a noisy construction site.

Senders need to pay attention to audience feedback, even solicit it if it is not forthcoming, since this response clarifies whether their message was perceived in the way they intended. Even with the best of intentions, sender and audience can misunderstand each other. A major aircraft company announced a ten percent pay reduction by means of individual letters to its employees signed by the president. The immediate effect was the opposite of what was expected. Employees greeted the message with amusement rather than disappointment: It had arrived at each employee's desk on April Fool's Day! Unfortunately, the company had to provide official verification to establish the true meaning—a pay cut.

Basic Forms of Communication

People communicate in many different ways. Some methods—calling a meeting of team members or writing a formal mission statement—are obvious. Others, ranging from gestures and facial expressions during a conversation to leaning forward when speaking to someone, are much less obvious, even though they can impact significantly the message being communicated. It is convenient to discuss communication based on the following forms: oral and written, formal and informal, verbal and nonverbal.

Oral Communication   As we saw earlier, managers spend a great deal of their time communicating orally, whether in person or on the phone. Some business people prefer to communicate this way, feeling that oral channels allow them to convey their true message more accurately. A vital component of oral

Forms of Communication

Form	Description	Example
Oral communication	Communication transmitted through speech	Personal conversations, speeches, meetings, voice mail, telephone conversations, videoconferences
Written communication	Communication transmitted through writing	Letters, memos, formal reports, news releases, e-mail, faxes
Formal communication	Communication transmitted through the chain of command within an organization to other members or to persons outside the organization	Internal—memos, reports, meetings, written proposals, oral presentations, meeting minutes; and external—letters, written proposals, oral presentations, speeches, news releases, press conferences
Informal communication	Communication transmitted outside formally authorized channels without regard for the organization's hierarchy of authority	Rumors spread through "the grapevine"
Verbal communication	Transmission of messages in the form of words	Meetings, telephone calls, voice mail, videoconferences
Nonverbal communication	Communication transmitted through actions and behaviors rather than through words	Gestures, facial expressions, posture, body language, dress, makeup

From gestures and body language to formal reports, communication transmits messages through an array of different channels.

communication is **listening,** *the skill of receiving a message and interpreting its genuine meaning by accurately grasping the facts and feelings conveyed.* While listening is the first communication skill we learn in life and the one we use most often, it is also the one in which we receive the least formal training.

It is tempting to think that listening is easy—after all, it seems to require no effort. This is deceptive, however. While the average person talks at a rate of roughly 150 words per minute, the brain can handle up to 400 words per minute. This discrepancy can lead to boredom, inattention, and misinterpretation. In fact, immediately after listening to a message, the average person can recall only half of it. Several days later, the percentage of the message that can be recalled falls to 25 percent or less.

Noise, interference with messages being transmitted, can occur as a result of physical factors—poor reception of a radio message or misunderstanding a conversation with a co-worker. In other instances, misinterpretations produce faulty communication. Insurance companies, such as Metropolitan, study auto accident-claim data in an attempt to spot problem areas and adjust coverage costs accordingly. Such data provide expected reasons for car accidents—excessive speed, alcohol, equipment malfunction, and inattentiveness,

among others. As the bulletin board shown below reveals, some explanations are bizarre.

Certain types of listening behaviors are common in both business and personal interaction. They include:

- *Cynical listening.* Defensive listening that occurs when recipients of a message feel its goal is to take advantage of them.
- *Offensive listening.* Listening to catch the speaker in a mistake or contradiction.

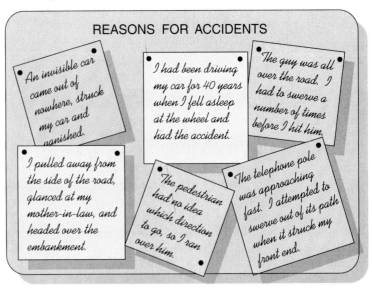

REASONS FOR ACCIDENTS

An invisible car came out of nowhere, struck my car and vanished.

I had been driving my car for 40 years when I fell asleep at the wheel and had the accident.

The guy was all over the road. I had to swerve a number of times before I hit him.

I pulled away from the side of the road, glanced at my mother-in-law, and headed over the embankment.

The pedestrian had no idea which direction to go, so I ran over him.

The telephone pole was approaching fast. I attempted to swerve out of its path when it struck my front end.

- *Polite listening.* Mechanical listening done to be polite rather than to communicate. Polite listeners are usually inattentive and spend their time rehearsing what they want to say when the speaker finishes. Former major-league baseball player Tom Paciorek was referring to this type of listening when he defined boredom as "having to listen to someone talk about himself when I want to talk about me."[20]

- *Active listening.* A form of listening that requires involvement with the information and empathy with the speaker's situation. In both business and personal life, active listening is the basis for effective communication.

> **THEY SAID IT**
>
> "My father gave me these hints on speech-making: Be sincere . . . be brief . . . be seated."
>
> *James Roosevelt (1907–) Son of President Franklin D. Roosevelt, business executive and politician*

Written Communication Effective written communication reflects its audience, the channel being used, and the degree of formality that is appropriate. When writing a formal business document, such as a complex report or an important letter, it is important to plan in advance and construct the document carefully. The process of writing a formal document can be divided into five stages: planning, research, organization, composition and design, and revision.

Written communication via electronic mail and computer networks may call for a less formal writing style. "The medium favors the terse," says Crawford Kilian, a writing teacher at Canada's Capilano College. "Short paragraphs, bulleted lists and one-liners are the units of thought here." Electronic writers often communicate through a combination of words, acronyms, and *emoticons,* little faces called "smileys" that are constructed with punctuation marks conveying some of the message's emotional content (see figure on the next page). While electronic mail may be more informal, it is still important to write well. "It's so competitive that you have to work on your style if you want to make any impact," says software designer Jorn Barger.[21]

Formal Communication Communication that follows a company's official organization chart reflects **formal communication channels,** *messages that flow within the chain of command or task responsibility defined by an organization.* The most familiar is probably *downward communication,* which occurs when someone who holds a senior position in the organization communicates with subordinates. Managers, for example, may communicate downward via electronic mail, formal presentations, policy manuals, notices posted on bulletin boards, and reports printed in company newsletters.

Written Communication: A Five-Stage Approach	
Stage	**Description**
Planning	Writer determines the objective of the document, assesses the audience's needs and current knowledge about the topic, and decides the best way to write the document. Although thorough planning takes time, it saves time in the long run by helping the writer focus on what really has to be communicated.
Research	Writer investigates the subject systematically to discover relevant facts, opinions, and beliefs. The amount of research needed depends on the nature of the document and the amount of information available. A simple memo often requires little or no research; a long report may call for extensive preparation.
Organization	Writer determines sequence in which ideas will be presented and the logical connections between those ideas. These choices will determine the format and overall approach of the document. Two often-used alternative approaches include showing a series of causes and effects or identifying a problem and then proposing a solution. The organization of the document should reflect the chosen alternative.
Composition and design	Writer composes a rough draft of the document. Draft will reflect decisions made about tone, writing style, and level of formality. Design issues involve decisions regarding how best to arrange information on the page and what design is more readable for the document's intended audience.
Revision	Through a series of revisions, the writer transforms the rough draft into a finished document. This stage includes assessing the document's wording, clarity, and readability; eliminating any errors; and rewriting as necessary. The writer also may decide to incorporate suggestions from other people, perhaps supervisors or co-workers, into the final draft.

The systematic five-step approach is a logical progression of the steps involved in converting an idea into a polished document.

EMOTICONS	
:-)	sarcastic; "Don't hit me for what I just said."
:-(	depressed or upset by a remark
:-I	indifferent
>:->	devilishly sarcastic
;-)	winking at a suggestive remark
:-7	wry
:-/	skeptical
:-&	tongue-tied
:-P	sticking out tongue
:-[	sour
:-D	laughing at someone
:-@	screaming
:[)	drunk
X-)	dead
+-:-)	a priest or minister
0:-)	like an angel
c=:-)	a chef
[:o)	a clown
:-Q	a smoker
:-?	a pipe smoker
:-E	a vampire
8-)	wearing sunglasses
::-)	wearing normal glasses
:-#	wearing braces
:-{}	wearing lipstick
(-:	left-handed

Writers on Internet, an international computer network, described in Chapter 1, use a variety of emoticons, or "smileys," in their messages. Note how much they resemble a face when you look at them sideways.

Informal Communication Informal communication channels *exist outside formally authorized channels without regard for the organization's hierarchy of authority.* A familiar example of an informal channel is the **grapevine,** *an internal information channel that conducts information through unofficial, independent sources.* Research shows that many employees cite the grapevine as their most frequent source of information. Grapevines are rapid disseminators of information. While a message sent through formal channels may take days to reach its audience, messages that travel via grapevines can arrive within hours. Grapevines also are surprisingly reliable. They pass on accurate information 75 to 96 percent of the time. However, even a tiny inaccuracy can distort an entire message.

At Quantum Health Resources, which provides medicines and services for people with chronic dis-eases, CEO Douglas Tickney uses informal communication channels to foster creativity. Tickney encourages employees to brainstorm during casual, impromptu get-togethers. "It's those Monday mornings or Friday afternoons—that's when you really need to create an atmosphere where people can say, 'Why aren't we thinking about going into thrombosis?' An idea like that might not come out during a formal planning meeting."[22]

Verbal and Nonverbal Communication So far, we have been considering different forms of verbal communication: communication that conveys meaning through words. Perhaps of equal importance is **nonverbal communication,** *communication that is transmitted through actions and behaviors.* Gestures, posture, eye contact, tone of voice, even the clothing we wear—all of these are nonverbal communication cues. Nonverbal cues become important during oral communication since they can distort the intended meaning of a message.

Nonverbal cues can have a far greater impact on our ability to communicate than we realize. One study, for instance, divided face-to-face conversations into three sources of communication cues: verbal (the actual words spoken), vocal (pitch, tone, and timbre of a person's voice), and facial expressions. The researchers found that the relative weights of these factors in message interpretation were as follows: verbal (7 percent), vocal (38 percent), and facial expressions (55 percent).

Even personal space—the physical distance between people who are engaging in communication—can convey powerful messages (see figure on the next page). A continuum of personal space and social interaction comprise the four zones: intimate, personal, social, and public. In the United States, most business conversations occur within the social zone, between roughly 4 to 12 feet apart. If one person tries to approach closer than that, the other is likely to feel uncomfortable or threatened.

Interpreting nonverbal cues from members of other cultures can be especially challenging. Concepts of appropriate personal space, to name just one example, can be quite different. Latin Americans insist on conducting business while standing closer than most Americans and Northern Europeans find comfortable. The result is that Americans back away to preserve their personal space, causing Latin Americans to perceive them as cold and unfriendly. To protect themselves from such a personal "threat," experienced Americans use desks or tables to separate themselves from their Latin American counterparts. "The result," explains cultural anthropologist Edward T.

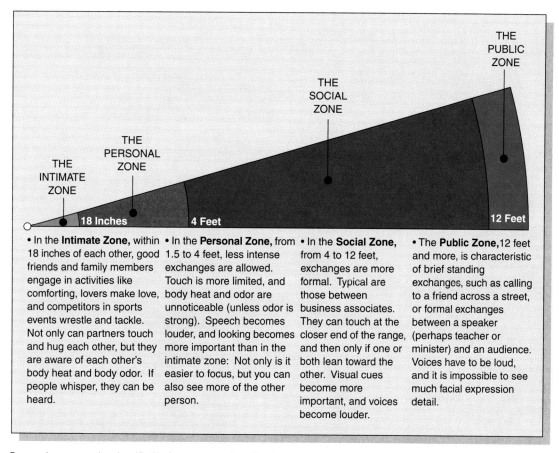

THE
PUBLIC
ZONE

THE
SOCIAL
ZONE

THE
PERSONAL
ZONE

THE
INTIMATE
ZONE

18 Inches   4 Feet   12 Feet

• In the **Intimate Zone**, within 18 inches of each other, good friends and family members engage in activities like comforting, lovers make love, and competitors in sports events wrestle and tackle. Not only can partners touch and hug each other, but they are aware of each other's body heat and body odor. If people whisper, they can be heard.

• In the **Personal Zone**, from 1.5 to 4 feet, less intense exchanges are allowed. Touch is more limited, and body heat and odor are unnoticeable (unless odor is strong). Speech becomes louder, and looking becomes more important than in the intimate zone: Not only is it easier to focus, but you can also see more of the other person.

• In the **Social Zone**, from 4 to 12 feet, exchanges are more formal. Typical are those between business associates. They can touch at the closer end of the range, and then only if one or both lean toward the other. Visual cues become more important, and voices become louder.

• The **Public Zone**, 12 feet and more, is characteristic of brief standing exchanges, such as calling to a friend across a street, or formal exchanges between a speaker (perhaps teacher or minister) and an audience. Voices have to be loud, and it is impossible to see much facial expression detail.

Personal space can be classified in four zones and can be viewed as a continuum.

Hall, "is that the Latin American may even climb over the obstacles until he has achieved a distance at which he can comfortably talk."[23]

People usually are sending nonverbal messages, even when they make a conscious effort not to do so. Sometimes nonverbal cues may serve to "leak" a person's true attitudes and thoughts. A discrepancy between verbal and nonverbal messages may indicate that someone is not being truthful. Generally, when verbal and nonverbal cues conflict, receivers of the communication tend to believe the nonverbal elements. Consider what happened when several employees at manufacturing firm Refuse Compactor told their plant manager, George Miller, that they wanted a pay raise, an extra week of vacation, and another paid holiday. Miller told them to put the request in writing so he could show it to company president Art Nevill. However, his nonverbal cues apparently did not fit his verbal message, since the employees interpreted this remark as a rejection. Shortly thereafter, they voted to join a union and went on strike.[24]

COMMUNICATION WITHIN THE ORGANIZATION

Internal communication involves *communication through channels within an organization*. Examples include memos, meetings, speeches, phone conversations, even a simple conversation over lunch. Internal communication may be relatively simple in small organizations since it is often face to face. Unclear instructions can be remedied by further conversation. But communication problems increase as the organization grows. Messages, many of which are transmitted in writing, often pass through several hierarchical layers in a formal organization. The distortion of the original message as it flows through several intermediaries is illustrated by the following:

Memo from Colonel to Executive Officer
Tomorrow evening, at approximately 2000 hours, Halley's Comet will be visible in this area, an event that occurs only once every 76 years. Have the troops fall out in the battalion area in fatigues, and I will explain this rare phenomenon to

them. In case of rain, we will not be able to see anything, so assemble them in the theater and I will show them films of the comet.

Executive Officer to Company Commander
By order of the Colonel, tomorrow at 2000 hours, Halley's Comet will appear above the battalion area. If it rains, fall the troops out in fatigues, then march to the theater where this rare phenomenon will take place, something that occurs only once every 76 years.

Company Commander to Lieutenant
By order of the Colonel, be in fatigues at 2000 hours tomorrow. The phenomenal Halley's Comet will appear in the theater. In case of rain, in the battalion area, the Colonel will give another order, something which occurs once every 76 years.

Lieutenant to Sergeant
Tomorrow at 2000 hours, the Colonel will appear in the theater with Halley's Comet, something which happens every 76 years. If it rains, the Colonel will order the comet into the battalion area.

Sergeant to Squad
When it rains tomorrow at 2000 hours, the phenomenal 76-year-old General Halley, accompanied by the Colonel, will drive his comet through the battalion area in fatigues.

The sender of the message continually must be aware of the recipient and make certain the message is both clearly written and likely to be interpreted correctly.

Computers and electronic mail, or e-mail, can facilitate internal communication within large organizations, and may even make companies less formal. "Businesses that have pervasive use of electronic mail operate differently," says Intel CEO Andrew Grove. "It squeezes all the slack out of the system."[25] It also removes time and geography constraints, improves the accuracy of information being exchanged, and can be an effective means of building customer relationships by maintaining customer–supplier contacts and supplying such information as product modifications and price changes. These benefits explain why North American businesses sent almost 6 billion e-mail messages last year. If each message had 50 words, it would be like sending 1,000 manuscripts the length of *War and Peace* every day.[26]

DID YOU KNOW?

Women now comprise one-third of the world's work force. More than half of all women between the ages of 18 and 64 work outside the home—59 percent in developed nations, 49 percent in developing regions.

While 20 million Japanese currently are enrolled in English-language classes, less than 50,000 U.S. students are learning to speak Japanese this year.

An interpreter for President Jimmy Carter translated his arrival speech in Poland by reporting: "The president says he is pleased to be here in Poland grasping your secret parts."

Kellogg renamed its Bran Buds cereal in Sweden after learning that the name translates into "burned farmer."

Certainly, electronic mail speeds up internal communications at Boston Chicken, the fast-growing restaurant chain. Managers use networking software to collaborate on team projects and develop menus, solve distribution problems, and plan the chain's expansion. Online records of sales and cost breakdowns help them monitor the business. President Bruce Harreld, along with other managers, pays particular attention to the database of customer gripes, which can be sorted by region or type of complaint. "We look for patterns," says Harreld. "The messages go back to the regional level and, as of this fall, back to the store itself electronically, so that everyone sees."[27]

Communicating in Teams

Communications in teams can be divided into two broad categories: centralized and decentralized. In a **centralized network,** *team members communicate through a single person to solve problems or make decisions.* In a **decentralized network,** *members communicate freely with other team members and arrive at decisions together.*

Which type of network is more effective? It depends on the nature of the problem or decision at issue. Research has shown that centralized networks usually solve simple problems more quickly and accurately. Members simply pass information along to the central decision maker. However, when problems are complex, a decentralized network actually works faster and comes up with more accurate answers. Team members pool their data, provide greater input into the decision, and emerge with a higher-quality solution. This research indicates that organizations should use centralized team networks to deal with simple problems, but should set up decentralized teams to handle more complex issues. Members of decentralized teams should be encouraged to share information with each other and generate as much input into the solution as possible.[28]

Decentralized teams work well for the complex process of new-product development. The decentralized structure of Thermos' Lifestyle team allowed team members to catch several design flaws in the Thermal Electric Grill before they resulted in manu-

CROSS-FUNCTIONAL ENVIRONMENT

The Triad Project

The Triad Project is an example of cutting-edge teamwork on an international scale. More than 100 scientists from three companies—Siemens AG of Germany, Toshiba Corp. of Japan, and America's IBM—are cooperating to design and develop a revolutionary new computer chip. Their laboratory is an IBM facility in the small town of East Fishkill in upstate New York.

Ordinarily, these three international giants would be fierce rivals in the computer-chip industry. But there are at least two good reasons for this unprecedented level of cooperation. The first is money. As research and development costs mushroom, more and more companies are pooling their financial resources, employees, and expertise for mutual benefit.

Money is not the only reason for the Triad team's international makeup. Research shows that diverse work teams—those combining men and women from a variety of cultures—reap important benefits from a broader range of viewpoints. Bringing together scientists from diverse backgrounds can help generate creative leaps that lead to new ideas and strategies.

While pursuing creative leaps, Triad team members also have learned a great deal about the work practices and communication styles of each other's cultures. Early in the project, Toshiba colleagues shocked Siemens co-workers when they closed their eyes and seemed to nap during meetings. Others in the team discovered that this was a common practice for harried Japanese managers when discussions turn to topics that don't involve them.

Japanese researchers, for their part, had to adjust their work style to IBM's building, with its layout of small offices. At Toshiba, teams of scientists work together in large rooms. Team members keep track of what everyone is doing by overhearing conversations. Managers constantly look over their shoulders to provide insights and feedback. Toshiba and IBM finally compromised by knocking out several office walls to enlarge rooms and promote the open communication Toshiba employees preferred.

Another adjustment centered on the delicate issue of how best to convey criticism and suggestions. American managers employ what Siemens workers call a "hamburger style" of criticism: managers start with small talk (the hamburger bun), slip in the criticism (the meat), and finish with

encouraging remarks (more bun). "With Germans, all you get is the meat," remarks cross-cultural trainer Alf Keogh. "And with the Japanese, it's all the soft stuff—you have to *smell* the meat." Siemens engineer Klaus Roithner has worked out his own communication strategy for making suggestions: "I indirectly suggest an idea to IBM engineers," he says, "and let them think they have come up with it themselves."

Despite the adjustments team members have had to make, the Triad Project is on schedule, even ahead of schedule in some areas. Participants note that they have learned a great deal, both about computer chips and communication.

SOURCE: E. S. Browning, "Side by Side," *The Wall Street Journal,* May 3, 1994, A1, A8.

facturing glitches. The first design for the grill featured custom-made tapered legs which would have required an expensive, time-consuming production process. In a centralized team, representatives from the manufacturing division might not even have seen

the design until late in the development process. However, the problem surfaced early, during informal discussions between designers and production staff, and the designers promptly replaced it with a new, straight-legged style. Says Frederick Mather, director

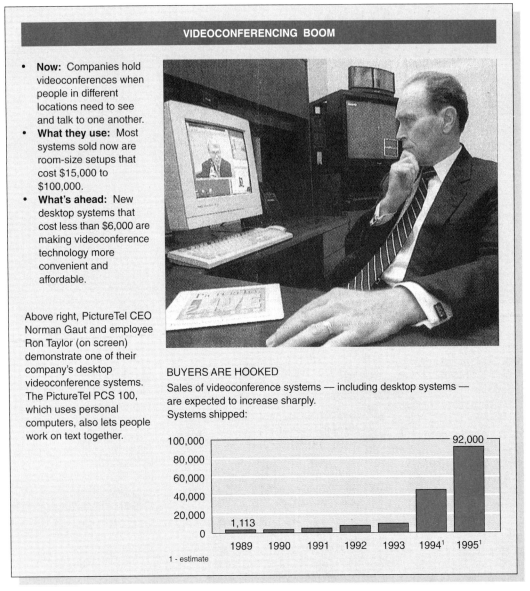

VIDEOCONFERENCING BOOM

- **Now:** Companies hold videoconferences when people in different locations need to see and talk to one another.
- **What they use:** Most systems sold now are room-size setups that cost $15,000 to $100,000.
- **What's ahead:** New desktop systems that cost less than $6,000 are making videoconference technology more convenient and affordable.

Above right, PictureTel CEO Norman Gaut and employee Ron Taylor (on screen) demonstrate one of their company's desktop videoconference systems. The PictureTel PCS 100, which uses personal computers, also lets people work on text together.

BUYERS ARE HOOKED

Sales of videoconference systems — including desktop systems — are expected to increase sharply.
Systems shipped:

100,000	92,000

1,113 at 1989; 1994¹ 1995¹

1 - estimate

Videoconferencing is a high-tech communication tool that is rapidly changing the way firms work.

of research and development, "If that mistake hadn't been caught, we would have lost three to four months doing re-work on the design."[29]

ProShare, an Intel Corp. division producing computer-based videoconferencing products, facilitates this sort of information sharing by allowing team members to view each other on their desktop computer screens as they work together on documents, spreadsheets, and other applications. One satisfied customer is Unisys's airline systems division, which sells computers and software to airlines. "Each time we go to the video, we'll probably save from $75 to $100," says Gary Hart, director of sales and marketing. "It's the kind of sale where a lot of people are involved—program managers, project managers, legal, marketing, as well as myself and the sales rep. The savings [from using videoconferencing] will come from eliminating overnight couriers when preparing proposals for an airline."[30]

COMMUNICATIONS OUTSIDE THE FIRM

External communication is *the meaningful exchange of information through messages between an organization and its major audiences,* such as customers, suppliers, other firms, the general public, and government officials. Businesses use external communication to keep their operations functioning and to maintain their position in the marketplace.

The central focus of a company's external communication, of course, is the customer, since the creation of goods and services that provide customer satisfaction is the ultimate purpose of business. Every interaction with customers—whether sales presentations, order fulfillment, routine dealings, or one-time transactions—should create goodwill and contribute to customer satisfaction.

Consider customer complaints. According to management authors Tom Peters and Nancy Austin, organizations tend to treat complaints in one of two ways. "The first, the most typical, views the complaint as a disease to be got over, with memory of the pain rapidly suppressed. The second views the complaint as a luscious, golden opportunity." Wise business people see a complaining customer as one who can be retained, once the complaint has been resolved.[31]

Effective communication can help a firm win back lost customers. When KFC Japan experienced a ten percent decline in business in a single year, Toshiki Nakata, deputy general manager, commissioned a market survey to find out why. A surprising number of respondents stated that, while they liked KFC's food, they thought it was very expensive. Nakata promptly announced a "value strategy" that targeted the chain's largest customer group in Japan: 18- to 26-year-olds who buy from urban outlets near railway and subway stations. KFC lowered the price on its biggest-selling meal by 16.8 percent to 500 yen at city stores. "We call it our one-coin price," says Nakata. KFC regained ten percent of its lost customers within a few months after the one-coin price took effect.[32]

We already have seen how personal computer-based videoconferencing facilitates internal communication. It offers similar benefits for communication outside the firm. Market Strategies, a small market research company in Portland, Oregon, shares its videoconferencing system with major customers to discuss new bids and current projects, and to resolve

Australian beer company Foster's uses communication differences in its "Speak Australian" advertising campaign aimed at American consumers.

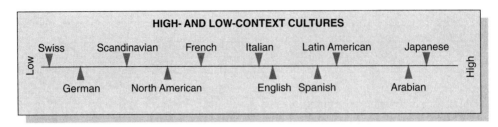

Eleven global regions denote a continuum of low- to high-context cultures.

any complaints before they can jeopardize a project. Says President Michael Malone, "The major benefit is the avoidance of misunderstanding. I can watch a customer and see how he or she is reacting to the material we're discussing."[33]

INTERNATIONAL BUSINESS COMMUNICATION

Pepsico marketers decided to build sales in China, so they created a promotional campaign based on the theme, "Come Alive with Pepsi." Sales were poor, which surprised them, until they discovered that the direct Chinese translation of their slogan was "Bring your ancestors back from the dead." Managers ordered a hasty rewrite.

As this example shows, business people who want to succeed in the international marketplace must ensure that their communications are linguistically and culturally appropriate. This holds true even when marketing products to subcultures within the United States, as Tropicana managers discovered when they tried to sell their orange juice to Miami's Cuban population. The juice was already popular in Puerto Rico under the label *jugo de China.* Tropicana put the same packages on Miami shelves, only to be surprised by the poor sales. Managers discovered that, while *china* meant "orange" to Puerto Ricans, it meant China to Cubans—and Cuban immigrants had no desire to buy Chinese juice.[34]

Communication snafus occur even among English-speaking countries. Most Americans know that the British refuse to call trucks *trucks*; they insist on calling them *lorries.* Brits call the hood of the car a *bonnet* and the garage attendant will search your back seat looking for a trunk. Translate trunk to *boot.* Windshields are *windscreens*, tire is spelled *tyre*, and the elevator is simply a *lift.* Little wonder that playwright George Bernard Shaw referred to the United States and Great Britain as "two countries separated by a common language."

It is helpful to understand the cultural context that surrounds and influences every attempt at international business communication. Anthropologists divide cultures into two basic types, low context and high context (see figure). *Communication* in **low-context cultures** *tends to rely on explicit written and verbal messages.* Examples include Switzerland, Germany, Scandinavia, and the United States. *Communication* in **high-context cultures,** however, *is more likely to depend not only on the message itself, but also on everything that surrounds it,* such as nonverbal cues and the personal relationship between the communicators.

Western business people must be careful to temper their low-context style to the expectations of colleagues and clients in high-context settings. While Americans tend to be direct, wanting to "get down to business" soon after shaking hands or sitting down to a meal, business people in Mexico or the Near East prefer to become acquainted first. When conducting business there, it is wise to allow time for relaxed meals during which business-related topics are avoided and business people can engage in small talk and discuss their families and countries. They may get together for several meetings before any business actually is transacted.

The ability to communicate cross-culturally is becoming more and more important in business. This may explain why so many successful American companies are managed by immigrant CEOs. Roberto Goizeuta, head of Coca-Cola, hails from Cuba; 3M's Livio DeSimone comes from Canada; and Wolfgang Schmitt, CEO of Rubbermaid, was born in Germany. An international viewpoint definitely leads to business success. As DeSimone says,

> ## THEY SAID IT
>
> "The first EDSer [Electronic Data Systems employee] to see a snake kills it. At GM, the first thing you do is organize a committee on snakes. Then you bring in a consultant who knows a lot about snakes. Third thing you do is talk about it for a year."
>
> *H. Ross Perot (1930–   ) American computer industry executive and presidential candidate*

The coming decade promises communication breakthroughs ranging from wristwatch-sized phones to wireless faxing of messages.

"Two-thirds of our top 100 managers have spent more than three years outside the United States. They are comfortable anywhere." Schmitt notes another advantage: "It gives you a certain empathy for minorities, because you've been one."[35]

COMMUNICATIONS TECHNOLOGY

We already have seen how various communications technologies—computers, videoconferencing, e-mail, and networks—can influence the communication process. And the numbers point to their contribution to the world of business. Since 1983, 25 million computers have been installed in U.S. offices; over 10 million fax machines and 26 million U.S. e-mail addresses have been added since 1987; and 11.9 billion messages were left on voice mailboxes last year.[36] Communication giants like AT&T are investing billions in new technologies aimed at making the process of exchanging information even simpler in the future.

These technological advances can improve the speed and efficiency of communication by making it easier to create, organize, and distribute messages. They also facilitate international transactions by minimizing time differences and making all areas of the world more accessible.

For example, communication throughout Europe is made easier by the continent's fast-growing wireless telecommunications networks. Indeed, Europe's networks far surpass those of the United States. Europe now has 1.8 million digital cellular subscribers, compared to only 100,000 in the United States, and the market continues to expand by 133 percent a year. Business people already can talk via digital cellular telephones in most of Europe's cities. By 1996, this will be possible in less-populated areas as well.[37]

In the next chapter, we will examine further the role of these and other communications technologies in business.

SUMMARY OF LEARNING GOALS

1. **Distinguish between the two major types of teams found in organizations.**

A team is a small number of people with complementary skills who are committed to a common purpose, set of performance goals, and approach, for which they hold themselves mutually accountable. There are two major types of teams: special-project problem-solving teams and work teams. Problem-solving teams are temporary combinations of workers who gather to solve a specific problem and then disband. Work teams consist of small numbers of people with complementary skills who perform the day-to-day work of the organization. A cross-functional team can be either a work team or a problem-solving team. It is made up of employees from different departments who work on specific projects, such as developing a new product or solving a particular problem.

2. **Identify the characteristics of an effective team and the different roles played by team members.**

Three important characteristics are the size of the team, the roles played by its members, and its diversity. Effective teams typically have between 5 and 12 members, with about 7 members being the ideal size. Team members can play task specialist, socio-emotional, dual, or nonparticipator roles. Ideally, teams contain a balance of the first three roles. Research indicates that diverse teams tend to display a broader range of viewpoints and produce more innovative solutions to problems.

3. **Summarize the stages of team development.**

A team goes through five stages of development: (1) *forming*, an orientation period during which team members get to know each other and find out what behaviors are acceptable to the group; (2) *storming*, during which participants' individual personalities emerge as they clarify their roles and expectations; (3) *norming*, when differences are resolved, members accept each other, and consensus is reached about the roles of the team leader and other participants; (4) *performing*, characterized by problem solving and a focus on task accomplishment; and (5) *adjourning*, where the focus is on wrapping up and summarizing the team's experience and accomplishments.

4. **Relate team cohesiveness and norms to effective team performance.**

Team cohesiveness is the extent to which team members are attracted to the team and motivated to remain in it. Generally, teams with a high degree of cohesiveness tend to be more productive. When cohesiveness is low, morale suffers.

5. **Describe the factors that can cause conflict in teams, and discuss conflict resolution styles.**

Conflict can stem from many sources: competition for scarce resources, personality clashes, conflicting goals, poor communication, unclear job responsibilities or team role assignments. Conflict resolution styles cover a continuum, from assertive to cooperative. The most effective resolution style varies according to the situation.

Resolution styles include: the competing style, the avoiding style, the compromising style, the accommodating style, and the collaborating style. A team leader can reduce conflict by focusing team members on broad goals, clarifying participants' respective tasks and areas of authority, acting as mediator, and facilitating effective communication.

6. **Explain the importance of effective communication skills in business.**

Communication can be defined as the meaningful exchange of information through messages, and it is essential to business. Managers spend 80 percent of their time in direct communication with others, and the other 20 percent on desk work, much of which is also communication in the form of writing and reading. Communicators need to pay attention to audience feedback, even solicit it, to determine whether their message was perceived in the way they intended.

7. **Compare the different types of communication.**

Communication takes many forms: oral and written, formal and informal, verbal and nonverbal. While some people feel oral channels allow them to convey their message more accurately, nonverbal cues can distort it. Effective written communication reflects its audience, its channel, and the degree of formality that is appropriate. Formal communication channels are those that flow within the chain of command or task responsibility defined by an organization. Informal communication channels are channels, such as grapevines, that exist outside formally authorized channels without regard for the organization's hierarchy of authority. Nonverbal communication plays a larger communication role than most people realize. Generally, when verbal and nonverbal cues conflict, the receivers of the communication tend to believe the nonverbal elements.

8. **Identify and explain several important considerations in international business communications.**

The ability to communicate cross-culturally is becoming more and more important in business. Communication in low-context cultures tends to rely on explicit written and verbal messages. In high-context cultures, however, it is more likely to depend not only on the message itself, but also on everything that surrounds it, such as nonverbal cues and the personal relationship between the communicators. American business people must temper their low-context style when in high-context cultures.

9. **Summarize important developments in communication technology and how they affect business communication.**

Various communications technologies—computers, videoconferencing, electronic mail, networks—can influence the efficiency of communication by making it easier to create, organize, and distribute messages. They also facilitate international transactions by minimizing time differences and making all areas of the world more accessible.

KEY TERMS QUIZ

problem-solving team
decentralized network
external communication
team
low-context culture
team cohesiveness
work team

listening
task specialist role
high-context culture
informal communication channels
nonverbal communication
conflict
team norm

centralized network
formal communication channels
socio-emotional role
communication
internal communication
grapevine

team

1. A small number of people with complementary skills who are committed to a common purpose, approach, and set of performance goals.

work team

2. A mid-1990s approach in which small numbers of people with complementary skills perform the day-to-day work of the organization.

problem-solving team

3. Temporary combinations of workers who gather to solve a specific problem and then disband.

task specialist role

4. Role played by leaders who devote time and energy to help the team accomplish its goals.

socio-emotional role

5. Role played by leaders who devote their time and energy to providing support for group members' emotional needs and social unity.

team cohesiveness

6. The extent to which team members are attracted to the team and motivated to remain a part of it.

team norm

7. A standard of conduct that is shared by team members and guides their behavior.

conflict

8. An antagonistic interaction in which one party attempts to thwart the intentions or goals of another.

communication

9. The meaningful exchange of information through messages.

listening

10. The skill of receiving a message and interpreting its genuine meaning by accurately grasping the facts and feelings conveyed.

formal communication channels

11. Messages that flow within the chain of command or task responsibility defined by an organization.

informal communication channels

12. Communication outside formally authorized channels without regard for the organization's hierarchy of authority.

grapevine

13. An internal information channel that transmits information through unofficial, independent sources.

nonverbal communication

14. Communication that is transmitted through actions and behaviors.

internal communication

15. System of communication through channels within an organization.

external communication

16. The meaningful exchange of information through messages between an organization and its major audiences.

centralized network

17. Communication of team members through a single person to solve problems or make decisions.

decentralized network

18. System in which members communicate freely with other team members and arrive at decisions together.

low-context culture

19. Communication that relies on explicit written and verbal messages.

high-context culture

20. Communication that depends not only on the message itself, but also on everything that surrounds it.

OTHER IMPORTANT TERMS

adjourning stage
audience
channel
context
cross-functional team

decoding
dual role
emoticons
encoding
feedback

forming stage
message
noise
nonparticipator role
norming stage

performing stage
self-managed team
sender
storming stage
virtual teams

REVIEW QUESTIONS

1. Distinguish among work teams, problem-solving teams, and cross-functional teams.
2. Is there an optimal size for a team? Identify the problems that often occur with large teams.
3. Which team roles are most important in achieving the goals of a team? Which role would you be most likely to assume on a team?
4. Describe each of the five stages of team development. What happens during each stage?
5. List the factors that can lead to team conflict. What resolution styles are identified in the chapter?
6. Draw a diagram of the communication process and label each element. Explain the concept of noise.
7. Compare the different types of communication discussed in the chapter, including oral, written, formal, informal, and nonverbal.
8. Explain why it is important to be an effective communicator in business.
9. Describe how computers and related technologies can impact business communication.
10. Discuss the factors that should be kept in mind when communicating internationally.

DISCUSSION QUESTIONS

1. Suppose that you have been asked to create a training program to help employees at a local company improve their teamwork and communication skills. Develop a plan that describes this program.
2. Interview someone from another nation who is visiting or living in the United States. What are this person's most vivid impressions of America and Americans? How do work practices and communication styles differ? Write a summary of the interview.
3. Think back to your most recent experience with being part of a team at work or school. Analyze the team's development. Can you recall specific examples of each stage of development? What were the norms of this group? How would you assess its degree of cohesiveness? How did this impact the team's effectiveness?
4. Keep a record of your communications for one day. Include phone conversations, personal conversations, and mail. Write a two-page report that summarizes your findings and include a description of your personal communication style and patterns.
5. More and more businesses are communicating with foreign customers, colleagues, and vendors via fax machines and electronic mail. Discuss the advantages and disadvantages of using these channels for international communication.

VIDEO CASE: American Worker—Japanese Boss

This video case compares the management styles of these two cultures and examines the differences in motivation techniques. It is included on page 417 of Appendix D.

Solution to Key Terms Quiz

1. team 2. work team 3. problem-solving team 4. task specialist role 5. socio-emotional role 6. team cohesiveness 7. team norm 8. conflict 9. communication 10. listening 11. formal communication channels 12. informal communication channels 13. grapevine 14. nonverbal communication 15. internal communication 16. external communication 17. centralized network 18. decentralized network 19. low-context culture 20. high-context culture

Information for Decision Making

Learning Goals

1. Explain the purpose of an information system and how it aids decision making in business.
2. List the major contributions and limitations of computers.
3. Distinguish among mainframe computers, minicomputers, and microcomputers.
4. Distinguish between computer hardware and software.
5. Discuss the role of telecommunications in business.
6. Explain the concept of an information superhighway and its implications for business.
7. Identify the major business applications of computers.
8. Summarize the major computer security issues that affect organizations.

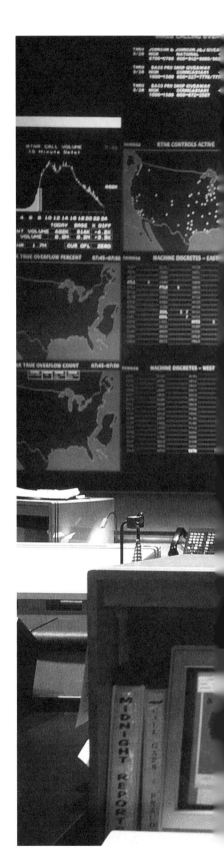

The U.S. government recently announced the ambitious goal of merging America's sprawling telecommunications, information, and data networks into a single, enormous pathway accessible to all businesses, not-for-profit organizations, and individual households. The Clinton administration views this so-called *information superhighway* as a crucial building block in the nation's long-term economic competitiveness.

Among the strongest proponents of this concept are the firms that make up the telecommunications industry. They are competing fiercely in an effort to make the United States the world leader in designing, building, managing, and servicing the various components that will make up this huge information pipeline.

No firm is competing harder than AT&T. Although many consumers equate American Telephone & Telegraph with long-distance telephone service, it is much more than a telephone company. Despite the fact that long-distance service still accounts for 62 percent of its $67 billion in annual sales, the New York-based giant is also the nation's largest producer of electronic cash registers, the world's largest maker of bank automated teller machines, and the third largest issuer of credit cards. The firm's management is attempting to combine these various businesses to become a superplayer on the superhighway. "AT&T is pursuing its 'communacopia' strategy," says investment analyst Robert Morris III. "It wants to be the horn of plenty for every conceivable information technology, and be to multimedia what Ma Bell was to telephones."

Despite its many strengths, AT&T must overcome two obstacles to achieve this goal. One hurdle in its path is that it does not make the products many consumers want from the information superhighway—movies, video games, or TV shows, for example. Another hurdle is that, because of the divestiture of the local Bell companies during the 1980s,

AT&T no longer possesses a direct link to individual homes and businesses. Like other long-distance phone carriers, AT&T must pay an access fee to the local telephone system in order to reach out and touch someone. Access fees cost the company $14 billion a year.

AT&T's management is tackling the first problem through a combination of acquisitions and strategic alliances. By acquiring a major financial interest in interactive computer maker 3DO Company and software producer General Magic, AT&T has expanded into the multimedia computing industry. A joint venture with Sega Enterprises allows opponents playing video games to compete long-distance over AT&T's phone lines.

One way to overcome the second obstacle is to bypass local phone companies in favor of cable TV operators. Through an alliance with cable-TV programmer Viacom, for instance, AT&T provides technologies for two-way video interaction, enabling Viacom customers to shop from home and receive movies on demand.

Wireless technologies are another way that AT&T can bypass local phone lines. Demand for wireless services is surging, thanks to the rapid development of digital technology, the steady decline in prices, and the growing mobility of American workers. AT&T's research shows that 74 percent of U.S. managers, professionals, and business owners—27.3 million workers in all—now spend 20 percent or more of their time away from their offices.

To enter the wireless market, AT&T has invested in firms that are developing wireless "personal communicator" devices with computer, facsimile (fax), and telephone capabilities. The company has created a wireless network, PersonaLink, which filters customers' electronic messages by identifying the most important ones and discarding the junk mail. It also has acquired McCaw Cellular Communications, the country's largest cellular telephone company. The McCaw deal, says analyst Morris, "will certainly enhance AT&T's opportunities to bypass the local phone systems."

AT&T is expanding aggressively overseas as well. The firm already generates one-fourth of its revenues outside the United States, and managers plan to earn still more by upgrading telephone systems in developing nations. The company has won contracts in Eastern Europe and China to build modern networks with advanced switches and microelectronics. "What's happening is that AT&T is becoming second supplier to the world," explains telecommunications analyst George Dellinger. "For example, if you're in Asia, you don't want to be dominated by the Japanese and NEC. If you're in Germany, you don't want to be dominated by the Germans and Siemens. So, all of a sudden, AT&T pops up as a high-quality, long-term second supplier offering good prices."

"AT&T wants all roads to lead to its electronic superhighway," says consultant Fritz Ringling. "It wants Johnny in Atlanta to play Sega video games with his cousin in Seattle; Mom to use the Universal [credit] card and have her purchases rung up on an NCR cash register that uses an AT&T fax to transmit credit-verification data; and Dad to send messages to his office while he's out on a sales call using his AT&T hand-held computer."

AT&T's strategy appears to be working; it ranks number one in *Fortune* magazine's Service 500, with the highest market value of any firm on the list.[1]

CHAPTER OVERVIEW

Someone once gave the recipe for effective decisions as "90 percent information and 10 percent inspiration." Clearly, obtaining the right information and knowing how to use it are vital to business success.

As the opening story shows, AT&T has prospered by finding new ways to deliver information to businesses and consumers all over the world. In this chapter, we will look at how information systems are transforming business and the process of decision making. To an ever-increasing extent, these systems rely on computers and related technologies to store, access, and manage the information that business people need.

MANAGEMENT INFORMATION SYSTEMS

THEY SAID IT

"Just try explaining the value of statistical summaries to the widow of the man who drowned crossing a stream with an average depth of four feet."

Anonymous

- "What is the sales potential for our brand in South Korea compared to Hong Kong?"
- "If we raise the price for the brand by two percent, how will it affect sales in both countries?"
- "How do our wage rates compare with similar firms in St. Louis?"
- "What are the storage costs for Model 238?"

Every day in business, people are asking questions such as these. An effective information system helps people to answer them. The **management**

information system (MIS) is *an organized method for providing past, present, and projected information on internal operations and external intelligence for use in decision making.* Large organizations typically assign *responsibility for directing the firm's MIS and related computer operations* to an executive called the **chief information officer (CIO).** Generally, the CIO reports directly to the chief executive officer (CEO).

Information from a variety of sources is needed to perform almost every company activity, whether internal or external. It can make the difference between staying in business or going broke. Keeping on top of changing consumer demands, competitors' actions, and the latest government regulations helps firms fine-tune existing products, develop new winners, and market them effectively.

Liz Greetham, a fund manager for the New York City firm of Weiss, Peck & Greer Venture Partners, must stay on top of the volatile financial industry—and she does it from Bermuda, thanks to a well-planned information system in her home there. Five phone lines and several computers connect her to the New York office, 700 nautical miles away. One computer provides live stock-market quotes; another contains spreadsheets that help Greetham calculate earnings projections for the pharmaceutical, health-care, and biotechnology firms in her $150 million stock portfolio. "I can track exactly how the market is moving on that little quote machine over there," says Greetham. "I have all my research on the portable PC over here. I have direct access to my trader by picking up the phone." This combination of resources helps her succeed in a highly competitive field—and still live in her island paradise. Over the past two years, her portfolio of stocks has risen 57 percent, much higher than the industry average of 22 percent.[2]

Liz Greetham

Databases

The heart of an information system is its **database**— *a centralized, integrated collection of the organization's data resources.* Databases, the subject of our focus on technology in Chapter 2, are designed to meet the particular information processing and retrieval requirements of decision makers. They serve as electronic file cabinets, capable of storing massive amounts of data and retrieving needed data within seconds. Databases also help firms target their direct marketing efforts by finding out more about prospective customers. Kimberly-Clark, maker of Huggies diapers, has a database of over ten million new mothers.

Firms that cannot afford to create and maintain their own databases can subscribe to services that provide databases on specific topics. In addition to such broad-based databases as Prodigy, CompuServe, and Lexis, specialized commercial databases are available to meet the specific needs of businesses. If a company is interested in exporting its products to Germany, for instance, it can pay to access ABC der Deutschen Wirtschaft, which carries data on 76,000 manufacturers in Germany. Its listings include such helpful items as each firm's name, address, phone number, products, and number of employees, as well as its industry classification and its bankers.

CONTRIBUTIONS AND LIMITATIONS OF COMPUTERS

The English mathematician William Shanks spent one-third of his life computing pi to 707 decimal places— only to make a mistake at the 528th place! Today, computers can duplicate Shanks' work without error in less than five seconds.

A **computer** is *a programmable electronic device that can store, retrieve, and process data.* Once considered exotic, these machines have become indispensable to business; 71 percent of everyone employed in the finance, insurance, and real-estate industries use a computer on the job. In all, three of every eight U.S. employees now use computers regularly at work (up from 25 percent a decade ago).[3]

Computers offer many advantages to business. They are fast, accurate, capable of storing large quantities of information in a small space, can make volumes of data available quickly, and can perform the mechanical, often boring work of recording and main-

Computer systems, such as those provided by Unisys Corp., are indispensable to contemporary business.

taining incoming information. The tremendous speed of computers can save time when correcting problems, implementing solutions, and taking advantage of business opportunities. These machines can perform repetitive tasks, such as adding endless strings of numbers or comparing collected data against established standards, that would soon wear out human beings.

As is the case with any time- or labor-saving device, the advantages of using computers are compounded by a number of potential problems. Computer equipment and software specifically designed to meet a firm's particular needs can be expensive. In addition, computers can make disastrous mistakes when programmed incorrectly. Consider when, a few years ago, a computerized defense system almost tried to shoot down the moon. At about the same time, an amazed magazine subscriber received 700 copies of the same issue in the mail. Computers also have the potential of becoming a crutch rather than a tool in decision making when they are relied on too heavily.

Finally, computers can alienate customers if they are used to the extent that the human element in customer contact is eliminated. To overcome consumer resentment toward the typical depersonalized computer letter, a Charleston, West Virginia, hospital uses this message:

Hello there. I am the hospital's computer. As yet, no one but me knows that you have not been making regular payments on this account. However, if I have not processed a payment from you within ten days, I will tell a human, who will resort to other means of collection.

Hardware and Software

Computer **hardware** consists of *all the tangible elements of the computer system*—the input devices, the machines that store and process data and perform the required calculations, and the output devices that provide the results to the information user. Computer hardware includes all machinery and electronic gadgets that make up the computer installation.

In order to work, however, hardware requires **software,** which consists of *sets of instructions that tell the hardware what to do.* Computer languages and computer programs—including custom-designed as well as "off-the-shelf" commercial software packages—are both considered software. Over the years, MS-DOS software and its upgrades have remained the number one choice of businesses. Other leading software packages include Microsoft Windows, WordPerfect, Quicken for Windows, and QEMM.[4]

MAINFRAMES, MINICOMPUTERS, AND MICROCOMPUTERS

Based on their memory capacity and processing speeds, computers can be divided into three broad categories: mainframes, minicomputers, and micro- computers. The *mainframe computer* is the largest type of computer sys- tem, with the greatest amount of storage capacity and the fastest pro- cessing speeds. Some observers, noting IBM Corp.'s fall from grace over the past five years, argue that mainframes are the dinosaurs of the twenty-first century computer in- dustry. After all, IBM, a name that is synonymous with *computer* and that built most of its fame and reve- nue base on mainframes, has seen its mainframe revenues drop by nearly half since 1990. However, these gi- ant computers are not destined for extinction, primarily due to their ability to handle *T. rex*-sized tasks. In fact, they continue to evolve as new applications are discovered for these massive machines.[5]

The growth of the smaller mini- and micro- computers is due to their ever-increasing capability to handle many of the functions that mainframes performed 20 years ago. The *minicomputer* is an intermediate-sized computer—more compact and less expensive than mainframes, but is also slower and has less memory. These intermediate computers often are used in universities, factories, and research labs.

Most people are familiar with the **micro- computer,** *the smallest type of computer,* since it is so widely used in business today. A microcomputer, typ- ically called a personal computer or PC, has a *video display terminal (VDT)* that displays output on a TV- like screen.

The distinctions among these three types of com- puters are blurring due to rapid developments in tech- nology. Today's microcomputers can handle as much work as the huge mainframes of the 1970s. Other ma- chines, called supercomputers, are especially powerful tools that can handle extremely rapid, complex cal- culations involving thousands of variables. Super- computers are most commonly used for scientific research.

These advances were made possible by the de- velopment of powerful *computer chips*—thin silicon wafers on which integrated circuits (networks of tran- sistors and circuits) are assembled—and the *micro- processor*—a fingernail-sized chip that contains an entire CPU. "Intelligent" features available in today's

Chips: The miniature brains of the computer.

new cars, toys, and watches also rely on microproces- sors. Additional chips containing instructions and data memory then are added to convert the microprocessor into a microcomputer.

As technology continues to improve, computers continue to get smaller. Laptop computers are micro- computers that are lightweight enough to be easily portable, and small enough that they can be used on your lap when no desk is avail- able. Notebook computers are small enough to slip into a briefcase, and palmtops fit in a shirt pocket and run on ordinary AA batteries. An- other hot development in miniatur- ized computers is the notepad computer, which can "read" hand- written letters, numbers, and drawings.

Small computers, such as note- books, lag about three years behind microcomputers in terms of tech- nology, but the increasing mobility of American work- ers makes them popular. Roughly one-third of the people who buy Compaq Computer's notebooks, for example, are replacing desktop machines. Typical of this market is Dallas telephone technician Robert Mears, who recently bought his notebook computer because he does not want to be tied down to his office microcomputer. "I need more portability than that," he says.[6]

The future will produce even smaller PCs. Hewlett-Packard has introduced its new OmniBook, the first subnotebook on the market. Industry tech- nologists are developing a credit-card-sized computer that is expected to enable users to access information on office networks from hotel rooms or home. These new technologies are stifled by the need for frequent battery recharging and difficulties in upgrading trans- mission services, but will soon become state of the art in personal computing.[7]

Hewlett-Packard's OmniBook weighs less than three pounds and measures a small 11 by 6 by 1½ inches.

TELECOMMUNICATIONS AND THE INFORMATION SUPERHIGHWAY

Information technologies are changing the business world rapidly and in numerous ways. One of the fastest-growing segments of the information industry today is in **telecommunications**—*any system in which information or data are sent over a distance through some type of transmission medium.* Telecommunications can involve not just computers, but also such diverse technologies as telephones, television, fax machines, and wireless communications.

These new technologies impact contemporary business in three primary ways. First, the timeliness and quantity of information makes decision-making faster and often more effective. Second, accurate, nonbiased data are available to all interested parties. Finally, since more and more consumers have computers connected to online services, such as travel agents or brokerage houses, it presents the potential to eliminate many intermediaries.

Thousands of businesses, both large and small, are changing supplier–buyer relationships by combining computers and communications networks. Information gathered and stored on networks allow retail stores, for example, to analyze customer and sales data and spot trends in the industry. All network members benefit; however, those not connected to the network frequently are eliminated from the chain. For example, insurance companies now provide policyholders with an 800 number to make a claim. That number also connects the policyholder with a network repair shop. However, if a repair shop is not on the insurance company's computer network, it has no access to these customers. When the Globe Glass & Mirror Co. chain created a network for Allstate Corp. in 1990, hundreds of small shops in the $2.3 billion replacement-glass industry found themselves shut out of the market.

In much the same way, retail stores can gather customer data that can be used to analyze sales and spot trends. Accurate, unbiased information about recorded music sales is now available from an independent source that collects data from 14,000 retailers. Among the recent findings: Country music is more popular than many record executives had assumed and small rap labels such as Priority Records are getting more rack space because the numbers show the demand is there. The result, according to an industry researcher, is that information technology is "helping make marketplaces operate closer to how classical

economic theory says they should," by giving the industry better information on which to act.[8]

As we saw in the opening story, the Clinton administration supports the development of an **information superhighway**, *merging telecommunications, information, and data networks into a single, enormous pathway accessible to all consumers and businesses.* Thanks to telecommunications media supplied by local cable or telephone companies, a growing number of businesses and residences have access to libraries, databases, and teleconferencing, as well as many other services.

The information superhighway affects business in many ways. It reduces the time necessary to transmit data and speeds up the pace of work. Some experts suggest, for example, that it will reduce employers' health-care costs as much as 20 percent by speeding up medical claims processing. It will overcome geographic barriers, since branch offices located in different countries can share information as if they were all in the same city. Business people can conduct international meetings electronically, rather than having to spend hours and dollars traveling. An information superhighway also will benefit business relationships by allowing more producers to deal directly with their customers instead of having to go through wholesalers and other intermediaries.[9] By installing order-taking computer terminals in the stockrooms of large hospitals, Baxter Healthcare Corp. has become the

Billboard magazine uses information gathered at Camelot Music checkout counters to rank what's hot and what's not in its weekly surveys.

TECHNOLOGY

Fiber Optics and the Information Revolution

Fiber optics technology, the "asphalt of the information superhighway," eventually will provide users with worldwide information connections. Optic fibers are strands of glass no thicker than a human hair that enable billions of bits of data to move from one continent to another in seconds. The National Academy of Engineering lists fiber optic communication as one of the most important scientific engineering achievements of the last 25 years. Fiber optic networks currently are used primarily for long-distance telephone connections, but in the very near future they will carry not only voice messages, but video images as well. Businesses are the major users of this new technology now, but soon businesses will be connected with homes via fiber optics across the United States and around the world. They will provide businesses with opportunities never before imagined, such as digitalizing television pictures, which will make HDTV (high-definition TV) as outdated as 45 rpm records.

Fiber optics is gathering speed as each new network is added. The next step consists of replacing old copper-wire information networks with new fiber optic technology. For several years, Sprint was the leader in this technology, but more recently MCI and AT&T are trying to bypass outdated systems and the multitude of regulations left over from earlier days of information processing and transmission. Federal communications policies are a major roadblock to the use of new fiber optic technology.

Another problem that must be overcome involves traffic jams and bottlenecks. AT&T and MCI are conducting research to eliminate many of the problems created by slower electronic switches. In the future, computer chips will combine the logic capabilities of electronics with the transmission capacity of fiber optics.

Fiber optics technology will allow the immense amount of accumulated data to be transformed into useable information for decision making. Efficiently processing and dealing with information will be advantageous in any application—research, education, economic development, and medicine, to name just a few.

During the 1980s, the promise of a network of information superhighways was just an idea; today, it is a reality in state-of-the-art communication. In recent decades, the process of collecting information has resulted in an abundance of data that has not been organized successfully for productive applications. Vice President Albert Gore, Jr., explains the situation this way:

> *Years ago, I created a new word called "ex-formation," information that exists outside the conscious awareness of any living being but that exists in such enormous quantities that it changes the context and the weight of any problem one addresses. The problem is to convert "ex-formation" into information, and then to convert the information into knowledge, and eventually to distill the knowledge into wisdom, the hardest process of all.*

SOURCES: "Advanced Fiber Optics," *U.S. News & World Report,* May 2, 1994, 58; and Albert Gore, Jr., "Information Superhighways: The Next Information Revolution," *The Futurist,* January–February 1991, 21–23.

---

dominant firm in the hospital supply business. The terminals not only eliminate the need to place orders through salespeople, they are more convenient to use and produce faster, more efficient service for the hospitals.[10]

Computer Networks

The information superhighway will play a greater role in business as more and more applications are developed. An important development involves **computer networks,** *systems that interconnect numerous computers so they function individually or communicate with each other.* The network can include one or a combination of mainframes, mini-, and microcomputers.

Currently, intercompany computer networks are having the greatest impact in the area of electronic purchasing. An estimated 40,000 U.S. companies routinely exchange electronic invoices and other business forms directly from one computer to another—a scheme called *electronic data interchange (EDI).* CommerceNet, a Silicon Valley electronic marketplace of 20 big companies, including Intel, Apple Computer, Hewlett-Packard, Sun Microsystems, and Pacific Bell, is designed to get purchase orders moving in the valley by helping companies conduct business electronically. The firm's $12 million computer-connection project—backed by federal, state, and private funds for developing software—is the prototype of how the superhighway will be paved.[11]

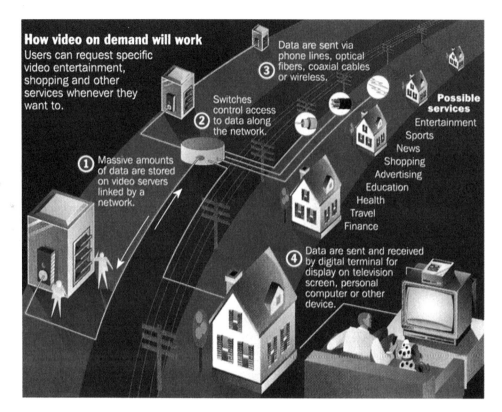

How video on demand will work
Users can request specific video entertainment, shopping and other services whenever they want to.

① Massive amounts of data are stored on video servers linked by a network.

② Switches control access to data along the network.

③ Data are sent via phone lines, optical fibers, coaxial cables or wireless.

Possible services
Entertainment
Sports
News
Shopping
Advertising
Education
Health
Travel
Finance

④ Data are sent and received by digital terminal for display on television screen, personal computer or other device.

The information superhighway—a dazzling range of choices. A national high-tech network would link everybody's computers, telephones, and television sets.

Computing in the 1980s was typically one person performing one task on a single system. Today, computer networks make it easier for people to obtain and share information, even if they are not in the same location. In fact, networks will become a required tool for business success in today's increasingly competitive environment.[12]

Many companies connect their different offices and buildings by creating a **local area network (LAN),** *a computer network that connects machines within a limited area* (such as one building or several buildings that are near each other). LANs are useful in many businesses because they can link microcomputers and allow them to share printers and information.

The development of powerful microprocessors means that LANs are starting to replace mainframes at many companies. Employees at Motorola's computer group, for example, used to do their computing on two large IBM mainframes. Today, that work is done on three local area networks that link more than 1,000 microcomputers and 25 to 30 minicomputers. The shift has saved Motorola money; while each of the huge mainframes cost the company $30,000 a month to program and maintain, the equivalent computing power in a network format costs just $10,000 a month. Motorola's MIS costs used to be 3.7 percent of sales; today they are down to 1.2 percent.[13]

Computer networks also allow various departments, such as purchasing, finance, and marketing, to make comparisons of actual sales with sales forecasts. The results of such comparisons may show a need

> **DID YOU KNOW?**
>
> Over 6,200 databases are available worldwide. The United States is the largest participant in database technology since it both produces and consumes more than 50 percent of them.
>
> Russian forecasters consider the most reliable information about their country and its economy to be that gathered by the U.S. Central Intelligence Agency.
>
> Your Edinburgh computer programmer will correct you if you call her Scotch. She's a Scot. (If she consumes alcoholic beverages, her drink of choice is likely to be scotch.) Her language and her terrier are called Scottish.
>
> Identical information often has different meanings in different countries. An inept translation once resulted in Schweppes tonic water being advertised in Italy as "bathroom water." In South America, Parker Pen Co. once unwittingly indicated that its product would prevent unwanted pregnancies.

to change production, finance, or marketing plans. Cakebread Cellars is a family-owned winery situated in the fiercely competitive wine-producing area of Napa Valley, California. Cakebread has fought for awards, name recognition, and shelf space in a crowded market and has won. The key to its success has been its information network that connects the vineyards to the barrel rooms to the business office.[14]

Computer networks have their disadvantages, too. It is important for organizations to plan and control networks. Otherwise, each division might develop its own system, and end up being unable to link up with other divisions. Issues of privacy and security also arise: Should everyone in the company be able to access all of the mainframe's data? What about confidential human resource files? Is it safe to give all employees access to the corporation's payroll system? Later in the chapter, we will examine several of these issues.

Cakebread Cellars uses computer information networks to obtain maximum productivity and the highest quality possible from its vines.

HOW COMPUTERS HELP BUSINESS

Computers have changed how people spend their days, the skills they need, and the leverage they can bring to their work. Software programs, such as ManagePro by Avantos, help management set goals, monitor progress, conduct reviews of personnel and sales, and give informal feedback. Richard Corea, vice president of IDS Financial Services, supervises 15 division vice presidents from his home office in Fairport, New York. Not only is Corea better organized and more efficient with the help of ManagePro, his stress level is a lot lower.[15]

Almost every industry has felt the impact of computers and information systems. Two popular business tools—fax machines and cellular phones—were discussed in the last chapter. Other important applications include word processing, desktop publishing, decision support systems, spreadsheets, electronic mail, executive information systems, expert systems, voice processing, multimedia computing, and interactive media.

Word Processing

One of the most popular business applications involves **word processing,** *the use of computers to type, store, retrieve, edit, and print various types of documents.* If you have ever used a typewriter to write a paper, you know the advantages of using a personal computer in revising what you have written, checking spelling, and correcting mistakes.

Word processing allows companies to handle huge volumes of correspondence, process numerous documents, and personalize form letters. Some firms may use special-purpose computers, called dedicated word processors, designed exclusively for this purpose. However, word processing more often involves using special word-processing software packages, such as AppleWriter, WordPerfect, MacWrite, or WordStar.

Desktop Publishing

A development that takes word processing a step further is **desktop publishing,** *a computer system that allows companies to design and produce printed material in-house.* Desktop publishing software combines high-quality type, graphics, and layouts to create output that looks as attractive as documents produced by professional publishers and printers. Advanced equipment can scan photos and drawings and duplicate them on the printed page. Desktop publishing systems often are used to print newsletters, reports, and form letters. Winning Forms, produced by Random House, is a book-disk package designed to work in conjunction with many of the major software packages, such as Word for Windows, WordPerfect, Lotus 1-2-3, and Quattro Pro. It provides templates for many office procedures, including mailing labels, invoices, purchase orders, expense reports, business cards,

How a Spreadsheet Works						
Fixed Costs			Fixed	Per-Unit	Sales	Breakeven
Manufacturing	Marketing	R&D	Cost	Variable Cost	Price	Point in Units
$80,000	$100,000	$170,000	$350,000	$4	$8.00	87,500
$80,000	$200,000	$170,000	$450,000	$4	$8.00	112,500
$80,000	$100,000	$170,000	$350,000	$3	$6.50	100,000

Making pricing decisions concerning a proposed product offers a good illustration of how a spreadsheet works. A relatively simple example demonstrates the ease with which a manager can use a spreadsheet to analyze alternative decisions. Assume a proposed new-product entry will be marked at $8 per unit and can be produced for $4 in variable costs. Total fixed costs of $350,000 include $80,000 for such manufacturing overhead outlays as salaries, general office expenses, rent, utilities, and interest charges; $100,000 for marketing expenditures; and $170,000 for research and development on the product. The spreadsheet calculation reveals that sales of 87,500 units are necessary to cover all costs and break even.

But what if the firm's marketing director persuades other members of the group to increase marketing expenditures to $200,000? A spreadsheet program automatically replaces the $100,000 with $200,000 and calculates the breakeven point. Similarly, the breakeven point can be determined quickly if there is a reduction in variable costs and a reduction in selling price. Complex spreadsheets may have 50 columns or more, but the spreadsheet makes new calculations as fast as the manager can change the variables.

resumes, and press releases.[16] Often firms' advertising and graphic arts departments use this type of software to create brochures and marketing materials. A good desktop publishing system can save a company money by allowing it to produce such documents in-house.

Decision Support Systems

A **decision support system (DSS)** is a *system that quickly provides relevant facts to help business people make decisions.* It includes software tools that help decision makers generate the information they need. DSS tools may vary from company to company, but they typically include software that helps people obtain needed information from a database, simulation software that lets employees create computer models to evaluate company performance under different conditions, and presentation software that lets them create graphs and charts.

Spreadsheets

An electronic **spreadsheet** is *the computerized equivalent of an accountant's worksheet.* Spreadsheet software *permits business people to manipulate decision variables to determine their impact on such outcomes as profits or sales.* Lotus 1-2-3 is a popular spreadsheet software package.

A spreadsheet presents a grid of columns and rows that allows information to be organized in a standardized, easily understandable format. As soon as the manager changes a variable, such as price or advertising outlays (see table), the computer immediately re-

calculates all figures to show the impact on expected unit sales or dollar revenues. Since the tedious chore of recalculating and revising figures by hand is done automatically by computer, the manager can analyze

E-mail systems like Microsoft Mail Remote allow global travelers to stay in touch with the home office.

the impact of dozens of "What if?" alternatives in a matter of seconds.

Electronic Mail

Another popular business use for computers is **electronic mail (E-mail),** *a system for sending and receiving written messages from one computer to another via phone lines.* If you want to send a message to co-workers, for instance, you would just type in the message, indicate who should receive it, and signal the computer to send it. The computer saves the message in a special file. When your co-workers sign on, they can retrieve the written note, read it on the screen, and dispose of it as they wish—either by printing a "hard copy" on paper, storing it electronically, forwarding it to other people, answering it with another E-mail message, or just deleting it altogether.

In an average year, more than 16 billion messages travel by E-mail. With the increase in usage, many business cards now include an E-mail address in addi-

> ### THEY SAID IT
>
> "There are three kinds of lies: lies, damned lies, and statistics."
>
> *Benjamin Disraeli (1804–1881) British novelist and prime minister*

tion to a phone and fax number.[17] Certainly it can help companies reduce paper waste, "telephone tag," and the time necessary to communicate with many different people. An obvious requirement is that employees must be able to use a computer in order to send or receive their mail. Furthermore, it still may be more convenient to send long letters on paper, either by fax or by traditional mail delivery.[18]

Executive Information Systems

Sometimes, specialized information systems are created to address the needs of specific levels of employees. An *executive information system (EIS)* allows top managers to access the firm's primary databases, often by touching the computer screen or using a piece of computer hardware called a mouse. EIS software typically produces easy-to-read graphics with full-color displays and charts. A typical EIS gives users a choice between many kinds of data, such as the firm's financial statements, sales figures, and stock-market trends for their

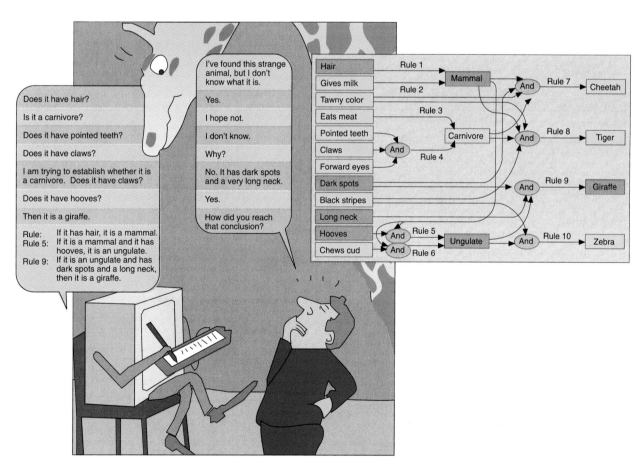

Expert systems help businesses make decisions by evaluating known data.

Common Business Uses of Voice Processing, Companies that Offer Each Service, and the Market Size

Business Uses	Description	Companies Offering the Service	Size of U.S. Market (in millions)
Voice-Mail Equipment	Allows users to record, store, forward, and broadcast voice messages with touch-tone phones.	Octel, AT&T, Northern Telecom, Rolm, VMX	$930
Voice-Mail Service	Instead of buying special equipment to handle voice mail, some companies prefer to use outside services.	Local phone companies, service bureaus, Baby Bell holding companies, long-distance carriers	363
Voice Response Gear	Responding to prerecorded cues, callers can instruct a computer to complete a transaction or recite information by pushing the correct key on a touch-tone phone.	AT&T, Syntellect, InterVoice, Dytel	406
Audiotex Service	Supplies recorded entertainment and information over the phone, sometimes with voice response capabilities.	Call Interactive, an AT&T-American Express joint venture; Universal Studios, MTV	900
Automatic Call Distributors	Parcel out incoming calls to operators.	Rockwell, AT&T, Rolm, Northern Telecom, Teknekron, Aspect, Solid State Systems	493
Speech Recognition	Lets computers "understand" and respond to the human voice.	AT&T, Texas Instruments, Kurzweil, Dragon, Verbex, Voice Control Systems	100

company and industry. Managers can start by looking at summaries and then request more detailed information if they wish.

Expert Systems

Expert systems are *computer programs that imitate human thinking through a complicated series of "if . . . then" rules.* These systems apply human knowledge to problems in specific subject areas in order to solve problems.

Alamo Rent-A-Car Inc. uses an expert system to help employees decide how to price its rental cars. The system continually compares Alamo's prices to those of competitors and identifies cases in which Alamo's rates are different. For instance, the demand for rental cars soars every October in Albuquerque, New Mexico, when the city hosts the international hot-air balloon races. Alamo's expert system signals employees when competitors' prices start rising to meet this peak demand, allowing Alamo to raise its prices, too. The system also catches data-entry errors and, by making employees more productive, enabled

Alamo to keep up with a 25 percent increase in business in one year without having to hire additional staff.[19]

Voice Processing

Voice processing involves technologies that use spoken language to send or receive information from a computer. Voice processing typically involves using the telephone. For example, an automated telephone ordering system can be used to order catalog merchandise from some retailers. Montgomery Ward uses voice processing to help customers find the store closest to them. Customers call an 800 phone number, enter their zip code, and a synthesized voice provides the location and phone number of the nearest store.

Voice processing also can improve customer service, while helping companies keep their costs down. Emerson Electric's In-Sin-Erator Division in Wisconsin offers a toll-free phone line with automated tips on fixing garbage disposals. Says customer service manager Julie Bezotte, "It's amazing how many people will call it at one, two, three o'clock in the morning." In the past, those calls would have gone unanswered because the company cannot afford to staff 24-hour specialists. The automated service provides a low-cost alternative.[20]

Speech recognition systems that allow computers to "understand" and respond to the human voice are still more common in science fiction than in business. At present, no commercially available system exists that instantly can understand a stranger's conversation. Systems first must be "trained" to understand specific individuals' voices and speech patterns. However, voice recognition systems, such as VoiceAssist, can, once trained, convert almost anything a certain speaker says to written text.[21]

Voice recognition systems can be a boon for the physically challenged. Three years ago, Don Dalton started Micro Overflow Corp., a Naperville, Illinois-based distributorship that adapts computer technology for the disabled. Dalton, who is paralyzed from the chest down, runs his computer by voice. Speaking into a microphone in a headset connected to a PC, he can activate all the computer's functions, type 100 words a minute, and manage the firm's finances and scheduling. Dalton expects sales to top $1 million this year, but he has another goal that is far more important to him. "I want the millions of people who are disabled and unemployed to be working for a living and be happy with themselves."[22]

Multimedia Computing

Multimedia computing refers to *the technologies that facilitate the integration of two or more types of media*, such as text, voice, sound, full-motion video, still video, graphics, and/or animation into a computer-based application. For example, *Compton's MultiMedia Encyclopedia* is an electronic reference work that includes 15,000 illustrations, many in full color, plus 45 animated sequences, an hour of audio clips of famous speeches and music, and *Webster's Intermediate Dictionary.*

Among the more promising business applications for multimedia computing are employee training and business presentations. Employees at Bethlehem Steel Corp., for instance, learn new steel production techniques from a video multimedia program that shows them how to analyze production, inventory, and sales statistics to control the availability of different types of steel. The multimedia approach has reduced training time at Bethlehem Steel 20 to 40 percent.[23]

Many multimedia applications are programmed on a *CD-ROM* (compact disk-read only memory), because the spiral-type storage is well-suited for retrieving continuous blocks of data, such as data converted

from music or animation. CD-ROMs are also useful because of their durability and large capacity. A single CD-ROM can store 680 megabytes of any kind of data—the equivalent of more than 1,000 floppy disks or a stack of books ten stories tall.[24]

Interactive Media and Groupware

While multimedia involves multiple technologies, interactive media is more focused on one technology with multiple applications. **Interactive media** involve *program applications that allow users to interact with computers to perform different functions at the same time.* For example, computer chip manufacturer Intel and Cable News Network are developing a system that allows people to view CNN broadcasts in a small window on their computer screens. In addition to simply watching the programs, viewers later can retrieve news clips by subject heading. "Instead of TV being something that happens to you, it can be something you control," says Steven McGeady, vice president of Intel's media delivery lab.[25]

Interactive media inevitably will change the way most people live their lives. Interactive video allows the TV viewer to select menu options using either a keyboard or remote control. The science fiction of yesterday's computerized world is closer to reality as the television becomes more than an entertainment medium—TV finally has grown to include an increasing number of business and educational applications. Out of 100 million U.S. households, one-third of

Interactive television allows viewers to choose between Seinfeld's weekly sitcom or the shopping channel. In addition, purchases can be made using an interactive remote control.

which own PCs, 7 million people already subscribe to interactive services such as CompuServe, Prodigy, and America Online. CEO Walter Forbes, of the Stamford, Connecticut-based CUC International shopping service, says: "This is virtual-reality inventory. We stock nothing, but we sell everything."[26]

An especially useful interactive medium is **groupware,** *computer software that combines and extends the concept of shared information (a database) with a method for moving data between users (E-mail).* Groupware is effective as a primary means of collaboration among users. Employees at the accounting and consulting firm Price Waterhouse use Lotus Development Corp.'s Notes groupware to keep in touch with more than 18,000 co-workers in 22 countries. Lotus Notes combines a sophisticated electronic mail system with a huge database containing work records and memos. Employees can consult over 1,000 *electronic bulletin boards* (public message centers that appear on computer networks) to learn about and obtain information on a variety of services and industries. They also can give their computers standing orders to locate and retrieve the latest news articles on specific topics.[27]

INFORMATION SYSTEMS AND SECURITY

As information systems become more important to business, they also become harder to replace. However, natural disasters, power failures, equipment malfunctions, and human error can wreak havoc with even the most sophisticated system. When computers are connected to a network, a problem at any location can affect the entire network. Organizations need to be prepared with backup plans so they can continue operating if their computer system fails.

While many of these security issues go beyond the scope of this textbook, we will discuss two important security threats: computer crime and viruses. These threats are so real that the Clinton administration is proposing the so-called Clipper Chip to be installed in telephones, faxes, computer modems, and any other equipment necessary for traveling the information superhighway. The Clipper is a digital scrambler that puts messages and data into a secret code so only the intended receiver has access to the information.[28]

Computer Crime

Computers can be an effective work tool. Unfortunately, they also can be an effective way to commit crimes. Computer crime falls into three general categories:

1. Data can be changed or invented to produce inaccurate information.
2. Computer programs can be changed to create false information or illegal transactions.
3. Unauthorized people can access a company's computer system and use it for their benefit.

Every year, U.S. companies lose over a half-billion dollars to computer crime. Often they are reluctant to admit it publicly, fearing the negative image this can give to the public.

Computer Viruses

A related problem involves *computer viruses,* programs that secretly attach themselves to other programs and change them or destroy the data kept on a disk. A virus

Information Controls	
Control	**Example**
Hardware	Restricting access to machines/terminals; checking for equipment malfunction.
Software	Requiring logs of operating-system activities; restricting unauthorized access to software programs.
Data security	Using passwords; restricting access to terminals to limit access to data files.
Operations	Establishing procedures for running computer jobs correctly; establishing backup and recovery procedures for abnormal or disrupted processing.
Systems development	Requiring management review and audit of each new information system project for conformity with budget, solution requirements, and quality standards; requiring appropriate technical and business documentation for each system.
Management	Establishing formal written policies and procedures; segregating job functions to minimize error and fraud; providing supervision and accountability.

General controls that organizations can use to protect their information systems.

IT'S THE LAW

A number of laws have been enacted to protect citizens' privacy. Many of these have a direct impact on business today.

1970 Freedom of Information Act Allows individuals to access any information about them that is stored in a government database.

1970 Fair Credit Reporting Act Gives consumers the right to review their credit records; prohibits credit bureaus from giving credit information to anyone but authorized customers.

1986 Electronic Communications Privacy Act Makes it illegal to intercept electronic communications.

1988 Computer Matching and Privacy Act Regulates computer matching of government data to verify people's eligibility for federal benefits programs and to identify delinquent debtors.

can reproduce by copying itself to other programs stored on the disk. It spreads as the owner of infected software exchanges software with other users, usually by an electronic bulletin board or by trading floppy disks. Viruses can be programmed to remain dormant for a long time, after which the infection suddenly activates itself.

Sometimes viruses result from pranks that get out of hand. One German student sent a Christmas greeting over a computer network which ended up spreading into IBM's international network and, within hours, attached itself to every mailing list it encountered.

Other viruses involve deliberate crimes. The Michelangelo virus, for example, erases data in computers that are used on March 6, the Italian artist's birthday. In one year, 18.2 percent of major U.S. companies reported being infected by this virus. Also

ETHICS AND SOCIAL RESPONSIBILITY

The Clipper Chip: Freedom of Speech or Restriction of Trade?

In 1993, the Clinton administration announced its plans for the Clipper Chip—a data encryption chip designed to scramble digital data, making it understandable only to the intended receiver. The Clipper, according to President Clinton, is necessary to protect privacy, both at home and abroad. With the growth of networks that have begun to envelope the globe, the government worries that, eventually, the country's defense will be endangered. Cryptography is included on the State Department's list of weapons that could compromise the nation's security.

Civil liberties leaders argue that the whole idea too closely resembles "Big Brother" and desktop surveillance. The government eavesdropped on 1.35 million conversations in 1991 and made 3,000 arrests as a result of court-authorized intercepts, according to a study by Computer Professionals for Social Responsibility.

The computer industry is the strongest opponent of the Clipper, since it faces the highest financial risk. While the controversy focuses on privacy, it has as much to do with controlling encryption technology and its market as anything else. The administration is proposing stringent regulations on exports of encryption technology, and only Clipper encryption is exempt. The problem is that U.S. manufacturers cannot meet foreign competition as a result of these proposed regulations. The Software Publishers Association counted 22 countries, including Britain, Germany, and Australia, that manufacture, use, and export some form of the encryption chip. Many of these chips are identical to encryption chips produced by U.S. producers. Digital Equipment lost sales of $70 million in 1993 because it couldn't provide the encryption customers wanted.

The best alternative for producers of encrypted software is to move production and operations outside the United States, robbing the nation of a potential leading role in tomorrow's technology.

SOURCES: James Aley, "How Not to Help High Tech," *Fortune,* May 16, 1994, 100–101; and Carol Levin, "Digital Privacy: Who Has the Right to Read Your Data?" *PC Magazine,* November 23, 1993, 29.

infected were computers in England, the Netherlands, Austria, and South Africa.

To protect against computer viruses, experts recommend the following steps:[29]

- Buy software only if it is in its original shrink-wrapping or sealed container.
- Make backup copies of all new software as soon as you open the package, and store the copies in a location away from the work place.
- "Quarantine" each new piece of software by reviewing it carefully on a computer that is not connected to a network.
- Restrict access to data and programs wherever possible.
- Check all programs regularly for changes in the amount of memory they use; any change could be a sign of tampering.
- Be cautious about using shareware or freeware programs (software that users on a network share with each other).
- Develop a plan for immediately removing from the computer system all copies of suspicious programs and related data.

Anti-viral programs are also available to help computer users detect and erase computer viruses.[30]

GOING GLOBAL ON THE INFORMATION SUPERHIGHWAY

In the past few years, the information superhighway has grown to resemble more closely an information *air*way, since it now spans the globe. France has swapped nearly all of its old-fashioned telephone switches for new digital ones. Singapore has built a state-of-the-art communications network to encourage international investment. And Nippon Telegraph & Telephone Corporation plans to interconnect every Japanese home, school, and business with fiber-optic cables by the year 2015. Is the United States ready to keep up with the traffic on this global highway?

New technology is expected to merge computers, television, telecommunications, and information systems into a single interactive information industry, one whose annual revenues could reach a staggering $3.5 trillion worldwide by 2001. President Clinton has

Japan-based Hitachi is a global provider of today's newest technology with a presence in hospitals, at construction sites, and even in the local hardware store.

Computer Aids for the Physically Challenged

For most PC users today, the greatest problem is knowing what key to push to get the results they want. But to thousands of physically challenged users, the seemingly simple task of *pushing* that key can be a major feat, let alone pushing a combination of two keys at once. That's where technology comes in.

While the typical daily computing jobs are taken for granted by many, they can be enormously painful and time consuming for a physically challenged user. Today, however, several programs and devices have been designed specifically to make computing easier for these challenged people. STAYDOWN, a utility program of Indianapolis-based Public Brand Software, enables key combinations, such as *alternate-F*, to be entered in two steps: first by pressing the alternate key and then the F key rather than having to use them simultaneously.

Concurrent keystrokes are only one obstacle for people with limited motor control. One function of the hardware installed in all IBM PCs and most of the other brands is that, if a key is held down for a period of seconds, an automatic repeat function kicks in until the key is released. Since utility programs, such as STAYDOWN and StickyKeys, are software, the user can override the repeat function by using DOS commands or purchasing a special software, such as NOREPEAT or DEBUG.

Another problem for physically challenged computer users is the inability to control how many times a key is pressed. Some users have a tendency to bounce keys—press a key twice when they meant to press it only once; other keys are struck by accident. Microsoft's RepeatKeys has a feature that allows the rate and delay interval of key strokes either to be set at specified intervals or eliminated entirely. SlowKeys ignores keystrokes that are not depressed for a specified period of time, and BounceKeys eliminates accidental repetitive keystrokes.

Another software package, Toggle-Keys, is designed for visually impaired users and provides an audible notification when lock keys, such as *Caps Lock, Num Lock,* or *Scroll Lock,* are on or off. Speech-recognition software is opening doors for many physically challenged PC users. Covox Voice Blaster can be attached to a Sound Blaster sound board to allow spoken commands to replace manually entered ones.

Although the number of software packages designed to help physically challenged computer users is increasing steadily, many people, including those with limited motor skills, are still unaware of how much of this type of computer technology is available. As these various software programs and devices become more familiar features in the computing world, it is highly likely that users other than the physically challenged will find applications for such packages.

SOURCE: Jeff Prosise, "Empowering Physically Challenged Users," *PC Magazine,* January 11, 1994, 261–263.

included $5 billion in the federal budget over the next few years specifically to develop equipment and software. AT&T, MCI, Sprint, and other telephone companies want to build the information highway and control what is transmitted over it. They are focusing on services that generate two-way traffic, such as video phones and long-distance library access—services that can be measured and billed by message units.

Computer companies like IBM and Hewlett-Packard are busy developing file servers that will store the information in video libraries. Computer software companies, such as Microsoft, are developing basic operating systems that will control the flow of information to each home. Entertainment companies are figuring out how to capture some of the $4 billion spent annually on video games, the $12 billion on video rentals, and the $70 billion on catalog shopping by offering these services in the home.

The U.S. computer industry has moved rapidly into international operations. Compaq, the world's leading producer of personal computers, has opened its first office in China, and Apple, AST, and IBM have plans to expand operations there as well. Motorola is perhaps the most internationally-based manufacturer in the computer industry. More than 50 years after H-P invented the Handie Talkie for American soldiers to lug through war-torn Europe, portable, wireless, two-way communication finally is becoming a medium for the masses. The Motorola Integrated Radio Service (MIRS) combines all the features of cellular phones, pagers, and two-way radios in a sleek, handheld device. Another state-of-the-art invention is the Motorola Envoy—a wireless device weighing under two pounds that will write and send a fax, retrieve E-mail, interface with online services, such as Internet and America Online, manage appointments, and keep financial records, to mention only a few of its features.

If Motorola continues its current rate of growth, it will gross $270 billion a year by 2013. The company already has gone beyond worldwide status with its sponsorship of Iridium, a $4 billion project to interconnect every square mile of the globe wirelessly via 66 satellites orbiting 420 miles above the earth.[31]

SUMMARY OF LEARNING GOALS

1. **Explain the purpose of an information system and how it aids decision making in business.**

   Information is a vital element in making business decisions. Effective decisions cannot be made without answers to questions about the internal operations of the firm and the external environment in which it operates. Progressive companies use a planned management information system (MIS) that provides past, present, and projected information on internal operations and external intelligence for use in decision making. Such information systems should aid all areas of the organization—production, accounting, marketing, human resources, purchasing, engineering, and finance—in carrying out their decision-making responsibilities.

2. **List the major contributions and limitations of computers.**

   In addition to speed and accuracy, computers provide many advantages over manual methods of data processing. They can store large amounts of data in a small space and quickly make this data available for decision makers. Also, by performing the mechanical, routine, boring work of recording and maintaining incoming information, they can free people for more challenging work. Limitations are that computers and software can be expensive, can make disastrous mistakes when programmed incorrectly, can become a crutch rather than a tool in decision making when they are relied on too heavily, and can alienate customers.

3. **Distinguish among mainframe computers, minicomputers, and microcomputers.**

   The primary basis for distinction among the three types of computers is size. Mainframes are the largest, with the greatest storage capacity and fastest processing speeds. Minicomputers are smaller (about the size of a small filing cabinet), less powerful, and less expensive. Microcomputers, the smallest type of computers, include desktops, notepads, and pocket computers that have limited storage systems but are portable. Each type—mainframe, minicomputer, and microcomputer—contains the basic elements of any computer system.

4. **Distinguish between computer hardware and software.**

   Computer hardware consists of all the tangible elements of the computer system. These include input devices, the machines that store and process data and perform required calculations, and output devices that communicate the results to the computer user. Software consists of computer languages and special programs that tell the computer what to do.

5. **Discuss the role of telecommunications in business.**

   Telecommunications refers to any system in which information or data is sent over a distance through some type of transmission medium. Telecommunications involves such technologies as computer networks, telephones, television, facsimile (fax) machines, and wireless communications. Telecommunications and computer networks are useful because they can link microcomputers and allow them to share printers and information. Computer networks make it easier for people to obtain and share information, even if they are not in the same location.

6. **Explain the concept of an information superhighway and its implications for business.**

   The term *information superhighway* refers to a single pathway that will merge telecommunications, information, and data networks and make them accessible to all consumers and businesses. This will give businesses and residences access to libraries, databases, teleconferencing, and many other services. The information superhighway will reduce the time necessary to transmit data and speed up the pace of work. It will overcome geographic barriers, and restructure business relationships by reducing the need for intermediaries.

7. **Describe the major business applications of computers.**

   Computers are used throughout the private and public sectors. It is difficult to imagine a modern organization operating without computers. Examples of important business applications include word processing, desktop publishing, decision support systems, spreadsheets, expert systems, electronic mail, executive information systems, expert systems, voice processing, multimedia computing, and interactive media.

8. **Summarize the major computer security issues that affect organizations.**

   Important computer security issues include natural disasters, power failures, equipment malfunctions, human error, computer crime, and computer viruses. When computers are connected to a network, a problem at any location can affect the entire network. Organizations need to be prepared with backup plans so they can continue operating if their computer system fails.

KEY TERMS QUIZ

chief information officer (CIO)	electronic mail (E-mail)	computer network
hardware	local area network (LAN)	database
spreadsheet	word processing	multimedia computing
microcomputer	management information system (MIS)	computer

expert system	desktop publishing	interactive media
telecommunications	decision support system (DSS)	information superhighway
groupware	software	

MIS _____ 1. Organized method of providing information for decision making.

CIO _____ 2. Top-management executive responsible for directing a firm's management information system and related computer operations.

Computer _____ 3. Programmable electronic device that can store, retrieve, and process data.

hardware _____ 4. All of the tangible elements of the computer system.

software _____ 5. Programmed instructions that tell the computer what to do.

microcomputer _____ 6. Desktop, laptop, and pocket-sized portable computers.

telecommunication _____ 7. Any system in which information or data is sent over a distance through some type of electronic transmission system, typically a telephone line.

information superhighway _____ 8. System in which interconnected computers either can function individually or communicate with each other.

computer network _____ 9. A single, enormous network merging telecommunications, information, and data that can be assessed by any individual or organization.

LAN _____ 10. A computer network that connects machines within a limited area.

word prossesing _____ 11. Use of computers to write, store, retrieve, edit, and print text materials.

desktop publishing _____ 12. Software designed to print documents with high-quality type, graphics, and layouts.

DSS _____ 13. Computer system that quickly provides relevant facts for use in decision making.

spreadsheat _____ 14. Special computer software permitting manipulation of decision variables to determine their impact.

E-mail _____ 15. Systems for sending and receiving written messages through computers.

data dase _____ 16. A centralized, integrated collection of the organization's data resources.

expert system _____ 17. Computer programs that imitate human thinking through the use of "if . . . then" rules.

multimedia computing _____ 18. The technologies that facilitate the integration of two or more types of media.

interactive media _____ 19. Program applications that allow users to interact with computers to perform different functions at the same time.

groupware _____ 20. Computer software that combines and extends the concept of shared information (a networked database) with a method for moving data between users (E-mail).

OTHER IMPORTANT TERMS

CD-ROM	mainframe computer
computer chips	minicomputer
computer virus	mouse
electronic bulletin boards	video display terminal (VDT)
microprocessor	voice processing

REVIEW QUESTIONS

1. Explain the purpose of a management information system and its functions in an organization.
2. What are the major contributions made by computers? What potential problems are involved with their use? Suggest steps to minimize each of these problems.
3. Categorize each of the following as either hardware or software and defend your choices:
   a. CD-ROM
   b. Computer instruction manual
   c. Line printer
   d. A company's customer database
   e. Keyboard
   f. Word processing program
   g. Groupware
4. Differentiate among the mainframe, minicomputer, and microcomputer.
5. What is telecommunications? Describe its impact on business operations.

230 PART THREE / Management: Empowering People to Achieve Business Objectives

6. List at least two computer applications for each of the following areas of business:
   a. Physical distribution
   b. Production and inventory control
   c. Human resources
   d. Marketing
   e. Finance and accounting
   f. Legal
   g. Customer service

7. Explain the term *information superhighway*. Which industries are likely to profit from such a pathway? Which might suffer financially from it?
8. What is multimedia computing? Give several examples.
9. Discuss how groupware might change business procedures and working relationships.
10. Explain why business people need to be aware of computer security and possible threats to their information system.

DISCUSSION QUESTIONS

1. Keep a diary for two or three days, recording each time a computer affects your life. Discuss what you learn from the exercise.
2. Discuss how your college or university uses information systems.
3. Ragnar Vanderhorn, a computer programmer at Tandum Computers, was doing contract work for a San Diego-based software publisher when he accidentally acquired a disk infected with a computer virus. Unsuspecting, he ran the infected disk on his office computer. Later, he reviewed one of the publisher's programs on the same computer and, unknowingly, infected his own company's program. When Ragnar returned the program to the publisher, they, in turn, copied the infected program into their nationwide system. Discuss ways to prevent instances of this nature.
4. Interview someone who has started using a computer at work. Ask this person to compare his or her job to the way it was before the computer was introduced. How has the job changed? Does this employee feel the computer is an asset, a drawback, or both? Why?

5. The Clinton administration wants U.S. companies to begin installing an encryptor—a digital scrambler that puts messages into secret code—in various information system components, including computers, telephones, and fax machines. The encryptor, called the Clipper Chip, would make users secure from computer hackers and competitors, who would be unable to crack the code. However, law enforcement agencies, with a court order, would be able to monitor these chips. FBI Director Louis Freeh defends the encryptor concept as a necessity in an age where conventional wire-tapping is fast becoming obsolete. However, many U.S. manufacturers claim that this would hurt their sales, especially in fast-growing overseas markets.

   Do you feel the government should require U.S. companies to install such a device? Defend your answer.

VIDEO CASE: Sea World

The video case for this chapter vividly demonstrates the impossibility of operating these aquatic theme parks—or of keeping their main attractions healthy—without a functioning information system. It is included on page 418 of Appendix D.

Solution to Key Terms Quiz

1. management information system (MIS) 2. chief information officer (CIO) 3. computer 4. hardware 5. software 6. microcomputer 7. telecommunications 8. information 9. computer network 10. local area network (LAN) 11. word processing 12. desktop publishing 13. decision support system (DSS) 14. spreadsheet 15. electronic mail (E-mail) 16. database 17. expert system 18. multimedia computing 19. interactive media 20. groupware superhighway

Production and Marketing

CHAPTER 11

Marketing Management and Customer Satisfaction

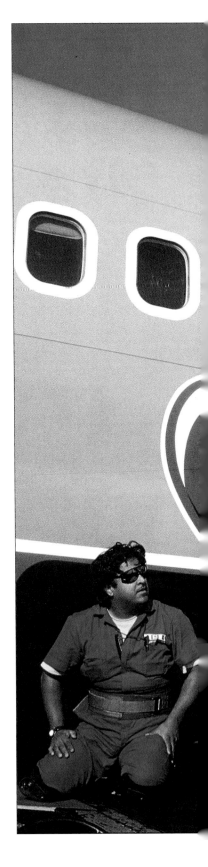

Learning Goals

1. Discuss how marketing's role in the exchange process creates utility.
2. List the major functions of marketing.
3. Explain the importance of the marketing concept and customer satisfaction in achieving success in the marketplace.
4. Outline methods for obtaining customer feedback and measuring customer satisfaction.
5. Outline how a marketing strategy is developed.
6. Explain the concept of a market.
7. Discuss why the study of consumer behavior is important to marketing.
8. Describe the marketing research function.
9. List and explain the bases used to segment markets.
10. Explain the concept of relationship marketing.
11. Identify the major components of the marketing environment.

The man was definitely having a bad day. Racing to catch his Southwest Airlines flight, he panted through the airport and ran down the jet way toward the waiting plane. He was too late; the plane already had pushed back and was about to depart. But the pilot spotted him, noted his anguished expression—and returned the plane to the gate to pick up the ecstatic passenger. Says Colleen Barrett, Southwest's executive vice president for customers, "It broke every rule in the book, but we congratulated the pilot on a job well done."

Putting customers first and breaking rules when necessary: this is what is known at Southwest Airlines as P.O.S. (Positively Outrageous Service). According to Barrett, "It's a level of service that's unexpected, delivered at random, out of the ordinary, and out of proportion for the circumstances. It generates word-of-mouth advertising and builds customer loyalty. Whether it's a small, individual act of kindness or an entire marketing concept, it creates pleasant memories and leaves the customer feeling good."

One Southwest reservations clerk in Dallas, for example, booked a flight for an 88-year-old woman who was flying to St. Louis. When the elderly woman's son worried that she would be unable to handle the change of planes in Tulsa, the clerk reassured him: "I'll fly with her as far as Tulsa and make sure she gets safely aboard the St. Louis flight."

P.O.S. helps Southwest turn negative situations into positive experiences for its customers. Recently, when an unusually severe winter delayed many planes, Southwest employees found themselves facing large crowds of disgruntled passengers who were stuck waiting for late flights. The employees came up with the idea of the LUV cart—a small cart stocked with coffee, soft drinks, and snacks. After passing out complimentary goodies, employees passed the time by playing games with passengers and holding impromptu contests. Customers received prizes for having the biggest hole in their socks, for warbling the Southwest Airlines ad jingle over the public-address system, or for answering trivia questions. The LUV cart became so popular that Southwest began using it whenever flights were delayed.

Southwest's customer service strategy is based on solid marketing research. Survey after survey shows that low fares and on-time flights are what matter most to air travellers, so the airline's management concentrates on providing them.

Rigorous cost-cutting helps Southwest maintain its bargain fares, which are often one-third those of the competition. Unlike other airlines, Southwest is not connected to the computerized reservation systems used by travel agents; nearly half of its tickets are sold directly to passengers, which saves the company about $30 million a year. The airline uses only one type of aircraft, the Boeing 737, which saves more money by simplifying employee training and plane maintenance. Southwest passengers do without assigned seating, and they dine on peanuts and crackers rather than full meals.

Southwest's enviable record of on-time performance is made possible by its efficient use of aircraft. Rather than using the hub-and-spoke routes of competitors, Southwest planes make frequent flights between pairs of cities that are located relatively close to each other; planes average ten flights a day, more than twice the industry average, and the usual flight is only 375 miles. The airline also prefers secondary airports in metropolitan areas; in Chicago, for example, it uses Midway rather than the crowded O'Hare airport. This helps ground crews turn around a plane at the gate in 15 to 20 minutes, compared to an hour for other airlines.

This attention to customer service has won Southwest both awards and more customers. For the past two years, the airline has received the U.S. Department of Transportation's Service Triple Crown—the most on-time flights, the best baggage handling, and the highest customer satisfaction rating. When Southwest enters a market, its low fares attract both passengers who ride on competing airlines and travellers who otherwise would take a bus or drive. Around 8,000 people used to fly between Louisville and Chicago every week, for example; now that Southwest offers flights on that route, about 26,000 travellers take to the air weekly.

Perhaps no one appreciates Southwest's P.O.S. more than a recent passenger who discovered, while boarding, that he couldn't bring his large, irascible dog with him. To placate the angry pet-owner, a customer service agent offered to take care of the animal—for the rest of the flier's two-week vacation. As Colleen Barrett says, "Rules are great, programs are great, but the bottom line is to do the right thing."[1]

CHAPTER OVERVIEW

All organizations—profit-oriented or not-for-profit—must serve consumer needs if they are to succeed. Perhaps J. C. Penney expressed it best when he told his store managers, "Either you or your replacement will greet the customer within the first 60 seconds." Marketing is the link between the organization and the consumer. It is the way in which consumer needs are determined and the means by which consumers are informed that the organization can meet those needs.

In addition to selling goods and services, marketing is also used to advocate ideas or viewpoints, and to educate people. For example, the American Diabetes Association mails out questionnaires that ask, "Are you at risk for diabetes?" and then lists risk factors and common symptoms as well as describing the work of the association.

The American Marketing Association defines **marketing** as *the process of planning and executing the conception, pricing, promotion, and distribution of ideas, goods, and services to create exchanges that satisfy individual and organizational objectives.* In this chapter we examine the role of marketing in organizations and describe how organizations develop a marketing strategy. We also will look at customer satisfaction as a key to organizational profitability and will discuss techniques for obtaining customer feedback and measuring customer satisfaction.

> **THEY SAID IT**
>
> "The only pretty store is one full of people."
>
> William Dillard
> (1914–   )
> Founder and chairman, Dillard's Department Stores

To convince consumers to make an exchange, for example, money for dishes, the marketer must convince them that they will gain from the transaction.

THE EXCHANGE PROCESS

Marketing activity begins when the exchange process becomes important to society. **Exchange** *is the process by which two or more parties trade things of value, so that each party feels it is better off after the trade.* For example, a consumer "trades" a check for $396.96 to Circuit City in exchange for a new color TV. But where does marketing fit in?

Consider a preindustrial society consisting of two families that each produce their own food and clothing. One of the families is expert at producing clothing; the other consists of skilled farmers. The exchange process allows the two families to concentrate on what they do best and to trade clothing for food and vice versa. This specialization and division of labor leads to increased total production and a higher standard of living for both families. The exchange process could not occur, however, unless each family marketed its products. Marketing is clearly a prime determinant of the overall standard of living. In fact, in advanced societies, marketing costs range between 40 and 60 percent of selling prices.

> **THEY SAID IT**
>
> "Marketing is merely a civilized form of warfare in which most battles are won with words, ideas, and disciplined thinking."
>
> *Albert W. Emery (1923–) American advertising agency executive*

FUNCTIONS OF MARKETING

Marketing is more than just selling—it is a complex activity that affects many aspects of an organization and its dealings with consumers. We can think of the functions of marketing in terms of *utility*, which is the want-satisfying power of a good or service. The production function is responsible for creating *form utility* by converting raw materials and other inputs into finished goods and services. The marketing function creates three other types of utility: time, place, and ownership. *Time utility* is created by having a good or service available when the consumer wants to purchase it. A bank with hours on Saturday illustrates this concept. *Place utility* is created by having a good or service available in the right place when the consumer wants to purchase it. The location of convenience stores and video-rental outlets suggest the importance of place utility. Arranging for an orderly transfer of ownership creates *ownership utility*. Retailers create ownership utility by accepting currency or credit-card payments, making it easier for customers to purchase merchandise.

Marketing adds to the utility of goods and services by performing some basic functions: buying, selling, transporting, storing, standardization and grading, financing, risk taking, and providing market information.

Buying and selling are the exchange functions of marketing. Marketers must study why consumers buy certain goods and services. Indeed, this study of consumer behavior is critical to the firm's overall success.

Transporting involves the physical movement of the product from the seller to the buyer, and storing involves the warehousing of goods until they are needed for sale. Standardization and grading deals with standardizing the description of goods; many industries, such as agricultural products or the tire industry, have specific grading standards for their goods. The financing function involves extending credit to consumers, wholesalers, and retailers.

Risk taking takes into account uncertainties about future consumer behavior; marketers must be entrepreneurial risk takers in many instances. For example, several major manufacturers currently are spending a lot of time and money developing refrigerators that use less energy and emit fewer CFCs. Marketers of these companies are betting that consumers will choose a more environmentally friendly refrigerator. Finally, marketers collect and analyze market information to determine what will sell and who will buy it.

THE MARKETING CONCEPT AND CUSTOMER SATISFACTION

In Chapter 6, we discussed the importance of quality in all functions of an organization. In the marketing function, the marketing concept is an important expression of quality. The **marketing concept** can be defined as *adopting a consumer orientation in order to achieve long-term success.* All of the organization's efforts, whether profit-oriented or not-for-profit, are geared to satisfying consumer needs.

Customer satisfaction directly affects a company's profitability. In fact, it is crucial to an organization's continued existence, since a company that fails to provide the same level of customer satisfaction as its competitors will not stay in business for very long. Boosting customer loyalty by just five percent translates into a significant increase in lifetime profits per customer. The profit increases range from 35 percent in the software industry to a whopping 95 percent for advertising agencies.

Today's savvy customers want the satisfaction of acquiring goods and services that go beyond the ordinary. They are demanding more than just a fair price; they are seeking an added value. *A good or service with* **added value** *attains increased worth by delivering more than expected—something of personal significance to the customer.* If marketers want to compete in today's marketplace, they need to conform to the customer's mind set and standards. In other words, companies have to work harder to make a sale and to satisfy the customer.

Consider the new check-in procedure at Marriott hotels. Hotel guests often complain about the time-consuming process of check-in, so Marriott decided to compete by streamlining it. Hotel employees collect important information, such as credit-card number and arrival time, when reservations are first made; this cuts the time guests must spend at the registration desk from an average 3 minutes to 1.5 minutes. Marriott now is working on ways to reduce

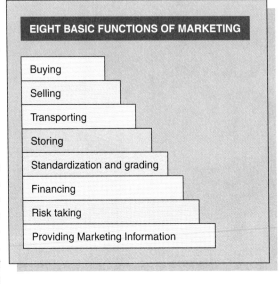

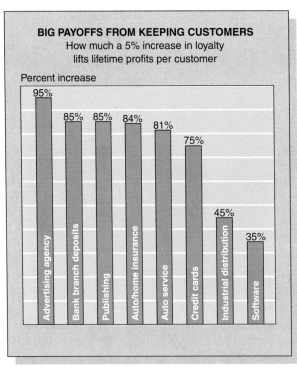

The Hyatt chain offers added value to its business customers by providing services such as copiers and in-room faxes.

this time even further by issuing electronic "smart cards" that will enable guests to register and locate their rooms automatically. Says Stephen Weisz, senior vice president of sales and marketing, "We don't want to just satisfy our customers—we want to delight them."[2]

Obtaining Customer Feedback

It is imperative for a company to obtain customer feedback. "It is important to get the voice of customers, to capture their words, in order to really understand what they want," remarks consultant Jennifer Brotman.[3] This is often a challenging task, as it can be difficult to determine the best way to obtain and measure clients' feedback.

Most firms use reactive methods, such as toll-free customer service telephone lines, to monitor customer feedback. Far fewer companies use proactive approaches—visiting clients, calling them, or sending out written surveys—to find out how satisfied their

customers really are. An example of a proactive approach is that used by the health maintenance organization Kaiser Permanente. Kaiser hires research firms to call Kaiser members to record and evaluate specific responses to lengthy questionnaires. Thus, consumer reactions are monitored to determine the satisfaction levels of HMO participants. A few companies may even go to the length of hiring a *mystery shopper*, a professional investigator who poses as a "shopper" and visits or calls a business in order to evaluate the services rendered.

Any method that makes it easier for customers to complain is to a firm's advantage. Customer complaints offer organizations the opportunity to overcome problems and prove commitment to service. Customers often have a stronger commitment to a company after a conflict has been resolved than they would have had they never complained at all. Businesses benefit from treating complaints as welcome resources and opportunities to gain innovative ideas for improvement. After all, studies show that while 95 percent of customers don't complain to the company, they end up telling 11 friends and/or business acquaintances about any negative experiences.[4]

Measuring Customer Satisfaction

Once it has obtained feedback, a firm may initiate a **customer satisfaction measurement (CSM) program,** *a procedure for measuring customer feedback against customer satisfaction goals and developing an action plan for improvement.* These programs can be quite sophisticated, and may require the aid of an outside specialist.

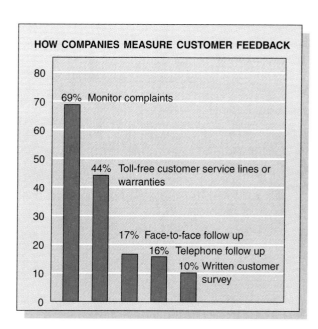

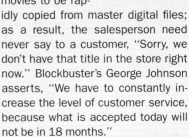

TECHNOLOGY

Customer Service Goes Hi-Tech

Along with the revolution in technology of the late twentieth century has come a revolution in customer service. In fact, *Business Week* reported that approximately 70 percent of 782 large companies surveyed in the United States and Europe said that their main goal in updating their technology was to improve customer service. Businesses use computers, voice mail, databases, speech recognition systems, cellular telephones, artificial intelligence, and point-of-sale scanners to achieve that aim.

Some uses of technology are relatively simple. WordPerfect, Microsoft, and Lotus all use phone systems that allow a "hold jockey" to amuse callers waiting to speak to customer support personnel. By interspersing music with information about how much longer callers are likely to have to wait, the "hold jockey" makes the customer's experience more agreeable.

Databases allow businesses to hone their services to match customer preferences exactly. Dell analyzed the buying patterns of computer users and discovered that the small hard drives didn't meet their needs; Dell switched to larger hard drives, with great success. A customer ser-vice database saved Whirlpool much aggravation when the company easily tracked down defective washing machines they had already sold and fixed them before the buyers even knew there was a problem. A & P uses its customer information to match the food at each of its stores to the predilections of the neighborhood shoppers.

The salespeople of F. D. Titus & Son, which distributes medical supplies, use "personal communicators," which include pen-based computers, fax capability, and a cellular phone. Through these "communicators," salespeople can access the Titus catalogue and database from wherever they are, allowing them to answer customer queries and meet customer needs promptly and accurately.

Even more sophisticated technology is being developed constantly. The Universal credit card division of AT&T plans a "Personal Servant," a speech recognition-artificial intelligence hybrid that will respond to instructions via phone or computer to purchase airline tickets, pay bills, and balance checkbooks. AT&T even intends to let each user choose the voice and attitude of the personal servant.

Blockbuster Entertainment aims to stay on the cutting edge of customer service through distribution-on-demand retailing and rental. This technology will allow music and movies to be rapidly copied from master digital files; as a result, the salesperson need never say to a customer, "Sorry, we don't have that title in the store right now." Blockbuster's George Johnson asserts, "We have to constantly increase the level of customer service, because what is accepted today will not be in 18 months."

Even old-fashioned services like providing a place to sleep are rushing into the future, as hotel chains such as Marriott provide computers and fax machines for their guests, switch to credit card-sized "smart cards" or speech recognition systems rather than door keys, and plan eventually to have videoconferencing facilities on site or perhaps in every room.

One day technology will even assist the customer desperate to talk to a plain old human being, as video technology matures to allow face-to-face interaction over the phone.

SOURCES: John Verity, "The Gold Mine of Data in Customer Service," *Business Week,* March 21, 1994, 113–114; Mark D. Fefer, "Taking the Pain Out of Holding Patterns," *Fortune,* January 10, 1994, 20; and Faye Rice, "The New Rules of Superlative Service," *Fortune,* Autumn–Winter 1993, 50–53.

CSM programs vary widely, but most include the following steps:

1. Determine what areas are critical to the business and what measurement systems currently are being used.
2. Probe a representative group of customers to learn what factors, or attributes, are important to their use of a good or service.
3. Conduct research to determine the company's performance on the selected attributes.
4. Analyze results to develop action plans.

For instance, GTE embarked on a customer satisfaction measurement program by focusing on its telephone division, which brings in four-fifths of the corporation's $20 billion annual revenues. The company measured customer satisfaction by evaluating how quickly its repair staff responded when customers called to report problems on their phone lines. The feedback was not encouraging. Customers wanted to have their problems solved while they were still on the phone to GTE, and this happened only once in 200 calls. Research showed that many of the delays occurred because each "trouble ticket" not only had to be filled out by a repair clerk but also had to be processed by several other employees before the line actually was tested and repaired. Based on these findings, GTE managers developed an action plan that called for establishing a "customer care center" where repair clerks have switching and testing equipment at their desks and receive regular training on how to use it. These days, repair clerks can solve customers' problems while they're on the line in three out of ten calls, and GTE eventually hopes to increase this success record to seven out of ten.[5]

Marketing in Not-for-Profit Organizations

The not-for-profit sector consists of some 900,000 organizations, including museums, colleges and universities, symphony orchestras, religious and human services organizations, government agencies, political parties, and labor unions. Like profit-seeking firms, not-for-profit organizations may market a tangible good or an intangible service, or both. The U.S. Postal Service, for example, offers stamps (a tangible good) and mail delivery (an intangible service).

Atlanta has been the focus of event marketing throughout this decade as the city prepares for the 1996 Olympics.

Five types of not-for-profit marketing are person marketing, place marketing, cause marketing, event marketing, and organization marketing. **Person marketing** *refers to a program designed to enhance the favorable opinion of an individual by selected others.* The marketing of a political candidate is an example. Campaign managers conduct marketing research to identify voters and financial supporters and then design promotions, such as advertising, fund-raising events, and political rallies, to reach voters and donors.

Place marketing *refers to attempts to attract people to a particular area, such as a city, state, or nation.* In addition to marketing themselves as a general vacation destination, some areas advertise to specific market segments. For instance, Jamaica, Bermuda, and Puerto Rico place ads in bridal magazines to catch the attention of brides-to-be who are planning their honeymoons.

Cause marketing *refers to the marketing of a social cause or issue.* Cause marketing covers a wide range of issues, including gun control, birth defects, child abuse, physical fitness, overeating, and alcoholism.

Event marketing is *the marketing of sporting, cultural, and charitable activities to selected target markets.* It includes the sponsorship of such events by firms seeking to increase public awareness and bolster their images by linking themselves and their products to a specific event. The worldwide recognition received by official sponsors and marketing partners of the recent World Cup soccer championship is an example of event marketing on a very large scale.

Organization marketing *attempts to influence others to accept the goals of, receive the services of, or contribute in some way to an organization.* The Smithsonian Institution in Washington, D.C., tries to attract new members by offering free three-month trial memberships. Temporary members receive complimentary issues of *Smithsonian* magazine and qualify for discounts on special tours and items sold through the museum gift shops.

> **THEY SAID IT**
>
> "I solemnly promise and declare that every customer that comes within ten feet of me, I will smile, look them in the eye, and greet them, so help me Sam."
>
> *Employee pledge, Wal-Mart Stores*

Developing a Marketing Strategy

All organizations, whether profit oriented or not-for-profit, need to develop a marketing strategy to reach customers effectively. This involves analyzing the market, selecting a target market, and developing a marketing mix.

Often a company will develop a marketing plan, which is a written document that expresses the firm's marketing strategy. Target market, sales and revenue goals, marketing budget, and timing of the marketing mix elements are included in the marketing plan.

A **market** consists of people with purchasing power and the authority to buy. Markets can be classified by the types of products they handle, whether consumer or business products. **Consumer products** are those goods and services purchased by the ultimate consumer for his or her own use. Examples include such familiar items as toothpaste, shoes, and CDs. **Business products**—*sometimes called organizational or industrial products—are goods and services purchased to be used, either directly or indirectly, in the production of other goods for resale.* Sometimes an item can be either a consumer or business product, depending on who buys it and why. The computer you bought for your own use at home is a consumer product; but that same computer, if purchased by a company for use by its office staff, becomes a business good.

Marketers must be familiar with a market's buying patterns and the purchasing behavior of those involved. This knowledge is critical when marketers deal with consumer and business goods and services.

Having analyzed the market, the next step is to select a **target market**—*the group of consumers toward whom a firm will direct its marketing efforts.* Consumer needs and wants vary considerably, and no single organization has the resources to satisfy everyone. Sometimes an organization chooses several target markets for a given good or service. A college or university might select several target markets for its fund-raising campaign: alumni, wealthy benefactors, foundations, and local businesses.

The final step is creating a marketing mix to satisfy the needs of the target market. The **marketing mix** *is a combination of the firm's product, pricing, distribution, and promotion strategies;* it is the mechanism that

DID YOU KNOW?

Hoover is such a well-known brand in the United Kingdom that the British use *hoover* as a verb for vacuuming. Similarly, Middle Easterners call laundry detergents *tide.*

One American firm, seeking an African market for its baby food, packed its jar labels with product information and a picture of a smiling baby. But many of the potential customers cannot read and write. Unable to read the print on the label, they assumed that what was on the outside of the jar was what was inside it—babies.

White is the color of mourning in Japan. The color purple is associated with death in Latin America.

Most American hotels have somehow managed to eliminate the thirteenth floor.

A computer can be either a consumer product or a business product, depending on how the buyer uses it. As more people work out of their homes, it increasingly becomes both.

Nike uses print advertising to reach its target markets.

allows organizations to match consumer needs with product offerings. We will discuss the marketing mix in more detail in Chapter 13.

RELATIONSHIP MARKETING

An important trend in marketing centers on the concept of relationship marketing. **Relationship marketing** is *an organization's attempt to develop long-term, cost-effective links with individual customers for mutual benefit.*

Good relationships with customers can be a vital strategic weapon for a firm. By identifying current purchasers and maintaining a positive relationship with them, organizations can target their best customers more efficiently. As Mitch Kurz, president of ad agency Wunderman Cato Johnson, says, "That's where the money is. . . . Without exception, every client's profits are drawn from a relatively small number of its current users." Furthermore, studying current customers' buying habits and preferences can help marketers identify potential new customers and keep in touch with them on an ongoing basis.

Information technologies, such as computers, databases, and spreadsheets, help make effective relationship marketing possible. Marketers can maintain databases on current customers' tastes, price ranges, and lifestyles, and can obtain names and other information about good prospects quickly. Spreadsheets allow marketers to answer "what if" questions related to prices and marketing performance.

Service industries, including retailers and airlines, have been in the forefront of relationship marketing, since their staffs often meet customers personally. Sears, for instance, builds loyalty and repeat business through its Best Customer plan. "Best customers" are those who come to Sears at least six times a year, spend a large amount there annually, and shop in a variety of departments. According to Al Malony, senior marketing manager for customer marketing, there are 7.2 million best customers, each of whom is worth five to six times more to Sears than a new customer. The plan retains their patronage by offering benefits and privileges, such as guaranteed response to a service call within 24 hours. It has boosted Sears' retention rate by

Sears' "best customers" receive personalized attention aimed at keeping them loyal to the chain.

11 percent and increased sales to the best-customer group by 9 percent.

Air France attempts to build an ongoing relationship with passengers who ride the Concorde several times a year by offering periodic gifts. While this target market may consist of only a few hundred people, they are responsible for $25 million to $30 million of the airline's annual revenues. It is important, of course, to tailor such gifts to the tastes of the market; as Mitch Kurz notes, "These are not the kind of people who are going to be looking for a coupon for $50 off their next $6,000 trip." Instead, Air France offers more upscale freebies, such as videocassettes of French director Jean Cocteau's film *Beauty and the Beast.*[16]

THE MARKETING ENVIRONMENT

In selecting a target market and developing a marketing mix, marketers must consider the environmental forces described as competitive, political and legal, economic, technological, social, and cultural. As the following figure illustrates, these five external forces provide the framework for planning product, pricing, distribution, and promotion strategies aimed at the target market.

To some extent, all organizations are affected by the external forces in the marketing environment over which they have little or no control. Marketers must monitor these factors and assess the impact they will have on goods, services, and marketing practices, adjusting marketing strategy accordingly.

Competitive Environment

Marketers must monitor the marketing activities of their competitors continually in order to devise a strategy that will give them a competitive edge. An old marketing tool that is becoming increasingly im-

portant again is the *satisfaction guarantee*, which many firms use to distinguish themselves from the competition. Xerox, for example, promises that if you are not satisfied with your Xerox equipment within three years after you buy it, the company will exchange it for an identical model or a comparable machine. Mannington Resilient Floors, which sells vinyl flooring, offers a "no questions asked" one-year warranty for its top-of-the-line Mannington Gold brand; if you don't like the new floor for any reason, the company will rip it out and replace it—free of charge. If the staff at a Hampton Inn cannot satisfy a disgruntled guest, the customer gets to spend the night there for free.[17]

Political and Legal Environment

Federal, state, and local governments pass laws that regulate many marketing activities, ranging from package labeling to product safety. These laws are designed to maintain a competitive environment and protect consumers. Marketers must be aware of them in order to comply with them, and noncompliance can result in fines, bad publicity, and even lawsuits. Sometimes government regulations can have an unexpected negative impact on a business. New England lobster marketers lost a sizable portion of their export market to Japan when the states increased the minimum size of a legally caught lobster to 3¼ inches from 3³⁄₁₆ inches. Canada kept the lower limit, one that matches a one-pound lobster. Japanese consumers prefer smaller lobsters, so the 1-pound Canadian exports were well received there.[18]

The marketing environment consists of competitive, political and legal, economic, technological, and social and cultural components.

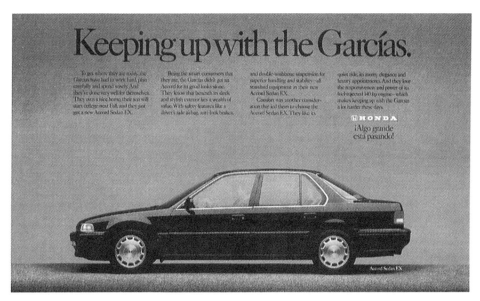

Honda attempts to reach middle-class Hispanics by playing on the familiar "keeping up with the Joneses" theme. Marketers use a number of strategies, including Spanish language or combined Spanish–English ads to reach the Hispanic market.

Economic Environment

Economic factors, such as inflation, unemployment, and business cycles, influence how much consumers are willing and able to spend as well as what they buy. Marketers' understanding of how economic factors influence consumer buying behavior allows them to adjust their marketing-mix strategies. For example, during a recession, consumers are more apt to buy basic products with low prices. Marketers might respond by lowering prices and increasing promotional spending to stimulate demand. Different strategies apply during prosperous times, when consumers are willing to purchase higher-priced goods and services. Marketers then might consider raising prices, expanding distribution, and increasing product lines.

Technological Environment

Changes in technology have a significant impact on how marketers design, produce, price, distribute, and promote their goods and services. New technology can make a product obsolete. For example, calculators wiped out the market for slide rules. Technological adaptations can give an organization a competitive advantage and create new marketing opportunities. Again consider the case of the U.S. lobster industry. Since it is difficult to ship live lobsters to Japan, the industry is now looking into "relay pounds" in Hawaii where Maine lobsters could be revived in saltwater before continuing the journey to Japan.[19]

Social and Cultural Environment

Consumer values change, and marketers must keep abreast of these changes to ensure that their marketing strategies are effective. Many companies are realizing that standard English-language advertisements are not reaching all Americans. "Minorities were the majority of population growth in the 1980s," notes *American Demographics* publisher Peter Francese. "In some products," says the founder of an Hispanic advertising agency, "Hispanics are 30 percent to 35 percent of sales." There is a growing multilingual mass market in the United States, and savvy marketers are finding ways to tap into America's rich cultural diversity. In a new ad on English-language TV stations, for instance, a cast of Hispanic-Americans praise Diet Coke in both English ("Just one calorie!") and Spanish (*"Por su sabor refrescante"*).[20]

Marketing Products Abroad: Standardization versus Adaptation

Marketing a good or service overseas means choosing between standardization—selling the same product to every market—and adaptation—modifying products to fit each market.

The advantages of standardizing include better marketing performance and lower costs. This approach seems to work best with business goods, such as steel, chemicals, and farm equipment, which tend to be less dependent on each nation's culture.

Adaptation, on the other hand, lets companies adapt more effectively to local competition, consumer behavior patterns, and government regulations. Consumer goods generally require product adaptation because they tend to be more culture-dependent than business products.

Increasingly, companies even are trying to build adaptability into standardized goods and services. You can have a beer with your Burger King Whopper in France. In Holland, Heineken beer sells at about the same price as mineral water and soft drinks. However, overseas, Heineken has determined that its overseas target market will pay a premium price for the product.[6]

CONSUMER BEHAVIOR

Consumer behavior *consists of actions that are involved directly in obtaining, consuming, and disposing of products, including the decision processes that precede and follow these actions.*[7] This definition includes both consumers and business purchasers. By studying consumer behavior, marketers can identify consumers' attitudes toward their products and how they use the items. This, in turn, helps marketers develop more effective marketing strategies for reaching these people.

Frito-Lay conducts extensive market research to see what people want in a potato chip. The company also studies how, when, and why people eat chips. Sixty-five percent of all chips, it has found, are eaten in private. "When one is alone on a Friday night, potato chips confer some of the merriment and excitement of snacks eaten previously at a party or other fun event," suggests one psychologist.[8] Responding to consumers' concerns about fatty foods, Frito-Lay now promotes its reduced-oil Lite Ruffles chips. "Less than that, they taste lousy, and consumers won't sacrifice taste for health in snacks," says Dwight Riskey, Frito-Lay's vice president of market research. A typical adult eats about 72 potato chips (four ounces) in one sitting. Frito-Lay discovered this by renting theaters and offering thousands of moviegoers free tickets and unmarked bags of chips. The company collected the bags when people left and counted the uneaten chips. The result? People apparently felt a bit guilty about eating such an openly unhealthy snack. The tests showed that consumers eat about one-third more chips at a sitting than they admit to in interviews.[9]

Both personal and interpersonal factors influence consumer behavior. The personal influences on consumer behavior include people's needs and motives,

> ### THEY SAID IT
> "Fifty percent of Japanese companies do not have a marketing department, and ninety percent have no special section for marketing research. The reason is that everyone is considered to be a marketing specialist."
>
> *Hiroyuki Takeuchi*
> *(1934–)*
> *Educator and*
> *business writer*

perceptions, attitudes, learned experiences, and self-concepts. Marketers frequently use psychological techniques to understand what motivates people to buy products and to study consumers' emotional reactions to goods and services. Frito-Lay researchers, for example, show consumers photographs of people in various situations, and ask whether these people are likely to eat potato chips. Some answers: construction workers and people with umbrellas are unlikely to eat chips, while someone playing softball is slightly more likely to eat them. Most likely of all is a person watching television. From such responses, Frito-Lay assembles videotapes depicting "typical" consumers of various Frito-Lay products. Munchers of Lay's potato chips are "affectionate, irresistible, casual, and a fun member of the family." The Dorito tortilla chips video depicts people talking about dating and love; the singer formerly known as Prince takes off his shirt, and an unknown person writes "I want" on a blackboard. Customers who prefer Ruffles potato chips are portrayed as "expressive, aware, confident enough to make a personal statement." The videos are shown to copywriters who prepare ads for the company's different product lines.[10]

The interpersonal determinants of consumer behavior include cultural influences, social influences, and family influences. Such factors often will vary in different countries—even countries that speak the same language, such as the United States and Great Britain.

In its American ads, Pet Inc. brags that its Old El Paso taco shells are less likely to break apart than those of the competition. In Britain, such claims are meaningless, for a very simple reason: most Britons don't know what a taco is. Indeed, all "finger foods" are much less common in Europe. During Pet's market-research interviews, many Brits asked for a knife and fork prior to eating a taco. Pet's British ads now explain what tacos are and how to make (and eat) them. Today, Old El Paso leads the British taco market.[11]

Purchasers of business products face a variety of organizational influences as well as their own personal preferences, since many people can play a role in a business purchase. A design engineer may be instrumental in setting the specifications that potential vendors must satisfy. A purchasing manager invites selected companies to bid on the purchase. A production supervisor is responsible for evaluating the operational aspects of the proposals that are received, and the vice president of manufacturing may make the final decision.

MARKETING RESEARCH

Marketing research *is the information function that ties the marketer to the marketplace.* It provides the information about potential target markets that is necessary to design effective marketing mixes. Marketers conduct research for five basic reasons:

1. to identify marketing problems and opportunities;
2. to analyze competitors' strategies;
3. to evaluate and predict consumer behavior;
4. to gauge the performance of existing products and package designs and assess the potential of new ones; and
5. to develop price, promotion, and distribution plans.

Marketing research involves more than just collecting information. Researchers also must decide how to collect the information, interpret the results, and communicate the interpretation to managers for their use in decision making.

Marketing research started in a humorous way. In the early 1900s, Charles C. Parlin was trying to sell advertising space in the *Saturday Evening Post* to Campbell Soup Company. But the soup company resisted, saying that its product was sold to upscale consumers who paid a pricey ten cents per can. The *Saturday Evening Post*, by contrast, was viewed as being sold to a working-class audience.

Parlin eventually overcame Campbell Soup's sales resistance by counting empty soup cans in the garbage from different neighborhoods. He soon found that more soup cans came from working-class neighborhoods than from wealthier areas. Parlin reasoned that well-to-do people had servants who made soup from scratch. Campbell Soup soon became an advertiser in the *Saturday Evening Post*, and Parlin became the head of the first marketing research department established in the United States.

Marketers occasionally use short-hand names developed by their customers in their advertising—or even in their brand names. McDonald's advertising often incorporates the teenager's reference to "Mickey-D's." Overnight delivery pioneer Federal Express Corporation went even further in adopting the FedEx abbreviation commonly used by its customers.

Obtaining Marketing Research Data

Marketing researchers are concerned with both internal and external data. *Internal data* are generated within the organization. A tremendous amount of useful information is available from financial records, such as changes in accounts receivable, inventory levels, customers, product lines, profitability of particular divisions, or comparisons of sales by territories, salespeople, customers, or product lines.

External data are generated outside the firm and can be obtained from previously published data. Trade associations, for example, publish reports on activities in particular industries. Advertising agencies collect information on the audiences reached by various media. National marketing research firms offer information to organizations on a subscription basis. Citicorp, for example, offers information from customer files on 30 million Citibank Visa and MasterCard cardholders. The service, called CitiProfiles, helps marketers create consumer profiles using 15 categories of data, including age, income, ZIP code, shopping frequency, and average purchase amounts. Credit-card databases like this can provide valuable information on what consumers actually buy as opposed to what they say they can buy—which is not always the same.[12]

Federal, state, and local government publications are the marketing researcher's most important data sources. The most frequently used government statistics are census data, available on population characteristics, such as age, sex, race, education levels, household size and composition, occupation, employment status, and income. Such information helps marketers to assess the buying behavior of certain segments of the population, anticipate changes in their markets, and identify markets with growth potential.

In addition to using published data, marketing researchers also gather information by conducting

ETHICS AND SOCIAL RESPONSIBILITY

Equal-Access Advertising

As recently as 1980, the only commercials that featured disabled people were charity fund-raisers. Businesses feared that showing deaf people, blind people, people with Down Syndrome, or people in wheelchairs in their ads would distract attention from their products. They also worried that the commercials might be perceived as maudlin, manipulative, or unattractive.

In 1984, Levi Strauss, often a ground-breaker in social issues, produced a spot featuring an actor in a wheelchair. Little by little, other advertisers followed suit. Vietnam veteran, basketball player, and amputee Bill Demby stars in a DuPont ad; IBM, Apple, Nordstrom, and Target pieces depict people in wheelchairs; and deaf architect Eliza Rubins uses sign language to "talk" about Dr. Scholl's Clear Away, a wart remover. Recently, a Budweiser commercial focused on a wheelchair athlete lifting weights, completing a marathon, and flirting with his girlfriend.

This evolution was motivated in part by disability activists who fought for better representation in the media and by the Americans with Disabilities Act, which mandates equal access for the disabled to businesses, public transportation, and schools—thereby bringing disabled people more into the public eye. In addition, during the 1980s, corporations came to realize that 43 million American consumers are disabled. Says Sandra Gordon of the National Easter Seal Society, "Companies have started seeing that there are disabled people out there who are working and have money."

Toys "R" Us devotes an entire catalogue to disabled children. The 22-page "Toy Guide for Differently-

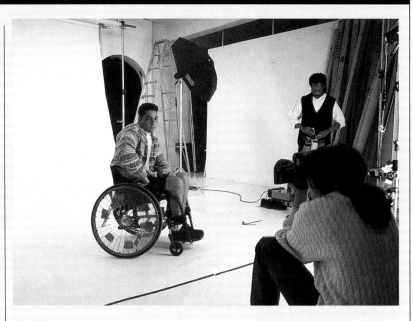

Abled Kids!" uses a series of colored symbols, such as a yellow ear for "auditory" and an orange sneaker for "gross motor," to help parents match toys to their children's particular needs. For instance, the Tonka "Preschool Dump Truck" is accompanied by the symbols for visual, thinking, gross motor, and fine motor benefits. The "Little Tikes Place," a doll house with dolls and furniture, offers a wheelchair ramp and a little boy doll in a wheelchair, sold separately from the main set. The models in the catalogue, or different ethnic backgrounds and both sexes, sit in wheelchairs or wear glasses or hearing aids. Writes Charles Lazarus in the front of the catalogue, "As founder of Toys 'R' Us, I am dedicated to providing toys for all children everywhere."

Not all responses to disabled people in ads and catalogues have been positive. A Spray 'N Wash Stain Stick commercial starring Halley Ewing, who has Down Syndrome, was called "crassly contrived" by *Advertising Age,* and McDonald's creative direc-

tor Susan Leick says that McDonald's occasionally gets letters from customers who "are uncomfortable" seeing disabled people in McDonald's ads.

Despite some complaints, it is likely companies will continue to hire disabled actors and models. "Our ads featuring the disabled have performed equal to or better than our other ads," explains Bob Thacker, vice president of retail discounter Target. And there are other benefits as well: "People thank us for acknowledging a previously anonymous group. Many are touched that we've given their children an example to aspire to."

SOURCES: Toys "R" Us, *Toy Guide for Differently-Abled Kids!* 1994; Bruce Horovitz, "Caught in a Delicate Balance," *Los Angeles Times,* May 22, 1993, 1, 14–15; Bernice Kanner, "Equal-Opportunity Advertising," *New York,* May 25, 1992, 22–23; Elizabeth Roberts and Annetta Miller, "This Ad's for You," *Newsweek,* February 24, 1992, 40.

observational studies and surveys. In *observational studies*, researchers actually view the actions of the respondents, either directly or through mechanical de-

vices. Traffic counts can be used to determine the best location for a new fast-food restaurant. *People meters* (electronic, remote-control devices that record the viewing habits of each household member) are used to check television audience viewership, thereby setting advertising rates.

Some information cannot be obtained through simple observation. When information is needed about attitudes, opinions, and motives, researchers must ask questions by conducting a *survey.* Survey methods include telephone interviews, mail surveys, personal interviews, and focus groups. In a *focus group interview,* 8 to 12 people are brought together in one location to discuss the subject being researched. Ideas generated during focus group interviews are especially helpful to marketers in developing new products, improving existing products, and creating effective advertising campaigns.

Applying Marketing Research Data

The information collected by researchers is valuable only when it can be used to make decisions within the framework of the organization's strategic plan. The more accurate the information collected by researchers, the more effective are the marketing strategies that result. Sometimes market research can be very specific indeed, even focusing on various individual purchase patterns. Waldenbooks has enrolled 3.7 million members in a program that rewards people who buy books frequently with discounts and extra service. In addition to increasing store visits by club members by 43 percent, the program allows the retailer to keep track of who buys what. The company then promotes books on particular topics to consumers who have shown interest in those subjects in the

past. Sales of books promoted in this way are up as much as 25 percent.[13]

MARKET SEGMENTATION

Market segmentation *is the process of dividing the total market into several relatively homogeneous groups.* Both profit-oriented and not-for-profit organizations use market segmentation to help define their target markets.

The figure shows that markets can be segmented on a variety of bases. Consumer marketers may divide markets according to demographic characteristics, such as sex, age, and family life-cycle stage; geographic factors; psychographic variables, which involve behavioral and lifestyle profiles; and product-related variables, such as the benefits that consumers seek when buying a product, or the degree of brand loyalty they feel toward it.

Segmentation strategies are important worldwide. In Europe, for instance, Volvo used psychographic research as the basis for developing a small, sporty-style coupe for career women. In Holland, an Amsterdam retailer has taken a product-related approach to segmentation. Witte Tanden-Winkel (translated "White Tooth Shop") sells only dental products like toothbrushes and floss.[14]

In the past several years, mainstream companies have begun marketing directly to gays and lesbians. Recent print ad campaigns by Benetton, American Express, and Met Life use same-sex couples, and viewers in some television markets saw two men picking out home furnishings together in an IKEA commercial.[15]

Alternative Methods of Segmenting Consumer and Business Markets

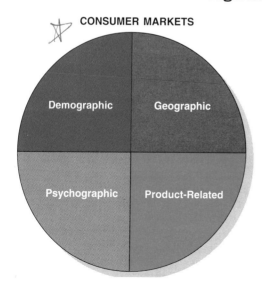

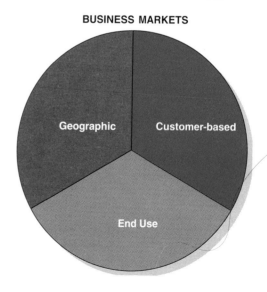

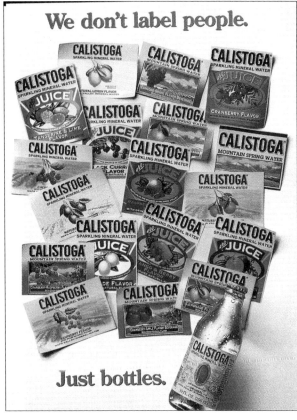

Companies are using several types of promotion to tap into the gay market: Calistoga Mineral Water runs print ads with a message of acceptance in gay and lesbian magazines; PLWC sponsored Stonewall 25, a commemoration of the New York City riot that started the gay liberation movement.

Miller Lite has become a corporate sponsor of the Gay Rodeo after many years of sponsorship by individual distributors. Gay and lesbian couples, who tend to be childless, are seen as consumers with disposable income to burn. A 1991 survey by Overlooked Opinions, a Chicago marketing firm, estimated gay spending power at $500 billion, although this has recently been disputed.[16] Up until now, much of that money was spent within the community at gay-owned businesses. It remains to be seen how far acceptance will go—Martina Navratilova or Greg Louganis on a Wheaties box is still in the future. What is clear, however, is that lesbian and gay consumers, long overlooked, are not being ignored any longer.

Business marketers segment markets according to three criteria: geographic characteristics; customer-based specifications for products; and end-use applications, or the precise way in which the business purchaser will use the product.

SUMMARY OF LEARNING GOALS

1. Discuss how marketing's role in the exchange process creates utility.

Exchange is the process by which two or more parties give something of value to one another to satisfy felt needs. Marketing is closely linked with the exchange process. It creates utility—the want-satisfying power of a good or service—by having the product available when and where the consumer wants to buy it and by arranging for an orderly transfer of ownership. While production creates form utility, marketing creates time, place, and ownership utility.

2. List the major functions of marketing.

The eight basic functions of marketing are buying, selling, transporting, storing, standardization and grading, financing, risk taking, and acquiring market information.

3. Explain the importance of the marketing concept and customer satisfaction in achieving success in the marketplace.

In the marketing function, the marketing concept—adopting a consumer orientation in order to achieve long-term success—is an important expression of quality. Customer satisfaction—the ability of a good or service to meet or exceed buyer needs and expectations—is the true measure of quality. Customer satisfaction directly affects a company's profitability. It is crucial to an organization's continued existence, since a company that fails to provide the same level of customer satisfaction as its competitors will not stay in business for very long.

4. **Outline methods for obtaining customer feedback and measuring customer satisfaction.**

Companies can obtain customer feedback in many ways, including monitoring complaints; monitoring feedback from warranties and from toll-free phone service lines; visiting clients; calling them; sending out written surveys; or hiring "mystery shoppers." To measure customer satisfaction, a firm may initiate a customer satisfaction measurement (CSM) program. CSM programs involve determining what areas are most critical to the business and what measurement systems are currently being used; probing a representative group of customers; conducting research to determine the company's performance; and analyzing results to develop action plans.

5. **Outline how a marketing strategy is developed.**

All organizations, whether profit oriented or not-for-profit, need to develop a marketing strategy to effectively reach customers. This involves analyzing the market, selecting a target market, and developing a marketing mix. Often a company will develop a marketing plan that expresses the firm's marketing strategy.

6. **Explain the concept of a market.**

A market consists of people with purchasing power and the authority to buy. Markets can be classified on the basis of the types of products they handle. Consumer products are those goods and services purchased by the ultimate consumer for his or her own use. Business products (also known as industrial or organizational goods) are products purchased to be used, directly or indirectly, in the production of other products for resale.

7. **Discuss why the study of consumer behavior is important to marketing.**

Consumer behavior consists of actions that are directly involved in obtaining, consuming, and disposing of products, including the decision processes that precede and follow these actions. This definition includes both consumers and business purchasers. By studying consumer behavior, marketers can identify consumers' attitudes toward their products and how they use the items. This in turn helps marketers develop more effective marketing strategies for reaching these people.

8. **Describe the marketing research function.**

Marketing research is the information function that links the marketer to the marketplace. It provides the information about potential target markets that is necessary to design effective marketing mixes. Marketers conduct research for five basic reasons:

1. to identify marketing problems and opportunities;
2. to analyze competitors' strategies;
3. to evaluate and predict consumer behavior;
4. to gauge the performance of existing products and package designs and assess the potential of new ones; and
5. to develop price, promotion, and distribution plans.

It involves more than just collecting information; researchers must also decide how to collect the information, interpret the results, and communicate the results.

9. **List and explain the bases used to segment markets.**

Consumer marketers may divide markets according to demographic characteristics, such as sex, age, and family life-cycle stage; geographic factors; psychographic variables, which involve behavioral and lifestyle profiles; and product-related variables, such as the benefits that consumers seek when buying a product, or the degree of brand loyalty they feel toward it. Business marketers segment markets according to three criteria: geographic characteristics; customer-based specifications for products; and end-use applications, or the precise way in which the business purchaser will use the product.

10. **Explain the concept of relationship marketing.**

An important trend in marketing centers on the concept of relationship marketing—an organization's attempt to develop long-term, cost-effective links with individual customers for mutual benefit. Good relationships with customers can be a vital strategic weapon for a firm. By identifying current purchasers and maintaining a positive relationship with them, organizations can target their best customers more efficiently. Information technologies, such as computers, databases, and spreadsheets, help make effective relationship marketing possible.

11. **Identify the major components of the marketing environment.**

The major components of the marketing environment are the competitive, political and legal, economic, technological, social, and cultural environments.

KEY TERMS QUIZ

customer satisfaction measurement (CSM) program
added value
business products
consumer behavior
consumer products
cause marketing
marketing concept

relationship marketing
event marketing
exchange
market segmentation
marketing
market
marketing mix

target market
marketing research
organization marketing
place marketing
person marketing

marketing 1. The planning and executing of the conception, pricing, promotion, and distribution of ideas, goods, and services in order to create exchanges that satisfy individual and organizational objectives.

exchange 2. Refers to the process by which two or more parties give something of value to one another to satisfy felt needs.

marketing concept 3. Consumer orientation designed to achieve long-run success.

added value 4. The increased worth resulting from better-than-expected performance.

CSM 5. The procedure for measuring customer feedback against customer satisfaction goals and developing an action plan for improvement.

person marketing 6. Refers to marketing efforts designed to attract the attention, interest, and preference of a target market toward a specific person, such as a political candidate.

place marketing 7. Refers to marketing efforts designed to attract people to a particular geographic area.

cause marketing 8. Refers to marketing efforts designed to promote a cause or social issue.

event marketing 9. The marketing of sporting, cultural, and charitable activities to selected target markets.

organization marketing 10. Refers to the marketing efforts designed to influence others to accept the goals of, receive the services of, or contribute in some way to an organization.

market 11. Refers to people with purchasing power and authority to buy.

consumer products 12. Goods and services purchased by the ultimate consumer for his or her own use.

buissnes products 13. Items purchased to be used directly or indirectly in the production of other goods or for resale.

target market 14. A group of consumers toward which a firm decides to direct its marketing efforts.

market mix 15. Refers to the combination of a firm's product, pricing, distribution, and promotional strategies focused on selected consumer segments.

consumer behavior 16. Consists of actions that are involved directly in obtaining, consuming, and disposing of products, including the decision processes that precede and follow these actions.

marketing reaserch 17. The information function that links the marketer to the marketplace.

market segmentation 18. Refers to the process of dividing the total market into several relatively homogeneous groups.

relationship marketing 19. An organization's attempt to develop long-term, cost-effective links with individual customers for mutual benefit.

OTHER IMPORTANT TERMS

customer satisfaction	mystery shopper	place utility
external data	observational studies	survey
focus group interview	ownership utility	time utility
internal data	people meters	

REVIEW QUESTIONS

1. What type of utility is created by the following?
   a. Emery Air Freight's shipment of a fast-selling fad item
   b. A Kroger supermarket
   c. The finishing department of a furniture factory
   d. An escrow company that handles the details of a property transfer
2. List various examples of marketers who are performing each of the eight basic functions of marketing. What, if anything, does this list suggest?
3. Explain the relationship between customer satisfaction and profitability.
4. How successfully do you think the following organizations have adopted the marketing concept?
   a. Xerox
   b. The college you are attending

c. Texaco

d. Florida Power & Light

5. Explain the role of customer feedback in achieving customer satisfaction. What are primary methods of securing such feedback?

6. Identify the likely target markets of each of the following:
   a. Houston Rockets
   b. Midas Muffler
   c. ChemLawn
   d. NordicTrack
   e. Infiniti

7. Develop a marketing strategy for a Thai restaurant in your community. Defend your marketing strategy decisions.

8. What is meant by a *market*? Distinguish between consumer and business markets.

9. Distinguish between internal and external data.

10. Match the segmentation variables below with the following four bases of consumer market segmentation: (1) geographic segmentation, (2) demographic segmentation, (3) psychographic segmentation, and (4) product-related segmentation.
    a. Lifestyle
    b. Sex
    c. Urban/suburban/rural
    d. Cholesterol-free products

DISCUSSION QUESTIONS

1. Describe a situation in which you, as a customer, were not satisfied with either a good or a service. How did this experience affect your feelings toward the company? What advice would you give to that company?

2. While Cadillacs are popular with consumers who are over 60 years of age, younger car buyers feel the vehicle is not sporty enough for them. They are more likely to buy foreign-made luxury cars, such as the Lexus or BMW.[17] This fact concerns managers at General Motors, who want to reposition their upscale cars to appeal to younger consumers as well. Suppose that you are the marketing manager in charge of developing a plan to achieve this goal. What strategy do you think would be most effective for reaching this market segment? Why?

3. The chapter notes that all organizations, whether profit-oriented or not-for-profit—must serve consumer needs if they are to succeed, and that marketing is an important determinant of a nation's overall standard of living. Do you feel that more college students should be encouraged to take marketing classes? Would offering marketing courses at the secondary level help? Explain your answer.

4. Members of the baby boom generation (generally defined as those born between 1946 and 1961) are a popular target market because there are so many of them.[18] Ten years from now, the consumers in this sizable segment of the American population will be in their forties and fifties. Discuss how this demographic trend could affect specific goods and services, such as fast-food restaurants, cosmetics, leisure travel, and soft drinks. What other goods and services would you expect to be affected, and how? Explain your answer.

5. CUC International is starting an interactive video shopping service that lets consumers call to place telephone orders for roughly 250,000 products. Unlike most home shopping services, CUC customers can comparison-shop, via interactive video on their TV screens, for numerous models of the same item and compare prices against those of competitors. Manufacturers ship purchases directly to buyers. "This will go far beyond the Home Shopping Channel, since customers can call up and compare thousands of products," predicts CUC Chief Executive Walter Forbes. "The power of television is about to transform retailing forever."[19] Relate CUC's new venture to the chapter's discussion of utility. What type(s) of utility are being created?

VIDEO CASE: Global Marketing

The video case in this chapter discusses the rise of global marketing and its strengths and weaknesses. It is located on page 419 of Appendix D.

Solution to Key Terms Quiz

1. marketing 2. exchange 3. marketing concept 4. added value 5. customer satisfaction measurement (CSM) program 6. person marketing 7. place marketing 8. cause marketing 9. event marketing 10. organization marketing 11. market 12. consumer products 13. business products 14. target market 15. marketing mix 16. consumer behavior 17. marketing research 18. market segmentation 19. relationship marketing

CHAPTER 12

Creating and Producing World-Class Goods and Services

Learning Goals

1. Explain why product development is important to a firm.
2. List the stages of new-product development.
3. Explain how products are identified.
4. Explain the strategic importance of production and operations management in an organization.
5. Compare mass production with newer production techniques.
6. Discuss how computers and related technologies are revolutionizing product development and production.
7. Outline the major factors involved in choosing plant locations.
8. Describe the major tasks of production and operations managers.
9. Explain the importance of inventory control and just-in-time systems.
10. Discuss the benefits of quality control.

G eneral Electric is best known for making light bulbs and kitchen appliances. But this industrial giant is likely to take its place in the corporate hall of fame not for its famous products but, instead, for its contribution to management concepts and applications. The company's ability to identify and improve upon good ideas and change or discard failures has enabled GE to prosper when other corporate giants are failing.

In 1981, Jack Welch took over as CEO at General Electric. He has energized the company with a true sense of entrepreneurship. Welch's preference is for the simple, uncluttered, and informal systems found in smaller companies that seem better able to respond to customers' demands on a timely basis. Welch's attempts to adapt those small company attributes to his giant company have proven surprisingly successful.

Take GE Appliances, for example. This division invested millions to redesign its production operations to achieve the quality levels of Japanese products. GE even instituted a "quality circle" program since workers' suggestions and informal meetings were supposedly driving quality in Japanese companies. The programs produced marginal

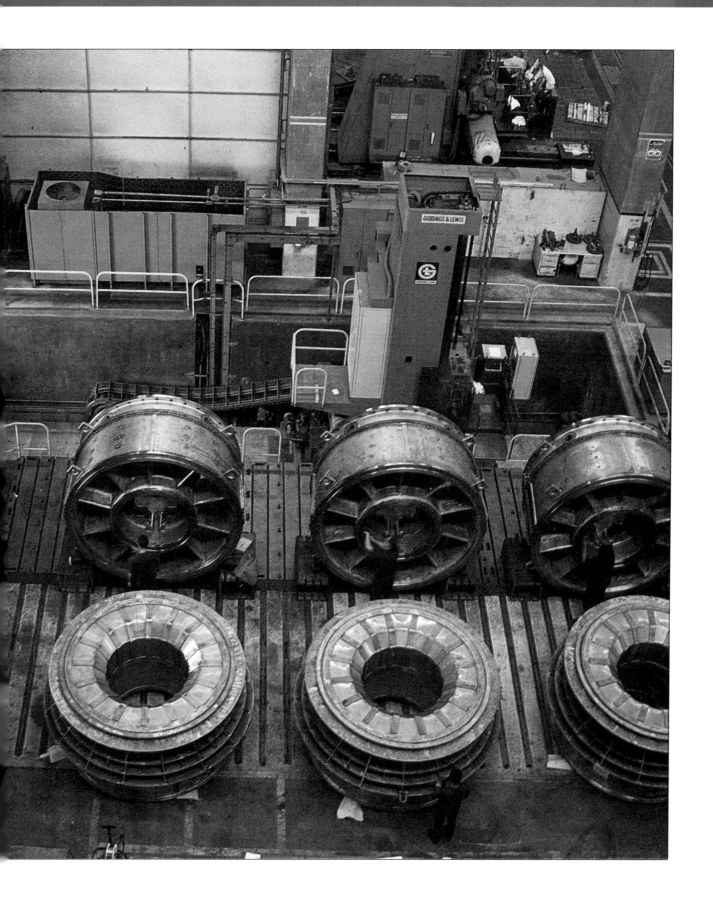

results for General Electric, which found them too restrictive for American workers. In1990, GE replaced the program with an Americanized version called Work-Out, in which managers and workers meet in a town hall setting. Workers are encouraged to offer radically new ideas regardless of cost. Managers then discuss the suggestions in the group setting.

Unlike quality circles, Work-Out recognizes individuals who contribute good ideas. One GE executive estimates that 90 percent of Work-Out ideas have been used. As a result of one suggestion, GE Appliances began building wire racks for their refrigerators rather than buying them from an outside source.

Another Japanese concept that didn't work well for General Electric was the just-in-time system. Under JIT, inventory levels are minimized by having all suppliers deliver parts on an as-needed basis. This system works well in Japan where suppliers' facilities are close to their customers. The Japanese invented the system to expose deficiencies in the manufacturing process. If production were kept error-free, inventories could be kept at a minimum.

Many American companies missed the point of JIT and concentrated on materials handling to reduce inventories. GE Appliances soon found that low inventory levels of needed parts—75 suppliers stock 475 parts— prevented the company from filling customer orders on a timely basis. The company recently increased its inventory of some component parts by 24 percent. GE now fills customer orders in 3.6 weeks, compared with a 1990 level of 18 weeks. The company is striving to reduce that number to only three days. Not only is the factory more attuned to customer needs, the benefit of a faster delivery system more than offsets the cost of the higher inventory levels.

What lesson can be learned from General Electric Appliances' experiences? A very important one: what works in one culture may not work in another. However, if a system proved unsuccessful for GE, the company either modified it to specifically fit its needs or discarded it entirely. GE's success is due, in large part, to flexibility: its willingness to experiment, to change, and to adapt.[1]

CHAPTER OVERVIEW

Products, which are discussed in more detail in the next chapter, can be defined as a bundle of physical, service, and symbolic attributes designed to satisfy consumer wants. The creation of new products is the lifeblood of an organization. Products do not remain economically viable forever, so new ones must be developed to assure the survival of an organization. Each year, thousands of new products are introduced. For many firms, these new products account for a sizable part of sales and profits.

By developing and producing desired goods and services, businesses create utility. *Form utility* is created through the conversion of raw materials and other inputs into finished goods or services. For example, fabric, thread, and zippers are converted into Levi's jeans. The firm's production function is responsible for creating form utility.

In this chapter we will describe the stages of new-product development and examine the strategic role of the production function. We will discuss the importance of product identification through brands and brand names. Finally, we will look at quality control and new technologies that are revolutionizing the production of goods and services.

> **THEY SAID IT**
>
> It used to be that people needed products to survive. Now products need people to survive.
>
> *Nicholas Johnson (1934–   ) American lecturer and writer*

STAGES IN NEW-PRODUCT DEVELOPMENT

New-product development is expensive, time consuming, and risky, since only about one-third of new products become success stories. Products can fail for many reasons. Some are not properly developed and tested, some are poorly packaged, and others lack adequate promotional support or distribution, or fail because they do not satisfy a consumer need or want.

Most newly developed products today are aimed at satisfying specific customer demands. New-product development is becoming increasingly efficient and cost-effective, because marketers use a systematic approach in developing new products.

The new-product development process has six stages:

1. generating new-product ideas
2. screening
3. business analysis
4. product development
5. test marketing
6. commercialization

Each stage requires a "go/no go" decision by management.

The starting point in the new-product development process is generating ideas for new offerings. Ideas come from many sources, including customers, suppliers, employees, research scientists, marketing research, inventors outside the firm, and competitive products. The most successful ideas are directly related to satisfying customer needs.

In the second stage, screening, ideas are eliminated if they do not mesh with overall company objectives or cannot be developed given the company's resources. Some firms hold open discussions of new-product ideas among representatives of different functional areas in the organization. In Japan, this cross-functional sharing of ideas within a firm is called *kaizen.*

During the business analysis phase, further screening is done. The analysis involves assessing the new product's potential sales, profits, growth rate, and competitive strengths, and whether it fits with the company's product, distribution, and promotional resources. *Concept testing*—marketing research designed to solicit initial consumer reaction to new product ideas before the products are developed—may be used at this stage. For example, potential consumers might be asked about proposed brand names and other methods of product identification.

Next, an actual product is developed, subjected to a series of tests, and revised. Tests measure both the product's actual features and how consumers perceive it.

During the test marketing stage, the item actually is sold in a limited area while the company examines both the product and the marketing effort used to support it. Cities or television coverage areas that are typical of the targeted market segments are selected for such tests. Test market results can help managers determine the product's likely performance in a full-scale introduction. Some firms choose to skip test marketing, however, because of concerns that the test could reveal their product strategies to the competition.

In the final stage, commercialization, the product is made generally available in the marketplace. Sometimes it is referred to as a product launch. Consider-

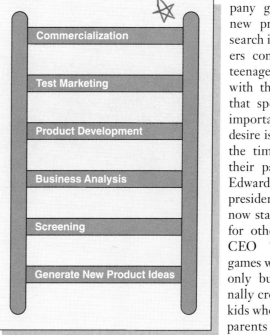

Steps in new-product development.

able planning goes into this stage, since the firm's promotional, distribution, and pricing strategies must all be geared to support the new product offering.

New-product development is vital to firms today. Consider Sega of America, which creates over 60 new video games every year. The company generates ideas for many new products by extensive research into the teen market; staffers conduct focus groups, visit teenagers' homes, and hang out with them at malls. Tests show that speed and novelty are all-important: "Kids' number one desire is to be up on new stuff all the time and know things that their parents don't know," says Edward Volkwein, senior vice president of marketing. Sega is now starting to develop products for other markets too. Explains CEO Tom Kalinske, "Video games will never again be a child-only business because we've finally crossed the threshold where kids who played Pong are now the parents of kids who play Sonic." The company has developed games on CD-ROM, 70 percent of which sell to adults. It also is targeting preteens; a new video game stars purple dinosaur Barney.[2]

PRODUCT IDENTIFICATION

As noted earlier, product identification is an important aspect of developing a successful new product. Products and services are identified by brands, brand names, and trademarks. A **brand** *is a name, term, sign, symbol, design, or some combination thereof used to identify the products of one firm and to differentiate them from competitive offerings.* Brands are important in developing a product's image. If consumers are aware of a particular brand, its appearance becomes advertising for the firm. Pepsi, Mountain Dew, and Slice are all soft drinks made by PepsiCo, but each brand possesses a unique combination of name, symbol, and package design that distinguishes it from the others. Successful branding is also a means of escaping some price competition, since well-known brands often sell at a considerable price premium over their competition.

A **brand name** is *that part of the brand consisting of words or letters included in a name used to identify and distinguish the firm's offerings from those of competitors.*

Although Sega's number one market is teens, adults are becoming a major customer base.

The brand name is the part of the brand that can be vocalized. Many brand names, such as Coca-Cola, McDonald's, American Express, and IBM, are famous around the world.

A **trademark** is *a brand that has been given legal protection.* The protection is granted solely to the brand's owner. Trademark protection includes not only the brand name, but also design logos, slogans, packaging elements, and product features such as color and shape. A well-designed trademark can make a definite difference in how consumers perceive a brand.[3]

Tropicana juices are marketed both in the United States and overseas under the same brand name.

Selecting an Effective Brand Name

Good brand names are easy to pronounce, recognize, and remember: Crest, VISA, and Avis, for example.

Global firms face a real problem in selecting brand names, since an excellent brand name in one country may prove disastrous in another. Most languages have a short "a," so Coca-Cola and Texaco are pronounceable almost anywhere. But an advertising campaign for E-Z washing machines failed in the United Kingdom because the British pronounce "z" as "zed." Fingos, the brand name for General Mills' meant-to-be-eaten-manually cereal, works well in the United States because it sounds like a play on the English word *fingers.* The name would be less successful in Hungarian, however, because it sounds like a common obscenity in that language.[4]

Brand names should give the right image to the buyer. Accutron suggests the quality of a high-priced, accurate timepiece. Federal Express suggests a fast delivery service that covers a broad geographic reach.

Sometimes, changes in the market's environment require changes to a brand name. Dep Corporation changed the brand name of Ayds diet candy to Diet Ayds because they were concerned that the old name would remind consumers of the AIDS virus.

Brand names also must be legally protectable. Trademark law specifies that brand names cannot contain words in general use, such as *television* or *auto-mobile*. Generic words—words that describe a type of product—cannot be used exclusively by any organization. On the other hand, if a brand name becomes so popular that it passes into common language and turns into a generic word, the company can no longer use it as a brand name. Once upon a time, aspirin and linoleum were exclusive brand names, but today they have become generic terms and are no longer legally protectable.

Brand Categories

A brand offered and promoted by a manufacturer is known as a **national brand,** or a manufacturer's brand. Examples are Tide, Jockey, Gatorade, Swatch, and DoveBar. But not all brand names belong to manufacturers; some are the property of retailers or distributors. A **private brand** (often known as a house, distributor, or retailer label) identifies *a product that is not linked to the manufacturer, but instead carries a wholesaler's or the retailer's label.* The Sears line of DieHard batteries and The Limited's Forenza label are examples.

IMAGE CONTRIBUTION – TEN BEST-PERFORMING LOGOS		
	Name	Logo
1.	Motorola	Ⓜ MOTOROLA
2.	Buick	BUICK
3.	US West	U S WEST
4.	Mercury	MERCURY
5.	Cadillac	Cadillac
6.	Nike	NIKE
7.	Borden	BORDEN
8.	Pennzoil	PENNZOIL
9.	Lexus	LEXUS
10.	Arm & Hammer	ARM & HAMMER

Logos are an important aspect of brand image.

National, private, and generic brands of non-dairy creamer.

Many retailers offer a third option, **generic products,** which *have plain packaging, minimal labeling, little if any advertising, and meet only minimum quality standards.* Generic products sell at a considerable discount from manufacturers' and private brands. Many consumer goods are available as generic products, such as paper towels, toilet paper, breakfast cereal, and pasta.

Another branding decision marketers must make is whether to use a family branding strategy or an individual branding strategy. A **family brand** is *a single brand name used for several related products.* KitchenAid, Johnson & Johnson, Xerox, and Dole use a family brand name for their entire line of products. When a firm using family branding introduces a new product, both customers and retailers recognize the familiar brand name. The promotion of individual products within a line benefits all the products because the family brand is well known.

Other firms utilize an **individual branding** strategy by *giving products within a line different brand names.* For example, Procter & Gamble has individual brand names for its different laundry detergents—Tide, Cheer, Dash, and Oxydol. Each brand targets a unique market segment. Consumers who want a cold-water detergent can buy Cheer rather than Tide or Oxydol instead of purchasing a competitor's brand. Individual branding builds competition within a firm and enables the company to increase overall sales.

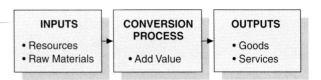

The production process converts inputs to outputs.

STRATEGIC IMPORTANCE OF THE PRODUCTION FUNCTION

Production is *the use of people and machinery to convert materials into finished goods or services.* Production is a broad term that includes manufacturing, nonmanufacturing, and service industries.

The task of **production and operations management** is *to manage the use of people and machinery in converting materials and resources into finished goods and services.* Services are intangible outputs of the production system and can include outputs as diverse as trash hauling, education, haircuts, and tax accounting. There are almost as many production systems as there are goods and services.

Like marketing, accounting, or human resource management, the production process is a vital business function. Indeed, without production, none of the other functions would exist. Without a good or service, a company cannot create profits. Without prof-

Typical Production Systems			
Example	**Primary Inputs**	**Transformation**	**Outputs**
Pet-food factory	Grain, water, fish meal, personnel, tools, machines, paper bags, cans, buildings, utilities	Converts raw materials into finished products	Pet-food products
Trucking firm	Trucks, personnel, buildings, fuel, goods to be shipped, packaging supplies, truck parts, utilities	Packages and transports goods from sources to destinations	Delivered goods
Department store	Buildings, displays, shopping carts, machines, stock goods, personnel, supplies, utilities	Attracts customers, stores goods, sells products	Marketed goods
Automobile body shop	Damaged autos, paints, supplies, machines, tools, buildings, personnel, utilities	Transforms damaged auto bodies into facsimiles of the originals	Repaired automobile bodies
County sheriff's department	Supplies, personnel, equipment, automobiles, office furniture, buildings, utilities	Detects crimes, brings criminals to justice, keeps the peace	Acceptable crime rates and peaceful communities

Mass production is efficient when producing a large number of the same items, as at this plant producing GE ovens in San Luis Potosi, Mexico.

its, the firm will fail quickly. Yet, the production process is just as crucial in not-for-profit organizations, since it is this good or service that justifies the organization's existence.

In short, the production function adds value to a company's inputs by converting them into marketable outputs. This added value turns the outputs into something that customers are willing to pay for. Thus, production and operations management plays an important strategic role. Effective management can lower the costs of production, boost the quality of products, and allow the firm to respond dependably to customers' demands. It also can help companies stay flexible, so they can respond more quickly when customers' demands change.

Developing nations, such as China, have come to recognize the economic importance of effective production. Indeed, the Chinese government has purchased several U.S. factories and is disassembling and moving them to China, where they will be reconstructed to begin operations anew. Purchases include a microchip facility from Pennsylvania, an auto-engine assembly line from Michigan, and a steel mill from California. "China could build a new steel mill like this one," explains Wang Shengli, who is supervising that particular move. "We bought this one because we can have it operating sooner than if we built our own."[5]

> **THEY SAID IT**
>
> Benjamin Franklin may have discovered electricity, but it was the man who invented the meter who made the money.
>
> *Earl Wilson (1907–1987) American newspaper columnist*

MASS PRODUCTION

The United States began as a colonial supplier of raw materials to Europe and evolved into an industrial giant. A major factor in this remarkable change has been **mass production,** *the manufacture of products in large amounts through the effective combination of specialized labor, mechanization, and standardization.* Mass production makes large quantities of products available at lower prices than would be possible if these products had been crafted individually.

Mass production has three key factors: specialization, mechanization, and standardization. *Specialization* involves dividing work into its simplest components so workers can concentrate on performing one task. Once jobs are separated into smaller tasks, managers can use *mechanization*, the use of machines to perform work previously performed by people, to increase workers' productivity. The third component of mass production—*standardization*—involves producing uniform, interchangeable goods and parts. Standardized parts make it easier to replace defective or worn-out components. If your car's windshield wipers wear out, for instance, you can buy replacement wipers at any auto supply store. Just think how long it would take—and how much more it would cost—if you had to have the replacements specially crafted!

A logical extension of the factors of specialization, mechanization, and standardization is the **assembly line.** This is *a manufacturing technique that involves placing the product on a conveyor belt that travels past a number of workstations where workers perform specialized tasks,* such as welding, painting, installing a part, or tightening a bolt.

NEW APPROACHES TO PRODUCTION

Although mass production has advantages for a firm, it has its drawbacks, too. While highly efficient for making large numbers of similar products, mass production is less efficient for making small batches of different items. Companies may focus on efficient production methods rather than on what customers really want. Furthermore, specialization can make workers' jobs boring because they do the same task over and over. To become more competitive, many firms are adopting new approaches, such as flexible

> **THEY SAID IT**
>
> Production is not the application of tools to materials, but logic to work.
>
> *Peter Drucker (1909–   ) American business philosopher and author*

production, customer-driven production, and the team concept. Mass production and new techniques are not mutually exclusive; many firms retain their mass-production systems but improve them by applying newer production techniques.

Flexible Production

At a Caterpillar plant in East Peoria, Illinois, two manufacturing systems operate side by side to manufacture 120 types of transmissions for Caterpillar equipment. The old system consisted of a long assembly line of 35 machine tools, each requiring a specialized worker to operate it. Since each machine can handle only one type of job at a time, the area around the assembly line was packed with parts waiting to be processed. When the line finished making one type of transmission, the operator spends from four hours to two days setting up the machines for the next batch, plus two or three trial runs to get things operating smoothly.

Meanwhile, the new system consists of machine units that are programmed to handle any type of transmission that the plant makes. It takes only seconds for workers to set up the machines to process a new batch; the system selects the right tools for the new job from a rotating belt and inserts them into spindles. Trial runs are not necessary, since the machines already are programmed to perform the new functions.

Many companies besides Caterpillar now recognize the advantages of flexible, so-called lean production methods that require fewer workers and less inventory. The table compares the traditional, mass-

Flexible Production versus Mass Production

Flexible Production	Mass Production
Can be profitable making small batches of products.	Profitable only when making large batches.
The product and the process for making it are designed concurrently.	The process is designed after the product has been designed.
Lean inventory turns over fast.	Fat inventory turns over slowly.
Suppliers are helped, informed, and kept close.	Suppliers are kept at arm's length.
Engineers search widely for ideas and technology.	Engineers are insular, don't welcome outside ideas.
Employees learn several skills, work well in teams.	Employees are compartmentalized.
The company stresses continuous small improvements.	The company looks for the big breakthroughs.
The customers' orders pull the products through the factory.	The system pushes products through to the customers.

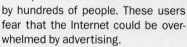

TECHNOLOGY

Online Services

From the quill pen to the fax machine, each step forward in information technology has brought vast changes—some predictable, some unexpected—in how business is done. It is too soon to identify the full ramifications of business use of online services, but it is safe to say that they will be significant.

Already, many businesses use online services to access information. America Online, CompuServe, Prodigy, GEnie, and Dow Jones News/Retrieval each feature databases and offer digital back issues of thousands of publications. Via computer, a researcher can access Lexis, an electronic law library; Biz*File, which features the phone numbers of more than ten million companies; or online encyclopedias.

These services are not without pitfalls. They can be quite expensive, particularly when used by employees who are not experienced and comfortable with computers. In addition, the size of the services makes quality control difficult, and some information retrieved from them may be outdated or incorrect.

It might seem obvious that online services, with their millions of subscribers, would be excellent venues in which to market products, but whether these services will be popular shopping forums remains to be seen. In a 1994 poll, only 32 percent of respondents said they would use "emerging interactive services" to buy goods and services, while a full 79 percent planned to seek information "on staying healthy and on diseases or related topics." The percentage of consumers shopping online may grow, however, and experts note that early public responses to technological advances often focus on lofty goals, while actual usage can be quite different than predicted.

While the commercial online networks offer shopping services, advertisers are not popular on the Internet, a noncommercial computer network that is the biggest online conglomeration of all. The purveyors of obvious ads on the Internet are "flamed" (that is, sent scathing e-mail) sometimes by hundreds of people. These users fear that the Internet could be overwhelmed by advertising.

Many questions remain to be answered. Will the average employee one day have online access, or will only specialists travel the information superhighway? Will online services put some people out of work, such as stockbrokers or librarians, or simply change the way they do their jobs? Will computer shopping ever replace malls? Will disadvantaged people have access to online services? The information superhighway is still being built, and only the future will reveal its ultimate shape.

SOURCES: Peter H. Lewis, "Poll Indicates Few Plan to Shop Electronically," *New York Times,* October 5, 1994; Jean Sherman Chatzky, "Warp Speed on the Information Highway," *Smart Money,* September 1994, 96–103; and Rick Tetzeli, "Is Going On-Line Worth the Money?" *Fortune,* June 13, 1994, 104–108.

production approach with the newer, more flexible methods. While mass production is most efficient at making large batches of similar items, flexible production can be cost effective with smaller batches, too. Flexible production methods also require new approaches to customers, inventory, design, and engineering.

Customer-Driven Production

With customer-driven production, customers' demands determine what retail stores stock and, in turn, what manufacturers make. Japanese firms have implemented this approach in many of their factories, with notable success. Several U.S. companies are testing computer linkups between their factories and retailers that will allow them to base production on retail sales.

Team Concept

Some production methods challenge the mass-production approach in which specialized workers perform repetitive tasks. The team concept combines employees from various departments and functions—such as design, manufacturing, finance, and maintenance—to work together on designing and providing products. The teams also may include people from outside the firm, such as suppliers and customers. This approach is sometimes called *concurrent engineering,* since engineering is done concurrently with design, production, and other functions.

Two years ago, General Electric Motors was ready to close its plant in Fort Wayne, Indiana, entirely; the factory had been losing money for years, while the cost of producing motors there continued to rise. New manager Dick Krause decided to apply the team concept by grouping employees into teams that followed the progress of each part from start to finish. Krause also began sharing facts and statistics about GE competitors and customers, and arranged for all workers to take classes in group dynamics. Today, the cost of producing a motor at the plant has fallen by 16 percent, elapsed time from order to shipment has shrunk from 55 days to 16, and quality has improved from 2,300 rejects per million to only 150 per million. Employees overwhelmingly support Krause's commitment to the team concept. Says one, "Krause doesn't think management is necessary in manufacturing, he thinks we can do it."[6]

TECHNOLOGY AND THE PRODUCTION PROCESS

Like other business functions, production has been greatly affected by computers and related technologies. In addition to making the production process more efficient, automation allows companies to redesign their current methods. Production can become more flexible, allowing companies to design and create new products faster, modify them more rapidly, and meet customers' changing needs more effectively. Important production technologies include robots, computer-aided design, computer-aided manufacturing, flexible manufacturing systems, and computer-integrated manufacturing.

Robots

To free people from boring, sometimes dangerous assignments, many production managers have replaced blue-collar workers with "steel-collar" workers: robots. A **robot** is *a reprogrammable machine capable of performing a variety of tasks requiring programmed manipulations of materials and tools.* Robots can repeat the same tasks over and over without varying their movements.

Boeing set up 238 teams to carry designs from their initial concepts through the design and manufacturing phases of Boeing 777 production. The teams included employees from across the company, as well as representatives from key suppliers and customers.

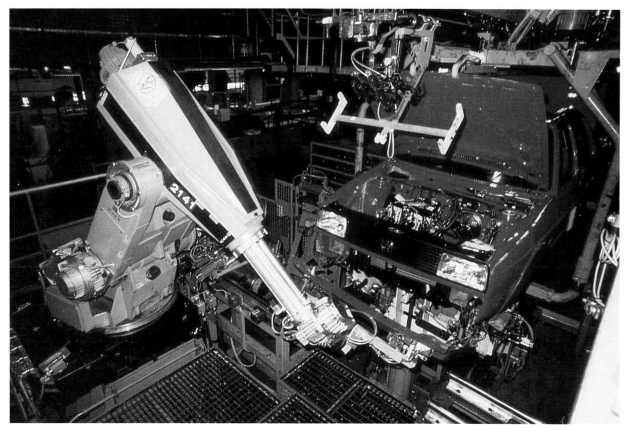

A robot assembles cars at Volkswagen's Frankfurt, Germany plant.

Initially, robots were most common in the automotive and electronics fields, but more industries are using them as technology continues to make them less expensive and more flexible. There are many different types of robots. The simplest kind is a *pick-and-place robot*, which moves in only two or three directions as it picks something up from one spot and places it in another. *Field robots* assist human workers in nonmanufacturing, often hazardous, environments, such as nuclear power plants, space stations, and battlefields.

Computer-Aided Design and Computer-Aided Manufacturing

A process called **computer-aided design (CAD)** *enables engineers to design parts and buildings on computer screens faster and with fewer mistakes than on paper.* Using a special electronic pen, engineers can sketch three-dimensional designs on an electronic drafting board or directly on the computer screen. The computer then can be used to make major and minor de-

sign changes and to analyze the design for certain characteristics or problems. Thus, through computer simulations, engineers can put a new car design through an on-screen road test to see how it performs. If they find a problem with weight distribution, for example, they can make the necessary changes on their computer terminal. Only when they are satisfied with all the structural characteristics of their design will they manufacture an actual car model. In a similar manner, aircraft designers can analyze the shape and strength of a proposed aircraft fuselage and wings under various conditions.

The process of **computer-aided manufacturing (CAM)** picks up where CAD leaves off. It *enables manufacturers to use special-design computers to analyze the necessary steps that a machine must perform to produce a needed product or part.* Electronic signals then are transmitted to the production processing equipment, instructing it to perform the appropriate production steps in the correct order.

Traditional methods of product design can be compared with the new computer-based approach used to create Timex's B-29 wristwatch. The traditional method involves more steps. Even as late as

DOING PRODUCT DESIGN BY HAND...

1 SKETCHING Using pencil and paper, the designer draws the idea

2 RENDERING The idea is drawn or painted on paper to give a more detailed idea of the product

3 MODELING A skilled craftsman makes a three-dimensional model of the product from wood or clay for evaluation by marketing and engineering

4 ENGINEERING/MANUFACTURING Engineers decide how to build the product. For the first time, the design is fed into a computer. Engineers, designers, and marketers make revisions. The design is then fed electronically into a CAD/CAM system and later manufactured

IMAGE OF A
TIMEX B-29
GENERATED
BY ALIAS

...AND BY 3-D COMPUTER SOFTWARE

1 SKETCHING, RENDERING, AND COMPUTER MODELING Using a workstation, the designer sketches an idea, then fleshes it out using rendering software. The computer generates a realistic 3-D model of the product on the screen. Because it's electronic, the design can be tweaked easily and cheaply. A physical mock-up can be made by transferring the design electronically to computerized milling equipment. But this entire step can often be skipped

2 ENGINEERING/MANUFACTURING Once all revisions have been made, data describing the computer-generated 3-D model are transferred directly to a CAD/CAM system and produced

DATA: BW

Traditional manufacturing versus computer-aided manufacturing.

step 4, errors can be discovered that require the whole process to begin all over again. With three-dimensional design, however, ideas can be tested—and changed if necessary—before the product becomes a physical reality.[7]

Flexible Manufacturing Systems

A *flexible manufacturing system (FMS)* is a facility that can be modified quickly to manufacture different products. The typical system consists of computer-

Automated guide vehicles at work carrying cloth at a Russell Athletics manufacturing plant.

controlled machining centers to produce metal parts, robots to handle the parts, and remote-controlled carts to deliver materials. All components are linked by electronic controls that dictate what will happen at each stage of the manufacturing sequence, even automatically replacing broken or worn-out drill bits and other implements.

Computer-Integrated Manufacturing

When robots, CAD/CAM, FMS, computers, and other technologies are combined, the result is **computer-integrated manufacturing (CIM),** *the use of computers to design products, control machines, handle materials, and control the production function in an integrated fashion.* CIM does not necessarily mean more automation and fewer people; it involves a different type of automation, organized around the computer. The key to CIM is a centralized computer system that integrates and controls various separate processes and functions.

Russell Corporation is an old company, founded 91 years ago, but its factories are anything but old-fashioned. The firm has spent over $500 million in the last five years to install computer-integrated manufacturing systems that have turned it into the nation's largest supplier of athletic uniforms. In its textile mills, seeing-eye computers sort fabrics by color, lasers cut the fabrics, robots sew seams together, and automated guided vehicles carry materials from one part of the plant to another. Since 1983, Russell's profits have more than tripled to reach $82 million; at the same time, its production costs have fallen from 69 percent of sales to 66 percent.

DID YOU KNOW?

A Goodyear advertisement demonstrated the strength of its 3T tire cord by showing a steel chain breaking. When the commercial was shown in Germany, however, it was perceived as an insult to steel chain manufacturers.

Many Japanese food stores are resupplied three times a day to ensure product freshness.

The owl logo symbolizes wisdom in the United States, but not in India where it is considered bad luck.

An American airline operating in Brazil decided to promote its luxurious "rendezvous lounges" on its jets. Management quickly learned that *rendezvous* in Portuguese means a room hired for lovemaking.

CHOOSING THE BEST LOCATION

One of the major decisions a firm will make is choosing the right place to build a plant. Factors involved in choosing the best location fall into three categories: transportation, human, and physical factors.

Transportation factors include the proximity to markets and raw materials, and the availability of transportation alternatives. Physical variables involve such issues as water supply, available energy, and options for disposing of hazardous wastes. Human factors include the area's labor supply, local regulations, and living conditions.

Many communities require a firm that wants to locate there to do an **environmental impact study** that *analyzes how the proposed plant would impact the quality of life in that area.* Regulatory agencies typically require the study to cover such topics as impact on transportation facilities; energy requirements; water and sewage treatment needs; effect on natural plant life and wildlife; and water, air, and noise pollution.

Labor costs and the availability of a qualified labor force are important issues. Many electronics firms, for example, are located in the San Jose, California, and Boston areas, which have high concentrations of skilled technicians. Many automakers, on the other hand, are moving their production operations to areas with low labor costs. Germany ranks highest among industrialized nations in average hourly labor

Factors in the Location Decision

Location Factor	Examples of Affected Businesses
TRANSPORTATION	
Proximity to markets	Baking companies or manufacturers of other perishable products, dry cleaners, hotels, or other services for profit
Proximity to raw materials	Mining companies
Availability of transportation alternatives	Brick manufacturers, retail stores
HUMAN FACTORS	
Labor supply	Auto manufacturers, hotels
Local regulations	Explosives manufacturers, welding shops
Community living conditions	All businesses
PHYSICAL FACTORS	
Water supply	Paper mills
Energy	Aluminum, chemical, and fertilizer manufacturers
Hazardous wastes	All businesses

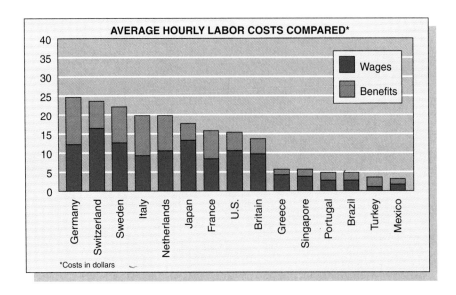

costs, which is why the country is losing an estimated 100,000 jobs a year. Many of these jobs are migrating to lower-cost labor areas, such as Spain, Portugal, Eastern Europe, and the United States. German automaker Daimler-Benz has moved much of its production out of Germany and now builds sport/utility vehicles in Alabama, vans in Spain, and Mercedes-style sedans in South Korea. Other German firms, such as BMW, Siemens, and Helima Helvetian International, are building plants in the United States.[8]

TASKS OF PRODUCTION MANAGERS

Production and operations management is responsible for overseeing the use of people and machinery to convert inputs (materials and resources) into finished goods and services. These managers have four major tasks. First, they must plan the overall production process. Next, they must determine the best layout for the production facilities and implement the production plan. Finally, they are responsible for controlling the production process to maintain the highest possible quality. Part of the control process involves continually evaluating results. If problems occur, managers should return to the first step and adjust the production process if necessary.

Marketing research studies are used to obtain consumer reactions to proposed products, to test prototypes of new products, and to estimate their potential sales and profitability. The production department is concerned primarily with (1) converting the original product concept into the final product and

> **THEY SAID IT**
>
> Production is the goose that lays the golden egg. Payrolls make consumers.
>
> *George Humphrey (1890–1970) American industrialist and U.S. secretary of the treasury*

(2) designing production facilities to produce this new product as efficiently as possible. The new item or service must not only be accepted by consumers, it also must be produced economically to assure an acceptable return on company funds invested in the project.

INVENTORY CONTROL

Inventory control *balances the need to have inventory on hand to meet demand with the costs involved in carrying the inventory.* The financial costs of carrying inventory are the funds tied up in it that cannot be used in other activities of the business. Among the expenses involved in storing inventory are warehousing, taxes, insurance, and maintenance. Too much inventory represents wasted money.

But a shortage of raw materials, parts, goods, or sales often means lost production—and delays in production mean unhappy customers if the delays result in late delivery. Firms lose business when they consistently are unable to meet promised delivery dates or when their shelves are empty. These two costs must be balanced to produce acceptable inventory levels; effective inventory control can save a great deal of money.

Just-in-Time System

Ten years ago, the typical American factory kept several weeks' worth of parts and supplies on hand, while

BUSINESS STRATEGY

Cummins Engine Co.

A few years ago, the Cummins Engine Company shut down its factory and laid off all its employees in Columbus, Indiana, citing the plant's high costs and poor quality. Recently, the factory got a second chance when Cummins decided to expand production of its midrange engines, and the Columbus employees are making the most of their new opportunity. To head off quality problems from the beginning, Cummins tested all job applicants' math ability and interviewed them extensively for teamwork skills. Those who were hired received 250 hours of training in quality control, engine mechanics, and mathematics. Quality control is an ongoing process, as workers and managers meet regularly to review product defects found during inspections and to devise solutions. As quality has improved, so has the plant's production rate, from 150 engines a day a few years ago to 180 today. This new attention to quality, says Executive Vice President for Operations Tim Solso, has enabled the plant to "beat every single [target] since the day it opened." Production worker Randy Acton puts it simply: "We work smarter."

SOURCE: Robert Rose, "Humming Mills," *The Wall Street Journal*, January 3, 1994, A1, A38.

---

a similar factory in Japan would have had no such inventory backlog. The Japanese plant then and now may have only enough supplies to keep it going for a day. This shortage is not accidental; it is an essential ingredient of the Just-in-Time (JIT) System used by major Japanese corporations for years and now widely used in American firms.

In reality, **JIT** is *a broad management philosophy that reaches beyond the narrow activity of inventory control and influences the entire system of production and operations management.* JIT is an approach that seeks to eliminate all sources of waste—anything that does not add value in operations activities—by providing the right part at the right place at the right time. This results in less inventory, lower costs, and better quality goods and services than the traditional approach.[9]

When applied to inventory control, a JIT system supplies parts to the production line on an as-needed basis. This approach lowers factory inventory levels and inventory control costs. The JIT system also lets firms respond quickly to changes in the market, and employ only the most essential personnel to maintain the inventory. Manufacturers in many industries have adopted JIT, saving billions of dollars. This benefits the economy, since this money can be invested, spent on new-product development, or returned to shareholders as dividends. Says Alan Dawes, who heads operations at GM's auto components group, "There's absolutely no way we're going away from just-in-time."[10]

JIT shifts much of the responsibility for carrying inventory to suppliers operating on forecasts, since they are forced to keep more on hand to be responsive to manufacturers' needs. Suppliers who cannot keep enough high-quality parts on hand often get dropped in favor of suppliers who can.

Use of bar codes and other automated systems have enabled businesses to keep better track of inventory and lower their carrying costs.

THE IMPORTANCE OF QUALITY

Quality, a concept discussed in Chapter 6, is just as vital in the product development and production functions as it is in other areas of business. More companies are realizing that if they build quality into product design from the very beginning, they are more likely to end up with quality products, which are an important aspect of customer satisfaction. Investing more money up front in quality design and development ultimately decreases "costs of quality," or those costs that result from not making the product right the first time. These costs average at least 20 percent of the sales revenues for most companies. Some typical costs of quality include downtime, repair costs, rework, and employee turnover. Systems must be set up to track and reduce such costs. If management concentrates on producing a quality product that satisfies the needs of its customers, a byproduct will be lower costs of quality.

Quality control involves *measuring goods and services against established quality standards.* Such

checks are necessary to spot defective products and to see that they are not shipped to customers. Devices for monitoring quality levels of the firm's output include visual inspection, electronic sensors, robots, and x-rays. A high rejection rate is a danger signal that quality standards are not being met.

But companies cannot rely solely on inspections to achieve quality. A typical U.S. factory can spend up to half of its operating budget to identify and fix mistakes. This is both costly and time-consuming. A company instead must identify all processes involved in producing products and work to make them as efficient as possible. This can be done by finding the cause of problems in the processes and eliminating them. If a company concentrates its efforts on improving the processes, a quality product will result.

SUMMARY OF LEARNING GOALS

1. Explain why product development is important to a firm.

The creation of new products is the lifeblood of an organization. Products do not remain economically viable forever, so new ones must be developed to assure the survival of an organization. For many firms, new products account for a sizable part of sales and profits.

2. List the stages of new-product development.

The new-product development process has six stages: (1) generating new-product ideas, (2) screening, (3) business analysis, (4) product development, (5) test marketing, and (6) commercialization. Some firms skip the test marketing stage because of concerns that the test could reveal their product strategies to the competition.

3. Explain how products are identified.

Goods and services are identified by brands, brand names, and trademarks. A brand is a name, term, sign, symbol, design, or some combination thereof used to identify the products of one firm and to differentiate them from competitive offerings. A brand name is that part of the brand consisting of words or letters included in a name used to identify and distinguish the firm's offerings from those of competitors. A trademark is a brand that has been given legal protection.

4. Explain the strategic importance of production and operations management in an organization.

Like marketing, accounting, or human resource management, the production process is a vital business function. Without a good or service, a company cannot create profits, and it would fail quickly. The production process is also crucial in not-for-profit organizations, since it is this good or service that justifies the organization's existence. Production and operations management plays an important strategic role by lowering the costs of production, boosting the quality of products, and allowing the firm to respond flexibly and dependably to customers' demands.

5. Compare mass production with newer production techniques.

Mass production is the manufacture of products in large amounts through the effective combination of three key factors: specialization, mechanization, and standardization. Mass production makes large quantities of products available at lower prices than would be possible if these products had been crafted individually. However, while highly efficient for making large numbers of similar products, it is less efficient for making small batches of different items. Furthermore, specialization can make workers' jobs boring. To become more competitive, many firms are adopting new approaches. Flexible production methods require fewer workers and less inventory and are cost effective with smaller batches too. With customer-driven production, customers' demands determine what stores stock and, in turn, what manufacturers make. The team concept combines employees from various departments and functions—such as design, manufacturing, finance, and maintenance—to work together on designing and building products.

6. **Discuss how computers and related technologies are revolutionizing product development and production.**

   Automation allows companies to design and create new products faster, modify them more rapidly, and meet customers' changing needs more effectively. Important design and/or production technologies include robots, computer-aided design (CAD), computer-aided manufacturing (CAM), flexible manufacturing systems (FMS), and computer-integrated manufacturing (CIM).

7. **Outline the major factors involved in choosing plant locations.**

   Factors involved in choosing the best location fall into three categories: transportation, human, and physical factors. Transportation factors include proximity to markets and raw materials, and availability of transportation alternatives. Physical variables involve such issues as water supply, available energy, and options for disposing of hazardous wastes. Human factors include the area's labor supply, local regulations, and living conditions.

8. **Describe the major tasks of production and operations managers.**

   Production and operations managers are responsible for overseeing the use of people and machinery to con-vert inputs (materials and resources) into finished goods and services. This involves four major tasks. First, they must plan the overall production process. Next, they must determine the best layout for the production facil-ities and implement the production plan. Finally, they are responsible for controlling the production process and evaluating results in order to maintain the highest possible quality.

9. **Explain the importance of inventory control and just-in-time systems.**

   Inventory control balances the need to have inventory on hand to meet demand with the costs involved in car-rying the inventory. Too much inventory represents wasted money, but a shortage of raw materials, parts, goods, or sales often means lost production and un-happy customers. The just-in-time (JIT) system is a philosophy that seeks to eliminate all sources of waste—anything that does not add value in operations activi-ties—by providing the right part at the right place at the right time. This results in less inventory, lower costs, and better quality goods and services.

10. **Discuss the benefits of quality control.**

    Quality control involves measuring goods and services against established quality standards. Such checks are necessary to spot defective products and to see that they are not shipped to customers. Devices for moni-toring quality levels of the firm's output include visual inspection, electronic sensors, robots, and x-rays. Quality is just as vital in product development; invest-ing more money up front in quality design and devel-opment ultimately decreases the "costs of quality."

KEY TERMS QUIZ

mass production
brand name
computer-aided design (CAD)
generic product
just-in-time (JIT) system
robot
individual branding

national brand
brand
quality control
trademark
family brand
assembly line
inventory control

computer-aided manufacturing (CAM)
production and operations management
private brand
computer-integrated manufacturing (CIM)
production
environmental impact study

1. A name, term, sign, symbol, or design used to identify the goods or services of a firm.
2. The words or letters that identify the firm's offerings.
3. The brand that has been given legal protection exclusive to its owner.
4. The brand that is offered and promoted by a manufacturer.
5. The brand name owned by a wholesaler or retailer.
6. The nonbranded item with plain packaging and little or no advertising support.
7. The brand name used for several related products or the entire product mix.
8. Giving each product in a line its own brand name.
9. The use of people and machinery to convert materials into finished goods or services.

[handwritten: productions and operations management] 10. Managing people and machinery used in converting materials and resources into finished goods and services.

[handwritten: mass production] 11. The manufacture of goods in large quantities as a result of standardization, specialized labor, and mechanization.

[handwritten: assembly line] 12. The manufacturing technique wherein the product passes through several workstations, each with a specialized task.

[handwritten: robot] 13. A reprogrammable machine capable of performing numerous programmed tasks by manipulating materials and tools.

[handwritten: Computer added design] 14. Interaction between a designer and a computer resulting in a product, building, or part that meets predetermined specifications.

[handwritten: Computer added manufacturing] 15. Computer analysis of a CAD to determine steps in producing the design and electronic transmission of instructions to production equipment used in producing the part or product.

[handwritten: computer integrated manufacturing] 16. The use of computers to design products, control machines, handle materials, and control the production function in an integrated fashion.

[handwritten: environmental impact study] 17. The analysis of the impact of a proposed plant location on the quality of life in a specific area.

[handwritten: inventory control] 18. Used when deciding whether to manufacture, purchase, or lease a needed product, component, or material.

[handwritten: Just in time system] 19. The continuously updated listing of items in inventory.

[handwritten: quality control] 20. The measurement of goods and services against established quality standards.

OTHER IMPORTANT TERMS

concept-testing
concurrent engineering
field robots
flexible manufacturing system (FMS)
form utility

mechanization
pick-and-place robot
specialization
standardization

REVIEW QUESTIONS

1. Why is product development important?
2. Identify and explain the stages in new-product development. Illustrate each stage with a hypothetical example.
3. Differentiate among the terms *brand*, *brand name*, and *trademark*. Cite examples of each.
4. Suggest types of form utility that the following firms might produce:
   a. delivery service   c. airline
   b. sugar refinery   d. family counseling center
5. Explain why effective production and operations management can provide a strategic advantage for a firm.
6. Describe a mass production system. What are its advantages and disadvantages?
7. Explain the concept of a flexible manufacturing system.
8. Distinguish among CAD, CAM, and CIM.
9. What problems are associated with having too much inventory? With having too little inventory?
10. Relate the tasks of production and operations managers to each of the following. Give specific examples of each component.
    a. major league sports facility in the Tampa Bay area
    b. convenience food store
    c. fish processing facility
    d. color television assembly plant

DISCUSSION QUESTIONS

1. Evaluate your city or county as a prospective industrial site and suggest organizations that would be well suited to the location.
2. Suggest a brand name for each of the following new products and explain why you chose each name:
   a. a development of exclusive homesites
   b. a low-price term life insurance policy sold by mail
   c. an airline's improved business-class service on Asian routes
   d. a lawn edger that is more durable than its competition
3. Choose a service organization in your community—perhaps a restaurant or an office at your school—and evaluate its production process. How efficient is it? Does the resulting good or service meet your standards? Are there any quality-control standards that you might wish to suggest?

4. Collect four advertisements for the same product in different countries. (Possibilities might be Coca-Cola, Pepsi, or McDonald's.) Assess the trademark and image shown in the ads; are they different or similar? If they are different, explain in what ways. How does the company identify this product in each market?
5. What is quality control? Suggest ways in which each of the following firms could practice it.
   a. local bank
   b. city hospital
   c. amusement park
   d. clothing manufacturer that exports 50 percent of its goods abroad

VIDEO CASE: Stewart-Warner

The video case for this chapter discusses Stewart-Warner's decision to close a plant in Chicago and move the work to Texas and Mexico. It can be found on page 420 of Appendix D.

Solution to Key Terms Quiz

1. brand 2. brand name 3. trademark 4. national brand 5. private brand 6. generic product 7. family brand 8. individual branding 9. production 10. production and operations management 11. mass production 12. assembly line 13. robot 14. computer-aided design (CAD) 15. computer-aided manufacturing (CAM) 16. computer-integrated manufacturing (CIM) 17. environmental impact study 18. inventory control 19. just-in-time (JIT) system 20. quality control

CHAPTER 13

Designing and Implementing Customer-Driven Marketing Strategies

Learning Goals

1. Explain what a product is and list the components of product strategy.
2. Identify the classifications of consumer products, business products, and services.
3. Discuss the product mix and the stages of the product life cycle.
4. Describe the importance of pricing strategy.
5. Identify the major components of distribution strategy.
6. Outline the various types of distribution channels, and discuss the factors that influence channel selection.
7. Explain the importance of customer service.
8. Explain how advertising, sales promotion, and public relations are used in promotional strategy, and identify the factors that influence the selection of a promotional mix.
9. Discuss the factors that influence international promotion.

Grupo Elektra got its start from a family feud. In 1907, two brothers-in-law, Benjamin Salinas and Joel Rocha, opened a furniture store in Mexico City. The years passed and the lone furniture shop became one of Mexico's largest department-store chains. Although the company still was called Salinas y Rocha, the Salinas family did not enjoy any of the profits; the Rochas ousted Hugo Salinas in the late 1950s.

Annoyed, Hugo Salinas started his own business, an electronics retailing store called Elektra that competed successfully with Salinas y Rocha in assembling and selling radios. For 30 years, Grupo Elektra prospered, until the Mexican debt crisis of the 1980s devalued the country's monetary system and drove the retailer into bankruptcy.

Enter Hugo's grandson, Ricardo Salinas, who had earned an M.B.A. degree in the United States and had experience with managing several of Elektra's retail stores. One of Salinas' most cherished memories is a day he spent with Sam Walton, founder of the discount chain Wal-Mart. The young manager found the visit enlightening: "He asked me a lot of questions I didn't know the answers to," Salinas recalls. "He asked me about my gross margin return on inventory. I didn't know what that was."

Salinas saw clearly that, in order to survive bankruptcy and prosper again, Grupo Elektra would have to develop an entirely new marketing strategy. First, he invested in computer systems that modernized the company's operations and made it possible to answer Walton's questions. Then, he zeroed in on a new target market, Mexico's poor and lower-middle-class consumers, who, for the most part, were ignored by Elektra's competitors.

To better serve his target market, Salinas introduced several retailing innovations to Mexico. He cut costs by reducing the number of product lines carried by Grupo Elektra stores; this enabled him to lower prices to a level that attracted low-income consumers. Grupo Elektra became the first Mexican retailer to offer credit to low-income customers; they could pay for their electronics purchases a week at a time, at annual interest rates averaging 60 percent. In three years, credit sales grew to account for more than half of the company's revenues.

The new strategy has proved highly successful; Grupo Elektra is now the country's largest home electronics and appliance retailer. While many Mexican retailers are suffering, Elektra's sales have gone up. Salinas notes that Elektra stores have taken a great deal of business from the higher-priced Salinas y Rocha chain. "I feel my family has finally been vindicated," he says with a smile.

As an astute businessman, however, Salinas knew that even the most successful marketing strategy has to change with the times. He realized that the rapid modernization of Mexico's economy would lead to greater competition, which would ultimately drive down interest rates and make his retail stores less profitable. The answer, he felt, was to diversify Grupo Elektra by expanding into Mexico's media industry. As a first step, he acquired Television Azteca, a government-owned company that operated two TV networks, 168 TV stations, a movie theater chain, and a production studio.

Television Azteca was an underdog. Its two channels compete against the hugely successful Grupo Televisa, which controls four TV networks and 90 percent of Mexican companies' advertising budgets. To make things worse, programming had languished under government ownership; Mexicans joked that anyone who wanted to get away with murder simply should commit the crime in front of Azteca's cameras—the shows were so dull that no one would be watching anyway.

To boost viewership, Salinas licensed TV programs produced in other countries. During weekdays, his Channel 13 targets women by broadcasting aerobics workouts and soap operas produced in Argentina, Venezuela, and Brazil. On weekends, the focus shifts to male viewers, as Channel 13 beams World Cup soccer and U.S. professional basketball and baseball games. Meanwhile, Television Azteca's Channel 7 targets younger viewers with U.S. shows, such as *The Simpsons* and *The Wonder Years*, dubbed in Spanish.

The new Television Azteca has started to attract big-name advertisers, including The Coca-Cola Company, General Motors, Telmex, and Bancomer, Mexico's largest bank. Unsold air time does not go to waste; Salinas uses it to advertise Elektra products and Azteca's chain of movie theaters.

When Salinas bought Television Azteca, its market share of the prime-time viewing audience was a paltry four percent. These days, it stands at 16 percent and continues to grow. Popular shows like *Los Simpson*, reach over 6 million consumers—more than the circulation of all of Mexico's newspapers combined. Salinas plans to make Grupo Elektra into a global media empire by selling stock and taking on international partners. "We will be a force," he vows.[1]

CHAPTER OVERVIEW

In this chapter we will discuss ways in which organizations can design and implement marketing strategies that address customers' needs and wants. We begin by describing the classification of goods and services, the product mix, and the product life cycle. We examine the four elements of the marketing mix— product, pricing, distribution, and promotional strat- egy—and the role of customer service in developing successful marketing strategies.

THE MARKETING MIX

As we saw in Chapter 11, any customer-oriented or- ganization begins its marketing strategy by studying its **target market**—*the group of people toward whom a*

MARKETING
MIX

Product Strategy

Pricing Strategy

Distribution Strategy *place*

Promotion Strategy

The appropriate blend of product, pricing, distribution, and promotion strategies is the firm's marketing mix.

firm markets its goods, services, or ideas with a strategy designed to satisfy their specific needs and preferences. For Contempo Casuals, the target market consists of fashion-minded women aged 18 to 25 years; Saab targets well-educated, 30- to 40-year-old professionals with household incomes of $50,000 to $100,000.

After selecting a target market, an organization develops an appropriate marketing mix. The **marketing mix** is *a blending of the four strategy elements of marketing decision making*—product, price, distribution, and promotion—to satisfy chosen consumer segments. These elements are described in the sections that follow. Each strategy is a variable in the mix; the combination of the variables determines the degree of marketing success.

PRODUCT STRATEGY

As noted in Chapter 12, marketers broadly define a **product** as *a bundle of physical, service, and symbolic attributes designed to satisfy consumer wants.* Therefore, *product strategy* involves considerably more than just producing a good or service. It also includes decisions about package design, brand name, trademarks, warranties, product image, new-product development, and customer service. Think, for instance, about your favorite soft drink. Do you like it for its taste alone, or do other attributes, such as clever ads, attractive packaging, and overall image also attract you? These other

attributes may influence your choice more than you realize.

Classifying Goods and Services

Marketers have found it useful to classify goods and services as either *consumer* or *business*, depending on the purchasers of the particular item. These classifications can be subdivided further, and each type requires a different competitive strategy.

Classifying Consumer Goods The classifications most typically used for consumer goods are based on consumer buying habits. *Convenience products* are items the consumer seeks to purchase frequently, immediately, and with little effort. Items stocked in 7-Eleven stores, vending machines, and local newsstands are usually convenience products—for example, newspapers, chewing gum, and bread.

Shopping products are those typically purchased only after the consumer has compared competing products in competing stores. Someone intent on buying a new television set may visit many stores, examine perhaps dozens of sets, and spend days making the final decision. *Specialty products* are those that a purchaser is willing to make a special effort to obtain. The purchaser is already familiar with the item and considers it to have no reasonable substitute. The nearest Lexus dealer may be 100 miles away, but if you have decided that you want one, you will make the trip.

Note that a shopping product for one person may be a convenience item for someone else. Majority buying patterns determine the item's product classification.

Televisions and other home-entertainment equipment are typical shopping products.

BUSINESS STRATEGY

Marketers Target Generation X

Advertisers trying to reach Generation X soon come up against a major roadblock: no one knows exactly who Generation X is. Generation X includes people born from 1965 to 1974—or 1975, or 1976, or 1978, or 1979, depending on who's talking. They have been described as slackers, interested only in watching *Brady Bunch* reruns—and as the most conservative, hard-working generation since people born during the Depression. Some experts interpret Generation X demographics as meaning that X-ers are serious about marriage, while others see Generation X as reluctant to make commitments. X-ers include the widest variety of ethnic backgrounds in U.S. history, yet the media often present them as middle-class whites. And while X-ers are often characterized as cynical and whining, 48 percent of Americans between the ages of 18 and 24 do volunteer work.

Perhaps the most salient feature of the X-ers is that they don't identify with the label "Generation X," calling it "a media fabrication." An MTV poll found that only ten percent of respondents would ever use the phrase.

No matter what they are called, 46 million 16- to 31-year-olds make up a huge consumer base, and an entire industry has sprung up to explain them to advertisers. Douglas Coupland, who named Generation X in his novel of the same title, charges $8,000 to $10,000 a speech. Consulting firm Popeye Chauvel offers videotapes of X-ers in their "natural habitats," and X-Fests feature daylong arrays of speakers such as Richard Linklater, director of *Slacker*, a "Generation X movie."

It is not surprising that advertisers are seeking help; ads aimed at X-ers have not been particularly successful. Subaru failed to impress Generation X with an Impreza commercial that featured a pseudo-grunged-out guy likening the car to punk rock, and a Bud commercial that included banter about *Gilligan's Island* was scorned by its target audience. Nor have movies aimed at Generation X done well; *Reality Bites*, *P.C.U.*, *Singles*, and *Bodies, Rest, and Motion* all performed poorly at the box office.

One suggested approach to X-ers is to appeal to their sense of irony and even self-depreciation and to take into account their media savvy, since X-ers grew up surrounded by TV. Using this strategy, a Converse sneaker ad trumpeted, "We don't want to live in a beer commercial," while Hyundai dropped their "World-Class Value" tag line for "Cars that make sense."

Although Deroy Murdock, a "Generation X consultant," says, "Everybody's doing a lot of gymnastics in order to figure out something that's really very amorphous," the immense buying power of the "twenty-somethings" will continue to tempt advertisers. And Marion Salzman, president of BKG Youth, is already using "Generation Why" to describe the next batch of customers: people born between 1975 and 1981.

SOURCES: Charlie Green, "Take This McJob and Shove It," *Business Week*, July 11, 1994, 8; Judy Harrigan and J. J. Gilmartin, "Xers Are Misnamed; How About 'Cocoes'?", *Advertising Age*, June 27, 1994; Jeff Giles, "Generations X," *Newsweek*, June 6, 1944, 62–71; and Damon Darlin, "Ugly Chic," *Forbes*, September 13, 1993, 200.

Classifying Business Goods   While consumer products are classified by buying habits, business products are classified based on how they are used and by their basic characteristics. Products that are long-lived and usually are purchased with large sums of money are called *capital items.* Less costly products that are consumed within a year are referred to as *expense items.*

Installations are major capital items, such as new factories, heavy equipment and machinery, and custom-made equipment. Installations are expensive and often involve buyer and seller negotiations that may last several years before a purchase actually is made. *Accessory equipment* includes capital items that are usually less expensive and shorter-lived than installations; examples are hand tools and fax machines.

Component parts and materials are finished business goods that become part of a final product, such as disk drives that are sold to computer manufacturers or tires that are sold to automakers. *Raw materials* are farm and natural products used in producing other, final products; examples include cotton, milk, and iron ore. *Supplies* are expense

Timber, harvested in the Pacific Northwest and made into boards or pulp in Japan, is a raw material.

Relationship between Consumer Products Classification and Marketing Strategy			
Marketing Strategy Factor	**Convenience Product**	**Shopping Product**	**Specialty Product**
Store image	Unimportant	Very important	Important
Price	Low	Relatively high	High
Promotion	By manufacturer	By manufacturer and retailers	By manufacturer and retailers
Distribution channel	Many wholesalers and retailers	Relatively few wholesalers and retailers	Very few wholesalers and retailers
Number of retail outlets	Many	Few	Very small number; often one per market area

items used in a firm's daily operation that do not become part of the final product, such as paper clips, light bulbs, and copy paper.

Classifying Services   Services can be classified as either consumer or business services. Child-care centers and shoe-repair shops provide services for consumers, while the Pinkerton security patrol at a factory and Kelly Services' temporary office workers are examples of business services. In some cases, a service can accommodate both consumer and business markets. For example, when ServiceMaster cleans the upholstery in a home, it is a consumer service, but when it spruces up the painting system and robots in a manufacturing plant, it is a business service.

Marketing Strategy Implications

The consumer product classification is a useful tool in marketing strategy. For example, once a new lawn edger has been classified as a shopping good, marketers have a better idea of its promotion, pricing, and distribution needs. The impact of the consumer products classification on various aspects of marketing strategy is shown in the table above.

Each group of business products, however, requires a different marketing strategy. Because most installations and many component parts are marketed directly from the manufacturer to the buyer, the promotional emphasis is on personal selling rather than on advertising. By contrast, marketers of supplies and accessory equipment rely more on advertising since their products often are sold through an intermediary, such as a wholesaler. Producers of installations and component parts may involve their customers in new-product development, especially when the business product is custom made. Finally, firms marketing sup-

plies and accessory equipment place greater emphasis on competitive pricing strategies than do other business products marketers, who concentrate on product quality and servicing.

THE PRODUCT MIX

A **product mix** is *the assortment of goods and services a firm offers consumers and business users.* Although Borden Inc. may be best known for its dairy products, the firm's product mix also includes pasta, snack items, niche grocery products (Gallina Blanca dry soups and ReaLemon juice), nonfood consumer goods (Krazy Glue, Elmer's Glue, wallpaper), and specialty business chemicals (plastic film, forest product adhesives, food-wrap items).

The product mix is a combination of product lines and individual offerings that make up the product line. A **product line** is *a series of related products.* Borden's product line of frozen dairy desserts, for example, includes Eagle Brand ice cream, Lady Borden ice cream sandwiches, Meadow Gold frozen yogurt and yogurt pops, and Turtles frozen novelties.

Marketers must assess their product mix continually to ensure company growth, to satisfy changing consumer needs and wants, and to adjust to competitors' offerings. To remain competitive, marketers look for gaps in their product lines and fill them with new products or modified versions of existing ones. A helpful tool used by marketers in making product decisions is the product life cycle.

Product Life Cycle

Once a product is actually on the market, it often goes through a series of four stages known as the **product**

> **THEY SAID IT**
>
> "Marketing is the delivery of a standard of living."
>
> *Paul Mazur (1892–1979) American investment banker*

life cycle—*introduction, growth, maturity, and decline.* Industry sales and profits will vary depending on the life-cycle stage of a product.

Product life cycles are not set in stone: not all products follow this progression precisely, and different products may spend different periods of time in each stage. The concept, however, helps the marketing planner anticipate developments throughout the various stages of a product's life. Profits assume a predictable pattern through the stages, and promotional emphasis must shift from dispensing product information in the early stages to heavy brand promotion in the later ones.

Stages of the Product Life Cycle

In the *introduction stage*, the firm tries to promote demand for its new offering, inform the market about it, and explain its features, uses, and benefits. New-product development and introductory promotional campaigns, though important, are expensive and commonly lead to losses in the introduction stage. A new product can cost

Coca-Cola has expanded its product line in recent years with the addition of Cherry Coke, New Coke, and caffeine-free Diet Coke.

millions of dollars to introduce, but such expenditures are necessary if the firm is to profit later.

During the *growth stage*, sales climb quickly as new customers join the early users who now are repurchasing the item. Word-of-mouth referrals and continued advertising by the firm induce others to make trial purchases. At this point, the company begins to earn profits on the new product. Unfortunately, this encourages competitors to enter the field with similar offerings, and price competition appears.

Industry sales at first increase in the *maturity stage*, but eventually reach a saturation level at which further expansion is difficult. Competition also intensifies, increasing the availability of the product. Firms concentrate on capturing competitors' customers, often dropping prices to further their appeal. Sales volume fades late in the maturity stage, and some of the weaker competitors leave the market. During this stage, firms promote mature products aggressively to protect their market

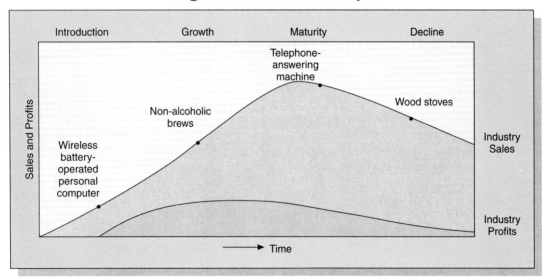

Products should be evaluated to see where they fall in the product life cycle.

share and to distinguish their products from those of competitors.

Sales continue to fall in the *decline stage*, the fourth phase of the product life cycle. Profits decline and may become losses as further price-cutting occurs in the reduced market for the item. The decline stage usually is caused by a product innovation or a shift in consumer preferences.

Marketing Strategy Implications of the Product Life Cycle

The product life cycle is a useful concept for designing a marketing strategy that will be flexible enough to accommodate changing marketplace characteristics. For instance, knowing that the advertising emphasis will change from informative to persuasive as the product faces new competitors during its growth stage helps the marketer anticipate competitive actions and make necessary adjustments. These competitive moves may involve developing new products, lowering prices, increasing distribution, creating new promotional campaigns, or any combination of these strategies.

In general, the marketer's objective is to extend the product life cycle as long as the item is profitable. Indeed, some products can be highly profitable during the later stages of their life cycle, since all of the initial development costs already have been recovered.

One strategy for extending the life cycle is to increase customers' frequency of use; persuading homeowners that they need to have more smoke alarms and flashlights may result in increased purchases by each household. Another strategy might be to add new users; Gerber Products increased the size of its babyfood market by creating specialty foods for foreign consumers, such as strained sushi for Japanese babies and strained lamb brains for Australian infants. Arm & Hammer used a third approach, finding new uses for its product. Arm & Hammer baking soda's original use in baking has been augmented by its newer uses as a

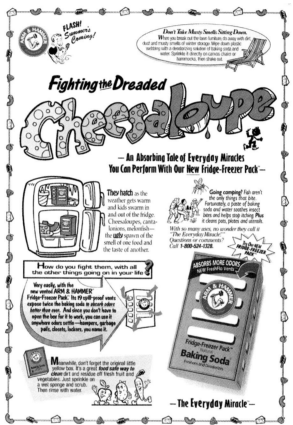

Arm and Hammer has successfully extended its product life cycle by promoting new uses for its baking soda.

toothpaste, refrigerator freshener, and lame extinguisher. A fourth strategy—changing package sizes, labels, and product designs—works well for Timex Corporation, which supplements traditional wristwatches with new designs, such as The Lefty and Gizmoz for kids and the large-numbered Easy Reader for people with failing eyesight.

Package and Label

Packaging and labels play an important role in product strategy. Packaging affects the durability, image, and convenience of an item, and is responsible for one of the biggest costs in many consumer products. Cost-effective packaging is one of industry's greatest needs.

Choosing the right package is especially crucial in international marketing, since marketers must be aware of many variables. One variable is cultural preference: African nations, for instance, often prefer bold colors, but flag colors may be preferred (or frowned upon), and red often is associated with death or witchcraft. Package size can vary according to the purchasing patterns and market conditions of a country. In countries with little refrigeration, people may want to buy their beverages one at a time rather than in six-packs. Package weight is another important issue, since the cost of shipping often is based on weight.[2]

Labeling is an integral part of the packaging process as well. In the United States, labeling must meet federal requirements as set forth in the Fair Packaging and Labeling Act (1966) and the Nutrition Labeling and Education Act (1990), which require companies to provide enough information to allow consumers to make value comparisons among competitive products. Marketers who ship products to other countries have to comply with labeling requirements in those nations: Should the labels be in more than one language? Should ingredients be specified? Do the labels give enough information about the product to meet government standards?[3]

Nutrition Facts

Serving Size 30 Crackers (30g)
Servings Per Container About 7

Amount Per Serving

Calories 140   Calories from Fat 45

	% Daily Value*
Total Fat 4.5g	**8**%
Saturated Fat 1g	**5**%
Cholesterol 0mg	**0**%
Sodium 280mg	**12**%
Total Carbohydrate 19g	**6**%
Dietary Fiber Less than 1g	**3**%
Sugars Less than 1g	
Protein 4g	

Vitamin A **	•	Vitamin C **	
Calcium 4%	•	Iron 6%	
Thiamine 10%	•		
Riboflavin 8%	•	Niacin 6%	

** Contains less than 2 percent of the daily value of these nutrients

* Percent Daily Values are based on a 2,000 calorie diet. Your daily values may be higher or lower depending on your calorie needs:

	Calories:	2,000	2,500
Total Fat	Less than	65g	80g
Sat Fat	Less than	20g	25g
Cholesterol	Less than	300mg	300mg
Sodium	Less than	2,400mg	2,400mg
Total Carbohydrate		300g	375g
Dietary Fiber		25g	30g

The new labeling mandated by the Food and Drug Administration has cost manufacturers millions of dollars to implement.

Another important aspect of packaging and labeling is the *Universal Product Code (UPC)*, the bar code read by optical scanners that print the name of the item and the price on a receipt. For many stores, these identifiers are useful not just for packaging and labeling, but also for evaluating customers' purchases and controlling inventory.

PRICING STRATEGY

The second element of the marketing mix is *pricing strategy*. **Price** is *the exchange value of a good or service.* An item is worth only what someone else is willing to pay for it. Pricing strategy deals with the multitude of factors that influence the setting of a price.

Prices help direct the overall economic system. A firm uses various factors of production, such as natural resources, labor, and capital, based on their relative prices. High wage rates may cause a firm to install labor-saving machinery, and high interest rates may lead management to decide

against a new capital expenditure. Prices and volume sold determine the revenue received by the firm and influence its profits.

Consumer Perception of Prices

Marketers must be concerned with the way consumers perceive prices. If a buyer views a price as too high or too low, the marketer must correct the situation. Price–quality relationships and psychological pricing are important in this regard.

Research shows that the consumer's perception of product quality is related closely to the item's price: the higher the price, the better its perceived quality. Most marketers believe this perceived price–quality relationship exists over a relatively wide range of prices, although extreme prices may be viewed as either too expensive or too cheap. Marketing managers need to study and experiment with prices because the price–quality relationship can be of key importance to a firm's pricing strategy.

Many marketers use psychological pricing, because they believe certain prices are more appealing than others to buyers. Many retailers believe that consumers are attracted to uneven amounts, so they use prices such as $19.98 or $9.99, rather than $20 or $10. Some stores use prices ending in 1, 2, 3, 4, 6, or 7 to avoid the look of more common prices like $5.95, $10.98, and $19.99.

Place DISTRIBUTION STRATEGY

The third element of the marketing mix, *distribution strategy*, deals with the marketing activities and institutions involved in getting the right good or service to the firm's customers. Distribution decisions involve modes of transportation, warehousing, inventory control, order processing, and selection of marketing channels. Marketing channels are made up of institutions such as retailers and wholesalers that move a product from producer to final consumer.

The two major components of an organization's distribution strategy are distribution channels and physical distribution. **Distribution channels** are *the paths that products—and title to them—follow from producer to consumer.* They are the means by which all organizations distribute their goods and services. **Physical distribution** is *the actual movement of these products from the producer to the user.* Physical distribution covers a broad range of activities, including customer service, transportation, inventory con-

CROSS-FUNCTIONAL ENVIRONMENT

Team Compensation

Teamwork may be easy to embrace—who's against cooperation, after all? But it's tough to reward.

Companies looking to form sales teams or cross-functional groups have to consider two key compensation questions: How do you reward all players equitably and fairly? How do you ensure that hyper-competitive top performers, who are used to fat rewards, aren't demotivated by egalitarian pay schemes?

"Every compensation plan has a weakness," says Mark Blessington, national director, sales force effectiveness, for Sibson & Company, a consulting firm headquartered in Princeton, New Jersey. "With team compensation, the weakness is that the slackers receive the same rewards as contributors."

Nevertheless, most team programs reward players equally. Blessington helped develop a plan for an automobile equipment company in which salespeople work in regional teams, and commissions generated by those teams are divided equally among reps. (Regional managers and district managers get greater shares.) "In this system, when you've got 30 reps, some may try to hide in the weeds, or ride on the backs of hard-charging sellers," Blessington says. "But since everyone has a share of the rewards, peer pressure comes into play. If someone is at 50 percent of quota, a top seller may start to work with him, go with him on calls, and try to get him up to speed. Team rewards motivate people to help each other and share ideas."

Dun & Bradstreet, an information-services company based in Murray Hill, New Jersey, uses a similar compensation plan for its cross-functional teams—groups of five to 120 employees that usually include sellers, marketing staffers, and data-collection people, among others. If a team hits 100 percent of quota, all members equally divide a ten percent commission. "Rewarding people this way says that everyone is responsible for pulling their weight and helping the team meet its goal," says George Martin, executive vice president, U.S. sales. "If you give certain people the lion's share of rewards, then you have disharmony or discontinuity. Some people may not want to participate."

But is Martin worried about disarming a team's top guns? "A lot of great sellers are creative and independent, and you always have to worry about turning them off," he says. "But top performers also love the way a team gives them more arms and legs to generate sales. That means more money for everyone. Who doesn't want that?"

SOURCE: Reprinted from Geoffrey Brewer, "Team Selling: Keys to Dividing the Spoils," *Sales & Marketing Management,* August 1994, 61.

---

trol, materials handling, order processing, and warehousing.

Distribution Channels

Distribution channels consist of **marketing intermediaries** (also called *middlemen*), *the channel members that operate between the producer and the consumer or business user.* Marketing intermediaries perform various functions that help the distribution channel to operate smoothly, such as buying, selling, storing, and transporting products; sorting and grading bulky items; and providing information to other channel members. The two main categories of marketing intermediaries are wholesalers and retailers.

Wholesalers **Wholesaling intermediaries** are *distribution-channel members that sell primarily to retailers, other wholesalers, or business users.* For instance, Sysco is a wholesaler that buys food products from manufacturers and resells them to restaurants, hotels, and other institutions in the United States and Canada.

Wholesaling is a crucial part of the distribution channel for many products, particularly consumer goods. Wholesaling intermediaries can be classified on the basis of ownership; some are owned by manufacturers, some by retailers, and others are independently owned. Most U.S. wholesalers are independent wholesalers who account for about two-thirds of all wholesale trade.

Retailers **Retailers,** by contrast, are *distribution-channel members that sell goods and services to individuals for their own use rather than for resale.* Consumers usually buy their food, clothing, shampoo, furniture, and appliances from some type of retailer. The supermarket where you buy your groceries may have bought some of its items from Sysco and then resold them to you.

Retailers are the final link in the distribution channel. Since they are often the only channel

> **THEY SAID IT**
>
> "In our factory, we make lipstick. In our advertising, we sell hope."
>
> *Charles Revson (1906–1975)
> Chairman, Revlon, Inc.*

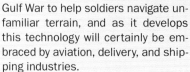

TECHNOLOGY

Putting Technology on the Map

The human race has long relied on maps, although they've always had limitations. The parchment charts that ancient voyagers perused featured areas marked "here be dragons," and today's awkward, large, multifolded printed sheets make drivers wish they possessed longer arms and magnifying glasses. Luckily, geographical information system (GIS) technology soon will make the maps stuffed into glove compartments as outmoded as primitive globes of a world lacking North America.

Geographic information systems are computer programs that specialize in spatial data, from maps to aerial photographs to satellite images. These systems already are utilized to manage natural resources and examine pollution patterns, but their once exorbitant costs have limited their use to government agencies and a few large corporations. As with all things digital, however, prices have decreased to a fraction of what

they once were, and a complete set of street maps and census information for the United States is now available for less than $1,000—although the equivalent data would once have run $50,000 or more. These price changes have made geographic information systems more widely available, and it seems that every type of business on earth has a use for one.

Sylvania combines GIS technology with a customer database to develop maps of bulb-buying habits by neighborhood, allowing their salespeople to show owners of retail stores exactly why they should stock Sylvania lightbulbs. McDonalds uses GIS data to choose restaurant locations. And real estate agents use GIS maps to show house hunters which neighborhoods are near bus lines, which they can afford, and even which have light traffic patterns.

A particularly valuable relative of GIS is the global-positioning system (GPS). Using satellites, the GPS can inform any person carrying the appropriate receiver of his or her ex-

act location. The Army used GPS devices in the Gulf War to help soldiers navigate unfamiliar terrain, and as it develops this technology will certainly be embraced by aviation, delivery, and shipping industries.

Imagine a salesperson hitting a few keys on the car computer and immediately being presented with a detailed map of a section of the city. Even one-way streets are labeled, saving time. Most important, even if the salesperson is completely lost, no street sign in sight, a flick of a switch adds a "You Are Here" component to the map—no matter where on earth. As the price of GIS technology decreases, such fantasies will come true.

SOURCES: Bruce Auster, "A New Way to Shop," *U.S. News & World Report,* July 11, 1994, 16; Ben Marsh, "Map II 1.5," *Mac World,* May 1994, 67–68; Michael Antoniale, "Mapping Software Can Take Your Business in a New Direction," *Real Estate Today,* May 1994, 24–28; and Rick Tetzeli, "Mapping for Dollars," *Fortune,* October 18, 1993, 91–96.

members that deal directly with consumers, it is essential they remain alert to customers' needs. It is also important that they keep pace with developments in the fast-changing business environment.

There are two categories of retailers: nonstore and store. *Nonstore retailing* includes direct selling, such as Tupperware and Amway; direct-response retailing, such as catalogs and television shopping; and automatic merchandising, which includes vending machines. The second category of retailers, *store retailing,* accounts for about 90 percent of total retail sales; there are about 2 million retail stores in the United States. The following table lists the different types of store retailers, with examples of each type. Clearly, there are many ap-

Best Buy, which competes with Circuit City in the home-electronics market, has a no-frills approach that keeps its overhead low and its prices down.

proaches to retailing and a variety of services, prices, and product lines.

Retailers are subject to constant change as new stores replace older establishments. In a process called the *wheel of retailing,* new retailers enter the market by offering lower prices made possible through reductions in service. Supermarkets and discount houses, for example, gained their initial market footholds through low-price, limited-service appeals. These new entries gradually add services as they grow, and ultimately become targets for new retailers. The wheel of retailing shows that business success involves the "survival of the fittest." Retailers that fail to change fail to survive.

Types of Store Retailers		
Type of Retailer	**Description**	**Examples**
Variety Store	Offers a variety of low-priced merchandise.	F.W. Woolworth, Ben Franklin
Department Store	Offers a wide variety of merchandise sold in departmentalized sections (furniture, cosmetics, clothing) and many customer services.	Dillard's, Bon Marche, Marshall Field's, JC Penney
Specialty Store	Offers a complete selection in a narrow range of merchandise.	Kinney Shoes, Joel's Camera, jewelry stores
Convenience Store	Offers staple convenience goods, long store hours, rapid checkouts, adequate parking facilities, and convenient locations.	7-Eleven, Circle K, Dairy Mart, gasoline stations
Discount Store	Offers a wide selection of merchandise at low prices and few services.	K-mart, Target, Wal-Mart
Off-Price Store	Offers designer or brand-name merchandise of many manufacturers at discount prices.	T.J. Maxx, Marshall's, Loehmann's
Factory Outlet	Manufacturer-owned store selling seconds, production overruns, or discounted lines.	Nike outlet store
Catalog Store	Sells discounted merchandise from showrooms that display samples of products detailed in catalogs mailed to consumers.	Service Merchandise, Zales, Gordon Jewelry
Supermarket	Large, self-service store offering a wide selection of food and nonfood merchandise.	Winn-Dixie, Kroger, Lucky, Safeway, Super Fresh, Albertson's
Hypermarket	Giant store (at least three times the size of the average supermarket) offering food and general merchandise at discount prices.	Hypermart USA, Bigg's, Meijer, Carrefour, Fred Meyer, Omni
Warehouse Club	Large warehouse-style store that sells food and general merchandise at discount prices to people who are part of its associated club membership.	Sam's Club, Price/Costco

Wal-Mart has succeeded by staying on top of this fast-moving industry. The discount chain is already the top retailer in the United States; sales reached $84 billion in 1994, and industry analysts predict that they will continue to grow 18 percent annually through the rest of this decade. Now Wal-Mart is expanding rapidly in other countries. Through a joint venture with Mexican retailer Cifra S.A., the company opened 100 stores in Mexico by 1995—a mix of supercenters, Sam's Club warehouse clubs, and Bodega discount outlets. Recently, Wal-Mart also acquired 91 Pace warehouse clubs from K-Mart and 122 Woolco stores in Canada. Wal-Mart also opened stores in Brazil and Argentina in 1995.[4]

Vertical Marketing Systems (VMS)

Some companies have developed *vertical marketing systems (VMS)*, which are planned distribution channels organized to reduce channel conflict and improve distribution efficiency. In Japan, for example, it is common for businesses to form alliances dominated by one channel member. Japanese retail outlets are often just showrooms for a particular manufacturer or wholesaler; even their employees may work for the manufacturer and depend on bonuses received from that firm.

Types of Distribution Channels

Manufacturing and service industries may use hundreds of channels to distribute their output. Canned foods usually pass through wholesalers and retailers before they reach the grocery store. Some vacuum cleaners and encyclopedias may be sold directly to you at your home. No one channel is right for every product. The best channel depends on the circumstances of the market and on consumer needs, and it may change over time. In order to stay competitive, marketers must keep their distribution methods up to date.

There are six primary channels of distribution. The first four channels typically are used to distribute consumer goods and services, while the last two

The Primary Channels of Distribution

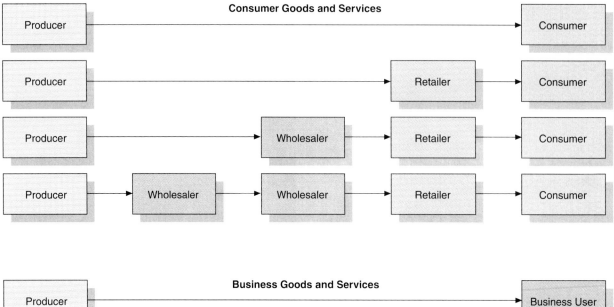

The primary channels of distribution involve a variety of marketing intermediaries.

commonly are used for business goods and services. Also, a low-priced product usually goes through more intermediaries than a similar product with a higher price tag.

Selecting a Distribution Channel

The best distribution channel depends on several factors: the market, the product, the producer, and the competition. These factors often are interrelated.

Market factors may be the most important consideration in choosing a distribution channel. Companies must select the degree of market coverage that is most appropriate for their products. Changes in consumer buying behavior may necessitate a change in distribution channel strategy. If a product can be sold to more than one market segment, more than one distribution channel may be necessary. In fact, some companies are finding that multiple distribution channels help them sell more, period, so they sell their products through retailers, mail order, and on-line computer catalogs. In addition to selling mattresses through stores, for example, bedding manufacturers Sealy, Simmons, and Serta market their products through a toll-free phone number (1-800-MATTRES) and through computer

network CompuServe (users type GO BEDS into the computer).[5]

In general, products that are complex, expensive, custom made, or perishable move through shorter distribution channels. Producers that offer a broad product line, with the financial and marketing resources to distribute and promote it, are more likely to choose a shorter channel of distribution. A builder of large supercomputers, nCube Inc., sells its products directly to corporations; Bell Atlantic recently bought three for $25 million.[6] Inexpensive or standardized products typically are sold through longer channels.

Performance is a key consideration when choosing a distribution channel. A producer loses customers if its intermediary falls down on the job in promoting or delivering its products. Sometimes a producer may switch channels if distribution is becoming too difficult or complex.

New technologies are opening up new channels of distribution for some industries. Clothing manufacturers, which have long distributed their products through retailers and catalogs, now distribute them via television as well; home shopping channels generate $2 billion in sales each year, and the audience continues to grow. TV has certain advantages over more traditional distribution channels; during bad weather, for

CompuServe has expanded distribution channels for bedding manufacturers.

instance, sales at malls decline, but TV sales hold steady or even rise.[7]

Physical Distribution

Physical distribution, the other component of distribution strategy, involves the actual movement of goods from producer to user. Physical distribution is important for two reasons. First, such activities account for, on average, one-fifth the cost of a manufactured product; reducing the cost of physical distribution can improve productivity and make a company more competitive. Physical distribution is also important because customer satisfaction, to a large extent, depends on reliable movements of goods.

Physical distribution covers a broad range of activities, including warehousing, materials handling, inventory control, order processing, and transportation. *Warehousing* is the physical distribution activity that involves the storage of products. *Materials handling* is the physical distribution activity of moving items within plants, warehouses, transportation terminals, and stores. *Inventory control* involves managing inventory costs, such as storage facilities, insurance, taxes, and handling. The physical distribution activity of *order processing* includes preparing orders for shipment and receiving orders when shipments arrive.

The form of transportation used to ship products depends primarily on the kind of product, the distance, and the cost. The physical distribution manager has a number of companies and modes of transportation from which to choose. The five major modes of transportation are railroads, trucks, water carriers, pipelines, and air freight. The faster methods typically cost more than the slower ones. Speed, reliable delivery, shipment frequency, location availability, handling flexibility, and cost are all important considerations when choosing a mode of transportation.

Order processing and the other physical distribution activities performed by distribution channel members ensure that customers receive the right products at the right time and the right place. Manufacturers, wholesalers, and retailers have reduced the costs of many physical distribution functions by applying computer-based electronics and automation. Computer linkups that let channel members share information speed up order processing and delivery and help reduce inventory on hand.

Customer Service

Customer service is a vital component of product and distribution strategy. **Customer service standards** *measure the quality of service a firm provides for its customers.* Managers frequently set quantitative guidelines—for example, that all orders be processed within 24 hours after they are received or that salespeople approach shoppers within two minutes after they enter the store. Sometimes customers set their own service standards and choose suppliers that meet or exceed them. The service standards set by companies for their suppliers are rising, as U.S. companies gear up to compete more effectively on a global basis.

As more and more consumer goods are distributed through home shopping channels, some traditional retail channels may contract or disappear.

		Factor				
Comparing Modes of Transportation						
Mode	**Percent of Domestic Intercity Volume**	**Speed**	**Dependability in Meeting Schedules**	**Frequency of Shipments**	**Availability in Different Locations**	**Cost**
Rail	37%	Average	Average	Low	High	Medium
Water	16	Very Slow	Average	Very Low	Low	Very Low
Truck	25	Fast	High	High	Very High	High
Pipeline	24	Slow	High	High	Very Low	Low
Air	0.33	Very Fast	High	Average	Average	Very High

The customer service components of product strategy include warranty and repair service programs. A *warranty* is a firm's promise to repair, refund money paid, or replace a product if it proves unsatisfactory. The Magnuson-Moss Warranty Act (1975) authorizes the Federal Trade Commission to establish warranty rules for any product covered by a written warranty and costing $15 or more. This law does not require warranties, but it does say they must be understandable and that a complaint procedure for consumers must be in place.

Repair services are also important. Consumers want to know that help is available if something goes wrong. Those who shop for home computers, for example, often choose retailers who offer repair services and telephone "help lines."[8] Products with inadequate service backing quickly disappear from the market as a result of word-of-mouth criticism.

PROMOTIONAL STRATEGY

Promotional strategy, the final marketing mix element, is the function of informing, persuading, and influencing a consumer decision. It is as important to a not-for-profit organization, such as the American Heart Association, as it is to a profit-oriented company like Colgate-Palmolive.

Components of the Promotional Mix

The **promotional mix** is *the firm's combination of personal selling and nonpersonal selling designed to achieve promotional objectives.* **Personal selling** is *a promotional*

DID YOU KNOW?

Eyeball of lamb is a delicacy in Saudi Arabia.

In Japanese department stores, the bargain "basement" is located on an upper floor.

Feet are regarded as despicable in Thailand. Athlete's foot remedies with packages featuring a picture of feet will not be well received.

presentation made on a person-to-person basis with a potential buyer. Telemarketing is personal selling conducted entirely by telephone. Many firms use this method if it is too difficult or too expensive to have salespeople meet all potential customers in person. **Nonpersonal selling** consists of *advertising, sales promotion, and public relations.* Marketers attempt to develop a promotional mix that effectively and efficiently communicates their message to target customers.

For book retailer Barnes & Noble, the optimal promotional mix involves a wide range of goods and services designed to encourage customers to stay for hours. Cafes in its superstores serve espresso and sandwiches, a minitheater presents puppet shows for kids, and handy window seats and comfortable chairs encourage browsers to relax. Software and multimedia sections attract those interested in nonbook media. Barnes & Noble's promotional strategy represents the fastest-growing trend in book retailing.[9]

Advertising

For many firms, advertising is the most effective type of nonpersonal promotion. **Advertising** is *a paid, nonpersonal sales communication usually directed at a large number of potential customers.* While consumers in the United States often think of advertising as an American industry, three of the world's five largest advertising agencies are headquartered outside the United States. They include the British agencies WPP Group and Saatchi & Saatchi, and Tokyo-based Dentsu Inc.[10]

All marketers face the question of how best to allocate their advertising budgets. Cost is an important consideration, but it is equally important to choose the media best suited for the job. All media have their advantages and disadvantages.

Sales Promotion

Sales promotion is *a form of promotion designed to increase sales through one-time selling efforts, such as displays, trade shows, or special events.* Traditionally viewed as a supplement to a firm's sales or advertising efforts, sales promotion now has become an integral part of the promotional mix. Its expenditures total about $250 billion each year. Sales promotion techniques include point-of-purchase advertising displays in stores; specialty advertising, such as items imprinted with a company's name and logo; trade shows; samples; coupons; premiums; and contests.

Public Relations

Public relations refers to *an organization's communications with its customers, vendors, news media, employees, stockholders, government, and the general public.* Many of these communication efforts have a marketing purpose. IBM, for example, has received Thailand's prestigious Garuda Award, which recognizes significant contributions to that country's social and economic development. IBM provides personnel and equipment to Thai universities and donates funds to the nation's environmental protection agency.[11]

SELECTING A PROMOTIONAL MIX AND PROMOTIONAL STRATEGY

Developing the right promotional mix is one of the toughest tasks confronting marketers. The following questions provide some general guidelines for allocating promotional efforts and expenditures among personal selling, advertising, sales promotion, and public relations.

1. *What is your target market?* For instance, a drill press is sold to the business market, so the manufacturer's strategy must emphasize an effective sales

Barnes & Noble's Dallas superstore encourages browsers to linger over a cup of coffee.

Comparing the Advantages and Disadvantages of Advertising Media		
Media	**Advantage**	**Disadvantage**
Newspapers	Tailored to individual communities; readers can refer back to ads	Short life span
Television	Mass coverage; repetition; flexibility; prestige	High cost; temporary message; public distrust; lack of selectivity
Direct Mail	Selectivity; intense coverage; speed, flexibility; complete information; personalization	Expensive; consumer resistance; dependent on effective list
Radio	Immediacy; low cost; flexibility; targeted audience; mobility	Short life span; highly fragmented audience
Magazines	Selectivity; quality reproduction; long life; prestige	Lack of flexibility
Outdoor Advertising	Communicates simple ideas quickly; promotes local goods and services; repetition	Two brief; environmental concerns

force. By contrast, Scope mouthwash is sold to consumers, so an appealing advertising campaign is more important.

2. *What is the value of the product?* Most companies cannot afford to emphasize personal selling in marketing low-priced items like toothpaste, cosmetics, soft drinks, and candy, so they choose advertising instead. Higher-priced items in both business and consumer markets rely more on personal selling. Examples include time-share vacation condominiums and Boeing aircraft.

3. *What time frame is involved?* Advertising usually is needed to precondition a person for a sales presentation. An effective and consistent advertising theme may influence people favorably when they are approached by a salesperson in a store. But, except for self-service situations, a salesperson typically is involved in completing the actual transaction. Advertising often is used again after the sale to assure consumers of the correctness of their selection and to precondition them for repeat purchases.

4. *Should you spend your promotional budget on advertising or personal selling?* Once this decision is made, you need to determine the level of sales promotion and public relations efforts necessary to market your product.[12]

Push versus Pull Promotional Strategies

The promotional mix choice is related directly to the promotional strategy the firm will employ. The marketer has two alternatives available to meet these goals: pushing strategy or pulling strategy. A **pushing strategy** *is a sales-oriented approach. The product is marketed to wholesalers and retailers in the distribution channels.* Sales personnel explain to them why they should carry this particular product. The marketing intermediaries usually are offered special discounts, promotional materials, and cooperative advertising allowances. In the last case, the manufacturer shares the cost of local advertising of the product or line with the wholesaler or retailer. All these strategies are designed to motivate the intermediaries to "push" the good or service to their customers.

A **pulling strategy** *attempts to generate consumer demand for the product, primarily through advertising and sales promotion appeals.* Most advertising is aimed at the ultimate consumer, who then asks the retailer for the product, who in turn requests the item from the supplier. The marketer hopes that strong consumer demand will "pull" the product through the marketing channel by forcing marketing intermediaries to carry it.

Most marketing situations require the use of both pushing and pulling strategies, although the emphasis can vary. Consumer products are usually dependent on a pulling strategy and business products depend on a pushing strategy. John Stollenwerk, head of Wisconsin-based shoe company Allen Edmonds, used both pushing and pulling strategies to break into foreign markets. When Stollenwerk first bought the company, it had no sales outside the United States. Stollenwerk began displaying Edmonds shoes at trade shows in Italy, Germany, and France for several years, until a European retailer finally agreed to begin carrying his products. This pushing strategy did not work in Japan, however; Stollenwerk's applications for the Tokyo Trade Fair were rejected repeatedly by officials who politely told him that the fair was closed to foreigners. Then Stollenwerk discovered that several European firms had been invited to attend; "That really ticked us off," he says. He immediately packed his bags, flew to Tokyo, and called a press conference to discuss his products. The international press picked up the story and ran articles that drew the attention of Japanese consumers. Today, more than ten percent of Allen Edmonds sales are made abroad.[13]

INTERNATIONAL PROMOTIONAL STRATEGY

Cultural sensitivity and good homework are crucial when planning international promotional strategies. Strategies that are effective for promoting products to American audiences may not work in other countries due to differences in language and culture.

Different countries offer different media to advertisers. Television is the most widespread advertising medium in both Europe and Latin America; the most popular advertising spots in Latin America are on prime-time soap operas that are watched by consumers from Brazil to Mexico. In other countries, commercial TV and radio are limited, so print advertising is more common, as in

This gigantic Sony billboard is typical of the outdoor advertising used in China.

Oman, Norway, and Sweden. The major advertising media in China are outdoor posters and billboards, which usually are located near factories.

Another challenge for international marketers is the wide variety of national regulations. Sweden, for example, prohibits television advertising entirely; Germany allows it, but restricts it to 15 to 20 minutes each day, in blocks of 3 to 5 minutes. France and Italy limit the profits that state monopoly systems can make from advertising. U.S. computer manufacturers sometimes have waited up to 18 months to get air time on French television, which makes advertising this way almost useless for introducing new products.[14]

Cultural preferences, moral standards, educational levels, and language—all of these factors influence how ads will be perceived. IBM promoted its product line of Series 44 computers under that name in all countries except Japan, where they were given a different number because the Japanese word for *four* also sounds like the word for *death*. Kellogg renamed its Bran Buds cereal in Sweden, where the brand name sounded uncomfortably like the Swedish words for *burned farmer*. In most markets, ads for Kellogg's Rice Krispies show the cereal going "snap, crackle, and pop"; since these sounds are difficult for Japanese consumers to pronounce, Rice Krispies commercials in Japan go "patchy, pitchy, putchy."[15]

SUMMARY OF LEARNING GOALS

1. Explain what a product is and list the components of product strategy.

A product is defined as a bundle of physical, service, and symbolic attributes designed to satisfy consumer wants. The product concept includes choosing the brand, product image, warranty, service, packaging, and labeling, in addition to the physical or functional characteristics of the good or service.

2. Identify the classifications of consumer products, business products, and services.

Goods and services can be classified as consumer or business. Consumer goods are purchased by ultimate consumers for their own use. Business goods are those purchased for use either directly or indirectly in the production of other goods for resale. Consumer products can be classified as either convenience products, shopping products, or specialty products. This classification is based on consumer buying habits. Business goods can be classified as installations, accessory equipment, component parts and materials, raw materials, and supplies. This classification is based on how the items are used and on the product characteristics. Services can be classified as either consumer or business services.

3. **Discuss the product mix and the stages of the product life cycle.**

The product mix is the assortment of goods or services a firm offers consumers and business users. The four stages all products pass through in their product life cycle are introduction, growth, maturity, and decline. In the introductory stage, the firm attempts to elicit demand for the product. In the product's growth stage, sales climb, and the company earns profits on the product. In the maturity stage, sales reach a saturation level. In the decline stage, both sales and profits wane. Marketers sometimes can employ strategies that will extend the length of the product life cycle. These strategies include increasing the frequency of use, adding new users, finding new uses for the product, and changing the package size, label, or product quality.

4. **Describe the importance of pricing strategy.**

Price is the exchange value of a good or service. An item is worth only what someone else is willing to pay for it. Pricing strategy deals with the multitude of factors that influence the setting of a price. If a buyer views a price as too high or too low, the marketer must correct the situation. Price–quality relationships and psychological pricing are important in this regard.

5. **Identify the major components of distribution strategy.**

The two major components of an organization's distribution strategy are distribution channels and physical distribution. Distribution channels are the paths that products—and title to them—follow from producer to consumer. Physical distribution is the actual movement of these products from the producer to the user. Physical distribution covers a broad range of activities, including customer service, transportation, inventory control, materials handling, order processing, and warehousing.

6. **Outline the various types of distribution channels, and discuss the factors that influence channel selection.**

Distribution channels vary in length. Some channels are short, with goods and services moving directly from manufacturer to consumer. Others are longer, involving channel members, such as retailers and wholesaling intermediaries. Selecting a channel involves consideration of various factors, including the product, market, producer, and competition.

7. **Explain the importance of customer service.**

Customer service is a vital component of marketing strategy. Customer service standards measure the quality of service a firm provides for its customers and suppliers. The standards set by companies for their suppliers are rising, as U.S. companies gear up to compete more effectively on a global basis. Customer service components include warranty and repair service programs. Products with inadequate service backing quickly disappear from the market as a result of word-of-mouth criticism.

8. **Explain how advertising, sales promotion, and public relations are used in promotional strategy, and identify the factors that influence the selection of a promotional mix.**

Advertising is a paid, nonpersonal sales communication usually directed at a large number of potential customers. For many firms, advertising is the most effective type of nonpersonal promotion. Sales promotion consists of the one-time supporting aspects of a firm's promotional strategy. It includes point-of-purchase (POP) advertising, specialty advertising, trade shows, samples, premiums, trading stamps, and promotional contests. Public relations deals with the organization's communications with its various publics. Many of these communications have a marketing purpose. The first decision necessary in the development of a promotional mix is whether to use advertising and/or personal selling. Sales promotion and public relations efforts then are determined. The factors involved in these decisions are the type of product (business or consumer), the value of the product, and the timing of its use.

9. **Discuss the factors that influence international promotion.**

Cultural sensitivity and good homework are crucial when planning international promotional strategies. Effective strategies for promoting products to U.S. audiences may not work in other countries due to differences in media availability, audience characteristics, laws, and product regulations.

KEY TERMS QUIZ

personal selling	product	sales promotion
retailers	advertising	product mix
pushing strategy	public relations	product life cycle
nonpersonal selling	wholesaling intermediaries	product line
pulling strategy	customer service standards	marketing intermediaries
promotional mix	price	
distribution channels	physical distribution	

physical distribution 1. Refers to the movement of goods from producer to user.

product line 2. A series of related products offered by a firm.

nonpersonal selling 3. Advertising, sales promotion, and public relations.

product 4. Refers to a bundle of physical, service, and symbolic attributes designed to satisfy consumer wants.

price 5. Refers to the exchange value of a good or service.

wholesaling intermediaries 6. Distribution-channel members selling primarily to retailers, other wholesalers, or industrial users.

customer service standards 7. Refers to the quality of service that a firm's customers will receive.

public relations 8. An organization's communications with its customers, vendors, news media, employees, stockholders, government, and the general public.

retailers 9. Distribution-channel members selling goods and services to individuals for their own use rather than for resale.

product mix 10. An assortment of products offered by a firm.

marketing intermediaries 11. Distribution-channel members operating between the producer and the consumer or business producer.

distribution channels 12. Paths that goods and services and title to them follow from producer to consumer.

product life cycle 13. Refers to the four stages through which a successful product passes: introduction, growth, maturity, and decline.

promotional mix 14. A firm's combination of both personal and nonpersonal selling designed to achieve promotional objectives.

personal selling 15. Refers to the promotional presentation made on a person-to-person basis with a potential buyer.

pulling strategy 16. Refers to a promotional strategy utilizing advertising and sales promotion appeals to generate consumer demand for a product.

sales promotion 17. Refers to a form of promotion designed to increase sales through one-time selling efforts, such as displays, trade shows, special events, and other methods.

pushing strategy 18. Refers to a sales-oriented promotional strategy designed to motivate marketing intermediaries to push the product to their customers.

advertising 19. A nonpersonal sales presentation usually directed at a large number of potential customers.

OTHER IMPORTANT TERMS

accessory equipment	installations	shopping products
business good	inventory control	specialty products
capital items	materials handling warehousing	store retailing
component parts and materials	maturity stage	supplies
consumer good	shopping products	universal product code (UPC)
convenience products	nonstore retailing	vertical marketing systems (VMS)
decline stage	order processing	warranty
distribution strategy	promotional strategy	wheel of retailing
growth stage	raw materials	

REVIEW QUESTIONS

1. Differentiate among the following categories of consumer goods, business goods, and services:
   a. Convenience, shopping, and specialty products
   b. Installations, accessory equipment, component parts and materials, raw materials, and supplies
   c. Consumer and business services
2. What is meant by a product mix? Identify its primary components.
3. Suggest current products that represent each of the stages in the product life cycle. Why did you classify these products as you did?
4. Draw and explain the distribution channels for consumer products and for business products. How does a marketer select a specific channel?
5. Cite a local example (if one exists) of a variety store, department store, specialty store, convenience store, discount store, off-price store, factory outlet, catalog store, supermarket, hypermarket, and warehouse club.
6. List the various modes of transportation. Compare the modes on the basis of speed, dependability in meeting schedules, frequency of shipments, availability in different locations, and cost.

7. What promotional mix would be appropriate for the following products?
   a. Arc welder
   b. Personal computer
   c. Specialty steel products sold to manufacturers
   d. Landscaping service
8. What type of sales promotion techniques would you use in the following businesses?
   a. Independent insurance agency
   b. Jaguar dealership
   c. Family restaurant
   d. Hardware wholesaler
9. Explain how public relations might be used in the marketing strategy of the following:
   a. Natural gas utility
   b. Ford Motor Company
   c. Pittsburgh Pirates baseball team
   d. A local McDonald's franchise
10. What variables should be considered when selecting a promotional mix? Explain how each variable influences promotional strategy.

DISCUSSION QUESTIONS

1. Mountain Valley Spring Water Company bottles drinking water from a spring ten miles north of Hot Springs, Arkansas. The water, highly regarded for its purity, is consumed by the king of Saudi Arabia and has been served in the White House since the administration of Calvin Coolidge. Classify Mountain Valley Spring Water as a consumer product. Discuss why you classified it as you did.
2. Select a distribution channel for the following:
   a. A car seat for infants
   b. An income-tax preparation service
   c. Forklift trucks
   d. Pears

3. Select a transportation mode for the following:
   a. Sheet steel
   b. Natural gas
   c. Live lobsters
   d. Breakfast cereal
4. Describe the best television commercial you have seen in the past year. What made this commercial so effective?
5. Suppose that you are a business owner who wants to start promoting your consumer products in Latin America. Describe the factors that you should consider in planning your promotional strategy.

VIDEO CASE: Paint by Numbers

When is art art? When does it become a product? The video case for this chapter discusses the marketing efforts of Mark Kostabi, a well-known contemporary artist. It is located on page 422 of Appendix D.

Solution to Key Terms Quiz

1. physical distribution   2. product line   3. nonpersonal selling   4. product   5. price   6. wholesaling intermediaries   7. customer-service standards   8. public relations   9. retailers   10. product mix   11. marketing intermediaries   12. distribution channels   13. product life cycle   14. promotional mix   15. personal selling   16. pulling strategy   17. sales promotion   18. pushing strategy   19. advertising

Accounting and Financial Planning

CHAPTER 14

Accounting and Budgeting

Learning Goals

1. Explain the functions of accounting and its importance to the firm's management and to outside parties, such as investors, creditors, and government agencies.
2. Identify the three basic business activities involving accounting.
3. Contrast the roles played by public, private, government, and not-for-profit accountants.
4. Outline the steps in the accounting process.
5. Explain the functions of the balance sheet and the income statement and identify their major components.
6. Discuss how the major financial ratios are used in analyzing a firm's financial strengths and weaknesses.
7. Explain the role of budgets in business.
8. Explain the impact of exchange rates on international accounting and the importance of uniform financial statements for firms engaged in international business.

Giant supercenters such as Wal-Mart Stores and Kmart Corp. have taken a big bite out of market shares and profits of top grocery chains in the United States, Canada, and Mexico. But Kroger Co., the nation's largest grocery retailer, is fighting back. With over 1,200 stores in 24 states, Cincinnati-based Kroger netted a paltry $171 million on sales of $22 billion last year. This amounts to a minuscule eight cents on every $10 in sales—about half what the average grocery store earns.

Kroger's accounting statements tell the sad story of what happens when a firm takes on too much debt. Back in 1988, the firm fought off firms seeking to swallow it by borrowing $5.3 billion, then paying shareholders a $40-a-share dividend. Overnight, the debt-ridden chain became an unattractive takeover target. Since then, the major problem has been servicing all of this debt. Then there are the high labor costs from a unionized work force and a poor record of productivity.

Survival for Kroger meant generating enough cash to make huge mortgage payments; accounting data showed management where the cash could be found. Kroger decided to excel where supercenters lag—in high-profit perishables, like produce and meat. Every revenue and expense item was placed under the efficiency microscope. The 37-cent cake containers were replaced with a 25-cent version. Payroll expenses were trimmed by cutting corporate staff from 1,400 to 400.

Automated systems installed throughout the firm produced further savings. In the old days, employees had to count inventory on the receiving dock, check invoices by hand, and then send them to the accounting department. The new scanner technology accomplished the same tasks with 36 fewer people. Productivity improvements such as this made it possible for Kroger to reduce operating costs by $142 million.

The results already are showing up on the firm's accounting statements. In 1995, annual profits soared 43 percent above those of the previous year. Kroger employees are ecstatic about their ability to meet the challenges of a $5 billion debt load in a low-profit industry. As one employee pointed out, just because Wal-Mart moves next door, it doesn't mean that competition will automatically gobble up profits.[1]

CHAPTER OVERVIEW

The degree to which Kroger management depends on accounting to chart a course away from financial ruin is a single example of how today's organizations use this key information tool. The traditional stereotype of an accountant as a pale, bookish male dressed in a white shirt and narrow tie, seated behind a desk in a small office and making notations in a dusty ledger has been replaced by an image illustrated in the following scene:

Simone Reynolds carries a leather attaché case to her first meeting with the president and chief officials of Computer Controls Inc., the reportedly fast-growing company she is considering for acquisition as the eighth subsidiary of Reynolds Enterprises. She shakes hands with everyone at the meeting and quickly goes to her seat at the head of the long, polished, oak conference table. She immediately opens the attaché case and produces a folder containing a one-page computer printout. "Ladies and gentlemen," she begins, "let's get right to the point. Here is the information I need immediately."

The list is a short one:

1. *Did Computer Controls earn a profit last year?*
2. *What was the taxable income for the year?*
3. *How did Computer Controls raise money last year and how was it used?*
4. *What were the production costs of the firm's major products?*
5. *What were the costs involved in marketing the products?*
6. *How profitable and efficient was each of the firm's three major divisions?*
7. *What is the overall financial position of the company?*
8. *How did last year's operations and current financial position compare with plans made by management at the beginning of the year?*

The president of Computer Controls breathes a sigh of relief. "Thank goodness we've got a good accounting system," he says.

Today's accountants are international business people of both genders and from every ethnic background, equipped with personal computers and using sophisticated information. Never before have they been in such demand. In the United States alone, 1 million men and women list their occupation as accountant and 400,000 new accounting jobs are created every year. The availability of jobs and the relatively high starting salaries for talented accounting graduates have made accounting one of the most popular business majors on North American college and university campuses.

Accounting is the process of *measuring, interpreting, and communicating financial information to enable others inside and outside the firm to make informed decisions.* Like statistics, accounting is a language of business. Both profit and not-for-profit organizations are involved in business functions, such as financing, investing, and operating activities. Accountants gather, record, report, and interpret financial information that describes the status and operation of a firm and aids in decision making. They must accomplish three major tasks: scorekeeping, calling attention to problems and opportunities, and aiding in decision making.

This chapter begins by describing the three basic categories of business activities that all organizations are involved in or influenced by: financing, investing, and operating. The accounting process is explained, followed by a discussion of the development of accounting statements from financial transactions. Methods of interpreting these statements are described, and the role of budgets in planning and controlling is examined.

USERS OF ACCOUNTING INFORMATION

While accountants are the primary providers of financial information, many others are users. So, who are

> **THEY SAID IT**
>
> "My problem lies in reconciling my gross habits with my net income."
>
> *Errol Flynn (1909–1959) American actor*

the parties interested in a firm's accounting information? They are people both inside and outside the firm who rely on this information to help make business decisions. Inside the business, government agency, or not-for-profit organization, managers are the major users of accounting information, which helps them plan and control daily and long-range operations. Owners of the firm and boards of trustees of not-for-profit groups rely on accounting data to determine how well the firm or agency is being operated. Union officials use the data in contract negotiations, and employees refer to it in monitoring productivity and profitability.

Outside the firm, potential investors use accounting information to help them decide whether to invest in the company. Bankers and other current and potential lenders find that accounting information helps them determine a company's credit rating and gives them insight into a potential client's financial soundness. The Internal Revenue Service and state tax officials use it to evaluate a company's tax payments for the year. Citizens' groups and government agencies use such information in assessing the efficiency of a charitable group, local school system, or a city museum or zoo.

Accounting and the Environments of Business

Accountants not only play a fundamental role in business, but also in other aspects of society. Their work impacts each of the environments of business. The importance of

> ### DID YOU KNOW?
>
> Buying on credit is widely viewed by inhabitants of Germany and The Netherlands as living beyond one's means. *Schuld,* the German term for "debt," also means "guilt."
>
> The word budget comes from *bougette,* the French term for a small leather bag in which business people kept their money during the Middle Ages. Budgeting then consisted of counting the money in the bag to see if there was enough to pay expenses.
>
> The accounting system used in Russia makes it almost impossible for a manager to determine whether a single item in a product line makes a profit or not. Fixed and variable costs are lumped together and revenues and expenses are not matched.
>
> A customer in Rome, Italy, who receives a letter from the United States promising a shipment on 11-6-96 will expect delivery no later than June 11, 1996, six months before the American supplier complies. Unlike the U.S. practice of listing the month first when writing a date, the European dating system lists the day first, followed by the month, and then the year.

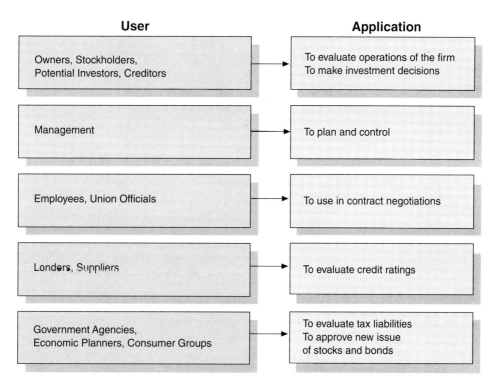

User	Application
Owners, Stockholders, Potential Investors, Creditors	To evaluate operations of the firm / To make investment decisions
Management	To plan and control
Employees, Union Officials	To use in contract negotiations
Lenders, Suppliers	To evaluate credit ratings
Government Agencies, Economic Planners, Consumer Groups	To evaluate tax liabilities / To approve new issue of stocks and bonds

Internal and external users need accounting information to help make effective decisions.

accounting information in aiding management in dealing with the competitive and economic environments is clear. Not so obvious is accounting's contributions to understanding, predicting, and reacting to the technological, regulatory, and social/cultural environments.

Accounting information and the interpretation of financial reports affect daily business decisions ranging from adjustments in inventory to employee work schedules. When NationsBank management decided to cut non-salary expenses by $100 million, the Charlotte-based bank's accounting records identified several areas for cost-savings:

- $81 million spent annually on travel
- Another $19 million spent on long-distance phone calls
- One copy machine for every ten employees—and $4 million spent keeping them filled with paper
- $67 million spent on office supplies, including $200,000 just for Post-It stickers.[2]

On a broader scale, such analyses may result in decisions, such as Kroger's plans to compete profitably in the grocery field by emphasizing high-margin departments and reducing costs. Similar analyses prompted B. F. Goodrich Co., whose name is almost synonymous with tires, to exit the tire business and focus on less competitive and more profitable chemicals and aerospace industries.[3]

Professional accountants often are called on to provide courts with information in litigation involving embezzlement, misrepresentation, fraud, and misuse of funds. In an increasingly automated accounting process, they must be adept in the use of computerized systems and in teaching managers and operative workers how to access this information. Twenty-first century accounting is far different from the bookkeeping stereotype of the past.

Catch what might otherwise go unnoticed.

Ektachrome Elite 100 film is Kodak's sharpest Ektachrome ever, with the finest grain of any 100-speed slide film. It delivers outstanding color accuracy, and details so sharp, nothing will go unnoticed. Not even a chameleon.

A Kodak Moment.

Kodak, which has 90 percent of the professional slide film market, demonstrates its regular film's clarity in this "find the chameleon" photo.

BUSINESS ACTIVITIES INVOLVING ACCOUNTING

The natural progression of a business begins with financing, involves investing, and leads to operating the business. All businesses, profit and not-for-profit, perform these three basic activities. Accounting plays a key role in each.

1. *Financing activities* are necessary to provide the funds to start a business and to expand it in the future. The implications of a firm's financial status go beyond the accounting statements. Kroger's $5 billion debt was used to pay $40-per-share stock dividends, but was also a strategy to prevent a hostile takeover of the company.

2. *Investing activities* are needed to provide valuable assets required to run a business. Kroger invested in scanner technology and automated systems; the return was a $142 million reduction in operating costs.

3. *Operating activities* focus on the sale of goods and services, but also consider expenses as an important part of sound financial management. By using a less-expensive cake container, Kroger slashed packaging costs by one-third.

For Eastman Kodak, the Rochester, New York-headquartered firm that gave birth to modern photography, financing activities result in the availability of funds needed to expand its international operations and compete with such firms as Japan's Fuji Photo Film Company. These funds are invested in production equipment, raw materials, and research and development activities that lead to new products such as Kodak's disposable camera. In addition, the firm seeks out the most efficient methods of producing and marketing its output. A current advertising campaign uses vivid images to illustrate the color accuracy and sharp details of its Ektachrome film.

TECHNOLOGY

Point-of-Sale Systems

Over the past two decades, the bar-code scanning point-of-sale (POS) terminal has become a familiar sight at retail giants ranging from Sears to Safeway stores. As technology and competition have pushed down prices, thousands of smaller companies have added these speedy, cost-saving devices to their operations. At the beginning of the 1990s, a mainframe POS system carried a $20,000 price tag. Today, a two-computer system can be installed for about $4,000 total investment.

But what does the business person get for the $4,000 outlay? In addition to replacing the traditional cash register, a simple bar-code scanner will update instantaneously a store's inventory records and accounting data while it performs error-free transactions. However, the real beauty of this technology lies in what it can do in collecting raw data and turning it into decision-oriented information.

Faced with the persistent dilemma of what styles of clothes he should order for his customers, Stephen Janus, owner of Maui-based Koala Blue retail stores, turned to Retail Engine, a Macintosh-based POS. Today, Janus studies the routine sales reports generated by the system, reviews the percentage of sales and recent sales trends for each clothing line, and makes his buying decisions ac-

cordingly. "Customer buying trends change quickly," Janus points out, "and now my inventory is in line with what the people want."

Further west across the Pacific, 7-Eleven Japan management already knew the benefits of a POS system in their small stores, each carrying a high percentage of perishable goods. During each transaction, the clerk swipes the bar code with a scanner to register the sale. Then two more bits of information are entered by touching a set of special keys: the sex and estimated age of the customer. This additional information

gives the manager a better understanding of what is being sold, when it is sold, and who is buying it. Armed with the data, the manager can adjust his or her buying practices almost immediately in response to any changes in buying patterns.

SOURCES: Gale Eisenstodt, "Information Power," *Forbes,* June 21, 1993, 44–45; and Larry Stevens, "Point-Of Sale Inventory Systems: Now Ready For Small Business," *Nation's Business,* December 1991, 11.

Taco Bell uses touch screens to give customers speedy, error-free service.

ACCOUNTING PROFESSIONALS

The 1 million accountants in the United States are employed in a variety of areas in business firms, government agencies, and not-for-profit organizations; others are self-employed.

Certified public accountants (CPA) *have demonstrated their accounting knowledge by meeting state requirements for education and experience and successfully completing a number of rigorous tests* in accounting theory and practice, auditing, and law. Accountants who meet specified educational and experience re-

quirements and pass certification exams carry the title certified management accountant (CMA) or certified internal auditor (CIA).

The various types of accounting professionals can be classified as public, private (or management), government, and not-for-profit.

Public Accountants

A **public accountant** *provides accounting services to individuals or business firms for a fee.* Most public accounting firms provide three basic services to clients: (1) auditing, or examining, financial records; (2) tax services; and (3) consulting services to management and small business. Since they are not employees of the firm for which they are providing services, public accountants are in a position to provide unbiased advice about the firm's financial condition.[4] The six largest public accounting firms, the so-called Big Six, are Arthur Andersen, Coopers & Lybrand, Deloitte & Touche, Ernst & Young, KPMG Peat Marwick, and Price Waterhouse.

Private (or Management) Accountants

An accountant employed by a business other than a public accounting firm is called a **private accountant.** Private, or management, accountants are responsible for collecting and recording financial transactions and preparing financial statements used by the firm's managers in decision making. In addition to preparing financial statements, private accountants play a major role in interpreting them.

Private accountants frequently specialize in different aspects of accounting. A *cost accountant*, for example, determines the cost of goods and services, and helps set their prices. A *tax accountant* seeks to minimize taxes paid and is in charge of the firm's federal, state, county, and city tax returns. An *internal auditor* examines the firm's financial practices to ensure that records are accurate and that company operations are in compliance with federal laws and regulations.

Government and Not-for-Profit Accountants

Federal, state, and local governments also require accounting services. **Government accountants** and those working for not-for-profit organizations are *professional accountants who perform services similar to those of private and public accountants.* But here, instead of the reporting emphasis being on measuring profit or loss, it is more concerned with determining how efficiently the organization is accomplishing its objectives. Among the many government agencies employing accountants are the Environmental Protection Agency, local police and fire departments, the FBI, the IRS, and many state and local governments. Not-for-profit organizations, such as churches, labor unions, political parties, charities, schools, hospitals, and universities also hire accountants. In fact, the not-for-profit sector is one of the fastest-growing segments of accounting practice.

THE ACCOUNTING PROCESS

Accounting deals with financial transactions between a firm and its employees, customers, suppliers, owners, bankers, and various government agencies. Weekly payroll checks result in cash outflows for the compensation of employees. A payment to a supplier results in the receipt of needed materials for the production process. Cash, check, and credit purchases by customers generate funds to cover the costs of operations and to earn a profit. Prompt payment of bills preserves the firm's credit rating and its ability to obtain future loans. This *procedural cycle, used by accountants in converting individual transactions to financial statements*, is called the **accounting process.** It involves recording, classifying, and summarizing transactions in order to produce financial statements for the firm's management and other interested parties.

> **THEY SAID IT**
>
> "If you owe $50, you're a delinquent account.
> If you owe $50,000, you're a small business person.
> If you owe $50 million, you're a corporation.
> If you owe $50 billion, you're the government."
>
> *L. T. White, Jr.*
> *(1907–1987)*
> *American historian*

The Impact of Computers on the Accounting Process

For hundreds of years, the recording, or posting, of transactions was entered manually in a *journal*, and then the information was transferred or posted to individual accounts listed in *ledgers.* However, the computer revolution of the twentieth century has simplified the accounting systems of thousands of firms, both industrial giants and neighborhood service providers. Fully automated systems, developed by firms such as NCR Corporation, have eliminated most of the recording, classifying, and summarizing tasks once done by hand. As *point-of-sale terminals* replace cash registers, a number of functions can be performed each time a sale is recorded. Not only can such a terminal recall prices from memory and maintain a perpetual inventory count of every item in stock, but it also automatically performs accounting data entries.

Accounting software programs, such as *Quicken* and *Turbo Tax*, are used widely in business today. They make possible a "do-it-once" approach, whereby each sale is converted automatically into a journal entry, which then is stored until needed. Up-to-date financial statements and financial ratios then can be requested when needed by the decision maker. The integration of accounting and computers in almost

Basic Data

> **Transactions**
> Receipts, invoices, and other source documents related to each transaction are assembled to justify making an entry in the firm's accounting records.

Processing

> **Record**
> Transactions are recorded in chronological order in books called journals. Brief explanations are given for each entry.
>
> **Classify**
> Journal entries are transferred, or posted, to individual accounts kept in a ledger. All entries involving cash are brought together in the ledger's cash account; all entries involving sales are recorded in the ledger's sales account.
>
> **Summarize**
> All accounts in the ledger are summarized at the end of the accounting period and financial statements are prepared from these account summaries.

Financial Statements

Balance Sheet	Income Statement	Statement of Cash Flows

The accounting process involves recording, classifying, and summarizing transaction data in order to create financial statements.

every organization requires accountants to be increasingly computer-literate.

But computers do more than record and organize data for statements; they help accountants make sound financial decisions quickly and effectively. In fact, the most important job of the typical private accountant is to communicate this information clearly and effectively for use in decision making.

THE FOUNDATION OF THE ACCOUNTING SYSTEM

In order to provide reliable, consistent, and unbiased information to decision makers, accountants follow guidelines, or standards, known as *generally accepted accounting principles (GAAP)*. These standards are principles that encompass the conventions, rules, and procedures necessary in determining acceptable accounting practices at a particular time. Accountants use GAAP to create uniform financial statements throughout an industry for comparison purposes. GAAP provide the basis for sound decision making.

Two accounting statements form the foundation of the entire accounting system: the balance sheet and the income statement. The information found in these statements is calculated using the accounting equation and the double-entry system.*

The Accounting Equation

Four fundamental terms are involved in the accounting equation: assets, equities, liabilities, and owners' equity. An **asset** is *anything of value owned or leased by a business.* Cash, accounts receivable and notes receivable (amounts owed to the business through credit sales), land, buildings, supplies, and marketable securities are all assets.

An **equity** is a *claim against the assets of a business.* The two major classifications of individuals who have

---

*A third statement, the statement of cash flows, is frequently prepared to focus specifically on the information related to sources and uses of cash for the firm from its operating, investing, and financing activities.

**WITH OUR FINANCIAL STRENGTH, YOU'LL BE GLAD
WE'RE ON YOUR SIDE.** *On the tough playing field of international business, you need
all the leverage you can get. That's why AIG's strength and stability are so important. We're one of the world's
strongest insurance and financial services organizations, with over $13 billion in shareholders' equity and*

*$17 billion in general insurance net loss and loss adjustment reserves. Our record of profitability is unsurpassed
in the industry, and we hold the highest ratings from the principal rating services. The AIG Companies have the
capacity to serve your needs through all kinds of market conditions. We're ready to throw our weight behind you.*

AIG WORLD LEADERS IN INSURANCE AND FINANCIAL SERVICES.
American International Group, Inc. – Dept. A, 70 Pine Street, New York, NY 10270.

$15 billion in stockholders' equity makes AIG a world player in insurance and financial services.

equity in a firm are creditors (liability holders) and owners. A **liability** of a business is *anything owed to creditors*—that is, the claims of the firm's creditors. When the firm makes credit purchases for inventory, land, or machinery, the creditors' claims are shown as accounts payable or notes payable. Wages and salaries owed to employees also represent liabilities (known as wages payable). The **owners' equity** represents the *investment in the business made by owners of the firm and retained earnings that were not paid out in dividends.*

A strong owners' equity position often is used as evidence of a firm's financial strength and stability. Insurance giant AIG features its owners' equity strength in its corporate advertising.

Because equities, by definition, represent the total claims of both owners and creditors against assets, then assets must equal equities:

Assets = Equities

The basic **accounting equation** states that *assets are equal to liabilities plus owners' equity*. It reflects the financial position of any firm at any point in time:

Assets = Liabilities + Owners' Equity

Since financing comes from either creditors or owners, the right side of the accounting equation also represents the financing structure of business.

The relationship expressed by the accounting equation is used to develop two primary accounting statements prepared by every business, large or small: the balance sheet and the income statement. These two statements reflect the current financial position of the firm and the most recent analysis of income, expenses, and profits for interested parties inside and outside the firm. They provide a fundamental basis for planning activities and are used in attracting new investors, securing borrowed funds, and preparing tax returns.

FINANCIAL ANALYSIS

Financial statements provide managers with essential information they need to evaluate the *liquidity* of the organization—its ability to meet current obligations and needs by converting assets into cash; the firm's

1 Current Assets
Cash and other liquid assets that can or will be converted to cash or used within one year.

2 Fixed Assets
Relatively permanent plant, property, and equipment expected to be used for periods longer than one year.

3 Current Liabilities
Claims of creditors that are to be repaid within one year.

4 Long-Term Liabilities
Debts that come due one year or more after the date of the balance sheet.

5 Owners' Equity
Claims of the proprietor, partners, or stockholders against the assets of a firm; the excess of assets over liabilities.

FIESTA POOLS
Balance Sheet
as of December 31, 199X

ASSETS

1 Current Assets

Cash	$ 8,000	
Marketable Securities	30,000	
Accounts Receivable	194,000	
Inventory	124,000	
Total Current Assets		$356,000

2 Fixed Assets

Store Equipment	$112,000	
Furniture and Fixtures	40,000	
Total Fixed Assets		$152,000
Total Assets		$508,000

LIABILITIES AND OWNERS' EQUITY

3 Current Liabilities

Accounts Payable	$ 82,000	
Current Installments of Long-Term Debt	30,000	
Accrued Expenses	14,000	
Income Taxes Payable	$ 12,000	
Total Current Liabilities		$138,000

4 Long-Term Liabilities

Long-Term Notes Payable	$ 60,000	
Total Long-Term Liabilities		$ 60,000
Total Liabilities		$198,000

5 Owners' Equity

Common Stock (160,000 shares @ $1)	$160,000	
Retained Earnings	150,000	
Total Owners' Equity		$310,000
Total Liabilities and Owners' Equity		$508,000

Fiesta Pools' balance sheet illustrates the accounting equation—assets equal liabilities plus owners' equity.

profitability; and its *overall financial health.* The balance sheet and income statement provide an outline from which management can base its decisions. By interpreting the data provided in these financial statements, the appropriate information can be communicated to internal decision makers and to interested parties outside the organization.

The Balance Sheet

The **balance sheet** shows the *financial position of a company as of a particular date.* It is similar to a photograph comparing a firm's assets with its liabilities and owners' equity at a specific moment in time. Balance sheets must be prepared at regular intervals, since a firm's managers

and other internal parties are likely to request this information on a daily, weekly, or at least once-a-month basis. On the other hand, external users, such as stockholders or industry analysts, typically use this information less frequently, perhaps every quarter or once a year.

It is helpful to keep the accounting equation in mind as a diagram that is explained by the balance sheet. Listing the various assets on the balance sheet indicates sources of the firm's strengths—where the money is coming from. These assets, shown in descending order of liquidity (convertibility to cash), represent the *uses* that management has made of available funds. On the other side of the equation, liabilities and owners' equity indicate the *sources* of the firm's assets. Liabilities reflect the claims of creditors—

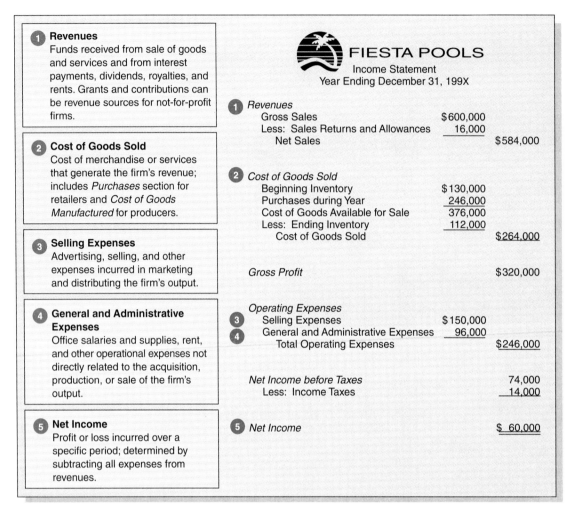

1 Revenues
Funds received from sale of goods and services and from interest payments, dividends, royalties, and rents. Grants and contributions can be revenue sources for not-for-profit firms.

2 Cost of Goods Sold
Cost of merchandise or services that generate the firm's revenue; includes *Purchases* section for retailers and *Cost of Goods Manufactured* for producers.

3 Selling Expenses
Advertising, selling, and other expenses incurred in marketing and distributing the firm's output.

4 General and Administrative Expenses
Office salaries and supplies, rent, and other operational expenses not directly related to the acquisition, production, or sale of the firm's output.

5 Net Income
Profit or loss incurred over a specific period; determined by subtracting all expenses from revenues.

FIESTA POOLS
Income Statement
Year Ending December 31, 199X

1 *Revenues*		
Gross Sales	$600,000	
Less: Sales Returns and Allowances	16,000	
Net Sales		$584,000
2 *Cost of Goods Sold*		
Beginning Inventory	$130,000	
Purchases during Year	246,000	
Cost of Goods Available for Sale	376,000	
Less: Ending Inventory	112,000	
Cost of Goods Sold		$264,000
Gross Profit		$320,000
Operating Expenses		
3 Selling Expenses	$150,000	
4 General and Administrative Expenses	96,000	
Total Operating Expenses		$246,000
Net Income before Taxes		74,000
Less: Income Taxes		14,000
5 *Net Income*		$ 60,000

Fiesta Pools' income statement shows the firm earned $60,000 on sales of $584,000.

financial institutions or bondholders that have made loans to the firm, suppliers that have provided goods and services on credit, and others to be paid, such as federal, state, and local tax officials. Owners' equity represents the owners' (stockholders', in the case of corporations) claims against the firm's assets or the excess of all assets over liabilities.

Income Statement

While the balance sheet reflects the financial position of the firm at a specific point in time, the income statement is a *flow* statement that reveals the performance of the organization over a specific time period. Resembling a motion picture rather than a snapshot, the **income statement** is a *financial record summarizing a firm's financial performance in terms of revenues, expenses, and profits over a given time period.*

The purpose of the income statement is to show the profitability of a firm during a period of time, usually a year, a quarter, or a month. In addition to reporting the profit or loss, it helps decision makers focus on overall revenues and the costs involved in generating these revenues. Not-for-profit organizations use this statement to see if the organization's revenues and contributions will cover costs involved in operating the firm. Finally, the income statement provides much of the basic data needed to calculate numerous ratios used by management in planning and controlling the organization.

The income statement (sometimes called a profit and loss—or P&L—statement) begins with total sales or revenue generated during a year, quarter, or

> **THEY SAID IT**
>
> "I gave him an unlimited budget and he exceeded it."
>
> *Edward Bennett Williams (1920–1988) Former owner, Washington Redskins football club (referring to former Head Coach George Allen)*

Wanted: Accounting Standards in Hungary

Many businesses today are looking to the former Soviet-bloc countries of Eastern Europe in hopes of finding a bargain bonanza for investment. Unfortunately, it is becoming apparent that the pitfalls frequently outnumber the opportunities for businesses operating in countries without an established, well-structured economic system. Because Hungary seemed the most likely country to achieve a free-market economy, several international firms chose it for their expansion. General Electric, for example, bought 50 percent of the Hungarian light-bulb maker, Tungsram, several years ago, but has yet to realize a profit.

One of the first tasks facing such firms is to establish a uniform accounting system within the country. Because established accounting systems typically do not exist in these countries, accounting fraud has become entrenched in day-to-day business operations. For example, Hungarian manufacturers record all production as revenue regardless of whether or not it has been sold. No records are kept on inventories either, and unpaid receivables never are accounted for. Many businesses already have been victims of this lack of accountancy—an estimated 60 percent of Hungary's industrial firms are insolvent. Their operations are dependent on government subsidies and free bank credits to stay afloat.

Annual sales of $400 million and still no profits at Tungsram.

U.S.-based accounting firm Price Waterhouse recently opened an office in Budapest. A primary mission was to establish a uniform accounting system. Hungarian balance sheets had to be converted to a format used by financial officers in corporations in the United States and Western Europe.

In addition to establishing acceptable and consistent accounting systems, other systems must also be instituted if free-market enterprises are to succeed in these countries. Since World War II, much of Eastern Europe has been operating on a barter system under the direction of the Council for Mutual Economic Assistance. Until a few years ago, this system allowed Hungary to obtain energy and raw materials at far below world-market prices from the former Soviet Union. Like other newly independent countries, Hungary now must acquire these commodities at world prices. This is producing a major strain on the country's economy.

Financial managers and consultants involved in international companies operating in these fledgling countries are challenged by the enormity of restructuring needed before foreign investors will see it as a viable and profitable investment alternative.

SOURCE: Adapted from Peter Fuhrman, "Doing Business in the Dark," *Forbes,* February 19, 1990, 50–54.

month, and then deducts all of the costs related to producing this *revenue.* Once all costs—administrative and marketing expenses, costs involved in producing the product, interest, and taxes, for instance—have been subtracted, the remaining *net income* may be distributed to the firm's owners (stockholders, proprietors, or partners) or reinvested in the company as retained earnings. *The final figure on the income statement—net income after taxes—*is the well-known **bottom line.**

Statement of Cash Flows

In addition to the income statement and the balance sheet, many firms prepare a third accounting statement. Since 1987 all companies listed on organized stock exchanges have been required to prepare a statement of cash flows as part of their annual registration information. In addition, major lenders often require it of all firms applying for business loans. As the name indicates, the *statement of cash flows* provides investors

CROSS-FUNCTIONAL ENVIRONMENT

Working Together for a Fatter Paycheck

A surprising number of people working at employee-owned companies would echo the words of cartoonist Marvin Townsend: "My mistake was buying stock in the company. Now I worry about the lousy work I'm turning out!" Employee-owners of Springfield Remanufacturing Corp. will be quick to tell you that people in different job areas will work together effectively when they control their own financial destiny.

A decade ago, SRC was losing $2 million a year and facing the prospect of going out of business. Today, the Missouri-based remanufacturer of diesel and gasoline engines enjoys a 40 percent annual growth rate and is one of the most successful small businesses in the United States. President Jack Stack and his 450 employee-owners turned the company around by first educating every

SRC employee, many with only a high-school education, about financial data—accounting statements, profit reports, cost-control analyses, and quality-control measures.

Employees meet weekly to receive information on operating income, expenses, cash flows, and other relevant data. In small group sessions, supervisors go over the figures, encouraging questions. Daily printouts detail the progress of every job, and the goal is to beat the numbers. After all, in an employee-owned company, beating the numbers means more money for everyone.

The game starts every Wednesday morning, when 25 managers and supervisors meet to pore over a detailed current financial statement. The first column of figures lists the income and expenses for last month. The next column gives projections for the current month based on the annual budget. As Stack records the variances on a chalkboard, the financial

statement shows them where they stand, the expected income figure, where the problem areas are, and the results necessary to trigger an employee bonus. That same afternoon, the information is shared with all employees.

Decentralizing cost-control decisions has had an unmistakable impact at SRC. For instance, first-line supervisors are involved actively in not only reducing costs in their own departments, but in helping solve problems in other areas, thereby affecting companywide expenses. Information is readily available, since there is one computer terminal in the plant for every three employees. Anyone can go to a terminal and secure information on incoming parts, costs, or engineering problems. Data on current labor, material, and overhead costs—and comparisons with expected costs—are immediately available. Individuals on the production line work with others in shipping or product set-up to remedy problems as they arise.

Keeping individuals and work groups involved with their own work and in assisting other functions that affect the overall bottom line is the key to SRC's success. There are no spectators. At SRC, only the people can make the numbers work, and they are the same people who set the numbers.

SOURCE: Nancy K. Austin, "When Honesty Is the Best Management Policy," *Working Woman,* May 1994, 25–26; Jack Stack, "Springfield Remanufacturing Bought the Company and Learned to Play the Game of Open-Book Management," *National Productivity Review* (Winter 1993): 39–52; and Timothy O'Brien, "Company Wins Workers' Loyalty by Opening Its Books," *The Wall Street Journal,* December 20, 1993, B1.

and creditors with relevant information about a firm's cash receipts and cash payments during an accounting period.

The fact that cash flow is the lifeblood of every organization is evidenced by the business failure rate. Of the more than 60,000 businesses that failed during a recent year, three of every five blamed economic factors linked to cash flow for their demise. More recent studies of small- and medium-sized companies reveal that one firm in four ranks inability to control cash flow as the firm's number one problem. Proponents of the statement of cash flows hope its preparation and scrutiny by affected parties will prevent financial disaster for otherwise profitable firms that are forced into bankruptcy due to a lack of funds needed to continue day-to-day operations.

Ratio Analysis

Accounting professionals are not simply responsible for preparing financial statements. Of ever greater importance is assisting managers in interpreting these documents by comparing the firm's activities to previous periods and with other companies in the industry. **Ratio analysis** is *one of the most commonly-used tools for (1) measuring the liquidity, profitability, extent of debt financing, and effectiveness of the firm's use of its resources and (2) permitting comparison with other firms and with past performance.* Ratios assist the manager by interpreting actual performance and making comparisons with what should have happened. They can be compared with those of similar companies to reflect company performance relative to that of competitors. These industry standards serve as important yardsticks in pinpointing problem areas as well as areas of excellence. Ratios for the current accounting period also may be compared with similar calculations for previous periods to spot any trends that might be developing. Ratios can be classified according to their specific purpose.

Liquidity Ratios   *A firm's ability to meet its short-term obligations when they must be paid is measured by* **liquidity ratios.** Highly liquid firms are less likely to face emergencies in raising needed funds to repay loans. On the other hand, firms with less liquidity may be forced to use high-cost lending sources to meet their maturing obligations or face default.

Small, poorly financed companies often are faced with liquidity crises. When Chicago-based Quality Croutons started business a few years ago, with McDonald's as its sole customer, it had no liquidity problem. After all, the fast-food giant has a pay-in-ten-days policy. But when the crouton supplier began taking on new customers, it learned that not everyone pays their bills as quickly. Company owners had to contribute additional operating funds when receipts began to lag behind by 30 to 45 days.

Two commonly used liquidity ratios are the current ratio and the acid-test ratio. The *current ratio* compares current assets to current liabilities, giving management information concerning the firm's ability to pay its current debts as they mature. The current ratio of Fiesta Pools can be computed as follows:

$$\text{Current Ratio} = \frac{\text{Current Assets}}{\text{Current Liabilities}} = \frac{\$356,000}{\$138,000}$$
$$= 2.6 \text{ to } 1$$

This means Fiesta Pools has $2.60 of current assets for every $1 of current liabilities. In general, a current ratio of 2 to 1 is considered financially satisfactory. This rule of thumb must be considered along with other factors, such as the nature of the business, the season of the year, and the quality of the company's management. Fiesta Pools' management and other interested parties are likely to compare this ratio of 2.6 to 1 to previous operating periods and to industry averages to determine its appropriateness.

The *acid-test* (or quick) *ratio* measures the ability of Fiesta Pools to meet its debt on short notice. It calculates quick assets, meaning highly liquid current assets, against current liabilities. It does not include inventory or prepaid expenses—only cash, marketable securities, and accounts receivable.

Fiesta Pools' current balance sheet lists the following quick assets: cash ($8,000), marketable securities ($30,000), and accounts receivable ($194,000). The firm's acid-test ratio is computed as:

$$\text{Acid-Test Ratio} = \frac{\text{Quick Assets}}{\text{Current Liabilities}} = \frac{\$232,000}{\$138,000}$$
$$= 1.7 \text{ to } 1$$

Because the traditional rule of thumb for an adequate acid-test ratio is 1 to 1, Fiesta Pools appears to be in a good short-term credit position. However, the same cautions as for the current ratio should be applied here. The ratio should be compared with industry averages and with previous operating periods in determining its appropriateness for Fiesta Pools.

Profitability Ratios   **Profitability ratios** *measure the firm's overall financial performance in terms of its ability to generate revenues in excess of operating and other expenses.* Earnings are compared with total sales or investment. Over a period of time, these ratios also may reveal the effectiveness of management in operating the business. Three commonly used profitability ratios are *earnings per share, return on sales,* and *return on equity.*

$$\text{Earnings per Share} = \frac{\text{Net Income after Taxes}}{\text{Common Shares Outstanding}}$$
$$= \frac{\$60,000}{160,000} = \$0.375$$

$$\text{Return on Sales} = \frac{\text{Net Income}}{\text{Net Sales}} = \frac{\$60,000}{\$584,000}$$
$$= 10.3 \text{ percent}$$

$$\text{Return on Equity} = \frac{\text{Net Income}}{\text{Total Owners' Equity}}$$
$$= \frac{\$60,000}{\$310,000} = 19.4 \text{ percent}$$

All of these ratios reflect positively on the current operations of Fiesta Pools. For example, the return-on-sales ratio indicates that the firm realized a profit of 10.3 cents for every dollar of sales. Although this ratio varies widely among business firms, Fiesta Pools compares favorably with retailers in general, that average about five percent return on sales. However, this ratio, like the other profitability ratios, should be evaluated in relation to profit forecasts, past performance, or more specific industry averages to better interpret the results. Similarly, while the firm's return of almost 20 percent on equity appears to be satisfactory, the degree of risk present in the industry also must be considered.

Profitability ratios, such as return on sales, are widely used indicators of a firm's success in its industry. Although the 29 Books-A-Million superstores are a tiny number in comparison with industry giants Barnes & Noble, K-mart's Borders-Walden Group, and Crown Books, the Birmingham-based retailer is succeeding financially by keeping its customers satisfied. Its 4.6 percent return on sales is three times that of Barnes & Noble and Crown and well above Waldenbooks' 2.2 ratio.[5]

Story time at one of Books-A-Million's Louisiana outlets.

Leverage Ratios   The third category of financial ratios, **leverage ratios,** *measure the extent to which a firm is relying on debt financing.* They are of particular interest to potential investors and lenders. If too much debt has been used to finance the firm's operations, problems may arise in meeting future interest payments and repaying outstanding loans. In addition, both investors and lenders may prefer to deal with firms whose owners have invested enough of their own money in the firm to avoid overreliance on borrowing. The *debt-to-owners'-equity* ratio provides answers to these questions.

$$\text{Debt to Owners' Equity} = \frac{\text{Total Liabilities}}{\text{Owners' Equity}}$$
$$= \frac{\$198,000}{\$310,000} = 64\%$$

Since a debt-to-equity ratio of greater than 1 would indicate the firm is relying more on debt financing than owners' equity, it is clear that Fiesta Pools' owners have invested considerably more than the total amount of liabilities shown on the firm's balance sheet.

Firms such as RJRNabisco that have acquired numerous companies through borrowing often find themselves in the position of having to sell off product lines and even whole divisions to reduce the interest costs that accompany heavy reliance on debt. Mobile, Alabama-based Morrison's recently sold its institutional foods subsidiary to improve its equity position. This placed the firm in a strong position to finance the expansion of its successful casual restaurants, including Ruby Tuesday's, Mozzarella, and Sweetpea's.[6]

Activity Ratios   The final category of financial ratios, **activity ratios,** *measure the effectiveness of the firm's use of its resources.* The most frequently used activity ratio is the *inventory turnover ratio,* which indicates the number of times merchandise moves through the business.

$$\text{Inventory Turnover} = \frac{\text{Cost of Goods Sold}}{\text{Average Inventory}}$$
$$= \frac{\$264,000}{\$121,000} = 2.2 \text{ times}$$

Average inventory for Fiesta Pools is determined by adding the January 1 beginning inventory of $130,000 and the December 31 ending inventory of $112,000 (as shown on the income statement) and dividing by 2. The 2.2 turnover rate can be compared with industry standards and used as a measure of efficiency. For retailers, such as furniture and jewelry stores, an annual turnover rate of 1.5 times is about average. For a supermarket, the turnover rate can be as high as once every two weeks.

The four categories of financial ratios relate balance sheet and income statement items to one another and assist management in pinpointing strengths and weaknesses. In large, multiproduct organizations operating in diverse markets, today's sophisticated information systems are capable of updating these financial ratios on a daily or even hourly basis. Consequently, management must decide on an appropriate review schedule to avoid the costly and time-consuming task of overmonitoring.

Recently, Harte & Co. CEO Axel L. Grabowsky concluded that the sheer volume of such information was consuming his working days, leaving him with little time to devote to "the future of business, to new-product development, acquisitions, and to short- and long-term planning." The New York-based manufacturer of plastic sheeting markets 12 major product categories in numerous domestic and international markets. Grabowsky's current monitoring involves a daily focus on sales, comparing actual sales to forecasts. Cash flows and profitability and activity ratios are evaluated each week. He concluded that monthly reviews are appropriate for ratios involving production costs, accounts receivable, and sales by major product category, territory, and major customers. However, Grabowsky expects managers from each area to monitor their own operations on a more frequent basis and supply him with detailed explanations for all important variations from budgeted performance within 24 to 48 hours.[7]

BUDGETING

Although the financial statements discussed in this chapter focus on what has occurred in the past, they are the basis for planning in the future. A **budget** is a *planning and control tool that reflects expected sales revenues, operating expenses, and cash receipts and outlays.* It is the quantification of the firm's plans for a specified future period. Since it requires management to estimate expected sales, cash inflows and outflows, and costs, it serves as a financial blueprint. The budget

becomes the standard against which actual performance can be compared.

Budget preparation is frequently time-consuming and involves many people from various departments of the firm. The complexity of the budgeting process varies with the size and complexity of the organization. Giant corporations, such as Walt Disney, Intel, and Boeing, tend to have more complex and sophisticated budgeting systems. Their budgets serve as a means of integrating the numerous divisions of the firm in addition to serving as planning and control tools. But budgeting by both large and small firms is similar to household budgeting in that the purpose is to match income and expenses so as to accomplish objectives and correctly time cash inflows and outflows.

Since the accounting department is the organization's financial nerve center, it provides much of the data used in budget development. The overall master, or operating, budget is actually a composite of numerous sub-budgets for each of the departments or functional areas of the firm. These typically include the

The K-Swiss operating budget includes expenses the firm expects to incur in the next fiscal period. The money that paid for this shoe ad was included in the budget as an advertising expense.

production budget, cash budget, capital expenditures budget, advertising budget, and sales budget.

The composite master budget for sports-shoemaker K-Swiss includes funds allocated in its marketing budget. The marketing budget, in turn, combines sub-budgets for such functions as transportation, storage, sales, and advertising. The $122,475 cost of a K-Swiss ad in *People* magazine is not surprising; the decision to use it was made months ago and its cost is reflected in the advertising budget.

Budgets usually are established on an annual basis, but may be divided monthly or quarterly for control purposes. Since some activities, such as the construction of new manufacturing facilities or long-term purchasing contracts, tend to involve activities extending over several years, longer-term budgets may be used in those cases.

INTERNATIONAL ACCOUNTING

As organizations become more involved with the global economy, accounting procedures and practices must be adapted to reflect an international environment. Nestle, the giant chocolate and food products multinational, operates throughout the world. A whopping 98 percent of its revenues come from outside Switzerland, its headquarters country. International accounting for this type of firm is concerned primarily with the need to translate the financial statement of a global firm's international affiliates, branches, and subsidiaries and to convert foreign currency transactions to dollars.

Exchange Rates

As defined in Chapter 3, an exchange rate is the rate at which a country's currency can be exchanged for other currencies or gold. Currencies can be considered goods that can be bought and sold. Like the price of any good or service, currency prices change daily according to supply and demand. Exchange rate fluctuations will affect accounting entries differently than would a single-currency transaction.

Accountants dealing with international transactions are concerned with recording foreign sales and purchases. Johnson & Johnson produces and markets Sundown sunblock to sun worshippers both here and abroad. Brazilian purchasers pay in *cruzeiros*, a currency that often fluctuates greatly in relation to U.S. dollars.

The international firm's consolidated financial statements must reflect any gains or losses that may

Careless Brazilians who fail to use sunblock may find their skin color resembling this reclining red pepper—"Done to a frizzle," as the copy reads. Johnson & Johnson's Sundown solution results in receipts of Brazilian currency—and an international currency issue for its accountants.

occur as a result of fluctuations in exchange rates during specific periods of time. Financial statements covering two or more countries also need to be consistent to allow for comparison.

International Accounting Standards

The International Accounting Standards Committee (IASC) was established in 1973 to provide worldwide consistency in financial reporting practices. The IASC is recognized as the sole body having responsibility and authority to issue pronouncements on international accounting standards. The International Federation of Accountants, formed in 1977, supports the work of the IASC and develops international guidelines for auditing, ethics, education, and management accounting. Every five years, an international congress is held to judge the progress in achieving consistency in standards. Its objective is to enhance comparability between nations and currencies. With the advent of a single European market and the North American trade bloc, the necessity for comparability and uniformity of international accounting standards is becoming widely recognized and soon will be a reality.

FIESTA POOLS
16853 Katy Freeway
Houston, Texas 78555

SAMPLE CASH BUDGET
January–June 199X

	January	February	March	April	May	June
Beginning Monthly Balance	$ 6,000	$ 6,000	$ 6,000	$ 6,000	$ 6,000	$ 6,000
Add: Cash Receipts (collections from customers, interest receipts, and other cash inflows)	4,000	14,000	12,000	10,000	8,000	18,000
Cash Available for Firm's Use	$ 10,000	$ 20,000	$18,000	$16,000	$ 14,000	$ 24,000
Deduct: Cash Disbursements (for payroll, materials, income taxes, utilities, interest payments, etc.)	10,000	8,000	10,000	12,000	6,000	14,000
Preliminary Monthly Balance	$ 0	$ 12,000	$ 8,000	$ 4,000	$ 8,000	$ 10,000
Minimum Required Cash Balance	6,000	6,000	6,000	6,000	6,000	6,000
Excess (or Deficiency)	(6,000)	6,000	2,000	(2,000)	2,000	4,000
Short-Term Investment of Excess			2,000		2,000	4,000
Liquidation of Short-Term Investment				2,000		
Short-Term Loan to Cover Deficiency	6,000					
Repayment of Short-Term Loan		6,000				
Ending Monthly Balance	$ 6,000	$ 6,000	$ 6,000	$ 6,000	$ 6,000	$ 6,000

This sample cash budget covers a six-month period. The firm has set a $6,000 minimum cash balance. The cash budget indicates the months in which excess funds will be invested to earn interest rather than remaining idle. It also indicates periods in which temporary loans will be required to finance operations. Finally, it produces a tangible standard for comparing actual cash inflows and outflows.

SUMMARY OF LEARNING GOALS

1. **Explain the functions of accounting and its importance to the firm's management and to outside parties, such as investors, creditors, and government agencies.**

   Accountants measure, interpret, and communicate financial information to parties inside and outside the firm for effective decision making. They are responsible for gathering, recording, and interpreting financial information to management. In addition, they provide financial information on the status and operation of the firm for use by such outside parties as government agencies and potential investors and lenders.

2. **Identify the three basic business activities involving accounting.**

   Accounting plays key roles in (a) financing activities, which are necessary to start a business and to expand it in the future; (b) investing activities, which provide the assets needed to run the business; and (c) operating activities, which focus on the sale of goods and services and the expenses incurred in operating the business.

3. **Contrast the roles played by public, private, government, and not-for-profit accountants.**

   Public accountants are independent organizations or individuals who provide accounting services, such as tax statement preparation, management consulting, and accounting systems design to other firms or individuals for a fee. Private, or management, accountants are responsible for collecting and recording financial transactions, preparing financial statements, and interpreting them for managers in their own firm. Government and not-for-profit accountants perform many of the same functions as a private accountant, but their emphasis is on how effectively the organization or agency is operating rather than on profits and losses.

4. **Outline the steps in the accounting process.**

   The accounting process involves the recording, classifying, and summarizing of accounting transactions and using this information to produce financial statements for the firm's management and other interested parties. Transactions are recorded chronologically in journals, posted in ledgers, and then summarized in accounting statements.

5. **Explain the functions of the balance sheet and the income statement and identify their major components.**

   The balance sheet shows the financial position of a company as of a particular date. The three major classifications on the balance sheet represent the components of the accounting equation: assets, liabilities, and owners' equity.

   The income statement shows the operations of a firm over a specific period. It focuses on the firm's activities—its revenues and expenditures—and the firm's profit or loss during the period. The major components of the income statement are revenues, cost of goods sold, expenses, and profits or losses.

6. **Discuss how the major financial ratios are used in analyzing a firm's financial strengths and weaknesses.**

   Liquidity ratios measure a firm's ability to meet short-term obligations. Examples are the current ratio and acid-test ratio. Profitability ratios assess the overall financial performance of the firm. Earnings per share, return on sales, and return on owners' equity are examples. Leverage ratios measure the extent to which the firm relies on debt to finance its operations, for example, the debt to owners' equity ratio. Activity ratios, such as inventory turnover, measure how effectively a firm uses its resources. Each of these ratios assists management and others by enabling a comparison of current company financial information with that of previous years and with industry standards.

7. **Explain the role of budgets in business.**

   Budgets are financial guidelines for future periods reflecting expected sales revenues, operating expenses, and/or cash receipts and outlays. They represent management's expectations of future occurrences based on plans that have been made. They serve as important planning and control tools by providing standards against which actual performance can be compared.

8. **Explain the impact of exchange rates on international accounting and the importance of uniform financial statements for firms engaged in international business.**

   An exchange rate is the rate at which a country's currency can be exchanged for other currencies or gold. The daily changes in exchange rates affect the accounting entries for sales and purchase transactions of firms involved in international markets. They create either a loss or a gain for the company, depending on whether they increase or decrease. Financial statements must be translated into the currency of the country in which the parent company resides. The International Accounting Standards Committee was established to provide worldwide consistency in financial reporting practices and comparability and uniformity of international accounting standards.

KEY TERMS QUIZ

public accountant
private accountant
accounting equation
government accountant
accounting
accounting process
asset

equity
liquidity ratios
balance sheet
income statement
budget
leverage ratios
profitability ratios

owners' equity
bottom line
ratio analysis
certified public accountant (CPA)
activity ratios
liability

_____accounting_____ 1. Measuring, interpreting, and communicating financial information for internal and external decision making.

public accountant 2. Professional who provides accounting services to other businesses and individuals.

private accountant 3. Professional employed by a business other than a public accounting firm.

_____(CPA)_____ 4. Accountant who has completed education and experience requirements and has passed a comprehensive examination.

government accountant 5. Professional employed by a government agency or not-for-profit organization.

accounting process 6. Method of converting individual transactions to financial statements.

_____asset_____ 7. Anything of value owned or leased by a business.

_____equity_____ 8. Claim against the assets of a business.

_____liability_____ 9. Claim of the firm's creditors.

owners/equity 10. Claims of the proprietor, partners, or stockholders against the assets of the firm; the excess of assets over liabilities.

accounting equation 11. Basic accounting concept that assets are equal to liabilities plus owners' equity.

balance sheet 12. Statement of a firm's financial position on a particular date.

income statement 13. Financial record of revenues, expenses, and profits of a company over a period of time.

bottom line 14. Overall profit or loss earned by a firm.

ratio analysis 15. Use of quantitative measures in evaluating a firm's financial performance.

liquidity ratios 16. Ratio measuring a firm's ability to meet its short-term obligations.

profitability ratios 17. Ratio measuring the overall financial performance of the firm.

leverage ratios 18. Ratio measuring the extent to which a firm relies on debt financing in its operations.

activity ratios 19. Ratio measuring the effectiveness of the firm's use of its resources.

_____budget_____ 20. Planning and control tool that reflects expected sales revenues, operating expenses, and cash receipts and outlays.

OTHER IMPORTANT TERMS

acid-test ratio
cost accountant
current ratio
debt to owners' equity
earnings per share
generally accepted accounting
   principles (GAAP)

internal auditor
inventory turnover ratio
journal
ledger
liquidity
net income
point-of-sale terminal

return on equity
return on sales
revenues
statement of cash flows
tax accountant

REVIEW QUESTIONS

1. Who are the major users of accounting information?
2. Describe the role that accounting plays in a firm's financing activities, its investing activities, and its operating activities.
3. Distinguish between public, private, government, and not-for-profit accountants. Why are approximately 50 percent of the nation's certified public accountants employed as private accountants?
4. Explain the steps of the accounting process and the impact of computerization on this process.
5. What is meant by the statement, "the balance sheet is a detailed expression of the accounting equation"?

6. Identify the primary purpose of each of the components of the balance sheet and the income statement. What are the major differences between the balance sheet and the income statement?
7. Identify the four categories of financial ratios discussed in the chapter, and describe specific ratios included in each category.
8. Explain the similarities and differences between budgeting and the development of accounting statements.
9. What are the primary purposes of budgets?
10. What financial statements are affected by exchange rates in international accounting? What are the benefits of uniform international financial statements?

DISCUSSION QUESTIONS

1. Many accountants show the values for the various items on their firm's income statements in percentages based on net sales rather than showing the actual figures involved. What additional insights would this approach make possible?
2. Identify the three types of assets and the two types of liabilities that appear on a typical balance sheet. Categorize the following account titles:
   a. Mary Ellen Beasley, Capital
   b. Mortgage Payable
   c. Patent
   d. Buildings
   e. Common Stock
   f. Prepaid Expenses
   g. Accounts Payable
   h. Marketable Securities
3. Match each of the accounts listed below with the appropriate accounting categories. Each account may be included in more than one category.

   ___ a. Net Sales
   ___ b. Accounts Receivable
   ___ c. Advertising Expense
   ___ d. Common Stock
   ___ e. Equipment
   ___ f. Marketable Securities
   ___ g. Long-Term Notes Payable
   ___ h. Salaries
   ___ i. Retained Earnings

   1. Current Asset
   2. Fixed Asset
   3. Current Liability
   4. Long-Term Liability
   5. Owners' Equity
   6. Revenue
   7. Expenses

4. Indicate the ratio that would provide information on:
   a. A firm's ability to meet short-term obligations
   b. A firm's ability to pay current debts
   c. A firm's ability to pay current debts on short notice
   d. A firm's overall financial performance
   e. The amount of profits earned for each share of common stock outstanding
   f. Net income compared to sales
   g. Owners' equity
   h. The firm's use of its resources
   i. The number of times merchandise moves through the business
   j. The extent to which a firm relies on financing
   k. The percentage of owners' investments to debt financing

5. At the end of the year, Jupiter Enterprises showed the following balances in its accounts:

Land	$ 80,000
Buildings	314,000
Inventory	100,000
Cash	10,000
Accounts Payable	90,000
Marketable Securities	36,000
Retained Earnings	300,000
Common Shares (80,000 shares @ $1)	80,000
Notes Payable	110,000
Equipment	40,000

   a. Prepare a balance sheet for Jupiter Enterprises.
   b. Calculate the current ratio, acid-test ratio, and debt to owners' equity ratio. What conclusions can be drawn from these ratios?

VIDEO CASE: Springfield Remanufacturing Corp.

This video case illustrates concepts discussed throughout the chapter with a graphic emphasis on the application of accounting methods used by this company. It is included on page 422 of Appendix D.

Solution to Key Terms Quiz

1. accounting 2. public accountant 3. private accountant 4. certified public accounting (CPA) 5. government accountant 6. accounting process 7. asset 8. equity 9. liability 10. owners' equity 11. accounting equation 12. balance sheet 13. income statement 14. bottom line 15. ratio analysis 16. liquidity ratios 17. profitability ratios 18. leverage ratios 19. activity ratios 20. budget

CHAPTER 15

Banking and Financial Management

Learning Goals

1. Identify the functions performed by a firm's financial manager.
2. Describe the characteristics a good form of money should have and list the functions of money.
3. Distinguish between money (M1) and near-money (M2).
4. Explain how a firm uses funds.
5. Compare the two major categories of sources of funds.
6. Identify likely sources of short-term and long-term funds.
7. Identify the major categories of financial institutions and the sources and uses of their funds.
8. Explain the functions of the Federal Reserve System and the tools it uses to increase or decrease the money supply.
9. Describe the institutions and practices that regulate bank safety.
10. Discuss the U.S. financial system in its global context.

U nlike most small privately owned company founders, Patrick Duffeler has been extremely successful in finding enough funds to open and operate his Williamsburg Winery. In just seven years, over $6 million has been raised to fund the winery's start-up and growth strategies. The success of these financial strategies stands as an example to many would-be entrepreneurs who, too often, find their greatest barrier is financing the business.

Duffeler emigrated from Brussels in 1959, earned a degree in economics and finance from the University of Rochester, and began a career track with major firms such as Eastman Kodak and Philip Morris. In these corporate environments, Duffeler learned techniques and strategies of financing new-product development, marketing, and the advantages of a lean management style. He was able to apply this experience and knowledge when he began managing the winery.

The wine industry is different in many ways from the typical business. Holding inventory is considered an investment rather than a cost to most wine producers since

they expect certain wines to appreciate in value over time. Weather is always an unknown environmental factor in growing any crop, but while the demand for grapes remains relatively stable from year to year, wine producers also must consider changing consumer tastes and the competition. For these reasons, owning a winery is considered a wealthy person's hobby, and a high-risk business for investors. Behind every $1 in revenues is an initial investment of $2 to $3 in land, grapes, barrels, and laboratory equipment. Says firm chairman S. Buford Scott, "There's a consensus among investors that you cannot make money in the wine business!"

In 1986, Patrick and Peggy Duffeler formed a limited partnership with $115,000 of capital from their retirement accounts and savings and $65,000 from friends and business colleagues. First they bought a 300-acre cattle and grain farm in Williamsburg, Virginia, and 2,500 grape plants. They paid the rental fees on the production equipment and entered the production-test phase. But the money quickly evaporated even before the winery entered real production.

Duffeler converted the partnership into a corporation and sold shares to the general public to raise more money for the fledgling winery. With this fresh cash infusion, he planted new fields, bought new fermenting devices, and acquired 60 wine barrels at $500 each. Most importantly, Duffeler hired a viticulturist to supervise the fields and a wine maker to oversee production processes.

By 1989, the Williamsburg Winery had shipped its first white wine, Governor White, and Duffeler continued building inventory and buying vines even though profits remained elusive. But investors become interested in businesses offering predictable, growing sales; secure cash flow; and the prospects of profitability. With production up to about 14,000 cases, Duffeler raised another $1.5 million by selling additional shares of ownership to existing investors.

But Duffeler grew tired of the continuing difficulty of obtaining loans from commercial banks; so in 1991 he turned to an outside advisor, John Jamison, formerly a general partner of brokerage giant Goldman Sachs. Jamison knew that Duffeler needed to "build a sophisticated and large capital base that would include debt and equity and would ultimately position the company to borrow from the right bank."

Ultimately, the Charlotte, North Carolina-based NationsBank provided the long-sought-after access to borrowed funds. The winery's credit line (its limit of preapproved borrowing) has risen from $300,000 to $1 million, which gives Duffeler the ability to buy grapes quickly in response to changing harvest conditions. With this financial backing, Duffeler explains, "We are finally positioned to go national."[1]

CHAPTER OVERVIEW

In this chapter, we will examine how companies like Williamsburg Winery develop and implement financial plans. Earlier in the text, two essential functions were discussed that a business must perform. First, it must produce a good or service, or contract with suppliers to produce it. Second, the firm must market its good or service to prospective customers. There is, however, a third function that is equally important: the company must ensure that it has enough money to continue performing its other tasks successfully, both now and in the future. Adequate funds must be available to buy materials and equipment, pay bills, purchase additional facilities, and compensate employees. This third function is **fi-**nance—*planning, obtaining, and managing the company's use of funds in order to accomplish its objectives most effectively.*

Organizational objectives include not only meeting expenses, but also maximizing the firm's overall value, which often is determined by the value of its common stock. More and more frequently, businesses designate a financial manager to be responsible for both meeting expenses and increasing profits for the firm's stockholders.

This chapter focuses on such topics as the role of financial managers, why businesses need funds, and the various types and sources of funds. We will discuss how the Federal Reserve System regulates the various institutions that make up the financial system in the United States. Finally, we will examine the role the U.S. financial system plays in a global context.

DID YOU KNOW?

Products that have served as money include fishhooks, tea, shells, feathers, salt (from which came "salary" and "being worth one's salt"), shark teeth, cocoa beans, wampum beads, and woodpecker scalps.

Nearly 900 U.S. banks have failed since 1987.

The rate of interest on your student loan is determined, in part, by bankers in Zurich and London.

An installment plan in China works this way: You make all the installment payments and then you get your bicycle.

Almost half of the federal government's annual budget is transferred electronically.

THE ROLE OF THE FINANCIAL MANAGER

In the modern business world, effective financial decisions are increasingly important to organizational success. Businesses are placing greater priority on measuring and reducing the costs of conducting business. As a result, **financial managers**—*those responsible for developing and implementing the firm's financial plan and for determining the most appropriate sources and uses of funds*—are among the most vital people on the corporate scene. Their growing importance is reflected in the number of chief executives who were promoted from financial positions. A recent study of major corporations reveals that nearly one in three chief executives has a finance or banking background.[2]

Possible job titles for high-ranking financial managers include vice president for finance and chief financial officer (CFO). The way a company's money is managed can reduce the need for financing as often or as much and, when money is needed, there is a better chance of getting it since investors can see how well the company is handling its finances.[3] In performing their jobs, financial managers continually seek to balance the risks involved with expected financial returns. *Risk* is the uncertainty of loss; *return* is the gain or loss that results from an investment over a specified period.

A heavy reliance on borrowed funds, however, may raise the return on the owners' or stockholders' investment. The financial manager strives to maximize the wealth of the firm's stockholders by striking a *balance between the risk of an investment and its potential gain.* This balance is called the **risk-return trade-off.** An increase in a firm's cash on hand, for instance, reduces the risk of unexpected cash needs. But cash is not an earning asset, and the failure to invest surplus funds in an earning asset (such as marketable securities) reduces potential return, or profitability.

Every financial manager must perform this risk-return balancing act. When Nicholas Graham founded his small custom necktie business, he quickly realized the importance of balancing risk with return. Using a sheet of plywood on top of his bed for a workbench, the 24-year-old entrepreneur cut and sewed unusual ties, then sold the finished products to specialty shops for cash. Even though overhead expenses were virtually nonexistent, Graham was not able to make and sell enough ties to earn a profit. So he decided to add underwear, which cost less to make and sold for more money, to his line. Although the new line forced Graham to add new equipment and buy additional materials, it also maximized returns. Today the firm known as Joe Boxer Corporation has 46 employees and earns $22 million a year.[4]

The Financial Plan

Financial managers develop the organization's **financial plan,** a *document that specifies the funds needed by a firm for a period of time, indicates the timing of inflows and outflows, and indicates the most appropriate sources and uses of funds.* It is based on *forecasts* of production costs, purchasing, and expected sales activities for the period covered. Financial managers use forecasts to determine the specific amounts and timing of expenditures and receipts. The financial plan is built on answers to three vital questions:

1. What funds does the firm require during the next period of operations?
2. How will the necessary funds be obtained?
3. When will more funds be needed?

Some funds will be obtained through selling the firm's goods or services. But funds are needed in different amounts at different times, and the financial plan must reflect both the amount and timing of inflows and outflows of funds. Profitable firms often face a financial squeeze as a result of the need for funds when sales lag, when the volume of credit sales increases, or when customers are slow in making payments. Cash inflows and outflows of a business are similar to those in a household; the members of a household may depend on a weekly or monthly paycheck for funds, but their expenditures vary greatly from one pay period to the next. The financial plan should indicate when the flows of funds entering and leaving the organization will occur and in what amounts.

A good financial plan also involves **financial control,** *a process that periodically checks actual revenues, costs, and expenses against the forecasts.* If significant differences exist between projected figures and reality, it is important to discover them early in order to take corrective action.

Steve Shaw and Ric Serrenho, owners of corporate communications firm Visual Concepts Media, discovered firsthand the importance of a good financial manager. When the Connecticut-based company was smaller, Shaw and Serrenho managed everything themselves—marketing, video production, and finance. But, as the firm began growing rapidly, operating costs shot up, and then the IRS conducted a

THEY SAID IT

"I've got all the money I'll ever need if I die by four o'clock."

Henny Youngman (1906–   ) American comedian

tax audit. The company founders soon realized they could not maintain financial control and decided to hire Randy LaVigne to develop a financial plan and perform needed financial analyses. LaVigne overhauled the financial system, purchased new financial management software, and taught Shaw and Serrenho how to use the financial reports. He also conducted "what-if" strategic analyses, such as determining how much money Visual Concepts Media could save if it consolidated its numerous video purchases throughout the year into one annual order. Having a financial manager has freed Shaw and Serrenho to concentrate on other aspects of the business. Says Shaw, "[Hiring LaVigne] will save us money and improve our management abilities."[5]

CHARACTERISTICS AND FUNCTIONS OF MONEY

Playwright George Bernard Shaw once said that the *lack* of money is the root of all evil. Many a business person would agree, for money is the lubricant of contemporary business. Firms require adequate funds to finance the company's operations and carry out the plans of management.

Characteristics of Money

Money is *anything generally accepted as a means of paying for goods and services.* Most early forms of money had a number of serious disadvantages. For example, a cow is a poor form of money for an owner who wants only a loaf of bread and a bottle of wine. Exchange involving the use of money can permit elaborate specialization and provide a general base for purchasing power if the money has certain characteristics. It must be divisible, portable, durable, difficult to counterfeit, and it should have a stable value.

Divisibility The dollar can be converted into pennies, nickels, dimes, and quarters. The British pound is worth 100 pence; the German deutsche mark can be traded for 100 pfennigs. These forms of money can be exchanged easily for products ranging from chewing gum to a car. Today, almost all economic activity is concerned with making and spending money.

Portability Modern paper currency is lightweight, which facilitates the exchange process. Portability is an important characteristic, since the typical dollar bill changes hands 400 times during its lifetime,

> **THEY SAID IT**
>
> "If you think nobody cares if you're alive, try missing a couple of car payments."
>
> *Earl Wilson (1907–1987) American newspaper columnist*

staying in the average person's pocket or purse less than two days.

Durability U.S. dollar bills have an average life of 17 months and can be folded some 4,000 times without tearing. Although coins and paper currency wear out over time, they are replaced easily with new money.

Difficulty in Counterfeiting The distribution of counterfeit money could undermine a nation's monetary system by ruining the value of legitimate money. For this reason, all governments make counterfeiting a serious crime and take elaborate steps to prevent it. A U.S. dollar bill, for instance, contains an interwoven security thread and microprinting on the portrait. The government has plans to redesign paper currency by making bills multicolored, adding a hologram, or using a watermark in order to make counterfeiting even more difficult.[6]

Stability A good money system should have a stable value. If the value of money fluctuates, people become unwilling to trade goods and services for it. Inflation is, therefore, a serious concern for governments. When people fear that money will lose much of its value, they begin to abandon it and look for safer means of storing their wealth. In the case of runaway inflation, where the value of money may decrease 20 percent or more in a single year, people increasingly return to a barter system, exchanging their output for the output of others.

A similar problem is faced by firms operating in Russia. During the 1980s, the Kama automotive factory, located 600 miles north of Moscow, turned out 150,000 heavy-duty trucks a year, equaling the entire U.S production. The wildly fluctuating ruble drove the firm to adopt the barter tactics of a bazaar. Today, a Kama truck may be traded to another firm for sheet metal, electrical parts, or glass components. The new truck even may be involved in a second- or third-hand exchange by purchasers who barter it for needed parts.[7]

Functions of Money

Money performs three basic functions. First, it serves primarily as a *medium of exchange*—a means of facilitating exchange and eliminating the need for a barter system. Second, it functions as a *unit of account*—a common denominator for measuring the value of all goods and services. Finally, money acts as a temporary *store of value*—a way of keeping accumulated wealth until it is needed to make new purchases. Money offers

BUSINESS STRATEGY

The End of the $1 Bill?

Does the $1 bill make economic sense? It buys what a quarter bought 25 years ago; the $5 bill does what the dollar bill did 35 years ago. These questions face the U.S. Congress as it wrestles with the decision of whether to replace the $1 greenback with a coin.

Although a $1 coin would cost an estimated 8 cents to produce—about twice the cost of producing a dollar bill—its 30-year average life makes it much more durable than paper money. In addition, automated counting machines can count coins at less than $2 per thousand dollars as compared with $22 per thousand for bills. The advantages of coins over small-denomination paper money led England to eliminate £ notes and replace them with a £ coin. Monetary experts predict a $400 million a year reduction in the federal budget if a $1 coin would be accepted by the American public.

But there's the rub. The last two efforts at introducing a dollar coin—the Eisenhower coin in 1971 and the Susan B. Anthony coin in 1979—

Replacing the U.S. dollar bill with a dollar coin might make pockets bulge, but would it save the U.S. government some $400 million a year?

were flops, the latter because people had trouble distinguishing it from a quarter. In both cases, people continued to have a choice, since paper dollars continued to be circulated. If Congress approves a change, expect to see an octagonally shaped, thicker, or gold-colored $1 coin—similar to the British pound shown here.

SOURCE: Peter Samuel, "Uncle, Can You Spare a Coin?" *Forbes,* November 8, 1993, 92–95.

---

one big advantage as a store of value: It is highly liquid, meaning it can be obtained and disposed of quickly and easily. The chief advantage of money is that it is immediately available for purchasing products or paying debts.

THE MONEY SUPPLY AND NEAR-MONEY

The U.S. money supply is divided into the following categories: coins, paper money, traveler's checks, demand deposits (checking accounts), interest-bearing NOW (negotiable order of withdrawal) accounts, and credit union share draft accounts. In government reports and business publications, the term *M1* often is used to refer to those items considered to be money.

In addition to the money supply, a number of *assets* exist *that are almost as liquid as cash or checking*

accounts but cannot be used directly as a medium of exchange. These are known as **near-money.** Time deposits (savings accounts), government bonds, money market mutual funds, and credit cards are considered near-money. These categories of near-money are commonly referred to as *M2.*

WHY ORGANIZATIONS NEED FUNDS

Organizations require funds for many reasons, including running day-to-day business operations, paying for inventory, making interest payments on loans, paying dividends to stockholders, and purchasing land, facilities, and equipment. The financial plan identifies the firm's specific cash needs and when they will be needed. Comparing these needs with expenditures and expected cash receipts (from product sales, payments made by credit purchasers, and other sources) will help the financial manager determine precisely

Credit Cards: The Next-Best Thing to Money

The era of "plastic money" has reached every aspect of modern society, from gas stations to grocery stores, and even churches. Parishioners at St. Mark's United Methodist Church in Lincoln, Nebraska, simply fill out a charge slip with their charge-card information and the amount of the donation and drop the merchant copy in the collection plate.

More and more people are using the credit card as a substitute for currency and checks. The popularity of credit cards is due to the convenience they offer and the growing willingness of merchants throughout the world to accept them. The use of credit cards grew steadily through the 1980s, and, by the mid-1990s, annual U.S. billings of credit-card purchases totaled $400 billion. While many cards are issued by banks, consumers also can obtain cards from manufacturers (such as General Motors), large retailers (such as Sears' Discover card), catalog and specialty retailers (Spiegel), groups (Diners Club), and competing firms (AT&T's Universal Card).

The monthly statement of card purchases is a tangible reminder that they are *credit* cards—not money.

The cards merely represent a special credit arrangement between the holder and the organization issuing them. The cardholder can repay the outstanding balance at the end of the billing period or, in the case of bank cards and retail cards, make a monthly payment of at least the stated minimum plus interest on the unpaid balance.

The 3,000-plus companies currently issuing credit cards love them because of their profit potential. Merchants typically pay fees of one to five percent for credit-card sales; cardholders frequently pay an annual fee and average interest charges of about 18 percent on unpaid balances. As a result, credit cards are the most profitable product in bank-

ing, often generating three times the profit of other bank loans. Today, 111.3 million Americans carry at least one card, and the average cardholder carries three. Americans use credit cards for everything from taxi rides to groceries. Sixty-eight percent of cardholders carry balances forward every month, and credit-card debt is expected to reach $4.4 trillion by the year 2000.

SOURCES: Geoffrey Brewer, "Don't Buy a Stapler Without It," *Sales & Marketing Management,* March 1994, 16; Larry Light and Leah Spiro, "The War of the Plastic," *Business Week,* April 14, 1991, 28–29; and Thomas McCarroll, "No Checks. No Cash. No Fuss?" *Time,* May 9, 1994, 60–62.

---

what additional funds must be obtained at any given time. If inflows exceed cash needs, the financial manager will invest the surplus to earn interest. On the other hand, if inflows do not meet cash needs, the financial manager will seek additional sources of funds.[8]

Generating Funds from Excess Cash

Most financial managers will choose to invest the majority of their firm's excess cash in marketable securities. These often are considered near-money since they are, by definition, marketable and easily converted into cash.

Three of the most common types are U.S. Treasury bills, commercial paper, and certificates of deposit. *Treasury bills* are one of the most popular marketable securities since, as issues of the U.S. government, they are considered virtually risk-free and easy to resell. While *commercial paper* (a short-term note issued by a major corporation with a very high credit standing and backed solely by the reputation of that firm) is riskier than a Treasury bill and does not have a well-developed secondary market for resale prior to maturity, it pays the purchaser a higher rate of interest. A *certificate of deposit (CD)* is a short-term note issued by a financial institution, such as a commercial bank, savings and loan,

Financial Planning Process

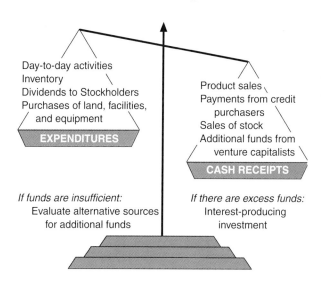

Day-to-day activities
Inventory
Dividends to Stockholders
Purchases of land, facilities, and equipment

EXPENDITURES

Product sales
Payments from credit purchasers
Sales of stock
Additional funds from venture capitalists

CASH RECEIPTS

If funds are insufficient:
Evaluate alternative sources for additional funds

If there are excess funds:
Interest-producing investment

The financial planning process aids managers in analyzing the firm's cash position and making decisions aimed at achieving objectives.

or credit union. The size and maturity date of a CD vary considerably and can be tailored to meet the needs of the purchaser. Large CDs in denominations of $100,000 can be purchased for periods as short as 24 hours. At the other extreme, ten-year certificates are available in denominations as low as $100 to $250.

SOURCES OF FUNDS

So far, we have focused on half of the definition of finance—the reasons organizations need funds and how they use them. But of equal importance to the firm's financial plan is the choice of the best sources of

needed funds. Sources fall into two major categories: debt and equity. **Debt capital** represents *funds obtained through borrowing*. **Equity capital** consists of *funds provided by the firm's owners by reinvesting earnings, making additional contributions, liquidating assets, issuing stock to the general public, or by soliciting contributions from venture capitalists.* Equity capital also is obtained from revenues from day-to-day operations and from liquidating some of the firm's assets.

When Walt Disney Co. executives decided to raise $400 million to rescue their troubled Euro-Disney theme park near Paris, they secured the funds from 27-year-old Prince Al-Walid of Saudi Arabia in exchange for 24 percent ownership.[9]

Cash needs vary from one time period to the next, and even established firms may not be able to generate sufficient funds from operations to cover all costs of a major expansion or a significant investment in new equipment. In these instances, the financial manager must evaluate the potential advantages and drawbacks of seeking funds by borrowing. The alternative to borrowing is equity capital, which may be raised in several ways. The financial manager's job includes determining the most cost-effective balance between equity and borrowed funds and the proper blending of short- and long-term funds.

Short-Term Sources of Funds

At numerous times throughout the year, an organization may discover that its cash requirements exceed available funds. For catalog retailers, such as Best Products, Service Merchandise, and Gordon Jewelry, 80 percent of their total annual sales are generated during the Christmas season. A store like Service Merchandise will generate surplus cash for most of the

Sources of Funds

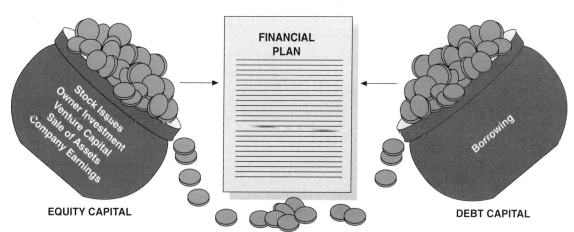

In financial planning, two basic sources of funds exist: debt capital and equity capital.

Comparison of Debt and Equity Capital		
Factor	**Debt**	**Equity**
Maturity	Has a specific date when it must be repaid.	Has no maturity date.
Claim on assets	Company lenders have prior claims on assets.	Stockholders have claims only after claims to lenders have been paid.
Claim on income	Lenders have prior claim on a fixed amount of interest, which must be paid before dividends can be paid to stockholders. Interest payments are a contractual obligation of the borrowing firm.	Stockholders have a residual claim after all creditors have been paid. Dividends are not a contractual obligation of the firm.
Right to a voice in management	Lenders are creditors, not owners. They have no voice in company affairs unless interest payments are not received.	Stockholders are the owners of the company, and most are given a voice in the operation of the firm.

Four factors are used in making financial decisions concerning whether to use debt capital or equity capital as the major source of funds.

year. But the buildup of inventory just before the Christmas season will require additional funds to finance it until it is sold. As sales occur during the Christmas season, the incoming funds can be used to repay the suppliers of the borrowed funds. In these instances, the firm's financial manager will evaluate short-term sources of needed funds. By definition, these sources must be repaid within one year.

Santa Monica Bank attracts loan customers by emphasizing personal attention.

The major short-term source of funds is *trade credit*, or making open-account purchases from suppliers. A second source is *unsecured bank loans*, for which the business does not pledge any assets as collateral. Another option is secured short-term loans, for which the firm must pledge collateral such as inventory. Large firms with unquestioned financial stability can raise money from a fourth source: by selling *commercial paper.* Commercial paper typically is sold in denominations of $100,000 with a maturity of 30 to 90 days. Issuing commercial paper to raise funds is usually one or two percent cheaper than borrowing short-term funds from a bank.

Long-Term Sources of Funds

Short-term sources of cash can be used to meet current needs for cash or inventory; but acquiring another company or making major purchases, such as land, plant, and equipment, will require funds for a much longer period. Unlike short-term sources, long-term sources can be repaid over a period of one year or longer.

A business firm has three long-term financing sources available. One is long-term loans issued by various financial institutions, such as banks, insurance companies, and pension funds. A second source is **bonds:** *certificates of indebtedness sold to raise long-term funds for corporations or government agencies.* A third source is not to borrow but to secure *equity funds,* ownership funds obtained from selling stock in the company, selling company assets, reinvesting company earnings, or from additional contributions by venture capitalists or the firm's owners.

Public Sale of Stocks and Bonds The sale of stocks and bonds represents a major source of funds for corporations. Such sales provide cash inflows for the firm and either a share in the ownership (for the stock purchaser) or a specified rate of interest and repayment at a stated time (for bond purchasers). Since stock and bond issues of many corporations are traded on organized securities exchanges, stockholders and bondholders can easily sell the shares they hold. The use of stock and bond issues to finance corporations is an important decision and is discussed in more detail in the next chapter.

Attracting Venture Capital The typical business begins operations with an investment of $10,000 or less. But Douglas Pihl and Duane Carlson, founders of computer peripherals maker NetStar, knew they had to raise $10 million. Had their business idea been of the $10,000 variety, they could have called the U.S. Small Business Administration at 800-ASK SBA and applied for one of the agency's "micro loans" of up to $25,000. But the computer hardware industry is capital-intensive, and the partners knew their capital needs exceeded SBA guidelines, so they turned to venture capital funds and brokerage houses and used every source available to them to reach their financial goal.[10]

Venture capital usually is provided by outside investors in exchange for an ownership share in the business. The venture capitalist may be a corporation, a wealthy individual, a pension fund, or a major endowment fund. In exchange for funds, the venture capitalist receives shares of the corporation's stock at relatively low prices and becomes a part-owner of the corporation. Apollo Advisors, a major venture capitalist firm, owns substantial shares of companies ranging from Perry Ellis clothing, Converse shoes, Samsonite luggage, and Chi-Chi's restaurants to the Telemundo international Spanish-language TV network.[11] For taking risks inherent in any struggling firm, the venture capitalist has the opportunity to earn substantial profit should the firm become successful and issue shares of stock to the general public.

There are virtually hundreds of venture capitalists in the United States today, and each typically receives dozens of proposals every month from busi-

Apollo Advisors owns 45 percent of Buster Brown, a well-known manufacturer of children's apparel.

nesses seeking funds. Most applications are rejected by these investors, who seek soundly managed firms with unique goods or services in a rapidly growing industry. In recent years, venture capitalists have concentrated in such industries as medical technology, computers, and environmental waste management. Often a venture capitalist provides management consulting as well as funds.

Leverage Raising needed cash by borrowing allows the firm to benefit from the principle of **leverage,** *a technique of increasing the rate of return on investment through the use of borrowed funds.* The concept of leverage can be related to a lever. Like the fulcrum on which a lever rests, the interest payments on borrowed funds are fixed. The key to managing leverage is ensuring that the company's earnings are larger than the interest payments, which increases the leverage on the rate of return on the stockholders' investments. Of course, if the company earns less than its interest payments, stockholders will lose money on their original investments.

As long as earnings exceed interest payments on borrowed funds, financial leverage will allow a firm to increase the rate of return on stockholders' investments. However, leverage also works in reverse. If, for example, Equity Corp. (see table) earnings drop to $5,000, stockholders will earn a five percent return on their investment. But, because Leverage Corp. must pay its bondholders $9,000 in interest, what appears to be a $5,000 gain is actually a $4,000 loss for Leverage stockholders. A second problem with overreliance on borrowed funds is that it reduces management flexibility in future decisions.

Hershey Foods Corp., the Pennsylvania-based candy and pasta company, has little debt. This fact, combined with a solid track record of steady profits and market leadership, also produces a sterling credit rating for the firm. Consequently, when Hershey decides to borrow funds, its managers encounter little difficulty in securing debt capital at rock-bottom interest rates. Two new plants are currently under construction. Hershey chose to finance them with a $100 million bond issue. The annual interest rate was at least one percentage point less than that paid by competitors with considerable debt.[12]

How Leverage Works			
Leverage Corp.		**Equity Corp.**	
Common stock	$ 10,000	Common stock	$100,000
Bonds (at 10% interest)	90,000	Bonds	0
	100,000		100,000
Earnings	30,000	Earnings	30,000
Less bond interest	9,000	Less bond interest	0
	21,000		30,000
Return to stockholders	$\frac{21,000}{\$\ 10,000} = 210\%$	Return to stockholders	$\frac{30,000}{\$100,000} = 30\%$

The Leverage Corp. obtained 90 percent of its funds from lenders who purchased company bonds. The Equity Corp. raised all its funds through the sale of company stock. Each company earned $30,000. However, Leverage Corp. paid $9,000 in interest to bondholders and earned a 210 percent return for its owners' $10,000 investment, while Equity Corp. provided only a 30 percent return on its stockholders' investments of $100,000.

THE U.S. FINANCIAL SYSTEM

Traditionally, the U.S. financial system has been divided into two categories: deposit institutions (which accept deposits from customers or members and provide some form of checking accounts) and nondeposit institutions. Deposit institutions are commercial banks, thrifts (savings and loan associations and savings banks), and credit unions. Nondeposit institutions include insurance companies, pension funds, and consumer and commercial finance companies.

Commercial Banks

Fundamental to the U.S. banking system are the approximately 12,200 **commercial banks,** *profit-making businesses that hold the deposits of individuals, business firms, and not-for-profit organizations in the form of checking or savings accounts and use these funds to make loans to individuals and businesses.* They also generate funds by selling certificates of deposit, by borrowing from the Federal Reserve System, and by charging a variety of fees for their services. These funds then are loaned to individuals, business firms, and not-for-profit organizations. By charging higher interest rates to borrowers than they pay to depositors and others who provide funds for lending, the banks generate revenue to be used in covering their operating expenses and to earn profits.

The number of competing banks and their average size vary greatly in different countries. About 11,000 commercial banks operate in the United States (many of them extremely small), as compared with less

than 20 giant banks in the United Kingdom.[13] In the half-dozen years since *perestroika*, over 2,500 banks have sprung up in Russia.[14]

Types and Services of Commercial Banks

Most U.S. commercial banks are *state banks*—commercial banks chartered by individual states. Approximately one-third of all commercial banks are chartered by the federal government and are referred to as *national banks.* These tend to be larger, and they hold approximately 60 percent of total commercial bank deposits. While the regulations affecting state and national banks vary slightly, in practice there is little difference between the two from the viewpoint of the individual depositor or borrower. The five largest U.S. banks are New York-headquartered Citicorp; Chemical Banking Corp. of New York; San Francisco's BankAmerica Corp.; NationsBank of Charlotte, North Carolina; and J. P. Morgan & Co. of New York.

"Full-service bank" is an accurate description of the typical commercial bank because of the dozens of services it offers its depositors. In addition to a variety of checking and savings accounts and personal and business loans, commercial banks typically offer bank credit cards, safe deposit boxes, tax-deferred individual retirement accounts (IRAs), discount brokerage services, wire transfers (which permit immediate movement of funds by electronic transfers to distant banks), and financial counseling. Most banks provide low-cost traveler's checks and overdraft checking accounts that automatically provide small loans at

> **THEY SAID IT**
>
> "Drive-in banks were invented so that automobiles could visit their real owners."
>
> *Anonymous*

Operations of a Commercial Bank

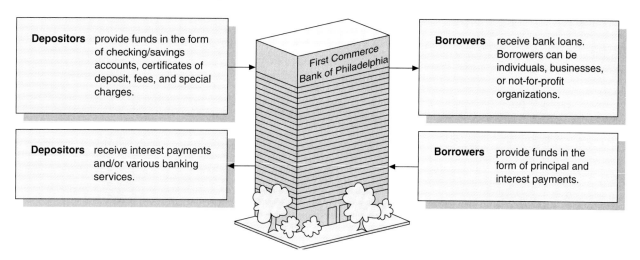

Depositors provide funds in the form of checking/savings accounts, certificates of deposit, fees, and special charges.

Depositors receive interest payments and/or various banking services.

Borrowers receive bank loans. Borrowers can be individuals, businesses, or not-for-profit organizations.

Borrowers provide funds in the form of principal and interest payments.

relatively low interest rates for depositors who write checks exceeding the balance on their account.

Banks have made themselves more accessible to customers by opening *automated teller machines (ATMs)*, electronic banking machines that permit customers to make banking transactions on a 24-hour basis by using an access code. In 1980, 20,000 ATMs processed 100 million transactions annually; today, over 87,000 machines handle more than 600 million transactions a year. Network systems now enable ATM users to access their bank accounts from other states and countries. Citibank has programmed its ATMs in 11 different languages to perform foreign currency transactions at branches in a dozen countries.[15]

More financial institutions are offering electronic banking through **electronic funds transfer systems (EFTS)**, *computerized systems for conducting financial transactions electronically.* Last year, companies paid more than 35

Growth of ATMs

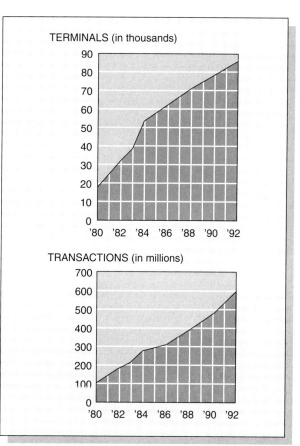

TERMINALS (in thousands)

TRANSACTIONS (in millions)

ATMs are one of the most popular ways to get cash when you need it.

million invoices electronically, a 59 percent increase over the previous year. Although this is still less than one percent of the 12 billion checks that U.S. corporations write each year, the use of electronic funds transfer is expected to increase rapidly. One reason is that EFTS saves money; estimates are that printing, mailing, and clearing paper checks costs U.S. firms more than $50 billion a year. Another reason is the wealth of data that can accompany electronic payments, including invoice numbers, whether discounts were taken, and which dividends are to be paid.[16]

Thrifts: Savings and Loan Associations and Savings Banks

Thrifts, as savings and loan associations and savings banks are commonly called, offer a variety of banking services at rates competitive with commercial banks, such as home mortgages, loans, passbook

A Check's Journey through the Federal Reserve System

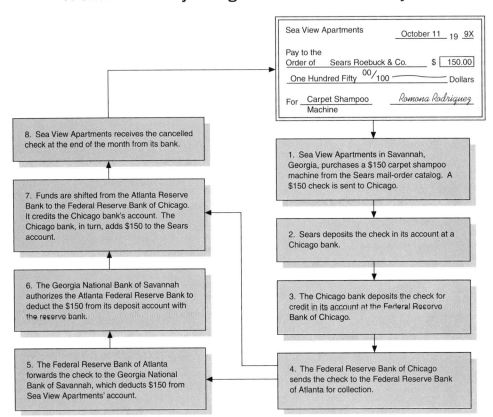

Check processing begins with a *check*—a piece of paper addressed to a bank or other financial institution on which is written a legal authorization to withdraw a specified amount of money from an account and to pay that amount to someone. In this instance, a purchasing agent for the Sea View Apartments buys a $150 carpet shampoo machine from Sears. The check used to pay for the machine authorizes the Georgia National Bank of Savannah, where Sea View has a checking account, to reduce Sea View's balance by $150. This sum is to be paid to Sears to cover the cost of the machine. If both parties have checking accounts in the same bank, check processing is easy. The bank simply increases Sears' balance by $150 and reduces Sea View's balance by the same amount.

However, this purchase was made from a Sears catalog and involves the firm's Chicago checking account. In this case, the Federal Reserve System acts as a collector for intercity transactions. It handles a large number of the 180 million checks written every business day. You can trace the route a check has taken by examining the endorsement stamps on the reverse side.

accounts, time deposits, traveler's checks, consumer leasing, trust services, and credit cards. A **savings and loan association (S&L)** is *a thrift institution offering both savings and checking accounts and using most of its funds to make home mortgage loans.* **Savings banks,** also known as mutual savings banks, are *state-chartered banks with operations similar to those of S&Ls.* They are concentrated in the New England states.

Credit Unions

A third type of deposit institution, the **credit union,** is *a member-owned financial cooperative that pays interest to depositors, offers share draft accounts, and makes short-term loans and some home-mortgage loans.* It typically is sponsored by a company, union, or professional or re-

ligious group. The nation's 12,800 federally insured credit unions can provide consumer loans at competitive rates for their members.[17] They also offer interest-bearing checking accounts (share draft accounts), long-term mortgage loans, life insurance, and financial counseling. While credit unions tend to be relatively small, with only 30 percent having assets of $5 million or more, they exist in every state and claim over 55 million members. Credit unions today have outstanding loans of almost $100 billion.[18]

Nondeposit Institutions

Other sources and users of funds include insurance companies, pension funds, and consumer and commercial finance companies. An *insurance company* provides financial protection for policyholders in return for premium payments. These firms use the funds generated by premiums to make long-term loans to corporations, for commercial real-estate mortgages, and to purchase government bonds.

A *pension fund* is a large pool of money set up by a company, union, or not-for-profit organization for the retirement income needs of its employees or members. Participants in the pension fund may begin to collect a monthly allotment upon retiring or at a certain age. Like insurance companies, pension funds invest in long-term mortgages on commercial property, business loans, government bonds, and common stock in major firms.

Consumer and commercial finance companies offer short-term loans to borrowers who pledge tangible items, such as inventory, machinery, property, or accounts receivable, as security against nonpayment. A *commercial finance company*, such as Commercial Credit or CIT, supplies short-term funds to businesses that pledge tangible items, such as inventory, machinery, or property, as collateral. *Consumer finance companies*, such as Household Finance, serve a similar role for personal loans. Consumer and commercial finance companies obtain their funds from the sale of bonds and from short-term loans from other firms.

Financial Supermarkets In the late 1990s, some nondeposit institutions are doing just about everything commercial banks do. The term *financial supermarket* describes a growing number of nonbank corporations that offer a wide range of financial services, including investments, loans, real estate, and insurance. A good example is GE Capital Services, which serves as both a commercial and consumer finance company. GE Capital insures home mortgages and municipal bonds, supplies the credit behind millions of retail charge cards, and includes an investment bank that has participated in over 100 corporate acquisitions and mergers.[19]

THE FEDERAL RESERVE SYSTEM

Since 1913, a growing number of financial institutions have been regulated by the **Federal Reserve System.** The Fed is *a network of 12 district banks, controlled by a board of governors, that regulates banking in the United States.* In practice, it acts as a clearinghouse for checks and regulates the commercial banking system.

The central bank of the U.S.

> **THEY SAID IT**
>
> "The next time you see a headline about the government spending a billion dollars on some project, think about it this way: If you spend $100,000 every day of the week, it would take you more than 27 years to spend a billion dollars."
>
> *Louis E. Boone*
> *(1941–)*
> *American educator*

While all national banks are required to be members of the Federal Reserve System, membership is optional for state-chartered banks. In all, there are approximately 5,500 member banks. The Fed has regulatory powers over all deposit institutions, whether Federal Reserve System members or not. They are required to maintain reserves against checking accounts, NOW accounts, and share draft accounts.

The Federal Reserve System's most powerful tool is the *reserve requirement*—the percentage of a bank's checking and savings deposits that must be kept in the bank or on deposit at the local Federal Reserve district bank. By changing the percentage of required reserves, the Fed can affect the amount of money available for making loans. However, changing the reserve requirement is a drastic means of changing the money supply, since even a one percent variation in the reserve requirement means a potential fluctuation of billions of dollars in the money supply. Because of this, other tools are used more widely.

10%

A far more common method used by the Federal Reserve System involves *open market operations*—the technique of controlling the money supply by purchasing and selling government bonds. If the Fed buys bonds, the money it pays enters circulation, increasing the money supply and making more money available to member banks. If the Fed sells government securities, the money generated from these transactions is taken out of circulation, reducing the money supply. Over the years, open market operations have been used increasingly as a flexible means of expanding and contracting the money supply.[20]

A third tool of the Fed, the *discount rate*, is the interest rate it charges on loans to member banks. This tool has been used often in recent years to control the money supply, stimulate economic growth, and match changes in discount rates made by central banks in such nations as Japan and Germany.[21] Even small changes in the discount rate can exert a large effect on the economy; raising it may motivate bankers to offer fewer new loans, while lowering it can stimulate the economy.[22]

The Federal Reserve System also has the authority to exercise *selective credit controls*, such as the power to set *margin requirements*—the percentage of the purchase price of a security that must be paid in cash by the investor—on credit purchases of stocks and bonds.

Transactions involving international markets also affect the U.S. money supply. On the **foreign**

Sources and Uses of Funds			
Institution	**Typical Investments**	**Types of Accounts Offered to Depositors**	**Primary Sources of Funds**
DEPOSIT INSTITUTIONS			
Commercial bank	Personal loans Business loans Increasingly involved in real-estate construction and home-mortgage loans	Checking accounts NOW accounts Passbook savings accounts Time deposits Money market deposit accounts	Customer deposits Interest earned on loans
Savings and loan association	Bond purchases Home mortgages Construction loans	Savings accounts NOW accounts Time deposits Money market deposit accounts	Customer deposits Interest earned on loans
Savings bank	Bond purchases Home mortgages Construction loans	Savings accounts NOW accounts Time deposits Money market deposit accounts	Customer deposits Interest earned on loans
Credit union	Short-term consumer loans increasingly involved in making longer-term mortgage loans	Share draft accounts Savings accounts Money market deposit accounts	Deposits by credit union members Interest earned on loans
NONDEPOSIT INSTITUTIONS			
Insurance company	Corporate long-term loans Mortgage of commercial real estate—major buildings/shopping centers Government bonds		Premiums paid by policyholders Earnings on investments
Pension fund	Some long-term mortgages on commercial property and business loans Government bonds Corporate securities		Contributions by member employees and employers Earnings on investments
Commercial and/or consumer finance company	Short-term loans to businesses (commercial finance companies) Individual consumer loans (consumer finance companies)		Interest earned on loans Sale of bonds Short-term borrowing from other firms

exchange market, *purchases and sales of one nation's currency are made for that of another country.* Billions of U.S. dollars are traded this way every day. The Fed can lower the exchange value of the dollar by selling dollars and buying foreign currencies; and it can raise the dollar's exchange value by doing the opposite—buying dollars and selling foreign currencies. When it buys foreign currencies, the effect is like buying securities, since it increases the U.S. banking system's reserves. Selling foreign currencies, on the other hand, is like selling securities, in that it depletes bank reserves.

IT'S THE LAW

1913 Federal Reserve Act
Created the Federal Reserve System, a network of 12 district banks and controlled by a board of governors currently headed by Alan Greenspan. The Fed regulates banking in the United States, holds deposits of member banks, and acts as a check clearinghouse.

1980 Banking Act of 1980
Formally titled the Depository Institution Monetary Control Act, this legislation deregulates financial institutions by permitting all deposit institutions to offer checking accounts, expanding services and lending powers of thrifts, and phasing out interest rate ceilings.

BANK SAFETY

Most family histories include stories of money lost due to a bank failure. To increase confidence in the security of financial institutions and to prevent so-called "runs" on banks by depositors seeking to withdraw their deposits in times of economic crises, specialized federal insurance programs have been created for most commercial banks, thrifts, and credit unions. For instance, deposits at all commercial banks that are members of the Federal Reserve System are insured by the **Federal Deposit Insurance Corporation (FDIC).** The FDIC *insures depositors' accounts up to a maximum of $100,000 per account and sets requirements for sound*

banking practices. Deposits at federally insured thrift institutions are covered by the federal Office of Thrift Supervision (OTS) and the Resolution Trust Corporation (RTC). Eighty-eight percent of U.S. credit unions are also federally insured by the National Credit Union Share Insurance Fund (NCUSIF).

The primary technique for guaranteeing the safety and soundness of commercial banks and thrifts is the use of unannounced inspections of individual institutions at least once a year by bank examiners. A **bank examiner** is *a trained representative who inspects the financial records and management practices of each federally insured financial institution.* Other commercial banks are inspected by examiners from

Federal Reserve Tools

	Action	Effect on Money Supply	Short-Term Effect on the Economy
General Tools			
Reserve requirements	Increase reserve requirements	Reduces money supply	Results in increased interest rates and a slowing of economic activity
	Decrease reserve requirements	Increases money supply	Results in reduced interest rates and an increase in economic activity
Discount rate	Increase discount rate	Reduces money supply	Results in increased interest rates and a slowing of economic activity
	Decrease discount rate	Increases money supply	Results in reduced interest rates and an increase in economic activity
Open market operations	Purchase government securities	Increases money supply	Results in reduced interest rates and an increase in economic activity
	Sell government bonds	Reduces money supply	Results in increased interest rates and a slowing of economic activity
Selective Credit Controls			
Margin requirements	Increase margin requirements		Reduced credit purchase of securities; negative impact on securities exchanges and on securities prices
	Reduce margin requirements		Increased credit purchase of securities; positive impact on securities exchanges and on securities prices

Is Your Loan Environmentally Safe?

Ecology. It has become a byword of this century, and carries with it an enormous burden of protection at a very high cost. In 1986, as a result of the Superfund Act of 1980, courts ruled that banks were liable for their customers' pollution. As a result, a would-be borrower is evaluated carefully before a loan is granted, including not only a financial audit but an environmental audit as well, and those that are too "dirty" are *greenlined*.

The superfund law, formally known as the Comprehensive Environmental Response, Compensation, and Liability Act (CERCLA), transfers the responsibility of paying for environmental cleanups from the government to the owners, past and present, of polluted property. The plot thickened in 1990, when a panel of federal judges ruled that if a bank, or any other secured lender, could "influence" management, it should be treated like an owner.

Dry cleaners, gas stations, auto-repair shops, and other small- and medium-size businesses in industries involved with dangerous chemicals or that produce contami-

nated waste are finding it more difficult to get bank loans. The ruling also affects companies involved in waste removal and hazardous waste sites. One Midwestern bank foreclosed on a boat-repair shop that went bankrupt on a $20,000 loan. The bank then discovered that the site had been a gas station 60 years earlier and found itself facing a $14,000 cleanup bill. Fleet Financial CEO Terrence Murray explains, "These are loans that were booked seven, eight, ten years ago, when we lacked the consciousness of environmental issues. . . . [Now] we may have a $200,000 loan and a $500,000 liability for cleanup."

The result of CERCLA was a loss of interest income for banks and a loss of an important source of funds for many U.S. small businesses. Legislators and federal regulators were forced to reexamine the law, and, in 1992, the Environmental Protection Agency (EPA) issued new regulations easing the financial burden on banks. It clarifies circumstances under which

a bank can foreclose on contaminated property or lend money to finance a cleanup *without* incurring the penalties of ownership.

Although new laws are helping to relieve the responsibilities placed on banks for cleaning up the environment, industry experts doubt that they will end the freeze on loans. As banker J. R. Jamison says, "We are skeptical of any real property lending that could have any contamination of any kind. No gas stations. No area that has ever had a paint gun on it. No areas with industrial activity."

SOURCE: Gary Hector, "A New Reason You Can't Get a Loan," *Fortune,* September 21, 1992, 107–108, 112.

the Comptroller of the Currency, the Federal Reserve System, or state regulatory authorities, such as the state's banking commission.

During the examination, which may take from a week to several months, the following areas are evaluated: ability of the bank's management, level of earnings and sources of earnings, adequacy of properties pledged to secure loans made by the bank, capital, and current level of liquidity.

If the bank examiners believe serious problems exist in one or more of these areas, they include the bank on a "problem list." Such

banks are viewed as candidates for failure unless corrective actions are taken immediately, such as emergency loans or management assistance. Sometimes the government may even replace the bank's directors with new managers. Needed improvements typically are discussed in the written examination report and in meetings with the bank's top management and board members. The problem list is confidential, and most depositors are likely to be unaware of such actions. Subsequently, more frequent examinations take place to see if these problems are being corrected. Should

The 12 nations of the European Union have agreed to replace their individual currencies by 1999 with a single currency unit called the Ecu. The new currency should facilitate money's functioning as a medium of exchange in Western Europe, as individuals and businesses will no longer need conversion tables to determine, for example, how many Italian lira are needed to acquire a French franc or an English pound.

the problems uncovered during an examination require immediate action, more drastic measures can be taken.

If the government cannot locate a satisfactory merger partner or buyer, the institution is closed. In such cases, officials secure control of the financial records and physical facilities. Typically, authorities take control after business hours on Friday and freeze accounts. By the following Monday, they either have allowed another bank to assume control or have paid off depositors up to the $100,000 limit of the deposit insurance. Any assets held by the failed institution are sold, and proceeds are divided among creditors and holders of accounts exceeding the $100,000 insurance maximum.[23]

THE U.S. FINANCIAL SYSTEM: A GLOBAL PERSPECTIVE

Financial services have become a global industry, and it is important to consider the U.S. financial system in its international context. Almost 43 percent of Citicorp's assets, for example, come from outside the United States, and it earns 56 percent of its net annual profit from its foreign operations. Sixty-three percent of the assets at Bankers Trust New York are foreign, and the company earns almost 78 percent of its net annual profit from abroad. In a typical year, GE Capital earns $150 million from outside the United States.

Even though most Americans consider large U.S. banks, such as BankAmerica and Citibank, global giants, no U.S. bank ranks among the world's twenty largest banks. Over half of the largest global banks are headquartered in Japan; France ranks second, with four in the top twenty.

Like the United States, most nations have a central banking authority that controls their money supply. In Germany, it is the Bundesbank, while in the United Kingdom the Bank of England is the central bank. Policymakers at these banks often respond to changes in the U.S. financial system by making similar changes in their own systems. When the Fed raised U.S. interest rates recently, interest rates in Japan and Germany also rose. These changes can impact countries around the world. Higher interest rates in the United States or Germany not only increase the cost of borrowing for American and German firms; they also reduce the amount of money available for loans to Asia and Latin America.

International banks and financial-service firms play an important role in global business. They help transfer purchasing power from buyers to sellers, and from lenders to borrowers. They also provide credit to importers and reduce the risks associated with exchange rates. GE Capital, mentioned earlier in the

While U.S. banks compete with 12,000 other domestic banks, the British banking industry consists of fewer than 15 banks. As a result, banks like National Westminster reap the benefits of large-scale operations.

chapter, is a prime source of funds for companies throughout the world. It is bringing new financial services to Malaysia through a joint venture with that nation's UMW Corporation. Recently, when financial problems at Swedish automaker Volvo made it difficult for the company to finance a leasing program for its vehicles, GE Capital stepped in. A joint venture between the two firms now lets Volvo offer competitive lease rates for its cars. Without GE Capital, admits Volvo car finance president Michael Duke, "We would have been pinched. . . . They're the first guys you turn to."[24]

SUMMARY OF LEARNING GOALS

1. **Identify the functions performed by a firm's financial manager.**

   The financial manager's major responsibility is to develop and implement a financial plan for the organization. The firm's financial plan is based on a forecast of expenditures and receipts for a specified period and reflects the timing of cash inflows and outflows. The plan includes a systematic approach to determining needed funds during the period and the most appropriate sources for obtaining them. In short, the financial manager is responsible for both raising and spending money.

2. **Describe the characteristics a good form of money should have and list the functions of money.**

   In order to perform its necessary functions, money should possess the following characteristics: divisibility, portability, durability, stability, and difficulty of counterfeiting. These characteristics allow money to perform as a medium of exchange, a unit of account, and a temporary store of value.

3. **Distinguish between money (M1) and near-money (M2).**

   Money, sometimes referred to as M1, is defined broadly as anything generally accepted as a means of paying for goods and services, such as coins, paper money, and checks. Near-money, or M2, consists of assets that are almost as liquid as money but that cannot be used directly as a medium of exchange, such as time deposits, government bonds, and money market funds.

4. **Explain how a firm uses funds.**

   Organizations require funds for many reasons, including running day-to-day business operations, paying for inventory, making interest payments on loans, paying dividends to stockholders, and purchasing land, facilities, and equipment. Most financial managers will choose to invest the majority of a firm's excess cash in marketable securities.

5. **Compare the two major categories of sources of funds.**

   Debt capital represents funds obtained through borrowing. Equity capital consists of funds from several sources, including stock issues, additional investments by the firm's owners, earnings that have been reinvested in the firm, contributions from venture capitalists, and cash obtained by liquidating some of the company's assets.

6. **Identify likely sources of short-term and long-term funds.**

   There are four important sources of short-term funds for business firms. The major short-term source is trade credit, or making open-account purchases from suppliers. A second source is unsecured loans; a third is secured loans, for which the firm must pledge collateral. Large firms with unquestioned financial stability can raise money from a fourth source, by selling commercial paper.

   Sources of long-term financing include long-term loans that can be repaid over one year or longer, bonds, and equity funds (ownership funds obtained from selling stock in the company, selling company assets, reinvesting company earnings, or from additional contributions by the firm's owners and venture capitalists).

7. **Identify the major categories of financial institutions and the sources and uses of their funds.**

   The U.S. financial system consists of deposit institutions and nondeposit institutions. Deposit institutions, such as commercial banks, thrifts, and credit unions, accept deposits from customers or members and offer some form of checking account. Nondeposit institutions include insurance companies, pension funds, and finance companies and represent sources of funds for businesses and provide mortgage funds for financing commercial real estate.

8. **Explain the functions of the Federal Reserve System and the tools it uses to increase or decrease the money supply.**

   The most essential function of the Fed is to control the supply of credit and money in order to promote economic growth and a stable dollar. Its tools include reserve requirements, open market operations, and the discount rate. Increases in the reserve requirement or the discount rate have the effect of reducing the money supply, while decreases have the opposite effect. Open market operations increase the money supply when bonds are purchased and decrease the supply by their sale. Selective credit controls and the purchase and sale of foreign currencies also can be used by the Fed in influencing the economy.

9. **Describe the institutions and practices that regulate bank safety.**

Deposits at all commercial banks that are members of the Federal Reserve System are insured by the Federal Deposit Insurance Corporation (FDIC). The FDIC insures depositors' accounts up to a maximum of $100,000 per account and sets requirements for sound banking practices. Deposits at federally insured thrift institutions are covered by the federal Office of Thrift Supervision (OTS) and the Resolution Trust Corporation (RTC). Eighty-eight percent of U.S. credit unions are federally insured by the National Credit Union Share Insurance Fund (NCUSIF). The primary technique for guaranteeing the safety and soundness of commercial banks and thrifts is the use of unannounced inspections of individual institutions at least once a year by bank examiners.

10. Discuss the U.S. financial system in its global context.

Many U.S. banks and financial companies earn substantial revenues from outside the United States. Like the United States, most nations have a central banking authority that controls the money supply. Policymakers at these banks often respond to changes in the U.S. financial system by making similar changes in their own systems; these changes can impact countries around the world. International banks and financial-service firms play an important role in global business. They help transfer purchasing power from buyers to sellers, and from lenders to borrowers. They also provide credit to importers and reduce the risks associated with exchange rates.

KEY TERMS QUIZ

near-money	debt capital	savings banks
financial manager	bonds	Federal Reserve System
risk-return trade-off	equity capital	credit union
financial plan	leverage	foreign exchange market
finance	electronic funds transfer system (EFTS)	bank examiner
financial control	commercial banks	Federal Deposit Insurance Corporation
money	savings and loan association (S&L)	(FDIC)

finance 1. Business function of effectively obtaining and managing funds.

financial manager 2. Individual in an organization responsible for developing and implementing the firm's financial plan and for determining the most appropriate sources and uses of funds.

risk-return trade-off 3. Balance between the risk of an investment and its potential gain.

_____ 4. Document that specifies the funds needed by a firm for a period of time, charts inflows and outflows, and outlines the most appropriate uses of funds.

_____ 5. Process that periodically checks actual revenues, costs, and expenses against the forecasts.

_____ 6. Anything generally accepted as a means of paying for goods and services.

_____ 7. Assets almost as liquid as checking accounts but that cannot be used directly as a medium of exchange.

_____ 8. Funds obtained through borrowing.

_____ 9. Funds provided by the firm's owners by plowing back earnings or making additional contributions, by stock issues to the general public, or by contributions from venture capitalists.

_____ 10. Certificate of indebtedness sold to raise long-term funds for corporations or government agencies.

_____ 11. Technique of increasing the rate of return on investment through the use of borrowed funds.

_____ 12. Profit-making business that holds deposits of individuals and businesses in the form of checking or savings accounts and uses these funds to make loans to individuals and businesses.

_____ 13. Computerized method for making purchases and paying bills by electronically depositing or withdrawing funds.

_____ 14. Thrift institution offering savings and checking accounts and using most of its funds to make home-mortgage loans.

_____ 15. State-chartered banks with operations similar to savings and loan associations.

_____ 16. Member-owned financial cooperative that pays interest to depositors, offers share draft accounts, and makes short-term loans and some home-mortgage loans.

_____ 17. Network of 12 regional banks that regulates banking in the United States.

_____ 18. Market where one nation's currency can be purchased with—or sold for—that of another nation.

_____ 19. Corporation that insures bank depositors' accounts up to a maximum of $100,000 and sets requirements for sound banking practices.

_____ 20. A trained representative who inspects the financial records and management practices of each federally insured financial institution.

OTHER IMPORTANT TERMS

automated teller machines (ATMs)	M2	selective credit controls
certificate of deposit (CD)	margin requirements	state banks
commercial finance company	medium of exchange	store of value
commercial paper	open market operations	thrifts
consumer finance company	national banks	trade credit
discount rate	pension fund	Treasury bills
financial supermarket	reserve requirement	unit of account
insurance company	return	unsecured bank loans
M1	risk	

REVIEW QUESTIONS

1. Explain the functions performed by the financial manager. What roles does forecasting play in these functions?
2. Identify the primary uses of cash in an organization.
3. What are the primary uses of short-term financing? Distinguish between unsecured and secured loans.
4. Distinguish between debt capital and equity capital. What are the primary sources of equity capital?
5. Identify the sources for long-term financing. Explain how borrowed funds produce leverage. What impact does borrowing have on a firm's financial performance?
6. Identify the components of the U.S. money supply. What functions are performed by these components?
7. Explain the concept of near-money. Why is it not included as part of the money supply?
8. Explain how the different types of financial institutions can be categorized, and identify the primary sources and uses of funds available in each institution.
9. Explain the functions of the Federal Reserve System. Give an example of how each of the following tools may be used to increase the money supply or to stimulate economic activity:
   a. open market operations
   b. reserve requirements
   c. discount rate
   d. selective credit controls
10. Summarize recent trends and developments in the electronic funds transfer system (EFTS).

DISCUSSION QUESTIONS

1. Joe Valdez timed the opening of his Sandia Mountain Tours to coincide with the annual International Balloon Festival. Valdez knew from the beginning that his enterprise was undercapitalized, but he hoped to cover his need for funds out of cash flow. Sandia Mountain Tours' annual sales volume grew quickly from $80,000 to $326,000, then $675,000 and $750,000. This rapid expansion of business involved the addition of many new services, such as overnight and week-long camping trips.

Cash flow was a constant problem and remains so today. Valdez remarked, "There's a limit to bootstrapping. If you wish to remain a mom-and-pop business, bootstrapping will work, but I wanted more than that. Now I know I should have taken more time and put together more capital before jumping in feet first."

Analyze and discuss Sandia Mountain Tours' financial-management problems. Do you agree with Valdez on "bootstrapping"? Why or why not?

2. Gift shops earn 70 percent of their annual volume just after Thanksgiving and on through Christmas. Given this simple statistic, chart and then explain the cash inflows and outflows for a new gift shop. When would it be most advisable to open a new gift shop? Discuss.

3. Investigate how one of the following firms originally was financed:
   a. Blue Bell Ice Cream (premium ice cream)
   b. Apple Computer
   c. Boston Chicken
   d. Snapple beverages
   e. The Body Shop (cosmetics and skin-care products)

4. Choose a business you would like to start. What short-term and long-term sources of funding would be needed? Why? Discuss what business needs are served by each source of funding.

5. Why was the Federal Deposit Insurance Corporation created? Explain its role in protecting the soundness of the banking system. What actions can it take in case of bank failure?

VIDEO CASE: Duracell International

The video case for this chapter examines how the battery-maker uses debt financing to fund its growth. It is included on page 423 of Appendix D.

Solution to Key Terms Quiz

1. finance   2. financial manager   3. risk-return trade-off   4. financial plan   5. financial control   6. money   7. near-money   8. debt capital   9. equity capital   10. bonds   11. leverage   12. commercial banks   13. electronic funds transfer system (EFTS)   14. savings and loan association (S&L)   15. savings banks   16. credit union   17. Federal Reserve System   18. foreign exchange market   19. Federal Deposit Insurance Corporation (FDIC)   20. bank examiner

CHAPTER 16

The Securities Market

Learning Goals

1. Distinguish between primary markets for securities and secondary markets.

2. Compare common stock, preferred stock, and bonds, and explain why investors might prefer each type of security.

3. Identify the four basic objectives of investors and the types of securities most likely to accomplish each objective.

4. Explain the process of selling or purchasing a security listed on the organized securities exchanges.

5. Describe the information included in stock, bond, and mutual fund quotations.

6. Explain the role of mutual funds in the securities field.

7. Evaluate the major features of state and federal laws designed to protect investors.

Fifteen years ago, Alan S. McKim started a nationwide environmental services company to transport, treat, and dispose of hazardous materials. His Boston-based Clean Harbors Inc. began with only four employees, but a lot of ambition. Although somewhat coincidental, it seemed appropriate that the office was located near the most polluted harbor in the United States.

McKim began operations using only equity capital, including his life savings of $13,000. The little firm grew rapidly, securing a contract in its first year from *Fortune* 500 giant Texaco. Within two years, its revenues reached $1.5 million; after another two years, they nearly tripled to $4.2 million; and in the next three years, revenues had reached an incredible $46.7 million.

McKim was quick to recognize that rapidly growing companies often consume cash at a faster rate than they generate it from operating revenues, since by this time he had incurred more than $11 million in long-term debt to finance Clean Harbors' growth. Since he still owned 100 percent of the company, McKim had to personally guarantee this huge debt. If Clean Harbors failed to generate enough revenue to cover this liability, he faced the very real possibility of personal bankruptcy.

McKim decided to spread the risk by using other people's money—he would sell shares of Clean Harbors stock to investors. This financial restructuring occurred in two steps. McKim's first move was a private placement sale of about 18 percent of the company to a group of Boston-based venture capital investors. While the sale reduced McKim's ownership share, it raised $5 million that could be used to repay debt and expand the company.

The private placement sale paved the way for McKim's second step: an *initial public offering (IPO)* of Clean Harbors stock. To handle the IPO, McKim and the venture capital investors chose an *underwriter,* a financial intermediary who specializes in selling new issues of stocks and bonds. Hiring an underwriter also gave the fledgling company credibility. As McKim explains, "Now an underwriter could say, 'Here's a company that also has recently done a private placement with a reputable firm, so they must be a *good* company.'"

San Francisco-based underwriting firm Robertson, Colman & Stephens, a specialist in emerging growth companies, first determined how many shares of Clean Harbors stock to sell and calculated an appropriate price. Numerous factors were considered, including the overall stock market, the financial ratios of Clean Harbors in relation to other firms in its industry, and general investment interest in the waste-management industry.

One million shares were offered at $9 per share, netting $8 million for Clean Harbors, which, combined with $5 million received a few months earlier from the venture capital investors, went to repay all outstanding debt. In one year, the firm saved $1.2 million by no longer having to pay interest on this debt. Funds that would have gone to lenders were added to corporate profits.

Clean Harbors has prospered since the IPO. Within two years, the firm's stock was being bought and sold at double the price of the initial public offering. McKim has expanded into the Midwest, opening branch offices in Chicago and Cleveland and securing several major contracts. Today the company has contracts with the Illinois Environmental Protection Agency (EPA) to conduct statewide household hazardous waste collections in the spring and fall, and with the Ohio EPA for cleanup of several hazardous waste sites. Another contract with the U.S. Coast Guard is a proactive one, specifying Clean Harbors as the agency to help clean up any major oil or chemical spill that might occur in Lake Michigan.

Recently, the company saw its quarterly revenues reach a record $52 million, 12 percent higher than those earned the previous year. This revenue growth benefits all Clean Harbors stockholders and investors, including McKim, whose 58 percent share of the company's stock is worth nearly $100 million.[1]

CHAPTER OVERVIEW

Many entrepreneurs entering business today are faced with the challenges of financing a new business. For Clean Harbors, an initial public offering of stock enabled the company to relieve its high debt burden and expand. In fact, the small company would not have become a leader in its industry without the inflow of additional funds.

In the previous chapter, we discussed two sources of funding for long-term financial needs: debt capital and equity capital. Long-term debt capital exists in the form of corporate bonds, U.S. government bonds, and municipal bonds. Equity capital takes the form of stocks—shares of ownership in the corporation. Stocks and bonds are commonly referred to as **securities** because both represent *obligations on the part of their issuers to provide purchasers with an expected or stated return on the funds invested or loaned.*

Stocks and bonds are bought and sold in two marketplaces. *In the* **primary market,** *securities are first sold to the public.* The secondary market is the one in which previously issued securities are bought and sold.

DID YOU KNOW?

More than 75 percent of shareholders have graduated from college. The average shareholder has 15 years of formal schooling; fewer than six percent have not received a high school diploma.

As many women as men own stock. Adult males constitute 48 percent of the total, and adult females account for 48 percent; the remaining 2 percent are held by children.

Almost half of the investor population has a portfolio worth less than $5,000; however, 21 percent own more than $25,000 worth of stock.

Only one of every 1,000 U.S. corporations is listed on the NYSE, but they control over 40 percent of the assets of American business.

More than 47 million people own shares in publicly traded corporations; this represents one out of every four U.S. households.

PRIMARY MARKETS

When a corporation needs capital to expand a plant, develop products, acquire a smaller firm, or for other business reasons, it may make a stock or bond offering. A stock offering gives investors the opportunity to purchase ownership shares in the firm and to take part in its future growth in exchange for current capital. In other instances, a corporation or a government agency may choose to raise funds by issuing bonds. Announcements of these stock and bond offerings appear daily in such business newspapers as *The Wall Street Journal* in the form of simple black-and-white announcements called *tombstones.* Governments also use primary markets to generate funds; U.S. Treasury bonds are sold to finance part of the federal deficit, while city bonds are issued for various projects such as funding a new city water system.

Although a corporation could market its stock or bond issue directly to the public, most large offerings are handled by financial specialists called investment bankers, or underwriters. An **investment banker** is *a financial intermediary who specializes in selling new issues of stocks and bonds for business firms and government agencies.* Investment bankers agree to acquire the total issue from the company or agency and then resell it to other investors. The investment banker underwrites the issue at a discount as compensation for services rendered (for risk incurred and to cover expenses).

For instance, Invemed Associates, the underwriter for IVI Publishing's 1.8 million-share offering, might have purchased the stock for $16.74 per share and now is selling them at $18 per share. In addition to locating buyers for the issue, the underwriter typically advises the issuer on such subjects as general characteristics of the issue, its pricing, and the timing of the offering. Often primary (or lead) underwriters do not take complete responsibility for the public sale. Instead, they may sell either all or part of the shares to other underwriters who, in turn, sell them to the

public. In the example described above, Invemed Associates acquired the issue at $16.74 per share and could have sold some of the shares to other underwriters, such as First Boston or Morgan Stanley, for $17.44. Ultimately, the public was offered this stock at $18 per share.

SECONDARY MARKETS

Daily news reports of stock and bond trading refer to **secondary markets,** *places where previously issued shares of stocks and bonds are traded.* Such markets are convenient locations for buyers and sellers to make exchanges. The issuing corporations do not receive proceeds from such transactions, and gains and losses affect only the current and future owners of the securities. The various secondary markets are discussed later in the chapter.

STOCKS

Stocks are units of ownership in a corporation. Although many corporations issue only one type of stock, two types exist: common stock and preferred stock.

Stock and Bond Announcements

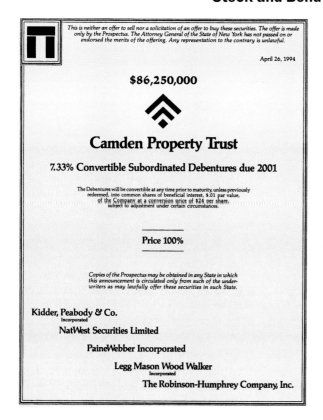 

These tombstone announcements alert investors to the completion of IVI Publishing's 1.8 million-share stock offering at $18 per share and Camden Property Trust's decision to acquire $86,250,000 in debt capital through the sale of bonds paying 7.33 percent annual interest and due in the year 2001.

Clean Harbors Stock Certificate

Type of stock

Name of corporation issuing the stock

State in which the company is incorporated

Par value of the stock is $.01 per share

Name and address of the stock's registered owner

Corporate officers

A stock certificate for Clean Harbors includes information such as the name and address of the registered owner, the type of stock, the number of shares represented by the certificate, the par value, the state in which the firm is incorporated, and the signatures of corporate officers.

Common Stock

The basic form of corporate ownership is **common stock.** Purchasers of common stock are the true owners of a corporation. In return for their investment, they expect to receive payments in the form of dividends and/or capital gains resulting from increases in the value of their stock holdings.

Holders of common stock vote on major company decisions, such as purchasing other companies or electing a board of directors. They benefit from company success, and they risk the loss of their investment if the company fails. Since creditors and preferred stockholders are paid before common stockholders, holders of common stock are said to have a residual claim to company assets. Common stock is sold on either a par or no-par value basis. *Par value* is the value printed on the stock certificate of some companies. In some states, par value is used as the basis for paying state incorporation taxes. Because the par value is highly arbitrary, most corporations now issue no-par value stock. In either case, the total number of shares outstanding represents the total ownership of the firm, and the value of an individual stockholder's investment is based on the number of shares owned and their market price rather than on an arbitrary par value.

Sometimes confusion results over two other types of value: market value and book value. *Market value*—the price at which a stock is currently selling—is determined easily by referring to the financial page of the daily newspaper. It usually varies from day to day, depending on company earnings and investor expec-

tations about future prospects for the firm. *Book value* is determined by subtracting the company's liabilities from its assets, minus the value of any preferred stock. When this net figure is divided by the number of shares of common stock, the book value of each share is known.

A common stock certificate includes the name and address of the registered owner and the number of shares represented by the certificate, the state in which the firm is incorporated, and the signatures of corporate officers.

Preferred Stock

In addition to common stock, many corporations issue **preferred stock**—*stock whose owners receive preference in the payment of dividends.* Also, if the company is dissolved, holders of preferred stock *have a claim on the firm's assets before any claim by common stockholders.*

In return for this privilege, preferred stockholders usually do not have voting rights and, even when voting rights do exist, they typically are limited to such important proposals as mergers, sales of company property, and dissolution of the company itself. Although preferred stockholders are granted certain privileges over common stockholders, they still are considered owners of the firm, and their dividends, therefore, are not guaranteed.

Preferred stock often is issued with a conversion privilege. This *convertible preferred stock* gives stockholders the option of having their preferred stock converted into common stock at a stated price. Owners of

Stock Certificates—Then and Now

A stock certificate is an important piece of paper. To the investor who buys it, the certificate represents ownership in the company. To the issuing company, though, the certificate is more— it is an extension of the company that conveys a message about its business.

Early certificates portrayed classical imagery, such as Greek gods and Roman warriors, to give investors a notion of the power and strength associated with the company. Until the 1950s, stock certificates, for the most part, could have any design the company chose. Following the suggestion of the New York Stock Exchange (NYSE), by 1963 all new stock certificates were required to feature some human form.

In the 1990s, many companies decided to change their certificate design. Playboy Enterprises' original stock certificates featured the nude Miss February 1971. Twenty years later, the certificates were changed to reflect the company's new international strategies. The new certificates feature a woman in a long dress holding the globe with Big Ben and the Eiffel Tower in the background.

Even more recent changes include the push by the General Accounting Office to have the Securities and Exchange Commission reduce the use of certificates. The reason is that the certificate system of stock transfers is risky and inefficient compared to the speed and accuracy of computerized systems. But stock certificates are not gone yet and, for many investors and collectors today, they are still another motivation for purchasing stocks.

SOURCE: Stock certificates courtesy Playboy Enterprises.

AMR's convertible preferred stock currently receive annual dividends equal to seven percent, compared with no dividend on AMR common stock. They also have the option of converting to common stock of parent company American Airlines at a stated price.[2]

Preferred stock usually is issued to attract conservative investors who want the margin of safety in having preference over common stock. Although preferred stock represents equity capital, many companies consider it a compromise between bonds and common stock.

BONDS

Bondholders are creditors, not owners, of a corporation. Chapter 15 described bonds as a means of obtaining long-term debt capital for the corporation and as sources of funds for municipal, state, and federal government units. Bonds are issued in denominations of $1,000, $5,000, and even $50,000. They indicate a definite rate of interest to be paid to the bondholder and the maturity date. Because bondholders are creditors of the corporation, they have a claim on the firm's assets before any claims of preferred and common stockholders in the event of the firm's dissolution.

Types of Bonds

The potential bondholder has a variety of bonds from which to choose. A **secured bond** is *backed by specific pledges of company assets.* For instance, mortgage bonds are backed by real and personal property owned by the firm, such as machinery or furniture, and collateral trust bonds are backed by stocks and bonds of other companies owned by the borrowing firm.

Since bond purchasers are attempting to balance their financial returns with the risks involved, bonds backed by pledges of specific assets are less risky than those without such collateral. Consequently, a firm will be able to issue secured bonds at lower interest rates than unsecured bonds.

However, a number of companies do issue these unsecured bonds, called **debentures**—*bonds backed only by the reputation of the issuing corporation or government unit.* Only governments and major corporations with extremely sound financial reputations, such as oil industry giant Mobil Corp., can find buyers for their debentures.

A *government bond* represents funds borrowed by the U.S. government. Because they are backed by the full faith and credit of the federal government, government bonds are considered the least risky of all debt obligations. A *municipal bond* is a debt issue of a

Mobil Corporation Bond

Name of corporation issuing the bond

Face value of bond

Registered bond

Type of bond

Annual interest rate

Maturity date

state or a political subdivision, such as a county or city. An important feature of municipal bonds is that interest payments are usually exempt from federal income tax and, in most cases, from taxes in the state and locality in which the bonds are issued. Because of this attractive feature, these bonds can be issued at significantly lower interest rates.

In order to entice more speculative purchasers, convertible bonds sometimes are issued by corporations. A *convertible bond* has the option of being converted into a specific number of shares of common stock. The number of shares of stock exchanged for each bond is included in the *bond indenture*—the legal contract containing all provisions of the bond. A $1,000 bond might be convertible into 50 shares of common stock. If the common stock is selling at $18 when the bonds are issued, the conversion privilege has no value. But if the stock rises in price to $30, this conversion privilege has a value of $1,500. Convertible bonds offer lower interest rates than those lacking conversion provisions and, therefore, reduce the interest expenses of the issuing firm. Some bond purchasers prefer such bonds, even at lower interest rates, due to the potential of additional gains if the price of the firm's stock increases.

Rating Bonds

When most people think of investing, they immediately think of the stock market. But it is not the only investment arena available. Investors seeking safe instruments in which to put their money often choose the bond market.

Two factors determine the price of a bond: the degree of risk and its interest rate. Since the bondholder is a creditor of the company, he or she has first claim on the firm's assets if it is liquidated. For this reason, bonds are generally less risky than stocks, although not always. To judge the degree of risk in a bond, ask yourself the following:

- Will the company or government agency issuing the bond be able to pay the principal when due?
- Is it able to make the interest payments?
- Is the bond already in default?

In general, the level of risk is reflected in a bond's rating, provided by the two bond-rating services, Standard & Poor's (S&P) and Moody's. The most risk-free bonds are rated AAA (S&P) and Aaa (Moody's), and the scales descend to the so-called *junk bonds*, and then on to the most speculative issues, usually in default.

Junk bonds attract investors because of the high yields they offer in exchange for the risk involved. Typically, the safer the bond, the higher the price. During periods of high interest rates, BB-rated bonds may earn six to seven percent more interest than AAA bonds. Of course, these higher returns also mean higher risk.

The second factor affecting the price of the bond is the interest rate. Other things being equal, the higher the interest rate, the higher the price at which

Moody's and Standard & Poor's Bond Ratings

Moody's	Interpretation	Standard & Poor's	Interpretation
Aaa	Prime quality	AAA	Bank investment quality
Aa	High grade	AA	
A	Upper medium grade	A	
Baa	Medium grade	BBB	
		BB	
Ba	Lower medium grade or speculative	B	Speculative
B	Speculative	CCC	
		CC	
Caa	From very speculative to near or in default	C	
Ca			
C		DDD	In default (rating indicates the relative salvage value)
		DD	
		D	

Moody's and Standard & Poor's bond ratings help investors balance risks and rewards when purchasing bonds.

a bond will be bought and sold. But everything else usually is not equal—the bonds may not be equally risky, or one may tie up money for longer periods of time than the other. Consequently, investors must evaluate the trade-offs involved. Another important rule is that when interest rates go up, bond prices go down. This is because bondholders are locked into relatively lower interest rates on their money.

How Bonds Are Retired

Because bonds have a maturity date, the issuing corporation must have the necessary funds available to repay the principal when the bonds mature. The two most common methods of repayment are serial bonds and sinking-fund bonds.

In the case of a *serial bond*, a corporation simply issues a large number of bonds that mature at different dates. For example, if a corporation decides to issue $4.5 million in serial bonds for a 30-year period, the maturity dates may be established in such a manner that no bonds mature for the first 15 years. Beginning with the 16th year, $300,000 in bonds mature each year until the bonds are repaid at the end of the 30 years. Serial bonds often are issued by city governments.

A variation of the concept of serial bonds is the *sinking-fund bond*. Under this plan, the issuing corpo-

ration makes annual deposits of funds for use in redeeming the bonds when they mature. These deposits are made with a *bond trustee*—usually a major bank with the responsibility of representing bondholders. The deposits must be large enough so that with accrued interest they will be sufficient to redeem the bonds at maturity.

A *callable bond* has a provision that allows the issuing corporation to redeem it before its maturity date if a premium is paid. For instance, a 20-year bond may not be callable for the first 10 years. Between 11 and 15 years, it can be called at a premium of perhaps $50, and between 16 and 20 years it can be called at its face value.

Why issue callable bonds? If a corporation issues 30-year bonds paying 14 percent annual interest and interest rates decline to 10 percent, it is paying more interest than it should. In this instance, it may decide to retire the 14 percent callable bonds and issue new bonds that pay a lower rate of interest. Such actions may be financially sound, even though the firm would incur additional costs in retiring the old bonds and issuing new ones.

SECURITIES PURCHASERS

Two general types of investors exist: institutional and individual. An **institutional investor** is *an organiza-*

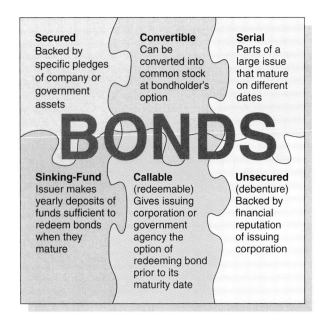

Six major types of bonds and their distinguishing characteristics.

tion that invests its own funds or those it holds in trust for others. Included in this definition are insurance companies, pension funds, mutual funds, commercial banks, and thrifts, as well as other investors, such as not-for-profit organizations and foundations.

Institutional investors buy and sell large quantities, often in blocks of at least 10,000 shares per transaction. Such block trading accounts for more than half the total daily volume on organized securities exchanges, and institutional investors account for approximately two-thirds of all trading volume. The number of investors who own shares through mutual funds or employers' pension plans is rising steadily, and the firms that manage their funds now control about 40 percent of all U.S. equities.[3]

Institutional investors have become the most important force in today's securities market. Since 1980, for example, the percentage of stocks held by individual investors has fallen from 71 percent to 50 percent. Mutual funds provide 96 percent of the money that goes into stocks.[4]

Despite the importance of institutional investors, however, individual investors still play a vital role. About 51 million Americans own stocks, either directly or by investing in stock mutual funds.[5] Furthermore, many institutional investments reflect the demands of individual investors.

It used to be that the typical individual investor was male, average age 55, and married, with an annual income of $80,000 or more. These days, however, women comprise a growing number of stock market participants, and one out of three investors is female. The median age also has declined as younger people

become investors. In fact, one out of nine investors today is under the age of 40. George Salem, banking analyst for Prudential Securities Inc., believes that the growing diversity among individual investors will encourage greater diversity in investment options. These investors, says Salem, "are not going to be satisfied with the three flavors of investments that banks offer. They'll want 50 or 100 flavors."[6]

Investment Motivations

Why do people and institutions invest? For some, the motivation is **speculation**—*the hope of making a large profit on stocks within a short time.* Speculation may take the form of acting on a corporate merger rumor or simply purchasing high-risk stocks, such as low-priced penny stocks (so called because they sell for less than $1 per share).

A second motivation is growth. According to the National Association of Investment Clubs, investors who choose growth as a primary goal should invest in fast-growing companies. An example is Wal-Mart, where earnings have grown 30 percent annually over the past five years. Today, a share of Wal-Mart costs over $25 and, if the present trend continues, that same share could cost at least $37.25 within 12 months.[7]

Growth-minded investors are also likely to benefit from stock splits, which typically occur in fast-growing companies such as Wal-Mart. A *stock split*, a recapitalization in which a single share is divided into multiple shares, lowers the price of the stock and makes it easier for new investors to buy.

Still another investment motivation is to use stocks and bonds to supplement income. *The income*

Slicing the Institutional Investment Pie

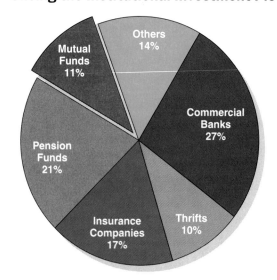

received from securities investments is called the investor's return, or **yield.** Yield is calculated by dividing dividends by market price. The yield from any particular security varies with the market price and the dividend payments.

Investors motivated primarily by income concentrate on the dividends of prospective companies. An investor with enough foresight to purchase ten shares of General Motors Corp. stock in 1940 for $468 would have received dividend payments of more than $8,000 by the mid-1990s. Because dividends are paid from company earnings, investors consider the company's past record for paying dividends, its current profitability, and its prospects for future earnings. Purchasers of income stocks are likely to own shares of companies in industries such as banking, insurance, and public utilities.

Investors whose primary objective is safety for their original investments are likely to purchase high-quality bonds and preferred stocks. These securities offer substantial protection and are likely to continue paying a good return on the long-term investment.

Most investors have more than one investment goal. Investors who emphasize safety of principal may buy preferred stocks, which can grow in market value. Those who buy growth stocks may choose stocks paying at least a three percent yield in order to receive some short-term return on the investment.

Liquidity and Taxes In addition to these primary investment goals, investors have two other factors to consider: liquidity and taxes. Since the prices of securities can vary widely, investors cannot count on making a profit whenever they decide to sell. If liquidity (the speed at which assets can be converted to cash) is important, investors should choose securities that tend to remain stable in price.

Taxes also can influence the investment decision. The tax that has the greatest impact on investments is the federal income tax, which is levied on investment income and on capital gains (increases in the value of assets such as stocks and bonds). Taxes on wealth, such as the federal estate tax or property taxes, also can affect specific types of investments. Some investments, like the purchase of gold or antiques, also may be subject to sales taxes.

SECURITIES EXCHANGES

Securities exchanges are the marketplaces for stocks and bonds. At a **stock exchange,** *stocks and bonds are bought and sold.* Although corporations' securities are

> **THEY SAID IT**
>
> "Never invest in anything that eats or needs repainting."
>
> *Billy Rose (1899–1966) American theatrical impresario*

traded, the corporations are not involved directly, and they receive no proceeds from the sales. The securities traded at organized exchanges already have been issued by corporations. The sales occur between individual and corporate investors.

The New York Stock Exchange

When investors talk about the stock market, they usually are referring to the New York Stock Exchange (NYSE). The "Big Board," as it is sometimes called, is the largest and best known of all stock exchanges. To do business at the NYSE, a firm must be a member. Currently, 2,089 companies are listed as members, with 115.8 billion shares worth $4.04 trillion. Potential members must purchase their seats from current members and be approved by the exchange. Memberships have varied considerably in price. Their cost has grown from a mere $17,000 each in 1942 to $431,000 in recent years.[8]

The American and Regional Stock Exchanges

The second national exchange operating in the United States is the American Stock Exchange (AMEX). The AMEX, also located in New York, is smaller than the NYSE and handles smaller firms with national followings.

To be listed on the NYSE or AMEX, a firm must meet a number of requirements. The less strict requirements for listing on the AMEX make it an attractive seasoning board for firms not ready to be listed on the Big Board. In fact, many of the firms now listed on the NYSE were originally part of the AMEX, and transferred to the Big Board only after achieving larger earnings and size.

Long-Term Investment Objectives of Securities			
	Investment Objective		
Type of Security	**Safety**	**Income**	**Growth**
Bonds	Best	Very steady	Usually none
Preferred stocks	Good	Steady	Variable
Common stocks	Least	Variable	Best

Stocks and bonds can be evaluated on the basis of three long-term investment objectives.

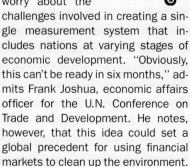

ETHICS AND SOCIAL RESPONSIBILITY

Investing in the Environment

The private enterprise system has many strengths, competition being one of the most far-reaching. Competition drives companies to improve their products, develop new ones, and constantly refine their customer service. But recently the private enterprise system has been challenged by state, federal, and international agencies, including the United Nations, to become active in preserving the environment.

A growing number of scientists contend that the pollution emitted by cars, factories, and power generators collects in our atmosphere, trapping solar heat as it reaches the earth. As the ability of the earth to cool down diminishes, the effects of solar heat increase. Within 50 years, this global warming process is predicted to contribute to coastal flooding, severe storms, and dangerous droughts. The question today is what can be done to reduce the pollution?

The United States was one of the first countries to deal with the problem by passing the 1990 Clean Air Act, which set up a market-based system to encourage companies to reduce their sulfur dioxide emissions by selling and buying *allowances*. These allowances allow a company to emit a prescribed amount of pollution; if a firm has a low rate of emissions, it may have extra allowances that it can sell to another firm with higher emission rates. The U.S. Environmental Protection Agency predicts the program will cut sulfur dioxide pollution in half by the year 2000.

The United Nations is using the U.S. model to create a global Environmental Protection Agency. This worldwide EPA would administer a global system, permitting businesses to buy and sell pollution allowances, or rights. The plan would allow companies to trade pollution rights in the same way securities currently are traded. For example, a single allowance of carbon dioxide would permit a firm to emit one ton of the chemical pollutant each year.

The global EPA would control the number of allowances issued, and gradually reduce them over a period of years. This would motivate inefficient companies that produce large amounts of such pollutants as carbon dioxide to clean up their act and avoid ever-steeper payments. Meanwhile, companies that do not pollute could make a profit by selling their extra allowances on the open market. Countries that generate the most pollution would be targeted first. In the case of carbon dioxide, the top polluters are the United States, Great Britain, Germany, and most of the industrialized Eastern European nations.

The U.N.'s proposal remains controversial. Some environmentalists feel it is unethical to let companies buy the right to pollute. Others worry about the challenges involved in creating a single measurement system that includes nations at varying stages of economic development. "Obviously, this can't be ready in six months," admits Frank Joshua, economic affairs officer for the U.N. Conference on Trade and Development. He notes, however, that this idea could set a global precedent for using financial markets to clean up the environment.

In fact, pollution allowances may become the next major innovation of the securities industry. After all, the commodities industry, once limited to agricultural items like grain and livestock, has adapted to trading less homespun products such as foreign currencies. Private markets, including the Chicago Board of Trade, already are developing plans for running the sulfur dioxide market in the United States. Says Richard Sandor, an economist and director of the CBOT, "Air and water are simply no longer the 'free goods' that economists once assumed. They must be redefined as property rights so that they can be efficiently allocated."

SOURCE: Adapted from Jeffrey Taylor, "Global Market in Pollution Rights Proposed by U.N.," *The Wall Street Journal,* January 31, 1992, C1, C10.

In addition to the NYSE and AMEX, several regional exchanges operate in the United States. These include the Midwest, the Pacific, and the Philadelphia exchanges. Originally established to trade the shares of smaller firms operating in limited geographic areas, the regional exchanges now list many major corporations as well. The largest regional exchange is the Midwest, located in Chicago, which handles about eight percent of all trades in NYSE-listed stocks.[9] Roughly half of the companies listed on the NYSE are listed on one or more regional boards also.

Even though they are regional rather than national, the Midwest and the Pacific exchanges actually trade more than the AMEX does in total market value. They still are dwarfed, however, by the NYSE and Tokyo stock exchanges.

Foreign Stock Exchanges

Stock exchanges are not unique to the United States. In fact, the world's oldest board is the Amsterdam Stock Exchange, which began operations in 1611. The London Stock Exchange, which lists more than 7,000 securities, traces its beginnings to pre-American Revolution times.

Foreign exchanges are gaining market share when it comes to global trading. Unlike the NYSE, where overseas listings account for only five percent of its trades, foreign exchanges actively trade shares from numerous companies around the world. Of the 2,510 securities traded on the Geneva, Switzerland, exchange, 257 shares and 933 bonds are non-Swiss. Some U.S. firms are listed both at home and abroad. In fact, London's stock exchange trades more than 20 million shares daily of NYSE-listed stocks—over ten percent of the NYSE's volume. Other American companies prefer to list with foreign exchanges to avoid the Big Board's strict listing requirements.

Overseas trading volume of securities is rising three times faster than U.S. trading, as stock exchanges in both Europe and Asia grow rapidly. Paris's MATIF market is a popular trading center that averages 3,000 contracts every night. Frankfurt and Paris are competing to set up a trading system that would include almost 300 of Europe's top companies.[10]

In Shenzhen, China's special economic zone outside Hong Kong, millions of dollars in shares were traded in the first few months after it opened. American-trained investment experts recently started a nationwide computerized trading system, uniting numerous trading centers in several major Chinese cities. Shanghai has long had an "informal" stock market. In fact, that's how Yang "Millions" Huading became a millionaire. The former steelworker earned his nickname from trading government treasury bills and corporate bonds. When Shanghai opened its first official exchange, Yang celebrated in his own way: he bought a personal computer to better track the market.

THEY SAID IT

"It is not the return *on* my investment that I am concerned about; it is the return *of* my investment."

Will Rogers
(1879–1935)
American actor
and humorist

How does China's conservative government feel about securities trading? Says one economist, "The securities market is a matter of economic necessity. It is inevitable." While many of China's politicians are wary of western ways, they like the prosperity that accompanies them. In the bustling city of Shekou, for instance, a huge government-sponsored billboard exhorts passersby to "Build the prosperity of China for the next 100 years." Meanwhile, professional investors like Yang sidestep the political issues and concentrate on building their portfolios. "We are neither capitalists nor communists," declares Yang. "Buying stocks now is patriotic."[11]

Global Securities Trading

International stock exchanges are becoming a reality. GLOBEX, an international 24-hour trading system, links traders from around the world to MATIF and other exchanges. GLOBEX recently received permission to add terminals in Japan, since its trading now tops 15,000 contracts each session and continues to rise. The 12 major exchanges in the European Union are working toward forming one unified exchange. In the process, they will have to overcome significant differences between different nations' business methods. For instance, Paris's stock market reveals volumes and prices within seconds of a trade, while investors in Milan may have to wait until the following day.

A big step toward unifying the different markets is Eurolist, a cross-listing of firms of over 250 major European companies. While some European firms

Stock Exchange Listing Requirements		
Requirements	New York Stock Exchange	American Stock Exchange
Number of shares held by the general public	1,100,000	400,000
Number of stockholders owning 100 or more shares	2,000	1,200 (of which 500 must own 100 to 500 shares)
Pretax income for latest fiscal year	$ 2,500,000	$ 750,000
Pretax income for preceding two years	$ 2,000,000	
Minimum aggregate value of shares publicly held	$18,000,000	$ 300,000
Tangible assets	$16,000,000	$4,000,000

A number of requirements limit the stocks that can be listed on the NYSE and AMEX.

already list their stock on more than one exchange, this is not cheap to do. One company that trades on six different markets estimates that its annual listing fees total almost $60,000, and the cost of meeting all the different disclosure requirements comes to nearly $1 million a year. Eurolist reduces listing charges to a single fee and allows firms to qualify for listing just by meeting their home country's requirements.[12]

The NASDAQ Market System

In addition to both domestic and foreign stock exchanges, investors have another option: the *over-the-counter (OTC) market*, an informal method for trading securities through market makers who fill customers' buy and sell orders.

Unlike traditional stock exchanges, the OTC market has no trading floor on which securities are bought and sold. Instead, buyers and sellers are brought together by computers, teletype, fax machines, and telephones. Dealers involved in these transactions keep in regular contact with one another, and the prices of the securities they trade are established by supply and demand. They "make a market" by quoting a *bid*—what they will pay for a security—and an *asked*, or *selling, price*. Investors who decide to purchase OTC stocks and bonds contact their brokers, who contact the dealers handling the security in order to search for the best price. When the investor and dealer agree on a price, a market is made. Over 500 market-maker firms are operating, including such well-known brokerage firms as Merrill Lynch and Goldman Sachs.

At the heart of the OTC market is the **National Association of Securities Dealers Automatic Quotation (NASDAQ)** system, *a nationwide OTC network.* About 4,100 companies, including Clean Harbors, list their securities with NASDAQ. In a typical year, it trades over 48 billion shares, with a total market value of $890.8 billion.[13]

NASDAQ was a pioneer in using computers to trade securities. All trades in the NASDAQ system are reported within seconds, providing immediate access to current market systems. Also, since stockbrokers have immediate access to bid and ask prices on their automatic desktop quotation machines, the NASDAQ system is not noticeably different from securities trading on national or regional exchanges. However, transactions involving the less actively traded OTC securities are reported less frequently, typically at the end of each trading day.

Many of the firms whose stocks are traded on OTC markets have too few shares to be listed on the NYSE or AMEX. Others have too few stockholders, and still others do not have sufficient earnings to qualify for listing. Also, the OTC market includes the shares of most insurance companies and banks and the bonds issued by many city and state government units. A number of major corporations have chosen not to list their stocks and bonds on the national and regional exchanges, opting instead for NASDAQ listings. Well-known firms that are listed on NASDAQ include Apple Computer, MCI Communications, Lotus Development, Microsoft, and TCI Cable, the largest cable company in the United States.

NASDAQ International Service Recently the NASD began operating the world's first intercontinental OTC market. In a two-year pilot program, NASDAQ International Service offers a trading session, based in London, that runs from 3:30 A.M. to 9:00 A.M. (EST) every U.S. business day. Any NASD-member firm or approved United Kingdom affiliate can participate in this service. To accommodate international differences in regulations and time zones, NASDAQ International has slightly different reporting requirements from domestic NASDAQ trades. For instance, all international transactions must be reported within three minutes, as opposed to 90 seconds for U.S. trades.

HOW SECURITIES ARE BOUGHT AND SOLD

For the most part, securities transactions involve a *stockbroker*, a financial intermediary who buys and sells securities for individual and institutional investors.

Placing an Order

An investor wanting to purchase Exxon common stock typically would contact a stockbroker, who would convey the order to the firm's member at the NYSE, who would go directly to the location on the floor of the exchange where Exxon is traded and attempt to make the purchase.

An investor request to buy or sell stock at the current market price is a *market order.* The NYSE representative would carry out the order on a best-price

IT'S THE LAW

1933 Securities ("Truth in Lending") Act
Federal law designed to protect investors by requiring full disclosure of relevant financial information by companies desiring to sell new stock or bond issues to the general public.

1934 Securities Exchange Act
Created the Securities and Exchange Commission (SEC) to regulate the national stock exchanges and established strict rules for trading on organized exchanges. A 1964 amendment extended the authority to the SEC to the over-the-counter market. Brokerage firms, individual brokers, and dealers selling OTC stocks are regulated by the SEC, and brokers engaged in buying and selling securities are required to pass an examination.

1938 Maloney Act
Amended the Securities Exchange Act of 1934 to authorize self-regulation of OTC securities operations. This led to the creation of the National Association of Securities Dealers (NASD), which is responsible for regulating OTC businesses. Written examinations now are required of all new brokers and dealers selling OTC securities.

1940 Investment Company Act
Brought the mutual fund industry under SEC jurisdiction. Mutual funds now are required to register with the SEC. The state and federal laws mentioned protect investors from the securities trading abuses and stock manipulations that occurred before the 1930s.

1970 Securities Investor Protection Act
Created the Securities Investor Protection Corporation (SIPC), a not-for-profit corporation that insures the accounts of brokerage firm clients up to $100,000 in cash in case of dealer or broker insolvency. The loss of securities is insured up to $500,000.

1990 Securities Enforcement Remedies and Penny Stock Reform Act
Expanded the SEC's role in dealing with securities violations. The law created three tiers of fines based on the severity of the violation.

basis. On the other hand, an investor request to buy or sell stock at a specified price is a *limit order.* In this case, a notation of the limit order is made at the post that handles the stock transactions, and, if the price reaches the specified price, the order is carried out.

Stock trading is conducted in quantities of 100 shares, called *round lots.* Investors can purchase fewer than 100 shares, however, by buying in *odd lots*—purchases or sales of fewer than 100 shares of stock that are grouped together to make up one or more round lots. The stocks then are distributed to the various odd-lot purchasers when the transaction is completed.

Two frequently mentioned stock market terms refer to investor attitudes. A **bull** is *an investor who expects stock prices to rise.* Bulls buy securities in anticipation of the increased market prices. When stock market prices continue to rise, market observers call it a bull market.

A **bear** is *an investor who expects stock prices to decline.* Bears are likely to sell their securities in antic-ipation of the increased market prices. When stock market prices continue to rise, market observers call it a bull market.

Cost of Trading

When securities are purchased through a stockbroker, commission fees are charged. They vary among brokerage firms, generally ranging from one to two percent of the total value of the stock transaction.

Discount brokerage firms compete with traditional full-service brokers by offering fewer services and charging lower commissions. For instance, while full-service broker Merrill Lynch might collect a $70 commission for selling 100 shares, discount broker Lombard Institutional Brokerage charges a $34 commission.[14] The greater the amount of the purchase, the greater the savings on commissions with a discount broker, since the commissions as a percent of the amount invested declines as the cost of the investment rises.

COMPUTERIZED TRADING

Securities traders at NationsBank Corp. do not even need to speak when placing a buy or sell order, which may range from $15 million to $500 million in any given day. Instead, they log their orders directly onto computers, which execute the trade. Perhaps the most useful feature of this approach, according to Mary Primm, senior vice president of NationsBank, is the direct electronic communication between the computerized trading system and other computer systems at the bank. "The portfolio manager now has the ability to execute a trade electronically by entering it into the system and is assured that the system automatically will update the information to the accounting and custodial systems," she explains.[15]

As much as ten percent of today's stock trading now is done through computer networks like NationsBank's, a percentage that is certain to rise. Electronic systems have revolutionized securities trading by creating vast networks that deliver lightning speed, low overhead, and anonymity. Commissions charged for using such systems average about two cents per share, less than half the typical rate that large institutions pay on traditional trades through stockbrokers. Furthermore, computerized trading operates around the clock—unlike the NYSE, which limits trading to a 6½-hour trading day.[16]

The rise of computerized systems causes many analysts to question the future of the New York Stock Exchange and its armies of brokers. Since 1980, the NYSE's shares of trades in NYSE-listed stocks has fallen from 85 percent to 68 percent. Meanwhile, regional exchanges and electronic markets are gaining business. "Pit trading is archaic," says long-time trader Scott Schumer, who, after spending 17 years at a conventional exchange, now uses the GLOBEX electronic system. "If everything else is done over computer, eventually pit trading will be, too."[17]

The "Fourth Market"

Another reason for the erosion of the NYSE's market share is the rise of the so-called *fourth-market* systems that match buyers with sellers, bypassing both NASDAQ and stock exchanges. For example, one privately owned electronic trader, Bernard L. Madoff

Investment Securities, handles about ten percent of all trades in NYSE-listed stocks. Other fourth-market systems include Instinet and the Crossing Network, both electronic-trading subsidiaries of Reuters Holdings PLC; Quotron Systems, owned by Citicorp; and Dow Jones' Telerate Inc.[18]

Business people appreciate the convenience and low cost that such systems provide. "Our preferred method of trading is the internal marketplace, with no intermediaries," notes Donald Luskin of Wells Fargo/Nikko Investment Advisers. Wells Fargo starts by looking for low-cost trading routes through networks such as Instinet, and move to the traditional method of brokers and a stock exchange only as a last resort.[19]

An even more direct system for purchasing securities exists for a growing number of major corporations. If one would like to acquire common stock in such U.S. industrial giants as Exxon, W. R. Grace, Texaco, and Johnson Controls, one can purchase them directly from the company. The price is set at the closing price on the day they are purchased. Best of all, most companies charge no fees.

> ### THEY SAID IT
>
> "Now I'm in real trouble. First, my laundry called and said they lost my shirt and then my broker said the same thing."
>
> *Leopold Fechtner*
> *(1916–   )*

READING THE FINANCIAL NEWS

At least two or three pages of most major daily newspapers are devoted to reporting current financial news, which typically focuses on the previous day's securities transactions. Stocks and bonds traded on the NYSE and AMEX are listed alphabetically in the newspaper. Information is provided on the volume of sales and the price of each security.

Stock Tables

To understand how to read the stock tables found in most daily newspapers, it is necessary to interpret the symbols in the various columns. The symbol in the left-most column is the 52-week indicator. The *U* means this stock hit its 52-week high during the day. Column 2 gives the stock's highest and lowest trading prices during the past 52 weeks, and column 3 contains the abbreviation for the company's name. The next column (column 4) contains stock footnotes, which provide information about the stock, such as whether it is new, preferred, or in bankruptcy. Column 5 lists the dividend, usually an annual payment based on the last quarterly or semiannual declaration. Column 6 presents the yield, the percentage return from a dividend based on the stock's closing price.

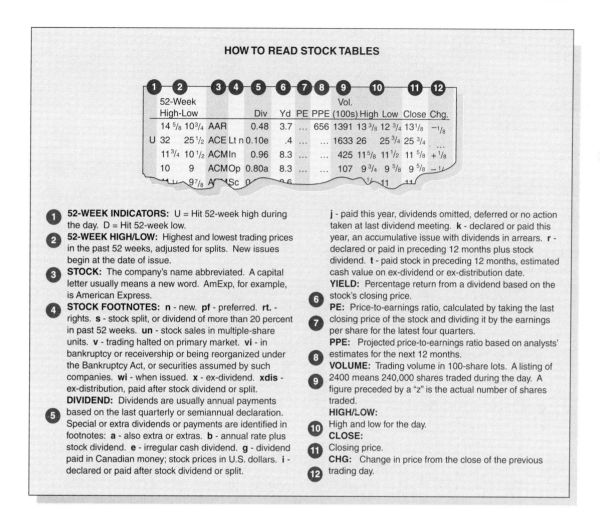

HOW TO READ STOCK TABLES

	52-Week High-Low		Stock		Div	Yd	PE	PPE	Vol. (100s)	High	Low	Close	Chg.
	14 5/8	10 3/4	AAR		0.48	3.7	...	656	1391	13 3/8	12 3/4	13 1/8	−1/8
U	32	25 1/2	ACE Lt	n	0.10e	.4	...	...	1633	26	25 3/4	25 3/4	
	11 3/4	10 1/2	ACMIn		0.96	8.3	...	...	425	11 5/8	11 1/2	11 5/8	+1/8
	10	9	ACMOp		0.80a	8.3	...	...	107	9 3/4	9 5/8	9 5/8	−1/

1 52-WEEK INDICATORS: U = Hit 52-week high during the day. D = Hit 52-week low.

2 52-WEEK HIGH/LOW: Highest and lowest trading prices in the past 52 weeks, adjusted for splits. New issues begin at the date of issue.

3 STOCK: The company's name abbreviated. A capital letter usually means a new word. AmExp, for example, is American Express.

4 STOCK FOOTNOTES: n - new. **pf** - preferred. **rt.** - rights. **s** - stock split, or dividend of more than 20 percent in past 52 weeks. **un** - stock sales in multiple-share units. **v** - trading halted on primary market. **vi** - in bankruptcy or receivership or being reorganized under the Bankruptcy Act, or securities assumed by such companies. **wi** - when issued. **x** - ex-dividend. **xdis** - ex-distribution, paid after stock dividend or split.

5 DIVIDEND: Dividends are usually annual payments based on the last quarterly or semiannual declaration. Special or extra dividends or payments are identified in footnotes: **a** - also extra or extras. **b** - annual rate plus stock dividend. **e** - irregular cash dividend. **g** - dividend paid in Canadian money; stock prices in U.S. dollars. **i** - declared or paid after stock dividend or split.

j - paid this year, dividends omitted, deferred or no action taken at last dividend meeting. **k** - declared or paid this year, an accumulative issue with dividends in arrears. **r** - declared or paid in preceding 12 months plus stock dividend. **t** - paid stock in preceding 12 months, estimated cash value on ex-dividend or ex-distribution date.

6 YIELD: Percentage return from a dividend based on the stock's closing price.

7 PE: Price-to-earnings ratio, calculated by taking the last closing price of the stock and dividing it by the earnings per share for the latest four quarters.

8 PPE: Projected price-to-earnings ratio based on analysts' estimates for the next 12 months.

9 VOLUME: Trading volume in 100-share lots. A listing of 2400 means 240,000 shares traded during the day. A figure preceded by a "z" is the actual number of shares traded.

10 HIGH/LOW: High and low for the day.

11 CLOSE: Closing price.

12 CHG: Change in price from the close of the previous trading day.

The **price-earnings (P/E) ratio,** *the current market price divided by the annual earnings per share,* is listed in column 7. Next (column 8) is the projected price-earnings (PPE) ratio, which is based on analysts' estimates for the next 12 months. The stock's trading volume in 100-share lots is in column 9, and the stock's highest and lowest prices for that day are in column 10. Column 11 gives the closing price for that day, and column 12 summarizes the stock's change in price from the close of the previous trading day.

Bond Quotations

To learn how to read bond quotations, pick a bond listed on the NYSE and examine the columns of information (see figure on the next page). Most bonds are issued in denominations of $1,000; thus, bond prices must be read differently from stock prices. Although the closing price of a stock might read 107¾, this does not mean $107.75. Because bond prices are quoted as a percentage of the $1,000 price stated on the face of the bond, 107¾ means $1,077.50.

The notation next to the bond name, such as "11s11," indicates the bonds pay an annual interest rate of 11 percent and have a maturity date of 2011. The first figure is the interest rate; the second is the maturity date. Assuming a bond is selling above its original $1,000 face value, the current yield is 10.2 percent, almost a full percentage point less than the 11 percent stated interest rate. Bonds with the notation *cv* are convertible bonds.

The next column indicates the total trading volume during that day. The closing bond price is listed next, followed by the percentage of net change in the price of the bond since the previous day's closing.

STOCK AVERAGES

A feature of most daily television and radio newscasts is the report of current stock averages. The most familiar average is the **Dow Jones Averages** (the Dow). However, most people are also familiar with the

HOW TO READ BOND TABLES

Bonds	Cur Yld	Vol	Close	Net Chg
❶ ❷ ❸	❹	❺	❻	❼
PhilEl 11s11	10.2	22	$107^3/_4$	$+ \ ^1/_4$
PhilP $12^1/_4$	11.2	18	$109^5/_8$	$+ \ ^5/_8$
PhilP $11^1/_4 13$	10.3	5	$108^7/_8$	$+ 1^3/_4$
PierOn dc $11^1/_2 03$	11.3	150	$101^7/_8$	...
Pittstn 9.2s04	CV	59	100	$- \ ^1/_4$
PopeTl 6s12	CV	11	88	$+ 1$
PorG $8^3/_4 07$	8.7	9	$100^1/_8$	...
PotEl $8^3/_8 09$	8.3	5	$100^5/_8$	$- \ ^5/_8$
PotEl $9^1/_4 \ 16$	8.8	9	105	...
PotEl 7s18	CV	15	$97^1/_2$	$+ \ ^1/_2$
viPrmM $6^5/_8 11f$	CV	30	$17^7/_8$	$- \ ^1/_8$

❶ **BOND:** Abbreviation of company name.

❷ **ANNUAL INTEREST RATE:** Annual percentage rate of interest specified on the bond certificate.

❸ **MATURITY DATE:** Year in which the bond issuer will repay bondholders the face value of each bond.

YIELD: Percentage return from interest payment calculated on the basis of the bond's closing price; **cv** indicates a bond that is convertible into shares of common stock at a specified price.

VOLUME: Number of bonds traded during the day.

CLOSE: Closing price.

❼ **CHG:** Change in the price from the close of the previous trading day.

Standard & Poor's Index. Both indexes have been developed to *reflect the general activity of the stock market.*

The Dow is actually three different indexes based on the market prices of 30 industrial, 20 transportation, and 15 utility stocks. The more broadly based Standard & Poor's Index is developed from the market performance of 400 industrial, 40 financial, 40 utility, and 20 transportation stocks.

The Dow Jones industrial average has been used as a general measure of changes in overall stock prices and a reflection of the U.S. economy since its appearance in 1896. The term *industrial* is a misnomer since the index is comprised of both industrial corporations, such as General Motors, Union Carbide, and Boeing, and such nonindustrial firms as American Express, McDonald's, and Sears. The Dow remains the most widely reported barometer of stock-market activity, although some financial analysts claim it overrepresents the market's capital goods and energy sectors, while underrepresenting financial and service firms.[20]

MUTUAL FUNDS

Many investors have neither the time nor the knowledge to continually analyze stock market developments. These people may choose another investment option, called **mutual funds**—*financial organizations that pool investment money from purchasers of their secu-*

rities and use the money to acquire a diversified portfolio of securities. Investors who buy shares of stock in a mutual fund become part owners of a large number of companies, thereby lessening the individual risk. Mutual funds are managed by trained, experienced professionals whose careers are based on success in analyzing the securities markets and specific industries and companies.

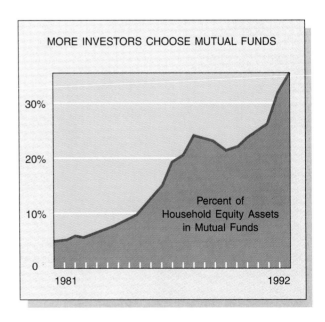

MORE INVESTORS CHOOSE MUTUAL FUNDS

Percent of Household Equity Assets in Mutual Funds

1981 — 1992

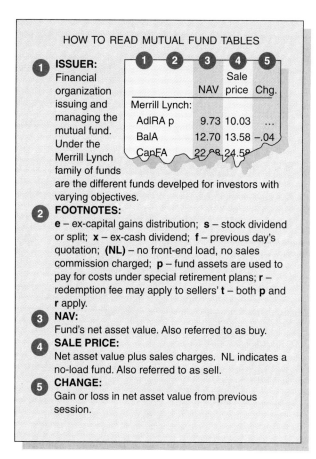

HOW TO READ MUTUAL FUND TABLES

1 ISSUER:
Financial organization issuing and managing the mutual fund. Under the Merrill Lynch family of funds are the different funds develped for investors with varying objectives.

2 FOOTNOTES:
e – ex-capital gains distribution; **s** – stock dividend or split; **x** – ex-cash dividend; **f** – previous day's quotation; **(NL)** – no front-end load, no sales commission charged; **p** – fund assets are used to pay for costs under special retirement plans; **r** – redemption fee may apply to sellers' **t** – both **p** and **r** apply.

3 NAV:
Fund's net asset value. Also referred to as buy.

4 SALE PRICE:
Net asset value plus sales charges. NL indicates a no-load fund. Also referred to as sell.

5 CHANGE:
Gain or loss in net asset value from previous session.

		NAV	Sale price	Chg.
Merrill Lynch:				
AdIRA p		9.73	10.03	…
BalA		12.70	13.58	–.04
CapFA		22.98	24.59	

The percentage of household equity assets held by mutual funds has risen sharply since 1981, from roughly 5 percent to 35 percent. Approximately 38 million people in the United States currently own shares in mutual funds. There are over 81 million accounts, which house $2 trillion in total assets.[21]

Reading mutual fund tables is relatively simple. The first column lists the fund's net asset value (NAV). Column 2 lists the sales price (the net asset value plus sales charges). The last column shows the change in the fund's asset value from the previous trading session. Footnotes may present additional information, such as whether the fund is a no-load fund, or whether a redemption fee or contingent deferred sales load may apply.

LEGAL AND ETHICAL ISSUES IN SECURITIES TRADING

Unethical practices typically lead to the passage of laws aimed at restricting such practices in the future. Both the federal government and all state governments have enacted legislation regulating the sale of securi-

ties. State laws typically require that most securities sold in the state be registered with an appropriate state official, usually the secretary of state, and that securities dealers and salespeople have annual licenses. In addition, several federal laws regulate interstate sales of securities.

The past two decades will be remembered as one of the most scandalous periods in Wall Street during the twentieth century. Jailed insider traders, such as Ivan Boesky and junk-bond pioneer Michael Milkin, made headlines for months. Financial portfolios filled with junk bonds led to the failure of hundreds of financial institutions; and dozens of corporate giants made drastic financial decisions in an attempt to ward off hostile takeovers. These events created a growing awareness of legal and ethical problems in these areas. Ethical issues in securities trading include illegal bond bids, program trading, insider trading, and abuses of the small-order execution system.

By law, no single company can buy more than 35 percent of the Treasury bonds on the market. However, loose trading practices have allowed some companies to make illegal bond bids, cornering as much as 90 percent of the Treasury notes offered during an auction and costing traders and investors millions of dollars. The government has announced plans to regulate the $2.2 trillion government securities market more closely in the future.

Program trading is *a controversial practice in which computer systems are programmed to buy or sell securities if certain conditions arise.* Program trading started as a type of portfolio insurance that allowed market players to hedge their bets with automatic buy or sell orders whenever their stock prices reached a certain level. The practice has become controversial since many people blamed it for the 1987 stock market crash, when the market value of the nation's leading stocks dropped 23 percent in one day. In fact, program trading accounted for only 15 percent of that day's trades. However, it can result in significant price swings in individual stocks when there are numerous buy and sell orders involved, and, for this reason, many people have suggested that it be banned.

Insider trading refers to *illegal securities trading by persons who profit from their access to nonpublic information about a company,* such as a pending merger or a major oil discovery. While this practice is prohibited by the Securities Exchange Act of 1934, Securities and Exchange Commission (SEC) analysis of stock trading patterns before major announcements has uncovered many cases of insider trading. The Insider Trading Act of 1984 expanded the authority of the SEC to investigate insider trading.

THEY SAID IT

"There are two times in a man's life when he should not speculate: when he can't afford it and when he can."

Mark Twain (1835–1910) American author

SUMMARY OF LEARNING GOALS

1. Distinguish between primary markets for securities and secondary markets.

The primary market is used by businesses and government units to sell new issues of securities. The secondary market includes transactions of previously issued securities.

2. Compare common stock, preferred stock, and bonds, and explain why investors might prefer each type of security.

As owners, common stockholders have voting rights, but they have only a residual claim on the firm's assets. Preferred stockholders receive preference in the payment of dividends and have first claim on the firm's assets after debts have been paid, but usually do not have voting rights. Bondholders are creditors, not owners, of a corporation, not-for-profit organization, or government unit.

3. Identify the four basic objectives of investors and the types of securities most likely to accomplish each objective.

The four basic objectives of investors are speculation, growth in the value of the investment, income, and safety. Common stocks are the most risky, but offer investment growth. Preferred stocks have limited growth opportunities, but are reasonably safe and offer a steady income.

4. Explain the process of selling or purchasing a security listed on the organized securities exchanges.

Securities purchases and sales are handled by a trained specialist, called a stockbroker. Once the broker receives a customer's order, it is conveyed to the stock exchange through a communications terminal. The firm's floor broker executes the sale, and a confirmation is communicated to the broker, who notifies the customer that the transaction has been completed.

5. Describe the information included in stock, bond, and mutual fund quotations.

Information in NYSE stock quotations includes: the 52-week indicator, highest and lowest trading prices during the past 52 weeks, the company's name, stock footnotes, dividend, yield, price-earnings (PE) ratio, projected price-earnings (PPE) ratio, volume, the stock's highest and lowest prices for that day, closing price for that day, and the stock's change in price from the close of the previous trading day. Bond quotations include maturity date and interest rate, current yield, volume, high, low, and closing price for the day, and a comparison of the closing price with that of the previous day. Tables of mutual funds list the fund's net asset value (NAV), sale price, and change in the fund's asset value from the previous session.

6. Explain the role of mutual funds in the securities field.

Mutual funds are professionally managed investment companies that own shares in many different companies and allow the investor to purchase their shares of the mutual fund, thereby creating a diversified investment portfolio. The percentage of household equity assets held by mutual funds has risen sharply since 1981, from roughly 5 percent to 35 percent.

7. Evaluate the major features of state and federal laws designed to protect investors.

The Securities Act of 1933, Securities Exchange Act of 1934, and individual state securities acts regulate organized securities exchanges and over-the-counter markets and protect investors by requiring disclosure of financial information from companies issuing securities. The Securities and Exchange Commission (SEC), created by the Securities Exchange Act of 1934, enforces the legislation and regulates brokers, brokerage firms, and mutual fund transactions. The Securities Investor Protection Corporation (SIPC) insures brokerage firm accounts in the event of dealer or broker insolvency. The Insider Trading Act of 1984 expanded the authority of the SEC to investigate insider trading. The Securities Enforcement Remedies and Penny Stock Reform Act of 1990 expanded the SEC's role in dealing with securities violations and created three tiers of fines based on the severity of the violation.

KEY TERMS QUIZ

debenture	preferred stock	securities
National Association of Securities Dealers Automatic Quotation (NASDAQ) system	investment banker	bear
	Dow Jones Averages	program trading
speculation	insider trading	price-earnings (P/E) ratio
secured bond	yield	institutional investor
primary market	mutual funds	bull
secondary market	common stock	stock exchange

_____ 1. Stocks and bonds representing obligations of the issuer to provide purchasers with an expected or stated return on investments.

_____ 2. New issues of securities sold publicly for the first time.

_____ 3. Sales of previously issued shares of stocks and bonds.

_____ 4. Specialist in selling new issues of securities for business and government.

_____ 5. Stock providing owners voting rights but only a residual claim to company assets.

_____ 6. Stock providing owners preferential dividend payment and first claim to assets after debts are paid, but seldom includes voting rights.

_____ 7. Bond backed by specific pledges of company assets.

_____ 8. Bond backed by the reputation of the issuing corporation.

_____ 9. Organization that invests its own funds or funds held in trust.

_____ 10. Purchasing stocks in anticipation of making large profits quickly.

_____ 11. Income received from securities; calculated by dividing dividends by market price.

_____ 12. Location at which stocks and bonds are bought and sold.

_____ 13. Nationwide over-the-counter network.

_____ 14. Investor who expects stock prices to rise along with market prices.

_____ 15. Investor who expects stock prices to decline along with market prices.

_____ 16. Current market price divided by annual earnings per share.

_____ 17. Averages based on market prices of 30 industrial, 20 transportation, and 15 utility stocks that reflect general market activity.

_____ 18. Financial organizations that use investors' money to acquire a portfolio of securities.

_____ 19. Computer systems programmed to buy or sell securities to take advantage of price differences that sometimes occur between stock futures and current stock prices.

_____ 20. Illegal securities trading by persons who profit from their access to nonpublic information about a company.

OTHER IMPORTANT TERMS

asked (selling) price	government bond	round lots
bid	initial public offering (IPO)	serial bond
bond indenture	junk bonds	sinking-fund bond
bond trustee	limit order	Standard & Poor's Index
book value	market order	stockbroker
callable bond	market value	stock split
convertible bond	municipal bond	tombstones
convertible preferred stock	odd lots	underwriter
discount brokerage firms	over-the-counter (OTC) market	
fourth market	par value	

REVIEW QUESTIONS

1. In what ways is the secondary market different from the primary market? With which market are investment bankers involved? What role do they play in financial decisions?

2. What is common stock? Explain the alternative methods for evaluating common stock.

3. Explain the major types of bonds issued by corporations and government units. What are the primary methods used in retiring bonds?

4. Identify the four major goals of investors, and suggest an appropriate mix of securities to achieve these goals.

5. Distinguish between the following:
   a. market orders and limit orders
   b. round lots and odd lots
   c. bulls and bears
6. How does the New York Stock Exchange operate? Compare NYSE operations with those of foreign and international markets and the NASDAQ market system.
7. What are stock averages? How do they affect securities trading? Would you expect the Standard & Poor's Index of 500 stocks to be a better indicator of overall market activity than the Dow Jones Industrial Average?

8. How does an investor place an order for common stock? Explain how computerized trading is revolutionizing the securities industry.
9. Discuss the purchase of shares in mutual funds as an alternative to purchasing stocks and bonds.
10. Explain the major laws affecting securities transactions. Include the primary purpose of each law and how it affects individual investors as well as the securities industry.

DISCUSSION QUESTIONS

1. Assume you just inherited $20,000 from your uncle and his will stipulates that you must invest all the money until you complete your education. Prepare an investment plan for the $20,000 inheritance.
2. Assume you are an investment counselor who has been asked to set up general investment goals for the following individuals, each of whom has adequate current income and about $30,000 to invest. Prepare a short report outlining the proposed investment goals for each person with general suggestions of an appropriate mix of securities:
   a. 56-year-old retired Army officer
   b. 40-year-old divorced woman with two children
   c. 19-year-old college student receiving $200 weekly for the next ten years in survivors' insurance benefits
   d. 26-year-old unmarried person earning $24,000 annually
3. The chapter notes that the NYSE's market share is slipping. Discuss the domestic and global developments that you feel are related to this trend.
4. How do bond ratings affect bond prices? What impact does a bond rating have on its yield? How might a bond rating determine the likely purchasers of a bond?
5. A married couple in their late twenties, with two small children and joint earnings of $45,000, have decided to invest in stocks that promise growth with a steady return in the form of dividends. They have narrowed the choice of stocks to five and have assembled the following data from the past three years.

Year	Company Designation	Average Price per Share	Earnings per Share	Average Dividend per Share
1992	A	$ 60	$ 5.12	$ 2.70
	B	268	13.35	10.00
	C	42	2.17	.05
	D	6	.12	.08
	E	30	3.06	1.70
1993	A	$ 59	$ 7.98	$ 2.80
	B	275	15.94	10.00
	C	45	2.74	.06
	D	8	.22	.10
	E	29	3.20	1.80
1994	A	$ 72	$ 9.00	$ 3.00
	B	320	17.50	10.00
	C	60	3.40	.10
	D	11	.80	.12
	E	42	3.75	2.00

Calculate the dividend yield and price-earnings ratio for each stock for each of the three years. Based on your analysis of the data and the risks and rewards involved, recommend one of the five stocks for the couple to purchase.

VIDEO CASE: The Tokyo Stock Market Crash

The video case for this chapter focuses on the tremendous growth of the Tokyo Stock Exchange and its decline by almost 50 percent by the early 1990s. Reasons for this decline's failure to generate a predicted subsequent decline on Wall Street and other securities exchanges around the globe are examined. It appears on page 426 of Appendix D.

Solution to Key Terms Quiz

1. securities   2. primary market   3. investment banker
4. secondary market   5. common stock   6. preferred stock
7. secured bond   8. debenture   9. institutional investor
10. speculation   11. yield   12. stock exchange   13. National
Association of Securities Dealers Automatic Quotation (NASDAQ)
system   14. bull   15. bear   16. price-earnings ratio   17. Dow
Jones Averages   18. mutual funds   19. program trading
20. insider trading

Risk Management and Insurance

Risk is a fact of life for all of us, both individuals and businesses. Sixty-seven people died in the most recent major San Francisco earthquake. Thousands of Rwandans lost their lives in the 1994 civil war. In addition to lives, risk threatens property. Losses from flooding along the Mississippi River during 1993 included lives and billions in property damage. Similar losses occurred the following year in Alabama, Georgia, and Florida in the wake of flooding caused by a tropical storm.[1]

Risk is present in our daily lives, too. Although motor vehicle accidents resulting in death have declined from 54,633 in 1970 to 40,300 last year, it is still the fourth leading cause of death in the United States. In a typical year, over 36,000 deaths involving firearms occur; of these, almost 19,000 are suicides and just over 16,000 are homicides. The total number of murders committed using a firearm in the United States has risen sharply from 10,895 in 1988 to 15,377 in 1992.[2]

Companies also face various forms of risk each day. Employees may be injured in job-related accidents. Faulty products can lead to lawsuits and lost business. Changing consumer tastes can turn profits into losses. Employee dishonesty can rob a firm of badly needed revenue.

If managers are to carry out their responsibilities of achieving organizational objectives, they must understand the types of risks they face and develop methods for dealing with them. One important method of dealing with risk is to shift it to specialized firms called *insurance companies.* This appendix discusses the concept of insurance in individual firms. We will begin by defining the meaning of risk.

DEFINING RISK

Risk is the *uncertainty about loss or injury.* The business firm's list of risk-filled decisions is long. The factory or warehouse faces the risk of fire, burglary, water damage, and physical deterioration. Accidents, judgments due to lawsuits, and nonpayment of bills by customers are other risks. Two major types of risk exist: speculative risk and pure risk.

In the case of **speculative risk,** the firm or individual has the *chance of making either a profit or a loss.* Purchasing shares of stock on the basis of the latest hot tip can result in profits or losses. Expansion of operations in a new market may mean higher profits or the loss of invested funds.

Pure risk, on the other hand, *involves only the chance of loss.* Automobile drivers, for example, always face the risk of accidents. Should they occur, the driv-ers (and others) may suffer financial and physical loss. If accidents do not occur, however, there is no gain. Insurance often is used to protect against the financial loss resulting from pure risk.

DEALING WITH RISK

Because risk is an unavoidable part of business, management must find ways of dealing with it. Recognition of its presence is an important first step. Once this occurs, the manager has four methods available for dealing with risk: avoiding it, reducing its frequency and/or severity, self-insuring against it, or shifting the risk to insurance companies.

Many factors must be considered in evaluating risk when conducting business at home and abroad: a nation's economic stability, social and cultural factors (such as language), available technologies, distribution systems, and government regulations. Risk is lowered in countries with stable economic, social/cultural, technological, and political/legal environments.

Avoiding Risk

Some firms are willing to take high risks for potentially high rewards, while others are unwilling to risk the costs involved in developing new and untried products. Although avoiding risk may ensure profitability, it stifles innovation and, as a result, risk-averse companies are rarely leaders in the industry.

Reducing Risk

Many types of risk can be reduced or even eliminated by removing hazards or taking preventive measures. Many companies develop safety programs to educate employees about potential hazards and the proper methods of performing certain dangerous tasks. Guard dogs and security guards offer protection from risk for many other firms. Preventive maintenance is yet another way to reduce risk.

All these actions can reduce the risk involved in business operations, but they cannot eliminate risk entirely. Most major business insurers assist their clients in avoiding or minimizing risk by offering them a thorough review prepared by their loss-prevention experts. These safety and health professionals evaluate customers' work environments and recommend procedures and equipment to help firms minimize worker injuries and property losses.

Self-Insuring Against Risk

Instead of purchasing insurance against certain kinds of pure risk, some multiplant, geographically scattered firms accumulate funds to cover possible losses. A **self-insurance fund** is a *special fund created by setting aside cash reserves on a periodic basis to be drawn upon only in the event of a financial loss resulting from the assumption of a pure risk.* The regular payments to the fund are invested in interest-bearing securities, and losses are charged to it. These funds typically are accompanied by risk-reduction programs aimed at minimizing losses.

Before the price of business insurance soared during the early years of this decade, self-insurance ac-

Risk-reduction reviews by Travelers Insurance Co.'s loss-prevention experts have helped save American business over $300 million.

counted for only 25 percent of the total insurance market. Today it accounts for over 33 percent. Self-insurance is most useful in cases where a company faces similar risks and the risks are spread over a broad geographic area.

Shifting Risk to an Insurance Company

> **THEY SAID IT**
> "To win you have to risk loss."
> Jean-Claude Killy
> (1943–   )
> French skier

Although steps can be taken to avoid or reduce risk, the most common method of dealing with it is to shift it to others in the form of **insurance**—*the process by which a firm, for a fee, agrees to pay another firm or individual a sum of money stated in a written contract when a loss occurs.* The fee the insured party pays the insurance company for coverage against losses is called a *premium.* Thus, insurance is the substitution of a small known loss—the insurance premium—for a larger unknown loss that may or may not occur. In the case of life insurance, the loss—

death—is a certainty; the uncertainty is the date of occurrence.

It is important for the insurer to understand the customer's business, risk exposure, and insurance needs. Many small- and medium-sized firms choose to do business with insurers, such as Maryland Casualty, who specialize in providing insurance coverage for companies of this size.

BASIC INSURANCE CONCEPTS

The premiums accumulated by insurance companies are designed to cover eventual loss. The returns from insurance-company investments may be used to reduce premiums, generate a profit for profit-seeking insurance companies, or both. Insurance companies represent a major source of long-term financing for other businesses.

Insurance companies are professional risk takers. For a fee, they accept the risk of loss or damage to businesses and individuals. Three basic principles operate in insurance: the concept of insurable interest, the concept of insurable risks, and the law of large numbers.

Insurable Interest

In order to purchase insurance, applicants must demonstrate that they have an **insurable interest** in the property or life of the insured. That is, *the policyholder must stand to suffer loss, financial or otherwise, due to fire, accident, death, or lawsuit*. However, for life insurance, a friend or relative may have an insurable interest even though no financial loss occurs in the event of the insured's death.

Because top managers are important assets to a firm, the corporation can purchase key executive insurance. But a business person cannot collect on insurance to cover damage to the property of competitors when no insurable interest exists. Nor can an individual purchase an insurance policy on the life of the president of the United States, since an insurable interest is not present.

Insurable Risks

Insurable risk refers to *the requirements a risk must meet in order for the insurer to provide protection against*

DID YOU KNOW?

In the Caucasus Mountains dividing Russia and Georgia, people pay their doctor as long as they remain healthy. They stop payment when they get ill.

In the Orient, two-thirds of adult males smoke. By contrast, smokers number less than 30 percent of U.S. adult males.

Product liability claims against Piper Aircraft's two-seater Cub plane have caused the company to close.

---

its occurrence. The following are five basic requirements of insurable risk:

1. The likelihood of loss should be predictable.
2. The loss should be financially measurable.
3. The loss should be fortuitous or accidental.
4. The risk should be spread over a wide geographic area.
5. The insurance company has the right to set standards for accepting risks.

Law of Large Numbers

Insurance is based on the law of averages, or statistical probability. Insurance companies have studied the occurrence of deaths, injuries, lawsuits, and all types of hazards. From their investigations, they have developed the **law of large numbers**—*a probability calculation of the likelihood of the occurrence of perils on which premiums are based*. They also use actuarial tables to predict the number of fires, automobile accidents, plane crashes, and deaths that will occur in a given year.

The following example demonstrates how we can use the law of large numbers to calculate insurance premiums. Previously collected statistical data on a small city with 50,000 homes indicates the city will experience an average of 500 fires a year, with damages totaling an average of $30,000 per occurrence. What is the minimum annual premium an insurance company would charge?

To simplify the calculations, assume the premiums charged would not produce profits or cover any of the insurance company's operating expenses. In total, the claim would be $15 million (500 homes damaged multiplied by $30,000). If these losses were spread over all 50,000 homes, each homeowner would be charged an annual premium of $300 ($15 million divided by 50,000 homes). In reality, though, the insurance company would set the premium at a higher figure to cover its operating expenses and to earn a reasonable return.

A **mortality table** is *used to predict the number of people in each age category who will die in a given year.* It is based on past experience with large numbers of male and female policyholders of different ages. Once the death rate is determined, the premiums for a life insurance policy can be calculated to provide sufficient income to pay death benefits and cover the

Mortality Tables Aid Insurers in Setting Premiums

| | | Expectation of Life in Years | | | | | Expected Deaths per 1,000 Alive at Specified Age | | | | |
| | | White | | African American | | | White | | African American | | |
Age	Total	Male	Female	Male	Female	Total	Male	Female	Male	Female
At Birth	74.9	72.3	78.9	64.9	73.4	9.99	9.55	7.47	19.19	16.26
1	74.7	72.0	78.5	65.2	73.6	0.70	0.73	0.55	1.17	0.88
5	70.8	68.1	74.6	61.4	69.8	0.30	0.30	0.23	0.54	0.40
10	65.9	63.2	69.7	56.5	64.9	0.17	0.17	0.13	0.24	0.25
15	61.0	58.3	64.8	51.6	60.0	0.64	0.85	0.38	1.07	0.38
20	56.3	53.6	59.9	47.0	55.1	1.09	1.51	0.51	2.47	0.72
25	51.6	49.0	55.0	42.7	50.4	1.19	1.57	0.52	3.22	1.13
30	46.9	44.4	50.2	38.4	45.7	1.35	1.69	0.61	4.14	1.58
35	42.2	39.8	45.4	34.3	41.1	1.73	2.05	0.82	5.91	2.30
40	37.6	35.2	40.6	30.3	36.6	2.22	2.60	1.21	7.49	3.22
45	33.0	30.7	35.8	26.5	32.2	3.17	3.65	1.95	9.54	4.39
50	28.6	26.3	31.2	22.8	28.0	4.98	5.74	3.26	13.16	6.48
55	24.4	22.2	26.8	19.4	24.0	7.96	9.57	5.37	17.62	9.77
60	20.5	18.4	22.6	16.2	20.3	12.61	15.64	8.63	25.31	15.19
65	16.9	14.9	18.7	13.4	16.9	18.72	23.60	13.17	35.26	21.26

insurance company's operating expenses. For example, insurance premiums for a 30-year-old African American male are usually greater than for a 20-year-old African American male because the number of deaths per thousand increases from 2.47 to 4.14. As the age of the insured increases, the length of expected life decreases and life insurance premiums rise. The same type of calculation also is made to determine premiums for automobile or fire insurance. The law of large numbers is the basis of all insurance premium calculations.

THEY SAID IT

"Make every decision as if you owned the whole company."

Robert Townsend (1920–) American business writer

MATCHING PREMIUMS TO DIFFERENT DEGREES OF RISK

Although insurance companies use the law of large numbers to design policies, they often divide individuals and industries into different risk categories and attempt to match premiums to the risk involved.

An example with which you may be familiar is automobile insurance. Young men often pay higher premiums for automobile insurance than young women do. While this may seem unfair, insurance statistics show there is a reason: male drivers are involved in fatal accidents 29 percent more than female drivers. Furthermore, young drivers of both sexes have more than their fair share of accidents. Drivers under age 21 account for just 7.1 percent of the nation's licensed

drivers, but they have 15 percent of all fatal accidents. Drivers aged 20 to 24 hold one-tenth of all licenses, but are involved in one of every six accidents.

SOURCES OF INSURANCE

The term **insurance company** includes both *private companies*, such as Prudential, John Hancock, State Farm, and Travelers, *and a number of public agencies that provide insurance coverage for business firms, not-for-profit organizations, and individuals.*

Public Insurance Companies

A *public insurance company* is a government agency established at the state or federal level to provide specialized insurance protection for individuals and organizations. It provides protection in such areas as job loss (unemployment insurance), work-related injuries (workers' compensation), pension plans (social security), and specialized programs ranging from flood insurance to depositor protection at commercial banks.

Unemployment Insurance Every state has an *unemployment insurance* program that assists unemployed workers by providing financial benefits, job counseling, and placement services typically for a period of

OTHER TYPES OF PUBLIC INSURANCE

- **Federal Deposit Insurance Corporation (FDIC)** and **National Credit Union Share Insurance Fund (NCUSIF)** provide insurance protection for deposits in commercial banks and credit unions.
- **Federal Housing Administration (FHA)** provides mortgage insurance to lenders as protection against possible default by home purchasers.
- **National Flood Insurance Association** protects against flooding and mud slides for properties located in flood-prone areas.

- **Federal crime insurance** is available for owners of property located in high-crime areas who might not be able to purchase such insurance from private insurance companies.
- **Federal Crop Insurance Corporation** insures farmers' crops.
- **Pension Benefit Guaranty Corporation** insures the assets of pension plans to prevent loss of retirement benefits for employees should an employer go out of business or declare bankruptcy.

26 to 39 weeks. The amounts vary depending on the worker's previous income and the state in which the worker files the claim. These insurance programs are funded by payroll taxes paid by employers.

Workers' Compensation   Under state law, employers provide *workers' compensation insurance* to guarantee payment of wages and salaries, medical-care costs, and such rehabilitation services as retraining, job placement, and vocational rehabilitation to employees who are injured on the job. Workers' compensation exists in all 50 states and Puerto Rico. Pittsburgh spends more than $20 million a year compensating municipal workers; nationwide, such costs are up 150 percent since 1980. In addition, workers' compensation provides benefits in the form of weekly payments or a single lump sum to survivors of workers who die as a result of work-related injuries. Premiums are based on the company's payroll, and rates depend on the hazards present on the job and on the employer's safety record.[3]

Social Security   The federal government is the largest insurer in the United States. Its social security program, officially titled *Old-Age, Survivors, Disability, and Health Insurance (OASDHI)*, grew out of the Social Security Act of 1935. In 1965, *Medicare*, a form of health insurance for persons 65 years or older and certain other social security recipients, was added to the OASDHI program. More than nine out of ten U.S. employees and their dependents are eligible for retirement benefits, life insurance, health insurance, and disability income insurance under this program.

Private Insurance Companies

Much of the insurance in force in the United States and other countries is provided by private insurance

companies. These companies typically are categorized by ownership: stock companies and mutual companies. Insurance companies, whether stock or mutual companies, have the objective of minimizing the premiums necessary to cover operating expenses and to pay for personal or property losses.

Both Prudential and Metropolitan—the nation's two largest insurance companies—are mutual companies.

Stock Companies The *stock insurance company* is operated for profit. Stockholders do not have to be policyholders; they invest funds in the firm by purchasing the firm's stock in order to receive dividends from earnings and/or to benefit from increases in stock prices. Profits earned by the company come from two sources: (1) insurance premiums in excess of claims and operating costs, and (2) earnings from company investments in mortgages, stocks, bonds, and real estate.

There is no clear indication that the insurance premiums of stock companies are higher than those of mutual companies. Stock companies dominate the insurance industry, with the exception of life insurance, which is controlled by mutual insurance companies.

Mutual Companies The *mutual insurance company* is a type of cooperative; it is owned by its policyholders. The mutual company is chartered by the state and governed by a board of directors elected by the policyholders. Prudential Insurance Company of America, the nation's largest insurer, is a mutual company.

Unlike the stock company, the mutual company earns no profits for its owners. Because it is a not-for-

profit organization, any surplus funds remaining after operating expenses, payment of claims, and establishment of necessary reserves are returned to the policyholders in the form of dividends or premium reductions.

TYPES OF INSURANCE

Although hundreds of insurance policies are available for purchase by individuals and businesses, we can divide them conveniently into three broad categories: (1) property and liability, (2) health, and (3) life insurance.

Property and Liability Insurance

Property and liability insurance is a general category of insurance that provides protection against a number of perils. **Property losses** are *financial losses resulting from interruption of business operations or physical damage to property as a result of fires, accidents, theft, or other destructive occurrences.* **Liability losses** are *financial losses suffered by a business firm or individual should the firm or individual be held responsible for property damage or injuries suffered by others.*

> **THEY SAID IT**
>
> "Insurance is death on the installment plan."
>
> *Philip Slater
> (1927–   )
> American author*

Solving the Property and Liability Insurance Puzzle

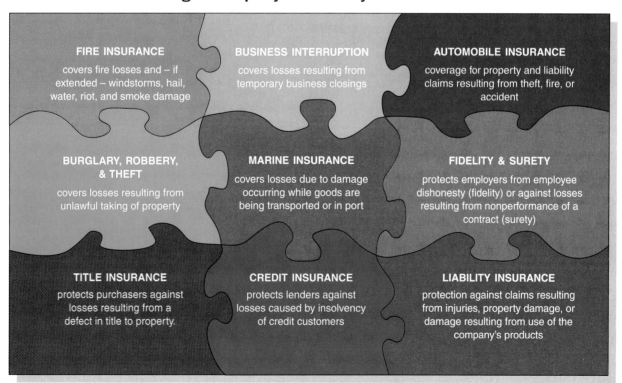

Types of Health Insurance	
Hospitalization Insurance	Health insurance designed to pay for most hospital costs.
Surgical and Medical Payments Insurance	Health insurance designed to pay the costs of surgery, fees of medical specialists, and physicians' care in the hospital during the patient's recovery.
Major Medical Insurance	Insurance that protects the insured against catastrophic financial losses by covering expenses that exceed the coverage limits of basic policies.
Dental Insurance	Insurance designed to pay a specified percentage of dental expenses.
Disability Income Insurance	Health insurance designed to protect against loss of income while the insured is disabled as a result of an accident or illness.

Health Insurance

Unfortunately, we all face the risk of getting sick or being injured in some way. To guard against this risk, one can purchase some form of **health insurance**—insurance that provides *coverage for losses due to sickness or accidents*. With soaring costs in health care, this type of insurance has become an important consideration of businesses and individuals in the late 1990s.[4]

Most businesses and not-for-profit organizations offer health and accident insurance for their employees as part of a benefit package. These *group policies* are similar to individual coverage, but are offered at a lower premium price.

Private insurance companies, such as Provident Insurance of Chattanooga, Tennessee, offer group health packages to employees. The not-for-profit Blue Cross/Blue Shield plans, which currently insure about 68 million people, are another option.

A **health maintenance organization (HMO)** is a *prepaid medical expense plan that provides a comprehensive set of health services and benefits to policyholders* for a monthly fee. It employs its own physicians and health-care specialists and often owns hospitals and clinical facilities. Among the largest HMOs are Kaiser Permanente, the Health Insurance Plan of New York, and the Group Health Cooperative of Seattle. Federal law requires employers to offer such plans to employees as an alternative to a group insurance plan in areas where HMOs are available.

The *preferred provider organization (PPO)* negotiates reduced prices from hospitals and physicians and then offers their health insurance packages to employers. Employees typically enjoy lower premiums with this type of insurance than under conventional plans.

Five major types of health insurance are available: hospitalization, surgical and medical payments, major medical, dental, and disability income insurance (see table at left).

LIFE INSURANCE

Life insurance is different from all the other types of insurance that we have discussed so far, because it deals with a risk that is certain—death. The only uncertainty is when it will occur. Life insurance is a common employee benefit in most firms because its purchase provides financial protection for the family of the policyholder and, in some instances, an additional source of retirement income for employees and their families. An immediate estate is created by the purchase of a life insurance policy. Because the need for financial security is great in most households, some 156 million people—two of every three U.S. citizens—are covered by life insurance.

The three major types of life insurance are term, whole life, and endowment (see table on the following page). A company can choose one type or a combination of them as part of its total fringe benefit package for its employees.

What Is a Life Worth?

When IBM Vice President Don Estridge was killed in a plane crash, a federal jury concluded his life was worth $7,975,000. The jury based its award on how much the man responsible for IBM's personal computer would have earned over his lifetime. The Estridge case raises the complex question of how much life insurance one should carry.

Life insurance policies can be purchased on an individual basis for almost any amount. Unlike property and liability insurance, life insurance purchases are limited only by the amount of premiums people can afford to pay, provided that purchasers qualify medically.

The average family has too little insurance to provide true financial security. While life insurance experts recommend that the average adult with family

Types of Life Insurance	
Term Insurance	Insurance that pays a death benefit if the policyholder dies within a specified period of time; it has no value at the end of that period.
Credit Life Insurance	Term insurance that repays the balance owed on a house or other major purchase if the policyholder dies.
Whole Life Insurance	Combines protection and savings for the individual who pays premiums throughout a lifetime. Policy includes a cash surrender value, which represents the savings portion of the policy.
Endowment Policy	Insurance that provides coverage for a specified period, after which the face value is refunded to the policyholder.
Variable Life Insurance	Hybrid form of whole life insurance in which policyholders can decide how to invest the cash surrender value.
Universal Life Insurance	Hybrid form of life insurance combining term insurance with a tax-deferred savings account.

responsibilities purchase insurance coverage amounting to a minimum of four to five times his or her annual salary, most people have no more than two years' protection.

Various government agencies have set widely varying values on a human life. The Department of Transportation and the Federal Aviation Administration say the figure is $1 million. The Consumer Product Safety Commission says it is $2 million. The Occupational Safety and Health Administration values human life at between $2 million and $5 million. The Environmental Protection Agency has a still broader range, from $475,000 to $8.3 million.

The death of a sole proprietor, partner, or a key executive is likely to result in financial losses to an organization. **Key executive insurance** *is life insurance designed to reimburse the organization for the loss of the services of an important executive and to cover the expenses of securing a qualified replacement.*

CHALLENGES FACING THE INSURANCE INDUSTRY

One of the principal problems facing the insurance industry today is the soaring cost of medical care. With the higher costs come higher premiums and sometimes less coverage. Obviously, the present health-care system in the United States needs to be reformed, but there is still debate over the best way to accomplish it. Some lawmakers want to make it mandatory for employers to provide health-care coverage for all workers. Others suggest having companies pay a percentage of their profits into a government-financed health plan. The Health Insurance Association of America proposes standardizing health insurance premiums by industry and the age mix of companies' employees. All insurers would contribute to a reinsurance system that would foot the bills for serious cases.[5]

Health Reform in the United States

President Clinton's health-care reform has five goals. First, basic medical coverage must be available to all Americans. Second, employers must bear a majority of employees' insurance costs. Third, the federal government will not get into the medical business. Fourth, flexibility must be given to the states to customize health programs to meet the needs of its citizens while staying within a budget. Finally, medical costs must be controlled.

At the center of the health-reform package is "managed competition" where everyone is part of a big insurance pool. These pools, representing tens of thousands of citizens, then would be strong enough to negotiate lower rates and improved benefits with doctors and hospitals. With lower rates, employers will be expected to provide basic coverage for their employees.

Physician practice standards will be established to help cut down on the litigation costs and malpractice premiums doctors pay. The standards will be generally accepted rules on how doctors should treat patients in any given circumstance. Thus, doctors would not rely on "defensive" medicine where many unnecessary tests are run to protect the doctor from malpractice suits. The estimated annual cost of defensive medicine alone is $100 billion.

Not everyone is happy at the prospect of a national health-care system. Small businesses maintain that, even with lower rates, insurance costs are still too high to provide coverage for all workers and their dependents.

Confronting the AIDS Crisis

Acquired immune deficiency syndrome (AIDS) has become a worldwide health crisis since the first cases were diagnosed. The disease also has become a crisis for the insurance industry. Nationwide, AIDS deaths account for less than two percent of all deaths, but the insurance paid to AIDS victims accounts for a higher percentage, and it continues to rise. The average size of an individual AIDS death claim for life insurance soared 44 percent in one recent year. By the end of this century—in less than five years—AIDS could account for 20 percent of all life insurance claims.

One year of medical treatment for a person with AIDS costs around $38,000; for a person with HIV, around $10,000. One drug costs $200 per dose. Private insurance companies have paid out more than $250 million in AIDS-related claims, and the number keeps rising as more cases are diagnosed.

The AIDS crisis is an example of the law of adverse selection—that is, persons with actual or potential health disabilities and those in dangerous occupations are more likely to purchase and renew health and life insurance. Research shows that most AIDS claims occur within the first two years of coverage. To protect itself against the antiselection process, insurance companies often require blood tests for the presence of the AIDS virus for people who are applying for life insurance. Application questions also may try to screen out those who belong to high-risk groups.

Numerous public protests and lawsuits resulted from the insurance industry's attempts to avoid antiselection of high-risk groups. Eighteen states prohibit insurance companies from denying AIDS benefits. AIDS testing was outlawed in the District of Columbia, where insurance companies stopped writing policies. The district has revised its law to permit the HIV antibody test, provided the applicant has consented. In California, the use of antibody tests is not permitted in determining eligibility for health insurance. However, such tests are allowed for life and disability-income insurance applications.

While the debate continues, insurance companies have adopted a variety of responses to the AIDS crisis. New York Life funded $8.5 million to AIDS research. Guardian Life discontinued coverage for hair stylists. Provident Indemnity Life limits AIDS claims on small business policies to $5,000 per year and $20,000 lifetime. By contrast, Golden Rule Insurance has a policy that offers full

coverage without AIDS testing, but it requires that the buyer remain free of AIDS symptoms during the first year the policy is in force. All of these responses suggest how the law of adverse selection plays a major role in today's insurance decisions.

SOURCES: Charles Culhand, "AIDS Costs One More Reason for Health Reform," *American Medical News,* January 11, 1993, 3; and Susan Pulliam, "Fateful AIDS Test on Magic Johnson Was for Insurance," *The Wall Street Journal,* November 8, 1991, A1, A7.

Big businesses support health-care reform, but only if it is on a national basis. If states are allowed the flexibility to change some aspects of a federal plan, some corporations could be faced with 50 sets of guidelines on required benefits packages and their respective funding. Any reform to the health-care system is bound to alienate one or more powerful interest group, such as doctors, drug companies, insurance companies, or patients.

Equal Care for All

Another important health-care issue involves delivering the same quality of care to all U.S. citizens.

A recent study found that white Medicare patients are three and one-half times more likely to have life-saving heart-bypass surgery than are African-American patients. Previous reports also have shown that minorities have less access to medical care. These studies focused on a lack of health-care insurance as the reason for the discrepancy in quality of care. The difference between surgery rates emphasizes the need to make quality medical care available to everyone who needs it. Perhaps the most surprising statistic in the U.S. insurance industry is that of the 37 million Americans without insurance, almost 4 million have family incomes of over $50,000.[6]

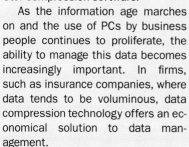

TECHNOLOGY

Data Compression

Insurance agents at Metropolitan Life loved their laptop computers. In fact, they found so many uses for them that they began to run out of storage space on their PC hard drives and asked management for more powerful—and more expensive—replacements. Faced with the expense of replacing 13,000 laptops for their field agents, Met Life managers turned to technology for the answer to their data-compression problem.

Computer files contain considerable blank space following periods, surrounding individual words, and between paragraphs. Data compression uses special mathematical formulas to compress these files. It also substitutes coded symbols in place of frequently used words. Moreover, this "shorthand" approach can be used to facilitate the transfer and storage of photographs, printed illustrations, and video by compressing the digitized images. This procedure often doubles a computer's storage capacity.

Although data compression was introduced in the mid-1980s, the software used produced numerous complaints because it resulted in slower-running programs. Today's data compression software achieves the objective of increasing computer storage capacity without compromising the computer's speed.

This technology is an economical alternative to purchasing additional storage devices. Hard drives cost about $30 per megabyte (MB) of memory. Compression software, such as DoubleDensity and Stacker 2.0, can turn a 50-MB hard drive into one that can accommodate up to 100 MB of data. Met Life agents doubled their PC capability and saved the company thousands by using Super-Stor compression software.

As the information age marches on and the use of PCs by business people continues to proliferate, the ability to manage this data becomes increasingly important. In firms, such as insurance companies, where data tends to be voluminous, data compression technology offers an economical solution to data management.

SOURCES: William J. Cook, et al., "25 Breakthroughs That Are Changing the Way We Live and Work," *U.S. News & World Report,* May 2, 1994, 46–60; Paula Rooney, "Insurance Giant Adds New Life to Its Laptops," *PC Week,* April 27, 1992, 35–36; and Patrick Marshall, "Data Control," *Inc.,* Fall 1992, 49–53.

KEY TERMS QUIZ

mortality table	law of large numbers	health maintenance organization (HMO)
liability losses	property losses	pure risk
key executive insurance	insurable risk	speculative risk
risk	insurance company	insurance
insurable interest	health insurance	self-insurance fund

_____ 1. Uncertainty about loss or injury.

_____ 2. Type of risk involving the choice of either profit or loss.

_____ 3. Type of risk involving only the chance of loss.

_____ 4. An account set up to cover losses from the assumption of pure risk.

_____ 5. Process by which an insurer, in exchange for a fee, agrees to reimburse firms or individuals for losses up to specified limits.

_____ 6. Insurance concept wherein the policyholder must stand to suffer loss.

_____ 7. Requirements a risk must meet in order for the insurer to provide protection against its occurrence.

_____ 8. Probability calculation of the likelihood of the occurrence of perils on which premiums are based.

_____ 9. Table used to predict the number of persons in each age category who will die in a given year.

_____ 10. Private companies and public agencies that provide insurance coverage for business firms, not-for-profit organizations, and individuals.

_____ 11. Financial losses resulting from interruption of business operations or physical damage to property as a result of fires, accidents, windstorms, theft, or other destructive occurrences.

_____ 12. Financial losses suffered by a business firm or individual should the firm or individual be held responsible for property damage or injuries suffered by others.

_____ 13. Insurance designed to provide coverage for losses due to sickness or accidents.

_____ 14. Prepaid medical expense plan that provides a comprehensive set of health services.

_____ 15. Life insurance designed to compensate the organization for loss of an important executive.

ASSIGNMENTS

1. Differentiate between speculative and pure risk.
2. Identify and give an example of each of the four methods of dealing with risk.
3. Outline the three basic principles of insurance. What requirements are necessary for an insurable risk?
4. Define the major types of property and liability, health, and life insurance.
5. What are the benefits of group insurance plans to the employee? To the employer?

VIDEO CASE A: Insurance Risks

This video case discusses how lack of insurance availability can damage research on new, untried drugs—even extremely promising ones. It appears on page 426 of Appendix D.

Solution to Key Terms Quiz

1. risk 2. speculative risk 3. pure risk 4. self-insurance fund 5. insurance 6. insurable interest 7. insurable risk 8. law of large numbers 9. mortality table 10. insurance company 11. property losses 12. liability losses 13. health insurance 14. health maintenance organization (HMO) 15. key executive insurance

APPENDIX B

Fundamentals of Business Law

What is Delaware's Chancery Court, and why are we starting this appendix by talking about it? The Chancery Court is small (five chancellors), busy (it hears about 1,000 cases a year), and efficient (many cases are decided in less than a week). Unlike the popular courtroom dramas you see on TV, this court (a descendant of medieval English courts) does not use juries or award money damages. Yet, this tiny court, located in Wilmington's Rodney Square, is quietly setting many precedents for the business world. Landmark cases decided there determine how major firms—Paramount Communications, Viacom, Texas Instruments, QVC, Revlon—conduct their corporate affairs. Delaware's governor says the Chancery Court "has become America's corporate battleground."

The reason for the court's importance is simple: almost 50 percent of the companies listed on the New York Stock Exchange are incorporated in Delaware. As early as 1913, many firms, attracted by Delaware's lower corporate taxes, began relocating from New Jersey. Another draw is the fact that Delaware updates its corporation laws on a regular basis. The Corporate Law Council, with members drawn from many of the state's largest law firms, periodically reviews trends in corporate law and recommends changes.

Yet another plus is Delaware's Division of Corporations, which has been quick to adopt new technologies and add extra services. For instance, the division uses a computerized imaging system to store pictures of all documents, even envelopes; it also maintains a 4 P.M.-to-midnight shift to process documents and assist West Coast companies that need help after the close of business hours on the East Coast.

Perhaps the main reason why many firms choose to incorporate in Delaware, however, is the Chancery Court itself, a 200-year-old institution that specializes in issues related to corporate governance. "The Delaware Chancery Court is a well-respected court," says attorney David King. "The judges are especially conversant in business. . . . A judge is not hearing a divorce or custody case in the morning before moving on to a big takeover case in the afternoon."

A growing trend in Chancery Court decisions has been to favor the rights of corporate shareholders. This approach to business law emphasizes that a company is obligated to get the best deal possible for those who own stock in it. In some cases, for example, the court has forced company directors to accept the highest bidder in a takeover war, even if they would prefer to sell to another. Several recent takeover verdicts have mandated that management must choose the most profitable option if this proves to be in the shareholders' best interests.

In other cases, the court has mandated that companies must reimburse shareholders who did not receive full value for their money. One case involved Home Shopping Network, which placed a notice on shares warning that their value could decrease, depending on the outcome of pending litigation. As a result, share prices plummeted, and the company repurchased them at a cheaper rate. Bondholders complained, and the court ruled against the company. Another time, Enserch Corporation shareholders claimed that the company had failed to compensate those who exchanged Enserch Exploration Partners stock for Enserch shares; the court ordered Enserch Corporation to pay an extra $3.42 per share.

As you can see, the impact of Delaware's Chancery Court goes far beyond the boundaries of Rodney Square; the decisions made there today could affect the company where you will be working tomorrow. A knowledge of business law is crucial to business success. In this appendix, we will look at basic legal terms and concepts, and explain why they are important.[1]

IMPORTANCE OF BUSINESS LAW

One cannot conduct any type of business activity without reference to business law. All business decisions must take into account their legal consequences. Sometimes in-depth planning and review of the law are necessary; other times it is a simple matter to check the legality of a proposed action. Executives learn how to apply legal standards to their decisions in much the same manner as they develop any other business skill: through constant practice and ongoing study. If they lack the experience and judgment to determine the legality of a matter, they should consult an attorney.

Law *consists of the standards set by government and society in the form of either legislation or custom.* The broad body of principles, regulations, rules, and customs that governs the actions of all members of society, including business people, is derived from several sources. **Common law** *refers to the body of law arising out of judicial decisions related to the unwritten law the United States inherited from England.* This unwritten law is based on customs and court decisions made in early England.

Statutory law, or written law, *includes state and federal constitutions, legislative enactments, treaties of the federal government, and ordinances of local governments.* Statutes must be drawn in a precise and reasonable manner in order to be constitutional (and thus enforceable), but courts frequently are called upon to interpret the intention and meaning of the laws. The court rulings often result in statutory laws being expanded, contracted, modified, or even discarded altogether.

As U.S. investments in foreign countries grow, and as more U.S. firms form joint ventures offshore, a knowledge of international law becomes crucial. **International law** *refers to the numerous regulations governing international commerce.* These laws arise from many sources. Companies must be aware of the domestic laws of trading partners, the rules set by the international trading community, and the guidelines established by regional and international organizations.

For example, since 1970, international trade in art and cultural artifacts has been regulated by the guidelines of the United Nations Convention. The U.S. State Department and the International Institute for the Unification of Private Law are negotiating a new agreement, to be known as Unidroit (French for "one law"). Under Unidroit, it will be more difficult to transport art from its native country. Supporters of the new law hope that it will help prevent looting and smuggling of rare art works. Others oppose the law, however, because they fear it will impact negatively on the multi-million dollar international industry of art dealing.[2]

NATURE OF BUSINESS LAW

In a broad sense, all law is business law because all businesses are subject to the entire body of law, just as individuals are. But, in a narrower sense, **business law** *consists of those aspects of law that most directly influence and regulate the management of various types of business activity.* Specific laws vary widely from business to business and from industry to industry. Laws affecting small firms are different from those governing large corporations. The legal interests of the automobile industry, for example, differ from those of real-estate developers.

State and local statutes also have varying applications. Some state laws effectively regulate all businesses operating in a particular state, regardless of the size or nature of the enterprise. Workers' compensation laws, which govern payments to workers for injuries incurred on the job, are an example. Other state laws control only certain businesses or business activities. For example, states have specific licensing requirements for businesses like law firms, funeral homes, and hair styling salons. Many local ordinances also deal with specific business activities. For example, many communities regulate the size and type of signs that businesses display.

COURT SYSTEM

The **judiciary,** or court system, *is the branch of government charged with deciding disputes among parties through the application of laws.* The judiciary is comprised of several types, or levels, of courts, each with a specific jurisdiction. Court systems are organized at the federal, state, and local levels. Administrative agencies also have some limited judicial functions, but these agencies are regarded more properly as belonging to the executive or legislative branches of government.

Trial Courts

At both the federal and state levels, the **trial court**—*a court of general jurisdiction*—hears a wide range of cases. Unless a case is assigned by law to another court or to an administrative agency, a court of general jurisdiction is empowered to hear it. The majority of cases, both criminal and civil, are heard by these courts. Within the federal system, the trial courts are known as *U.S. district courts*, and at least one such court exists in each state. In state court systems, the general jurisdiction courts usually are called *circuit courts*, and in most states there is one for each county. Some states call their general jurisdiction courts by other names, such as *superior courts, common pleas courts*, or *district courts*.

The state judiciary systems also include a wide range of courts with lesser or more specific jurisdiction. These courts have limited jurisdiction in that they hear only a certain size or type of case, as set forth by statute or constitution. In most states, decisions of the lesser courts can be appealed to the general jurisdiction courts. Examples of lesser courts are *probate courts* (where deceased persons' estates are settled) and *small claims courts* (where people can represent themselves in suits involving limited amounts of damage).

Appellate Courts

Appeals from general trial courts are heard by an **appellate court,** *a process that allows a higher court to review the case and correct any lower-court error* complained of by the *appellant*, the party making the appeal. Both the federal and state systems have appellate courts. An appeal usually is filed when the losing party feels that the case was decided wrongly by the judge or jury.

The federal appeals system, together with those of most states, consists of two tiers of courts. Federal courts at the intermediate level are called *U.S. circuit courts of appeals*, which hear appeals from the U.S. district courts. The intermediate level of state appellate courts—if it exists—is known as the *court of appeals*, or the *district court of appeals*, in most states.

Appeals from the U.S. circuit courts of appeals can go to the nation's highest court, the U.S. Supreme Court. Appeals from the state court of appeals are heard by the highest court in each state, usually called the state supreme court. In states without intermediate courts, the state supreme court hears appeals directly from the trial courts. Parties not satisfied by the verdict of a state supreme court can appeal to the U.S. Supreme Court and may be granted a hearing if grounds for such an appeal exist, and if the Supreme Court considers the case significant enough to be heard.

It is unusual for a case to go all the way to the Supreme Court; in an average year, the Court may hear less than 200 of the thousands of cases that are filed. One business case that did end up there involved two rival Mexican-food restaurant chains in San Antonio. When the Two Pesos chain began building restaurants that were nearly identical to Taco Cabana outlets, Richard Cervera, president of Taco Cabana, sued. The two companies fought the issue all the way to the Supreme Court, which ruled against Two Pesos; its management was told to pay Taco Cabana $3.7 million in damages and redesign its restaurants. Cervera took the money and then proposed a novel solution: he offered to buy out the Two Pesos chain and assume its debts. The Two Pesos managers accepted his offer and, no doubt, are glad they did; the Taco Cabana stock they received as part of the deal has risen almost 60 percent since the acquisition.[3]

While the great majority of cases are resolved by the system of courts described here, certain highly specialized cases require particular expertise. Such cases are assigned to special courts by constitutional provisions or statutes. Examples of specialized federal courts are the U.S. Tax Court (for tax cases) and the U.S. Court of Claims (which hears claims against the U.S. government itself). Similar specialized courts exist at the state level.

Administrative Agencies

Administrative agencies, also known as *bureaus, commissions*, or *boards*, exist at all levels of government to decide a variety of cases. Their powers and responsibilities sometimes are derived from constitutional provisions, but usually they come from state or federal statutes. Technically, they conduct hearings or inquiries rather than trials. The opposing parties often are represented by attorneys, evidence and testimony are included, and the agency issues legally binding decisions based on the regulations involved.

Examples of federal administrative agencies with extensive powers are the Federal Trade Commission, the National Labor Relations Board, and the Federal Energy Regulatory Commission. Examples at the state level include public utility commissions and boards that govern the licensing of various trades and professions. At the city or county level are zoning boards, planning commissions, and boards of appeal.

MAJOR COMPONENTS OF BUSINESS LAW

The cornerstones of U.S. business law are contract law; sales law; the Uniform Commercial Code; negotiable instruments; property law; the law of bailment; agency law; tort law; bankruptcy law; patents, trademarks, and copyrights; and tax law. We will discuss the key provisions of each of these legal concepts.

Contract Law

Contract law is important because it affects most aspects of a business operation. It is the legal foundation on which business dealings are conducted. A **contract** *is a legally enforceable agreement between two or more parties regarding a specified act or thing.*

Contract Requirements

The four elements of an enforceable contract are agreement, consideration, legal and serious purpose, and capacity. There must be an *agreement* among the parties as to the act or thing specified. In order for such an agreement, or contract, to be valid and legally enforceable, *consideration*—the value or benefit that a party provides to the others with whom the contract is made—must be furnished by each party to the contract. Legal consideration for a contract exists when, for example, A agrees to work for B, and B agrees to pay A a stated salary. The contract is just as valid if B actually pays A at the time A agrees to work. Similarly, valid consideration exists even if no promises are exchanged but A works for B, and B pays A for the work.

In addition to consideration, an enforceable contract must involve a *legal and serious purpose.* Agreements made in a joking manner, related to purely social matters, or involving the commission of a crime are not enforceable as legal contracts. An agreement between two competitors to fix the prices for their products is not enforceable as a contract because the subject matter is illegal and carrying out the agreement would violate the law.

The last element of a legally enforceable contract is *capacity*, the legal ability of a party to enter into agreements. The law does not permit certain persons, such as those judged to be insane, to enter into legally enforceable contracts.

Contracts are used in almost all types of business activities. Generally, they are created and executed by firms with minimal concern on the part of the contracting parties. Examples of valid contracts are purchase agreements with suppliers, labor contracts, group insurance policies for employees, franchise agreements, and sales contracts.

Breach of Contract

A *violation of a valid contract is called a* **breach of contract.** The injured party can go to court to enforce the contract provisions and, in some cases, collect **damages**—*financial payments made for a loss and related suffering.*

For instance, defense contractors McDonnell Douglas and General Dynamics Corporation filed suit against the Navy after it canceled its contract for a new bomber, the A-12. The military claimed that the contractors defaulted on the project by falling behind schedule and running up large cost overruns. The companies, for their part, charged that the Pentagon illegally canceled the order after withholding crucial technical information from the development team. They also claimed that they were told to proceed with the project even though Pentagon officials supposedly knew the deadlines were unrealistic. The lawsuit, which is expected to take the entire decade to resolve, probably will be the most expensive federal lawsuit of all time; overall litigation costs average $60 million a year.[4]

Sales Law

The law of sales derives from contract law, since a sales agreement, or sales transaction, is a special kind of contract that is entered into millions of times each day. **Sales law** *involves the sale of goods or services for money or on credit.* As economic transactions, sales can be of services or real estate as well as products, but the law of sales is concerned only with the transfer of tangible personal property. The law involved with intangible personal property and real estate will be examined later.

Sales law has evolved in a distinct manner. It goes back to ancient English law that consisted largely of the customs of merchants and included a system of merchant courts to resolve disputes. Many of these customs and practices were adopted in the United States as part of common law. Later, the Uniform Commercial Code provided uniformity in all commercial laws, including sales law.

Uniform Commercial Code (UCC)

The Uniform Commercial Code (UCC) is the basis for commercial law in the United States. It has been adopted by all states except Louisiana, which has adopted only part of it.[5] The UCC covers the law of sales as well as other specific areas of commercial law.

Article 2 of the UCC specifies the circumstances under which sales contracts are entered into by the seller and buyer. Ordinarily, such agreements are based on the express conduct of the parties. Under the UCC, enforceable sales contracts must also generally be in writing if products worth more than $500 are involved. The formation of the sales contract is quite flexible because certain missing terms in the written contract or other ambiguities do not keep the contract from being legally enforceable. A court will look to past dealings, commercial customs, and other standards of reasonableness to evaluate whether a legal contract exists.

These variables also will be considered by a court when either the buyer or the seller seeks to enforce his or her rights in cases where the sales contract has *not* been performed, has been only partially performed, or where performance has been defective or unsatisfactory. The UCC's remedies in such cases consist largely of monetary damages awarded to the injured party. The UCC defines the rights of the parties to have the contract specifically performed, to have it terminated, and to reclaim the goods or have a *lien*—a legal claim—placed against them.

Warranties

Article 2 of the UCC also sets forth the law of warranty for sales transactions. There are two basic types of warranties. An *express warranty* is a specific representation made by the seller regarding the product, while an *implied warranty* is one legally imposed on the seller. Generally, unless implied warranties are disclaimed by the seller in writing, they are automatically effective. Other provisions of Article 2 govern the rights of acceptance, rejection, and inspection of products by the buyer; the rights of the parties during manufacture, shipment, delivery, and passing of title to products; the legal significance of sales documents;

and the placing of the risk of loss in the event of destruction or damage to the products during manufacture, shipment, or delivery.

Negotiable Instruments

A **negotiable instrument** *is a form of commercial paper that is transferable among individuals and businesses.* The most common example of a negotiable instrument is a check; drafts, certificates of deposit, and notes also sometimes are considered negotiable instruments.

Article 3 of the UCC specifies that a negotiable instrument must be written and must

1. be signed by the maker or drawer;
2. contain an unconditional promise or order to pay a certain sum of money;
3. be payable on demand or at a definite time; and
4. be payable to order or to bearer.

Checks and other forms of commercial paper are transferred when the payee signs the back of the instrument, a procedure known as endorsement. The four kinds of endorsements described by Article 3 of the UCC include the following:

1. *Blank endorsement* consists only of the name of the payee. All that is required to make a blank endorsement is to sign the back of the instrument, which makes the check payable to the bearer. A blank

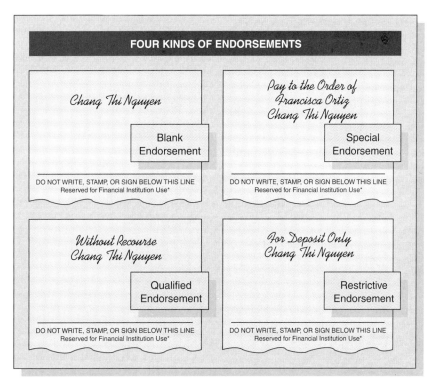

endorsement should not be used if the instrument is to be mailed.

2. *Special endorsement* specifies the person to whom the instrument is payable. With this kind of endorsement, only the person whose name appears after "Pay to the order of . . ." can profit from the instrument.

3. *Qualified endorsement* contains words stating that the endorser is not guaranteeing payment of the instrument. The qualified endorsement of "Without Recourse (signed)" limits the endorser's liability if the instrument is not backed by sufficient funds.

4. *Restrictive endorsement* limits the negotiability of the instrument. One of the most common restrictive endorsements is "For Deposit Only." It is useful if an instrument (usually a check) is lost or stolen, because it means that the instrument only can be deposited to the indicated bank account; it cannot be cashed.

Property Law

Property law is a key feature of the private enterprise system. *Property* is something for which a person or firm has the unrestricted right of possession or use. Property rights are guaranteed and protected by the U.S. Constitution.

Property can be divided into several categories. *Tangible personal property* consists of physical things, such as equipment, supplies, and delivery vehicles. *Intangible personal property* is property that most often is represented by a document or other written instrument, although it may be as vague and remote as a computer entry. You probably are familiar with certain intangible personal properties, such as checks and money orders. Others are less well known, but nonetheless are important to the businesses or individuals who own and utilize them. Examples are stocks, bonds, Treasury bills, notes, letters of credit, and warehouse receipts. Mortgages are also technically intangible personal property.

A third category of property is *real property*, or real estate. Some real-property customs have been formalized in statutes. There is also case law to guide real-property owners in their transactions and conduct. All firms have some concern with real-estate law because of the need to own or occupy the space or building where business is conducted. Some companies are created to serve these real-estate needs. Real-estate developers, builders, contractors, brokers, mortgage companies, and architects all deal with various aspects of real-property law.

Law of Bailment

The *law of bailment* is concerned with the surrender of personal property by one person to another when the property is to be returned at a later date. The person delivering the property is known as the *bailor*, and the person receiving the property is the *bailee*. Some bailments are for the benefits of the bailee, others are for the benefit of the bailor, and still others provide mutual benefit. Most courts now require that reasonable care be practiced in all bailment situations. The degree of benefit received from the bailment is used as a factor in determining whether a reasonable care standard was met.[6]

Rules exist for settling bailment disputes, which commonly arise in business settings, such as hotels, restaurants, banks, and parking lots. The law focuses on actual delivery of an item. For example, if a patron in a restaurant hangs a coat on a hook, there has been no actual delivery to the restaurant's proprietor. Therefore, the proprietor is not liable for theft or damage. On the other hand, if the restaurant has a coat-checking room and the patron receives a claim check, the coat has been delivered and the proprietor is liable for theft of, or damage to, the coat.

Law of Agency

Agency refers to *a legal relationship whereby one party, called a* principal, *appoints another party, called the* agent, *to enter into contracts with third parties in the principal's behalf.*[7] While the agency relationship can be as simple as one family member acting on behalf of another, the legal concept is most closely associated with commercial activities. All types of firms conduct business affairs through a variety of agents, such as partners, directors, corporate officers, and sales personnel.

The law of agency is based on common law principles and case decisions of state and federal courts. Relatively little agency law has been enacted into statute. The law of agency is important because the principal generally is bound by the actions of the agent.

The legal basis for holding the principal liable for acts of the agent is the Latin maxim of *respondeat superior* ("let the master answer"). In cases involving agency law, the courts must decide the rights and obligations of various parties. Generally, the principal is held liable if an agency relationship existed and the agent had some type of authority to do the wrongful act. The agent in such cases is liable to the principal for any damages caused to that person.

Law of Torts

A **tort** (French for "wrong") refers to *a civil wrong inflicted on other people or their property.*[8] The law of torts is closely related to the law of agency, because the business entity, or principal, can be held liable for the torts committed by its agents in the course of business dealings. Tort law differs from both criminal and contract law. While criminal law is concerned with crimes against the state or society, tort law deals with compensating injured persons who are the victims of noncriminal wrongs.

Types of Torts A tort may be intentional, or it may be caused by negligence. Assault, slander, libel, and fraud are examples of *intentional torts*. Businesses can become involved in such cases through the actions of both owners and employees. The security guard who roughly handles a suspected shoplifter and holds the suspect in the manager's office for questioning may be committing a tort if his or her conduct is excessive or otherwise unjustified. Under agency law, the store owner can be held liable for any damages or injury caused by the security guard.

The other major group of torts is *negligence*. This type of tort is based on careless, rather than intentional, behavior that causes injury to another person. Under agency law, businesses are held liable for the negligence of their employees or agents. The delivery truck driver who kills a pedestrian while delivering goods creates tort liability for his or her employer if the accident results from negligence.

Product Liability

An area of tort law known as **product liability** has been developed by both statutory and case law that *holds businesses liable for negligence in the design, manufacture, sale, and/or use of products.* Some states have extended the theory of tort to cover injuries caused by products regardless of whether the manufacturer is proven negligent. This legal concept is known as *strict product liability.*[9]

Some business people feel that the concept of product liability has been carried too far. For example,

product-liability lawsuits have caused many manufacturers of single piston-engine airplanes to go out of business. In 1978, U.S. companies made 17,000 light aircraft; today, only a few hundred are manufactured each year. Companies have been held liable even for old planes and obsolete designs; the average age of a plane in these suits was 22 years, and Cessna Aircraft was sued for an accident involving a 47-year-old plane of a type it no longer makes.[10] As a result, Congress passed the General Aviation Revitalization Act in 1994. This legislation limited lawsuits involving small aircraft to those less than 18 years old.[11]

Bankruptcy Law

Bankruptcy, *the legal nonpayment of financial obligations,* is a common occurrence in contemporary society. The term *bankruptcy* is derived from *banca rotta,* or "broken bench," since creditors in medieval Italy would break up the benches of merchants who did not pay their bills.[12]

Federal legislation passed in 1918 and revised several times since provides for an orderly handling of bankruptcies by the federal court system. The legal process of bankruptcy has two purposes. One is to protect creditors by providing a way to seize and distribute debtors' assets. The second goal, which is almost unique to the United States, is to protect debtors too, allowing them to make a fresh start and thus benefiting society in general.[13]

Two types of bankruptcies are recognized. Under voluntary bankruptcy, a person or firm asks to be judged bankrupt because of an inability to pay off creditors. Under involuntary bankruptcy, creditors may request that a party be judged bankrupt.

Personal Bankruptcies Two primary options are available to individuals under bankruptcy law.[14] Chapter 13 of the bankruptcy law—the wage-earner plan—allows a person to set up a three-year debt-repayment plan (the bankruptcy judge can extend the time to five years). Debtors often end up repaying only a portion of what they owe. The bankrupt party's current income is considered in determining the repayment schedule. Chapter 13 is available only if unsecured debts do not exceed $100,000 and secured debts do not exceed $350,000, although Congress is considering legislation that would raise these limits. About 70 percent of all bankruptcies, however, are resolved by the other alternative, Chapter 7, a liquidation plan under which the bankrupt person's assets are sold by a trustee and the proceeds are divided among creditors. Judges can deny the use of Chapter 7, but the initial choice of Chapter 13 does not preclude a later switch to Chapter 7.

Under Chapter 7, certain property is exempt from the claims of creditors:

1. home equity of $7,500;
2. motor vehicle equity of $1,200;
3. an amount of $200 on each personal item, such as household furnishings, clothes, and books, up to a maximum of $4,000;
4. an amount of $500 on personal property;
5. another $400 on any other property; and
6. tools of one's trade or prescribed health items up to $750.

Husbands and wives filing jointly can double the amounts noted above. Some states set different allowances than those specified in Chapter 7. Missouri, for example, exempts only $8,000. Florida offers the most liberal exemptions: its homestead law exempts up to 160 acres in rural areas and half an acre in a city. The sunshine state also exempts all wages, annuities, partnership profits, pension plans, and property owned jointly with a spouse.[15]

A third personal bankruptcy option, Chapter 12, allows farmers with debts up to $1.5 million to set up a repayment plan. This supersedes the debt limit set by Chapter 13.

Business Bankruptcies   Businesses also can go bankrupt. The specific provision under which this is done is known as Chapter 11, which allows a firm to reorganize and develop a plan to repay its debts. Chapter 11 also permits *prepackaged bankruptcies*, in which a company enters bankruptcy proceedings after obtaining most (as opposed to all) of its creditors' approval. The terms then are imposed on all creditors. Often, companies that take the "prepackaged" route can emerge from bankruptcy much sooner than those who opted for conventional bankruptcy proceedings.

Congress is considering revisions to the Chapter 11 code that would streamline the process and make it less expensive. The legislation also would raise the ceiling on personal debts from $350,000 to $1 million, which would make Chapter 11 court-approved repayment plans available to more business owners.[16]

Ironically, declaring bankruptcy under Chapter 11 may keep a company in business. Consider the Federated chain of department stores, which filed for bankruptcy after taking on too much debt. The chain's 45,000 creditors were grouped into 77 classes of debt. In 26 months, the company was reorganized into 14 units, 24 of the creditor groups received full payment, and Federated's 80,000 employees were able to keep their jobs.[17]

Trademarks, Patents, and Copyrights

Trademarks, patents, and copyrights provide legal protection for key business assets by giving a firm the exclusive right to use those assets. A **trademark** consists of *words, symbols, or other designations used by firms to identify their products.* The Lanham Act (1946) provides for federal registration of trademarks. Intel Corporation, for instance, broadens awareness of its computer chips through its "Intel Inside" logo in advertisements. When competitor Cyrix Corporation parodied the logo by using a similarly shaped logo labeled "Ditto," Intel's lawyers promptly sued Cyrix, its ad agency, and the ad agency's two partners. Ironically, the lawsuit promoted Cyrix far more effectively than its ads did. Indeed, says ad agency owner Frank Priscaro, "We were sort of worried that they wouldn't sue. We never could have generated the publicity and coverage they could generate by suing us. It probably generated $1 million worth of publicity."[18]

Oddly enough, if a product becomes too well known, this can create problems: once a trademark becomes part of everyday usage, it is no longer a legal trademark. Consider the fate of the terms *aspirin, nylon, kerosene, linoleum,* and *milk of magnesia.* All of them were once the exclusive property of their manufacturers, but have passed into common language, and now anyone can use them. Companies often attempt to forestall this by advertising that a term is actually a registered trademark. For example, the National Association of Realtors® is a federally registered trademark, and Triangle Publications Inc. has done the same for TVGUIDE®.

A **patent** *guarantees inventors exclusive rights to their invention for 17 years.* Copyrights and patents have a constitutional basis; the Constitution specifies that the federal government has the power "to promote the progress of science and useful arts by securing for limited times to authors and inventors the exclusive rights to their respective writings or discoveries." Patent owners sometimes license the use of their patents to others for a fee.

A **copyright** *protects written material,* such as this textbook, designs, cartoon illustrations, photos, computer software, and so on. Copyrights are filed with the Library of Congress. Authors or their heirs hold exclusive rights to the published or unpublished works for the author's lifetime, plus 50 years. Works for hire and anonymous or pseudonymous works receive copyright protection for a period of 75 years from the date of publication or 100 years from creation, whichever is shorter.

As firms do more business overseas, the law regarding trademarks, patents, and copyrights is growing more complex; while these protections may be registered in the United States, they may be fair game in other countries. Manufacturers in China have been known to blatantly copy foreign trademarks, brand names, and patents. Shoppers in China can buy Kongalu Corn Strips cereal in a box sporting a rooster reminiscent of Kellogg's Corn Flakes. Also available are "Cologate" toothpaste in a familiar bright-red package and "Cream Style Corn" in Del Monte-like green cans. Ray Ban sunglasses are renamed "Ran Bans," and bootleg copies of Madonna albums are sold for $1. Brand names sometimes resurface in unexpected ways; one company markets Rambo facial tissues in delicate hues of pink or blue.[19] More legal issues of this type, no doubt, will develop as business becomes increasingly global.

Tax Law

The branch of law that affects every business, employee, and consumer in the United States is tax law.

Taxes *are the assessments used to raise revenue for government units.* Federal, state, and local governments and special taxing authorities all levy taxes.

The percentage of federal taxation as a share of the United States gross domestic product (GDP) is currently about 20 percent; it has fluctuated between 18 and 20 percent since 1960. The share of GDP consumed by state and local taxes has remained stable—roughly 12 percent—since the early 1970s.[20]

How Taxes Are Levied Some taxes are paid by individuals and some by businesses. Both have a decided impact on contemporary business. Business taxes reduce profits within the firm, and personal taxes cut the disposable income that individuals can spend on the products of businesses. But governments get revenue from taxes and buy industry's goods and services. Governments also act as a transfer agent, moving tax revenue to other consumers and transferring Social Security taxes from the working population to retired or disabled persons.

Taxes can be levied on several different bases: income, sales, business receipts, property, assets, and so on. The type of tax varies from one taxing authority to the other. The individual income tax is the biggest source of revenue for the federal government. Many states rely on sales taxes. In addition to a sales tax, some cities collect a tax on earnings. Finally, community college districts often get the bulk of their revenue from real-estate or property taxes.

KEY TERMS

agency
appellate court
bankruptcy
breach of contract
business law
common law
contract

copyright
damages
international law
judiciary
law
negotiable instrument
patent

product liability
sales law
statutory law
taxes
tort
trademark
trial court

ASSIGNMENTS

1. The American Bar Association predicts that, by the middle of this decade, there will be an attorney for every 290 people in the United States. How does this ratio compare to other nations? What is the impact, both beneficial and

detrimental, of this high ratio of attorneys? Does the United States need this many lawyers?
2. The appendix referred to a case in which defense contractors McDonnell Douglas and General Dynamics

have filed suit against the Navy for canceling its contract for the A-12 bomber. The lawsuit appears likely to become the most expensive one that has ever involved the federal government. Attorneys for McDonnell Douglas and General Dynamics estimate that each company is paying $30 million a year in legal fees. The government has announced that it will not be ready to go to trial for four more years; it has hired a law firm to provide an estimated $8 million in legal support. The Justice Department has asked Congress for a budget increase to cover the cost of taking hundreds of depositions and reviewing roughly 70 million pages of classified documents. The lawsuit is expected to take the entire decade to resolve, and could result in a total bill of $1.5 billion in legal bills and interest costs.[21] Discuss the implications of this case. Do you feel that these costs are justified? How would you suggest resolving this dispute?

3. Privately owned companies are becoming more common in China. At the same time, the number of bankruptcies in that country also has grown.[22] Explain the relationship, if any, between these two facts. What purpose does bankruptcy law serve? Explain your answer.

4. Managers at U.S. software manufacturer Microsoft estimate that copyright and trademark violations in China cost the company about $30 million a year. The Motion Picture Association states that almost all laser-disk and videotape sales in China involve fakes rather than U.S.-made products. Beijing Jeep Corporation, a joint venture with Chrysler, has found more than 2,000 vehicles that are designed to resemble the Jeep Cherokee.[23] What legal steps, if any, might the United States take to protect trademarks and copyrights in China?

5. United States bankruptcy law permits bankrupt parties to retain a good deal of personal property. Discuss the concept behind this exemption.

Your Career in Business

Edward Shrager recently lost his job as the systems and financial director for an air freight company. Within a few hours, he had started his job search: he read through the help wanted ads in the newspaper, updated his resume, and scanned his rolodex for possible contacts. One day, he noticed an ad from the Boston courier company Eastern Connection, which had an opening for a director of information technology. Shrager forwarded his resume, went in for an interview, and was hired in less than two weeks.

Peg Donovan also was looking for work, so a friend sent her resume to Nike. While Donovan liked the idea of working for the athletic-shoe manufacturer, she figured there was no point in getting too excited; her credentials would, no doubt, join a paper mountain of other unsolicited resumes. But, surprise: a Nike recruiter called to invite her to an interview. Within ten days, Donovan had a new job as assistant to the corporate controller.

Terry Carroll worked full time as a computer designer while attending law school part time. When he lost his job, he immediately let his contacts know that he was looking for new work. Within 24 hours, he heard about six full-time openings, and also got leads on several free-lance assignments.

What do all these successful job-seekers have in common? They found their opportunities through computerized career services. "Electronics is changing the whole employment game," says Joyce Lain Kennedy, career consultant and author of *Electronic Job Search Revolution*, who notes that she knows of at least 30 such services, with more starting every day. Marvels Peg Donovan, "This was one of the shortest job searches I have ever had."

Computerized career services can take several different forms. Shrager, for example, logged onto his computer daily to access nine electronic bulletin boards and online services. Electronic bulletin boards allow job hunters to post messages, search for openings, and contact potential employers. Many online services, such as Prodigy, America Online, and CompuServe, offer "forums"—bulletin boards devoted to particular professions or areas of interest. Job hunters who want more information about marketing, computer consulting, or aviation—to name just a few—can take advantage of bulletin boards specializing in those fields. Most bulletin boards also include areas for posting resumes.

Electronic bulletin boards and forums can be a good place to showcase your own knowledge and to network with potential employers. Terry Carroll corresponded electronically with colleagues on CompuServe's legal forum; his contributions on copyright law led to several free-lance assignments and job offers.

Peg Donovan benefited from another computer-related trend in corporate hiring: her paper resume was scanned into a database. More companies are starting to file applicants' credentials electronically rather than stuffing them into forgotten file drawers. In the past, admits Nike employment specialist Karen Cross, "nobody ever looked at the resume files because they were just too huge." Since the company began storing resumes in a database, however, Cross can locate appropriate resumes by searching the system for job-related key terms. It takes only a few keystrokes to pull up a list of qualified applicants—one of whom happened to be Donovan.

Some firms, like Nike, maintain their own files of applicants; others contract with outside database services to match candidates with job openings. Job hunters who lack their own computer can subscribe to a service that will send updated databases on disk to employers. Subscribers to *New York Times* FasTrak, for example, pay $40 to post their resumes for six months in an employer-searched database.

Career consultants caution that job seekers should not rely solely on electronic career services. Time-tested approaches, such as advertising, requesting informational interviews, and visiting employment offices, are still crucial. In this appendix, we will discuss career strategies that will help you get the most from these and other job-hunting tools. However, computerized career services certainly can enhance your job search. Just ask Craig Baugher, director of quality for automotive products manufacturer Uniflow Corporation, who has hired several candidates he met online. Says Baugher, "I feel that anyone using [electronic] bulletin boards is already a cut above the rest. It is a great way to stand out."[1]

IMPORTANCE OF YOUR CAREER DECISION

Selecting a career may be the most important decision you will ever make. In the pages that follow, we will first examine the best way to approach career decisions and how to prepare for your first **entry-level job**—that is, *your first permanent employment after leaving school.* Then we will introduce the reader to a range of business careers by profiling five people who are performing very different kinds of jobs. Following each profile is a career section featuring employment opportunities in fields that are related to each major part of the text. In many cases, Bureau of Labor Statistics employment projections to the year 2000 also are included. You can use these sections as a starting point in evaluating your career plans.

First, you should become aware of employment projections and trends. According to the Bureau of Labor Statistics, over the next decade, the number of new jobs in every major occupational category will grow. During the same period, the number of American workers aged 25 to 34 will fall by 2.9 million men and almost 1 million women. These trends translate into exciting opportunities for those entering the work force. To quote Alan Reynolds, director of economic research at the Hudson Institute, "Young Americans will be in a strong position to enjoy rapid increases in real incomes over the next two decades."[2]

Education will improve your prospects of finding and keeping the right job. As you can see by comparing the median earnings of three groups of American adults—those who have completed high school, those with a bachelor's degree, and those who hold a master's degree—the more education you have, the more you are likely to earn. This trend holds true throughout an American's working life. In 1979, only

47 percent of the nation's best-paid workers (those in the top ten percent income bracket) had college degrees; today 64 percent of them do.[3]

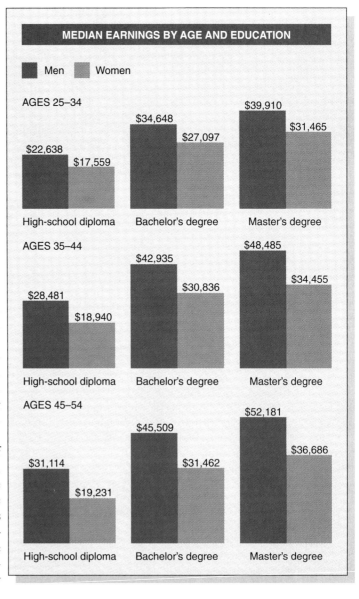

MEDIAN EARNINGS BY AGE AND EDUCATION

Men   Women

AGES 25–34

High-school diploma: $22,638 / $17,559
Bachelor's degree: $34,648 / $27,097
Master's degree: $39,910 / $31,465

AGES 35–44

High-school diploma: $28,481 / $18,940
Bachelor's degree: $42,935 / $30,836
Master's degree: $48,485 / $34,455

AGES 45–54

High-school diploma: $31,114 / $19,231
Bachelor's degree: $45,509 / $31,462
Master's degree: $52,181 / $36,686

In addition to maximizing your educational opportunities, you should try to gain related experience, either through working at a job or participating in campus organizations. Cooperative education programs, internships, or work-study programs also can give you "hands-on" experience while you pursue an education.

SELF-ASSESSMENT FOR CAREER DEVELOPMENT

You are going to spend a lot of time during your life working—so why not enjoy your job? In order to choose the line of work that is best for you, you must first understand yourself. Self-assessment can be difficult, because it involves answering some tough questions. But remember, it does pay off by helping you find a career that will be enjoyable and rewarding. The following are some of the questions you need to think about:

1. What motivates me to do something?
2. What type of lifestyle do I want?
3. What do I want to be doing in 5 years? In 10 years? In 20 years?
4. What activities do I enjoy?
5. What activities do I dislike?
6. What personal values do I hold?
7. What is my honest opinion of myself?

Here are a couple of exercises that will help you assess your skills and interests. First, make a list of 5 to 10 accomplishments that you have enjoyed the most, and of which you are the most proud. (They don't have to relate to a job; they can be volunteer work, leisure activities, hobbies, sports.) Analyze the list to see what these achievements have in common. Did they all involve working with people, for instance, to meet a common goal? Or did you work independently to achieve your own personal goals? Do most of them relate to a particular field, or involve doing certain kinds of tasks? This list can serve as a guide to show you what you enjoy doing and what talents you have.

Now, picture yourself in your dream job. Look at your work situation in this job. What are you doing? Are you surrounded by people and interacting with them, or are you working alone on your own project? Are you indoors or outdoors? What's the subject matter of your work: computers? cartoons? chromosomes?[4] There are a lot of resources available to help you choose and plan your career. They include school libraries, career guidance and placement offices,

counseling centers, and online job search services. You also may wish to talk with graduates from your school who are working in fields that interest you.

Another option is to arrange an **informational interview,** *a session designed to get more information about a company or an occupation,* rather than to apply for a job. If you are interested in a particular company, for example, perhaps you could arrange an informational interview with someone who works there to find out what it is really like. Or, if you are curious about a profession but are not sure it is for you, arrange an informational interview with someone who does that job. Find out what it really involves.

JOB SEARCH GUIDELINES

Once you have chosen a career that you feel is right for you, get your job search under way. Good entry-level positions are highly sought after, and the competition is intense. The first step is to locate available positions that interest you. Then, be resourceful! Your success depends on gathering as much information as possible. Register at your school's placement office. Establish a permanent, or credentials, file including letters of recommendation and supporting personal information. Most placement offices send out a periodic list of new job vacancies, so be sure your name and address are on their mailing list. Become familiar with the process your placement office follows to allocate limited interview slots with popular employers.

Preparing Job Placement Materials

Most placement or credentials files include the following information: (1) letters of recommendation from people who know you—instructors, employers, and others; (2) transcripts of academic work to date; (3) a personal data form reporting factual information; and (4) a statement of career goals. The placement office will provide special forms to be used in developing your placement file. Complete these forms neatly and accurately, since employers are extremely interested in your ability to communicate in writing. Keep a copy of the final file for later use in preparing similar information for other employment sources. Check back with the placement office to make sure your file is in order.

Letters of reference are very important. Be selective in securing recommendations, and try to include a business instructor in your list of references. Always ask people personally if they will write a letter of recommendation for you. Be prepared to give them a brief outline of your academic preparation along with information concerning your job preferences and career objectives. This will help them prepare the letter and may enable them to respond quickly. But remember that these people are usually busy. Allow them enough time to prepare their reference letters, then follow up on missing ones.

Finding Employment Sources

The next step—identifying job openings—involves seeking out additional job sources, such as educational placement offices, private and public employment agencies, and computer services.

Educational Placement Offices   Your school placement office is a good place to begin. If you have completed formal academic course work with more than one school, check with each of them about setting up a placement file. Some colleges have an agreement that permits a student who has completed course work at several different schools to establish a file with each placement office.

Private Employment Agencies   Other useful sources to consider are private employment agencies. These firms, which often specialize in certain types of jobs, perform several services for both employers and job candidates that are not provided elsewhere. For example, some private agencies interview, test, and screen job applicants.

Private employment agencies usually charge the prospective employer a fee for finding a suitable employee. In some cases, the job seeker is expected to pay a fee. Be sure you understand the terms of any agreement you sign with a private employment agency.

State Employment Offices   Still another source of job leads is the employment offices of your state. However, in many states, these public agencies process unemployment compensation along with other related work. Because of the mix of duties, some people view state employment agencies as providing services for semiskilled or unskilled workers. But these agencies also list jobs in many professional categories.

Computer Services   As we saw in the opening story to this appendix, online job services include electronic bulletin boards, job banks, and database services that distribute applicants' resumes on disk to

---

COMPUTER SERVICES THAT CAN HELP WITH YOUR JOB SEARCH

Prodigy (800) 776-3449. $14.95 monthly plus $3.60 an hour after first two hours of bulletin-board use. Speed: up to 9,600 bits.*

Compuserve (800) 848-8199. $8.95 monthly plus charge for forum use: $4.80 an hour for up to 2,400 bits, $9.60 an hour for 9,600 or 14,400 bits.

America Online (800) 827-6364. $9.95 monthly plus $3.50 an hour after first five hours. Speed: up to 9,600 bits.

Contractors Exchange (415) 334-0733 voice, (415) 334-7393 modem. Speed: up to 2,400 bits. Free.

FedWorld (703) 487-4608 voice, (703) 321-8020 modem. Speed: up to 9,600 bits. Free.

Internet Through many companies and local universities free or through "gateway" services like Delphi (800/695-4005). One Delphi package costs $10 a month plus $3 a month to access the Internet and $4 an hour after the first four hours. America Online and CompuServe plan access to the Internet.

Online Career Center Through Internet.

Help Wanted–USA Through Internet and America Online.

Online Opportunities (215) 873-2168 voice, (215) 873-7170 modem. Speed: up to 14,400 bits. Free. Two months of Help Wanted–USA, $20.

New York Times FasTrak (800) 340-5627.

University ProNet (800) 726-0280.

Career Database (508) 487-2238.

*Refers to modem speeds in bits per second.

---

potential employers. Before signing up for a service, find out how many companies subscribe to it; it may be a good idea to use more than one.[5]

Other Sources   A variety of other sources can help in identifying job openings. They include (1) newspaper employment advertisements (the Sunday edition of metropolitan newspapers is often a rich source of job leads); (2) trade journals or magazines; (3) college instructors and administrators; (4) community organizations, such as the local chamber of commerce; and (5) family and friends.

Another approach is to identify all the organizations where you think you might like to work. Mail a letter of inquiry and your resume to these companies. If possible, direct your mailings to a specific person who has the authority to hire new employees. The letter should ask briefly about employment opportunities in a particular line of work. It also should request a personal interview.

WRITING A RESUME

Regardless of how you identify job openings, you must learn how to develop and use a **resume,** *a written summary of your personal, educational, and professional achievements.* The resume is a very personal document covering your educational background, work experience, career preference, major interests, and other information. It must include such basic information as your address and telephone number.

The primary purpose of a job resume is to highlight your qualifications, usually on one page. An attractive layout facilitates the employer's review of your qualifications. The following figures illustrate traditional resumes using chronological, functional, and results-oriented formats.

There are several ways to prepare a resume. Some use narrative sentences to explain job duties and career goals; others are in outline form. If the job resume is being sent with a credentials file, the resume can be quite short. Remember, too, that it should be designed around your own needs and objectives.

If you use a computer service in your job search, you may want to create a resume that can be scanned and sent electronically to prospective employers. The figure summarizes tips for creating an effective electronic resume.

TIPS FOR WRITING AN EFFECTIVE ELECTRONIC RESUME

1   Scan from an original resume printed on a letter-quality printer, rather than from a photocopy.
2   Use standard-sized paper (8-1/2 x 11 inches) and don't fold the resume, since words printed in a crease will not scan well.
3   Print on white or beige paper, rather than darker colors, to maximize the contrast between letters and background.
4   Use 12-point type or larger; smaller print may not scan correctly.
5   Avoid unusual typefaces, underlining, and decorative graphics.
6   Avoid double columns, since scanners read from left to right.
7   Include jargon appropriate to your profession, since a computer search of resumes often targets key terms.

STUDYING EMPLOYMENT OPPORTUNITIES

You should carefully study the various employment opportunities you have found. Obviously, you will like some more than others, but you should consider each of the following factors when assessing each job possibilities: (1) actual job responsibilities, (2) industry characteristics, (3) nature of the organization, (4) geographic locations, (5) salary and advancement opportunities, and (6) the job's contribution to your long-run career objectives.

Too many graduates consider only the most striking features of a job, perhaps the location or the salary. However, a comprehensive review of job openings should provide a balanced perspective of the overall employment opportunity, including long-run as well as short-run factors.

THE JOB INTERVIEW

The first objective of your job search is to obtain an appointment for an interview with prospective employers. Once you have the appointment, begin planning for the interview. You will want to enter the interview equipped with a good understanding of the company, its industry, and its competition. Prepare yourself by researching the following essential information about the company:

How was the company founded?
What is its current position in the industry?
What is its financial status?
In which markets does it compete?
How is the firm organized?
Who are its competitors?
How many people does it employ?
Where are its plants and offices located?

This information is useful in several ways. First, it helps give you a feeling of confidence during the interview. Second, it can keep you from making an unwise employment decision. Third, it can impress interviewers, who often try to determine how much applicants know about the company as a way of evaluating their interest level. Candidates who do not make the effort to obtain such information often are eliminated from further consideration.

Where do you get this pre-interview information? First, your school placement office or employment agency should have information on prospective employers. Business instructors at your school also may

Chronological Resume

Beatrice Conner
4256 Pinebluff Lane
Cleveland, Ohio 44120
216-555-3296

OBJECTIVE

Challenging office management position in a results-oriented company where my organizing and people skills can be applied, leading to an operations management position.

WORK EXPERIENCE

1987–Present ADM Distribution Enterprises, Cleveland, Ohio

Office Manager of leading regional soft-drink bottler. Coordinating all bookkeeping, correspondence, scheduling of 12-truck fleet service to 300 customers, promotional mailings, and personnel records, including payroll. Installing computerized systems.

1985–1987 Merriweather, Hicks & Bradshaw Attorneys, Columbus, Ohio

Office Supervisor and Executive Secretary for Douglas H. Bradshaw, Managing Partner. Supervising four clerical workers and two paraprofessionals. Automating legal research and correspondence functions, improving filing and dictation systems, and assisting in coordinating outside services and relations with other firms and agencies. From Secretary, promoted three times in one year to Office Supervisor.

1981–1985 Conner & Sons Custom Coverings, Cleveland, Ohio

Secretary in father's upholstery and awning company. Performing all office functions over the years, running the office when the manager was on vacation.

EDUCATION

Mill Valley High School, Honors, Certificate 1984

McBundy Community College, Office Management, Automated Office Systems, Associate Degree 1986

Telecom Systems, Word Processing Seminar Series, Certificate 1987

PERSONAL

Member of various professional associations; avid reader; enjoy sports, such as camping, cycling, scuba diving, skiing; enjoy volunteering in community projects.

Functional Resume

Antonio Alvarez
Two Seaside Drive
Los Angeles, CA 90026
213-555-7092

OBJECTIVE
Joining a cohesive team effort in county government that has a positive impact on the quality of life in constituent communities, particularly in terms of traffic management and control.

EXPERIENCE

Administration
Coordinating multi-level projects within fixed time frame and budget restrictions; maintaining smooth and frequent communications under adverse conditions of competing political party interference; sustaining loyalty throughout.

Planning
Preparing strategic, long- and intermediate-range plans using latest computer models; gaining participation and commitment of all key groups in planning processes; establishing reporting points and methods for all milestones in statewide political campaign; integrating planning for financial, strategic actions, capital items, and breaking issues on an ongoing basis.

Problem Solving
Writing position papers for contingencies and for direct appeal in State Representative campaign; facilitating 50 discussion groups to reach consensus; contributing to strategy sessions on three campaigns; and four months of coordinating community traffic pattern hearings.

Leadership
Acting as a spokesperson with print and broadcast media and grassroots elements; establishing focus on common issues bringing differing factions together; setting standards and models for operating in various environments.

Traffic Management
Establishing computer-based modeling capability for 10,000 residents in a community traffic-control project; assisting in implementing a three-tiered measuring system for tracking inbound traffic volume in a high-risk neighborhood; submitting three proposals, now under consideration, for traffic reform in targeted communities.

WORK HISTORY
1988–Present	Valley Systems Research Co.
1988	Whittier Community Traffic Study Project
1987–1988	Federal Traffic Studies Grant
1982–1987	Part-time staff of four political campaigns
1978–1982	U.S. Navy Lieutenant

EDUCATION
Currently enrolled	UCLA mid-program, M.S. Communications
1986	University of Oregon, B.S. Political Science
1982	Loma Linda Junior College, A.S. Journalism

PERSONAL
Held various leadership positions in school and in community action groups. Special recognition for five years' work on city and college task forces. U.S. Navy reservist.

Results-Oriented Resume

T. L. Janecek
3609 N.W. 57th Street
St. Louis, MO 63166
314-555-2394

OBJECTIVE

To apply my expertise as a construction foreman to a management role in an organization seeking improvements in overall production, long-term employee relationships, and the ability to attract top talent from the construction field.

EXPERIENCE

DAL Construction Company, St. Louis, Missouri, 1989–Present
   Established automated on-site record-keeping system, improving communications and morale between field and office, saving 400 work hours per year, and reducing the number of accounting errors by 20 percent. As foreman, developed a crew selected as "first-choice crew" by most workers wanting transfers. Completed five housing projects ahead of deadline and under budget.

St. Louis County Housing Authority, St. Louis, Missouri, 1987–1988, Summers
   Created friendly, productive atmosphere among workers enabling first on-time job completion in four years and one-half usual materials waste. Initiated pilot materials delivery program with potential savings of 3.5 percent of yearly maintenance budget.

Jackson County Housing Authority, Kansas City, Missouri, 1986
   Produced information pamphlet, increasing applications for county housing by 22 percent. Introduced labor–management discussion techniques, saving jobs and over $21,000 in lost time.

Carnegie Brothers Construction Company, West Palm Beach, Florida, 1984–1985
   Introduced expediting methods, saving five percent of overhead cost on all jobs and attracting a new $1.6 million client. Cut new worker orientation time in half and on-site accidents by one-fourth through training and by modeling desired behavior.

Payton, Durnbell & Associates Architects, Kansas City, Kansas, 1983
   Developed and monitored productivity improvements, saving 60 percent on information-transfer costs for firm's 12 largest jobs.

EDUCATION

1988–1989   Washington University, B.S. English
1986–1987   Central State Missouri State University, English Major

PERSONAL

Highly self-motivated manager. Single and willing to relocate. Avid reader and writer.

provide tips. Your school or community library should have various references to help you investigate a firm, or you can write directly to a company. Many firms publish career brochures as well as annual reports. Finally, ask friends and relatives for input. Often they, or someone they know, may have had experience with the company.

There are two main reasons for poor performance in an interview. Interviewers report that many students fail due to ineffective communication, either because of inadequate preparation for the interview or a lack of confidence. Remember that the interviewer first will determine whether you can communicate effectively. You should be specific in answering and asking questions and should clearly and positively express your concerns. The questions interviewers ask most often include the following:

Why do you want this job?
Where do you see yourself ten years from now?
What are your strengths?
What are your weaknesses?
Why should I hire you?

It is important to know who is doing the interviewing and who will make the final hiring decision. Most people who conduct initial job interviews work in the firm's human resources division. They are in staff positions, which means that they can make recommendations to other managers about which individuals should be employed. Generally, line managers get involved in interviewing later in the hiring process. In some instances, the decision is made by human resources personnel and the immediate supervisor of the prospective employee. More likely, it is made entirely by the immediate supervisor. Rarely does the human resources department have sole hiring authority for professional jobs.

A typical format is the **open-ended interview** *in which the interviewer does not talk much, forcing you to talk about yourself and your goals.* If you appear unorganized, the interviewer may eliminate you on that basis alone. When faced with this type of situation, be sure to express your thoughts clearly and keep the conversation on target. Talk for about ten minutes, then ask some specific questions of the interviewer. (Come prepared with questions to ask!) Listen carefully to the responses. Remember that if you are prepared for a job interview, it will involve a mutual exchange of information.

If you do well in the first interview, you probably will be invited to come back for another interview. Sometimes you will be asked to take a battery of tests. Most students do very well on these tests because they have had plenty of practice in college!

THE EMPLOYMENT DECISION

By this time, the employer knows a lot about you from your placement file, resume, and first interview. You, in turn, should know a lot about the company. The primary purpose of further interviews is to determine whether you can work effectively within the organization.

If you create a positive impression during your second or later interviews, you may be offered a job. Again, your decision to accept the offer should depend on how well the career opportunity matches your career objectives. Make the best entry-level job decision you can, and learn from it. Learn your job responsibilities as quickly and thoroughly as possible; then start looking for other ways to improve your performance and that of your employer.

THE NONTRADITIONAL STUDENT

Once, it seemed as if colleges and universities served a market of mostly 18- to 22-year-olds. It was this age group that primarily sought to break into the job market. Times certainly have changed. *More people are returning to school to obtain their degrees, and more people who already have college degrees are returning for more education—these students often are referred to as* **nontraditional students.** Although the term is used to define any student who does not fit into the 18- to 22-year-old age group (the "traditional" clients of higher education), it is actually inaccurate, since older students have become the norm on many campuses. In any case, nontraditional students have two other characteristics: they work, either full time or part time; and college is often only one of their daily responsibilities. Many are married, and many, regardless of marital status, have children.

Most nontraditional students come from one of the following groups:

1. The **displaced homemaker**—*a full-time homemaker who returns to school or joins the work force because of divorce, widowhood, or economic reasons.*
2. The military service veteran—another major segment of nontraditional students, many of whom lack practical job skills.
3. The **technologically displaced worker**—*one whose job was lost to automation or industry cutbacks.* Recently, some middle- and upper-level managers have joined the ranks of displaced workers as their companies cut costs by eliminating their jobs.[6]
4. The older full-time employee—one who seeks additional education to enhance career prospects or for personal satisfaction.

Challenges Faced by Nontraditional Students

Nontraditional students often face challenges that are different from those encountered by younger students. One is scheduling; often, older students must juggle the responsibilities of work, school, and family. Studying may have to be done at odd times: during meals, while commuting, or after the kids have gone to bed. Another challenge is that nontraditional students may be trying to change careers. This means that they must learn skills in a different field, as well as work toward breaking into that field with a new job.

But take heart—nontraditional students also have a very important advantage going for them: experience. Even if it is in an unrelated field, experience is a plus. Older students know how organizations operate. Often they have developed useful skills in human relations, management, budgeting, and communications. And often, through observing other people's mistakes (and learning from their own!), they know what *not* to do.

Like other students, nontraditional students need to assess their accomplishments, skills, likes, and dislikes. The same exercises and resources that we suggested earlier can help both traditional and older students assess their strengths and determine their career goals.

YOUR CAREER: A LONG-RANGE VIEW

Throughout your career, it is important to stay flexible and continue learning; challenging new skills will be required of managers and other business people during the next decade. Remain open to unexpected changes and opportunities that can help you learn and develop new skills. "Don't get into this 1950s 'I am going to stay here forever' mindset," advises executive recruiter Kenneth Kelley. "In the next 20 or 30 years, you may have three different positions." Develop work skills that will transfer easily from one job to the next, such as computer literacy and good communication skills.

Jonathan Webb, for example, earned a bachelor's degree in banking and finance at Morehouse University and obtained an entry-level position as a securities analyst. He wanted to move into a sales position, however, so he took classes in investment banking and began selling securities to institutional investors, such as banks and insurance companies. Today, Webb is a vice president of regional institutional sales at a major brokerage division, and he appreciates the importance of

learning a wide variety of work skills. "If you work as a lending officer, you have to prepare a lot of numbers and sell it internally first so your client outside is not misled," he explains. "You need strong communication and sales skills."[7]

The most important skill to learn may be just that: the ability to learn. James Challenger, an outplacement consultant in Chicago, notes that employers want workers who can collect and analyze both verbal and numerical information. His advice to students is, "Study what you like, and learn to think." Lew Shumaker, manager of college relations for Du Pont, emphasizes the importance of flexibility and the talent to function well in a culturally diverse work place. "Over the past few years, 60 percent of our new hires have been women or members of minority groups," says Shumaker. "So we are looking for graduates who have shown that they value those who are different from themselves."[8]

A FINAL NOTE . . . THE AUTHORS' VIEW

We believe that choosing a career is one of the most important decisions you ever will make. Choosing wisely and staying open to new opportunities can help make it a happy decision, too. Just imagine the satisfaction of getting paid to do something you enjoy doing!

Do not procrastinate or trust others to make this decision for you. Follow the steps outlined here and in other sources, and make your own decision. Your instructors, parents, friends, and advisors will be willing to help in a multitude of ways. But, in the end, the bottom line is that it is your own decision.

We hope this textbook has presented a panorama of career options for you. And, whatever your decision, be sure it is right for you. As the old saying goes, "You pass this way only once." Enjoy!

In the rest of this appendix, we will present five career profiles and a selection of possible jobs related to the themes of the five major parts of the book.

PART ONE: CAREERS IN BUSINESS

Some specific jobs related to Part One of the text are discussed here. The Bureau of Labor Statistics estimates that the demand for managers and statisticians will grow about as fast as the average for all occupations, while the demand for economists of all kinds will grow faster than average, primarily in business rather than in academic settings.

PART ONE CAREER PROFILE: VERONICA FREKAUTSANU

Veronica Frekautsanu was born and raised in Moldova, a former republic in the Soviet Union. "Since I grew up under a communist regime, I always wondered what it was that produced all of these items and kept everything running in a free-market economy," she recalls. "To me the free-market economy was a big secret, but I wanted to learn the answer."

Veronica first came to the United States as an exchange student in high school, and later won a scholarship to the University of Alaska Anchorage. She plans to graduate with a bachelor's degree in business administration, majoring in finance with an international emphasis.

"It's very important to understand international business and finance," she emphasizes. "Students have to know how other cultures and legal systems operate. American companies want to diversify into foreign markets to minimize their risk, but if they don't know the markets they're going into, they

may end up losing more than if they had stayed home." She cites cereal as an example: "In the United States, people eat cereal for breakfast. But in Europe, they use cereal to feed animals. Imagine how these people feel when an American company tries to sell them cereal for themselves!"

Veronica enjoys applying what she learns in her business classes; in a recent internship, she implemented a new computerized system for the university library's accounting department. After graduation, she plans to earn a master's degree in business administration and learn more, she says, "about all aspects of business."

"Success comes from knowledge," she explains. "The more you learn, the more powerful you become. It's important to go to college, learn, and apply that knowledge."

SOURCE: Telephone interview with Veronica Frekautsanu, September 3, 1994.

ECONOMISTS

Economists often conduct research that will assist managerial decision making. They are employed in the private, public, and non-profit sectors. Academic preparation in economic theory and research methodology is necessary. Recent employment statistics reveal that 36,000 economists work in the United States alone.

Job Description

Economists study the ways a society uses scarce resources (land, labor, raw materials, machinery) to produce goods and services. They research subjects such as comparative wage rates, the impact of economic factors on consumer demand, and the balance of trade. Their findings are reported to the management of corporations, banks, trade associations, labor unions, government departments, and others.

Career Path

Junior-level economists assist senior-level personnel in their research. Advancement to the ranks of top management is possible.

Salary

Median annual earnings average $41,200.[9]

INSPECTORS AND COMPLIANCE OFFICERS

Inspectors and compliance officers are responsible for enforcing the rules and regulations that protect the public in such matters as health, safety, trade, and immigration. Recently, 130,000 people were employed as inspectors and compliance officers.

Job Description

Health inspectors work in the areas of consumer safety, food, agricultural quarantine, and environmental health. Regulatory officers work in the areas of immigration; customs; postal service; aviation safety; railroads; motor vehicles; occupational safety and health; mines; wage and hour compliance; and alcohol, tobacco, and firearms. Agricultural quarantine officers inspect shipments and people entering the country in order to protect U.S. farming industries. Immigration officers examine those seeking to enter the United States. Customs officers enforce the various laws and taxes dealing with exports and imports.

Career Path

Because their functions are so diverse, qualifications for these jobs differ greatly. A qualifying exam generally is required. Successful candidates receive on-the-job training. A career ladder with regular promotions is available to all employees.

Salary

Entry level salaries vary according to the activity involved. The national median salary is $26,700; the federal average varies greatly, from $20,100 to $55,800.

INDUSTRIAL DEVELOPMENT SPECIALISTS

Most industrial development specialists are state government employees, but a few industrial development specialists also work for utility companies. The aim of industrial development is to create jobs and increase the tax base of a state.

Job Description

These specialists work with businesses in an attempt to persuade them to locate within a state. They work with the state's tax department to provide corporate tax incentives and with other government agencies to provide adequate facilities for offices and plants. Industrial development specialists, especially in high-tech companies, also seek the cooperation of educational institutions, which can offer businesses qualified employees.

Career Path

Industrial development specialists often gain experience working in state commerce department offices. They must have a strong background in finance as well as strong negotiating skills.

Salary

Salaries vary from state to state and with levels of experience.

IMPORT-EXPORT SPECIALISTS

Import-export specialists plan and supervise the flow of products to and from other nations. They are important contributors to international businesses.

Job Description

Import-export specialists deal with various aspects of international trade; domestic customers and shippers, such as international freight haulers; and shipping, receiving, and billing activities. They are also responsible for compliance with the various legal requirements of international trade.

Career Path

Entry-level employees assist import-export managers in performing their functions. Import-export managers are usually middle-management positions reporting to an international manager.

Salary

Salaries for import-export specialists vary according to the responsibilities of the specific position, and among companies and industries. Average starting salaries fall between $20,000 and $25,000; with experienced managers earning over $37,000.

INTERNATIONAL EXECUTIVES

Companies often set up a separate international unit to handle overseas affairs. International executives manage this unit and oversee its operations.

Job Description

The exact job requirements for international management positions vary from firm to firm. These people perform all the tasks expected of other managers at their particular level.

Career Path

International managers can be drawn from any department in an organization. They must be knowledgeable in international marketing, finance, law, and production. There are various levels of international management, usually ranging from middle management to top management. Many companies believe all candidates for top management slots should have international experience.

Salary

Salaries of international managers vary by company and industry.

LOBBYISTS

Large firms with important interests in local, state, or federal laws hire lobbyists to represent their positions. Lobbyists are typically attorneys or have backgrounds in public relations.

Job Description

Lobbyists must monitor legal developments and legislative developments that affect their clients. Most of their work is done when the relevant legislative body is in session. They keep legislators up-to-date on their clients' interests and needs and provide them with the information to justify positions, such as studies and research reports. They have formal and informal contacts with legislators and work to build relationships with those most important to their clients' interests.

Career Path

Many lobbyists start with a public relations firm, which handles the public affairs of a number of firms. Others are attorneys with law firms that represent clients with interests in pending legislation. They begin by doing research or handling smaller issues. With experience, they take on larger and more important clients. Top lobbyists often start their own firms.

Salary

Earnings vary widely according to the size and number of clients. Successful lobbyists average $91,300 annually.[10]

PART TWO CAREER PROFILE: MICHAEL BIELINSKI

Notice the cover of this textbook? This graphic, which incorporates a hidden three-dimensional image, is the product of a small Texas-based firm called NVision Grafix. And NVision Grafix is the product of two friends, Michael Bielinski and Paul Herber, who met while attending the University of Texas at Arlington. Mike graduated with a B.S. in computer science engineering and a B.A. in Russian studies and went to work as a software engineer. After college, he and Paul kept in touch, and they decided to start their own company in 1992. "Paul talked me into it," recalls Mike. "We developed computer software that could take input data and arrange it into abstract patterns. The basic technology has been around since the 1970s, but no one saw its potential as an art form. Paul said, 'Let's give this a try.'"

The pair began by creating posters, but soon expanded into calendars, prints, postcards, a book, and a computer screensaver. Their distinctive artwork was an immediate success, and, within seven months, both Mike and Paul quit their engineering jobs to concentrate full time on NVision. Today, the firm has about 25 employees, and it continues to expand into advertising, promotions, and other types of graphic art. Successful promotions have included such well-known brands as Budweiser, Zima, and Cap'n Crunch cereal.

NVision now has expanded overseas; its products are sold in over 50 countries. "Our images appeal to a wide range of cultures," notes Mike, "so we rarely change our designs to fit foreign markets. We do adjust our sizing, however; we have to sell in metric sizes, and some people, like the Japanese, prefer smaller-sized prints. We form strategic alliances with local distributors, because they're much more familiar with their markets than we are."

What does Mike like most about running his own business? "The constant challenge," he says promptly. What does he like least? "Same answer," he smiles. "Owning your own company is like going through finals week every week of your life—you're always preparing, always performing. It's great to have control, but at the same time, your job isn't something you can walk away from. In a way, the company owns you."

SOURCE: Interview with Michael Bielinski, October 3, 1994.

PART TWO: CAREERS IN BUSINESS

Small business is a crucial part of the U.S. economy, since it creates two-thirds of our gross domestic product. Retail stores, service firms, and high-technology companies are among the most common small businesses. Franchising, an important aspect of small business, employs millions of people working in businesses that range from muffler-repair shops to dental offices and from fast-food restaurants to employment agencies.

In this section we will investigate some specific jobs in small business and franchising, as well as the attorneys and legal assistants who help people set up businesses.

SMALL BUSINESS OWNERS

Small business owners usually are involved in the conception, financing, and day-to-day operation of their enterprises.

Job Description

Many small business owners are people who saw a consumer need for a specific good or service and decided to go into business to fill that need. Judging the marketability of a product involves conducting market research into such areas as location and pricing. Small business owners also must find ways to finance their enterprises, which often involves working with banks, setting up partnerships, and submitting business plans to the Small Business Administration. The day-to-day operation of a business entails keeping records, managing employees, advertising, and dealing with customers.

Career Path

Many owners gained their experience working in other small businesses. Others worked for large corporations and decided they would rather work for themselves.

Salary

The earnings of small business owners vary widely.

SMALL BUSINESS CONSULTANTS

Many small business owners employ consultants to help them put their businesses on a sound footing.

Job Description

Small business consultants help firms develop a financial plan to attract investors or secure business loans. They also set up a marketing plan and an accounting system to meet a firm's day-to-day financial needs. In addition, consultants work with owners to establish employee benefit packages or provide needed advice on management techniques.

Career Path

Many people in this field are employed by large consulting firms, while others operate their own consulting firms. Most business consultants have degrees in business. Many gain experience and develop a network of business contacts working for an established firm before becoming consultants.

Salary

Earnings vary widely, depending on personal efforts and level of experience and contacts.

FRANCHISE DIRECTORS

Franchise directors, also known as franchisors, run operations on a local, state, or national level. They work with franchisees, who sell their good or service to the public.

Job Description

Franchisors provide the franchisee with a proven product, management and marketing know-how, training, ongoing assistance, standardized operating procedures, and a common identity. Franchise directors need a sound background in finance and marketing. They must be able to work with state and local governments to ensure that the franchise operation complies with applicable disclosure requirements.

Career Path

Many franchise directors gain experience in the franchise field by first working for other franchisors. Others start successful small businesses that have the potential for growth. They believe the best way to achieve this growth is through franchising.

Salary

The earnings of franchise directors often are tied to the up-front fees collected by franchisors when the franchisees buy into the operation, ongoing royalties, and fees for various authorized parts and services. Their incomes typically depend on the number of franchises in operation and their business success.

FRANCHISEES

Franchisees buy into ongoing franchise operations, which become their own small businesses.

Job Description

Franchisees are independent business people who finance and manage their own firms. Because buying into an established franchise chain is often costly, franchisees must be prepared to work with banks and financiers to raise funds. Once the business is in operation, they face the same responsibilities as other small business owners. They also must establish an effective working relationship with a franchisor.

Career Path

Franchisees share similar backgrounds to those engaged in other small businesses. One major difference is that the franchisee buys into an established business whose products are often already known to the public, while the small business owner goes into business without this support.

Salary

Earnings vary depending on the success of the franchise.

VENTURE CAPITALISTS

Venture capitalists provide an essential financing service to small business owners.

Job Description

Entrepreneurs in need of start-up money often turn to venture capitalists for funds. Venture capitalists see ideas that might turn into profitable businesses and decide to back the entrepreneur with needed financing in exchange for a percentage of the business. Venture capitalists work closely with banks and other financing sources. They also work closely with entrepreneurs, who present financial and business plans for review.

Career Path

Venture capitalists must have a strong background in finance. Many have worked in the finance department of large corporations.

Salary

Earnings depend on the number of businesses venture capitalists finance and the success of these enterprises.

TRAVEL AGENTS

Travel agencies are a rapidly growing type of small business. These firms make travel arrangements for both business and individual clients. The Bureau of Labor Statistics expects faster-than-average growth in this employment field in the years ahead.

Job Description

Travel agents provide an important service to their clients, saving both time and money in planning and arranging their trips. Travel agents must be very detail oriented and able to work on a number of projects at once. Travel agencies use computer reservation systems to obtain airline tickets and hotel rooms. Agents also take phone calls from clients to determine their needs and contact vendors to work on special arrangements.

Career Path

Beginning travel agents might work directly for airlines as reservation agents or in travel agencies handling relatively uncomplicated bookings. Their responsibility increases with experience and ability. At the top of the ladder, travel agents set up their own agencies.

Salary

In a recent year, experienced travel agents earned, on average, $23,800.[11]

ATTORNEYS

Businesses have many legal needs that primarily are filled by attorneys specializing in corporate law. In a recent year, 582,000 lawyers were in the American work force, with much-faster-than-average growth forecast through the year 2000.

Job Description

About four-fifths of all attorneys go into private practice to represent small business people and other firms that require their assistance. Their practices often cover a range of commercial law.

Career Path

New law-school graduates generally do research for experienced attorneys and handle small cases. As they gain experience, they take on increased responsibility. A law-firm partnership is the ultimate career step for attorneys in private practice.

Salary

Median annual salaries of lawyers average $60,500.[12]

LEGAL ASSISTANTS

Legal assistants, or paralegals, work with attorneys in providing legal services to individuals and busi-

nesses, including many small businesses. Currently, about 83,000 people are employed as legal assistants throughout the United States.

Job Description

Paralegals are supervised by an attorney. Most of their work involves legal research, but they also file court papers, help develop legal arguments, and assist with affidavits. Legal assistants working directly for firms assist attorneys with their specific areas of responsibility.

Career Path

Beginning paralegals are given routine tasks and are monitored closely. As they acquire experience, they are assigned more challenging responsibilities. Some paralegals become office managers and supervise other staff.

Salary

Median annual salaries for legal assistants average $27,900.[13]

PART THREE: CAREERS IN BUSINESS

Many of you eventually may select careers in human relations, human resource management, labor relations, or management. A variety of careers also exists in the fields of computers and management information systems, and these job opportunities are expanding rapidly. The Bureau of Labor Statistics forecasts that job opportunities for systems analysts, computer programmers, and telecommunications professionals will all grow much faster than the average for all occupations.

ARBITRATORS

Arbitrators use their knowledge of the law, as well as their own common sense to mediate and settle disputed issues.

PART THREE CAREER PROFILE: RANDI BREVIK

As we read in the preceding chapters, managers must perform a wide variety of tasks. Consider Randi Brevik, manager of administration at Community Services for Children in Bethlehem, Pennsylvania.

Community Services for Children is a private, not-for-profit agency that runs children's programs in the Lehigh Valley area. Eighteen employees report to Randi, who is responsible for facilities planning and management. She also oversees important administrative and human resources functions, such as supervising computer services, maintaining personnel files, advertising job openings, recruiting applicants, and hiring personnel. In addition, she manages the agency's transportation program, which includes a fleet of 18 vehicles that transports 700 Head Start children.

Even though Community Services is a not-for-profit organization, Randi notes, it must operate like any other business. "We set up budgets and allocate expenses just like a for-profit company," she explains. "For instance, certain expenses, such as outgoing mail and duplicating must be put against the proper budget line to credit the appropriate program. When it comes to interviewing and hiring people, we deal with the same issues that a private company faces."

The agency serves an increasingly diverse population; Latino families have grown to comprise almost 40 percent of its clientele. Randi feels it is important to recruit and maintain a work force that reflects clients' cultural diversity, so she advertises many openings in Spanish and African-American publications.

Randi holds a bachelor's degree in psychology from St. Olaf College and did graduate work in counseling at the University of Missouri. She currently is taking undergraduate business courses at Allentown College; eventually she plans to enroll for a master's degree in business administration. She just finished taking an introducton to business class and enjoyed it because of the added dimension it brought to her work. "It crystallized what I've learned on the job," she says.

SOURCE: Telephone interview with Randi Brevik, August 12, 1994.

Job Description

Many arbitrators specialize in labor relations, providing an alternative to costly lawsuits as a means of solving disputes for businesses, unions, and other parties. They analyze the information submitted to them by their clients (both parties in a dispute) and either render a judgment on the proper settlement or counsel the opposing parties in an effort to guide them to a mutually agreeable settlement.

Career Path

Arbitrators often have a background in law and psychology. They generally begin with simple cases and, as they gain experience, graduate to more complicated ones.

Salary

Earnings vary with experience and the types of cases decided. Financial success often is based on an arbitra-tor's ability to build a client base. Just as attorneys must bring in new clients, arbitrators must win the confidence of and compete for cases from insurance companies, corporations, and private individuals with legal issues in dispute.

OUTPLACEMENT CONSULTANTS

Outplacement consultants help people who are losing their jobs to develop new job skills and find new work.

Job Description

The services offered by outplacement consultants vary widely. Some provide temporary offices and secretarial services for clients; others offer job-hunting seminars, skills assessment, and help with resumes. Some offer professional development programs for employees who still have jobs but must take on the duties of those who have left.

Career Path

A bachelor's degree and business experience are important; many consultants also have a master's degree in business administration. Outplacement consultants may work for large consulting firms or small companies, or they may establish their own offices. Career paths vary according to the size of the company.

Salary

Entry-level salaries average $50,000; top-level consultants may earn $125,000 annually. Free-lancers can earn up to $300 a day.[14]

COLLEGE RECRUITERS

College recruiters visit college campuses and search for qualified job applicants.

Job Description

Recruiters travel to campuses with a list of job openings for their companies and the qualifications needed for each job. Recruiters talk with students about job openings, analyze their resumes, interview those who are qualified, and arrange for further interviews at the company's offices for promising candidates.

Salary

Salaries vary widely depending on the size and location of the firm and its type of business. The median salary in a recent year was $26,500.

EMPLOYEE-ASSISTANCE PROFESSIONALS

More than 90 percent of *Fortune* 500 companies have employee-assistance programs to counsel or refer workers who are experiencing problems.

Job Description

Employee-assistance professionals work closely with clients by offering counseling and referrals to special-

ized services. They may focus on specific issues, such as substance abuse, financial problems, or marital stress.

Career Path

Professionals might be on-staff or work for an outside firm. The career path will vary depending on the setting.

Salary

Entry-level salaries average $20,000 to $25,000; top-level salaries average $50,000.[15]

HEALTH SERVICES MANAGERS

Health services managers are the business management level of the health-care industry. They work in hospitals, health maintenance organizations, clinics, public health departments, nursing homes, and other health-oriented units. The chief administrator typically reports to the board of directors or trustees of the unit. Currently, 177,000 health services managers are employed in the United States.

Job Description

Health services managers direct the full range of activities of a health-care facility. The professional medical staff makes treatment decisions concerning patients, but most of the operational decisions for the facility are made by its administrator. Health services managers also are involved in budgeting, fund-raising, planning, and interacting with the public served by the unit. It also should be noted that individuals in the fields of long-term care or nursing homes must pass a licensing examination.

Career Path

Trainee and assistant administrator positions are available. Promotion comes with experience and effective performance.

Salary

Median annual earnings of a hospital administrator are $36,000.[16]

RETAIL MANAGERS

The retail sector is comprised of a wide variety of store types: department stores, discounters, specialty shops, and so on. Thousands of managers are needed to operate these stores.

Job Description

Store managers must perform a variety of tasks. They supervise personnel, plan the work schedule, oversee merchandising, make pricing decisions, and design promotions. They often work long hours and have the ultimate responsibility in many crucial business decisions.

Career Path

Retail managers often begin as assistant managers, handling one department in a larger store. They can move up into areas such as merchandising or into managing an entire store or a number of stores.

Salary

Retail salaries vary widely, depending on the size of the retailer and the responsibilities held. In a recent year, beginning salaries for college graduates at large stores typically ranged between $16,000 and $21,000, while managers at smaller stores earned less. Supermarket managers earned between $13,000 and $30,000.

SALES MANAGERS

Sales managers supervise all or part of a company's sales force. Sales managers exist in every firm that requires a sales force and at all levels in the distribution channel: production, wholesale, and retail.

Job Description

Sales managers recruit, hire, train, organize, supervise, and control sales organizations. They report to the top marketing executives or to general management. Their job is to produce the company's revenue. Effective interaction with sales personnel and customers is an important aspect of the job.

Career Path

Sales managers begin as sales representatives. Successful experience may lead to being designated a senior salesperson or sales supervisor. Upon promotion to district or division manager, the individual breaks away from selling per se and becomes a manager. It is possible to be promoted to even higher levels of sales management with additional responsibilities. A vice president of sales, or national sales manager, heads the entire sales organization.

Salary

Sales managers' salaries in a recent year ranged up to more than $52,500, with a median salary of $36,500. Salaries between $75,000 and $100,000 are not uncommon, and many sales managers also earn bonuses. Regional sales managers' salaries averaged $64,500.

SYSTEMS ANALYSTS

Systems analysts are computer experts who plan and develop the computer-based information systems required by an organization. They work in all types of business organizations, governments, and consulting and service firms. Currently, there are some 403,000 systems analysts working in the United States.

Job Description

Systems analysts determine what information is needed to solve a problem and how best to obtain it. Once management approves the recommendations, the systems analyst instructs the organization's computer programmers in how to implement the decisions.

Career Path

Trainee positions are available in this career. Trainees work under the direction of senior personnel. Additional responsibilities come with experience. Management slots in this field may come later.

Salary

Entry-level salaries average $26,000 to $34,000; top-level systems analysts earn $40,000 to $60,000.[17]

TELECOMMUNICATIONS MANAGERS

The growth of computer networks and the development of the information superhighway makes it important for firms to hire people who understand how to tailor these technologies to the company's needs.

Job Description

A telecommunications manager is responsible for selecting and managing the various technologies that serve a firm's information needs: data, images, voice and video signals.

Career Path

A bachelor's degree in telecommunications or business is necessary, along with technical knowledge. The growing importance of telecommunications can make successful managers candidates for executive positions.

Salary

Entry-level salaries average $36,000 to $42,000; top-level salaries average $60,000 to $110,000.[18]

COMPUTER PROGRAMMERS

Computer programmers carry out the instructions of systems analysts. Programmers are required in computer installations in both the private and public sectors. Some 519,000 programmers are currently at work in the United States.

Job Description

Working with the systems analyst's overall plan, computer programmers write the programs that provide the required information to run a program. Once it is tested and verified, the programmer turns the program over to computer operating personnel.

Career Path

Entry-level programmers are assigned basic tasks, while experienced personnel work on more complex assignments. Advancement to supervisory positions is possible.

Salary

Median annual earnings are $38,000.[19]

PART FOUR: CAREERS IN BUSINESS

Advertising, marketing research, retailing, personal selling, and physical-distribution management are some of the exciting career fields in marketing. Many beginning marketers start as sales personnel, then move into other positions as they gain experience; others remain part of the sales force.

MARKETING RESEARCH ANALYSTS

Marketing research is one of the fastest growing fields in business. Marketing research analysts study what consumers will and will not buy. Currently, about 29,000 of them are employed throughout the United States.

Job Description

Marketing research analysts use a variety of techniques, such as surveys, personal interviews, and test markets, to assess consumer perceptions and interests. They try to learn, for example, what consumers think of a company's product and how it is used in the home. These conclusions then are reported to marketing executives, who use them in their decision making. Marketing researchers work in all kinds of businesses, government, non-profit organizations, advertising agencies, and marketing research firms.

Career Path

Entry-level jobs in marketing research usually involve clerical duties or data-collection tasks. Once the individual is established as a marketing research analyst, he or she is assigned specific research projects. Advancement to supervisory positions is possible. Ul-

PART FOUR CAREER PROFILE: MARK MADDOX

As we saw in this unit, business-to-business marketing can be a complex process. Just ask Mark Maddox, manager of sales and marketing for Energy TRACS (Technology Resources and Computer Systems).

A Houston-based subsidiary of Tenneco Gas, Energy TRACS develops and markets computer systems for gas pipelines and local distribution companies. These systems manage companies' commercial activities, including transportation, allocation of gas, contracting, billing, rate assignments, and gas storage.

As manager of sales and marketing, Mark handles product introduction, trade shows, advertising, sales presentations and demonstrations, and contract negotiations. "A computer system this complex is a high-dollar product," he explains, "so we have a long sales cycle of about six to nine months. We send teams of people—technical experts, business experts, system designers—to explain what we can do for the client." Mark and his team give sales presentations to various decision makers and con-

duct a feasibility study to determine how best to serve a company's needs. Even when a customer decides to buy, the team's job isn't over. Since every client operates differently, the computer system must be customized; the team is responsible for creating a detailed design of the customized product. After the contract is signed, Energy TRACS continues to provide system maintenance and customer service.

Mark earned a bachelor's degree in finance, with a minor in economics, from Louisiana State University. He held jobs in a variety of departments at Tenneco, including accounting, gas marketing, pipeline operations, and special projects, before moving to his present position.

Mark finds his broad background helpful. "Companies hire a person, not a degree," he says. "Employers look for well-rounded students who have demonstrated an ability to learn."

SOURCE: Telephone interview with Mark Maddox, August 16, 1994.

---

timately, one may become director of marketing research or achieve an even higher management position.

Salary

In a recent year, median annual salaries of full-time analysts averaged $35,000. The salary range of a marketing research director for a large firm is between $100,000 and $150,000.

PUBLIC RELATIONS SPECIALISTS

Public relations jobs are found in businesses, trade associations, government, and other entities, such as colleges. The mission of the public relations specialist is to create a favorable public image for his or her employer. Currently, some 91,000 public relations specialists are employed in the United States.

Job Description

Public relations specialists deal with individuals and businesses that interact with their employers. For in-

stance, they send out press releases to newspapers, magazines, radio stations, and television news departments; prepare promotional materials; and write speeches for executives.

Career Path

Trainee positions are available in public relations. Senior people are given specific responsibilities depending on their employer and the nature of the task. Supervisory positions are the next level in the public relations career.

Salary

Median annual earnings are $31,900. Public relations professionals who specialize in particular professions—such as accounting, engineering, and law—can earn $80,000 and up.[20]

ADVERTISING AGENTS

Many jobs are available in advertising. These include copywriter, account executive, artist, media buyer, and production coordinator. Advertising employees can be found in company advertising departments, advertising agencies, and even government. More than 250,000 people currently are employed in advertising.

Job Description

The entry-level job is often involved with a specific activity, such as copywriting for an ad agency. Advertising copywriters sell an image of a good or service to the public. They are responsible for the written text of ads that appear in magazines and newspapers and for scripts for radio and television commercials.

Career Path

Entry-level positions are available in various phases of advertising. Success in these positions can lead to management positions. For instance, a junior copywriter might advance to senior copywriter and then to chief copywriter. Eventually, the person might become creative director of an advertising agency.

Salary

In a recent year, advertising agencies paid the following average salaries: account executive, $31,400; copywriter, $35,900; art director, $34,000; production manager, $31,000; and media buyer, $23,500. Salaries of advertising workers are usually higher in consumer product firms than in industrial product companies.

BUSINESS SERVICES SALES REPRESENTATIVES

As more companies outsource tasks, such as computer programming, advertising, and recruiting, to outside contractors, these firms need salespeople to promote them to potential customers.

Job Description

Business services sales representatives promote their employer's services to other companies. Many positions involve selling computer-related services, such as payroll, inventory control, and consulting.

Career Path

Successful sales representatives can move up to become regional managers and directors of sales and marketing.

Salary

Pay often includes commissions, which means it can vary widely. Entry-level salaries average $39,000; top performers can make $84,000 and more.[21]

PART FIVE: CAREERS IN BUSINESS

All businesses and many individuals require financial services. As a result, the areas of banking, finance, investments, and insurance provide lots of career opportunities that are not only exciting and challenging, but also provide excellent advancement possibilities.

BANK MANAGERS

Bank managers administer the various activities of their units. Currently, about 200,000 bank officers and managers are employed in the United States.

Job Description

Bank managers are part of the executive level of the rapidly changing banking industry. They must be familiar with all banking policies, procedures, and practices, and they must keep up with the many changes that occur. Bankers also must be knowledgeable about the legal framework of their industry. The American Bankers Association offers courses to help keep banking employees current.

Career Path

College-educated candidates usually begin in a management training program. This usually involves rotating among the various bank departments to familiarize candidates with all aspects of banking. Good performance in a junior-level position may lead to an appointment as a bank officer or manager.

Salary

In large banks, branch managers earn up to $52,000, depending on the size of the branch and assets of the

PART FIVE CAREER PROFILE: ERIN FINLEY

Erin Finley has some advice for today's college students: "College is your chance to learn and grow as much as you can. Use the opportunity to challenge yourself, and enjoy it!"

As an undergraduate at the University of Texas–Austin, Erin certainly followed her own counsel. She took classes in a wide variety of subjects, from communications to urban planning, before deciding to major in accounting. She participated in student clubs and activities, in addition to working part time all through school, before graduating in 1992 with a bachelor's degree in business administration.

After graduation she worked at the "Big Six" accounting firm Coopers & Lybrand, before moving to her present position as a financial analyst at Dallas-based Hat Brands Inc. Erin is responsible for maintaining the corporation's bank accounts for all of its various companies. The company manufactures western hats, baseball and golf caps, and western jewelry. The raw materials to make the company's wide range of products come from more than ten countries, and Erin is responsible for maintaining the letters of credit to pay each vendor. She establishes a letter of credit with every supplier and coordinates payments with the bank, based upon verification of shipping documents and customs statements. Timeliness is a crucial issue here, she notes; since goods aren't released until payment is made, it is important not to keep supplies sitting on the dock. Her other tasks include recording all non-sales-related cash to Hat Brands' accounts, reconciling approximately 15 bank accounts every month, filing the necessary forms to comply with customs regulations, and making sure the payments that go in and out of the department are recorded properly.

Erin already has passed the certified public account (CPA) exam, and currently is working to complete the experience requirements necessary to become a licensed CPA. She feels her broad academic background, extracurricular involvement, and accounting expertise are "really a plus" on her job. Next, she plans to attend evening classes working toward a master's degree in business administration; her long-range goal is to start her own company.

SOURCE: Telephone interview with Erin Finley, August 11, 1994.

bank. The average salary is $30,400. In smaller banks, the salaries are several thousand dollars less. The salaries of other banking executives vary by position, location, and size of the bank.

SECURITIES SALES REPRESENTATIVES

Securities sales workers, also known as registered representatives, account executives, or brokers, link investors to the securities industry. Through securities salespeople, investors buy and sell stocks, bonds, shares in mutual funds, and other financial products. In a recent year, more than 200,000 securities and financial salespeople were employed in the United States.

Job Description

Securities sales representatives transmit customer orders to buy and sell securities to the market in which the trade occurs. They also offer clients a range of financial counseling services, including advice on the purchase of mutual funds, annuities, life insurance, and other investments.

Career Path

Before being allowed to work with clients, securities sales reps must pass a series of examinations given by the state, the Securities and Exchange Commission, the exchange on which they will trade, and often the brokerage firm for which they will work. On-the-job training is provided to help workers pass these tests. Once fully qualified, beginning securities sales reps concentrate on building their client contacts. As they gain experience, the number and size of the accounts they handle usually increase. Some experienced reps also take on managerial duties and supervise other salespeople.

Salary

While they are being trained, beginning securities salespeople earn minimal salaries. Experienced workers depend on commissions rather than salary. Median annual earnings are $40,700.[22]

TAX ACCOUNTANTS

The growing complexity of tax law creates a need for more accountants who can interpret it.

Job Description

Tax accountants prepare a company's tax returns and advise managers on the tax consequences of their decisions. Many specialize in particular areas, such as health care or real estate.

Career Path

Some tax accountants work in-house; others are employed by accounting firms. Career paths vary according to the setting.

Salary

Entry-level salaries average $26,000 to $30,000; top-level salaries average $75,000 and up.[23]

ACTUARIES

Actuaries provide the statistical information needed by the insurance industry. They also work in areas like pension planning.

Job Description

Actuaries gather the data needed to determine the risk of losses of various job types and perform the statistical analyses that make such data usable to the insurance industry. They calculate the probability that people will die during the term of their life insurance policy, for example, and calculate the premium necessary for the company to insure them profitably. Some actuaries work for consulting firms or pension funds rather than for insurance companies.

Career Path

Advancement in the actuarial industry depends on experience and on successfully passing a series of exams

given by the actuarial societies, which are broken down by specialty. Depending on the society, there are either nine or ten exams to pass, which usually take five to ten years to complete.

Salary

Average starting salaries for those not having taken their actuarial exams were $22,000 to $26,000 recently. Those who had taken one exam averaged $24,000 to $28,000. Actuaries who become associates of the Society of Actuaries earned from $35,000 to $48,000, and Fellows of the Society earned from $47,000 to $57,000 a year.

UNDERWRITERS

Underwriters analyze the risks to which insurance applicants are exposed. In a recent year, there were 103,000 underwriters in the United States. Faster-than-average employment growth is expected through the year 2000.

Job Description

Underwriters use the information provided by applicants for insurance, in conjunction with statistics provided by actuaries and other specialists, to assess the risk to which the applicant is exposed. They use this information to set the terms of the policy, premiums, and so forth. The underwriter makes sure the company does not assume too much risk (causing it to lose money) but that it also remains competitive with other insurance firms by not turning down too many policies.

Career Path

New underwriters generally are supervised closely and are required to take further courses in underwriting. They first work with routine applications and move to more demanding applications as their ability grows. This career ladder extends to supervisory positions or to top management.

Salary

In a recent year, median salaries for underwriters ranged between $23,400 and $25,900, depending on their area of insurance. Supervisors' salaries averaged about $40,200.

CLAIMS REPRESENTATIVES

Claims representatives, or claims adjusters, assess insurance claims and determine how much the applicant will be paid. They study all available evidence about a loss situation and determine the insurance company's liability. Currently, about 70,000 people work as claims representatives throughout the United States.

Job Description

Most claims representatives are in property and liability insurance and tend to fall into two classes. Claims adjusters examine physical evidence of loss and witness testimony. Claims examiners investigate questionable claims and work in the field, interviewing experts and witnesses. Both groups determine the validity of a claim, whether the insurance company is liable, and how much of the loss is covered.

Career Path

Beginning claims representatives are supervised by senior-level personnel and usually are limited to small claims. As the person gains experience, he or she acquires responsibility for larger claims. Supervisory positions in the claims department cap this career.

Salary

Entry-level salaries average $15,000 to $18,000; top-level salaries average $40,000 and up.[24]

KEY TERMS

displaced homemaker	nontraditional student	technologically displaced worker
entry-level job	open-ended interview	
informational interview	resume	

ASSIGNMENTS

1. Construct your own resume following the procedures outlined in this appendix. Ask your instructors, friends, relatives, and associates to critique it. What did you learn from this exercise?
2. Conduct an informational interview with someone in your community who is working in a profession that interests you. (Remember that this person is busy. Call first to request an appointment. The interview should take no more than 15 to 20 minutes; come prepared with questions to ask.) Discuss with the class what you learned from the interview.
3. Discuss how you would answer each of the questions interviewers most often ask.
4. Choose a partner and take turns interviewing each other for a job in front of the class. (Use the interview questions mentioned in this chapter.) After the interview, ask the class to give you feedback on how you looked and acted during your interview. Would they advise you to do or say anything differently?
5. Discuss what you can do to prepare yourself to become a successful manager who possesses the skills necessary to succeed in the next decade.

INTRODUCTION TO "CAREER DESIGN EXERCISES"

Competition among graduating students for entry-level jobs is intense. Students who know what careers they want to pursue will enjoy a dramatic advantage. The best way to ensure that you land the right job when you graduate is to start your career preparations now. Begin by learning how to match your individual abilities and interests to specific career alternatives. Based on this knowledge, you will be able to create an academic plan that will result in securing that first job in your career path. Your instructor, the "Career Design Exercises," and the accompanying software will help you to accomplish this.

INTERESTS AND FASCINATIONS

This is the first and one of the most important exercises in this course, although it may not seem that way now. You will discover, as the course progresses, that anything that interests you is an important clue about your career direction.

When you are asked to list your interests, take the program's advice and type in as many of your interests as you can, regardless of whether or not you think they are job related. Since this introductory course provides a unique opportunity to discover what areas of business fascinate you, start this exercise by reviewing the chapters you have completed so far and write down any topics that interest you. Then add these to your "Interests and Fascinations" list on the computer.

This Exercise Will Help You to

- discover and keep track of your interests throughout the course,
- understand that choosing a career that interests you can result in better pay and job satisfaction, and
- get a start in choosing a major.

How to Locate the Exercise

When you see the main menu for the Career Design, select "What Do I Want?" Then select "Interests and Fascinations" to begin this exercise.

BUSINESS ADVENTURE

Now that you have completed the "Interests and Fascinations" exercise, here is another one that will help you discover even more about what you want. This exercise will stimulate your imagination about the things you would like to do in the field of business. The more you write, the better.

This Exercise Will Help You to

- discover some of your interests in the business world,
- feel encouraged to actively pursue your dreams,
- clarify your goals and determine what areas of life are important to you, and
- stimulate your thinking about what you want to accomplish in your life.

How to Locate the Exercise

When you see the main menu for Career Design, select "What Do I Want?" Then select "Business Adventure" to begin this exercise.

SKILLS

At the end of Part One, you learned that your interests are very important in choosing a career. You may have thought that there were many things that interested you, but that you were not capable of doing. This exercise will help you discover your skills and talents, and you will be surprised at the number of skills you possess. In fact, it is not unusual for students to uncover 50 or more skills in this exercise.

By the way, this is not a time to be modest. If you think you have a skill, type it in. Your professor may help you to verify if you truly possess the skills you listed.

This Exercise Will Help You to

- identify many of your skills and talents,
- discover you possess far more skills than you realize, and
- improve your awareness of your value to a potential employer.

How to Locate the Exercise

When you see the main menu for Career Design, select "Who Am I?" Then select "Skills."

ENTREPRENEURIAL QUOTIENT

Have you ever thought that you might want to start your own business some day? This exercise will help you determine whether you have what it takes to become an entrepreneur. Your professor also may follow up with some important things to consider in deciding if a new business idea is worth pursuing.

This Exercise Will Help You to

- develop a realistic picture of what it takes to become an entrepreneur, and
- gain some personal insights into your inclination toward starting your own business.

How to Locate the Exercise

When you see the main menu for Career Design, select "Who Am I?" Then select "Entrepreneurial Quotient."

PART THREE CAREER DESIGN EXERCISES

SURVEYING

Before making any decisions about something important—such as choosing a major or deciding on a career—you first need to gather a lot of information. That way, you will feel more confident that your choice is a good one.

To make an informed decision, it is necessary not only that you read about your topic of interest, but that you talk with people who are involved personally. For example, you could uncover many facts about a career interest in the *Occupational Outlook Handbook*. However, to get an idea about what it is really like on the job, you would need to visit with people who actually do the work. This process is called "surveying."

In your survey of an important topic, you will complete three sections: "Preparing a Plan," "Conducting a Survey," and "Evaluating Results."

This Exercise Will Help You to

- get the exact information you need to make good decisions,
- learn how to research any topic of interest,
- discover a method for making valuable contacts, such as potential employers, and
- verify that you have enough information before you make decisions.

How to Locate the Exercise

When you see the main menu for Career Design, select "How Do I Get There?" Then select "Surveying."

WORK PREFERENCES

Have you ever thought about what makes a job appealing or unappealing? Obviously, the actual work you do plays a big part, but there are many other factors. In fact, you may have talked to someone who said, "I don't really like what I'm doing, but this is such a great place to work that I don't want to quit." In this exercise, you will find out what kind of working conditions you want on the job.

This Exercise Will Help You to

- develop a clear picture of exactly what working conditions are important to you, and
- learn that your working environment can be just as important to job satisfaction as the work itself.

How to Locate the Exercise

When you see the main menu for Career Design, select "Who Am I?" Then select "Likes and Dislikes." Once you have the "Likes and Dislikes" menu, choose "Likes and Dislikes in Working Conditions."

PEOPLE PREFERENCES

Here is an exercise about which you probably will have some strong feelings. Have you ever thought about how you enjoyed a certain job—or hated one—because of the people at work? In this exercise, you will list all the things you like and dislike about people you have encountered in the work place. You even will decide which of those characteristics are so important that the next job you take has to have co-workers who possess them.

This Exercise Will Help You to

- develop a clear picture of exactly what kinds of people you prefer to encounter in your work setting, and
- learn that the people with whom you work can have a significant impact on job satisfaction.

How to Locate the Exercise

When you see the main menu for Career Design, select "Who Am I?" Then select "Likes and Dislikes." Once you have the "Likes and Dislikes" menu, choose "Likes and Dislikes in People."

PART FOUR CAREER DESIGN EXERCISES

BUSINESS WEEK ARTICLE

It is 20 years in the future. As a result of your successful business career, one of the most prominent business magazines in the world has decided to do a story about you! Even better, they will allow you to write the story.

This is your chance to imagine what you want to accomplish in the years ahead. This article is excellent publicity for you, and it has two distinct advantages over advertising: readers probably will find it more believable than an ad, and it is free!

This Exercise Will Help You to

- clarify how you might want to participate in the world of business, and
- start to create a picture of your career direction.

How to Locate the Exercise

When you see the main menu for Career Design, select "What Do I Want?" Then select "*Business Week* Article."

BILLBOARD

One of the most visible forms of advertising is a billboard. Suppose you had the opportunity to put a message of your choice on the most prominent billboard in town. This brief exercise asks you to create that message.

This Exercise Will Help You to

- examine your personal priorities, and
- consider what kinds of activities or businesses in which you might want to become involved.

How to Locate the Exercise

When you see the main menu for Career Design, select "What Do I Want?" Then select "Billboard."

PART FIVE CAREER DESIGN EXERCISE

PERSONAL FINANCES

As you learned in Chapter 15, one of the responsibilities of a financial manager is to assist the business in determining the amount of money it needs to pursue its goals, and then help it raise any needed funds. You experience some of these same responsibilities on a much smaller scale with your own personal finances. First, you determine how much money is needed to pay for your education, housing, food, and miscellaneous expenses. Second, you raise the money you need through employment, family, government aid, or other resources.

When you graduate, your goals certainly will change. You probably will have much higher expectations about your standard of living than you do now as a student. It is important to determine exactly what those expectations are and what is required, both financially and professionally, to meet them.

This Exercise Will Help You to

- determine what level of compensation you will need upon graduation to attain the lifestyle you want, and
- determine whether a given career direction will meet those financial expectations.

How to Locate the Exercise

When you see the main menu for Career Design, select "How Do I Get There?" Then select "Personal Finances."

Video Cases

CHAPTER 1
Lincoln Electric

In company after company, the key word in the 1990s is *competitiveness*. In the worldwide battle for sales and profits, progressive firms—large and small—know the value of highly trained, highly motivated human resources in producing a successful operation. Even though Lincoln Electric, a Cleveland-based manufacturer of arc welding equipment, is a relatively small component of the market, it attracts 800 visitors a year from such industrial giants as Motorola, TRW, 3M, and Ford. Both company and union leaders make the trek to the shores of Lake Erie to learn how a medium-sized company like Lincoln can be so successful in such a cyclical industry.

Today, Lincoln remains profitable by creating an environment in which its employees turn out consistently high-quality products while controlling costs. Profit-sharing plays an important role in the quality–cost equation. By making paychecks heavily dependent on the company's success, Lincoln shares the risks and rewards of business with its staff. Every year, profit-sharing bonus checks almost double the salary of each employee. The firm's explicit no-layoff policy, dating from 1958, encourages company loyalty. During the past five years alone, Lincoln's annual sales more than doubled to reach $800 million.

Lincoln Electric is strictly a no-frills firm. There are no paid holidays, no sick days, no dental insurance, and the employees work in a facility with neither windows nor air-conditioning. (They do get paid vacations.) Earnings are based on individual output and on bonuses from company profits. Turnover rates are often as high as 25 percent during the first few months as new employees are exposed to hard work and see employees competing for bonus money. After 90 days on the job, an employee is covered by the firm's no-layoff policy and turnover rates plummet. Donald F. Hastings, company president, sums up employee attitudes about his pay-for-performance system: "An employee has to *want* to be in a system like this."

The firm's philosophy is illustrated by Hastings' activities at a recent trade show in Germany. After noticing that the first day of the event had produced almost no business, he gathered the staff together and

explained that the pay-for-performance approach applied to them. In his words, "If you and your colleagues don't sell tomorrow, there will be no work the following day." The pep talk worked and the Essen show resulted in the sale of 1,762 products, far more than Hastings had hoped.

Each employee is evaluated every six months in four distinct areas: output, quality, dependability, and idea generation and cooperation. These evaluations serve as the basis for a year-end discretionary bonus that represents about 90 percent of each employee's total compensation. This approach prompts employees to manage their work as efficiently as possible. Highly productive workers, who don't mind overtime, have been known to earn more than $80,000 in a single year.

The result of the Lincoln approach is a stable, highly motivated, and extremely productive work force. There are no seniority rights at Lincoln, and everyone must be willing to be switched to other jobs when necessary. Employees are encouraged to air their complaints to company management. In fact, workers once voted down a dental plan because it might have reduced year-end bonuses.

Questions

1. Explain why the employees of Lincoln Electric have been able to compete with the Chinese and Mexican import markets.
2. How have the Lincoln Electric profit-sharing and incentive programs contributed to the company's productivity?
3. Explain how the private enterprise system permits Lincoln Electric to manage the company successfully and to produce and market its product to a worldwide market.
4. Relate the concepts of empowerment and teamwork to Lincoln Electric's focus on productivity and product quality.

CHAPTER 2
Is There Cash in Our Trash?

We all agree that recycling is vital. As we consume more and more of the world's resources, and as our landfills become clogged with more and more garbage, recycling becomes key to preserving our environment. And, in fact, recycling is catching on; today some 3,000 U.S. communities now have a curbside recycling program.

How are our recycling programs working? Let's look at the economics of the process. New York City could be called the "capital of trash" since it generates so much. The Big Apple is such a fertile trash producer, in fact, that it only has one landfill left. When this landfill towers to 500 feet, it will be full and the huge city will have to find somewhere else—farther away and much more expensive—to stash its trash.

New York is working to postpone this dreaded day by operating the country's largest recycling program. The city tries to turn its trash into cash by selling garbage to firms for reuse in manufacturing other products. Plastics are recycled by companies that make lumber, carpet, and other plastic products such as ketchup bottles. Old newspaper goes to mills that de-ink and recycle it at 75 percent to 80 percent of what it would cost to make paper from virgin wood pulp.

But the sad truth is that this recycling program, though extensive, is not economical. It costs New York City $300 a ton to collect plastic, but the city only nets $10 a ton when it sells it for recycling. The city also pays dearly for its newspapers to be hauled away. Many old newspapers end up being shipped to Taiwan and Korea, where trees are scarce but where recyclers buy them for much less than New York's shipping bills. The only recycled product that pays its way is aluminum, which is expensive to make from scratch.

These problems are not unique to New York. Around the country, the supply of trash to be recycled is growing faster than the demand for it. If you recycle plastic, glass, and paper, chances are that your garbage is piling up somewhere. After all, recycling consumes environmental resources, too; witness the gas and labor necessary to transport trash to recyclers. Unfortunately, it is still cheaper for most paper and plastics makers to craft their products from raw materials.

So what can we do? One solution is closed-loop recycling, in which companies create their own markets for their own recycled trash. A good example is McDonald's, which until recently produced 2 million pounds of garbage per day. The fast-food chain teamed up with the Environmental Defense Fund to develop an effective recycling program and the company replaced its "clamshell" polystyrene package with paper wrapping. McDonald's tries to recycle its waste into other products; for instance, it transforms cardboard boxes into take-out bags.

Other companies also are trying to close the recycling loop. GM's Saturn plant in Tennessee ships foundry sand—a waste by-product generated from

making engine blocks—to a firm that uses it to make concrete blocks. GM's wooden shipping pallets go to a distillery where they fire boilers. Cosmetics retailer Body Shop International gives customers a 25 cent discount on their next purchase if they bring their plastic bottles back to be refilled. When Florida Power replaces outdated streetlights with new models, it ships the old lights to Mexico, where they are installed in areas previously left dark. And France's state-owned electricity company is studying ways to generate power by burning household trash.

Another solution is to get the federal government involved. Some suggest that the government should regulate a nationwide program by requiring a minimum level of recycling from all companies. Alternatively, the government could serve as a "matchmaker" to bring creators and users of recycled products together. In Taiwan, for instance, companies that make plastic products have pledged to buy all recycled plastic and convert it to different products. Even schoolchildren are taught to buy only items made from recycled materials. In other words, Taiwan has "closed the loop" on a national basis.

Would a similar tactic work in the United States? Probably not, since business—and the general population—would see it as too much government interference. Unfortunately, in the near future, there won't be much cash in trash.

Questions

1. Explain why recycling often is not very economical.
2. Does business have a social responsibility to recycle its trash, even if it loses money on the deal? Explain your answer.
3. Discuss how a successful recycling program might affect the ecological problems described in this chapter.
4. Hold an in-class debate on the pros and cons of the following statement: "The federal government should take immediate steps to regulate a nationwide recycling program."

CHAPTER 3
Jamaica—Paradise Lost?

The International Monetary Fund (IMF) was created in 1944 to promote worldwide trade by stabilizing foreign exchange rates and establishing freely convertible currencies. The IMF lends money to many underdeveloped countries to strengthen their economies and bring them into the world marketplace.

The IMF's methods are controversial. Before making loans to debtor nations, it typically imposes an "austerity program," requiring higher taxes, reduced government spending, and curbs on credit. Some critics feel its strict, market-driven approach is actually harmful. Think-tank Hudson Institute published a pamphlet with the telling title, "The IMF's Destructive Recipe of Devaluation and Austerity." Other analysts feel that, while the IMF may not be perfect, overall it has upgraded the economies of many small countries and brought them into the global marketplace.

Let's look at how well the IMF's policies are succeeding in one nation that's borrowed heavily from it: Jamaica.

Jamaica is a high-risk land for foreign business because its financial policies change with each new government. Jamaica's current leaders, however, believe strongly in the IMF and its free-market reforms. The nation's prime minister is working to introduce the IMF's "four commandments" for solving the country's debt problems.

Commandment 1: Put government-run businesses under private ownership. At the IMF's urging, Jamaica has sold many state-owned companies to private business people. Often this action boosts profits and makes companies more competitive. An added benefit is that Jamaica's workers learn new business skills.

Commandment 2: Cut government subsidies. While the economy benefits from extra funds, this reduces social services in a nation with a history of helping its poor. Reductions in social services have affected public education, medical care, and quality of life for poverty-stricken families. All too often, this triggers rising crime and other problems, leading to what one Jamaican minister predicts will be a "social meltdown."

Commandment 3: Encourage exports to bring in foreign money. In addition to the usual exports, such as sugar and bauxite, Jamaica's government encourages the building of factories to make products for export. Workers making 70 cents an hour create T-shirts and other products for foreign markets. Unfortunately, the IMF encourages many Third World countries to export similar items, which could pose a potential problem. It is also doubtful whether such low-skill industries can help Jamaica prosper.

Commandment 4: Discourage imports by devaluing Jamaica's currency (so that imported goods cost Jamaicans more) and by raising taxes on imports. Sound logical? Not to Jamaica's many *higglers* (smugglers). Smuggling is a time-honored tradition in Jamaica. According to one government official, "Smugglers see themselves as valiant entrepreneurs who defy the restrictions on international trade being imposed by their countries. They are the heroes of capitalism." Smuggling, in fact, is so profitable that the Jamaican government legalized the profession so that it could tax it. Smugglers have their own association, the Independent Commercial Importers, as well as two professional groups that defend their interests to lawmakers. For smugglers, the IMF's fourth commandment is a barrier to business.

Even without the problems posed by outraged higglers, the IMF's fourth commandment doesn't go over well in Jamaica. Because Jamaicans prefer imported goods, they view locally made products as inferior.

So far, the IMF reforms have had mixed results. Jamaica's leaders admit that the evolution to a market-driven economy will be long and painful. However, they hope that following the IMF commandments will ultimately reduce the nation's debt and revive its economy.

Meanwhile, many Jamaicans who don't want to wait have flocked to the United States—creating "Little Jamaica" in New York City. The money they earn flows back into Jamaica's economy, boosting the country's gross domestic product beyond the official figures. The extra money doesn't just buy goods and services: it also buys time for the government as it waits to see if the IMF programs will work.

Questions

1. Explain how the IMF's four commandments are affecting Jamaica.
2. What comparative advantage(s), if any, does Jamaica have for producing goods for export? Explain.
3. Does Jamaica have a trade surplus or a trade deficit? How does the government want to change its balance of trade?
4. Refer to this chapter's discussion of obstacles to international business. What obstacles do foreign companies face in Jamaica?
5. Would you describe Jamaica's government as predominantly communist, socialist, or capitalist? Relate Jamaica's economic changes to the trends discussed in Chapter 1.

CHAPTER 4
Ampex

Forty years ago, both Ampex Corp. and American industry were riding high. The name Ampex was synonymous with audio recording. Moreover, the firm had developed the technology that eventually would lead to videotape. But already there were signs that short-term thinking was blurring Ampex's focus on technology.

Ampex, like much of American industry during this era, was beginning to play to its stockholders. Its new management was making quick profits by selling the world's first audio-tape recorder to anyone who could afford the $20,000 machine.

When a group of Ampex engineers invented the video recorder, the company saw a second source of short-term profits. It sold the huge, expensive machines to television networks but ignored the mass market. Providing cheap, reliable home-video recording seemed to be too many years in the future.

By contrast, Japanese managers were interested in the video recorder's long-term potential. In the 1950s, some Japanese asked to see Ampex's new video plant. They did not steal American ideas, but they did build on them, since they understood—better than the Americans—how technology progressed (and got cheaper if you worked at it long enough).

Japan's usual approach to the high-tech race is to take the long view. American companies often lead in basic scientific research, but research is not the same as development—that is, taking a new technology step-by-step to the marketplace. In high-tech markets, that can require a very long-term approach.

And the Japanese could afford to be farsighted. First of all, Japan's top executives—unlike many American senior managers—can see the long-term potential of technology. Second, Japanese companies do not have to rely on the stock market because Japanese investors will wait for their returns—in other words, money was available so that Japanese firms could invest for the future. Third, Japanese companies and their design engineers were committed to each other for the long haul. And fourth, Japan had a production-oriented economy with dedicated employees who earned relatively low wages, took few vacations, and generally sacrificed for the long-term good of the group. American companies, on the other hand, were satisfying short-term investors with short-term profits.

By the 1960s, Ampex had developed a new, more compact video recorder. At $15,000, it was still very expensive, but several of Ampex's engineers believed that the same technology could be used to make a small, inexpensive machine. However, approval to work on the project never came from upper management. In fact, it was Ampex's rivals, the Japanese engineers, who got the go-ahead from senior management and the money to redesign and remanufacture this American product.

Even so, by the 1970s, a video breakthrough had been made by a group of Ampex engineers—the world's first videocassette recorder (VCR). For Ampex, unfortunately, the breakthrough came too late. With its audio business on the wane, the company felt it needed quick profits—not long-range products. The firm invested (and lost) millions of dollars in "quick-fix" ventures it knew too little about. When it had no funds left to invest, Ampex abandoned the VCR.

So, in the 1980s, Ampex was the last American-owned videotape-equipment manufacturer. Late in the decade, the company that invented the video recorder dropped out of the $15 billion VCR market.

Ampex subsequently was purchased in a leveraged buyout involving millions of dollars worth of borrowed funds. With such a buyout came high interest payments. This made it even more difficult for the firm's new management to invest in the future potential of new products.

Ampex's owner, President and Chief Operating Officer Ed Bramson, has three chief goals for the company:

1. Quell the uneasiness about layoffs (in 1991, the company laid off 700 employees—about ten percent of its work force).
2. Implement a more decentralized management style.
3. Redirect product-development teams.

Ampex gave new-product development greater attention in the early 1990s. The level of research and development funding (ten percent of sales), however, remained the same. New-product development teams were formed, but Ampex declined to give details on those teams' missions.

Historically, Japan's strength has been the development of American technology, but today Japan is challenging the United States in basic research as well. High-definition television (HDTV) is a prime example. Japanese companies have been investing in HDTV research for more than ten years. This should cause great concern not only for Ampex but for all U.S. electronics firms. If Japan can pull ahead in both high-tech research and in development, America may not be able to catch up.

Questions

1. How do organizational objectives differ for Ampex and Japanese companies? How are they similar?
2. If you could go back to Ampex in the 1950s, how would you change its strategic and tactical plans?

3. If supervisory managers are evaluated daily, middle managers weekly, and top managers monthly, why would anyone be concerned about the long term?
4. Would you be willing to invest in a business that might not repay the investment for more than ten years? Why or why not?

CHAPTER 5
Samuel Adams Boston Lager

Small business is a vital segment of our society, producing two-thirds of the gross domestic product and employing half of the U.S. work force. An entrepreneur is a risk taker in the private enterprise system. He or she seeks a profitable opportunity and takes the necessary risks to set up and operate a business.

Jim Koch (pronounced Cook), the founder of Samuel Adams Boston Lager, is an entrepreneur and a fifth-generation brewmaster with a consuming desire to make the best glass of beer. He is "passionate about brewing beer and sophisticated about selling it."

Koch earned three degrees at Harvard, including one from the prestigious business school, and became a business strategy consultant. But his real desire was to start a brewery. Perhaps he learned even more watching his father run four different little breweries (that all went broke) than he did in the more formalized post-secondary educational setting.

While working as a business strategy consultant, Koch kept an eye on the brewing business, looking for any development that might provide him the opportunity to enter the market. His strategy was to find a niche, a distinctive corner of the overall U.S. beer market.

Just 20 to 30 years ago, the beer industry was crowded with small regional breweries. In the 1950s, most beers were regional, and the products' claims were pretty much the same because the products were pretty much the same. By the 1960s, however, some companies got big enough to brew, distribute, and advertise nationally. The national products were advertised more heavily, available everywhere, and cheaper to produce. Soon these national brands were able to beat their regional rivals to the mass market. In 1960, Anheuser-Busch had less than 10 percent of the market. Today it has almost 40 percent.

Koch knew he couldn't compete with the giants like Anheuser-Busch, so he targeted a different, smaller, and (he thought) very vulnerable segment of the beer market—the imports. Imports such as Becks, Heineken, Molson, and St. Pauli represented a very distinct niche and the only growing segment of the American beer market.

While foreign beer ads and sales were based on snob appeal, Koch wanted an American beer, with an American name, to be sold as an American beer. The name Samuel Adams was chosen because Adams was a patriot who instigated and nurtured the American Revolution. He was responsible for throwing the foreigners out of a young America and, most significant of all, was a brewer himself.

In 1985, Samuel Adams Boston Lager produced about 2,000 barrels of beer a month (one barrel holds 31 gallons). This is a mere "drop in a bucket" compared with Anheuser-Busch's five million barrels a month.

To market this product, Koch took his beer to Boston's hottest night spots, pitting his beer against the big-name brands. Samuel Adams Boston Lager has a distinct advantage over the competition: it is much darker than many of the imports, has more body, and is more bitter and aromatic. This advantage—looking and tasting different—became the strategy Koch used to fight the competition.

The next step was to get the public to notice the beer. With a tight advertising budget, Koch used every stunt and gimmick he could think of—beer-tasting events, seminars, and promotion nights. "He stumped for his beer like a latter-day evangelist."

Samuel Adams Boston Lager found a niche. The beer was positioned as the highest-priced, highest-quality, American alternative to foreign beers. But was a loyal, local following enough?

In the 1990s, beer may not have snob appeal, but many of the small breweries have real style. While some Americans still seek a beer with fewer calories, others have developed a liking for beers with traditional good taste. There are now about 200 microbreweries in the United States making these distinctive beers available.

Jim Koch may have been even wiser than he thought. Samuel Adams Boston Lager now is distributed in Chicago by the Pacific Wine Company and the beer has debuted in the U.S. Virgin Islands of St. Thomas and St. Croix. In 1992, Samuel Adams Boston Lager was even spotted at an Albertson's supermarket in Fort Worth, Texas.

Questions

1. Explain how an entrepreneur differs from a small-business manager.
2. What are the advantages and disadvantages of Samuel Adams Boston Lager being a small business?
3. Should Jim Koch try to export his beer to Europe? Why or why not?
4. Would a "light" Boston Lager be successful? Why or why not?

CHAPTER 6
The Japanese Distribution System

Ever wonder why the typical Japanese tourist spends so much money on U.S. products during a stateside vacation? After all, the products of the Land of the Rising Sun almost have become synonymous with quality over the past two decades.

Part of the answer is contained in our discussion of exchange rates in Chapter 3. Basically, for the past five years, Japanese shoppers have been able to buy U.S. dollars with fewer and fewer yen. The result is that the United States has become a bargain bonanza for the Japanese.

But there is more to it than just exchange rates. The Japanese, so well known for their quality products and productivity, are decidedly inferior when it comes to distribution efficiency in their own country. The result of these inefficiencies is higher prices for the Japanese consumer.

Just consider these statistics. In a downtown Tokyo grocery store, a watermelon costs $55 and grapes sell for $46 a box. A square foot of land costs $22,000, a cramped three-bedroom apartment is valued at $3 million. And even though Japan's factories turn out high-quality, price-competitive cars, Japanese households pay twice as much to buy and maintain an automobile.

Why do Japanese consumers tolerate these domestic prices? The answer lies in the country's history and priorities. After World War II, Japan was in an economic shambles. At that point, the country had one overriding goal—to achieve economic security. As part of its program, the government created jobs for all Japanese citizens, giving everyone a stake in the system.

Today, economic security is still a vital goal for the Japanese. The question is whether the price tag for this security is too high. One outspoken critic is Chinook Ohmae, a renowned Japanese economist and business consultant, who claims that the Japanese are, in effect, victims of their own success. Ohmae has become a popular figure in his native country, thanks to his economy-bashing books and TV appearances. His question to the Japanese people can be summarized this way: "If we're so rich, why don't we live rich?"

The answer, according to Ohmae, lies in Japan's distribution system. The $55 watermelon was grown in the United States and traveled to Japan via a Japanese importer. Once in Japan, the watermelon passes through a long series of wholesalers and other marketing intermediaries. Eventually it reaches a distributor, who often subcontracts the physical distribution to yet another intermediary. At every step of the way, there is a markup added to the cost.

Finally, the watermelon lands in a retail store. But, unlike in the United States, the Japanese government restricts the number of big stores, so there are relatively few large supermarkets or discount shops. A Japanese retailer is more likely to be a small family-owned business that is free to place a final hefty markup on the melon's price.

American critics call this distribution system inefficient. However, it all comes down to how we define *efficiency*. While the Japanese system is inefficient at keeping prices low, it is highly efficient at preserving employment. About 20 percent of Japan's entire labor force is involved with distribution, and reducing the number of intermediaries would throw millions of people out of work. Similarly, many of Japan's retailers are small mom-and-pop outlets; the government restricts the growth of large stores to protect these small businesses. Again, the overriding goal is job security. In effect, much of Japan's distribution chain operates as an informal welfare system—and it is financed by consumers.

The ultimate culprit, argues Ohmae, is the Japanese government, which shelters special interest groups, encourages protectionist trade surpluses, and discourages imports. The result is that, while everyone has job security, Japanese citizens are forced to lead needlessly grim, austere lives. Few families can afford $55 watermelons or $3 million apartments. Instead, they buy Japanese-grown food (which is often lower in quality) and endure long commutes from small suburban apartments to their urban jobs.

While Ohmae thinks many Japanese consumers are fed up with high prices, he doubts whether they would be willing to accept the costs of lowering them. The power of special interest groups, combined with the large numbers of workers involved, makes it unlikely that Japan will overhaul its distribution system any time soon. In the meantime, Japanese consumers must continue to be content with a first-rate economy—and a third-rate lifestyle.

Questions

1. What are the chief benefits and drawbacks of the Japanese distribution system?
2. Which of Deming's 14 points for quality are reflected in this case?
3. Describe how benchmarking might be used to identify inefficiencies and suggest improvements for the Japanese distribution system.
4. Which types of U.S. firms would be most likely to be victimized by the inefficient Japanese distribution system if they decide to enter that market? Explain your answer.

CHAPTER 7
Middle Management:
Twenty-first Century Dinosaur?

A sad fact of economic recessions is that many people may lose their jobs. One way in which the American recession of the early 1990s differed from earlier economic downturns was that the shirt collars of many victims were white, not blue. Layoffs in previous recessions largely involved blue-collar and hourly workers. More recently, however, when corporations have downsized, they have been more likely to cut higher-ranking staff. An especially tempting target has been middle management. Although middle managers make up only five to eight percent of America's work force, they suffered 16 percent of recent layoffs. Says Bill Cheney, an economist with John Hancock Financial Services in Boston, "It's not that this was just a white-collar recession, but it did spread to the white-collar sector. Employers economized on lower levels of labor through the 1980s. This trend finally worked its way up. There had to be cuts at a higher level."

Some of these cuts became necessary, say economists, due to the increasing impact of overhead—that elusive, hard-to-measure, and even-harder-to-control drain on a company's profits. "The labor content of a product today is probably less than 15 percent," claims William Fife, Jr., chairman of machine-tool maker Giddings & Lewis Inc. "I don't care how much I cut labor, it's not going to get to the bottom line. We have to get at overhead costs." Dexter Baker, head of Air Products & Chemicals Inc., agrees that high overhead is "why you're now seeing so much cutting of white-collar work forces and delayering of management." Indeed, a survey conducted by Boston University found that overhead at U.S. manufacturing firms equaled 26 percent of sales—compared to a slim 21 percent for Western Europe's companies and a skinny 18 percent in Japan.

Terrifying though it is to lose one's job, a layoff can actually signal the start of a new career. William Morin, chairman of outplacement firm Drake Beam Morin, recommends that laid-off managers stay flexible: "They should learn to identify with their careers rather than with the company for which they worked," he says. "They must think in broader terms of what they can do—of the transferable skills they have." Many managers find new opportunities in small- and medium-sized firms. ("You'd be surprised at the number of $100 million companies you've never heard of that are just around the corner," remarks a Minneapolis executive recruiter.) Others start their own companies, free-lance as contract managers, or set up shop as consultants.

But layoffs have other, less-visible victims, too. What about the employees who are left behind? The legacy of middle-management layoffs, says Eric Greenberg of the American Management Association, "creates a shadow that looms over those employees who are still working." These folks are expected to keep things running with smaller staffs and shrinking budgets. The result, all too often, is a group of frantic employees who take on new jobs while still trying to do their old ones. One Massachusetts consultant notes that managers who remain with downsized companies often are forced to work 80-hour weeks and carry two beepers just to maintain the status quo. Under these circumstances, overhead may go down, but so will employees' morale and productivity.

Clearly, just cutting jobs is not enough; smart firms realize that they also need to rethink the ways in which they do business. Companies have not just been downsizing, they have been merging, consolidating, and delayering. The result of these drastic reorganizations is that many of the old white-collar jobs no longer exist. Since the mid-1980s, roughly 2 million middle-management positions have been eliminated permanently, and this trend looks like it will continue. Eric Greenberg believes that, while the 1980s was a decade of long, slow economic expansion, "the 1990s may prove to be a period of long, slow contraction." Agrees the chairman of one executive search firm, "Minimal management and minimal administration will be with us for at least a decade."

What companies emphasize instead of traditional management jobs are positions that clearly influence the firm's financial health—the "bottom line," as William Fife, Jr., put it—such as marketing and sales. Kenneth Stancato, a vice president at Weyerhaeuser Co., recommends that companies analyze their work processes and try to eliminate as many "redundancies and non-value-added activities" as possible.

One way to identify redundancies is to track costs via activity-based accounting. This approach assigns costs to each task that employees perform, including such seemingly inexpensive activities as answering phones and opening mail. Activity-based accounting helps pinpoint areas of waste within an organization.

How can companies boost the productivity of their remaining managers? Ironically, one effective method is to empower the people who report to them. Some firms organize workers into self-supervised teams, freeing managers from supervisory functions. Others train staffers to perform quality-control tasks, reducing the need for inspectors. Still others, such as General Electric, solicit suggestions for improvement from employees at all levels. It holds large corporate "town meetings" at which junior employees—and even some customers—can question upper-level management and suggest ways to improve efficiency.

Questions

1. What function(s) do middle managers traditionally perform in an organization?
2. What advice would you give to a middle manager who has been laid off?
3. Discuss how the elimination of middle managers' jobs can affect the employees who were not laid off.
4. If a firm eliminates whole layers of management, how could this affect its corporate culture?

CHAPTER 8
Strength in Diversity: Xerox

In this chapter we emphasized the importance of employee training. During the 1990s, American business faces two human resource challenges that make effective training especially crucial. One issue is the changing nature of the labor force. Between now and the year 2000, 85 percent of new workers will be women, minorities, and immigrants. The other challenge involves a looming shortage of qualified employees. Says one CEO, "Workers are going to be so few and far between that you are going to have to utilize everybody. . . . You will find a way to use each individual, either as a future resource or by training them for something else."

Xerox Corp. has found a way to get the most from its work force by capitalizing on cultural diversity. In one sense, of course, this is a purely practical response to the undeniable trends in the U.S. population. As one manager notes, America is engaged in an "economic war," and it cannot win this war by using only one-third of its population.

But, more importantly, Xerox sees cultural diversity as a competitive advantage. By combining people with different backgrounds, experiences, and skills, Xerox feels it can create a more successful work force. The company's top management believes diversity is a strategic advantage that fosters flexibility and innovation.

How does Xerox turn employee diversity into a competitive weapon? A key ingredient is staff training, both formal and informal. Minority members are encouraged to help each other through groups like the Black Caucus Network (BCN). African-American executives teach after-hours classes in management and other work skills to incoming staffers. In these sessions, seasoned pros pass on practical tips for getting ahead in the work place: How does one handle a

hostile subordinate? What is the best way to quiet hecklers when giving a presentation?

Minority employees also support and train each other informally through mentoring. Experienced BCN professionals meet with newer workers to discuss their experiences and problems, and advise them on strategies for job success. Sometimes these sessions simply involve answering work-related questions. At other times, mentors may find themselves handing out more personal advice—for instance, how can a minority woman, just transferred to a new position in a mostly white town, best balance her social and professional lives?

While Xerox's cultural diversity programs have been highly successful in its marketing division, minorities have made fewer inroads in some other areas of the company. One holdout is in the engineering division, where a shortage of qualified minority applicants for technical positions continues to exist and many managers are still white males. In this case, the company's goal is to encourage "majority" managers to shed any stereotypes and work more effectively with non-whites. Managers attend half-day training sessions that address management issues related to diversity and sensitize supervisors to situations faced by minority subordinates. Through a technique called "training theater," participants role-play and resolve actual problems that occur on the job.

Xerox's diversity programs don't just help people at Xerox; the company also encourages employees to help the community. Past and present African-American managers have formed a team called the "Road Show" to talk to student, community, and professional audiences about the importance of cultural diversity. Their message: Don't just cope with diversity—capitalize on it. One Road Show member has informally adopted 70 minority teenagers and meets with them regularly to discuss school and work. It is important, he notes, for minority teens to have role models and realize that professional sports are not the only way to get ahead. Even if they are not basketball stars, they still can be successful.

Diversity programs pay off in hiring and retaining qualified minority workers. At Xerox, 25 percent of the employees are minorities; 12,000 of them are African Americans. Eleven percent of managers and nine percent of top managers are black. Compare this to the nationwide average: less than six percent of middle-level managers and a scant 0.5 percent of top managers in the United States are African American. Employees note, however, that the impact of these programs goes far beyond sheer statistics. They credit these efforts with creating a strong sense of loyalty and corporate community within Xerox. In fact, BCN and the Road Show have been so successful that other minorities and women are forming their own self-help groups.

Employees aren't the only ones who appreciate what Xerox has done. Recently, *Hispanic* magazine included the company on its list of corporations that offer Hispanics the greatest opportunity. The magazine praised Xerox's long-term commitment to minority hiring, promotion, and community groups.

Questions

1. Describe Xerox's cultural diversity programs.
2. Do you think diversity programs like Xerox's should be part of the human resource management function at all companies? Defend your answer.
3. Discuss the pros and cons of having separate self-help groups for African Americans, women, and other minorities. What can Xerox do to minimize any disadvantages?
4. What types of employee training are included in Xerox's programs? What other kinds, if any, would you suggest Xerox add?

CHAPTER 9
American Worker—Japanese Boss

Almost half a million Americans now work for Japanese-owned firms in the United States. While multinational ventures frequently create conflicts in human relations, Japanese–American work places in particular pose their own challenges. Japanese firms have been accused of racism, sexism, and just plain prejudice. Some American workers have even taken their Japanese bosses to court.

Why do Americans find it hard to work for the Japanese? Perhaps because the employer and the employee come from such vastly different cultures. Japanese society is built upon a strict social hierarchy that carries over into business life; Japanese culture also emphasizes group loyalty. The United States, however, was founded as a frontier society of immigrants from diverse backgrounds and with a strong emphasis on individualism and the family. Japanese culture often mystifies Americans, so much so that a market has developed for English-language publications that explain Asian practices to Westerners. "Puzzled by Japanese business?" asks an ad for one such newspaper, which promises to reveal to bemused Americans "the truth about how Japanese business people think and behave."

Like anyone moving halfway around the globe, Japanese employers who come to America bring "cultural baggage" with them. Some Asian practices, such as work teams and morning exercise sessions, translate

well. Hundreds of firms have transplanted Japanese manufacturing techniques to the United States successfully. Other practices, however, may not be so well received. Take employee evaluations: Japanese firms often evaluate staffers not through one-on-one meetings, but by using form letters. In Japan, where it is considered rude to press your views on someone else, form-letter evaluations seem polite and respectful. In the United States, however, they come across as cold and distant. At one Japanese-owned company, an American manager tried to persuade his Asian boss to evaluate the staff through personal, American-style interviews, but without success.

One of the greatest on-the-job mysteries for American employees is the Japanese approach to corporate power. In Japan, organizational power comes from interpersonal networks formed by a lifetime of working for the same company. Those within the network are the decision makers, while those outside the network are just that—outsiders. American managers in Japanese-run firms often complain about butting their heads against a "glass ceiling" of invisible but powerful discrimination. They tell of "shadows," Japanese execs who stay in the background but make the real decisions. Often it is the middle-level managers who feel the greatest frustration, as they find themselves wielding power in name only. Both turnover rates and employment discrimination lawsuits are prevalent among white-collar American employees in Asian-owned firms.

Japanese interpersonal networks don't just breed power; they also determine which employees keep their jobs. Some Americans who formerly worked for Japanese bosses complain bitterly of the nation's "no-layoff policy." They claim that, when hired, they were promised lifetime employment—a promise that was later broken. One ex-manager tells of being hired to fulfill a "five-year plan," only to be dismissed. Outraged employees may demand explanations, only to be told that "Tokyo has decided" they should go. Outsiders, says one, are considered "talented specialists" who are expendable if profits sag.

Of course, American companies fire employees, too, and it doesn't make the news. Part of the problem is that many Americans romanticize the idea of Japanese management, and when they go to work for Asians, they have high expectations that turn out to be unrealistic. One ex-manager admits that when a Japanese firm offered him a job, he found it "kind of neat" that in 50 years the two nations could go from being enemies to friends. Today he is suing his former employer for discrimination based on national origin.

For their part, the Japanese admit that they view American employees as outsiders. They also feel they are justified, because they think Americans are not willing to make a lifetime commitment to one firm. One Japanese consultant notes that U.S. workers often stay with one company for a few years, then look around for a better job. Who can blame Japanese managers, he asks, for withholding power from people they know will leave?

Questions

1. Evaluate differences and similarities between American and Japanese management styles.
2. Discuss communication issues that arise when American employees work for Japanese managers.
3. What needs might constitute "self-actualization" for an American employee? For a Japanese employee?
4. Apply your answer from Question 3 to the challenge of motivating employees. Would a manager motivate American employees differently from Japanese workers? Explain.
5. What advantages and disadvantages do you see in the Japanese reliance on interpersonal networks?

CHAPTER 10
Sea World

In Chapter 10, you learned about many functions that computers serve in business. But here is one you probably did not read about: using computers to generate and analyze data needed to monitor pregnancies in killer whales. However, if your business happens to be Sea World, a division of St. Louis-based Anheuser-Busch, with aquatic theme parks in California, Florida, Ohio, and Texas, you might well use computers to secure the information required to boost family life among your killer whale population. Computers also might be used to help you learn how Antarctic penguins keep their cool in the Florida heat. You certainly would be likely to use them to make sure that your factory-made "sea water" is close enough to the real thing to keep sharks smiling.

Few businesses, of course, face the types of challenges that Sea World does. However, the theme-park company depends on its computer system just as any other firm does. Indeed, while some might think of technology and ecology as natural enemies, the information systems at Sea World show that technology sometimes can be the environment's best friend.

While Sea World uses computers for less exotic functions (such as accounting, tracking attendance, and billing), the park would not last long without its computerized systems for habitat management. These systems monitor and adjust living conditions in the various habitats (native environments) that make up Sea World's exhibits. They also advise the park's employees on the health and needs of their aquatic friends.

Take those Antarctic penguins. How can birds from a freezing wilderness survive in the sultry heat of a Florida summer? The answer is a computer-managed climatic balancing act. Sensors constantly measure the temperature and air quality in the penguins' new home. If the readings fall even slightly below the ideal measurements stored in computer memory, the computer triggers a condenser that makes snow and drops it on the birds. This is just fine with the penguins, who are used to lots of snow anyway.

Sea World's extensive database on animal characteristics and needs also helps it manage the popular Shark Encounter exhibit. When visitors first enter the three-part exhibit, they find themselves looking down on a pool filled with sharks, with an occasional glimpse of those famous fins slicing the water. Then they view a short film that, unlike Hollywood movies, presents the facts on these much-misunderstood creatures. "The film," notes the fish curator, "dispels many myths about sharks. It explains that they are not just eating machines, but an important part of the ocean's food chain." The final portion of the exhibit is a clear acrylic tube, 3½ inches thick, at the bottom of the sharks' pool. Visitors move through the tube and enjoy a breathtaking underwater view. Says the curator, "I can think of no better, closer way to see sharks without getting wet."

Like the penguin exhibit, Shark Encounter would not be possible without constant help from computers. The "sea water" in which the sharks swim is actually artificial, created by a careful mixing of water, salt, and other ingredients. Sensors continually monitor water quality, since the hot summer sun can evaporate water quickly and leave the pool too salty. When this happens, the sensors trigger a computer program that operates filters, valves, and circulation equipment to return the pool to its shark-ideal state.

Perhaps Sea World's best-known habitat-management program involves its killer whales. A few years ago, the Orlando park hosted an event that caused a big stir in scientific circles. Shamu, its killer whale star, gave birth to the first killer whale born in captivity. The successful birth was a tribute to Sea World's carefully controlled aquatic environment: after all, Shamu would not have felt like breeding if her man-made habitat did not resemble her natural surroundings. The birth also provided an incredible opportunity for scientists to study the gestation, birth, and growth of killer whales—research almost impossible to conduct in the wild.

Immediately after Shamu's pregnancy was discovered, Orlando Sea World staffers and visiting scientists began keeping careful track of her progress. Researchers constantly collected data that were fed into computers. Some staffers sat poolside and recorded Shamu's behavior and activities on laptop computers. Others measured her body weight and shape at frequent intervals, while a sonogram unit bounced sound waves off the whale fetus to measure its shape and heartbeat via sound-wave imaging. Still other researchers took regular blood samples from Shamu and fed them into a blood serum analyzer. Using a light pen, the researcher could scan a list of bar-coded computer programs and select a specific diagnostic test. The computerized test analyzed the whale's blood and logged the results.

All of this information was fed into computers, which analyzed the raw data for patterns and trends. Researchers correlated the computerized data with their observations of Shamu in her pool. Scientists around the world shared their findings via electronic mail.

This round-the-clock monitoring has greatly increased our knowledge of killer whales. More importantly (to Shamu, no doubt), it produced a healthy baby whale. Since then, Sea World's killer whale breeding program has resulted in five more calves, born in theme parks across the United States.

Questions

1. Describe some of the functions that information systems serve at Sea World.
2. Which of these functions are similar to the functions of information systems at other companies? Which are different?
3. Describe several of the hardware and software components of Sea World's information system.
4. Could Sea World operate without a computerized information system? If so, how would it have to modify its business operations? Explain your answer.

CHAPTER 11
Global Marketing

Are people the same everywhere? It's a simple question—with a complicated answer. Business professors, marketers, and consumers have been arguing over this one for years. At stake are billions of dollars in potential markets, waiting to be tapped all over the globe. Also at stake, perhaps, is the marvelous mosaic of cultural diversity.

If you are an American business person, how do you market your products to consumers in Nigeria, or Thailand, or Brazil? The traditional wisdom would tell you to employ a multinational marketing strategy, which involves tailoring your marketing mix to the culture, characteristics, and competitive situations in each country. Kraft, for instance, uses a multinational approach in promoting its cheese to different nations. Advertisements in Belgium show cheese being spread on toast for breakfast, while ads for the Spanish market depict the same brand of cheese combined with asparagus as an hors d'oeuvre.

During the 1980s, however, a new marketing strategy arose: global marketing. Harvard Business School professor Theodore Levitt started writing articles with titles like "The Globalization of Markets." Levitt argued that nations all over the world were becoming more like each other. He predicted that cultural differences would gradually vanish, and that smart organizations would begin standardizing their marketing strategies. This would allow them to take advantage of economies of scale, lowering their costs of doing business and allowing them to cut prices. Said Levitt, "What is needed is a confident global imagination that sees the world as a single marketplace entity."

Ken Levin, another Harvard professor, agrees: "Increasingly, all over the world, you find the same markets and market segments repeated over and over again." Why are cultural differences disappearing? Levitt and Levin credit the change to technology—improved global communications, increased international travel, and the growing influence of international media, such as television and movies. Privatization of media also has helped. Until recently, many TV stations in foreign countries were owned by the government, which placed strict limits on advertising. As the media were deregulated, more time has been made available for American advertising. Another important factor is travel, which exposes people to different cultures.

Benetton is an example of a company that successfully uses a global marketing strategy. It markets its cosmetics and knitwear to the same type of consumer worldwide—young, affluent, trendy—by using a common theme, "United Colors of Benetton," and images with a broad visual appeal. The only change is in the translating of advertising copy into different languages.

Food and beverage marketers are also fond of the global approach. Coca-Cola is developing a long-term strategy that will incorporate movies, sporting events, and popular music into its global marketing. Says one Coke executive, "American culture broadly defined—music, film, fashion, and food—has become the culture worldwide." A recent Coke advertisement, called "General Assembly," features teenagers from 200 countries singing the virtues of the soft drink. The ad has been translated into 16 languages and broadcast in over 50 nations.

Not everyone likes the idea of a worldwide marketplace. Some people see global marketing as a serious threat to the multicultural flavors that make our world so interesting. They claim that one small industry—advertising—is attempting to force American lifestyles and values on the rest of the globe, destroying native cultures in the process. Protests by the French against Euro Disneyland represent one highly publicized example.

Even some marketers warn that global marketing strategies may be assuming too much, too soon. Nationalism remains a powerful emotional force in many countries, and marketing campaigns that try to force foreign attitudes on consumers could backfire. Where possible, say these marketers, multinational firms should put overseas operations under the control of local managers who respect and understand their own markets and customers.

Some marketers prefer to hedge their bets, realizing that people around the world may be similar in some ways, but very different in others. When Scott Paper started marketing its wares in Europe, its market research showed that the same image—a Labrador puppy—would be effective across the continent in creating a warm, "soft but strong" feeling. While the puppy starred in all its European ads, however, Scott was careful to customize the commercials to local environments. British ads showed the puppy in a traditional English country garden, while in Spain the setting switched to a living room with Spanish-style furniture.

Questions

1. Summarize the factors that are helping to create a global marketplace.
2. Describe several products that might be more suited to the multinational marketing approach.
3. Do global marketing strategies force American values on the people of other countries? Explain your answer.
4. Stage an in-class debate on the pros and cons of multinational versus global marketing.

CHAPTER 12
Stewart-Warner

Migration is a habit that dates back to the dawn of time. People and animals moved across the land be-

cause resources, such as water, climate, good land, and vegetation, dried up, and they settled in areas with abundant amounts of natural resources. Migration is evident today, not only in nature but in business as well. Companies are heading north, south, east, and west because resources are no longer available, the land and the cost of doing business has become too expensive, or they want to consolidate existing facilities.

Stewart-Warner, a manufacturer of speedometers and other instruments for cars, was bought out by BTR, a British conglomerate, a few years ago. In 1991, BTR decided to close down one of the two Stewart-Warner production facilities in Chicago and move the work to Texas and Mexico. The reasoning was simple. According to a BTR source, "Because most of our competitors obtain their products from lower-cost areas of the world, we have to move our operations in order to survive." The average wage in Chicago was $10 an hour. In Texas it was $8 an hour and in Mexico less than $1 an hour. Moving would save the company $17 million a year.

But this move affected more than just business economics. Closing the plant would impact not only the workers but their community and the local tax structure. By using data from previous plant shutdowns, it was possible to calculate what the Stewart-Warner plant closing would really cost.

First, the employees would lose jobs averaging $10 an hour plus benefits, and few, if any, other employment opportunities existed in the area. Second, many family members worked at the plant. So not only would one worker per family be displaced but whole families would be out of work. Finally, displaced elderly employees are seldom able to reenter the work force.

The community also would be affected by the increased costs of maintaining the social safety net. The plant closing would increase unemployment compensation costs by more than $11 million and general assistance (welfare) by another million. The number of food-stamp dependents would increase, and government revenues (taxes) would decline. Also hit hard would be the local businesses where the laid-off Stewart-Warner employees used to shop.

The plant closing also could be expected to result in higher rates of stress-related diseases, including cardiovascular problems, heart attacks, high blood pressure, ulcers, and alcoholism. Chronically unemployed workers are more prone to commit suicide, abuse their spouses and children, suffer more mental health problems, and be involved in criminal activities.

There is some relief for plant closings provided by government regulations. The Plant-Closing Notification Act of 1988 requires employers with more than 100 employees to give workers and local officials warning 60 days prior to a shutdown or mass layoff. This allows both the employees and the local community a little time to plan and adjust for the plant closing. A Worker Readjustment Program assists workers displaced as a result of plant closings. It provides job search, placement, and counseling services, as well as educational opportunities and, when necessary, child care, community assistance, and personal financial counseling.

An alternative to the plant closing was legislation introduced by a Chicago alderman. He recommended a new approach to the doctrine of *eminent domain* in which the city of Chicago would seize the plant from BTR and sell it to local investors.

While eminent domain law in the abstract strikes an equitable balance between private rights and public needs, current interpretations and applications of the just-compensation clause raise significant legal, ethical, and economic issues. The Fifth Amendment establishes eminent domain as an inherent power of government by providing that no person shall be deprived of life, liberty, or property without due process of law; nor shall private property be taken for public use without just compensation.

But the use (proper or improper) of eminent domain could be economically self-destructive. An interpretation might be that if Chicago doesn't like the decision a company makes, the city will seize the business's assets and sell them to somebody else. That interpretation would discourage companies from bringing future jobs to the city of Chicago.

Questions

1. Frequently when a business closes a plant or operational facility, only economic items are considered. What additional items should be evaluated?
2. If a company does decide to shut down, what responsibilities does it have to its workers?
3. Suppose a business wants to locate its plant where you live. Would you want any guarantees from the business? Explain.
4. What items must managers analyze before deciding where to put a new plant?

CHAPTER 13
Paint by Numbers

What is art? (Bet you didn't expect to find that question in a business textbook!) Some people see art as a highly personal, even inspired, expression of the artist's thoughts and feelings. Many of us think of artists as underfed, suffering types who struggle to express their artistic inspiration against all odds.

Take Vincent van Gogh as an example. A psychologically tortured nineteenth-century artist who symbolizes the idea of art as inspiration, Van Gogh firmly believed that art was the only thing that made his life worthwhile. In fact, he finally committed suicide because increasing episodes of mental illness kept him from painting.

Van Gogh lived—and died—in poverty because the art critics of his day thought his paintings were even stranger than he was. But here's an ironic twist: Today, 100 years after his death, his works sell for millions of dollars at auction houses.

This brings us to another definition of art. Some people view it as a product, just like any other commodity, which can be bought and sold. In fact, many collectors today prize art for its monetary value rather than its aesthetic value.

No one could be more different from Vincent van Gogh than, say, Mark Kostabi. While van Gogh sacrificed everything for art, some would say that Kostabi cheerfully sacrifices art for higher ends—like money and publicity.

Kostabi started out in suffering-artist style, studying art in California and selling his small drawings for whatever he could get. Soon, however, he realized the importance of marketing. Kostabi moved to Manhattan and worked to increase his visibility with potential customers. He invaded corporate offices, handed out free copies of his drawings, and talked wealthy executives into buying the originals. He crashed gallery openings and parties, introducing himself to anyone who would listen. Brags Kostabi, "I stayed up till 3 A.M. in clubs, just collecting business cards." When he realized that wealthy investors were more interested in big paintings than small drawings, he enlarged his works and began charging up to $5,000 apiece for them. When galleries starting competing with each other to sign him, Kostabi cheerfully exploited his newly minted marketability: "I played dealers off on each other, infuriating them."

It wasn't long before Kostabi had another idea. Rather than spending his own well-paid time in painting, why not hire cheap labor to do the work? The result: Kostabi World, a Manhattan "art factory" that employs about 21 painters, canvas stretchers, designers, and support staff. Working in assembly-line fashion, two shifts of employees produce about six "Kostabi originals" a day; the boss's participation is usually limited to inspecting the finished products and signing his famous name to them. Kostabi World's employees earn between $4.50 to $10.50 per hour; their creations sell for $4,000 to $30,000 apiece. Says Mark, "This way, you don't even have to be able to draw or paint to make art. You can just hire people to execute your ideas."

How do Kostabi's employees feel about this? Some are philosophical. Says one, "It's a fun job compared to being a waiter. And I don't feel that I need recognition. It's his artistic statement, his name, his reputation." Others feel used. One woman worked there for six months and stormed out sobbing. "I realized that I was being exploited beyond my imagination," she says. "In the first two months I put out 300 drawings, and I wasn't earning enough to support myself. I found out recently that one of my drawings was turned into a painting that is now in the Guggenheim [a prestigious New York museum]."

Kostabi dismisses such criticisms: "Legally they are my paintings. The artists work on my time, and they're paid for it." While the artists create the canvases, Kostabi develops his image and markets Kostabi World's products—activities that he feels are a much better use of his time and talents.

Mark took his hands-off management style to new lengths for a recent exhibit in Moscow. To avoid customs and shipping costs, he faxed instructions to Russian artists, who created the paintings. Kostabi then flew to Moscow, inspected the paintings, and signed them just before the show.

As you might imagine, Kostabi is a controversial figure in the art world. Sniffs one reviewer, "Kostabi's paintings are so bad that they even subvert the good name of 'bad painting.'" But others admire his unorthodox approach. Says one defender, "Mark has staked out a valid conceptual idea of art, dealing with status and the hypocrisy of the art world." Still others point out that Kostabi's "art factory" approach is not new. Vincent van Gogh was the exception rather than the rule; so-called old masters like Rubens and Monet were highly practical businessmen who painted what their customers wanted to buy.

So, returning to our earlier question: what is art? Is it simply a product? Mark Kostabi says yes, and he feels that this approach opens new doors for creative people. "In the '90s, kids won't have to be considered pansies or wimps when they tell their parents they want to be artists," he says. "Now everyone can see that art is actually a respectable business."

Questions

1. Into what product classification(s) would you place Kostabi's paintings? Van Gogh's paintings?
2. Analyze Kostabi's product strategy. Why do you feel it is successful?
3. What type of pricing strategy does Kostabi use?
4. Do you feel Kostabi's approach is ethical? Explain your answer.

CHAPTER 14
Springfield Remanufacturing Corp.

"We continually challenge people to tell us where they want to go, what they want to do with their lives. When you do that, you open a lot of doors. You get rid of a lot of the frustrations people have. You also take their excuses away, which is essential."

Who's talking here—a travel agent? A job counselor? A therapist? Actually, this quote comes straight from Jack Stack, president and CEO of Springfield Remanufacturing Corp. (SRC). Stack believes strongly that the best work force is an informed work force. In fact, he says, SRC's "real business" is not machinery, but education. "We teach people about business. . . . When people come to work at SRC, we tell them 70 percent of the job is disassembly—or whatever—and 30 percent of the job is learning. What they learn is how to make money, how to make a profit."

SRC places great importance on the company's financial data as an educational tool. Let's take a closer look at just how Stack and SRC's other managers use accounting information to educate and motivate their employees. Stack offers these general guidelines:

- *Start with the income statement.* Stack feels the ever-changing income statement is the best way to draw employees into the excitement of treating business as a game. At meetings, he likes to use these statements as an overall view of the game's action and each employee's role in it.
- *Highlight the categories in which the firm spends the most money.* Stack encourages employees to keep a close watch on these areas.
- *Break down categories into controllable elements.* Help employees see that these categories are not just columns on a page—they are expenses that can make or break the company. For instance, a trucking firm could separate the categories of maintenance, gas, and repairs; a sales organization could specify such elements as travel, hotel bills, and client entertainment.
- *Use the income statement to help employees understand the balance sheet.* While the income statement shows the action of the game, the balance sheet gives the overall score: how much wealth the company has created, where it is weak, and how secure people's jobs are. Show how changes in the income state-

ment translate into changes in the balance sheet, and what this means for the company.

At SRC, the financial statements present specific costs involved in manufacturing: materials, labor, overhead, and job performance. Almost everything in the entire company is quantified, from the amount spent on receptionists' note pads to the amount of overhead involved every time a worker grinds a crankshaft. Labor ratios are calculated daily for all employees. The latest figures on sales (broken down by both customer and product) are posted for everyone to see—who the customers are, what they buy, and how they buy it.

Clearly, SRC's work force is educated about the meaning and significance of accounting information. So how do Stack and other managers use this information to motivate workers?

An important motivator for any employee is the recognition represented by a bonus—money, in addition to his or her regular salary, that is linked directly to exceptional productivity or performance. Many firms use bonuses to motivate employees. At SRC, however, the difference is that employees are involved in calculating their bonuses from the very beginning. Says Stack, "A bonus system like ours allows us to hold base salaries at a level that gives people a great deal of job security but shares with them, through bonuses, whatever additional money they generate. The more they generate, the bigger the bonuses."

In setting up the bonus system, Stack meets with employees to set profit targets and maximum bonus payouts. This involves agreeing on a baseline and top target for profits, as well as the highest level of bonuses employees can receive by achieving both income-statement and balance-sheet goals. Having agreed on these figures, the group calculates how much additional profit employees might generate, and how much they should earn as bonuses if they meet all their targets.

Next, the group decides on a balance-sheet goal. The object here is to make sure the firm has enough cash—sufficient liquidity—to pay the bonuses employees earn.

The third step is to establish the targets for this balance-sheet goal. The group plugs various projections into the balance sheet to determine the target that would bring extra profits for workers.

Finally, the group measures the effect these goals will have on the value of SRC's stock. This, for Stack, is the bottom line of business: "the generation of wealth in the form of equity." Says the CEO, "Everything we do is based on a common understanding that job security is paramount—that we are creating a place for people to work not just this year or five years from now, but for the next 50 years and beyond. We owe it to one another to keep the company alive."

This concern for equity has paid off. When SRC employees first bought the then-struggling firm from Navistar, its stock was worth 10 cents a share. By the early 1990s, the stock price had soared to $18.30—an increase of 18,300 percent in eight years.

While Stack is proud of this achievement, he's even prouder of something else. Those years sometimes have been rocky for SRC; during one memorable year the little company lost a contract totaling 40 percent of its annual sales. But, brags Stack, SRC has never laid off a single employee.

Questions

1. Distinguish between the income statement and the balance sheet. What role(s) does each play at SRC?
2. Relate Jack Stack's management style to the concepts discussed earlier in Chapters 4 and 7. What management function(s) would Stack say are the most important? What type of organizational structure would he advocate?
3. Would you want to work for a company that used SRC's "business as a game" approach? Explain your answer.
4. How could SRC's approach be applied to the company where you work? (If you aren't employed presently, think of a company with which you are familiar.) What would change? What would stay the same?

CHAPTER 15
Duracell International

Merger mania was the wave of the 1980s. Huge amounts of money were involved, and many businesses ignored the possibility that all of these combinations could be unhealthy. Insider trading of merger and acquisition targets was rampant, and individuals like Ivan Boesky got rich and then went to jail, convicted of illegal activities. Michael E. Milken, of Drexel Burnham Lambert, provided many takeover firms the bonds needed to raise the billions required for these deals. But these bond issuers (and purchasers) are now paying the price. During the early 1990s, corporate bankruptcies increased to almost 60,000 a year, many of which are the result of debt loads taken on during the previous decade.

A leveraged buyout (LBO) is the use of borrowed money to purchase a company or division. The acquired unit's assets typically are used as collateral for the loan, which sometimes can amount to 90 or

95 percent of the leveraged buyout price. Because of the huge amount of leverage (debt) used in LBOs, two important issues must be addressed. First, will the acquired firm be able to generate enough cash to pay its bills and to pay off the loan? Second, is the LBO good for the long-term health of the company? For example, will the company become more efficient and competitive?

There were, however, some successes with LBOs during the previous decade. One of them was the purchase of battery maker Duracell International by Kohlberg Kravis Roberts and Company (KKR) in 1988. Duracell originally had been acquired by Kraft as part of a $2.5 billion merger with Dart Industries in 1980. But the combined companies simply did not mesh. Being part of Kraft placed Duracell in a company with too many other product lines. Duracell was stuck in a far-off division that was not part of the corporate family. After all, Kraft was food, and Duracell was batteries.

Duracell's president, C. Robert Kidder, was frustrated with Kraft's bureaucratic higher-ups. Duracell was treated as just small potatoes in the corporation. It needed cash to invest in new technology, such as batteries made from lithium, but Kidder was not able to shake loose the needed research and development money from Kraft.

In 1988, bad news for Kraft resulted in an ideal situation for Duracell. Philip Morris decided to attempt a takeover of Kraft. To raise capital to thwart the Philip Morris takeover, Kraft put Duracell on the block. While the $1.8 billion price was high, KKR saw an opportunity in batteries and organized the LBO of Duracell.

Of the $1.8 billion needed for the leveraged buyout, 50 percent was borrowed from banks, 30 percent was provided in the form of junk bonds, and the remaining 20 percent came directly from KKR (along with $6 million from management). The LBO freed Duracell from Kraft's corporate hierarchy, allowed KKR to put up only 20 percent of the purchase price to get control of the entire firm, and gave management an entrepreneurial incentive because of the change in company ownership.

Duracell has become more efficient since then. Its lithium technology research has advanced, and the company has become more focused. Charles Perrin, president of Duracell North America and the person who heads up the company's marketing efforts, says, "We want to be the worldwide leader in consumer batteries." By 1995, Duracell's worldwide sales were exceeding the $1.5 billion mark, the company held 43 percent of the U.S. alkaline battery market, and it owned the only battery brand name with worldwide recognition and acceptance.

Duracell also has responded quickly to consumer needs. The company was the first manufacturer to put freshness dates on battery packages. It has provided consumers with the Copper Top Tester—a free, reusable, energy-sensitive, plastic strip used to see how much life is left in batteries.

Duracell presently is spending record levels on research and development and contends that R&D increases will continue at a level at least equal to its current percentage of annual sales. And what about the huge debt-servicing requirements of the LBO? Well, Duracell has an answer for that, too. In 1991, Duracell International went public through an initial public offering (IPO). The stock opened at $15 a share on the New York Stock Exchange and, in less than a week, ran up to $21.60. In 1995, the stock was approaching $45 per share.

Duracell's future looks even brighter. The demand for alkaline batteries—which make up 80 percent of sales—is expected to grow eight to ten percent each year. Of equal importance, the company has managed to pay off $790 million of its LBO debt over the last three years. This has reduced Duracell's annual interest cost by $150 million.

Questions

1. What are the advantages and disadvantages of using debt financing for business expansion? Relate your answer to Duracell's experience.
2. Should leveraged buyouts continue to be used for business acquisition? Why or why not?
3. Who ultimately pays for an LBO's failure? Explain.
4. What are the advantages and disadvantages of using equity financing for business expansion?

CHAPTER 16
Tokyo Tumble

As we pointed out in this chapter, securities trading is going global. More nations are joining in, and their economies grow ever more interconnected. Given these facts, it would seem logical that an economic disaster in one country would inevitably trigger unpleasant side effects in the markets of major trading partners. Makes sense, doesn't it? During the 1980s, in fact, as Japan's stock market expanded enormously, respected economists and business journalists worried that a financial crash in Tokyo would lead to major shock waves in the United States.

But, in the murky world of securities trading, common sense doesn't always prevail. Japan's stock market crashed, its shares losing 33 percent of their value since 1989. But so far the predicted problems have failed to appear overseas. Let's look at why Japan's stock market rose and fell, and how this has affected—or failed to affect—U.S. markets.

Traditionally, one of Japan's primary strengths has been the country's unified approach to business: an attitude that some journalists label "Japan Inc." Until recently, Japanese workers willingly accepted low wages so that companies could earn greater profits, many of which were reinvested in the companies so the firms could, in turn, reap still greater earnings. The typical Japanese citizen saves almost 25 percent of his or her annual salary, storing the money in safe—but low-yielding—bank accounts.

During the 1980s, however, even the patient Japanese got restless. The country's business investments were paying off and cash came flooding in. Families who once stored their savings in banks decided to move them into securities. Between 1985 and 1989 Japan's stock market soared a staggering 197 percent. It was a great time to be a stockbroker in Tokyo; one broker recalls the boom times as "*hidari uchiwa* [literally, sitting comfortably and fanning yourself with your left hand]. . . . Things were so comfortable. You were so relaxed. You made money without really trying."

By 1990, Japan's economy—barely half the size of America's—had "made money" until it had swollen to almost twice that of the United States. Helping to fuel its growth was an almost total lack of government regulation. Rules did exist, but few brokers abided by them.

Despite its impressive growth, Japan's market was seriously overextended. Its price–earnings ratio averaged a staggering 65 to 1. By way of comparison, the average price–earnings ratio for firms listed on the New York Stock Exchange at that point averaged 13 to 1. Investors could continue to make money only if stock prices kept rising. And, in turn, stock prices rose only if people kept buying.

But, as any stockbroker will tell you, this kind of growth could not last forever. Investors got nervous as they watched the market bubble expand, and decided to sell their holdings before the bubble burst. Edgy brokers advised clients to invest in less risky American and German securities. Finally, the crash came: within a few months the market fell 25 percent and lost $1 trillion in value. In 1992 the Nikkei Index fell to its lowest point in almost six years. By 1995, it had recovered to above the 20,000 mark—still one-third below its pre-crash high.

Did the crash echo around the globe, as predicted? Not really. Over a two-year period, while Japan's stock market continued to drop, U.S. stock indexes rose to new highs. As Tokyo slowly recovers from its painful overexpansion, market analysts in other countries are measuring its effects on their own trading floors. So far, the results are mixed—but far from the global catastrophe many economists had foretold.

Perhaps the biggest impact has been on bank loans and the banking industry. Lower stock prices have reduced the amount of cheap capital that Japanese banks can lend. This in turn could limit the availability of loans in the United States. About 40 percent of the assets in Japan's big commercial banks are overseas loans. In California, about $1 out of every $4 in business loans comes from a Japanese bank. Says Robert Glauber, former undersecretary of the Treasury for Domestic Finance, "I think we'll get a dose of what it's like to have our banking system influenced by foreign banks."

Even this, however, ultimately could prove beneficial to the U.S. economy. During the 1980s, cheap capital helped Japanese firms to expand abroad and best other countries in international competition, just as it helped Japanese banks become financiers to the world. As Japanese banks retrench and cut back on foreign lending, this may give American banks and companies an opportunity to expand into new markets.

The Japanese market crash may, in fact, boost U.S. exchanges, since wary investors are likely to sell off Japanese holdings in favor of less risky U.S. stocks. At the same time, the huge price declines in Japanese share prices are beginning to attract "bottom fishers"—Western investors betting on a recovery of the Tokyo Stock Exchange. However, they usually buy through Western brokerage firms, not their Japanese counterparts. One analyst notes that "the combined share of all 14 top [Japanese] brokers . . . is weakening, signaling a gain in market share for the foreign brokers."

No one would deny that, around the world, nations' economies are getting more global. But, apparently, the U.S. and Japanese markets, says Richard Breeden, chairman of the U.S. Securities and Exchange Commission, "aren't linked in a manner that would cause an automatic impact on one market because of economic events in the other."

And, for Japanese-owned companies in the United States, business goes on as usual. A spokesperson for tire maker Bridgestone/Firestone Inc., the North American unit of Japan's Bridgestone Corporation, says there's been "absolutely no effect" from the Tokyo market's decline: "We regard ourselves as an independent company operating in America. Our performance is entirely due to our efforts."

Questions

1. Explain why Japan's stock market grew so rapidly.
2. Describe the factors that caused its stock market to crash.
3. Discuss how the decline of Japan's stock market could affect the U.S. economy. Are the effects likely to be positive, negative, or mixed? Explain.
4. Are there any lessons that U.S. investors can learn from Japan's stock market crash? Explain.

APPENDIX A
Insurance Risks

Coming down with a serious illness is bad enough. But what if you couldn't get medicine for your condition because companies were afraid to make it? This is the tragic situation in which some desperately ill people are trapped. Drug manufacturers would love to develop, produce, and market medicines to help them. However, many are reluctant to create and test experimental drugs and vaccines. The reason is product liability.

One lost product liability lawsuit can bankrupt a company because the amount of damages involved in such lawsuits has soared. In 1975, only nine product liability cases resulted in an award of $1 million or more; ten years later, the number had risen to more than 85 and continues to go up each year.

Companies can, and do, purchase product liability insurance to protect themselves against risk. But this is not an ideal answer, since premiums for product liability insurance are rising along with the lawsuit awards. A U.S. Department of Commerce study reveals that U.S. firms must pay 20 to 50 percent more for liability insurance than manufacturers in other countries. Ultimately, these higher premiums come back to haunt all of us in the form of higher prices on products.

Even more disturbing than the prospect of higher prices, however, is the possibility that the threat of a major lawsuit stops many companies from taking risks. Studies show that the risk of product liability discourages firms from investigating new leads, and sometimes causes them to stop work on promising but risky innovations. One example: the development of an AIDS vaccine.

AIDS is a serious worldwide health crisis that is spreading all too rapidly. The virus that causes the fatal disease first was isolated back in 1983, and a number of universities, private research labs, and companies around the world are working on ways to curtail the epidemic. A vital part of this research involves de-

veloping a vaccine that can protect people from AIDS. The good news is that research into an AIDS vaccine continues; the bad news is that the specter of product liability has slowed the development and testing of possible vaccines. Many researchers, in fact, feel that we would be much further along in the quest if drug companies were not so worried about the risk of lawsuits. Early tests on humans probably will involve volunteers who are at high risk for getting the disease anyway. Even the best vaccines aren't 100 percent effective, and some volunteers could end up being infected with the virus. Should that occur, drug makers fear, volunteers might blame it on the vaccine and go to court.

The problem appears to affect AIDS research at several companies. One is Oncogen, a subsidiary of Bristol-Myers Squibb, which has conducted promising experiments with a vaccine called HIVAC-le. Oncogen researchers demonstrated that HIVAC-le, when injected into humans, strengthens the body's immune response (an important part of warding off infection). They also used the vaccine to prevent four monkeys from getting AIDS after being exposed to the virus. One expert hailed Oncogen's clinical trials as the most promising yet.

Despite the enthusiastic response, however, Oncogen has stopped producing HIVAC-le. Officially, the firm denies that this is due to product liability fears. A company spokesperson simply states that, "We met our obligation to provide HIVAC-le for clinical trials, which are now over." Privately, some company researchers claim that fear of lawsuits is the real reason. "Bristol is short-sighted in terms of research," says one staffer. "We're not even supposed to mention the dreaded V-word."

Another company, Immune Response Corp. (IRC), also has seen its research bogged down by liability worries. For years, IRC has been testing an experimental vaccine in people who already are infected with the AIDS virus. No major liability issues have resulted from these tests; however, IRC hasn't yet been able to test a vaccine for healthy people—because it can't find a manufacturer willing to make it. "We, as a company, are quite willing to go forward," says a member of IRC's board.

Often researchers have been unable even to get funding for their experiments. When it comes to vaccines, pediatrician Stanley Plotkin has a great track record. He helped develop them for many diseases, including polio, chicken pox, and rabies. But he ran into a dead end when he wanted to produce a similar vaccine for AIDS. Many companies and other researchers thought his methods were just too risky, and no one in the United States would provide the necessary money. Plotkin believes that "the re-viewers—in addition to their scientific criticisms—must have had liability in mind."

Today, Plotkin still is working toward finding an AIDS vaccine—but not in the United States. He recently joined the staff at Pasteur-Merieux-Connaught in France.

Questions

1. Discuss how the risk of product liability lawsuits could affect research and development of experimental drugs.

2. Do drug manufacturers have an ethical responsibility to assume the risks of providing medicine to people with serious illnesses, such as AIDS? Explain your answer.

3. Hold an in-class debate in which half the class represents the insurance industry, while the other half represents a major drug manufacturer. Discuss the issue of product liability insurance and what can be done to keep premiums at a manageable level.

ENDNOTES

Chapter 1

1. Russell Mitchell, "Managing by Values," *Business Week*, August 1, 1994, 46–52; Russell Mitchell, "A Mild-Mannered Maverick Puts His Brand on Levi's," *Business Week*, August 1, 1994, 51; and Faye Rice, "How to Make Diversity Pay," *Fortune*, August 8, 1994, 78–86.
2. Theresa Howard, "Checkers' Mattei Quits; Segment Facing Big Test," *Nation's Restaurant News*, March 21, 1994, 1.
3. Tom Morrison, "Discovery Zone Finds Niche in Fun Center Market," *Amusement Business*, November 8, 1993, 35.
4. Andrew Serwer, "Lessons from America's Fastest-Growing Companies," *Fortune*, August 8, 1994, 42–62.
5. *Ibid.*
6. Edmund Faltermayer, "Competitiveness: How U.S. Companies Stack Up Now," *Fortune*, April 18, 1994, 52–64.
7. Resa W. King, "Women Entrepreneurs," *Business Week*, April 18, 1994, 104.
8. Thomas Stewart, "Managing in a Wired Company," *Fortune*, July 11, 1994, 44–56.
9. Rob Norton, "Strategies for the New Export Boom," *Fortune*, August 22, 1994, 124–130.
10. Otis Port, "So Much for Declining U.S. Competitiveness," *Business Week*, July 23, 1994, 82.
11. Myron Magnet, "The Productivity Payoff Arrives," *Fortune*, June 27, 1994, 79–84; and Gene Koretz, "Productivity: The U.S. Remains Leader of the Pack," *Business Week*, December 21, 1993, 18.
12. Richard Morais, "Hong Kong of Europe," *Forbes*, June 20, 1994, 69–70.
13. Marlene Piturro, "Capitalist China?" *Brandweek*, May 16, 1994, 23–27.
14. Myron Magnet, "The New Golden Rule of Business," *Fortune*, February 21, 1994, 60–64.
15. *Ibid.*
16. *Ibid.*
17. "Southwest No. 1 in Quality," *Mobile Press Register*, April 12, 1994, 5B.
18. Thayer C. Taylor, "Coming of Age," *Sales & Marketing Management*, August 1994, 67.
19. Stewart, "Managing in a Wired Company," 44–56.
20. Jonathan Berry, "What Is an Ad in the Interactive Future?" *Business Week*, May 2, 1994, 103; and Kathy Rebello, "Digital Pioneers," *Business Week*, May 2, 1994, 96–103.
21. Paul Wiseman, "The Internet Snares More Businesses," *USA Today*, July 7, 1994, A1.
22. *Ibid.*
23. Richard Daft, *Management*, 3d ed. (Fort Worth, TX: The Dryden Press, 1993), 635–636.
24. Thomas Stewart, "Rate Your Readiness to Change," *Fortune*, February 7, 1994, 106–110.
25. Neil Gross, "Who Says Science Has to Pay Off Fast?" *Business Week*, March 21, 1994, 110.
26. Louis E. Boone, *Quotable Business* (New York: Random House, 1992), 146.
27. Robert Langreth, "Gates & McCaw Propose Launching 840 Satellites," *Popular Science*, July 1994, 32; and Mark Lewyn, "He's No Mere Satellite-Gazer," *Business Week*, April 4, 1994, 39.
28. Nancy Totten, "Teaching Students to Evaluate Information," *RQ*, Spring 1990, 348.
29. Eugene Carlson, "Clarence Birdseye Found Profit in Deepfreeze," *The Wall Street Journal*, March 21, 1989, B2.
30. Serwer, "Lessons from America's Fastest-Growing Companies," 42–62; and Daft, *Management* 3d ed., 362–386.
31. Brenton Schlender, "Matsushita Shows How to Go Global," *Fortune*, July 11, 1994, 159–166.
32. Denise Topolnicki, "You'd Be Surprised What Folks Will Do for Money Today," *Money*, August 1994, 12–13.
33. Catherine Yang and Christina Del Valle, "In a Sweat over Sweatshops," *Business Week*, April 4, 1994, 40.
34. Tim Carrington, "Gender Economics," *The Wall Street Journal*, June 22, 1994, A1, A4.

Chapter 2

1. Laurie Jones, "Flap over Data on Nicotine's Addictiveness," *American Medical News* (April 18, 1994): 7; Alicia Mundy, "Blowing Smoke," *ADWEEK Eastern Edition*, April 11, 1994, 24; Rachel Nowak, "Key Study Unveiled—11 Years Late," *Science*, April 8, 1994, 196; Charles Culhane, "Group Backs $2-a-pack Federal Excise Tax on Cigarettes," *American Medical News* (February 1, 1993): 4; "Waxman Bill Prompts Protests," *ADWEEK Eastern Edition*, November 29, 1993, 42; Sandra Gottfried, *Biology Today* (St. Louis: Mosby-Year Book, 1993), 189; Henry Waxman, "Tobacco Marketing: Profiteering from Children," *JAMA, The Journal of the American Medical Association* (December 11, 1991): 3185.
2. Thomas Stewart, "Welcome to the Revolution," *Fortune*, December 13, 1993, 66–77.
3. Stratford Sherman, "Are You as Good as the Best in the World?" *Fortune*, December 13, 1993, 95–96.
4. Stewart, "Welcome to the Revolution," 66–77; Sherman, "Are You as Good as the Best in the World?" 95–96.
5. Sherman, "Are You as Good as the Best in the World?" 95–96.
6. Stewart, "Welcome to the Revolution," 66–77.
7. Peter Fuhrman and Michael Schuman, "Now We Are Our Own Masters," *Forbes*, May 23, 1994, 128–138.
8. "General Motors," *Business Week*, May 30, 1994, Special Advertising Section.

9. Rahul Jacob, "The Big Rise," *Fortune*, May 30, 1994, 74–90; and Fuhrman and Schuman, "Now We Are Our Own Masters," 128–138.

10. Gene Bylinsky, "Genetics: The Money Rush Is On," *Fortune*, May 30, 1994, 94–108.

11. Stephanie Losee, "Women's Wire," *Fortune*, July 11, 1994, 118–120.

12. Charles Watson, "Managing with Social Integrity: Social Responsibilities of Business as Seen by America's CEOs," *Business Horizons*, July–August 1991, 99–109.

13. Lynn Sharp Paine, "Managing for Organizational Integrity," *Harvard Business Review* (March–April 1994): 106–117; and Robert McGarvey, "Do the Right Thing," *Entrepreneur*, April 1994, 64–67.

14. Sandra Gottfried, *Biology Today*, 189.

15. *Ibid.*, 227–229.

16. *Ibid.*, 705–706.

17. *Ibid.*, 699–700.

18. David Woodruff with Larry Armstrong and John Carey, "Electric Cars," *Business Week*, May 30, 1994, 104–114; and David Woodruff with Gail DeGeorge and Gregory Sandler, "The Not-So-Big Wheels Leading the Charge," *Business Week*, May 30, 1994, 114.

19. Roberta Maynard, "Meet the New Law on Family Leave," *Nation's Business*, April 1993, 48.

20. Margaret Jacobs, "Men's Club," *The Wall Street Journal*, June 9, 1994, A1, A8; and Anne Fisher, "Sexual Harassment: What to Do," *Fortune*, August 23, 1993, 84–88.

21. Emily MacFarquhar, "The War Against Women," *U.S. News & World Report*, March 28, 1994, 42–48.

22. Richard Klonowski, "Foundational Considerations in the Corporate Social Responsibility Debate," *Business Horizons*, July–August 1991, 9.

Chapter 3

1. Bill Saporito, "How U.S. Soccer Hopes to Score," *Fortune*, June 27, 1994, 126–128.

2. Richard Lacayo, "America's New Competitive Muscle," *Time*, November 29, 1993, 28.

3. *Ibid.*

4. Edwin Dolan and David Lindsey, *Economics* 7th ed. (Fort Worth, TX: The Dryden Press, 1994), 280–284.

5. Subrata Chakravarty, "For Want of a Lever," *Forbes*, February 14, 1994, 18.

6. Amy Borrus and Joyce Barnathan, with Bruce Einhorn and Stewart Toy, "China's Gates Swing Open," *Business Week*, June 13, 1994, 52–53.

7. Michael Czinkota and Ilkka Ronkainen, *International Marketing* (Fort Worth, TX: The Dryden Press, 1993), 17–18.

8. Jolie Solomon, "Mickey's Trip to Trouble," *Newsweek*, February 14, 1994, 34.

9. "Labels to Tell Origin of Automobile," *Mobile Register*, July 19, 1994, 7B.

10. James Walsh, "Peace Finally at Hand," *Time*, February 14, 1994, 34–36.

11. Czinkota and Ronkainen, *International Marketing*, 645–646.

12. *Ibid.*, 139.

13. Louis Richman, "What's Next After GATT's Victory?" *Fortune*, January 10, 1994, 66; Rich Thomas, "The ABCs of the GATT Pact," *Newsweek*, December 27, 1993, 36; and Jay Branegan, "Put Up or Shut Up," *Time*, December 20, 1993, 46.

14. Borrus and Barnathan, with Einhorn and Toy, "China's Gates Swing Open," 52–53; and Richman, "What's Next After GATT's Victory?" 66.

15. Richman, "What's Next After GATT's Victory?" 66.

16. Geoffrey Brewer, "New World Orders," *Sales & Marketing Management*, January 1994, 5963; Susan Greco, ed., "The NAFTA Factor," *Inc.*, March 1994, 134; "Congress Passes NAFTA," *Deloitte & Touche Review* (November 29, 1993): 1–3; and "The NAFTA Vote: What's At Stake," *USA Today*, November 17, 1993, 8A.

17. Art Weinstein, "A Primer for Global Marketers," *Marketing News*, June 20, 1994, 4–5; and Allyson Stewart, "Europeans Embrace Tastes of Ethnic Food," *Marketing News*, January 17, 1994, 10.

18. Jerry Flint, "One World, One Ford," *Forbes*, June 20, 1994, 40–41.

19. Richard Lacayo, "America's New Competitive Muscle," *Time*, November 29, 1993, 28.

Chapter 4

1. Richard Brandt, "Bill Gates's Vision," *Business Week*, June 27, 1994, 56–62; Richard Brandt, "Microsoft Hits the Gas," *Business Week*, March 21, 1994, 34–35; and Amy Cortese, Catherine Yang, and Richard Brandt, "Gunning for Microsoft: The Feds' New Weapon," *Business Week*, May 9, 1994, 90.

2. Sharon Nelson, "Put Your Purpose in Writing," *Nation's Business*, February 1994, 61–64.

3. *Starbucks Mission Statement*, copyright 1993.

4. Starbucks Coffee, "The Story of Good Coffee from the Pacific Northwest" (Seattle, Washington, Starbucks Coffee).

5. See also Kathy Heine, "How We Measure Performance," *Monsanto Magazine*, April 1992, 7–11; and Peter Drucker, *The Practice of Management* (New York: Harper & Bros., 1954), 128–129.

6. Matt Rothman, "Into the Black," *Inc.*, January 1993, 59–65.

7. R. Lee Sullivan, "It's First Class Here, Man," *Forbes*, March 14, 1994, 102.

8. "Sega! It's Blasting Beyond Games and Racing to Build a High-Tech Entertainment Empire," *Business Week*, February 21, 1994, 66–72.

9. Marvin W. Tucker and David A. Davis, "Key Ingredients for Successful Implementation of Just-in-Time: A System for All Business Sizes," *Business Horizons*, May–June 1993, 59–65.

10. "Manufacturing," *Modern Materials Handling* (April 1994): 34.

11. George Newman, "As Just-in-Time Goes By," *Across the Board*, October 1993, 7–8.

12. Jim Bessen, "Riding the Marketing Information Wave," *Harvard Business Review* (September–October 1993): 150–160.

13. John Huey, "Nothing Is Impossible," *Fortune*, September 23, 1991, 134–140.
14. Ronald Henkoff, "How to Plan for 1995," *Fortune*, December 31, 1990, 70–79.
15. John A. Byrne, "Here's What to Do Next: Dow Corning," *Business Week*, February 24, 1992, 33.
16. John Carey, "Getting Business to Think about the Unthinkable," *Business Week*, June 24, 1991, 104–107.
17. Brian Dumaine, "The Bureaucracy Busters," *Fortune*, June 17, 1991, 36–50.
18. *Ibid.*; Becton Dickinson *1990 Annual Report*, 9; and Naomi Freundlich, "Reaching for Cancer's On–Off Switch," *Business Week*, May 23, 1994, 62.
19. Hugh Sidey, "When Mickey Comes Marching Home," *Time*, March 21, 1994, 61; William Heuslein, "The Mouse That Roars and Roars," *Forbes*, January 3, 1994, 174; and "The Man Who Would Destroy American History" (advertisement).
20. Brandt, "Bill Gates's Vision," 56–62.
21. Nada R. Sanders and Karl B. Manrodt, "Forecasting Practices in U.S. Corporations: Survey Results," *Interfaces* (March–April 1994): 92–100.

Chapter 5
1. Don Boroughs, "Cannondale Pedals Its Way to the Top," *U.S. News & World Report*, January 10, 1994, 53–54; Andrew Tanzer, "Just Get Out and Sell," *Forbes*, September 28, 1992, 68–72.
2. "Alternatives for Organizing a New Business," *Deloitte & Touche Review* (May 2, 1994): 7–8.
3. *Ibid.*
4. *Ibid.*; and William McCullough, "Limited-liability Companies," *Business Times*, October 25, 1993, 5.
5. Brigid McMenamin, "Help Wanted," *Forbes*, November 2, 1993, 186.
6. Del Jones, "Employees Call Shots in Friendly Skies," *USA Today*, July 13, 1994, B1, B2.
7. Brian O'Reilly, "The New Face of Small Business," *Fortune*, May 2, 1994, 82–88.
8. *Ibid.*
9. "The State of Woman-Owned Start-Ups," *Inc.*, November 1993, 34.
10. Peter Henrys, "Look before You Leap," *Business Victoria*, August 1993, 5.
11. Randall Lane, "Bathroom Humor," *Forbes*, June 6, 1994, 90–91.
12. "Debunking from Myths about Franchising," *Money*, September 1991, 34.
13. Peter Henrys, "Look before You Leap," 5.

Chapter 6
1. "Drake Introduces New Range of Receivers," *Satnews*, April 18, 1994; "International Markets for Satellite TV Remain Troublesome," *Satellite Week*, February 14, 1994, 7; and Seth Lubove, "Make a Better Mousetrap," *Forbes*, February 1, 1993, 56–57.
2. Douglas MacDonald, "A Conversation with Dr. Val Feigenbaum," *Tenneco Symposium*, Summer 1992, 20–24.

3. David Greising, "Quality: How to Make It Pay," *Business Week*, August 8, 1994, 54–59.
4. Louis Kraar, "Korea Goes for Quality," *Fortune*, April 18, 1994, 153; and Stratford Sherman, "Are You As Good As the Best in the World?" *Fortune*, December 13, 1993, 95–96.
5. William Keenan, Jr., "Making the Grade," *Sales & Marketing Management*, March 1994, 70.
6. Stratford Sherman, "Are You As Good As the Best in the World?" 95–96.
7. Leslie Brokaw, "ISO 9000: Making the Grade," *Inc.*, June 1993, 98–99.
8. Jerry G. Bowles, "Quality '92: Leading the World-Class Company," *Fortune*, Special Supplement, September 21, 1992.
9. Louis Kraar, "Korea Goes for Quality," *Fortune*, April 18, 1994, 153.
10. Brokaw, "ISO 9000: Making the Grade," 98–99.
11. Colleen Barrett, "Coworkers Are Customers, Too," *Sales & Marketing Management*, July 1994, 31–32.
12. William Marbach, "Quality: What Motivates American Workers?" *Business Week*, April 12, 1993, 93; and John Waggoner, "AT&T Card Aimed High from Start," *USA Today*, October 15, 1992, B1, B2.
13. Keenan, Jr., "Making the Grade," 70.
14. Michael Clements, "Granite Rock: Concrete Improvement," *USA Today*, October 15, 1992, B6.
15. "L. L. Summertime," *L. L. Bean 1994 Catalogue* (Freeport, ME: 1994), 3; Mark Henricks, "Satisfaction Guaranteed," *Entrepreneur*, March 1993, 48–51; and Julie Schmit, "Heavens to Betsy: Now Fliers Can Fax," *USA Today*, May 12, 1993, B1.
16. John W. Verity, "The Gold Mine of Data in Customer Service," *Business Week*, March 21, 1994, 113–114.
17. Mark Lewyn, "Teaching Computers to Tell a 'G' from a 'C'," *Business Week*, December 7, 1992, 118–119.
18. Verity, "The Gold Mine of Data in Customer Service," 113–114.
19. Stephanie Barlow, "Voice of Reason," *Entrepreneur*, March 1993, 52.
20. Rahul Jacob, "TQM: More than a Dying Fad?" *Fortune*, October 18, 1993, 66–72.
21. Louis E. Boone, *Quotable Business* (New York: Random House, 1992), 113.
22. Louis E. Boone and Dianne Wilkins, "The Role of Benchmarking in Total Quality Management," *International Journal of Management* (March 1995); Richard Gibson, "Pillsbury's Telephones Ring with Peeves, Praise," *The Wall Street Journal*, April 20, 1994, B1, B8; and Carl Quintanilla and Richard Gibson, "'Do Call Us': More Companies Install 1-800 Phone Lines," *The Wall Street Journal*, April 20, 1994, B1, B8.
23. Julie Schmit, "Ritz-Carlton: Room for Employees," *USA Today*, October 14, 1992, B6.
24. Cyndee Miller, "TQM Out; Continuous Process Improvement In," *Marketing News*, May 9, 1994, 5, 20.
25. Pamela Sebastian, "Pleasing Hospital Patients Can Pay Off," *The Wall Street Journal*, May 13, 1993, B1, B6.

26. Richard L. Daft, *Management* (Fort Worth, TX: The Dryden Press, 1994), 636.

27. Michael Hammer, "Reengineering Work: Don't Automate, Obliterate," *Harvard Business Review* (July–August 1990): 104–112.

28. Lynn Coleman, "Total Quality Management Prescribed as Cure for Health Care Ailments," *Marketing News*, May 11, 1992, 5, 8.

29. Jacob, "TQM: More than a Dying Fad?" 66–72.

30. Jeff Dewar, "Is 99.9% Good Enough?" *The Competitive Advantage* (1990): 6.

31. Susanne Hatherley, "Benchmarking for the Best Reasons," *Business Victoria*, April 1994, 12.

32. Louis E. Boone and Dianne Wilkins, "Benchmarking at Xerox: A Case Study," *Proceedings of the Academy of Business Administration London International Conference* (June 1994).

33. *Ibid.*

34. John Waggoner, "AT&T Card Aimed High from Start," *USA Today*, October 15, 1992, B1, B2.

35. William Keenan, Jr., "Training for Quality," *Sales & Marketing Management*, March 1994, 69.

36. Jacob, "TQM: More than a Dying Fad?" 66–72.

Chapter 7

1. Michelene Maynard, "Neon's Drive for Quality," *USA Today*, August 3, 1994, 3B; Michael Verespej, "Neon Warfare," *Industry Week*, February 7, 1994, 27; "Neon Rolls at Chrysler," *Machine Design*, April 18, 1994, 16; and Drew Winter, "Neon Is the Bright Sign of Chrysler Teamwork," *Ward's Auto World*, November 1993, 38.

2. Gilbert Fuchsberg, "As Costs of Overseas Assignments Climb, Firms Select Expatriates More Carefully," *The Wall Street Journal*, January 9, 1992, B1, B4.

3. Stefan Fatsis, "Amid Trouble, Companies Restructure Hierarchies," *Mobile Register*, December 27, 1992, 5E.

4. *Ibid.*

5. "Downsizing Often Costly Cut," *Mobile Register*, July 10, 1994, 1F, 2F.

6. *Ibid.*

7. John A. Byrne, "There Is an Upside to Downsizing," *Business Week*, May 9, 1994, 69; and Ronald Henkoff, "Getting Beyond Downsizing," *Fortune*, January 10, 1994, 58–64.

8. Stefan Fatsis, "Corporate America Retooling," *Seattle Post-Intelligencer*, December 26, 1992, B6.

9. Richard Knee, "Fujitsu Uses UPS as Hub in Europe," *American Shipper*, December 1993, 40.

10. "Out Is In," *Entrepreneur*, May 1994, 12.

11. John Huey, "The New Post-Heroic Leadership," *Fortune*, February 21, 1994, 42–50.

12. John Byrne, "The Horizontal Corporation," *Business Week*, December 20, 1993, 76–81; and "A Master Class in Radical Change," *Fortune*, December 13, 1993, 82–90.

13. Michelene Maynard, "Evaluations Evolve from Bottom Up," *USA Today*, August 3, 1994, 6B.

14. John Huey, "The New Post-Heroic Leadership."

15. *Ibid.*

16. *Ibid.*

17. Thomas J. Peters and Robert H. Waterman, Jr., *In Search of Excellence* (New York: Harper & Row, 1982).

18. Kevin Maney, "Giant Goes from Stodgy to Nimble," *USA Today*, May 18, 1994, 1B, 2B.

19. Toni Mack, "VPs of Planning Need Not Apply," *Forbes*, October 25, 1993, 84–85.

20. Alan Deutschman, "The CEO's Secret of Managing Time," *Fortune*, June 1, 1992, 135–146.

21. Walter Kiechel III, "Overscheduled, and Not Loving It," *Fortune*, April 8, 1991, 105–107.

22. Alison Sprout, "Saving Time around the Clock," *Fortune*, December 13, 1993, 157.

23. Brian O'Reilly, "The New Face of Small Business," *Fortune*, May 2, 1994, 82–88; and "Jobless at 50? It's Not Hopeless," *Business Week*, December 20, 1993, 82.

Chapter 8

1. Telephone interview with Tony Cook of Rhino Foods, Inc., August 12, 1994; and Michael P. Cronin, "Employee Swapping," *Inc.*, December 1993, 165.

2. Brian Dumaine, "Cool Cures for Burnout," *Fortune*, June 20, 1988, 78–84.

3. Anne Fisher, "Morale Crisis," *Business Week*, November 18, 1992, 78–80.

4. Alan Farnham, "How to Nurture Creative Sparks," *Fortune*, January 10, 1994, 94–100.

5. Toddi Gutner, "Meeting the Boss," *Forbes*, March 1, 1993, 126.

6. Robert La Franco, "Promote from Within," *Forbes*, February 28, 1994, 86–87.

7. Wade Lambert, "Have You Ever? New EEOC Guidelines for Job Interviewing Baffle Employers," *The Wall Street Journal*, July 15, 1994, B1, B6; and "How to Comply with the ADA," *Inc.*, August 1994, 104.

8. Thomas Toch, "Crafting the Work Force," *U.S. News & World Report*, August 19, 1991, 63–64.

9. Lewis Perelman, "Kanban to Kanbrain," *Forbes ASAP*, June 6, 1994, 85–95.

10. Jaclyn Fierman, "The Perilous New World of Fair Pay," *Fortune*, June 13, 1994, 57–64.

11. Sara Lamb, "Family Leave Law Leaves Many in the Dark," *Mobile Register*, August 3, 1994, E1.

12. Sue Shellenbarger, "Companies Help Solve Day-Care Problems," *The Wall Street Journal*, July 22, 1994, B1.

13. Aaron Bernstein, "Why America Needs Unions But Not the Kind It Has Now," *Business Week*, May 23, 1994, 70–82.

14. Brian Dumaine, "Payoff from the New Management," *Fortune*, December 13, 1993, 103–110.

15. Karen Peterson, "Job Stress, Satisfaction Can Co-Exist," *USA Today*, July 6, 1994, D1.

16. Sue Shellenbarger, "Firms Make the Most of Flexible Scheduling," *The Wall Street Journal*, April 12, 1994, B1.

17. Sue Shellenbarger, "Some Thrive, But Many Wilt Working at Home," *The Wall Street Journal*, December 14, 1993, B1, B10.

18. David Hage, "Unions Feel the Heat," *U.S. News & World Report*, January 24, 1994, 57–61.

19. Bernstein, "Why America Needs Unions," 70–82; and Kevin Salwen, "What, Us Worry? Big Unions' Leaders Overlook Bad News, Opt for Status Quo," *The Wall Street Journal*, October 5, 1993, B1.
20. "Unions Lose Power, Respect in Argentina," *Mobile Press Register*, March 23, 1994, 2E; and Hage, "Unions Feel the Heat," 57–61.
21. David Hage, "Unions Feel the Heat," 57–61.
22. Brian O'Reilly, "The New Deal," *Fortune*, June 13, 1994, 44–52.
23. Rochelle Sharpe, "Being Family Friendly Doesn't Mean Promoting Women," *The Wall Street Journal*, March 29, 1994, B1, B5.
24. Shellenbarger, "Firms Make the Most of Flexible Scheduling," B1.
25. Rochelle Sharpe, "The Waiting Game," *The Wall Street Journal*, March 29, 1994, A1, A10.
26. *Ibid.*
27. *Ibid.*
28. "Number of Part-Time Workers in U.S. Triples Since 1970," *Mobile Press Register*, June 1, 1994, 4E.
29. "Pared Firms Feed Temporary Work Force," *Mobile Press Register*, July 13, 1994, 1E, 2E.
30. John Huey, "The New Post-Heroic Leadership," *Fortune*, February 21, 1994, 42–50.

Chapter 9
1. Brian Dumaine, "The Trouble with Teams," *Fortune*, September 5, 1994, 86–92.
2. James Treece, "Improving the Soul of an Old Machine," *Business Week*, October 25, 1993, 134–136.
3. John A. Byrne, "The Horizontal Corporation," *Business Week*, December 20, 1993, 78–79.
4. Richard Daft, *Management*, 3d ed. (Fort Worth, TX: The Dryden Press, 1994), 584–591.
5. Brian Dumaine, "Payoff from the New Management," *Fortune*, December 13, 1993, 103–110.
6. William Cook, "The End of the Plain Plane," *U.S. News & World Report*, April 11, 1994, 43–46; and "What Now, Engineer?" *Flight Engineer*, April 20, 1994, 3.
7. Alan Farnham, "America's Most Admired Company," *Fortune*, February 7, 1994, 50–54.
8. Daft, *Management*, 591–594.
9. Faye Rice, "How to Make Diversity Pay," *Fortune*, August 8, 1994, 78–86.
10. *Ibid.*
11. Dumaine, "Payoff from the New Management," 103–110.
12. Dawn Baskerville, "Why Business Loves Workteams," *Black Enterprise*, April 1993, 85–90.
13. *Ibid.*
14. Daft, *Management*, 594–596.
15. David Woodruff, "Saturn: Labor's Love Lost?" *Business Week*, February 8, 1993, 122–124.
16. *Ibid.*
17. Kevin Salwen, "Workplace Friction," *The Wall Street Journal*, July 27, 1993, A1, A7.
18. Dumaine, "Payoff from the New Management," 103–110.

19. *Ibid.*
20. Louis E. Boone, *Quotable Business* (New York: Random House, 1992), 69.
21. Philip Elmer-Dewitt, "Bards of the Internet," *Time*, July 4, 1994, 66–67.
22. Andrew Serwer, "Lessons from America's Fastest-Growing Companies," *Fortune*, August 8, 1994, 42–60.
23. Louis E. Boone and David L. Kurtz, *Contemporary Business Communication*, (Englewood Cliffs, NJ: Prentice-Hall, 1994), 611.
24. Salwen, "Workplace Friction," A1, A7.
25. "The World According to Andy Grove," *Business Week/ The Information Revolution 1994*, 76–78. See also Ginger Trumfio, "The Case for E-Mail," *Sales & Marketing Management*, July 1994, 94–98; and Cheryl J. Goldberg, "Mail Call," *Entrepreneur*, August 1994, 36–39.
26. Suzy Parker, "E-Mail Explosion," *USA Today*, July 19, 1994, B1.
27. Serwer, "Lessons from America's Fastest-Growing Companies," 42–60.
28. Daft, *Management*, 568–570.
29. Dumaine, "Payoff from the New Management," 103–110.
30. Thayer Taylor, "Seeing Is Believing," *Sales & Marketing Management*, March 1994, 47–48.
31. Louis E. Boone and David L. Kurtz, *Contemporary Business Communication*, 8.
32. Jack Russell, "U.S. Fast-Food Giants in Japan Slice Prices," *Advertising Age*, June 13, 1994, 64.
33. Robert Mamis, "Desk-to-Desk Show-and-Tell," *Inc.*, July 1994, 100.
34. Michael Christie, "Slips of the Tongue Result in Classic Marketing Errors," *Advertising Age International*, June 20, 1994, 15.
35. Rahul Jacob, "America's Best?" *Fortune*, February 7, 1994, 54.
36. "The Infobog, By the Numbers," *Fortune*, July 11, 1994, 62.
37. Gail Edmondson, "Wireless Terriers," *Business Week*, May 23, 1994, 117–118.

Chapter 10
1. Justin Martin, "Services Show Their Muscle," *Fortune*, May 30, 1994, 196–197; Beth Freedman, "AT&T Bid to Buy McCaw Hits Minor Snag," *PC Week*, February 21, 1994, 96; "AT&T Taps Information Highway Potential through U.S. Trials," *Broadband Networking News*, January 24, 1994, 12; G. Christian Hill, "Look! No Wires!" *The Wall Street Journal*, February 11, 1994, R1, R5; Holt Hackney, "AT&T: Dialing for Dollars," *Financial World*, September 28, 1993, 17; William J. Cook, "The Levitation of a Giant," *U.S. News & World Report*, August 30, 1993, 58; Thomas McCarroll, "How AT&T Plans to Reach Out and Touch Everyone," *Time*, July 5, 1993, 44; and "AT&T, MCI, Sprint Back 'Information Superhighway' Plan," *Report on AT&T*, March 29, 1993, 7.
2. Jeffrey Young, "Sand, Sun, Mutual Fund," *Forbes ASAP*, October 1993, 156–157.

3. Lucy Howard and Ned Zeman, "Computerland," *Newsweek*, April 8, 1991.

4. "Top Retail Software," *PC Magazine*, January 11, 1994, 31.

5. "Mainframe Comeback?" *Forbes ASAP*, October 1993, 64–73. See also "IBM: There's Many a Slip . . ." *Business Week*, June 27, 1994, 26–27.

6. Kyle Pope, "Changing Work Habits Fuel Popularity of Notebooks," *The Wall Street Journal*, November 11, 1993, B1, B10.

7. Bill Howard, "You'll Love PCMCIA . . . Eventually," *PC Magazine*, November 23, 1993, 105; and John R. Quain, "HP's OmniBook: The Ultimate Subnotebook?" *PC Magazine*, July 1993, 37.

8. Zachary Schiller and Wendy Zellner, "Making the Middleman an Endangered Species," *Business Week*, June 6, 1994, 114–115.

9. "'Highway' Paves Path to Information Overload," *Mobile Register*, June 6, 1993, F1, F5; and "How Video on Demand Will Work," *U.S. News & World Report*, December 6, 1993, 66.

10. Louis E. Boone and David L. Kurtz, *Management*, 4th ed. (New York: McGraw-Hill, 1992), 504–506.

11. John W. Verity, "Truck Lanes for the Info Highway," *Business Week*, April 18, 1994, 112–114; Amy Cortese and Richard Brandt, "Microsoft's Network Wares Still Aren't Connected," *Business Week*, June 27, 1994, 60–61. See also Bart Ziegler, "Building the Highway: New Obstacles, New Solutions," *The Wall Street Journal*, May 18, 1994, B1, B3.

12. Michael J. Miller, "Networked PCs: Nothing Personal?" *PC Magazine*, January 11, 1994, 77–78.

13. Peter Nulty, "When to Murder Your Mainframe," *Fortune*, November 1, 1993, 109–120.

14. Michael S. Malone, "Smart Vineyard," *Forbes ASAP*, October 1993, 31–33.

15. Alison L. Sprout, "Using a PC to Be a Better Boss," *Fortune*, March 7, 1994, 107; and Jim Seymour, "Changing the Rules of the Game," *PC Magazine*, January 11, 1994, 97–98.

16. Carol Levin, "Ready-to-Run Resumes, Expense Reports, Newsletters, Flyers," *PC Magazine*, July 1993, 71.

17. Kevin Maney, "No E-Mail? Get With It!" *USA Today*, May 19, 1994, 2B.

18. Kenneth Laudon and Jane Laudon, *Business Information Systems*, 2d ed. (Fort Worth, TX: The Dryden Press, 1993), 241–242; and Owen Edwards, "The Grating Communicator," *Forbes ASAP*, October 25, 1993, 160–161.

19. Paul Desmond, "Alamo Builds Networked Expert System to Set Rates," *Network World*, September 3, 1990, 13–15.

20. Evan Schwartz and Keith Hammonds, "Your New Computer: The Telephone," *Business Week*, June 3, 1991, 126–131; "Here's Looking at Voice Processing," *Network World*, June 17, 1991, 1, 33–40; Chip Johnson, "Telephone Companies Hope Voice Mail Will Make Answering Machines Obsolete," *The Wall Street Journal*, July 23, 1992, B1, B8; and Mary Kathleen Flynn, "Take a Letter, Computer," *PC Magazine*, July 1993, 29.

21. Gregg Keizer, "$99 Voice Assist Listens to You," *PC Magazine*, November 23, 1993, 48.

22. Timothy O'Brien, "A PC Revolution," *The Wall Street Journal*, October 8, 1993, A1, A9.

23. Laudon and Laudon, *Business Information Systems*, 131–133.

24. Don Boroughs, "Profits on a Platter," *U.S. News & World Report*, April 2, 1994, 69–72; David Sullivan, *The New Computer User* (Fort Worth, TX: The Dryden Press, 1994), 60–70; and Evan Schwartz, "CD-ROM: A Mass Medium at Last," *Business Week*, July 19, 1993, 82–83.

25. Don Clark, "Intel and CNN to Test New Technology to Bring Television to Networks of PCs," *The Wall Street Journal*, April 22, 1994, B4.

26. Stratford Sherman, "Will the Information Superhighway Be the Death of Retailing?" *Fortune*, April 18, 1994, 98–108.

27. David Sullivan, *The New Computer User* (Fort Worth, TX: The Dryden Press, 1994), 279–285; David Kirkpatrick, "Groupware Goes Boom," *Fortune*, December 27, 1993, 99–106; and Mark Lewyn, "Lotus' Notes Get a Lot of Notice," *Business Week*, March 29, 1993, 84–86.

28. James Aley, "How Not to Help High Tech," *Fortune*, May 16, 1994, 100–101.

29 Laudon and Laudon, *Business Information Systems*, 576.

30. David Sullivan, *The New Computer User* (Fort Worth, TX: The Dryden Press, 1994), 331–335.

31. Ronald Henkoff, "Keeping Motorola on a Roll," *Fortune*, April 18, 1994, 67–78.

Chapter 11

1. Kenneth Labich, "Is Herb Kelleher America's Best CEO?" *Fortune*, May 2, 1994, 45–52; Colleen Barrett, "Giving Customers P.O.S.," *Sales & Marketing Management*, November 1993, 52; and Richard Teitelbaum, "Keeping Promises," *Fortune*, Autumn/Winter 1993, 32–34.

2. Faye Rice, "The New Rules of Superlative Service," *Fortune*, Autumn/Winter 1993, 50–53.

3. *Ibid.*

4. "Wining and Dining the Whiners," *Sales & Marketing Management*, February 1993, 73–75.

5. Thomas Stewart, "Reengineering: The Hot New Managing Tool," *Fortune*, August 23, 1993, 40–48; Charles Mason and Richard Karpinski, "Sculpting a New Industry Sculpture," *Telephony*, April 19, 1993, 88; and Peter Talberg, "Teamwork for Product Development," *Cellular Business*, April 1993, 54.

6. Art Weinstein, "A Primer for Global Marketers," *Marketing News*, June 20, 1994, 4.

7. James F. Engel, Roger D. Blackwell, and Paul W. Miniard, *Consumer Behavior*, 7th ed. (Fort Worth, TX: The Dryden Press, 1993), 4.

8. Robert Johnson, "In the Chips," *The Wall Street Journal*, March 22, 1991, B1–B2.

9. *Ibid.*, B1.
10. *Ibid.*, B2.
11. Cotton Timber Lake, "U.S. Goods Find Britain a Tough Sell," *Arkansas Democrat* (July 11, 1991), 10A.
12. Jon Berry, "Citicorp Opens Its Visa Database to Marketers," *ADWEEK's Marketing Week*, January 21, 1991, 6.
13. Kathleen Deveny, "Segments of One," *The Wall Street Journal*, March 22, 1991, B4.
14. "Gays Celebrate and Businesses Tune In," *Fortune*, June 27, 1994, 14.
15. Gary Boulard, "Numbers," *The Advocate*, October 4, 1994, 30–31.
16. Weinstein, "A Primer for Global Marketers," 4.
17. Tom Jensen, "Cadillac Comes Back in a Big Way with Its Seville STS Northstar," *The Business Journal* (November 22, 1993), 19A; and Jeff Rundles, "The Return of the American Car," *Colorado Business Magazine*, March 22, 1992, 25.
18. Marcy Magiera and Pat Sloan, "Levi's, Lee Loosen Up for Baby Boomers," *Advertising Age*, August 3, 1992, 9.
19. S.T., "Retailing's New Frontier," *Fortune*, Autumn/Winter 1993, 32.

Chapter 12
1. Amal Kumar Naj, "Some Manufacturers Drop Efforts to Adopt Japanese Technology," *The Wall Street Journal*, May 7, 1993, 1; and Amal Kumar Naj, "GE's Welch Extols Virtues of Being Big—and Small—in a Changing World," *The Wall Street Journal*, February 26, 1993, B5B.
2. P. S., "They Understand Your Kids," *Fortune*, Autumn/Winter 1993, 29–30.
3. Nancy Arnott, "To Know Brands Isn't Necessarily to Love Them," *Sales & Marketing Management*, December 1993, 25.
4. Alison Rogers, "Cherios Was Taken," *Fortune*, October 18, 1993, 11.
5. Jeffrey Rubin, "Industrial Flea Market," *Time*, January 24, 1994, 24.
6. David Hage and Linda Grant, "How to Make America Work," *U.S. News & World Report*, December 6, 1993, 48–54.
7. William Symonde, "Pushing Design to Dizzying Speed," *Business Week*, October 21, 1991, 64–68.
8. Jerry Flint, "The New Zeitgeist at Daimler-Benz," *Forbes*, December 6, 1993, 44–45. Michael McCarthy, "Unlikely Sites," *The Wall Street Journal*, May 4, 1993, A1, A12.
9. Norman Gaither, *Production and Operations Management*, 6th ed. (Fort Worth, TX: The Dryden Press, 1994), 39.
10. Howard Gleckman, with Zachary Schiller and James Treece, "A Tonic for the Business Cycle," *Business Week*, April 4, 1994, 57.

Chapter 13
1. Christopher Palmer, "Shotguns and Airwaves," *Forbes*, June 6, 1994, 50–51. "Mexican Government Completes Sale," *Broadcasting & Cable*, August 2, 1993, 22; and

"Group Led by Ricardo Salinas Pliego," *Television Digest*, July 26, 1993, 7.
2. Michael Czinkota and Ilkka Ronkainen, *International Marketing*, 3d ed. (Ft. Worth: The Dryden Press, 1993), 320–324.
3. *Ibid.*, 320.
4. Christopher Tobler, "Wal-Mart CEO Calms the Masses," *Arkansas Business*, June 13, 1994, 15; and Bill Saporito, "And the Winner Is Still . . . Wal-Mart," *Fortune*, May 2, 1994, 62–70.
5. Advertisement, "Buy a Bed on CompuServe," *CompuServe Magazine*, May 1994, 52.
6. Gary McWilliams with Robert Hof, "They Can't Wait to Serve You," *Business Week*, January 24, 1994, 92.
7. Elaine Underwood, "Marketers, Retailers Line Up to Ride Home Shopping's Highway," *Brandweek*, March 22, 1993, 8.
8. Gerry Khermouch, "Mail Order PC Channels Emerge from Boiler Room," *Brandweek*, June 6, 1994, 30–31.
9. Sunita Bhargava, "Espresso, Sandwiches, and a Sea of Books," *Business Week*, July 26, 1993, 81.
10. "World's Top 50 Advertising Organizations," *Advertising Age*, April 13, 1994, 12.
11. Czinkota and Ronkainen, *International Marketing*, 686–687.
12. This rule is noted in Harold C. Cash and W. J. E. Crissy, "The Salesman's Role in Marketing," *Psychology of Marketing*, vol. 12, Personnel Development Associates.
13. Czinkota and Ronkainen, *International Marketing*, 369–370.
14. Jeff Jensen, "TV Is Advertisers' Big Pick in Europe," *Advertising Age International*, June 21, 1993, I-19; and Czinkota and Ronkainen, *International Marketing*, 659–661.
15. Czinkota and Ronkainen, *International Marketing*, 154–160.
16. Tony Siciliano, "Relationship Marketing Must Be Personalized," *Marketing News*, Nov. 8, 1993, 4–5; Cyndee Miller, "Rewards for the Best Customers," *Marketing News*, July 5, 1993, 1, 6; and Theodore Smith and Ryen Johnson, "Facilitating the Practice of Relationship Marketing," (presentation at the 1993 American Marketing Association Summer Marketing Educators' Conference) August 1993, Boston, Mass.
17. Joshua Levine, "How'm I Doin'?" *Forbes*, December 24, 1990, 106–109.
18. Stephen Budiansky, "Hard Shell Hard Sell," *U.S. News & World Report*, July 29, 1991, 11.
19. *Ibid.*
20. Jon Berry, "The New 'Multilingual' Pitch," Adweek's Marketing Week, April 22, 1991, 35.

Chapter 14
1. Marcia Berss, "Cash Flow Joe," *Forbes*, June 6, 1994, 47.
2. Janet Fix, "NationsBank Checks Employee Waste," *USA Today*, June 10, 1994, B4.
3. Zachary Schiller, "Goodrich: From Tires to PVC to Chemicals to Aerospace . . ." *Business Week*, July 18, 1994, 86–87.

4. Kelley Holland and Larry Light, "Big Six Firms Are Firing Clients," *Business Week*, March 1, 1993, 76–77.

5. William M. Stern, "Southern Fried Reading," *Forbes*, June 20, 1994, 91–92.

6. "Morrisons Sells Institutional Food Division," *Mobile Register*, June 29, 1994, B1.

7. Axel L. Grabowsky, "What to Monitor to Stay in Control," *Inc. Magazine's Guide to Small Business Success* (New York: Inc., 1994).

Chapter 15

1. Jill Andresky Fraser, "Growth Capital: What to Do When You Need Big Money," *Inc.*, February 1994, 38–46.

2. Louis E. Boone, Janelle Emmert Goodnight, and Jeanne Harris, "Leading Corporate America in an Era of Change: A Statistical Profile of Chief Executive Officers," *USA Working Paper*, 1995.

3. Bruce J. Blechman, "Quick Change Artist," *Entrepreneur*, January 1994, 18–21.

4. Robert Mamis, "The Secrets of Bootstrapping," *Inc.*, September 1991, 52–70.

5. Jill Fraser, "Time to Hire a Controller," *Inc.*, May 1994, 153.

6. Janet Fix, "Currency to Get Face Lift, Maybe Dye Job," *USA Today*, May 10, 1994, A1.

7. "Strategy for Survival," *Time*, December 8, 1991, 36.

8. Jill A. Fraser, "Better Returns on Spare Cash," *Inc.*, June 1994, 115.

9. John Rossant, "How Disney Snared a Princely Sum," *Business Week*, June 20, 1994, 61–62.

10. Anne B. Fisher, "Raising Capital for a New Venture," *Fortune*, June 13, 1994, 99–101.

11. Matthew Schifrin and Riva Atlas, "Hocus-Pocus," *Forbes*, March 14, 1994, 81–83.

12. Matthew Schifrin and Riva Atlas, "Hocus-Pocus," *Forbes*, March 14, 1994, 81–83; and "The Tightwads Are Running the Show Now," *Business Week*, November 4, 1991, 114.

13. "Nation Has Fewer Banks," *USA Today*, June 24, 1994, B1.

14. Adi Ignatius and Neela Banerjee, "Russian Bankers Bring Triks of the Trade Home after U.S. Visit," *The Wall Street Journal*, May 23, 1994, A1, A10.

15. Margaret Mannix, "Paying the Price of ATM Convenience," *U.S. News & World Report*, July 5, 1993, 57; and "ATM Banking: New Prey for Thieves?" *Mobile Register*, June 6, 1993, 4F.

16. Fred Bleakley, "Fast Money," *The Wall Street Journal* April 13, 1994, A1, A5.

17. Gary Belsky, "Separating the Safe Federal Insurers from the Shaky Ones," *Money*, October 1991, 29–30.

18. *The World Almanac and Book of Facts: 1994* (Mahwah, NJ: Funk & Wagnals, 1994), 110.

19. Terrence Pare, "GE Monkeys with Its Money Machine," *Fortune*, February 21, 1994, 81–87; and Tim Smart, "GE's Money Machine," *Business Week*, March 8, 1993, 62–67.

20. Beth Belton and Desiree French, "Higher Rates Sideline Some Home Buyers," *USA Today*, June 1, 1994, B1.

21. William Meyers, et al., "Friendly Fire from the Fed," *U.S. News & World Report*, May 30, 1994, 46–47.

22. Owen Ullman and Dean Foust, "Inside the Fed," *Business Week*, May 2, 1994, 24–27; and Martin Crutsinger, "Interest Rates to Go Up Again," *Mobile Register*, May 17, 1994, A1.

23. Amy Barrett, "Backlash from the S&L Scandal," *Business Week*, July 4, 1994, 50.

24. Owen Ullman and Dean Foust, "Inside the Fed," *Business Week*, May 2, 1994, 24–27; Terrence Pare, "GE Monkeys with Its Money Machine," *Fortune*, February 21, 1994, 81–87; Tim Smart, "GE's Money Machine," *Business Week*, March 8, 1993, 62–67; and William Baumol and Alan Blinder, *Economics*, 6th ed. (Fort Worth, TX: The Dryden Press, 1994), 926–946.

Chapter 16

1. "Clean Harbors Inc. Sets Quarterly Review Mark," *Hazardous Waste News*, November 9, 1993, 44; Julie Lanza, "Legislature Limits Local Control of Waste Facilities," *Boston Business Journal*, April 20, 1992, 5; and "Clean Harbors Names Conrath Finance Manager," *PR Newswire*, September 17, 1991.

2. Antony J. Michels, "The New Appeal of Convertibles," *Fortune*, June 13, 1994, 32.

3. Rob Norton, "Who Owns This Company, Anyhow?" *Fortune*, July 29, 1991, 131–142.

4. Jeffrey Laderman with Geoffrey Smith, "The Power of Mutual Funds," *Business Week*, January 18, 1993, 62–68.

5. *NYSE Fact Book* (New York: New York Stock Exchange, April 1993), 2.

6. Laderman with Smith, "The Power of Mutual Funds," 62–68.

7. Lynn Asinof, "How to Find Good Stocks in a Dicey Market," *The Wall Street Journal*, April 29, 1994, C1, C10.

8. *NYSE Fact Book*, 8; and Gary Slutsker, "If You Can't Beat 'Em," *Forbes*, January 6, 1992, 48.

9. Slutsker, "If You Can't Beat 'Em," 48.

10. John Wicks, "The Bourse Joins Hands," *SwissBusiness*, July–August 1993, 22; and Steve Zwick, "GLOBEX Wins, Loses a Few," *Futures: Magazine of Commodities & Options*, May 1993, 12.

11. Rahul Jacob, "The Big Rise," *Fortune*, May 30, 1994, 74–90; and Frank Gibney and Peter McKillop, "Let a Thousand Bonds Bloom," *Newsweek*, December 24, 1990, 46.

12. Zwick, "GLOBEX Wins, Loses a Few," 12.

13. T. Patrick Harris, "Sixty Years—Over the Counter," *Security Traders Handbook* Vol. 20, No. 3 (March 1994): B10, B11; and *Statistical Abstract of the United States, 1993* (Washington, DC: GPO), 524.

14. "Advantage Lombard," *The Wall Street Journal*, April 12, 1994, C5.

15. Daniel Strachman, "NationsBank's Trading Software Slashes Compliance Costs," *American Banker*, March 28, 1994, A4.

16. David Nusbaum, "An Automated Argument," *Futures: Magazine of Commodities & Options*, February 1994, 52; and George Anders and Craig Torres, "The New Market," *The Wall Street Journal*, August 28, 1991, A1, A10.

17. Nusbaum, "An Automated Argument," 52; and Gary Slutsker, "If You Can't Beat 'Em," *Forbes* (January 6, 1992), 48.

18. Slutsker, "If You Can't Beat 'Em," 48.

19. Anders and Torres, "The New Market," A1, A10.

20. Gary Weiss, "What to Do about the Dow," *Business Week*, February 22, 1993, 82–83.

21. Garrison Wells, "Buy, Buy, Hold," *Denver Business Journal* (March 18, 1994): 12C.

Appendix A

1. Maria Mallory and Jonathan Ringel, "A Flood to Rival Sherman," *Business Week*, July 25, 1994, 36.

2. *The World Almanac and Book of Facts, 1994* (Mahwah, NJ: Funk & Wagnalls), 962–963.

3. Kevin Chappell, "Boss, I Feel Lousy. Where's My Check?" *U.S. News & World Report*, July 29, 1991, 25.

4. Mark D. Fefer, "Tailored Health Plans Take Off," *Fortune*, June 27, 1994, 12.

5. Matt Walsh, "Why Ronald Vessey Threw in the Towel," *Forbes*, July 4, 1994, 58–62.

6. Martin Anderson, "The Mystery of the 37 Million Americans without Insurance," *Mobile Register*, May 23, 1993, 7C.

Appendix B

1. Reinhardt Krause and Carol Haber, "Court Boots TI/Cyrix Suit to Texas Turf," *Electronic News*, March 28, 1994, 1; "Delaware Chancery Court is 'Key' to QVC's Chances of Buying Paramount," *Communications Daily*, November 12, 1993, 9; "Delaware Chancery Court," *The Oil and Gas Journal*, January 25, 1993, 50; and Michael Armstrong, "Small Wonder Delaware State Is Good Place to Incorporate," *Philadelphia Business Journal*, January 25, 1993, 4B.

2. Alexandra Peers, "Art World Shaken by Nations Seeking to Reclaim Items," *The Wall Street Journal*, June 21, 1994, C1, C18.

3. Christopher Palmeri, "The Great Taco Caper," *Forbes*, December 6, 1993, 106–109.

4. Andy Pasztor, "A-12 Bomber Suit May Be Biggest Ever," *The Wall Street Journal*, July 27, 1994, B2.

5. John R. Allison and Robert A. Prentice, *Business Law: Text and Cases in the Legal Environment*, 6th ed. (Fort Worth, TX: The Dryden Press, 1994), 81.

6. *Ibid.*, 301–302.

7. *Ibid.*, 628–629.

8. *Ibid.*, 160.

9. *Ibid.*, 447–450.

10. Malcolm Forbes, Jr., "Ending Airborne Ambulance Chasing," *Forbes*, March 14, 1994, 26; William Stern, "A Wing and a Prayer," *Forbes*, April 25, 1994, 42–43.

11. Howard Banks, "Cleared for Takeoff," *Forbes*, September 12, 1994, 116, 118, 122.

12. J. A. Simpson and E. S. C. Weiner, eds., *Oxford English Dictionary*, 2d ed., vol. 1 (Oxford: Clarendon Press, 1989), 934.

13. Jonathan Foreman, "The Freedom to Fail," *Audacity*, Winter 1994, 28–37.

14. Some of the information is from Michele Galen, "If Personal Bankruptcy Is Your Only Way Out," *Business Week*, January 21, 1991, 90–91.

15. David Corder, "Harsh Medicine," *The Kansas City Business Journal*, May 20, 1994, 16; Rosalind Resnick, "The Deadbeat State," *Forbes*, July 8, 1991, 62.

16. Olaf de Senerpont Domis, "Hopes Are High for Bankruptcy Reform," *American Banker*, July 15, 1994, 2; Corder, "Harsh Medicine," 16; Jim Wise, "Panel Approves Momentous Bankruptcy Code Changes," *Business Credit*, November–December 1993, 6.

17. Foreman, "The Freedom to Fail," 28–37.

18. Gerry Khermouch, "Nipping at Intel's Heels, Others Are in the Chips," *Brandweek*, June 6, 1994, 20–22.

19. Marcus Brauchli, "Chinese Flagrantly Copy Trademarks of Foreigners," *The Wall Street Journal*, June 20, 1994, B1, B5.

20. William Baumol and Alan Blinder, *Economics: Principles and Policy*, 6th ed. (Fort Worth, TX: The Dryden Press, 1994), 496–498.

21. Pasztor, "A-12 Bomber Suit May Be Biggest Ever," B2.

22. "Special Article Reviews Results of Bankruptcy Law," *China Intelligence Report*, May 11, 1994.

23. Brauchli, "Chinese Flagrantly Copy Trademarks of Foreigners," B1, B5.

Appendix C

1. Amy Saltzman, "An Electronic Job Hunt," *U.S. News & World Report*, March 28, 1994, 72–75; Julia Lawlor, "Job Seekers Going On–Line," *USA Today*, April 5, 1994, 4B; and Margaret Mannix, "Writing a Computer-Friendly Resume," *U.S. News & World Report*, October 26, 1992, 90–93.

2. Louis Richman, "The New Work Force Builds Itself," *Fortune*, June 27, 1994, 68–76.

3. "Americans' Changing Opportunities," *Money*, December 1993, 145.

4. Patsy Moore–Talbott, "Go with the Flow," *Managing Your Career* (College Edition of the National Business Employment Weekly), published by *The Wall Street Journal*, Spring 1991, 12–13.

5. Saltzman, "An Electronic Job Hunt," 72–75; Mannix, "Writing a Computer-Friendly Resume," 90–93.

6. Stratford Sherman, "Leaders Learn to Heed the Voice Within," *Fortune*, August 22, 1994, 92–100.

7. Caryne Brown, "Have I Got a Career for You," *Black Enterprise*, February 1993, 145–152.

8. Richman, "The New Work Force Builds Itself," 68–76; Lee Smith, "Landing that First Real Job," *Fortune*, May 16, 1994, 58–60.

9. J. G., "The Money Job Rankings," *Money*, March 1994, 72–73.

10. *Ibid.*

11. *Ibid.*

12. *Ibid.*

13. *Ibid.*
14. "Hot Tracks in 20 Professions," *U.S. News & World Report*, October 26, 1992, 104–110.
15. *Ibid.*, 106–112.
16. J. G., "The Money Job Rankings," 72–73.
17. J. G., "Hot Tracks in 20 Professions," 106–112.
18. *Ibid.*

19. J. G., "The Money Job Rankings," 72–73.
20. J. G., "Hot Tracks in 20 Professions," 106–112.
21. *Ibid.*
22. J. G., "The Money Job Rankings," 72–73.
23. J. G., "Hot Tracks in 20 Professions," 106–112.
24. *Ibid.*

absolute advantage Situation in which a country has a monopolistic position in the marketing of a good or produces it at the lowest cost.

accessory equipment Capital items, such as personal computers, that are less expensive and shorter-lived than installations.

accountability Individual's responsibility for results.

accounting Measuring, interpreting, and communicating financial information for internal and external decision making.

accounting equation Basic accounting concept that assets are equal to liabilities plus owners' equity.

accounting process Method of converting individual transactions to financial statements.

acid rain Rain containing sulfuric acid resulting from the burning of fossil fuels.

acid-test ratio Ratio measuring the ability of a firm to meet its current debt on short notice; calculated by dividing quick assets by current liabilities; also called quick ratio.

acquisition Procedure in which one firm acquires the property and assumes the obligations of another firm.

Active Corps of Executives (ACE) SBA program using volunteer consultants who assist people in small business through research and consulting activities.

activity ratio Ratio measuring the effectiveness of the firm's use of its resources.

adaptive planning Planning that allows changes in response to new developments in the business's situation and environment.

added value Increased worth resulting from better-than-expected performance.

adjourning stage Point at which a team focuses on wrapping up and summarizing the experience and accomplishments of the group before it disbands.

advertising Nonpersonal sales presentation usually directed at a large number of potential customers.

affirmative action program Program set up by businesses to increase opportunities for women and minorities.

allowances Rights allocated to a company to emit a prescribed amount of pollution; if a firm has a low rate of emissions, it may have extra allowances that it can sell to another firm with higher emission rates.

American Federation of Labor (AFL) National union made up of affiliated individual craft unions.

antitrust laws Acts that prohibit attempts to monopolize a market.

apprenticeship training Program wherein an employee learns job tasks by serving as an assistant to a trained worker for a relatively long time.

arbitration Process of bringing an impartial third party into a union–management dispute to render a legally binding decision.

asked (selling) price The price at which a security is offered.

assembly line Manufacturing technique wherein the product passes through several work stations, each with a specialized task.

asset Anything of value owned or leased by a business.

audience Receivers of verbal, nonverbal, and written messages.

authority Power to act and make decisions in carrying out responsibilities.

autocratic leaders Those who make decisions on their own without consulting others.

automated teller machine (ATM) Electronic banking machine that permits customers to make banking transactions on a 24-hour basis by using an access code.

automobile insurance Coverage for property and liability claims resulting from theft, fire, or accident.

balance of payments Flow of money into and out of a country.

balance of trade Relationship between a country's exports and imports.

balance sheet Statement of a firm's financial position on a particular date.

bank examiner A trained representative who inspects the financial records and management practices of each federally-insured financial institution.

bear Investor who expects stock prices to decline along with market prices.

benchmarking The process in which an organization continuously compares and measures itself against business leaders.

bid The amount a buyer will pay for a security.

board of directors Governing body of a corporation elected by the stockholders.

bond Certificate of indebtedness sold to raise long-term funds for corporations or government agencies.

bond indenture Legal contract containing all provisions of a bond.

bond trustee Financial institution or individual representing bondholders.

book value Value of stock determined by subtracting liabilities from assets, minus the value of any preferred stock.

bottom line Overall profit or loss earned by a firm.

boycott An attempt to keep people from purchasing goods or services from a company in dispute over a management practice.

brand Name, term, sign, symbol, or design used to identify the goods or services of a firm.

brand name Words or letters that identify a firm's offerings.

budget Planning and control tool that reflects expected sales revenues, operating expenses, and cash receipts and outlays.

bull Investor who expects stock prices to rise along with market prices.

burglary insurance Insurance coverage for losses due to the taking of property by forcible entry.

burnout A mental and physical state characterized by low morale and fatigue.

business All profit-seeking activities and enterprises that provide goods and services necessary to an economic system.

business ethics Standards of business conduct and moral values.

business interruption insurance Type of insurance designed to cover losses resulting from temporary business closings.

business plan Description of the business's goals and the means for achieving them.

business products Items purchased to be used directly or indirectly in the production of other goods or for resale.

buyer surveys Forecasting technique that collects information from potential buyers.

callable bond Bond allowing redemption by issuer before maturity.

capital Funds that finance the operation of a business.

cartel Monopolistic organization of foreign firms.

cash surrender value The savings portion of a life insurance policy.

cause marketing Marketing efforts designed to promote a cause or social issue.

CD-ROM Compact-disc-read-only memory; a popular computer disk for multimedia applications because it stores data in long spirals that are well-suited to retrieving continuous blocks of data.

centralized network Communication of team members through a single person to solve problems or make decisions.

certificate of deposit (CD) Short-term, high-interest note issued by a financial institution, such as a bank, savings and loan, or credit union.

certified public accountant (CPA) Accountant who has completed education and experience requirements and passed a comprehensive examination.

chain of command The set of relationships that indicates who gives direction to whom and who reports to whom.

channel Medium through which message sender and audience communicate.

chief information officer (CIO) Top management executive responsible for directing a firm's management information system and related computer operations.

classroom training Program that uses classroom techniques to teach employees difficult, high-skill jobs.

closed shop Illegal employment policy of refusing to hire nonunion workers.

coinsurance clause Insurance clause requiring that the insured carry fire insurance of some minimum percentage of the replacement value of the property to receive full coverage for a loss.

collective bargaining Negotiation between management and union representatives concerning wages and working conditions.

commercial bank Profit-making business that holds deposits of individuals and businesses in the form of checking or savings accounts and uses these funds to make loans to individuals and businesses.

commercial finance company Financial institution that makes short-term loans to businesses that pledge tangible items such as inventory, machinery, or property as collateral.

commercial paper Short-term note issued by a major corporation with high credit standing and backed solely by the reputation of that firm.

committee organization   The organization structure in which authority and responsibility are held jointly by a group of individuals.

common market   Form of economic integration that maintains a customs union and seeks to bring other trade rules into agreement.

common stock   Stock providing owners voting rights but only a residual claim to company assets.

communication   The meaningful exchange of information through messages.

communism   Economic theory, developed by Karl Marx, under which private property is eliminated and the means of production are owned in common.

comparative advantage   A country's ability to supply a particular item more efficiently and at a lower cost than it can supply other products.

competition   Battle among businesses for consumer acceptance.

competitive benchmarking   Comparisons with direct product competitors.

competitive differentiation   Any aspect of a company and its performance that makes it more successful than its competitors.

component parts and materials   Finished industrial products that become part of a final product.

compressed workweek   Scheduling work so workers spend fewer days on the job, but work approximately the same number of hours.

computer   Programmable electronic device that can store, retrieve, and process data.

computer-aided design (CAD)   Interaction between a designer and a computer resulting in a product, building, or part that meets predetermined specifications.

computer-aided manufacturing (CAM)   Computer analysis of a CAD to determine steps in producing the design, and electronic transmission of instructions to production equipment used in producing the part or product.

computer chips   Thin silicon wafers on which integrated circuits (networks of transistors and circuits) are assembled.

computer-integrated manufacturing (CIM)   Use of computer to design products, control machines, handle materials, and control the production function in an integrated fashion.

computer network   System in which interconnected computers either can function individually or communicate with each other.

computer viruses   Programs that secretly attach themselves to other programs and change them or destroy the data kept on a disk.

concept testing   Marketing research designed to solicit initial consumer reaction to new-product ideas before the products are developed.

conceptual skills   The ability to see the organization as a unified whole and understand how each part of the overall organization interacts with other parts.

concurrent engineering   Engineering done concurrently with design, production, and other functions.

conflict   An antagonistic interaction in which one party attempts to thwart the intentions or goals of another.

Congress of Industrial Organizations (CIO)   National union made up of affiliated individual unions.

conservation   Preservation of declining energy resources.

constraint   In SWOT analysis, the inability to respond to an opportunity.

consumer behavior   Actions that are involved directly in obtaining, consuming, and disposing of products, including the decision processes that precede and follow these actions.

consumer finance company   Financial institution that makes short-term loans to individuals, typically requiring collateral, also called a personal finance company or a small-loan company.

consumerism   Public demand for business to consider consumer needs in making decisions.

consumer products   Goods and services purchased by the ultimate consumer for his or her own use.

context   Every factor surrounding and affecting the transmission of a message.

contingency planning   Planning for emergencies.

contingency theory   Theory arguing that management should adjust its leadership style in accordance with the situation at hand.

contingent business interruption insurance   Insurance coverage for losses incurred as a result of a major supplier or customer being damaged by fire or for other specified property damage.

continuous process improvement   The process of constantly studying and making changes in work activities to improve quality, timeliness, efficiency, and effectiveness.

controlling   Evaluating the company's performance to determine whether it is accomplishing its objectives.

convenience products   Products that consumers seek to purchase frequently, immediately, and with a minimum of effort.

convertible bond Bond conversion option to a specific number of shares of common stock.

convertible preferred stock Preferred stock issued with a conversion privilege, giving stockholders the option of having their preferred stock converted into common stock at a stated price.

cooperative Organization that is operated collectively by its owners.

corporate culture The value system of an organization.

corporation Legal entity with authority to act and have liability separate and apart from its owners.

cost accountant Professional who determines the cost of goods and services and helps set their prices.

costs of quality The costs associated with poor quality, such as scrap, rework, and loss of customers.

countertrade International bartering agreement.

creativity The development of novel solutions to perceived organizational problems.

credit insurance Insurance to protect lenders against losses caused by insolvency of customers to whom credit has been granted.

credit life insurance Term insurance that repays the balance owed on a house or other major purchase if the policyholder dies.

credit union Member-owned financial cooperative that pays interest to depositors, offers share draft accounts, and makes short-term loans and some home mortgage loans.

critical success factors Those factors most important in gaining a competitive advantage and achieving long-term success.

critical thinking The process of determining the authenticity, accuracy, and worth of information, knowledge claims, or arguments.

cross-functional team Involves employees from different departments who work on specific projects, such as developing a new product or solving a particular problem.

current ratio Ratio measuring a firm's ability to pay its current debts as they mature; calculated by dividing current assets by current liabilities.

customer satisfaction The concept of a good or service pleasing buyers because it has met their emotional needs and quality expectations.

customer satisfaction measurement (CSM) program Procedure for measuring customer feedback against customer satisfaction goals and developing an action plan for improvement.

customer service Aspect of competitive strategy that refers to how a firm treats its customers.

customer service standards Quality of service that a firm's customers will receive.

customs union Form of economic integration in which a free trade area is established for member nations and a uniform tariff is imposed on trade with nonmember nations.

cycle time The time it takes to complete a work process or activity.

debenture Bond backed by the reputation of the issuing corporation.

debt capital Funds obtained through borrowing.

debt to owners' equity Ratio measuring the extent to which company operations are financed by borrowed funds; calculated by dividing total liabilities by owners' equity.

decentralized network System in which members communicate freely with other team members and arrive at decisions together.

decision making Recognizing that a problem exists, identifying it, evaluating alternatives, selecting and implementing an alternative, and following up.

decision support system Computer system that quickly provides relevant facts for use in decision making.

decoding The receiver's interpretation of the message.

delegation The act of assigning activities to subordinates.

Delphi technique Forecasting technique that uses an anonymous panel of individuals from both outside and inside the company.

demand Buyers' willingness and ability to purchase products.

democratic leaders Those who involve their subordinates in making decisions.

dental insurance Insurance designed to pay a specified percentage of dental expenses.

departmentalization The subdivision of work activities into units within the organization.

deregulation Elimination of legal restraints on competition.

desktop publishing Software designed to print documents with high-quality type, graphics, and layouts.

devaluation Reduction in value of a country's currency.

directing Guiding and motivating workers to accomplish organizational objectives.

disability income insurance Health insurance designed to protect against loss of income while the insured is disabled as a result of accident or illness.

discount brokerage firms Competitors of traditional full-service brokers that offer fewer services and charge lower commissions.

discount rate Interest rate charged by the Federal Reserve System on loans to member banks.

distribution channels Paths that goods and services and title to them follow from producer to consumer.

diversity The blend of persons of different genders, ethnic backgrounds, cultures, religions, ages, and physical and mental challenges.

Dow Jones Averages Averages based on market prices of 30 industrial, 20 transportation, and 15 utility stocks that reflect general market activity.

downsizing Management decisions to eliminate layers from the management hierarchy in an effort to reduce costs and make the firm more efficient.

dumping Selling goods abroad at a price lower than that charged in the domestic market.

earnings per share Profits earned by a corporation for each share of common stock outstanding; calculated by dividing net income after taxes by the number of common shares outstanding.

ecology Study of the relationship between living things and their environment.

economics Social science of allocating scarce resources.

electronic bulletin boards Public message centers that appear on computer networks.

electronic funds transfer system (EFTS) Computerized method for making purchases and paying bills by electronically depositing or withdrawing funds.

electronic mail (E-mail) System for sending and receiving written messages through computers.

embargo Ban on certain imported or exported products.

emoticons Little faces called "smileys," used in E-mail messages, that are constructed with punctuation marks, conveying some of a message's emotional content.

employee benefits Employee rewards, such as pension plans, insurance, sick-leave pay, and tuition reimbursement, given at all or part of the expense of the company.

employee involvement Practices that motivate employees to perform their jobs better through empowerment, training, and teamwork.

employee ownership Ownership and operation of an organization by its employees, usually under the supervision of the original corporate organization.

employers' association Cooperative efforts by employers to present a united front in dealing with labor unions.

empowering Giving employees additional decision-making authority and responsibilities.

empowerment The practice of giving employees the authority to make decisions about their work without supervisory approval.

encoding The translation of a message into understandable terms and in a form capable of being transmitted through the communication medium selected by the sender.

endowment policy Insurance that provides coverage for a specified period, after which the face value is refunded to the policyholder.

entrepreneur A risk taker in the private enterprise system, specifically a person who creates a new business.

entrepreneurship Taking risks to set up and operate a business.

Equal Employment Opportunity Commission (EEOC) Federal commission created to increase job opportunities for women and minorities and to help eliminate job discrimination.

equity Claim against the assets of a business.

equity capital (equity funds) Funds provided by the firm's owners by plowing back earnings, liquidating assets, making additional contributions, by stock issues to the general public, or by contributions from venture capitalists.

esteem needs Desire for accomplishment, a feeling of achievement, and the respect of others.

event marketing Marketing of sporting, cultural, and charitable activities to selected target markets.

everyday low pricing (EDLP) Retail practice of highly competitive prices and avoiding reliance on sales.

exchange Process by which two or more parties give something of value to one another to satisfy felt needs.

exchange control Allocation, expansion, or restriction of foreign exchange.

exchange rate Rate at which a country's currency can be exchanged for other currencies.

executive information system (EIS) User-friendly decision-oriented computer system used by senior management.

expert system Computer programs that imitate human thinking through the use of "if . . . then" rules.

exponential smoothing Form of trend analysis that considers recent historical data as more important than older data.

exporting Selling domestic goods abroad.

export management company Firm that performs international marketing services as commissioned representatives or distributors for other companies.

Export Trading Companies Act (1982) Legislation designed to encourage export trading companies.

export trading company Trading firm involved in importing, exporting, countertrading, investing, and manufacturing.

external communication The meaningful exchange of information through messages between an organization and its major audiences.

external customers People or organizations that buy or use another firm's good or service.

factors of production Basic inputs into the private enterprise system, including natural resources, labor, capital, and entrepreneurship.

Family and Medical Leave Act (1993) Legislation requiring covered employers to give up to 12 weeks of unpaid, job-protected leave to eligible employees.

family brand Brand name used for several related products or entire product mix.

family leave Giving employees a leave of absence from work in order to deal with family matters.

featherbedding Payment for work not done.

Federal Deposit Insurance Corporation (FDIC) Corporation that insures bank depositors' accounts up to a maximum of $100,000 and sets requirements for sound banking practices.

Federal Reserve System Network of 12 regional banks that regulates banking in the United States.

feedback Messages returned by the audience to the sender that may cause the sender to alter or cancel an original message.

fidelity bond Bond that protects employers from employees' dishonesty.

field robot Assists human workers in nonmanufacturing, often hazardous, environments, such as nuclear power plants, space stations, and battlefields.

finance Business function of planning, obtaining, and managing the company's use of funds in order to accomplish its objectives most effectively.

financial control Process that periodically checks actual revenues, costs, and expenses against the forecasts.

financial manager Individual in an organization responsible for developing and implementing the firm's financial plan and for determining the most appropriate sources and uses of funds.

financial plan Document that specifies the funds needed by a firm for a period of time, charts inflows and outflows, and outlines the most appropriate uses of funds.

financial supermarket Nonbank that provides financial services such as investments, loans, real estate, and insurance.

fire insurance Covers losses due to fire.

flexible benefit plan System of flexible benefits in which employees are provided with specific dollar amounts of benefits and are allowed to select areas of coverage.

flexible manufacturing system (FMS) Facility that allows production methods to be modified quickly when different products are manufactured.

floating exchange rates Exchange rates that vary according to market conditions.

forecasting The estimation or prediction of a company's future sales or income.

Foreign Corrupt Practices Act (1978) Legislation that prohibits bribery of foreigners by U.S. firms to secure sales.

foreign direct investment Investments in permanent foreign enterprises.

foreign exchange market Market where one nation's currency can be purchased with—or sold for—that of another nation.

foreign production Making goods and supplying services in a foreign country for sale there or in other countries.

foreign trade zones Sites where foreign goods may be held or processed and then re-exported without incurring further duties.

formal communication channels Messages that flow within the chain of command or task responsibility defined by an organization.

forming stage An orientation period during which team members get to know each other and find out which behaviors are acceptable to the group.

form utility Utility created through the conversion of raw materials and other inputs into finished goods and services.

fourth market Securities-trading systems that match buyers with sellers, bypassing NASDAQ and the stock exchanges.

franchisee Small-business person who is allowed to sell the goods or services of a supplier in exchange for some payment.

franchising Agreement that sets the methods a dealer can use to produce and market a supplier's good or service.

franchisor Supplier of a franchise that provides various services in exchange for a payment by the franchisee.

free-rein leaders Those who believe in minimal supervision and leave most decisions to their subordinates.

free trade area Form of economic integration in which participants agree to trade among themselves without tariffs or trade restrictions.

friendship, commerce, and navigation (FCN) treaties Agreements with other nations that include many aspects of international business relations.

functional benchmarking Comparisons made between the functions of firms in different industries.

gaps Differences between expected good or service quality and perceived good or service quality.

General Agreement on Tariffs and Trade (GATT) International accord that has sponsored a series of negotiations on tariffs and trade restrictions.

generally accepted accounting principles (GAAP) Standards that provide consistency concerning the conventions, rules, and procedures in accounting practices.

generic product Nonbranded item with plain packaging and little or no advertising support.

glass ceiling Arbitrary barrier that keeps women and minorities from advancing to top management.

global strategy Worldwide use of a standardized product and marketing strategy.

government accountant Professional accountant employed by a government agency or not-for-profit organization.

government bond Bond issued by the U.S. government.

grapevine An internal information channel that transmits information through unofficial, independent sources.

greenhouse effect Situation where carbon dioxide traps heat in the earth's atmosphere.

grievance Employee or union complaint that management is violating some provision of the union contract.

gross domestic product (GDP) Sum of all goods and services produced within a nation's boundaries.

group policies Insurance similar to individual coverage, but offered at a lower premium price.

groupware Computer software that combines and extends the concept of shared information (a networked database) with a method for moving data between users (E-mail).

hardware All of the tangible elements of the computer system.

health insurance Insurance that provides coverage for losses due to sickness or accidents.

health maintenance organization (HMO) A prepaid medical expense plan that provides a comprehensive set of health services and benefits to policyholders.

high-context cultures Cultures in which communication depends not only on the message itself, but also on everything that surrounds it.

hiring from within Organizational policy of first considering a company's own employees to fill job vacancies.

home-based work Program allowing employees to work at home, sometimes linked to their employers by terminals hooked to a central computer.

hospitalization insurance Health insurance designed to pay for most hospital costs.

human relations skills "People" skills involving the manager's ability to work effectively with and through people.

human resource management Process of acquiring, training, developing, motivating, and appraising a sufficient quantity of qualified employees to perform necessary activities; and developing activities and an organizational climate conducive to maximum efficiency and worker satisfaction.

human resources All the people employed in producing a good or service.

importing Buying foreign goods and raw materials.

import quota Limitation on the amount of certain products that can be imported.

incentive compensation An addition to a salary or wage given for exceptional performance.

income statement Financial record of revenues, expenses, and profits of a company over a period of time.

individual branding Giving each product in a line its own brand name.

informal communication channels Communication outside formally authorized channels without regard for the organization's hierarchy of authority.

information superhighway A single, enormous computer network merging telecommunications, information, and data that can be accessed by any individual or organization.

injunction Court order prohibiting some practice.

inland marine insurance Insurance coverage for losses of property due to damage while goods are being transported by truck, ship, rail, or plane.

insider trading Illegal securities trading by persons who profit from their access to nonpublic information about a company.

installations Expensive and long-lived major capital items, such as a new factory or heavy machinery.

institutional investor Organization that invests its own funds or funds held in trust.

insurable interest Insurance concept wherein the policyholder must stand to suffer loss.

insurable risk Requirements a risk must meet in order for the insurer to provide protection against its occurrence.

insurance Process by which an insurer, in exchange for a fee, agrees to reimburse firms or individuals for losses up to specified limits.

insurance company Private companies and public agencies that provide insurance coverage for business firms, not-for-profit organizations, and individuals in return for premium payments.

interactive media Program applications that allow users to interact with computers to perform different functions at the same time.

internal auditor Professional who examines the firm's financial practices to ensure that records are accurate and that company operations are in compliance with federal laws and regulations.

internal benchmarking Comparisons made between similar functions performed in different departments or divisions within the firm.

internal communication System of communication through channels within an organization.

internal customers Employees or departments within an organization that depend on the work of other people or departments to perform their jobs.

International Monetary Fund (IMF) Lender of foreign exchange to countries requiring assistance in international trade.

international union National union with membership outside the United States.

intrapreneurship Entrepreneurial-type activity within the corporate structure.

inventory control Function of controlling all costs associated with inventory.

inventory turnover ratio Ratio measuring the number of times merchandise moves through a business; calculated by dividing the cost of goods sold by the average amount of inventory.

investment banker Specialist in selling new issues of securities for business and government.

ISO 9000 International standards for quality management and quality assurance.

job enlargement Increasing the number of tasks a worker performs; may or may not be job enriching.

job enrichment Redesigning work to give employees more authority in planning their tasks, deciding how they are to be done, and allowing them to learn related skills or to trade jobs.

joint venture Partnership formed for a specific undertaking. Sharing of a foreign operation's costs, risks, and management with a foreign firm or government.

journal Book in which transactions are recorded in chronological order.

junk bonds The riskiest and lowest-rated bonds on the market.

jury of executive opinion Forecasting technique that averages the forecasts of top executives from all divisions.

just-in-time logistics (JIT) Management philosophy aimed at improving profits and return on investment by involving workers in the operations process and eliminating waste through cost reductions, inventory reductions, and quality improvements.

key executive insurance Life insurance designed to reimburse the organization for the loss of the services of an important executive.

labor union Group of workers united by common goals, such as wages, hours, and working conditions.

law of large numbers Probability calculation of the likelihood of the occurrence of perils on which premiums are based.

leadership The act of motivating or causing others to perform activities designed to achieve specific objectives.

leadership style The way in which a leader uses available power to lead others.

ledger Book containing individual account information obtained from the journal.

leverage Technique of increasing the rate of return on investment through the use of borrowed funds.

leverage ratio Ratio measuring the extent to which a firm relies on debt financing in its operations.

liability Claim of the firm's creditors.

liability insurance Insurance protection for businesses and individuals against claims caused by injuries to others or damage to the property of others.

liability losses Financial losses suffered by a business firm or individual should the firm or individual be held responsible for property damage or injuries suffered by others.

limit order Investor request that a stock purchase or sale be made at a specified price.

line-and-staff organization Combines the direct flow of authority present in the line organization with staff departments that serve, advise, and support the line departments.

line organization A direct flow of authority from the chief executive to subordinates.

liquidity Speed at which items can be converted to cash.

liquidity ratio Ratio measuring a firm's ability to meet its short-term obligations.

listening The skill of receiving a message and interpreting its genuine meaning by accurately grasping the facts and feelings conveyed.

local area network (LAN) A computer network that connects machines within a limited area.

local union Branch of a national union representing members in a specific area.

low-context cultures Cultures in which communication relies on explicit written and verbal messages.

mainframe computer Largest type of computer system, offers huge storage capacity and high processing speeds.

major medical insurance Insurance that protects the insured against catastrophic financial losses by covering expenses that exceed the coverage limits of basic policies.

management The achievement of organizational objectives through people and other resources.

management by objectives Program designed to improve motivation through employee participation in goal setting and defining factors used in performance evaluations.

management development program Training designed to improve the skills and broaden the knowledge of managers and potential managers.

management information system (MIS) Organized method of providing information for decision making.

margin requirement The percentage of the purchase price of a security that must be paid in cash by the investor.

market People with the purchasing power and authority to buy.

marketing Planning and executing the conception, pricing, promotion, and distribution of ideas, goods, and services to create exchanges that satisfy individual and organizational objectives.

marketing concept Consumer orientation designed to achieve long-run success.

marketing intermediaries Distribution channel members operating between the producer and the consumer or industrial producer.

marketing mix Combination of a firm's product, pricing, distribution, and promotional strategies focused on selected consumer segments.

marketing research Information function that links the marketer to the marketplace.

market order Investor request that a stock purchase or sale be made at the current market price.

market segmentation Process of dividing the total market into several relatively homogeneous groups.

market value Price at which a security is selling currently.

mass production The manufacture of goods in large quantities as a result of standardization, specialized labor, and mechanization.

matrix, or project management, organization Structure in which specialists from different parts of the organization are brought together to work on specific projects.

mechanization Use of machines to perform work previously performed by people, thus increasing workers' productivity.

mediation Process of settling union–management disputes through recommendations of an impartial third party.

Medicare Form of health insurance for persons 65 years old or older and certain other Social Security recipients.

merger Two or more firms that combine to form one company.

message Written, oral, or nonverbal communication transmitted by a sender to an audience.

microcomputer Desktop, laptop, and pocket-sized portable computers.

microprocessor A fingernail-sized chip that contains an entire computer processing unit (CPU).

middle management Those people responsible for developing detailed plans and procedures to implement the general plans of top management.

minicomputer Intermediate-sized computer.

mission statement Written explanation of a company's purpose and aims.

mixed economy Economic system having a mix of government ownership and private enterprise.

money Anything generally accepted as a means of paying for goods and services.

monopolistic competition Situation in which firms differentiate their products from those of competitors.

monopoly Market situation in which there are no direct competitors.

morale The mental attitude of employees toward their employer and job.

mortality table Table used to predict the number of persons in each age category who will die in a given year.

most favored nation (MFN) A country favored by the United States in trade relations. Benefits include low import duties.

motive Inner state that directs individuals toward the goal of satisfying a felt need.

mouse Computer hardware that allows easy access of on-screen information.

multicultural diversity Racial and cultural blend within a society.

multimedia computing The technologies that facilitate the integration of two or more types of media.

multinational corporation Corporation that operates on an international level.

multinational strategy Strategy whereby each national market is treated differently.

municipal bond Debt issue of a state or political subdivision that may be a general obligation bond or revenue bond.

mutual funds Financial organizations that use investors' money to acquire a portfolio of securities.

mutual insurance company Type of cooperative owned by its policyholders.

National Association of Securities Dealers Automatic Quotation (NASDAQ) system A nationwide over-the-counter securities-trading network.

national bank Commercial bank chartered by the federal government.

national brand Brand that is offered and promoted by a manufacturer.

national union Labor organization comprised of numerous local chapters.

natural resources Everything useful as a production input in its natural state.

near-money Assets almost as liquid as cash or checking accounts but that cannot be used directly as a medium of exchange.

need Lack of something useful; discrepancy between a desired state and the actual state.

net income Profit or loss incurred over a specific period; determined by subtracting all expenses from revenues.

no-fault insurance State laws that require claims to be paid by the policyholder's insurance company without regard to fault and that limit the right of victims to sue.

noise Anything that interferes with a message by distorting its meaning.

nonpersonal selling Advertising, sales, promotion, and public relations.

nonprogrammed decision Decision involving complex, important, and nonroutine problems of opportunities.

nonverbal communication Communication that is transmitted through actions and behaviors.

norming stage Point at which differences among team members are resolved, members accept each other, and consensus is reached about the roles of the team leader and other participants.

not-for-profit organization Organization whose primary objective is something other than returning profits to their owners.

objectives Guideposts in defining what the business aims to achieve in areas such as profitability, customer service, and social responsibility.

Occupational Safety and Health Administration (OSHA) Federal agency created to assure safe and healthy working conditions.

ocean marine insurance Insurance that covers shippers for losses of property due to damage to a ship or its cargo while at sea or in port.

odd lots Quantities of less than 100 shares of stock bought or sold.

Old-Age, Survivors, Disability, and Health Insurance (OASDHI)   Government insurance that is part of the Social Security program.

oligopoly   Market having few sellers and substantial entry restrictions.

on-the-job training   Training employees for job tasks by allowing them to perform tasks under the guidance of an experienced employee.

open market operations   Federal Reserve System method of controlling the money supply through the purchase and sale of government bonds.

open shop   Employment policy making union membership (with its dues) voluntary for all workers.

operational planning   Work standards and tasks that implement tactical plans.

organization   A structured grouping of people working together to achieve organizational objectives.

organization chart   The authority and responsibility relationships of most organizations.

organization marketing   Marketing efforts designed to influence others to accept the goals of, receive the services of, or contribute in some way to an organization.

organizing   Process of blending human and material resources through the design of a formal structure of tasks and authority.

outsourcing   Relying on outside specialists to perform functions previously performed by company employees.

over-the-counter (OTC) market   Method of trading securities through market makers who fill customers' buy and sell orders.

owners' equity   Claims of the proprietor, partners, or the stockholders against the assets of the firm; the excess of assets over liabilities.

ownership utility   Utility created by arranging for the transfer of ownership at the time of purchase.

partnership   Two or more persons who operate a business as co-partners.

par value   Value printed on stock certificates of some companies.

PDCA cycle   A step-by-step process of **p**lanning, **d**oing, **c**hecking, and **a**cting.

pension fund   Funds accumulated by a company, credit union, or not-for-profit organization for the retirement income needs of its employees or members.

performance appraisal   Defining acceptable employee performance levels, evaluating them, then comparing actual and desired performance to aid in determining, training, compensation, promotion, transfers, or terminations.

performing stage   Phase of team development characterized by problem solving and a focus on task accomplishment.

personal selling   Promotional presentation made on a person-to-person basis with a potential buyer.

person marketing   Marketing efforts designed to attract the attention, interest, and preference of a target market toward a specific person, such as a political candidate.

physical distribution   Movement of goods from producer to user.

physiological needs   Primary human needs for food, shelter, and clothing that must be satisfied before higher-order needs can be considered.

pick-and-place robot   Simplest robot that moves in only two or three directions as it picks something up from one spot and places it in another.

picketing   Workers marching at a plant entrance protesting some management practice.

place marketing   Marketing efforts designed to attract people to a particular geographic area.

place utility   Utility created by making products available where the consumer wants to purchase them.

planning   Anticipating the future and determining the best courses of action to achieve company objectives.

point-of-sale terminal   Machines linked to a bank's computer that allow funds to be transferred from the purchaser's account to the seller's account when purchases are made.

pollution   Tainting or destroying a natural environment.

power   The ability of one person to influence the behavior of another.

preferred stock   Stock providing owners preferential dividend payment and first claim to assets after debts are paid, but seldom includes voting rights.

premium   Fee paid by insured party to the insurer for coverage against losses.

price   Exchange value of a good or service.

price-earnings ratio   Current market price divided by annual earnings per share.

primary market   New issues of securities sold publicly for the first time.

private accountant Professional accountant employed by a business other than a public accounting firm.

private brand Brand name owned by a wholesaler or retailer.

private enterprise system Economic system in which success or failure is determined by how well firms match and counter the offering of competitors.

privatization Trend to substitute private ownership for public ownership.

problem In SWOT analysis, an external threat to a company weakness.

problem-solving team Temporary combinations of workers who gather to solve a specific problem and then disband.

product Bundle of physical, service, and symbolic attributes designed to satisfy consumer wants.

production Use of people and machinery to convert materials into finished goods or services.

production and operations management Managing people and machinery used in converting materials and resources into finished goods and services.

productivity The relationship between the number of units of goods and services produced and the number of inputs of human and other resources necessary to produce them.

product liability insurance Insurance protection for businesses against claims for damages resulting from the use of the company's products.

product life cycle Four stages through which a successful product passes: introduction, growth, maturity, and decline.

product line Series of related products offered by a firm.

product mix Assortment of products offered by a firm.

profitability ratio Ratio measuring the overall financial performance of the firm.

profits Rewards for the business person who takes the risks involved in blending people, technology, and information in creating and marketing want-satisfying goods and services that provide customer satisfaction.

programmed decision Decision involving routine, recurring problems for which well-established solutions exist.

program trading Computer systems programmed to buy or sell securities to take advantage of price differences that sometimes occur between stock futures and current stock prices.

promotional mix Firm's combination of both personal and nonpersonal selling designed to achieve promotional objectives.

property losses Financial losses resulting from interruption of business operations or physical damage to property as a result of fires, accidents, theft, or other destructive occurrences.

public accountant Professional who provides accounting services to other businesses and individuals.

public insurance company A government agency established at the state or federal level to provide specialized insurance protection for individuals and organizations.

public ownership Enterprise owned and operated by a governmental unit.

public relations An organization's communications with its customers, vendors, news media, employees, stockholders, government, and the general public.

pulling strategy Promotional strategy utilizing advertising and sales promotion appeals to generate consumer demand for a product.

pure competition Situation in which there are many firms in an industry and none individually can influence market prices.

pure risk Type of risk involving only the chance of loss.

pushing strategy Sales-oriented promotional strategy designed to motivate marketing intermediaries to push a product to their customers.

qualitative forecasting Forecasting based on subjective judgment and experience.

quality The degree of excellence or superiority of an organization's goods and services.

quality circle A small group of employees from one work area or department who meet regularly to identify and solve problems.

quality control Measurement of goods and services against established quality standards.

quantitative forecasting Forecasting based on mathematical models.

ratio analysis Use of quantitative measures in evaluating a firm's financial performance.

raw materials Farm and natural products used in producing other final products.

recycling Reprocessing of used materials for reuse.

reengineering   A process in which existing processes in the delivery chain are mapped out with detail, and technology is applied to key steps to reduce cycle time or errors.

regulated industry   Industry in which competition is either limited or eliminated, and government monitoring substitutes for market controls.

relationship marketing   An organization's attempt to develop long-term, cost-effective links with individual customers for mutual benefit.

research and development (R&D)   Scientific process of developing new commercial products.

reserve requirement   Percentage of a bank's checking and savings accounts that must be kept in the bank or on deposit at the local Federal Reserve district bank.

responsibility   Obligation of an employee to perform assigned duties.

retailers   Distribution channel members selling goods and services to individuals for their own use rather than for resale.

return   The gain or loss that results from an investment over a specified period.

return on equity   Ratio measuring company profitability by comparing net income and total owners' equity to assess the returns owners are receiving for their overall investment.

return on quality   Financial and customer satisfaction benefits derived from investment in quality improvement programs.

return on sales   Ratio measuring company profitability by comparing net income and net sales.

revenues   Funds received from sales of products and services and from interest payments, dividends, royalties, and rents.

right-to-work laws   State laws prohibiting compulsory union membership.

risk   Uncertainty about loss or injury.

risk-return trade-off   Balance between the risk of an investment and its potential gain.

robbery insurance   Insurance coverage for losses due to the unlawful taking of property from another person by force or by the threat of force.

robot   Reprogrammable machine capable of performing numerous programmed tasks by manipulating materials and tools.

round lots   Quantities of 100 shares of stock bought or sold.

safety needs   Second level of human needs, including job security, protection from physical harm, and avoidance of the unexpected.

salary   Employee compensation calculated on a weekly, monthly, or annual basis.

sales-force composite   A forecast based on sales-force estimates.

sales promotion   Form of promotion designed to increase sales through one-time selling efforts, such as displays, trade shows, special events, and other methods.

savings and loan association (S&L)   Thrift institution offering savings and checking accounts and using most of its funds to make home mortgage loans.

savings banks   State-chartered banks with operations similar to savings and loan associations.

secondary market   Sales of previously issued shares of stocks and bonds.

secured bond   Bond backed by specific pledges of company assets.

securities   Stocks and bonds representing obligations of the issuer to provide purchasers with an expected or stated return on investments.

selective credit controls   Federal Reserve System authority to regulate availability of credit by setting margin requirements on credit purchases of stocks and bonds and credit rules for consumer purchases.

self-actualization needs   Needs for fulfillment, for realizing one's potential, and for using one's talents and capabilities totally.

self-insurance fund   An account set up to cover losses from the assumption of pure risk.

self-managed team   A group of employees who work with little or no supervision.

sender   Participants in a transaction who communicate messages to an audience.

serial bond   Bonds issued at the same time, but with different maturity dates.

Service Corps of Retired Executives (SCORE)   Small Business Administration program using retired executives as consultants to assist small businesses.

sexism   Discrimination against either sex, primarily occurring against women.

sexual harassment   Inappropriate actions of a sexual nature.

shopping products   Products purchased only after the consumer has compared competing products in competing stores.

sinking-fund bond   Bond whose issuer deposits funds annually for redemption payment upon maturity.

small business Business that is owned and operated independently, is not dominant in its field, and meets certain size standards for its income or number of employees.

Small Business Administration (SBA) Principal government agency concerned with small U.S. firms.

small business investment company (SBIC) Federally funded investment group that makes loans to small businesses.

social (belongingness) needs Desire to be accepted by members of the family, other individuals, and groups.

social responsibility Management philosophy that highlights the social and economic effects of managerial decisions.

socialism Economic system that advocates government ownership and operation of all basic industries.

socio-emotional role Role played by leaders who devote their time and energy to providing support for group members' emotional needs and social unity.

software Programmed instructions that tell the computer what to do.

sole proprietorship Ownership (and usually operation) of an organization by one person.

specialization Involves dividing work into its simplest components so workers can concentrate on performing one task.

specialty products Products perceived to be so desirable that the buyer is willing to make a special effort to obtain them.

speculation Purchasing stocks in anticipation of making large profits quickly.

speculative risk Type of risk involving the chance of either profit or loss.

spreadsheet Special computer software permitting manipulation of decision variables to determine their impact.

Standard & Poor's Index Index based on market performance of 400 industrial, 40 financial, 40 utility, and 20 transportation stocks.

standardization Involves producing uniform, interchangeable goods and parts.

state bank Commercial bank chartered by an individual state.

statement of cash flows Information on a firm's cash receipts and cash payments that presents the sources and uses of cash for the firm.

statistical quality control A system of locating and measuring quality problems on production lines.

stockbroker Financial intermediary who buys and sells securities for individual and institutional investors.

stock exchange Location at which stocks and bonds are bought and sold.

stockholders People who acquire the shares of, and therefore own, a corporation.

stock insurance company Insurance company that is operated for profit.

stock split A recapitalization in which a single share is divided into multiple shares, lowering the price of the stock and making it easier for new investors to buy.

storming stage Point at which team participants' individual personalities begin to emerge as they clarify their roles and expectations within the team.

strategic alliance Partnerships formed by independent companies to create a competitive advantage.

strategic business units Divisions within a company, each with its own management, workers, objectives, products, and planning.

strategic planning Determining the overall strategy and resource allocations necessary to reach intermediate and long-term objectives.

strike Employee's temporary work stoppage until a dispute is settled or a contract is signed.

strikebreakers Nonunion worker hired to replace a striking worker.

subsidiary Corporation with all or a majority of its stock owned by another corporation.

supervisory management Those people directly responsible for the details of assigning workers to specific jobs and evaluating performance.

supplies Expense items needed in the firm's daily operation but not in part of the final product.

supply Sellers' willingness and ability to provide products.

surety bond Bond that protects individuals or companies against losses resulting from non-performance of a contract.

surgical and medical payments insurance Health insurance designed to pay the costs of surgery, fees of medical specialists, and physicians' care in the hospital during the patient's recovery.

SWOT analysis The analysis of a business based on its internal strengths and weaknesses and external opportunities and threats.

tactical planning Planning for short-term implementation of current activities and the related resource allocations.

target market   Group of consumers toward which a firm decides to direct its marketing efforts.

tariff   Tax levied against imported products.

task specialist role   Role played by leaders who devote time and energy to help the team accomplish its goals.

tax accountant   Professional who seeks to minimize taxes paid and is in charge of the firm's federal, state, county, and local tax returns.

team   A small number of people with complementary skills who are committed to a common purpose, approach, and set of performance goals.

team cohesiveness   The extent to which team members are attracted to the team and motivated to remain a part of it.

team norm   A standard of conduct that is shared by team members and guides their behavior.

technical skills   The manager's ability to understand and use techniques, knowledge, and tools of a specific discipline or department.

technology   The application to business of knowledge based on discoveries in science, inventions, and innovations.

telecommunications   Any system in which information or data is sent over a distance through some type of electronic transmission system, typically a telephone line.

term insurance   Insurance that pays a death benefit if the policyholder dies within a specified period of time; it has no value at the end of that period.

theft insurance   Insurance coverage for losses due to the unlawful taking of property.

Theory X   Managerial assumption that workers dislike work and must be coerced, controlled, or threatened to motivate them to work.

Theory Y   Managerial assumption that workers like work and, under proper conditions, accept and seek out responsibilities to fulfill their social, esteem, and self-actualization needs.

Theory Z   Management approach emphasizing employee participation as the key to increased productivity and improved quality of work life.

time management   The effective allocation of one's time among different tasks.

time utility   Utility created by making products available when the consumer wants to purchase them.

title insurance   Insurance protection for real-estate purchasers against losses incurred because of a defect in title to property.

tombstones   Black-and-white announcements of stock and bond offerings.

top management   The highest level of the management hierarchy staffed by executives who develop long-range plans and interact with the public and outside entities, like government.

total quality management (TQM)   An approach that involves a commitment to quality in achieving world-class performance and customer satisfaction as a crucial strategic objective.

trade credit   Short-term source of funds resulting from purchases made on credit or open account.

trademark   Brand that has been given legal protection exclusive to its owner.

Treasury bills   Short-term U.S. Treasury borrowings issued each week and sold to the highest bidder; virtually risk-free and easy to resell.

trend analysis   Mathematical approach to forecasting that assumes that the trends of the past will continue in the future.

unemployment insurance   Program that assists unemployed workers by providing financial benefits, job counseling, and placement services.

universal life insurance   Hybrid form of life insurance combining term insurance with a tax-deferred savings account.

unsecured loan   Short-term source of borrowed funds for which the borrower does not pledge any assets as collateral.

variable life insurance   Hybrid form of whole life insurance in which policyholders can decide how to invest the cash surrender value.

venture capitalist   Individual or business organization that invests in promising new businesses.

video display terminal (VDT)   A TV-like computer screen on which output can be displayed.

vision   The ability to perceive marketplace needs and what an organization must do to satisfy them.

voice processing   Technology that uses spoken language to send or receive information from a computer.

vulnerability   In SWOT analysis, the combination of an outside threat with an inside strength.

wages   Compensation based on the number of hours worked or the amount of output produced.

Webb-Pomerene Export Act (1918)   Exemption from antitrust laws for U.S. firms acting together to develop export markets.

whole life insurance   Combines protection and savings for the individual who pays premiums throughout a lifetime.

wholesaling intermediaries Distribution channel members primarily selling to retailers, other wholesalers, or industrial users.

word processing Use of computers to write, store, retrieve, edit, and print text materials.

worker buyout plan Financial incentive designed to encourage older employees to retire voluntarily.

workers' compensation insurance Insurance provided by employers under state law to employees injured on the job.

work team A mid-1990s approach in which small numbers of people with complementary skills perform the day-to-day work of the organization.

World Bank Organization that funds long-term national economic development projects.

yield Income received from securities; calculated by dividing dividends by market price.

ACKNOWLEDGMENTS

Photos

1 © Tony Stone Worldwide/Greg Pease
2–3 © Andy Freeberg
5 Courtesy Play It Again Sports
10 top © David A. Zickl
10 bottom © The Image Works
13 © Daniel Giry/Sygma
15 © Rich Mays
17 Courtesy SoftAd Group
18 © Michael Schumann/SABA
22 top left © Larry Downing/Sygma
22 top right © Wally McNamee/Sygma
22 bottom left © Jeffrey Markowitz/Sygma
22 bottom right © Arnie Schlissel/Sygma
28–29 © Tony Freeman/PhotoEdit
31 © Brian Smith, Miami, FL.
33 © C. Bruce Forster. Courtesy of PacifiCorp
37 © Lonnie Duka/Tony Stone Worldwide
38 © Krarit Phanvut/SIPA
41 © Alain-Hugues Bingen/Sygma
43 © Dan Peebles
48–49 © Philippe Caron/Sygma
58 top Courtesy Cole & Weber, Seattle
58 bottom © Pablo Bartholomew/Gamma Liaison
59 top © Giry-Sittler/REA/SABA
60 © Les Stone/Sygma
61 © Jean-Pierre Amet/Sygma
64 © M. Schumann/SABA
65 © Jim Frenek
69 © SuperStock, Inc.
70–71 © Erin Elder/SABA
77 © Michael Newman/PhotoEdit
84 © Charles Nes/The Gamma Liaison Network
92–93 © 1994 Scott Goldsmith
97 © Courtesy Leo Burnett, U.S.A,. Chicago
98 Photo © Tim Flach/Tony Stone Worldwide. Ad courtesy Adler, Boschette, Pebbles and Partners
101 © Ilene Erlich
102 © T. Matsumoto/Sygma
104 © Peter Korniss
108–109 Roger Ressmeyer-Starlight © 1990. All rights reserved.
111 Courtesy Burkhardt & Christy Advertising, Inc.
112 Courtesy National Institute of Standards & Technology

115 top, bottom © Kistone
116 Alen MacWeeney © 1990
118 bottom Courtesy UPS. Used with permission.
119 © 1994 Avis, Inc.
126 Courtesy Hewlett-Packard Company
133 Liaison International © PBJ Pictures
137 © John Katz. Printed with permission of Circle Ten Council, Dallas
141 © 1994 Brad Geller-Aerial Sports Photography, St. Louis, MO.
154 Courtesy Day Runner, Inc.
160–161 Used with permission of Rhino Foods, Inc.
171 © Steven Borns
175 right © Otto Greule/Allsport
176 Courtesy of Saturn Corporation
184–185 © Rich Frishman, Everett, WA.
187 Illustration by Rodica Prato
188 © 1994 James Schnepf
210 © Steve Chenn/Westlight
202 Tory Westnopfske/AP
203 Courtesy Molsen Brewing Company, USA
210–211 Photographed by Ted Hardin
213 © Anthony Edgeworth
214 Courtesy Bozell, NY
215 top Courtesy National Semiconductor
215 bottom Photo courtesy of Hewlett-Packard Company
216 © Peterson/SABA
218 Richard Gage/US News & World Report
219 © Christopher Irion
220 Reprinted with permission from Microsoft Corporation
223 Illustration by Tony Mikolajczyk
226 Hitachi/McCann-Erickson
231 © Paul Chesley/Tony Stone Worldwide
232–233 © 1994 Louis Psihoyos/Matrix
239 © 94 Rob Nelson/Black Star
242 © SABA
246 Gamma Liaison © Yvonne Hemsey
252–253 © Paulo Fridman/Sygma
256 top © Alan Levenson
256 bottom © David Carter
257 © Tony Freeman/PhotoEdit
259 © Keith Dannemiller/SABA
262 © 1994 Robbie McClaran
263 © R. Bossu/Sygma
264 bottom © 1994 Michael A. Schwarz

267 © Charles Gupton/Tony Stone Worldwide
270–271 © 1994 Nadine Markova
275 © Mark Peterson/SABA
276 © Tom Tracey/The Stock Market
278 © Tony Freeman/PhotoEdit
282 © Churchill & Klehr
285 © Najlah Feany/SABA
287 © 1994 Robb Kendrick. All rights reserved
289 © Adrian Bradshaw/SABA
293 © 90 Bill Binzen/The Stock Market
294–295 © David Young-Wolff/PhotoEdit
299 © 93 P. Saltonstall. All rights reserved
302 Courtesy of American International Group, Inc.
305 © Josef Polleros/JB Pictures
306 Courtesy of Craig Highbarger
308 © 94 Bryce Lankard
310–311 Used with permission by Sundown Sunblock, Johnson & Johnson, Brazil
316–317 © Claude Vasques
321 © Tony Freeman/PhotoEdit
322 © Tony Freeman/PhotoEdit
324 Team One Advertising, El Segundo, CA.
325 Courtesy Buster Brown Apparel, Inc.
332 top © 1993 AIUPPY Photography, P.O. Box 26, Livingstone, MT.
332 bottom © 1990 Phil Huber/Black Star
333 © Tony Freeman/PhotoEdit
338–339 Photo courtesy Dickenson Group, Boston
341 Invemed Assiciates, Inc.
342 Courtesy Clean Harbors, Inc.
343 Courtesy Playboy Enterprises, Inc.
344 Courtesy Mobil Corporation
361 Courtesy Travelers Insurance Companies
364 Courtesy Metropolitan Life Insurance Company, NY, NY. Peanuts © United Feature Syndicate, Inc.

Figures

6 Adapted from Edmund Faltermayer, "Competitiveness: How U.S. Companies Stack Up Now," *Fortune*, April 18, 1994, 54. © 1994 Time Inc. All rights reserved.

11 Reprinted from Gene Koretz, "Productivity: The U.S. Remains Leader of the Pack . . ." *Business Week*, December 21, 1992, 18. Data from C. V. Starr Center for Applied Economics, New York University. Reprinted with permission.

16 Reprinted from Thayer C. Taylor, "Coming of Age," *Sales & Marketing Management*, August 1994, 67. Data from *Los Angeles Times Mirror* Center for The People & The Press.

17 (bottom) Reprinted from Bob Laird, "Commerce in Cyberspace," *USA Today*, July 7, 1994, B1. Copyright 1994, USA Today. Reprinted with permission.

21 Adapted from Melisa Buchanan, "Just Kidding Around," *Entrepreneur*, May 1994, 126–132. Reprinted with permission from *Entrepreneur* Magazine, May 1994.
Adapted from Ricardo Sookdeo, "The New Global Consumer in Charts," *Fortune*, Autumn/Winter 1993, 71. © 1993 Time Inc. All rights reserved.

57 (bottom) Adapted from Susan Greco, ed., "Hands On: Sales & Marketing," *Inc.*, March 1994, 134. Research by Stephanie Gruner, data from U.S. Department of Commerce. Reprinted with permission, *Inc.* magazine March 1994. Copyright 1994 by Goldhirsch Group, Inc., 38 Commercial Wharf, Boston MA 02110.

73 Gilbert Fuchsberg, "Visioning Missions Becomes Its Own Mission," *The Wall Street Journal*, January 7, 1994, B1. Reprinted by permission of *The Wall Street Journal*, © 1994 Dow Jones & Co., Inc. All rights reserved worldwide.

74 (bottom) Adapted from *1990 General Electric Annual Report*, 3.

83 Adapted from discussion in Ramon J. Aldag and Timothy M. Stearns, *Management* (Cincinnati, OH: South-Western Publishing Co., 1991), 199–201.

94 Adapted from *State of Small Business: A Report of the President* (Washington, D.C.: U.S. Government Printing Office, 1990), 13.

100 Adapted from advertisement by Merrill Lynch. Data from U.S. Small Business Administration, Office of Advocacy, *The State of Small Business: A Report of the President*, 1992.

100 (top) Adapted from "Hands On: A Manager's Notebook," *Inc.*, September 1990, 130. Reprinted with permission, Inc. Magazine, September 1990. Copyright 1990 by Goldhirsch Group, Inc., 38 Commercial Wharf, Boston MA 02110.

101 (top) Adapted from John Hinge, compiler, "Owning the Business," *The Wall Street Journal*, November 22, 1991, R18. By permission of *The Wall Street Journal*, © 1991 Dow Jones & Co., Inc. All rights reserved worldwide.

114 (bottom) John Hillkirk, "On Mission to Revamp Workplace," *USA Today*, October 15, 1990, 4B. Copyright 1990, USA Today. Reprinted with permission.

120 Reprinted from Carl Quintanilla and Richard Gibson, " 'Do Call Us': More Companies Install 1-800 Phone Lines," *The Wall Street Journal*, April 20, 1994, B1. Reprinted by permission of *The Wall Street Journal*, © 1994 Dow Jones & Co., Inc. All rights reserved worldwide.

138 Adapted from Gilbert Fuchsberg, "As Costs of Overseas Assignments Climb, Firms Select Expatriates More Carefully," *The Wall Street Journal*, January 9, 1992, B1. Reprinted by permission of *The Wall Street Journal*, © 1992 Dow Jones & Co., Inc. All rights reserved worldwide.

149 Micheline Maynard, "Evaluations Evolve from Boss," *USA Today*, August 3, 1994, 6B. Copyright 1994, USA Today. Reprinted with permission.

163 Adapted from Delbert J. Duncan, Charles F. Phillips, and Stanley C. Hollander, *Modern Retailing Management* (Homewood, IL: Richard D. Irwin, 1972).

170 Reprinted from Christopher Farrell, Paul Magnusson, and Wendy Zellner, "The Scary Math of New Hires," *Business Week*, February 22, 1993, 70–71.

173 Adapted from *1992 World Almanac and Information Book*, 179–180.

178 From *The Wall Street Journal* study, March 29, 1994, 1. By permission of *The Wall Street Journal*, © 1994 Dow Jones & Co., Inc. All rights reserved worldwide.

191 Adapted from Dawn Baskerville, "Why Business Loves Workteams," *Black Enterprise*, April 1993, 90. Copyright *Black Enterprise* Magazine, April 1993. The Earl G. Graves Publishing Co., Inc. All rights reserved.

198 David Sullivan, *The New Computer User* (Ft. Worth, TX: The Dryden Press, 1994), 277.

199 From Peter March, ed., *Eye to Eye: How People Interact* (Topsfield, MA: Salem House, 1988), 42.

202 Bob Laird, in Julie Schmit, "High-Tech Tool Changing the Way Firms Work," *USA Today*, July 20, 1994, B1. Copyright 1994, USA Today. Reprinted with permission.

204 From Gene Boone and David Kurtz, *Contemporary Business Communication*, (Englewood Cliffs, NJ: Prentice Hall, 1994), 607.

218 (top) Reprinted from William J. Cook, "Science & Society," *U.S. News & World Report*, December 6, 1993, 66.

221 Adapted from Steven C. Lawlor, *Computer Information Systems* (Ft. Worth, TX: The Dryden Press, 1992), 400.

236 (bottom) Adapted from "Big Payoffs from Keeping Customers," *Fortune*, Autumn/Winter 1993, 57. © 1993 Time Inc. All rights reserved.

237 (bottom) Data reported in "How Do You Get Customer Feedback?" *Inc.*, January 1993, 31.

257 Nancy Arnott, "To Know Brands Isn't Necessarily to Love Them," *Sales & Marketing Management*, December 1993, 25.

264 (top) Reprinted from "Doing Product Design by Hand," *Business Week*, October 21, 1991, 68. By special permission copyright © 1991 by McGraw-Hill, Inc.

266 Some data taken from Amity Shlaes, "Anywhere but Germany," *The Wall Street Journal*, January 22, 1993, A10.

327 (bottom) Data from Bank Network News, Bank Administration Institute.

341 Invemed Associates, Inc.

342 Courtesy of Clean Harbors, Inc.

344 Courtesy Mobil Corporation.

346 (bottom) Data from *Business Week*, January 18, 1993, 65.

353 *The Dallas Morning News*, April 22, 1994, 5D. Reprinted with permission of *The Dallas Morning News*.

354 (bottom) From *Business Week*, January 18, 1993, 6b.

355 *The Dallas Morning News*, April 22, 1994, 8D. Reprinted with permission of *The Dallas Morning News*.

382 Adapted from "How You Stand on Income," *Money*, December 1993, 148.

384 Adapted from Amy Saltzman, "An Electronic Job Hunt," *U.S. News & World Report*, March 28, 1994, 74–75.

385 Adapted from Margaret Mannix, "Writing a Computer-Friendly Resume," *U.S. News & World Report*, October 26, 1992, 90–93.

Tables

65 (top) Reprinted from "The NAFTA Vote: What's at Stake," *USA Today*, November 17, 1993, 8A. Copyright 1993, USA Today. Reprinted with permission.

125 Adapted from Robert C. Camp, *Benchmarking: The Search for Industry Best Practices that Lead to Superior Performance* (Milwaukee, WI: ASQC Quality Press, 1989), 17.

222 Adapted from "The Voice Processing Business," *Business Week*, June 3, 1991, 128. (Data from Hambrecht & Quist Inc., Market Intelligence-Research Corp., Link Resources Inc., Northern Business Information, Probe Research Inc.).

224 Adapted from Kenneth C. Laudon and Jane P. Laudon, *Business Information Systems* (Ft. Worth, TX: The Dryden Press, 1991), 577.

258 (bottom) Adapted from Norman Gaither, *Production and Operations Management: A Problem Solving and Decision Making Approach*, 2d ed. (Ft. Worth, TX: The Dryden Press, 1994).

260 Adapted from *Fortune*, May 21, 1990, 60. © 1990. Time Inc. All rights reserved.

330 Data from the Federal Reserve System.

Video Cases

Chapter 1 Adapted from James Bredin, "Don Hastings Sparks Success," *Industry Week*, December 6, 1993, 21; Kenneth Chilton, "Lincoln Electric's Incentive System: Can It Be Transferred Overseas?" *Compensation and Benefits Review*, November–December 1993, 10–11; Carolyn Wiley, "Incentive Plan Pushes Production," *Personnel Journal* (August 1993): 86–92; and "Lincoln Electric Announces Executive Retirements and Forecasts Strong Second-Quarter Results," *PC Newswire*, July 21, 1994.

Chapter 2 Adapted from Rahul Jacob, "Change with the Market or Die," *Fortune*, January 13, 1992, 62–63; Bill Gifford, "The Greening of the Golden Arches," *Rolling Stone*, August 22, 1991, 34–37; Rahul Jacob, "What Selling Will Be Like in the '90s," *Fortune*, January 13, 1992, 63–64; Phyllis Berman, "McDonald's Caves In," *Forbes*, February 4, 1991, 73–74; and advertisement for Florida Power, *Today*, September 1991, 9.

Chapter 3 Adapted from Robert Hartley, "Russia's Economy Worth Fixing, If We Knew How," *The Wall Street Journal*, April 2, 1992, A14; Edwin Dolan and David Lindsey, *Economics*, 6th ed. (Ft. Worth, TX: The Dryden Press, 1991), 510, 959; H. Massaqquoi, "Ebony Interview with Jamaica Prime Minister Michael Manley," *Ebony*, February 1990, 110; William Glasgall with Elizabeth Wei-

ner, "The Global Rush to Privatize," *Business Week*, October 21, 1991, 49; Michael Czinkota and Ilkka Ronkainen, *International Marketing*, 3d ed. (Ft. Worth, TX: The Dryden Press, 1993), 29, 479; Philip Cateora, *International Marketing*, 7th ed. (Homewood, IL: Irwin, 1990), 61–62, 148, 583.

Chapter 4 Adapted from "Ampex Head Says Company Is Back on Track," *Broadcasting*, March 4, 1991, 66.

Chapter 5 Adapted from Ken Schles, "Top of the Hops," *Savvy Woman*, March 1990, 74–75; Eunice Fried, "The Best in Brews," *Black Enterprise*, July 1990, 77; and "Sam Travels from Boston," *Beverage World*, January 1992, 12.

Chapter 6 Adapted from A. G. Kefalas, review of Kenichi Ohmae, *The Borderless World: Power and Strategy in the Interlinked Economy* (New York: Harper Collings, 1990), in *Business Horizons*, September–October 1991, 73; and James Fallows, "The World According to Ohmae," *The Atlantic*, June 1988, 18.

Chapter 7 Adapted from Thane Peterson, "Can Corporate America Get Out from Under Its Overhead?" *Business Week*, May 18, 1992, 102; L. A. Winokur, "Job Seekers Are Counseled to Concentrate on Smaller Firms, Consider Relocating," *The Wall Street Journal*, February 10, 1992; and Bruce Nussbaum, "Downward Mobility," *Business Week*, March 23, 1992, 56–63.

Chapter 8 Adapted from Leon Wynter, "Making the Grade on Hispanic Concerns," *The Wall Street Journal*, March 24, 1992, B1; and Sheryl Tucker and Kevin Thompson, "Will Diversity = Opportunity + Advancement for Blacks?" *Black Enterprise*, November 1990, 50–60.

Chapter 9 Adapted from Allan Demaree, "What Now for the U.S. and Japan?" *Fortune*, February 10, 1992, 80–95; Akio Morita, "Why Japan Must Change," *Fortune*, March 9, 1992, 66–67; and Quentin Hardy, "Those Know-It-Alls Make Good Money in Japanese Media," *The Wall Street Journal*, March 31, 1992, A1, A5.

Chapter 10 Adapted from "Sea World May Get Two Whales," *Orlando Sentinel*, June 9, 1992, B3; and Susan Doerfler, "Close Encounters of the Shark Kind," *The Arizona Republic*, April 26, 1992, T5.

Chapter 11 Adapted from Alan Wolf, "Coke Says 'Call My Agent' as

Marketing Team Tires of Pepsi Stealing Center Stage," *Beverage World*, September 30, 1991, 1, 10; Philip Voss, Jr., "International Marketing Myopia," *Chief Executive*, January–February 1991, 30–33; "CCE Shakeup Creates 10 New Marketing Regions," *Beverage Industry*, March 1991, 4; "Olympic Gold for Coca-Cola," *Adweek* (eastern edition), March 9, 1992, 4; and Louis E. Boone and David L. Kurtz, *Contemporary Marketing*, 7th ed. (Ft. Worth, TX: The Dryden Press, 1992), 100–106.

Chapter 12 Adapted from "There's No Work for You," *Chicago Tribune*, July 20, 1991, 2, 9; Margaret G. Wilder and Joyce E. Stigler, "Rethinking the Role of Judicial Scrutiny in Eminent Domain," *Journal of the American Planning Association* (Winter 1989): 57–65; Glenn M. Gomes and James F. Morgan, "Unfair Just Compensation: Reforming Eminent Domain Law for Small Business," *Journal of Small Business Management* (October 1989): 17–25; and Julie Cohen Mason "Migrating Across the Land," *Management Review*, July 1991, 28–30.

Chapter 13 Adapted from Karen Thomas, "Giving Stars the Brush-Up," *USA Today*, October 8, 1991, D-1; Judd Tully, "Painting by the Numbers," *Washington Post*, August 18, 1991, G-1; "Art Celebrity Mark Kostabi Tries New Concept for Moscow Exhibit: The FAX," *PR Newswire*, March 14, 1990; and Michael Small, "Art for Whose Sake?" *People Weekly*, July 11, 1988, 97.

Chapter 14 Adapted from Jack Stack, "The Great Game of Business," *Inc.*, June 1992, 53–66.

Chapter 15 Adapted from Clint Willis, "Duracell International," *Money*, June 1992, 50; and Joyce Anne Oliver, "Duracell CEO Charged about His Company," *Marketing News*, November 11, 1991, 2.

Chapter 16 Adapted from David Wessel, Steven Lipin, and Michael Sesit, "Tokyo Tremors," *The Wall Street Journal*, April 9, 1992, A1; "Stock Plunge in Tokyo Isn't Shaking Up Substantial Japanese Operations in U.S.," *The Wall Street Journal*, April 30, 1992, A8; and Eric D. Randall, "Strong Earnings News Revives Japan's Market," *USA Today*, June 1, 1994, B1.

Appendix A Adapted from Jon Cohen, "Is Liability Slowing AIDS Vaccines?" *Science*, April 10, 1992, 168; and E. Thomas McClanahan, "Reform Product Liability," *Kansas City Star*, March 17, 1992, B6.

Terms in boldface are defined in text.

This index contains names of persons, products, publications, and organizations.

b = box
t = table
f = figure

Terms in boldface are defined in text.

Storming stage (in teamwork), 191, 192*f*
Strategic alliances, 13–14
Strategic business units (SBUs), 84
Strategic planning, 72, **79**–80
Strict product liability, 377
Strike, 175
Strikebreakers, 176–177
Subsidiary, 96
Substance abuse, 40
Superfund Act of 1980, 332*b*
Superior courts, 373
Supervisory management, 137, 150*f*
Supplies, 276
Supply, 36
Supply curve, 36
Supply and demand, law of, 36*f*
Sweden, 128*b*, 289
Switzerland, flextime in, 172
Switzerland, 310
SWOT analysis, 72, **83**–84, 83*f*
Systems analysts, 399 400

T
Tactical planning, 80, 80*t*
Taiwan, 282*b*
   recycling in, 411
Tall organizations, 142
Tangible personal property, 376
Target market, 241, 274, **275**
Tariff, 60
Task specialist role, 189
Tax accountants, 300, 404
Tax law, 379
Taxes, 347, **379**
Team, 186–187
Team cohesiveness, 192
Team concept in production, 261–262
Team norm, 192–193
Teamwork, 128, 186, 192*f*
   definition of team, 186–187
   diversity, 190
   problem-solving teams, 188
   processes, 190
      cohesiveness, 192
      norms, 192–193
      stages of team development, 191–192
   team characteristics, 188–189
   team conflict, 193
      causes of, 193–194
      conflict resolution, 194–195
   team roles, 189, 189*f*
   team size, 189
   types of teams, 187–188
   work teams, 188, 191*f*
Technical skills, 148
Technological environment, 37–38, 288–289
Technologically displaced worker, 389
Technology, 9, **15**–16, 289*b*
   interactive media, 16
   the Internet, 16–18
Tehran, 166*b*

Telecommunications, 215–**217**
   computer networks, 217–219
Telecommunications managers, 400
Telemarketing, 286
Television, 274, 288*t*, 289
Test markets, 85
Thailand, 286*b*, 287, 420
Theory X of management, **166**
Theory Y of management, **166**
Theory Z of management, **166**–167
Thrifts, 327 328, 346
Time management, 153–154
Time utility, 235
Title VII (Civil Rights Act), 35*t*, 43
Tobacco Education and Child Protection Act, 28, 30
Tokyo, 166*b*
Toll-free telephone lines, 120–121, 120*f*
Tombstones, 341
Top management, 137, 150*f*
Tort, 377
Total quality management (TQM), 77, **111**–112
   financial management and, 119–120
   human resource management and, 116
   information processes and, 118–119
   marketing and, 116–118
   production and, 115–116
   top management involvement, 114–115
   See also **Quality**
Trade credit, 324
Trade deficit, 54
Trade restrictions, 61
Trade surplus, 54
Trademark, 256, 378
Training, 127–138
Transportation of goods, 285, 286*t*
Travel agents, 395–396
Treasury bills, 322
Trend analysis, 85
Trial courts, 372, **373**
TRW Business Credit Profiles, 31*b*

U
Underwriters, 340, 404
Unemployment insurance, 363–364
Uniform Commercial Code (UCC), 374–375
Unit of account, 320
United Kingdom
   banking in, 333
   market for U.S. franchises in, 103
   unions in, 177
United States, 151*b*, 266
   apprenticeship programs in, 168
   exports, 50, 50*t*, 54*b*, 54*t*, 57
   flextime in, 172
   import quotas, 61
   Export-Import Bank of, 63
   Japanese managers in, 418–419
   job recruitment in, 166*b*
   labor unions in, 173, 173*f*

NAFTA and, 50, 64–65
part-time work force in, 178–179
personal computer ownership, 16, 16*t*
quality programs in, 112
service jobs in, 11, 11*f*
social and cultural environment in, 37
trade with Canada, 65*t*
trade deficit in, 54
trade with Mexico, 65*t*
work force in, 22
Universal Product Code (UPC), 280
Unsecured bank loans, 324
Uruguay Round (of GATT talks), 62
U.S. Court of Claims, 373
U.S. district courts, 373
U.S. Supreme Court, 373
U.S. Tax Court, 373
Utility, 235

V
Vaccine development, 427 428
Variation, reducing, 123
Venture capital, 325
Venture capitalists, 395
Verbal communication, 195–200, 196*t*
Vertical marketing systems (VMS), 283
Video display terminal (VDT), 215
Videoconferencing, 60*b*, 202, 202*b*
Vietnam, U.S. trade embargo against, 60–61
Vietnam Era Veterans Readjustment Assistance Act (1974), 43
Virtual personnel, 171*b*
Virtual reality, 17*b*
Virtual teams, 187
Virtual-reality theme parks, 77
Vision, 20
Vocational Rehabilitation Act, 35
Voice mail, 119
Voice processing, 222–223, 222*t*
Voluntary retirement, 177

W
Wages, 9, 169
Walkout, 175
Warehousing, 285
Warranties, 375
Warranty, 286
Warsaw, 166*b*
Waste, eliminating, 123–124
Webb-Pomerene Export Act, 62
Wheel of retailing, 282
Wheeler-Lea Act, 34
Wholesaling intermediaries, 281
Wireless technologies, 212
Women
   discrimination against in business, 43–44
   glass ceiling and, 177, 178
   in management, 178*t*
   small business opportunities for, 100–101, 101*f*